FROM PENTECOST TO PATMOS

AN INTRODUCTION TO
ACTS THROUGH REVELATION

CRAIG L. BLOMBERG

FROM PENTECOST TO PATMOS

AN INTRODUCTION TO ACTS THROUGH REVELATION

CRAIG L. BLOMBERG

ACADEMIC

NASHVILLE, TENNESSEE

Ten-Digit ISBN: 0-8054-3248-5
Thirteen-Digit ISBN: 978-0-8054-3248-0

Published by Broadman & Holman Publishers
Nashville, Tennessee

Dewey Decimal Classification: 225.6
Subject Heading: BIBLE. N.T.—STUDY AND TEACHING
BIBLE. N.T.—CRITICISM
Scripture quotations are from the Holy Bible, New International Version, copyright © 1973, 1978, 1984 by International Bible Society

1 2 3 4 5 6 7 8 9 10 11 12 • 15 14 13 12 11 10 09 08 07 06
LB

Dedication

τῇ Μαριάμ

ἀδελφῇ γνησίᾳ ἐν τῇ πίστει

Contents

PART 1

THE ACTS OF THE APOSTLES

PART 2

PAUL AND HIS LETTERS

PART 3

OTHER NEW TESTAMENT WRITINGS

Journal Abbreviations

ABR	Australian Biblical Review
AJT	Asia Journal of Theology
AUSS	Andrews University Seminary Studies
BBR	Bulletin for Biblical Research
BI	Biblical Interpretation
Bib	Biblica
BibRes	Biblical Research
BSac	Bibliotheca Sacra
BT	Bible Translator
BTB	Biblical Theology Bulletin
CBQ	Catholic Biblical Quarterly
CBR	Currents in Biblical Research
CT	Christianity Today
CTJ	Calvin Theological Journal
CTR	Criswell Theological Review
EJT	European Journal of Theology
EQ	Evangelical Quarterly
ET	Expository Times
ExAud	Ex Auditu
FN	Filología Neotestamentaria
GTJ	Grace Theological Journal
HBT	Horizons in Biblical Theology
HTR	Harvard Theological Review
Int	Interpretation
JAAR	Journal of the American Academy of Religion
JBL	Journal of Biblical Literature
JETS	Journal of the Evangelical Theological Society
JPT	Journal of Pentecostal Theology
JSNT	Journal for the Study of the New Testament
JTS	Journal of Theological Studies
LS	Louvain Studies
Neot	Neotestamentica
NovT	Novum Testamentum
NTS	New Testament Studies
PRS	Perspectives in Religious Studies
PSB	Princeton Seminary Bulletin
RB	Revue biblique
RestQ	Restoration Quarterly
RevExp	Review and Expositor
RevQ	Revue de Qumran

SJT	*Scottish Journal of Theology*
ST	*Studia Theologica*
STJ	*Stulos Theological Journal*
SWJT	*Southwestern Journal of Theology*
TrinJ	*Trinity Journal*
TS	*Theological Studies*
TynB	*Tyndale Bulletin*
USQR	*Union Seminary Quarterly Review*
VC	*Vigilae Christianae*
WTJ	*Westminster Theological Journal*
WW	*Word and World*
ZNW	*Zeitschrift für die neutestamentliche Wissenschaft*

Abbreviations of Series and Publishers

AB	*Anchor Bible*
ANTC	*Abingdon New Testament Commentary*
BBC	*Blackwell Bible Commentaries*
BECNT	*Baker Exegetical Commentary on the New Testament*
BNTC	*Black's New Testament Commentary*
BIP	*Biblical Institute Press*
BST	*Bible Speaks Today*
CBAA	*Catholic Biblical Association of America*
CUP	*Cambridge University Press*
ECC	*Eerdmans Critical Commentary*
HNTC	*Harper's New Testament Commentary*
ICC	*International Critical Commentary*
IVP	*Inter-Varsity Press*
IVPNTC	*Inter-Varsity Press New Testament Commentary*
JSOT	*Journal for the Study of the Old Testament*
LUP	*Leuven University Press*
NAC	*New American Commentary*
NCB	*New Century Bible*
NCBC	*New Cambridge Bible Commentary*
NIBC	*New International Biblical Commentary*
NICNT	*New International Commentary on the New Testament*
NIGTC	*New International Greek Testament Commentary*
NIVAC	*NIV Application Commentary*
NTC	*New Testament Commentary*
NTG	*New Testament Guides*
NTinCont	*New Testament in Context*
OUP	*Oxford University Press*
PIB	*Pontificio Istituto Biblico*
PNTC	*Pillar New Testament Commentary*
SAP	*Sheffield Academic Press*
SBL	*Society of Biblical Literature*
SBS	*Standard Bible Studies*
SCM	*Student Christian Movement*
SHBC	*Smyth & Helwys Bible Commentary*
SP	*Sacra Pagina*
SPCK	*Society for the Promotion of Christian Knowledge*
THNTC	*Two Horizons New Testament Commentary*
TNTC	*Tyndale New Testament Commentary*
UBS	*United Bible Societies*
UPA	*University Press of America*

WBC	*Word Biblical Commentary*
WJKP	*Westminster John Knox Press*
ZEC	*Zondervan Exegetical Commentary*

Acknowledgments

It may not take quite a village to create a book, but many people deserve thanks for helping this volume see the light of day. Of course, there are the classes of students, undergraduate and graduate, over a twenty-two-year period, in such diverse places as Palm Beach Atlantic College, West Palm Beach, Florida; Sangre de Cristo Seminary, Westcliffe, Colorado; the University of Colorado, Boulder; the Southern Baptist Theological Seminary, Louisivlle, Kentucky; Saint Petersburg Christian University, Russia; the Irish Bible Institute, Dublin; the Bible College of Victoria, Melbourne, Australia; Moore College, Sydney, Australia; and above all Denver Seminary, Englewood and Littleton, Colorado, who have interacted with previous versions of any or all of this material, helping me to see at least something of what was and was not important and what was and was not clear.

Then there is the Institute of Theological Studies in Grand Rapids, Michigan, whose invitation, via the late Harold van Broekhoven, to create a cassette-tape series with expanded syllabus for a correspondence course on the Epistles and Revelation, led to a predecessor to this volume, produced in 1995 and revised in 2000, slightly less than half the size of the current edition. Outreach, Incorporated, of which the ITS was a subsidiary, also graciously allowed me to retain the copyright for that material, reproduced in spiral-bound notebook form, precisely so that I might someday revise, supplement, and reuse it in updated form should the opportunity arise.

I am likewise grateful to the faculty and board of trustees of Denver Seminary, who granted me a sabbatical semester during the spring of 2004, which allowed me to do quite a bit of the additional research and writing necessary to produce this textbook-length edition (along with material on Acts, which had not previously been put into prose in any form). Dr. Philip Duce, theological books editor for Inter-Varsity Press in the United Kingdom, and his counterpart at B & H Publishing Group, Dr. John Landers, continued to be as helpful in the production of this volume as they were with the first. And, of course, neither editor works in isolation but surrounded by very competent and friendly staffs.

Numerous colleagues and students helped me in the mechanics of typing, editing, reference-checking, and proofreading, especially Mrs. Jeanette Freitag, assistant to the faculty; Professor Elodie Emig, instructor in Greek and New Testament; Mr. Michael Hemenway, MABS student and information services staff person; and Ms. Jennifer Foutz, who also worked as a grader for me in her final year as an M.Div. student. Jeanette has tirelessly, cheerfully, and with amazing promptness and astonishingly few mistakes completed just about any kind of editing I have requested on writing projects for longer than I can remember. Elodie meticulously double-checked countless quotations and footnotes for accuracy. Mike converted my PowerPoint slides into Word documents so I could merge them with my text, while Jenn proofread the entire manuscript and created the first draft of all the questions for review with remarkable skill. She also read a number of brand-new sources for me during the months between my submission of the manuscript and my receipt of the page proofs, highlighting points I might want to incorporate into this work, so that my final draft might be as up-to-date as possible. To them I am profoundly indebted for enabling me to complete this project far more quickly than I would have otherwise been able to do, and with greater accuracy and fluency as well.

The staff of the Denver Seminary Carey S. Thomas Library was uniformly helpful, as always. Mrs. Jeannette France, reference librarian, in particular continued to go above and beyond the call of duty to address more questions about how to find things than most library users ever ask her. Ms. Kim Backlund, our bookstore manager, and her staff were always cheery and quick to help in the ordering of new books I needed so that I could remain current with scholarship not yet available in local libraries or through interlibrary loan. Kim, in particular, went above and beyond the call of duty to point me to new materials I hadn't even yet discovered and to encourage me at key junctures during the research when I was feeling somewhat overwhelmed.

One individual, however, provided far more help than any other. I cannot express sufficient gratitude to the hopefully soon-to-be Dr. Mariam Kamell, my research assistant during the two academic years spanning 2003–05, for her tireless efforts on this project. Without her work on several fronts, especially in reviewing much of the recent scholarly literature on Acts through Revelation tucked away in journal articles, this book would (again) not have been ready nearly as soon as it was or marked by as thorough a survey of what scholars are saying *today,* frequently including perspectives quite different from mine. When I was afflicted for about three months in the spring of 2004 with the recurrence of a repetitive-stress injury, she took over a considerable part of my typing as well. She put up with my mood swings during the RSI and later graciously forgave one or two serious lapses in my patience, borne largely out of my frustration with my overcommitment to professional activities and my inability to control the speed of the completion of my projects. In 2004–06, she became a valued colleague, teaching as an adjunct professor for our New Testament department even while embarking on her Ph.D. in the University of Saint Andrews, Scotland. Her godly lifestyle and optimistic personality are an inspiration to many, not just to me. I therefore dedicate this book to Mariam, hoping that our Lord will supply her with at least as much fulfillment and joy in her career and ministry as a New Testament professor and scholar as he has given me in mine. But to God be all the glory.

Introduction

Many film producers create sequels to blockbuster movies. Most of these follow-up films are not crafted as carefully or artistically as their predecessors. Occasionally, exceptions emerge, in unusual cases generating long series of shows. The six-film Star Wars sequence, spanning three decades and distributed throughout the world, is undoubtedly the most famous contemporary example.

In 1997, I had the privilege of seeing my book, *Jesus and the Gospels: An Introduction and Survey,* appear in print.[1] This volume grew out of years of teaching a quarter-long class on this material first at the undergraduate and then at the graduate levels. What began as my own lecture notes had turned into detailed printed outlines that I distributed to my students and then into a spiral-bound booklet of prose commentary that added even more information. When Broadman & Holman Publishers were looking for an introductory textbook on precisely this topic, I was delighted to be able to expand the material once more and turn it into a publishable volume. I was also thrilled that Inter-Varsity Press in the United Kingdom was eager to publish a British edition.

At that time I did not imagine composing a sequel. Broadman & Holman had already contracted with John B. Polhill to produce a comparable introduction to Acts and Paul, and it appeared in 1999 as *Paul and His Letters,* an extraordinarily comprehensive, accurate, and user-friendly companion to my book. Nevertheless, I was greatly encouraged by the reception that *Jesus and the Gospels* was receiving. I discovered it was being used as a textbook in college and seminary classrooms around the English-speaking world and soon was translated into German as well.[2] Laypeople similarly volunteered the information that they found it helpful for serious, personal study apart from any educational institution or degree program.

Soon various individuals began to ask me what I used for textbooks when I taught Acts through Revelation. I explained that my class notes had begun a similar metamorphosis. In fact, in 1995, I had produced the first edition of a spiral-bound notebook of introduction to and commentary on "The Epistles and Revelation," for a cassette-tape series of lectures on those books produced for the Institute of Theological Studies' correspondence curriculum. For Acts, I still used handouts in outline form, but they had grown to a thirty-page stapled set of single-spaced notes. Early in the new millennium, therefore, I began seriously to contemplate a sequel to my first textbook. My two previous publishers expressed interest in the project, so my research moved forward. John Landers suggested the title *From Pentecost to Patmos.*

In the autumn semesters of 2004 and 2005, I had my students in "Understanding the Gospels and Acts" read drafts of my material on Acts. In the springs of 2005 and 2006, classes on "Understanding the Epistles and Revelation" worked through my writing on that half of the New Testament. Were our seminary still following

---

[1] Nashville: Broadman & Holman; Leicester: IVP.
[2] *Jesus und die Evangelien: Einführung und Überblick* (Nürnburg: VTR, 2000).

the quarter system, *Jesus and the Gospels* would fit perfectly for the first term and *From Pentecost to Patmos* for the second and third terms. But Denver Seminary, like many tertiary-level institutions in the U.S. in recent years, has shifted to the semester system, so the division becomes more awkward.

I am heartened by the fact that Ralph Martin's two-volume introduction to the New Testament has established a precedent for the division of labor represented here and managed to serve a generation of theological students quite well.[3] I do not envision authoring anything more that would create a longer series; I do not have the expertise, for example, in the Old Testament to create "prequels" as George Lucas did in the Star Wars series! But if those who have benefited from *Jesus and the Gospels* find the new volume a helpful companion, my time will have been well spent.

Like the first book, this one attempts to offer the reader a "one-stop shopping" guide to everything I would most want theological students to know about the biblical books covered. Classically, "introductions" have treated such background information as author, date, audience, provenance, purposes, genre, outline, theology, and the like, while "surveys" have sampled the contents of the books of Scripture sequentially, after the fashion of a miniature commentary, with only minimal background information. Increasingly, both kinds of works do some of each task, just in varying proportions. Recent introductions have recognized that a mastery of the contents and implications of biblical texts is often the more crucial need that theological students have today and are including more and more of that kind of information.[4] Some highlight more specialized forms of analysis that have been growing in popularity, particularly literary and sociological criticism,[5] or they may focus on theological issues more than has typically been the case—a task left in the past to "biblical theology" texts.[6] All of these approaches generally assume that lecturers will then supplement the textbooks with in-class treatments of the exegesis of important passages and discussions of interpretive controversies in more detail.

My experience has led me to a somewhat opposite procedure. What most interests most twenty-first century students and what they most often need for ministry and life is a detailed mastery of the meanings of the texts of Scripture themselves. All of these other topics are important but not as primary. So I have attempted to deal with the most crucial items of introduction in enough detail to provide the necessary background for correctly interpreting the New Testament books, with footnotes and bibliography indicating where more detailed discussions can be

---

[3] Ralph P. Martin, *New Testament Foundations,* 2 vols. (Grand Rapids: Eerdmans; Carlisle: Paternoster, 1975–78).

[4] E.g., Paul J. Achtemeier, Joel B. Green, and Marianne M. Thompson, *Introducing the New Testament: Its Literature and Theology* (Grand Rapids and Cambridge: Eerdmans, 2001); D. A. Carson and Douglas J. Moo, *An Introduction to the New Testament* (Grand Rapids: Zondervan, rev. 2005).

[5] See esp. David A. deSilva, *An Introduction to the New Testament: Contexts, Methods and Ministry Formation* (Downers Grove and Leicester: IVP, 2004).

[6] See esp. Carl R. Holladay, *A Critical Introduction to the New Testament: Interpreting the Message and Meaning of Jesus Christ* (Nashville: Abingdon, 2005).

found. I spend most of my time, however, on surveying the actual structure and contents of each book, the main points in each section, the distinctive exegetical cruxes, and several key items for contemporary application. Thus if students were never to attend class but know and understand, inside and out, what I have written, my conscience would be clear that they would have an excellent foundation in the biblical literature covered.

Of course, this seldom happens as well on its own as when students attend class too! So I use class time for a wide variety of activities: periodic quizzes as an incentive to learn the textbook material well; abbreviated reviews of the most crucial points in each section, supplemental "mini-lectures" to go into key issues in more detail than the book can or to introduce related issues that my text omits altogether; healthy intervals of time for follow-up discussions of reading, including question and answer (generated both by the students for me and by me for them), case studies, and other kinds of application. Slides, videos, and DVD clips can help make portions of the New Testament world come more alive; PowerPoint charts and presentations can clarify, illustrate, and reinforce key principles. International and minority students (and others with significant international or cross-cultural experiences) can highlight issues that most students might not consider, and so on.

As in *Jesus and the Gospels,* I adopt a broadly based evangelical perspective. A significant number of the sources in my bibliographies, especially under the commentary sections, come from evangelical authors. But I have read widely, interacted with a broad cross-section of scholarship, and tried to offer a representative sampling of approaches across a wide spectrum of theological commitments. When it comes to the more controversial passages and interpretive issues, it is almost impossible to do justice to all points of view, so I have discovered that students seem to learn best and appreciate most reading about my perspectives but hearing me repeatedly say that they are more than free to disagree with me. Class time and exegetical or topical papers can be used for exploring different options. I could hope that a wide variety of lecturers would find enough of value in my book that they would treat it similarly—not thinking that they must agree with an overwhelming majority of my views on specific issues to find the text valuable but rather using it as an opportunity for students to learn and understand one reasonably widespread, representative evangelical viewpoint on a topic. (I rarely adopt a position that only a small minority of commentators have held.) Then, in the other components of the class, they can supplement my perspectives with any others they would like.

The overall structure of the book is straightforward. Acts comes first because it appears immediately after the Gospels in canonical sequence and because it forms the narrative context into which many of the epistles may be inserted with greater understanding. The section on Paul's letters surveys his epistles in chronological order as best we can reconstruct it. These chapters are preceded by an introduction to Paul's life and ministry which includes, among many other things, an explanation of why his letters were arranged in our New Testament canon in a different sequence (pp. 106). The dating of the remaining epistles—Hebrews, James, 1 and 2 Peter, 1, 2 and 3 John, and Jude—is much less certain. But one possible chronology, which we have followed for the sequence of our discussions, is James, Hebrews, 1 Peter, Jude, 2 Peter, and 1, 2 and 3 John.[7] Revelation is almost certainly the last of the New Testament books to be written.

Throughout the history of the church, these letters have come to be called the "general" or "catholic" epistles (*catholic* originally just meant "universal"), because they were believed not to have been addressed to one specific church or group of churches. Today, this conviction has been almost universally discarded, as we shall explain when we introduce each of them. But this belief explains why they were treated together as one large section of the New Testament, just as Paul's letters were. After being located in a number of different places, the sequence followed today seems to have been dictated by two main factors. First, because Paul's importance and influence was so widespread since the earliest days of Christianity, his letters naturally came to be placed before the other epistles. Second, within the "general" epistles, the works again seem to have been arranged according to the importance of their authors in the first generation of church history. James was the first elder of the church in Jerusalem and the biological half brother of Jesus, Peter became the leader of the Twelve, John remained his close companion, while Jude was the least known of the four.

Hebrews contains no ascription of authorship in any of its oldest manuscripts. Some church fathers thought it came from Paul; many did not (cf. below, p. 411–12). So it eventually settled into the "gap" between the Paulines and the supposedly more general letters. Revelation, of course, is not a letter *per se,* though it includes seven letters in chapters 2–3 and partakes of certain other features of the epistolary genre (below, p. 513). But Revelation is more predominantly apocalyptic and prophetic literature. Given that its contents culminate with the events surrounding Christ's return, the end of human history, and a new heavens and earth, it was natural for it to wind up at the end of the Bible, regardless of its actual dating, though it probably is the last book to have been written chronologically as well.

The comments on each book will begin with introductory considerations. Then will follow abbreviated remarks in commentary form on the most central, interesting, relevant and/or controversial details of the book, and at last passage-by-passage (and at times even verse-by-verse) comments with footnotes to where specific concepts or quotations originate or to where fuller discussion of issues may be found. Finally, some brief remarks with respect to the contemporary application of each book and a selective bibliography of works for further study will appear. The bibliographies begin with commentaries arranged under three headings: advanced works, the understanding of which is usually enhanced (though not required) by some knowledge of Greek; intermediate-level items, which include detailed but not

---

[7] The most likely divergence from this chronology would come with the letter of Jude, which may be considerably earlier than all the other non-Pauline epistles except perhaps James. But because of the close literary relationship between Jude and 2 Peter, it makes sense to treat them together. See further below, pp. 461–62.

overly technical commentaries on the English text written with full knowledge of the original language and of current scholarship; and introductory volumes, which arc bricfer or more applicational in focus but still reflect sound, up-to-date scholarship evaluated in light of the original languages and texts of Scripture.

THE CANON OF THE NEW TESTAMENT	
Gospels	Matthew Mark Luke John
	Acts
	Letters of Paul to churches (decreasing length)
	Letters of Paul to individuals (decreasing length)
General Epistles	Hebrews James 1 and 2 Peter 1, 2, and 3 John Jude
	Revelation

In *Jesus and the Gospels,* I used the New International Version's Inclusive Language Edition (NIVI) published in the United Kingdom (London: Hodder & Stoughton, 1996) as my basic English-language translation from which I quoted. Since then, a partial equivalent published in the United States, called Today's New International Version (TNIV), has been completed (Colorado Springs: IBS; Grand Rapids: Zondervan, 2005). Unfortunately, a heated controversy has developed, largely limited to the United States, over these and similar recent translations that use inclusive language for humanity more so than older ones. Much of this debate involves misunderstandings and misrepresentations of these translations and the principles they followed, but some genuine theological issues are involved as well.[8]

Sadly, the debate obscures or ignores the fact that a significant majority of the changes made in the TNIV had nothing to do with gender issues but improved the

[8] See esp. D. A. Carson, *The Inclusive Language Debate: A Plea for Realism* (Grand Rapids: Baker, 2001).

NIV text by making it a more *literal* translation.[9] Nevertheless, as of this writing, the older, third edition of the NIV (Colorado Springs: IBS, 1984; Grand Rapids: Zondervan, 1985) continues to be the version of choice within the largest segment of English-speaking evangelicals worldwide. I have reverted, therefore, to citing its text (unless otherwise specified), so that the greatest number of readers possible will be able to follow me readily. At points where some might be misled into thinking a passage was gender exclusive, because of the NIV's uses of a masculine form originally intended to be generic, I have simply avoided quoting the Bible verbatim in any translation. If reference to the wording of the text is necessary for the clarity of my meaning, I then paraphrase the Scripture in my own words without using an actual quotation. Other principles regarding "politically correct" or "incorrect" language usage remain unchanged from my earlier volume, and I refer readers to my brief discussion included there.[10]

While reading widely the scholarship of several languages and cultures, with rare exceptions, I limit my footnotes and bibliography to English-language materials available to the introductory theological student. Italicized material, review questions at the end of each chapter, and maps, charts and diagrams are likewise designed to make the work more user-friendly.

In my previous volume, I concluded my introduction by inviting constructive critique from my readers, particularly regarding the book's usefulness as a set text for theological education. That invitation still stands. My goal is for readers to come to better understand first-century Christianity, the literature it produced that came to be treated as uniquely sacred, and through it a better appreciation of the Lord Jesus Christ, worshipped by this fledgling church, often in hostile circumstances and facing difficulties remarkably similar to those the church faces today throughout the world, despite the changes in cultural and technological forms in which those challenges may be cloaked.

---

[9] For detailed documentation, see Craig L. Blomberg, *"Today's New International Version*: The Untold Story of a Good Translation," in *Perspectives on the TNIV from Leading Scholars and Pastors* (Grand Rapids: Zondervan, 2004), 85–115; slightly updated for *BT* 56 (2005): 188–211.

[10] Blomberg, *Jesus and the Gospels*, 3.

PART 1

THE ACTS OF THE APOSTLES

Acts: The Gospel Moves Out

INTRODUCTION

THE UNIQUENESS OF ACTS

The fifth book of the New Testament proves unique in numerous ways. *First, it is the only intentional "sequel" in the canon.* No other Gospel besides Luke's proceeds to narrate the events of the first generation of Christian history. And while various epistles spawned follow-up letters, to our knowledge no two letters were ever conceived as a unity from the outset. Thus one cannot fully understand the book of Acts without first studying the Gospel of Luke.[1] As straightforward as this point may seem, it is often not realized because in the canonical process of grouping the four Gospels together, John's has intruded and come between Luke's first and second volumes.[2]

Second, the contents of Acts remain unique. It is the only book to treat the period between Jesus' crucifixion (probably in A.D. 30) and the end of Paul's ministry (or at least nearly the end, sometime in the 60s). It has often been observed that the traditional title ascribed to the book, "The Acts of the Apostles," is somewhat misleading because the only one of the original Twelve who plays a prominent role in this work is Peter. The most highlighted human character is Paul, who thought of himself as an apostle but was not one of the Twelve. Beyond that, we read a little about John, the other ten are listed, but the remaining characters are not apostles at all. Perhaps, then, we should think of the work as "The Acts of Peter and Paul," or better "The Acts of the Holy Spirit," since Luke clearly sees the work of the early church as "Spirit-directed."[3] Yet whatever the title, *this is the only existing work inside or outside the canon of Scripture to describe this first generation of church history.* Thus all appeals to the "New Testament church" as a model for Christian living in any other time and place sooner or later wind up scrutinizing Acts.

Third, this volume offers unique problems in application. Unlike the epistles, it gives few formal commands. Even the four Gospels, with their emphasis on Jesus' ethical instruction, have more explicitly didactic material than Acts. Most of its contents simply present various vignettes involving the characters Luke chooses to highlight. Subsequent readers frequently find themselves asking, "What is normative?" "What is a positive example to emulate or a negative one to avoid?" Or, "Are

---

[1] On which, see Craig L. Blomberg, *Jesus and the Gospels: An Introduction and Survey* (Nashville: Broadman & Holman, 1997), 140–55, and the literature there cited.

[2] Cf. I. Howard Marshall, "Acts and the 'Former Treatise,'" in *The Book of Acts in Its Ancient Literary Setting,* vol. 1, eds. Bruce W. Winter and Andrew D. Clarke (Grand Rapids: Eerdmans; Carlisle: Paternoster, 1993), 163–82.

[3] Justo L. González, *Acts: The Gospel of the Spirit* (Maryknoll: Orbis, 2001), 8.

certain events included for other reasons—perhaps just because they happened and remained important for explaining developments in the fledgling church?" *One fundamental hermeneutical axiom in answering these questions is to distinguish consistent patterns of behavior from multiple contexts within the book (and within the rest of the New Testament more generally) and patterns that vary from one context to the next.* Luke, as narrator, can also give indirect clues by noting God's blessing as the result of some activity—a further way of indicating its exemplary nature.[4]

Finally, the book of Acts appears in a unique position in the progress of God's revelation to humanity. The first Christian generation clearly formed a transitional period from the age of law to the era of the gospel. No one woke up the day after Pentecost to hear a Jerusalem town crier announcing the end of the old covenant and the inauguration of the new! The differences that Jesus made through his life, death, and resurrection only gradually dawned on his followers. Parallel to this development was the transformation of Jesus' first group of disciples from an exclusively Jewish sect centered in Jerusalem to what one generation later had become a predominantly Gentile movement scattered throughout the Roman Empire. Thus while many incidents in Acts reflect Christians, especially Jewish ones, still observing the law, Luke's own theological emphasis lies in highlighting how Christianity successively broke free from the law. It is this freedom (without using it as a license for sin) that remains normative after the end of this period of transition.[5]

AUTHORSHIP

Comparing the prefaces of Luke and Acts, along with the style of the two narratives overall, has convinced virtually all scholars that the author of these two volumes must be the same person. But who is he? Strictly speaking, Acts, like the four Gospels, is anonymous. As best we can tell, the titles to the books did not appear in the original documents and were probably first added in the second century as the various books of the New Testament began to be gathered together.[6] *The testimony of the ancient church fathers, however, unanimously affirmed that Luke, whom Paul calls his "beloved physician" (Col. 4:14 KJV), was the author,* a man who appears to have been a Gentile, since Paul refers to him only *after* mentioning "the only Jews among my fellow workers" who have remained with him (v. 11). Church tradition also accounts for those sections of Acts in which the author changes from third-person narrative to first-person plural (describing what "we" did) as due to Luke's presence with Paul on those occasions (16:10–17; 20:5–21:18; 27:1–28:16).[7] In modern times, however, scholars have proposed at least two other options. First, this "we material" could reflect the diary, memoirs, or oral recollection of an eyewitness and companion of Paul, which was consulted by someone else while writing the entire

---

[4] For an excellent treatment of this issue, see Walter L. Liefeld, *Interpreting the Book of Acts* (Grand Rapids: Baker, 1995).

[5] Craig L. Blomberg, "The Law in Luke-Acts," *JSNT* 22 (1984): 53–80.

[6] But see Martin Hengel (*The Four Gospels and the One Gospel of Jesus Christ* [London: SCM; Harrisburg: Trinity, 2000]), who argues for their originality.

[7] E.g., the Muratorian Canon; Irenaeus, *Against Heresies* 3.1.1, 3.14.1; Tertullian, *Against Marcion* 4.2; Eusebius, *Church History* 3.4.

book.[8] Alternately, some think this is an entirely artificial literary device based on allegedly similar practices, particularly in narrating travel accounts, especially by sea, of various characters in Greco-Roman stories, even when the author had no link to any participants in these adventures.[9]

In the late nineteenth century, William Hobart argued that distinctively medical vocabulary appeared throughout Luke-Acts, corroborating the tradition that a physician wrote these works.[10] But in the early twentieth century, Henry Cadbury demonstrated that this vocabulary appeared just as frequently in nonmedical works, demonstrating the inadequacy of Hobart's argument.[11] In more recent times, however, Loveday Alexander has shown that the closest parallels to the prefaces of Luke and Acts are found in Greco-Roman scientific treatises. While this does not prove that Luke was a "scientist," or more specifically a physician, it is at least consistent with the early church tradition.[12]

With the rise of modern biblical criticism, particularly in the nineteenth century, many followed the influential philosophy of Ferdinand Christian Baur, who built on Georg W. F. Hegel's dialectic view of history, in which a movement (thesis) was eventually opposed (antithesis) until a compromise between the two was achieved (synthesis). Baur believed that "Luke" mediated between the extreme Jewish Christianity of Peter and James and the extreme Gentile Christianity of Paul, creating a very late, mid-second-century synthesis. If the two works were this late, then of course no actual travel companion of Paul could have penned them. Today this approach has been all but abandoned.

Contemporary skepticism concerning Lukan authorship has focused far more on the apparent theological contradictions between Acts and the undisputed letters of Paul to argue that no close follower of Paul could have been the author of Acts. The classic exposition of this claim appears in a short article by Philipp Vielhauer, who pointed out four major differences: (1) Acts allows for a "natural theology" in which humans by general revelation may come to find God (esp. Acts 17:16–31), whereas Paul has an altogether negative view of the possibility of salvation apart from explicit faith in Christ (e.g., Rom. 1:18–32). (2) Paul's attitude to obeying the law is more positive in Acts, as compared especially with his tirade against those who would impose the law on Christians in his letter to the Galatians. (3) Paul's Christology in Acts, like that of other early Christian preachers, centers on the resurrection, whereas in 1 Corinthians 2:2 Paul refers to the crucifixion as the exclusive heart of his gospel.

---

[8] See esp. Stanley E. Porter, "The 'We' Passages," in *The Book of Acts in its Graeco-Roman Setting,* eds. David W. J. Gill and Conrad H. Gempf (Grand Rapids: Eerdmans; Carlisle: Paternoster, 1994), 545–74; A. J. M. Wedderburn, "The 'We'-Passages in Acts: On the Horns of a Dilemma," *ZNW* 93 (2002): 78–98.

[9] See esp. Vernon K. Robbins, "By Land and by Sea: The We-Passages and Ancient Sea-Voyages," in *Perspectives on Luke-Acts,* ed. C. H. Talbert (Danville, Va.: NABPR, 1978), 215–42. But see the response of Colin J. Hemer, "First Person Narrative in Acts 27–28," *TynB* 36 (1985): 79–109.

[10] William K. Hobart, *The Medical Language of St. Luke* (London: Longmans and Green, 1882).

[11] Henry J. Cadbury, *The Style and Literary Method of Luke* (Cambridge, Mass.: Harvard University Press, 1920).

[12] Loveday C. A. Alexander, *The Preface to Luke's Gospel* (Cambridge and New York: CUP, 1993). Alexander has also demonstrated that despite certain features of Acts that at first glance might have appeared fictitious, on more careful inspection Luke's style and genre show that he intended to write a book that was accepted as "fact" ("Fact, Fiction and the Genre of Acts," *NTS* 44 [1998]: 380–99).

(4) Finally, the eschatology of Luke appears to be "delayed," that is, the author recognizes a fair amount of time may elapse until Christ returns, whereas the Paul of the epistles still holds out a lively hope for an imminent parousia.[13]

There are valid observations in these summaries of key contrasts between Acts and the epistles, but they can be easily overdrawn. (1) Romans 1:19–20 agrees with Paul in Athens (Acts 17) that all humanity should recognize from the nature of creation that a creator exists. (2) Acts 13:39 makes clear, even in Acts, that Paul does not believe the law can save anyone, while 1 Corinthians 9:19–23 emphasizes Paul's willingness to put himself under the Law for the sake of winning his Jewish contemporaries. (3) Neither the crucifixion nor the resurrection represents Christ's entire salvific work, as Paul himself observes by stressing the necessity of the resurrection in 1 Corinthians 15. (4) Finally, a closer study of both Acts and the letters of Paul demonstrates strands of a lively expectation of Christ's near return, coupled with the possibility that it may in fact not happen for some time (cf., e.g., Luke 17:20–37; Acts 13:40–41, 47; 1 Thess. 4:13–5:10).

David Wenham thus rightly concludes that the differences between Acts and the epistles probably prove that Paul himself did not write Acts (though, of course, no one has ever claimed that)! But the differences do not demonstrate that an associate of his, himself theologically trained in the early Christian faith with his own emphases writing to a specific audience with particular needs, could not have authored this work.[14] Moreover, no convincing reason has ever been given for the early church to have uniformly latched on to such an otherwise obscure person as Luke and claimed him as author of either the Gospel or Acts if he were not the true writer of these works.

DATE

As noted above, it was popular in the mid-nineteenth century to date Acts to the early or even mid-100s. This late date allowed scholars to dismiss fairly easily the reliability of Luke's narrative as a tendentious presentation, concealing the serious differences that divided the first Christian generation. Petrine and Pauline Christianity were seen as profoundly different trajectories in the first century, with Luke's compromise only a much later development. Galatians 2:11–15, rather than Acts 15, seemed to reflect these early tensions better.

Today, however, a sizable majority of scholars dates Acts to sometime after A.D. 70 and before the mid-90s. The decade of the 80s proves most popular and could almost be spoken of as the consensus date among more liberal commentators. Later dates are rejected because by then Paul's letters were becoming widely known, so that the silence of Acts about them would be inexplicable. Because Acts follows the Gospel of Luke and many date Luke to a time after the fall of Jerusalem (particularly on the basis of Jesus' alleged "after the fact prophecy" in Luke 21:20), then Acts also

[13] Philipp Vielhauer, "On the 'Paulinism' of Acts," in *Studies in Luke-Acts,* eds. Leander E. Keck and J. Louis Martyn (Nashville: Abingdon, 1966; London: SPCK, 1978), 33–50.

[14] David Wenham, "Acts and the Pauline Corpus II. The Evidence of Parallels," in *The Book of Acts in Its Ancient Literary Setting,* eds. Winter and Clarke, 215–58. For a book-length study of *Paul in Acts,* see the work so entitled by Stanley E. Porter (Tübingen: Mohr, 1999; Peabody: Hendrickson, 2001).

would have to postdate 70. The supposed theological contradictions associated with Vielhauer (see above) likewise lead scholars to assume that some time has elapsed since the epistles were written in the 50s and 60s for further development in thought to have occurred.

On the other hand, *most conservatives still date Acts to the period between approximately A.D. 62 and 64.* The abrupt end of the book, with Paul awaiting the results of his appeal to Caesar in Rome, has suggested to many that Luke wrote almost immediately after these last events occurred. Given that Acts 21–28 has been narrating Paul's arrest, his various hearings and his imprisonments in considerable detail, all building toward his appeal to the emperor, it is hard to understand why Luke would not have recorded the outcome of that appeal if he had written at a late enough date to have known it. The two-year period of house arrest in Rome, with which the book of Acts ends, should probably be dated to 60–62 since Festus acceded to power in 59 and Paul was shipped to Rome that fall. If we allow some time for Luke to pen his Gospel, then we arrive at the date suggested above. What is more, if early church tradition is accurate that Paul was in fact freed as the result of this appeal (only to be arrested and martyred again later in the decade), this almost certainly must have occurred before Nero began persecuting Christians in 64 (see below, p. 77). As we discussed in our earlier volume, Luke 21:20 does not have to be seen as writing the events of history in the guise of prophecy after the fact. But if Luke 21:20 reflects a genuine prediction on Jesus' part, then it does not help us determine the date of Luke's writing one way or the other.[15]

Nevertheless, it is important to stress that the debate is not exclusively between conservatives opting for a pre-70 date and liberals preferring a post-70 date. Several prominent evangelical scholars opt for the later date, assuming that Luke meant to end his account with the gospel reaching Rome.[16] This was the heart of the empire from which it could truly go out to "the ends of the earth" (Acts 1:8) and may well have formed in Luke's mind a fitting climax, even if modern sensibilities want to know the outcome of Paul's appeal. The possible chiastic structure of Luke's two-volume work could also support this understanding. Beginning by setting God's plan of salvation in Jesus in the context of Roman history at the outset of the Gospel, Luke closes the Acts with the fulfillment of that plan in Rome. In a chiastic structure, the climax appears in fact at the center of the document, in this case the accounts of the resurrection of Jesus. There lies Luke's most crucial theological datum, and less urgency appears for the end of the work to be as climactic. Conversely, the well-known liberal English bishop in the 1970s, John Robinson, dated Acts (as he did all of the New Testament documents) prior to A.D. 70 for a variety of reasons, including his conviction that Luke 21:20 was too vague to be a description of the Roman sack of Jerusalem *ex post facto.*[17]

---

[15] See further Blomberg, *Jesus and the Gospels,* 151.

[16] E.g., David J. Williams, *Acts* (Peabody: Hendrickson, rev. 1990), 11–13; Ben Witherington III, *The Acts of the Apostles: A Socio-Rhetorical Commentary* (Grand Rapids and Cambridge: Eerdmans; Carlisle: Paternoster, 1998), 62.

[17] John A. T. Robinson, *Redating the New Testament* (Philadelphia: Westminster; London: SCM, 1976), 86–117.

AUDIENCE

Both the Gospels themselves and early church tradition typically give us the least information about the introductory topic of the audience to which each of the Gospels and Acts was addressed. In the opening verse of both of his works, Luke refers to *Theophilus,* a name that means "lover of God" and that some have taken as a generic reference to Christians. Most, however, recognize this was a proper name in the ancient Greek-speaking world and *probably refers to Luke's patron for his writing project,* given the time and cost involved in researching and dictating to a scribe an enterprise as ambitious as this one. Because of the preface to the Gospel (Luke 1:1–4), it would appear that Theophilus was either a new Christian or what we would call a "seeker," whom Luke wishes to instruct further in matters of the faith so that he could believe them with greater assurance. But the early church regularly understood all of the Gospels to be *written first of all for entire Christian communities and then quickly to be circulated for the benefit of the church at large.* Speculation concerning the location of Luke's congregation has ranged from Antioch, to Ephesus, to Philippi, with little way of being certain of any identification. Because of his interest in the theme of material possessions and his portrayal in Acts of a number of comparatively wealthy early believers, *it is also plausibly suggested that he may have been writing to a slightly more well-to-do Christian community somewhere in the predominantly Gentile and Greek-speaking eastern half of the empire.* But beyond that we can say little with confidence.[18]

PURPOSES

At least three main purposes dominate Acts, perhaps to an even greater extent than they did Luke's Gospel. *The first is clearly historical.* By being the only Gospel writer to pen a sequel, Luke obviously wanted to preserve a selective record of important events in the life of the first Christian generation. Despite a handful of apparent contradictions, which will be dealt with in the commentary section, countless names, places, customs, dates, and other details appear in the book of Acts, which can be corroborated by reference to non-Christian sources, and an even greater number can be harmoniously meshed with data from the epistles to form a plausible, detailed chronology of this roughly thirty-year period. A classic example involves the precise terms Luke uses for the political rulers in various cities and provinces, terms that include *proconsul, magistrate, governor, chief, city clerk, tribune, procurator,* and *politarch.* Some of these changed, even within the first century, yet in every case Luke gets the right term matched with the right community in the right period of time, hardly likely for someone unconcerned with careful historical reporting.[19]

Indeed, the archaeological support for the Gospels pales in comparison with the amount of information available from all of the sites treated in Acts. To this day tourists travel throughout Italy, Greece, Turkey, and the eastern Mediterranean, visiting modern cities as well as ancient ruins that fit well with a host of details

---

[18] Blomberg, *Jesus and the Gospels,* 150–52.

[19] Craig L. Blomberg, *Making Sense of the New Testament: Three Crucial Questions* (Grand Rapids: Baker; Leicester: IVP, 2004), 50–53.

in Luke's second volume. Over a hundred years ago, the British archaeologist Sir William Ramsay set out to disprove the historicity of Acts but, after extensive work, particularly in Turkey, became convinced of the book's reliability and converted to Christianity. His works still contain a wealth of valuable information,[20] but they must be supplemented by Colin Hemer's magisterial work *The Book of Acts in the Setting of Hellenistic History,* which contains the most extensive compendium of historical information by which one can evaluate the historicity of Acts.[21] Hemer comes to a most favorable verdict indeed. Also crucial in understanding the historical background more generally to virtually every location, development, and custom treated in Acts is the five-volume collection edited by Bruce Winter entitled *The Book of Acts in Its First-Century Setting.*[22]

However, even more fundamental than history to Luke's purposes were his theological motives. Luke is narrating not secular history but salvation history (Germ. *Heilsgeschichte*)—God's plan of redemption—as it unfolds during this key juncture between his old and new covenants. Thus God, especially through his Holy Spirit, appears as the primary agent who causes the events of the book to unfold. Particularly prominent is the geographical progress of the gospel as new churches are planted. Evangelistic efforts are highlighted, far more than the necessary subsequent work of "follow-up."[23] While the point has been exaggerated, it is fair to observe that Luke recognizes the end may not come immediately. Indeed, he may have been the first Christian (or at least the first Christian writer) to suspect that the church might continue long enough for such a theological history as his to prove valuable.[24]

The definitive recent survey of the major theological themes in Acts is edited by David Peterson and I. Howard Marshall.[25] A comprehensive evangelical compendium of studies of the theology of Acts, it includes contributions on topics such as the plan of God, Scripture and the realization of God's purposes, salvation history and eschatology, God as Savior, the need for salvation, salvation and health, the role of the apostles, mission and witness, the progress of the word, opposition and persecution, the preaching of Peter, the speech of Stephen, the preaching and defense of Paul, the spirit of prophecy, the new people of God, the worship of the new community, the Christian and the Law of Moses, mission practice and theology under construction, Israel and the Gentile mission, reciprocity and ethics, along with other more general or methodological essays.

Not exactly a theme but still centrally related to Luke's theological purpose is his apparent apologetic motive—defending the faith against critiques of various kinds.

---

[20] See esp. William M. Ramsay, *St. Paul the Traveller and Roman Citizen,* rev. Mark Wilson (London: Angus Hudson; Grand Rapids: Kregel, 2001 [orig. 1895]).

[21] Ed. Conrad H. Gempf (Tübingen: Mohr, 1989).

[22] In five volumes (Grand Rapids: Eerdmans; Carlisle; Paternoster, 1993–96). Cf. also Ben Witherington III, ed. *History, Literature and Society in the Book of Acts* (Cambridge and New York: CUP, 1996).

[23] See esp. Michael Green, *Evangelism in the Early Church* (Grand Rapids and Cambridge: Eerdmans, rev. 2004).

[24] See. esp. Daniel Marguerat, *The First Christian Historian: Writing the "Acts of the Apostles"* (Cambridge and New York: CUP, 2002).

[25] *Witness to the Gospel: The Theology of Acts* (Grand Rapids and Cambridge: Eerdmans, 1998).

If it is not merely Theophilus whom Luke wants to know the truth of the gospel with certainty (Luke 1:4) but all believers in the communities that will receive his writing, then Luke may well recognize that competing apocryphal traditions about characters and events in the first Christian generation had begun to circulate, if not yet in writing then at least by word of mouth. Even more probable is that there were external charges by both Jews and Romans that merited a Christian response. In various ways both groups thought that Christians were breaking their laws. Luke takes pains throughout the Acts to show that this is not the case. Luke may also be defending the faith to Gentiles, inside or outside the church, who began to wonder why this originally Jewish sect was becoming predominantly Gentile, with most Jews rejecting Christianity within thirty years of its inception. Luke thus shows how it is the natural and necessary outgrowth of Judaism and how it is the unbelieving Jews, rather than Christian believers, who have deviated from God's will.[26]

A third purpose, while no doubt subordinate to historical and theological interests, appears to be literary. Luke writes many of his stories in an artistic and adventurous manner. Who can read the account of the storm and shipwreck of Paul, in chapter 27, without feeling the suspense at numerous points? Who cannot help but chuckle at those praying in John Mark's home, in chapter 12, who refuse to believe that their prayers have been answered and Peter has been released from prison, even when the servant girl Rhoda tells them he is standing on their doorstep? Who cannot marvel at the great swings of superstition by the pagans in Lystra (chapter 14) or on the island of Malta (chapter 27), who at one moment think Paul is divine and at the next a condemned criminal? Luke repeats the stories that prove central for him, narrates speeches and episodes at greater length depending on their importance, uses the literary device of foreshadowing (e.g., with Saul's role at the stoning of Stephen), and, in general, seems to delight in recounting the works of God in his world with some aesthetic skill.[27]

A particularly controversial aspect of Luke's style of writing involves speeches or sermons attributed to various individuals. Thucydides, the ancient Greek historian, has often been quoted for explaining how he tried to acquire reliable sources when attributing speeches to his characters, but also conceded that he was not always able to do so. In such instances, he freely composed words he believed were likely to reflect the kind of thing most probably said on a given occasion (*Peloponnesian War* 1.22.1–2). Scholars of Acts have often cited one or the other of these two prongs of Thucydides's comments as accounting for the speeches in Acts.[28] Without a doubt the messages, like Jesus' teaching in the Gospels, were often drastically abbreviated. In keeping with completely acceptable historical and literary practice of the day, Luke would have felt free to put in his own words his understanding of the heart or

---

[26] Paul W. Walaskay, *"And So We Came to Rome": The Political Perspective of St. Luke* (Cambridge and New York: CUP, 1983).

[27] Cf. Richard I. Pervo, *Profit with Delight: The Literary Genre of the Acts of the Apostles* (Philadelphia: Fortress, 1987); with Leland Ryken, *Words of Life: A Literary Introduction to the New Testament* (Grand Rapids: Baker, 1987), 77–87. See also John Goldingay, "Are They Comic Acts?" *EQ* 69 (1997): 99–107.

[28] Stanley E. Porter, "Thucydides 1.22.1 and Speeches in Acts: Is There a Thucydidean View?" *NovT* 32 (1990): 121–42.

essence of what a given speaker uttered. That Luke regularly relied on eyewitness reports, trustworthy oral tradition, and shorter written sources for composing his Gospel makes it *prima facie* probable that he did so for the book of Acts as well.

The Roman historian Livy, for example, somewhat different from Thucydides, averred that he consistently relied on sources that he inherited, while Polybius censured those who fabricated history. At the same time, there are occasional written or oral addresses in Acts where it seems unlikely any Christian could have had access to them. A classic example is the letter from the commander Claudius Lysias to the governor Felix in 23:26–30, and Luke may even give hints on such occasions that he is recording information less literally (see below, pp. 70–71). But overall we have no reason to doubt the general accuracy of the speeches of Acts.[29]

LITERARY GENRE

"The ancient title *Praxeis* was a term designating a specific Greek literary form, a narrative account of the heroic deeds of famous historical or mythological figures."[30] Clearly Luke believes his characters to be historical. More specialized designations in recent studies devoted to the genre of Acts point out significant parallels between Luke's second volume and the "short historical monograph," "ancient intellectual biography," "apologetic historiography," and "biblical [i.e., Old Testament] history," while also recognizing that, as in the Gospels, the end product of Acts is a unique mixture of genres.[31] As the second volume in Luke's two-part work, Acts raises expectations of closely resembling the Gospels in genre. Yet because the focus is no longer on the one, central character of Jesus but on several early Christian leaders and the emerging church that they guided, the label need not be identical. If the Gospels are best described as theological biographies, then perhaps Acts is best described as a *theological history*.[32] And, as noted above, this does not exclude the fact that Luke writes in a very artistic and aesthetically pleasing fashion as well. Like the ancient historian Ephorus, Luke organizes a series of historical subjects along geographical lines,[33] while rhetorically Luke blends elements of the style of the Septuagint with characteristics of Greco-Roman orators.[34]

STRUCTURE

Of the many different outlines proposed for Acts, four take account of significant features in the text that must inform any proposal concerning the book's structure. *First, Acts 1:8* has regularly been seen as a programmatic statement of the book's outline. Here Jesus prophesies that *the disciples will be his witnesses, beginning in Jerusalem, moving out to Judea and Samaria and ultimately reaching the ends of*

---

[29] F. F. Bruce, *The Speeches in the Acts of the Apostles* (London: Tyndale, 1943) is still valuable, to be supplemented esp. by Conrad Gempf, "Public Speaking and Published Accounts," in *The Book of Acts in Its Ancient Literary Setting*, 259–303.

[30] Joseph A. Fitzmyer, *The Acts of the Apostles* (New York and London: Doubleday, 1998), 47.

[31] For these, along with less likely proposals, see the survey in Todd Penner, "Madness in the Method? The Acts of the Apostles in Current Study," *CBR* 2 (2004): 233–41.

[32] Craig L. Blomberg, "The Diversity of Literary Genres in the New Testament," in *Interpreting the New Testament*, eds. David A. Black and David S. Dockery (Nashville: Broadman & Holman, rev. 2001), 277–79.

[33] Witherington, *Acts*, 35.

[34] Howard C. Kee, *To Every Nation under Heaven: The Acts of the Apostles* (Harrisburg: Trinity, 1997), 20.

the earth. The three stages of chapters 1–7, 8–12, and 13–28 roughly correspond to this three-part outline. There is no question that topically Luke's progression of thought shows the fledgling Christian movement spreading ever further afield from its origins in Israel.

Second, chapters 1–12 and 13–28 broadly correspond to each other in that the Christian mission still operates predominantly in Jewish circles with Peter as the main character in the first "half" of the volume while with Paul in the second "half" the ministry turns predominantly to the Gentile world. More intriguingly, numerous specific parallels appear between the ministries of Peter and Paul. Both preach sermons replete with scriptural quotations fulfilled in Jesus. Both experience miraculous releases from prison. Both heal the sick and raise the dead. Both push the boundaries of Judaism by increasingly promoting a law-free gospel. Both are concerned for the poor and organize collections to meet their needs, and so on. There are also parallels between the ministries of one or both of these men and Jesus himself, as depicted in Luke's Gospel, a few of which include very precisely similar details (see e.g., below on Acts 9:32–43 or 19:21).[35]

Third, and helping to divide the book into shorter segments, *Luke records six summary statements,* all describing succinctly how the word of God grew and spread, the church was blessed and multiplied in numbers, and similar sentiments. Each of these appears at the end of a "panel" of texts that is reasonably homogeneous, geographically speaking—6:7; 9:31; 12:24; 16:5; 19:20; and 28:31.[36] Combining the insights of all three of these approaches leads to an outline as follows:

I. The Christian Mission to the Jews (1:1–12:24)
   A. The Church in Jerusalem (1:1–6:7)
   B. The Church in Judea, Galilee, and Samaria (6:8–9:31)
   C. Advances in Palestine and Syria (9:32–12:24)
II. The Christian Mission to the Gentiles (12:25–28:31)
   A. Paul's First Missionary Journey and the Apostolic Council (12:25–16:5)
   B. Paul's Second and Third Missionary Journeys (16:6–19:20)
   C. Paul's Final Travels to Jerusalem and to Rome (19:21–28:31)

In addition, it would appear that Luke and Acts together are arranged as an extended chiasm. The Gospel of Luke begins by setting the birth of Jesus in the context of world history and Roman rule. It proceeds to describe the adult Jesus exclusively in Galilee, moves him into Samaria and Judea through the large central section on travel narrative, and culminates with Jesus in Jerusalem. Only Luke among the Gospel writers limits the resurrection appearances to those that took place in Jerusalem and briefly refers to the ascension. Acts then summarizes the resurrection appearances and unpacks the ascension before describing the church moving out through Jerusalem, Judea and Samaria, and throughout the Gentile world, with the

---

[35] See esp. Andrew C. Clark, *Parallel Lives: The Relation of Paul to the Apostles in Lucan Perspective* (Carlisle: Paternoster, 2001); cf. Charles H. Talbert, *Reading Acts* (New York: Crossroad, 1997).

[36] Cf. Richard N. Longenecker, "Acts," in *The Expositor's Bible Commentary,* ed. Frank E. Gaebelein, vol. 9 (Grand Rapids: Zondervan, 1981), 244–47.

narrative ending with the preaching of the gospel by Paul extending as far as Rome.[37] The only sections that do not immediately seem to match are Jesus in Galilee paired with the church in the Gentile world, until we remember that from Isaiah's day onward Galilee was often known as "Galilee of the Gentiles" (cf. Isa. 9:1; Matt. 4:15) and that it contained a sizable Gentile population in the first century as well.[38]

TEXTUAL CRITICISM

Textual critics of the New Testament typically identify four major groupings of manuscripts that tend to follow recognizable patterns and are designated according to the parts of the Roman Empire in which they predominated. These four text types are the Alexandrian, the Caesarean, the Byzantine, and the Western. As its name suggests, the Western text particularly reflects manuscripts associated with Italy, including the earliest translations of the New Testament into Latin. The primary Greek uncial manuscript (from the earliest era in which writing was done entirely with capital letters) is Codex Bezae (often abbreviated simply as D and dating from the fifth century). While other parts of the New Testament remain less altered in Codex Bezae, *the Western text of Acts is about 10 percent longer than the other text types on which our various modern language translations are based.* It is possible that scribal notes originally written in the margins of texts were later copied into the narrative of Acts itself. What is particularly intriguing about the Western text in Acts is that a number of these insertions appear to give additional historical information, even if they do not reflect what Luke originally wrote. Perhaps the most famous of these appears in 19:9 (see below, p. 63). But an evangelical doctrine of Scripture relies only on what most likely appeared in the original copies of individual books, so we will not spend any additional time on this textual issue here.[39]

SOURCES

As already noted, it is probable that Luke used a variety of sources in compiling the book of Acts. Among recent writers, Fitzmyer has as elaborate a set of proposals as any.[40] Antioch is often assumed to be a place where a sizable amount of information could have been acquired, given its role as Paul's "home base" and a meeting point for various other apostles. When Luke accompanied Paul to Jerusalem at the end of his third missionary journey, he would have had even greater opportunity to interview eyewitnesses of the historical Jesus and of the early Christian movement, as well as to consult whatever shorter documents might have been produced covering events for which he was not personally present. With the Gospel of Luke we may

---

[37] Intriguingly, this outline could be correlated with Bruce Longenecker's ("Lukan Aversion to Humps and Hollows: The Case of Acts 11.27–12.25," *NTS* 50 [2004]: 185–204), which finds four interlocking "chain-links" as keys to Luke's structure, generating an outline of 1:1–8:3 (the church in Jerusalem); 8:4–12:25 (the persecution and spread of Christianity); 13:1–19:41(Paul's missionary journeys); and 20:1–28:31 (the series of events that take Paul from Jerusalem to Rome).

[38] Blomberg, *Jesus and the Gospels,* 142–44; and Kenneth Wolfe, "The Chiastic Structure of Luke-Acts and Some Implications for Worship," *SWJT* 22 (1980): 60–71.

[39] For details see Eldon J. Epp, *The Theological Tendency of Codex Bezae Cantabrigiensis in Acts* (Cambridge and New York: CUP, 1966); and W. A. Strange, *The Problem of the Text of Acts* (Cambridge and New York: CUP, 1992).

[40] Fitzmyer, *Acts,* 80–88.

develop some reasonable hypotheses because we have other Gospels with which to compare. Thus most scholars believe Luke relied in part on Mark, on a collection of Jesus' sayings (called Q—the largely didactic material that Matthew and Luke have in common not found in Mark), and possibly a shorter source accounting for some or all of Luke's distinctive material (L). But without parallel accounts of Acts, the source-critical enterprise proves far more subjective. Short of some new spectacular discoveries in the Middle East, *we probably never will be able to delineate the sources of Acts with any high degree of confidence.*[41]

CHRONOLOGY[42]

The most certain date in the book of Acts comes in 18:12, when Paul appears before Gallio in Corinth. From a stone inscription at Delphi, it appears that Gallio was proconsul there only from July of 51 to July of 52. The famine of Acts 11:27–30, according to Josephus, was actually a series of local famines that spanned 44–46, though its effect continued on for perhaps another two years. Acts 12:25–14:28 suggests that Paul's first missionary journey followed relatively soon after Paul's and Barnabas's return from Jerusalem to deliver famine relief for the poor.

In Galatians 1:18 and 2:1, Paul describes intervals of three and fourteen years, respectively, between his conversion and first two trips to Jerusalem. These trips seem most likely to correspond to Acts 9:28 and 11:30 (for more detailed defense see our treatment of Galatians below). The next step is to identify the specific dates for these two visits. Even if Paul's famine relief mission in 11:30 were as late as 47, this would push his conversion back to A.D. 30, a full seventeen years earlier, which is the most probable year of Christ's crucifixion. This would not seem to allow enough time for the events of Acts 1–8 in between the crucifixion and Paul's conversion and would not work at all if Christ's death were in A.D. 33, the next most common choice. As a result, some think that the three and fourteen years of Galatians 1:18 and 2:1 are to be taken as overlapping; that is, both are to be dated from Paul's conversion so that the total period of time from his becoming a Christian to his second trip to Jerusalem was only 14 years. This would allow for Paul's conversion to be as late as 33, but this does not seem to be as natural a meaning of the grammar of Galatians.

A better solution is to realize that ancient dating often employed "inclusive reckoning," with both first and last years of a period of time counted. Thus the "seventeen" years from Paul's conversion to his famine relief visit could have been as little as fifteen and a fraction years. This could place Paul's conversion shortly following Stephen's martyrdom in about A.D. 32, with his famine relief visit in 47. Paul's first trip to Jerusalem would then have been in 35 (32 plus the 3 years of Gal. 1:18).

Robert Jewett has vigorously argued that this time line is impossible and that the full historicity of the chronology of Acts cannot be salvaged. Jewett observes that Aretas IV was not given control over Damascus until 37, but he is the king from

---

[41] Cf. further Lewis R. Donelson, "Cult Histories and the Sources of Acts," *Bib* 68 (1987): 1–21; Justin Taylor, "The Making of Acts: A New Account," *RB* 97 (1990): 504–24.

[42] For full details, cf. esp. Rainer Riesner, *Paul's Early Period: Chronology, Mission Strategy, Theology* (Grand Rapids and Cambridge: Eerdmans, 1998). Documentation for select references in specific ancient sources appears in the appropriate places in our commentary below.

FIXED POINTS IN THE CHRONOLOGY OF ACTS

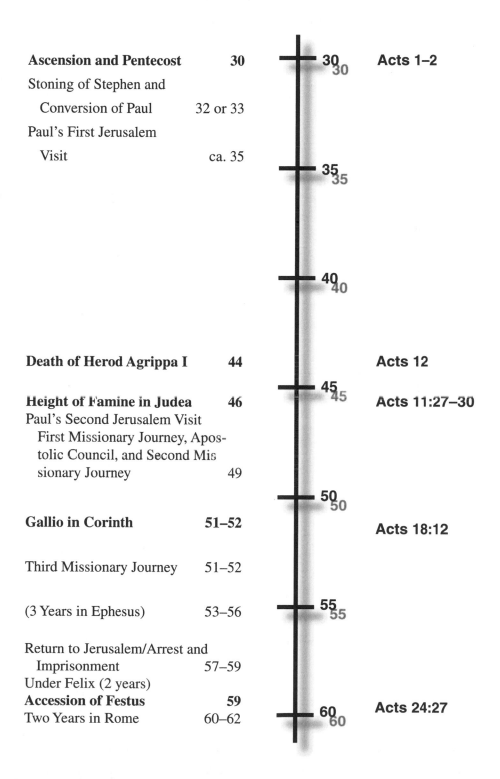

Ascension and Pentecost	**30**	**30** — Acts 1–2
Stoning of Stephen and		
Conversion of Paul	32 or 33	
Paul's First Jerusalem		
Visit	ca. 35	**35**
		40
Death of Herod Agrippa I	**44**	**Acts 12**
Height of Famine in Judea	**46**	**Acts 11:27–30**
Paul's Second Jerusalem Visit		
First Missionary Journey, Apostolic Council, and Second Missionary Journey	49	
		50
Gallio in Corinth	**51–52**	**Acts 18:12**
Third Missionary Journey	51–52	
(3 Years in Ephesus)	53–56	**55**
Return to Jerusalem/Arrest and Imprisonment	57–59	
Under Felix (2 years)		
Accession of Festus	**59**	**Acts 24:27**
Two Years in Rome	60–62	**60**

whom Paul fled before his first visit to Jerusalem (2 Cor. 11:32–33), which we are dating to 35.[43] On the other hand, we do not even know for sure that Aretas was given much control even in 37. It is merely a hypothesis since Caligula's reign as emperor began in 37 and he frequently gave client kings more extended powers than emperors usually bestowed. It seems better, therefore, to follow F. F. Bruce, who suggests that Aretas's influence was more unofficial, allowing for the earlier date. No Scripture actually gives him an official title as ruler in Damascus; Paul merely states that he fled from Aretas.[44]

Herod Agrippa I's death, described in Acts 12:19b–25, is dated by Josephus to 44. This makes the events of Acts 12 occur before those at the end of Acts 11, but this is no problem because Luke does not link the chapters chronologically. Chapter 12:1 reads merely "about this time" in the Greek, and in his Gospel Luke often arranges events in topical rather than chronological order. Here the topical link would be the common theme of events related to Antioch throughout 11:19–30. An early church tradition claims Peter stayed twelve years in Jerusalem after the crucifixion (*Acts of Peter* 5:22), which would mean that his imprisonment, miraculous release, and departure from the city, also narrated in Acts 12, happened in 42.

Paul's first missionary journey, the Apostolic Council, and his second journey up to his arrival in Corinth must then all be dated between 47 and 52. Since Paul was in Corinth at least a year and a half (18:11), apparently mostly all before his appearance before Gallio, he probably arrived in town already in late 50. The most common date for the Apostolic Council, therefore, is 49, but it could have been as much as a full year earlier. Paul's shorter, first missionary journey could have occurred in either or both of the years 48 and 49. Paul's third journey gives the impression of brief visits in cities previously evangelized, with the only extensive stop being his nearly three-year period in Ephesus (20:31). So these years would most likely be 52–55, or possibly 53–56.

The next fairly well established date involves the accession of Festus to the procuratorship in Judea. Based on a comparison of several passages in Eusebius and other early Christian writers, it would seem that Felix ruled from 52 to 59, though some dispute one or both of these dates. If accurate, the chronology would place Paul's arrest in Jerusalem in 57 since he spent two years in prison under Felix (24:27). This would allow up to a year or more for the rest of Paul's third missionary journey, a reasonable length of time, in which he revisited cities evangelized on the second missionary journey and then returned home to Jerusalem. Paul's hearings before Festus and Agrippa seem to have come soon after Festus's accession, with Paul's appeal to Caesar immediately thereafter. So the trip to Rome probably began in the fall of 59, with the arrival of the shipwrecked passengers who had wintered on the

---

[43] Robert Jewett, *Dating Paul's Life* (London: SCM, [= *A Chronology of Paul's Life* (Philadelphia: Fortress)] 1979), 30–33.

[44] F. F. Bruce, *Paul: Apostle of the Heart Set Free* (Grand Rapids: Eerdmans, 1977), 76–82, 475.

island of Malta, in the spring of 60. Paul's two years of house arrest in Rome (28:30) would then span 60–62.[45]

QUESTIONS FOR REVIEW

1. What are the unique features of the book of Acts, and what is their significance?
2. What are the arguments for and against Luke being the author of Acts?
3. What are the arguments for and against a date for Acts before A.D. 70?
4. What can we reasonably suggest about the audience of Acts?
5. What is the probable genre of Acts and its significance?
6. What appear to be the three main purposes of Acts, and how does each affect our interpretation of the book?
7. What textual clues enable us to propose various structures for Acts?
8. What unique features surround the study of the text and sources for Acts?
9. What are the most secure dates for various events within the book of Acts, and how do they help us arrive at other key dates for other events?

COMMENTARY

THE CHRISTIAN MISSION TO THE JEWS (1:1–12:24)

The Church in Jerusalem (1:1–6:7)   *Preface (1:1–5)*   The book of Acts begins with a preface very similar to the opening of the Gospel of Luke. Luke addresses the same patron, Theophilus, and refers back to his prior work in 1:1. Speaking of "all that Jesus began to do and to teach" suggests that this second volume reflects what Jesus is continuing to do and teach in the church through the Holy Spirit. Only here, in all of the New Testament, do we learn about *the forty-day period of time of Jesus' resurrection appearances* (vv. 2–5). At least three reasons for their inclusion may be discerned. First, they have *an apologetic value* in demonstrating repeatedly that Christ was truly alive in bodily form.[46] Second, they have *didactic or instructional value* because Jesus used this time to teach the disciples how all representative portions of the Old Testament were fulfilled in him (see Luke 24:25–27). Much early Christian preaching may have derived from what the apostles learned during this period of time. Third, the appearances have *predictive value,* outlining God's program for the coming ministry of the Holy Spirit.

The disciples must not begin their ministry immediately but wait for what John the Baptist had promised—*the baptism of the Holy Spirit.* This expression is used in many different ways in contemporary churches, but, if we are to remain faithful to the biblical use of the terminology, we will reserve it for the initial experience of the Spirit in a person's life. Of the other six uses of this phrase in the New Testament,

---

[45] Virtually all of these dates are tentative. Many scholars agree on the general outline, but vary the less secure dates a year or two in one direction or the other. A variety of more radical revisions has also been proposed from time to time, but none has commanded widespread support.

[46] The expression translated "convincing proofs" was, in fact, a technical term in Greek historiography. See David L. Mealand, "The Phrase 'Many Proofs' in Acts 1,3 and in Hellenistic Writers," *ZNW* 80 (1989): 134–35.

five of them (like this one) refer to John the Baptist's prediction of the role of the Spirit in the ministry of the coming Messiah. They thus refer to *Jesus' followers' first immersion into the power of the Spirit,* not to any subsequent "second blessing," significant and genuine as such an experience may be for various believers. The only other use of the "baptism of the Spirit" comes in 1 Corinthians 12:13, in which Paul speaks of everyone in the church having had this experience, presumably including the most immature of Christians. This again suggests that the expression refers to the time of one's conversion.[47]

Ascension (1:6–11)   The second introductory section of Acts narrates Christ's ascension (vv. 6–11). The disciples appear still to be looking for their Messiah to reign over an earthly kingdom of Israel (v. 6). Jesus does not deny that one day he might function in this capacity, but that time is not now. Instead, when the Spirit comes upon the disciples, they must fulfill the Great Commission (vv. 7–8; cf. Matt. 28:18–20). This passage provides a key warning against all supposed prophecy in any age that claims to know the time of Christ's return. The terms "times or dates" represent two of the most general words for periods of time in the Greek language (*chronos* and *kairos*) and do not permit us to claim to know even the generation in which Jesus will come back. Verse 8 forms a miniature outline of the rest of the book and the progress of the gospel that Luke will record. It has inspired Christians throughout the ages to begin evangelism at home and then move outward in ever widening circles.[48]

In verses 9–11, Jesus is taken up to heaven. This does not prove that heaven is a place up in the sky somewhere but rather indicates to the disciples that *the resurrection appearances have ended.* As the angels explain, the ascension also indicates the way in which Jesus will come back one day—publicly, visibly, on the clouds of heaven (cf. Matt. 24:24–27; Mark 14:62). For Jesus himself the ascension implies the *completion of his work of salvation* as he now returns to his heavenly Father.[49]

Waiting for the Holy Spirit (1:12–26)   The rest of chapter 1 describes the disciples waiting for the Spirit's coming. Verses 12–14 show them obeying verse 4 and highlight their unity.[50] Verse 15 gives us their number; interestingly, 120 people constituted a legitimate, separate community in Judaism.[51] Continuing to pray rather than to act precipitously, Peter leads the gathering in selecting a replacement for Judas. Verses 18–19 explain how Judas had taken his own life. Matthew 27:3–10 seems to give a quite different account of his death, but the two can be harmonized. The rope on the tree from which he hanged himself could have broken and the corpse fallen upon a rock, while the priests' purchase may have been reckoned as his by their agency.[52]

---

[47] See esp. James D. G. Dunn, *Baptism in the Holy Spirit* (London: SCM; Philadelphia: Westminster, 1970).

[48] E. Earle Ellis, "'The End of the Earth' (Acts 1:8)," *BBR* 1 (1991): 123–32.

[49] Cf. further John F. Maile, "The Ascension in Luke-Acts," *TynB* 37 (1986): 29–59.

[50] Indeed, a distinctive word throughout the early chapters of Acts is *homothumadon* ("with one accord"—KJV). See 1:14, 2:46, 4:24, 5:12, 7:57, 8:6, etc.

[51] *m. Sanhedrin* 1:6.

[52] I. Howard Marshall, *The Acts of the Apostles* (Leicester: IVP; Grand Rapids: Eerdmans, 1980), 65.

More importantly, Peter sees two key Psalms attributed to David, in which he contends against an archenemy (69:25, 109:8), as typologically in need of fulfillment in the first century as well (vv. 16–17, 20). Thus the group must choose a successor to Judas. While this passage became a prooftext for the doctrine of apostolic succession in the early church, nowhere else does the Bible ever describe one of the Twelve being replaced. Specifically, when James, the brother of John, is martyred (Acts 12:2), Luke gives no indication that anyone sought to fill his office. *It is apparently important for the leadership of the fledgling church to number twelve at the outset, to symbolize the church as the true Israel but not throughout its history.* At the beginning, in its entirely Jewish phase, the church has become the new or true Israel.[53]

The criteria for choosing the replacement also prove telling (vv. 21–22). The new apostle must have been a part of Jesus' larger group of followers, from the days of the ministry of John the Baptist onward, and a witness of the resurrection. Clearly, according to this definition of *apostle,* such an office could have existed only in the first century. On the other hand, Paul will use the word in his lists of spiritual gifts as one of the ways God endows his people in every age (see below, p. 190). The manner of choosing between the top two candidates is even more fascinating (vv. 23–26). As often in Old Testament times, the disciples cast lots, somewhat akin to our rolling of dice. Does this mean that believers today should use such a method in determining God's will? Probably not. The method is never used again in the New Testament, and "the coming of the Spirit soon gave the church a more certain guide to God's will."[54] At the same time, nothing in Luke's narrative suggests that the disciples employed a faulty approach on this occasion. While it is sometimes argued that we never hear of Matthias again and that Paul was God's "real twelfth" apostle, this overlooks the fact that, apart from Peter and John, we never hear from *any* of the other apostles again in the book of Acts.[55]

Pentecost (2:1–41)   Acts 2 introduces us to a momentous event, the significance of which can scarcely be overestimated. *Pentecost completes the sequence of events that began with Christ's death, included his resurrection and ascension, and now provides the opportunity for God to bestow his Spirit upon all his people.* In the Old Testament the Holy Spirit came upon certain Israelites temporarily for special acts of power and service; now he will permanently live within all believers. The occasion is a harvest festival celebrated fifty days after the Passover (Lev. 23:15–22). Already during the period between the Testaments, Jews had decided this festival marked the time of the giving of the law on Mount Sinai (*Jub.* 1:1). It was fitting, then, that just as the first covenant was established with signs and wonders, so too the new covenant would be heralded with dramatic events. Moreover, though God confused the languages of earth's inhabitants at the tower of Babel (Gen. 11), here he begins to undo that confusion.

---

[53] In detail, cf. Arie Zwiep, *Judas and the Choice of Matthias: A Study in Context and Concern of Acts 1:15–26* (Tübingen: Mohr Siebeck, 2004).

[54] Williams, *Acts,* 35.

[55] William J. Larkin Jr., *Acts* (Leicester and Downers Grove: IVP, 1995), 47.

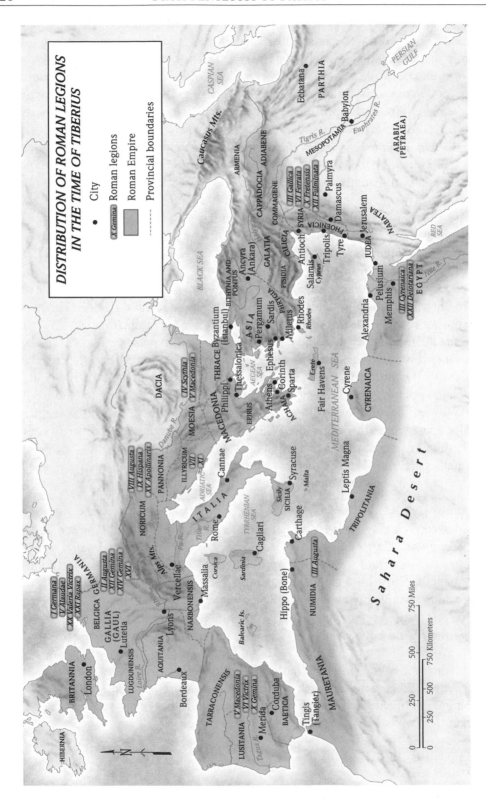

DISTRIBUTION OF ROMAN LEGIONS
IN THE TIME OF TIBERIUS

• City
X Gemina Roman legions
Roman Empire
Provincial boundaries

It is unclear what literally happened as the Spirit descended on the disciples (vv. 1–4). Luke uses similes to explain that there came a sound "like" rushing *wind* (the same word as for *spirit* in Hebrew and Greek) and tongues "as" of *fire* (the sign of divine judgment in the Old Testament). Miraculously, all of the Jewish visitors from other parts of the empire whose indigenous languages would have been other than Greek could now hear the apostles speaking in those tongues (vv. 5–12).[56] This miracle was hardly necessary to enable communication because all the people knew enough Greek to speak with one another and make sense of the festivities in the first place. Moreover, Peter subsequently addresses the crowd, explaining the phenomenon they have just experienced, and he speaks in Greek at that time as well. Rather, the miracle offers a dramatic confirmation of the divine origin and truth of the disciples' message. Here, too, Luke introduces the expression, being "filled with the Spirit," which for him is different from the baptism of the Spirit. *Whereas a person is baptized only once, at conversion, he or she may be filled repeatedly, that is, empowered for bold witness or other divine service* (e.g., Luke 1:15, 41, 67; Acts 2:4; 4:8, 31; 9:17; 13:9).[57]

Peter's first sermon (vv. 14–41) proceeds to interpret this first example of speaking in tongues in light of the prophecy of Joel 2:28–32. But what in the Old Testament came merely "afterward" (Joel 2:28) is now occurring explicitly "in the last days" (Acts 2:17). The New Testament consistently affirms that the last days or end-times began with Christ's first coming. The pouring out of God's Spirit, in turn, leads to his bestowing gifts upon his people (vv. 17–18). The cosmic signs that Joel foretold (vv. 19–20) can be taken somewhat figuratively and seen as fulfilled in the crucifixion (recall the eclipse of the sun in Luke 23:45) or understood as something that has not yet taken place.[58] In any event, Luke wants to quote Joel as far as the final promise that "everyone who calls on the name of the Lord will be saved" (v. 21). Here appears the first hint in Acts that the disciples understand that the gospel will eventually go to Gentiles as well. Verses 22–36 form the heart of Peter's message on this occasion and proceed according to the following logic. If the last days have come, then the Messiah must have appeared. He did; he was Jesus (vv. 22–24). The evidence is then marshaled from the Hebrew Scriptures. Psalm 16:8–11 (vv. 25–28) seems to suggest that David was speaking of himself, but clearly he was not immortal. Knowing that God had promised to establish his descendants on the Jewish throne forever (2 Sam. 7:12–16), David prophesied about the coming Messiah, believing that death could not ultimately bind him (see esp. v. 31).[59] As for Psalm 110:1 (vv. 34–35), Jesus himself had already interpreted this text as referring to his messianic role (Mark 12:35–37 pars.). Thus Peter's conclusion follows inexorably—God has

---

[56] "The specific regions catalogued in 2:9–11 form a box around Judea and Jerusalem, suggesting a broad sampling of peoples from the four corners of the earth" (F. Scott Spencer, *Journeying through Acts: A Literary-Cultural Reading* [Peabody: Hendrickson, rev. 2004], 44 [with chart]).

[57] On these and other ministries of the Spirit in Luke and Acts, see the various writings of Max Turner, esp. *Power from on High: The Spirit in Israel's Restoration and Witness in Luke-Acts* (Sheffield: SAP, 1996).

[58] F. F. Bruce, *The Book of the Acts* (Grand Rapids: Eerdmans, rev. 1988), 61–62.

[59] For a survey of approaches to Peter's use of Psalm 16 and a defense of the view that he understood it as a direct prophecy of the coming Messiah, see Gregory V. Trull, "Views on Peter's Use of Psalm 16:8–11 in Acts 2:25–32," *BSac* 161 (2004): 194–214, 432–48.

indeed raised Jesus, elevating him to the same exalted position in heaven that he had previously occupied, thus justifying the title "Lord" as well as "Christ" (Messiah) (v. 36).[60]

The response to Peter's sermon proves powerful, leading him to give what may be considered the first "altar call" in the history of Christian preaching (vv. 37–41). *Peter specifies two things his listeners must do (repent and be baptized) and makes two promises concerning what they will receive (forgiveness and the gift of the Holy Spirit). We may speak of these four elements as the Pentecostal package because they are considered as a unit, here and throughout most of the New Testament.* There will be three apparent exceptions in the book of Acts, which we will deal with when we come to them. Meanwhile, we need to define our terms. Repentance, as consistently in Scripture, means not just sorrow for sin but a noticeable change of behavior. Water baptism, well-known to Jews already from their practice of baptizing converts to Judaism as well as from the ministry of John the Baptist, was an outward sign and testimony to the inward change that God had begun in the person.[61] That such baptism was to be administered in the name of Jesus Christ does not contradict the Great Commission, in which a trinitarian formula appears (Matt. 28:19). Rather, it shows that there was no fixed formula for the words that had to be recited at a person's baptism this early in the history of the church.

At first glance it could appear that Peter is requiring water baptism for the forgiveness of sins, but this would contradict numerous texts that speak of salvation by God's grace alone. Even in chapter 3, in his very next sermon, Peter speaks of repentance without requiring baptism (v. 19). Probably, verse 38 forms a chiasm (A. B. B. A.), in which repentance is linked with forgiveness and baptism with the name of Jesus.[62] "The gift of the Holy Spirit" does not refer to a specific spiritual gift, as in Paul's lists of charisms (teaching, prophecy, giving, etc.). Instead it employs an appositional genitive—the gift "which is" the Spirit himself. As in verse 22, Peter again stresses that his offer is for everyone—"for you and your children" (v. 39)— both the current Jewish generation and their offspring—as well as to "all who are far off"—presumably implying Gentiles as well as Jews.

Communal Sharing (2:42–47)   The final paragraph of Acts 2 depicts the initial organization of those who responded to Peter's invitation and joined the 120 (vv. 42–47). Verse 42 is regularly cited as the earliest description of four central elements in Christian worship, which should characterize the church as it gathers in any time and place: *preaching or teaching God's word, fellowship, the Lord's Supper (Communion or the Eucharist) and prayer.* Fellowship is then further unpacked in verses 43–47 as far more than simply small talk over a meal! Rather, it involves communal sharing,

---

[60] "It was not that Jesus became *someone* different from who he was before, but that he entered a new stage in his career, or assumed new roles after the ascension" (Witherington, *Acts,* 149). For a balanced assessment of "Jesus as Lord in Acts and in the Gospel Message," see the article so entitled by Darrell L. Bock in *BSac* 143 (1986): 146–54.

[61] Striking corroboration for this comes from the testimony of Josephus, *Antiquities* 18.5.2.

[62] The shift from the plural form of "repent" to the singular for "be baptized" supports the idea that the two verbs are being treated differently. Cf. Luther McIntyre, "Baptism and Forgiveness in Acts 2:38," *BSac* 153 (1996): 53–62.

particularly of one's material possessions.[63] The imperfect tenses throughout these verses suggest a process of sharing, not a once-for-all, absolute renunciation of personal goods. This is not the modern system of contemporary communism, which is atheistic and coercive. The disciples pooled their resources out of love for God and one another in an entirely voluntary manner. At the same time, verse 45 does provide the foundation for the first half of Marx's famous manifesto—"to each according to his need." The other half will also appear in Acts—in 11:29 (see below, p. 46).

God's people should share with the poor and needy in their midst! Nor does this paragraph permit the interpretation that these practices were a mistake (based on the idea that the church's later poverty could have been avoided had it not given its money away). Luke, as narrator, makes clear that God approves of this scheme by concluding the passage stressing that God "added to their numbers daily those who were being saved."[64]

QUESTIONS FOR REVIEW

1. What is the significance of the resurrection and ascension narratives?
2. Which aspects of Acts 1:12–26 are normative and which are situation specific, and how can we tell?
3. What should we infer from the phenomenon of tongues at Pentecost, and what should we not infer?
4. Trace the logic of Peter's Pentecostal sermon and explain the Pentecostal "package" of 2:38. What is involved in each element of that package?
5. Which elements of Acts 2:42–47 are normative, and which are situation specific, and how can we tell?

A Healing in the Temple and Its Aftermath (3:1–4:31)   Acts 3:1–4:31 describes the first healing performed by the fledgling church, along with its aftermath. The account of the miracle itself spans 3:1–11. As at Pentecost, a remarkable incident gains a positive audience for the gospel. As when Jesus sent out the Twelve to reproduce his ministry (Matt. 10 and pars.), the apostles are enabled to reproduce his healing miracles. But they must do so "in his name," rather than commanding directly as he could. Verse 6 demonstrates the priority of spiritual over physical healing. At the same time the man's physical restoration to health enables him to work again and provide for his material needs in a better way than begging did.[65] And, as we have seen in 2:42–47, concern for one's financial state forms a key component of the early Christian communal arrangements.

---

[63] For the partially parallel arrangements in Qumran, see Brian Capper, "The Palestinian Cultural Context of the Earliest Christian Community of Goods," in *The Book of Acts in Its Palestinian Setting,* ed. Richard Bauckham (Grand Rapids: Eerdmans; Carlisle: Paternoster, 1995), 323–56.

[64] On this whole paragraph, see further Craig L. Blomberg, *Neither Poverty nor Riches: A Biblical Theology of Possessions* (Leicester and Downers Grove: IVP, 1999), 161–63.

[65] Marshall, *Acts of the Apostles,* 88. Cf., in detail, McGlory T. Speckman, "Healing and Wholeness in Luke-Acts as a Foundation for Economic Development: A Particular Reference to ὁλοκληρία in Acts 3:16," *Neot* 36 (2002): 97–109.

Peter's second sermon occupies 3:12–26. The structure closely follows the message from Pentecost and sets a pattern for Christian preaching throughout this book—a focus on Jesus, the Jewish leaders' role in his crucifixion, the resurrection and exaltation, a call to repentance, and support from the Old Testament to show all this as the fulfillment of prophecy. One key difference from Peter's previous sermon involves distinctive Christological titles not found often outside the early chapters of Acts. Thus in verse 13, Jesus is the suffering *servant* of Isaiah 52–53; in verse 14, he is the *Holy and Righteous One*. Likewise, Peter refers to him as the *author of life* (v. 15); while in verse 22, he is the *prophet* like Moses in fulfillment of Deuteronomy 18:15–18. Richard Longenecker discusses all of these titles in a work on the Christology of early Jewish Christianity, showing that these unique references support Luke's use of early, reliable tradition here.[66]

Peter's second sermon also offers additional hints that he has come to understand the disciples' mandate to go into all the world, even though he has not yet left Jerusalem. Verse 21 requires an interval of time for Christ's return to enable the mission to the Gentiles to go forward. This period of time also disproves the idea that, had the Jews uniformly responded to the gospel wholeheartedly, Jesus would have returned at once. The Great Commission was part of God's plan from the beginning, not merely a "plan B" after the Jewish leadership had rejected Jesus, as verses 19–20 by themselves have suggested to some. Ever since God had called Abraham and blessed him so that he might bless the nations, God's intention was that from Abraham's seed (and specifically, the Messiah) the word would go out to all peoples (v. 25).[67]

Not surprisingly, this same leadership, which only a few months earlier had crucified Jesus, was not going to allow this bold preaching to go on right under its nose for very long. Chapter 4, therefore, narrates the first postresurrection conflict between the disciples and the Sanhedrin. The primary opposition comes from the Sadducees, reflected in the leadership of the high priest and his family (vv. 5–6). We recall from the Gospels that certain prominent Pharisees had in fact sided with Jesus (e.g., Nicodemus; Joseph of Arimathea), and we will soon learn of another (Gamaliel). Indeed, throughout the book of Acts, whenever Christians are brought before Jewish authorities, their beliefs are described as causing an intramural debate within Judaism. The Pharisees believed in the coming resurrection of all people (Dan. 12:2), whereas the Sadducees did not (deriving binding doctrine solely from the five books of Moses). Thus throughout this book the distinctive belief of early Christianity is regularly portrayed as centering on the resurrection of Jesus (here see v. 2).

---

[66] Richard N. Longenecker, *The Christology of Early Jewish Christianity* (Naperville: Allenson; London: SCM, 1970). More broadly, Larry Hurtado (*Lord Jesus Christ* [Grand Rapids: Eerdmans, 2003]) demonstrates how a high Christology emerged at an astonishingly early date throughout the primitive church (against those who argue that it was a slow evolutionary development). On these opening chapters of Acts, see also Rainer Riesner, "Christology in the Early Jerusalem Community," *Mishkan* 24.1 (1996): 6–17.

[67] "Peter admits that God in mercy will pardon such Jews for what his Messiah has suffered, and especially that God will grant them a respite, i.e., times when they will be able to repent and convert before the end" (Fitzmyer, *Acts,* 288).

The interrogation of the disciples furnishes Peter with a third opportunity to preach publicly, in this case to the Jewish leadership (vv. 8–12). Interestingly, Luke has already described how the number of believers in Jerusalem has grown from three thousand after Pentecost to more than five thousand (v. 4). Some have used these statistics as biblical support for measuring church growth by the numbers of converts, which may or may not be a good idea in any particular context. With respect to the New Testament, however, it is worth pointing out that nowhere else are such numbers ever tallied. If there is a model to be imitated here, it is simply the bold preaching in the face of persecution and possible martyrdom that Peter and John exhibit, as they turn every opportunity to speak into a chance to point people to Jesus.

Luke's abbreviated summary of this message climaxes with the very exclusive claim of verse 12—that salvation is found in no other name. The word "name" throughout the Bible often refers to more than just a person's moniker and includes that person's power or authority. This verse, therefore, does not settle the debate over what happens to those who never hear about Jesus, but it does insist that all who are saved in any era receive salvation because of Christ's cross-work. Obviously, God's people in Old Testament times had not heard of the literal name *Jesus,* and animal sacrifices did not fully atone for their sins (see the book of Hebrews), yet they became right with God as he anticipated the complete atonement that Christ's crucifixion would accomplish.[68]

The disciples' faith and boldness in proclaiming the gospel amazes the Jewish leaders, particularly because they recognize that these are individuals without any formal education beyond the compulsory elementary-level schooling that Jewish boys received (v. 13). The two Greek words used in this verse (*agrammatos* and *idiōtēs*) have suggested to some that the disciples were actually illiterate, but in fact what they mean in this context is that Jesus' followers have not formally studied with a rabbi, beyond the age of twelve or thirteen when their schooling otherwise stopped.[69] Formal, theological instruction both then and now may enhance one's ability in ministry, but it is scarcely required for God to work powerfully through any person!

Equally significant in the response of the Sanhedrin to the disciples' bold witness is their inability to muster any successful counterarguments. Instead, the council simply forbids these preachers from continuing to proclaim their message (vv. 14–17). In turn, Peter and John provide one of the Bible's classic paradigms of civil disobedience (vv. 19–20). *Whenever human laws contradict God's laws, God's people must be prepared to break the laws of the land.*[70] In this instance, the authorities

---

[68] On the several major orthodox approaches throughout church history to the issue of those who have never heard the gospel, see John Sanders, *No Other Name: An Investigation into the Destiny of the Unevangelized* (Grand Rapids: Eerdmans, 1992).

[69] Witherington, *Acts,* 195. *Idiōtēs* elsewhere in the New Testament means "layperson." *Agrammatos,* not found elsewhere in Scripture, can in ancient Greek refer to those who can read or write but not in a cultured way, or who can read or write one language but not another. See Thomas J. Kraus, "'Uneducated,' 'Ignorant,' or Even 'Illiterate'? Aspects and Background for an Understanding of ἀγράμματοι (and ἰδιῶται) in Acts 4.13," *NTS* 45 (1999): 434, 441–42.

[70] Ajith Fernando (*Acts* [Grand Rapids: Zondervan, 1998], 221) gives a good list of criteria for how civil disobedience can be carried out in as tactful a way as possible and only as a last resort.

cannot decide how to proceed, so they release the disciples (vv. 21–22). Remarkably, the release leads the little band of Jesus' followers to praise God and pray for further boldness in testimony to characterize their ministry (vv. 23–31).[71] They continue to see Scripture fulfilled both in the opposition against them and in the inability of that opposition to prevail, citing Psalm 2:1–2 in particular (vv. 25–26).

More Communalism—Good and Bad (4:32–5:11)   In 4:32–5:11, Luke returns to the model of communal sharing.[72] Verses 32–35 provide the second summary statement of the church's activity. Verses 32 and 34 show that personal property was retained but sold as necessary. Verse 33 demonstrates that social concern or economics did not replace the preaching of the gospel; rather it made it possible or at least more effective. Luke next presents a positive model of one who sold a field and donated the proceeds to the "common pot" (vv. 36–37). His name is Joseph Barnabas; the latter name was actually his nickname, meaning "son of encouragement."[73] He will later become better known for being a great encouragement to the apostle Paul, but it is telling that it is for his financial generosity that he is first described with this label.

In contrast to Barnabas's exemplary behavior, Ananias and Sapphira provide a negative model (5:1–11). After pretending to give the entire proceeds from the sale of a piece of property when, in fact, they were holding back some of their earnings, God strikes this couple dead. The most pressing exegetical question surrounding this passage obviously is why God took such drastic action when throughout history he normally leaves far more serious sins unpunished, at least in this life. At least nine replies to this question may be offered.

(1) The verb "kept back" (from the Greek root *nosphizō*) carries the strong sense of "swindled" and occurs only one other time in the entire Greek Bible, in the story of Achan's sin in Joshua 7:1. In both cases God was establishing a covenant people, and stricter discipline may have been needed at the outset to ensure that the community survived. (2) Both Ananias and Sapphira committed their sins consciously as premeditated acts. Tellingly, Sapphira was not able to plead that she was simply submitting to or obeying her husband![74] (3) Some have argued that this couple was demon possessed, based on the language of verse 3. But "Satan has so filled your heart" is probably a Semitic idiom for "Satan has made you dare."[75] Nevertheless, the language is strong and suggests an extremely serious sin. (4) The lie was not just to the church but to the Holy Spirit, who is directly equated with God (vv. 3–4), so some kind of spiritual warfare between God and Satan seems probable. (5) The sin was not in refusing to give all of the money the couple earned but in claiming that

---

[71] Throughout Acts, "release *from* prison" is "also a release *for* proclamation" (John B. Weaver, *Plots of Epiphany: Prison-Escape in Acts of the Apostles* [Berlin and New York: de Gruyter, 2004], 286).

[72] On which, see esp. Richard J. Cassidy, *Society and Politics in the Acts of the Apostles* (Maryknoll, N. Y.: Orbis, 1987).

[73] Perhaps from the Hebrew *bar nabi*—"son of a prophet"—with the prophetic ministry of exhortation or encouragement in view here.

[74] As Ivoni Richter Reimer (*Women in the Acts of the Apostles* [Minneapolis: Fortress, 1995], 24) explains, "The husband does the action; the wife knows of it, but she does nothing to oppose this corrupt and corrupting deed." Thus "she becomes equally guilty and ultimately endangers herself as well."

[75] Bruce M. Metzger, *A Textual Commentary on the Greek New Testament* (New York and London: United Bible Societies, rev. 1994), 285.

they were doing so. (6) In fact, nothing compelled this pair to give away *any* of their money, for the process was entirely voluntary.

(7) It may even be too strong to say that God supernaturally struck them down, though of course this is possible. But it has often been suggested that they were so shocked by the confrontation and exposure of their sin that perhaps they experienced something like a heart attack. (8) Despite the tragedy these events had a powerful effect, coupled with other "signs and wonders" that enabled the church to grow even more (vv. 5, 11–12, 14). (9) Even though the two died, there is no reason to question their salvation. They are depicted as believers who lost merely their physical lives. Compare those who died after profaning the Lord's Supper in 1 Corinthians 11:29–30.

Yet even after enumerating these nine mitigating circumstances, the harshness of God's verdict remains. Perhaps the most important final comment, therefore, is simply that every situation in which God does *not* punish sin as seriously is a testimony to his marvelous grace because the wages of all sin is death (Rom. 6:23).

Further Growth and Conflict (5:12–42) The rest of chapter 5 describes further growth and conflict in the life of the church in Jerusalem. Not surprisingly, few people wanted to get too close to the apostles in light of the way that God worked through them with Ananias and Sapphira (vv. 12–13). Yet God continued to bless the church with growth, even using popular superstition to work healings and exorcisms (vv. 14–16).[76] The local authorities again arrest the apostles, but the Lord miraculously opens the jail doors enabling them to escape. Instead of going into hiding, they simply return to the temple, proclaiming the message about Jesus (vv. 17–26). Enraged with this behavior, the high priest again confronts the Twelve, commanding them to desist, but once more they refuse (vv. 27–32), insisting they must obey God rather than even the highest human authorities when they conflict (v. 29). At this point, Gamaliel intervenes and saves their lives (vv. 33 40).

This noted rabbi was probably the grandson of Hillel and thus from the more liberal wing of Pharisaism. Unfortunately his advice (v. 39) has often been applied in other settings to the detriment of believers. Not all religious movements whose origins are other than divine automatically shrivel and die if left alone. Simply because God providentially used Gamaliel's advice to free the believers does not mean that his counsel was based on timeless principles.[77] Belief in Scripture's inerrancy and authority does not imply that everything spoken by every character in the Bible is true, merely that everything spoken is what those people actually said!

A more difficult problem with Gamaliel's speech involves his reference to Theudas in verse 36. According to Josephus, Theudas led his revolts in A.D. 44, after the time of the events in Acts 5 and well after Judas's rebellion in A.D. 6 (v. 37), which Gamaliel seems to think came later (cf. *Antiquities* 20.97, 102, 171; *Jewish*

---

[76] "Parallels of a sort can be cited, but it is probably correct to say that in ancient thought it mattered little whether a miracle was worked by the shadow, the hands, or the words of the miracle-worker. In any case the agent here is God" (C. K. Barrett, *Acts: A Shorter Commentary* [Edinburgh: T & T Clark; New York: Continuum, 2002], 74).

[77] Witness the rapid growth of Islam, often by coercive force, in numerous eras of its history, including today. More generally, William J. Lyons, "The Words of Gamaliel (Acts 5.38–39) and the Irony of Indeterminacy," *JSNT* 68 (1997): 23–49.

War 2.259–64). Of course, Josephus may be wrong, as he demonstrably is on oc-casion (though not often), or perhaps Gamaliel knows of a different Theudas. The name was fairly common, and Josephus does refer to numerous such revolts. But a completely satisfactory resolution has yet to be discovered.[78] It is unlikely, though, that Luke would attribute to Gamaliel a comparison between Jesus and would-be revolutionaries, thereby risking confusion over Jesus' mission, unless Christ had been perceived in this way by leading opponents.[79]

Hebrews and Hellenists (6:1–7)   The final segment of the first panel in this second volume of Luke brings us to 6:1–7. The church has confronted opposition from without and has had to deal with one couple's rebellion from within, but now it faces the first full-fledged church split. The two groups involved are described literally as "Hebrews" and "Hellenists" (v. 1). A lively scholarly debate has tried to determine if the differences between these two groups were purely linguistic or cultural as well.[80] *At the very least we are meant to understand that the Hebrews spoke Aramaic as their native tongue, while the Hellenists, from outside of Israel, spoke Greek as their first language. But because some Jews living in the Diaspora assimilated to Greek culture, while others retained more distinctive practices and even continued speak-ing Aramaic and/or Hebrew, it is quite possible that cultural differences divided the two groups as well.* Paul, for example, could call himself a Hebrew (Phil. 3:5), even though he was brought up in his earliest years in Tarsus in Cilicia.

The problem that triggered the tension between the two groups is described as the Hebrews overlooking the Hellenist widows in the daily distribution (NIV adds "of food" in v. 1). This may well have been a form of charity to provide food for the neediest in the commune; but, based on Jewish analogies, it may also have involved the distribution of money. Either way, the apostles, as leaders of the Hebrews, del-egate the responsibility to the Hellenists to choose corresponding leaders from their own midst to address the problem (vv. 2–6). In so doing, they recognize a distinc-tion of ministries—some who preach the word and others who "wait on (*diakonein*) tables"—a distinction that would form the precedent for the later establishment of the office of deacons as separate from the elders of a church. At the same time, it is important to observe that the criteria for selecting these new leaders are every bit as spiritual as those for elders ("full of the Spirit and wisdom"—v. 3; cf. 1 Tim. 3:1–7). While there may be some sense that the seven play a more practical role, they must be equally mature believers. Interestingly, the only actual activities that Luke de-scribes any of these men undertaking are the entirely spiritual ministries of teaching and healing (by Stephen and Philip in 6:8–8:40).[81]

---

[78] Cf. Fitzmyer (*Acts*, 334): "The fact that Luke's background information can so often be corroborated may sug-gest that it is wiser to leave this particular matter open rather than to condemn Luke of a blunder."

[79] Jeffrey A. Trumbower, "The Historical Jesus and the Speech of Gamaliel (Acts 5.35–9)," *NTS* 39 (1993): 500–17.

[80] The classic work arguing for cultural differences is Martin Hengel, *Between Jesus and Paul* (London: SCM; Philadelphia: Fortress, 1983); an important response arguing for merely linguistic differences is Craig Hill, *Hellenists and Hebrews* (Minneapolis: Fortress, 1992).

[81] On this paragraph, see further Blomberg, *Neither Poverty nor Riches,* 167–69.

Several other principles emerge from 6:1–7, too. When linguistic or ethnic differences separate groups of Christians trying to work together, leadership should be delegated so that both groups are fairly represented. It also makes sense that congregations choose their own leaders, so long as godly criteria are employed. It would have been easy for the Hebraic apostles to appoint the leaders *for* the Hellenists, but instead they insisted that the Hellenists choose them for themselves (v. 3). This text has thus been used as support for a congregational form of church government. But we will also see different models elsewhere in Acts. Moreover, all seven of the names of the men they choose are Greek ones, suggesting that they picked people from their own midst. Indigenous leadership is also an important practice for the church in every age.[82]

Verse 6 reflects a commissioning ceremony known already in Judaism—the laying on of the hands—which was used to set apart or consecrate various individuals for leadership roles. But neither in the Judaism of the day nor in New Testament Christianity does a clear division between "clergy" and "laity" appear, nor any specified "offices" that require ordination in the modern sense of that term. In fact, there is some irony in the observation that seven was the number specified for *ad hoc* Jewish boards or committees,[83] whereas today the diaconate has in some circles become an entrenched office with numerous unalterable traditions attached to it. At any rate, the important thing Luke wants to leave us with as he ends the first sixth of his book is that the word of God spread and God blessed the activity of the new church greatly. Even many priests, who were mostly Sadducees and thus the church's strongest opponents, came to faith (v. 7).

QUESTIONS FOR REVIEW

1. Compare and contrast the miracles and sermons in Acts 2 and 3.
2. What are the most important exegetical observations concerning the church's conflict with the Sanhedrin in Acts 4:1–31?
3. What new information about the communal sharing of the early church do we learn from 4:32–35?
4. How can we account for God's severity in judging Ananias and Sapphira?
5. Comment on the nature of Gamaliel's advice and historical accuracy.
6. Who were the Hebrews and the Hellenists? What was the problem between them? How was it resolved? What abiding principles for the church today can we deduce from the resolution?

The Church in Judea, Galilee, and Samaria (6:8–9:31) *The Ministry and Martyrdom of Stephen (6:8–8:3)* The second panel portrays the church beginning to move out from Jerusalem. The initial impetus comes from the ministry and martyrdom of Stephen, one of the first "deacons." Speaking powerfully and working

---

[82] But not at the expense of the *unity* of the church. See Eckhard J. Schnabel, *Early Christian Mission,* vol. 1 (Downers Grove and Leicester: IVP, 2004), 654–55.

[83] Marshall, *Acts,* 126.

miracles, he attracts the attention and censure of the authorities (vv. 8–14). They charge him with blasphemy against Moses and God, claiming he is trying to change the customs Moses handed down (vv. 11, 13). In other words, they believe Stephen is in some way teaching others to break *the law*. Second, they claim he does not stop speaking against "this holy place" (vv. 13–14), which at the very least referred to *the temple* but may well have had *the entire land of Israel* in view as well. Although Luke refers to these charges as false, they undoubtedly contained at least half-truths—"false more in nuance and degree than in kind."[84]

Stephen is arraigned before Caiaphas probably within two years of Christ's crucifixion (recall our discussion of chronology). At first glance his "defense speech" (7:2–53) seems more like a modern filibuster as he reviews well-known biblical history before the high court. Is he hoping they'll forget the question they have asked him? On further inspection it becomes clear that Stephen has carefully chosen and structured his reply. Luke knows well how to abbreviate long speeches, so the space he devotes to this one shows its significance for him, no doubt in illustrating the transition from an exclusively Jewish church in Jerusalem to a more Hellenistic and geographically diverse movement.[85] *Stephen's defense refers, in turn, to each of the three possible charges against him.* In verses 2–18, he points out how all the patriarchs served God faithfully, but none ever fully inherited the promised land.[86] In verses 18–43, he reviews at length key events from the life of Moses, focusing particularly on how Moses himself predicted the coming of a prophet like him (the Messiah) whom the people had to follow (v. 37; quoting Deut. 18:15). Jesus was that prophet; therefore, the Jews should listen to him. Stephen's message is thus the true fulfillment of the law. As for the temple, verses 44–50 point out that the tabernacle rather than the temple represented God's initial plan for his people. The Israelites had rejected that plan, clamoring for a temple just like the nations that surrounded them. One of the dangers of an immovable temple, as contrasted with the more portable tabernacle, was that people might begin to think God was confined to one special location—thus Stephen's quotations from Isaiah 66:1–2 in verses 49–50.

Stephen's "Old Testament survey" thus shows that it is the unbelieving Jews who have consistently disobeyed God. *He* is not a lawbreaker but *they* are, and their current treatment of him matches this historic pattern (vv. 51–53). Ben Witherington describes this speech as an exemplary model of nonviolent resistance.[87] It also appears to reflect a more radical understanding of this fledgling religion than the apostles'

---

[84] Longenecker, "Acts," 335. At the same time we must avoid the temptation to see Stephen as hostile to the temple; he simply recognizes that its role in salvation history has been superseded. See James P. Sweeney, "Stephen's Speech (Acts 7:2–53): Is It as 'Anti-Temple' as Is Frequently Alleged?" *TrinJ* 23 (2002): 185–210.

[85] For a full-length study of this speech, see John Kilgallen, *The Stephen Speech: A Literary and Redactional Study of Acts 7, 2–53* (Rome: Biblical Institute Press, 1976). For a brief, updated précis, cf. idem, "The Speech of Stephen, Acts 7:2–53," *ET* 115 (2004): 293–97.

[86] Several minor discrepancies between Stephen's narrative and the Hebrew text of the relevant Old Testament texts appear and have been variously explained. But again, as with Gamaliel's speech, a high view of Scripture does not commit us to claiming that Stephen himself remembered everything exactly during his defense. Rather it means that Luke has recorded an accurate account of what Stephen said. See Rex A. Koivisto, "Stephen's Speech: A Theology of Errors?" *GTJ* 8 (1987): 101–14.

[87] Witherington, *Acts*, 275.

previous perspective. Jesus' followers are moving in the direction of being emancipated from Judaism in a way they did not previously imagine.

Far from being convinced, the Jewish leaders become outraged and begin to stone Stephen (7:54–8:3). Under Roman law, they had no right to enforce a death sentence in this kind of situation (John 18:31), but the narrative reads more like the actions of a violent mob unconcerned with legal restrictions. Stephen has already provoked them further by looking to heaven and claiming to see the glory of God and Jesus, the Son of Man, standing at his right hand (vv. 55–56).[88] Interestingly, this is the only place outside of the Gospels where "Son of Man" as a title appears.[89] As he is dying, Stephen further imitates his Lord by praying for Jesus to receive his spirit and not hold the authorities' sin against them (vv. 59–60; cf. Luke 23:34, 46).

STEPHEN'S BREAKTHROUGH (ACTS 6–7)

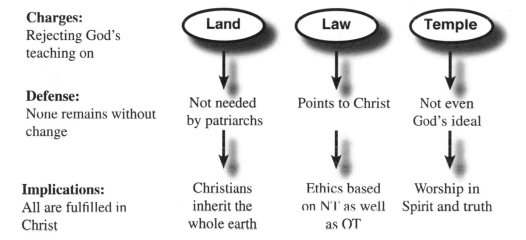

Charges: Rejecting God's teaching on	Land	Law	Temple
Defense: None remains without change	Not needed by patriarchs	Points to Christ	Not even God's ideal
Implications: All are fulfilled in Christ	Christians inherit the whole earth	Ethics based on NT as well as OT	Worship in Spirit and truth

In this context Luke reminds us again that Saul is present—a foreshadowing device to prepare readers for the prominent role he will play (as Paul) later in the book (8:1). One might have expected this first Christian martyrdom to deter the preaching of the word, but precisely the opposite occurs. As Tertullian would comment more than a century later, the blood of the martyrs often becomes the seed of the church (*Apology* 50). Although in 8:1 Luke says that "all except the apostles were scattered," he may be using the apostles as representatives of the Hebrews more generally.[90] If Stephen, as a representative of the Hellenists, had a more radical understanding of how following Jesus broke from the Jewish law, the authorities may have been even more intolerant of him than of the Hebrews, who seemed up to this point to be

---

[88] Barrett (*Acts*, 110) plausibly suggests "that the Son of man is standing because he is about to come—to the martyr at the time of his death as at the end he will come to all men."

[89] Kee (*To Every Nation under Heaven*, 103) notes what might be called the "trinitarian vision" after Stephen's speech: Stephen is full of the Holy Spirit, sees the glory of God and then sees Jesus standing next to him.

[90] Richard Bauckham, "James and the Jerusalem Church," in *The Book of Acts in Its Palestinian Setting*, ed. Bauckham, 429.

reasonably law-abiding. This could also explain Saul's anger and persecution of the church (v. 3), which again sets the stage for his dramatic conversion still to come.

The Ministry of Philip the Evangelist (8:4–40)   Chapter 8 turns from Stephen to Philip, another of the seven leaders of the Hellenists. Here Luke narrates two vignettes involving this "deacon" who becomes better known as an evangelist (and who is to be distinguished from the apostle by the same name). In verses 4–25, we read of Philip's encounter with a group of Samaritans and their ringleader, Simon Magus. Numerous theological debates arise from this intriguing episode, which we will discuss momentarily. In so doing, however, we must not lose sight of what for Luke was surely *the main point—the gospel is now leaving Jerusalem, even Judea, and moving to Samaria, the province populated primarily by descendants of the unlawful marriages between Jews and Gentiles centuries earlier.* The Samaritan was the despised half-breed, often disliked even more than the fully "other." In Christ, these human hostilities are breaking down.[91]

But what are we to make of Simon? He appears to believe (v. 13), yet he tries to buy the power of the Holy Spirit and is strongly condemned by Peter in response (vv. 18–23). The early church tradition was almost unanimous in its conviction that Simon was never saved (see esp. Irenaeus, *Against Heresies* 1:23; Justin Martyr, *Apology* 1:26), while the Gnostic sect of the Simonians traced its origin to this man (though there is no actual proof of their claim).[92] Peter certainly reacts harshly enough to suggest that he does not believe Simon is saved at this juncture. In fact, verse 20 more literally reads as in J. B. Phillips's paraphrase: "To hell with you and your money!" Likewise Peter's statement that "you have no part or share in this ministry" seems more absolute than what would be appropriate if Simon were a true believer, however misguided. Those who believe true Christians can lose their salvation often apply that belief to Simon here; those who affirm "eternal security" typically argue that his initial "belief" was merely superficial—more a part of his astonishment at Philip and his message than true commitment (v. 13).

Two grammatical observations could support this latter approach. The term for "astonished" is the same Greek verb used in verse 11 and translated as "amazed." But the amazement of the Samaritans in watching Simon hardly needs to imply full allegiance to him. Second, both the Samaritans in general and Simon in particular "believed Philip" (v. 12), whereas the more normal expression in the New Testament for saving faith is that people believe (in) Jesus—perhaps a tip-off to something less than true trust in the Lord here.[93]

An even thornier exegetical question may be the apparent delay of the arrival of the Holy Spirit. Why does he not come upon the Samaritans when they first believe and are baptized rather than only after Peter and John arrive from Jerusalem? Historically, Roman Catholics and some Protestants have used this interval in time

---

[91] John T. Squires, "The Function of Acts 8.4–12.25," *NTS* 44 (1998): 608–17.

[92] For a thorough analysis of the biblical and extrabiblical material about Simon Magus traditions and a demonstration of the theological ambiguities surrounding them, see Stephen Haar, *Simon Magus: The First Gnostic?* (Berlin and New York: de Gruyter, 2003).

[93] For both of these points, see Dunn, *Baptism*, 64–65.

to justify infant baptism separated from adolescent confirmation. But neither of these rites is depicted in this passage at all. Pentecostals often view this as a classic paradigm of a "second blessing." But if the Spirit did not come at first, then this is only a "first blessing"! Many Protestants and probably most Evangelicals among them simply deny that this passage provides a normative pattern, citing the unique situation of the extension of the gospel to the Samaritans. Without endorsement by the leadership of the church and the Hebraic Jewish Christians more generally, reconciliation between Jews and Samaritans in Christian circles might never have taken place.

On the other hand, two small grammatical observations may again suggest a different approach. Adopting the interpretation of Simon's "believing Philip" noted above suggests that the Samaritans had not truly converted at the time of their water baptism either. Moreover, the word order of verse 16 ("they had simply been baptized into the name of the Lord Jesus") suggests that the contrast is between being baptized into the name of Jesus and some other action directed toward Jesus (such as belief).[94] Thus if the Samaritans did not truly believe until Peter and John arrived, then there is no conflict with the pattern of Pentecost observed earlier.

The other episode in chapter 8 involving Philip is described more briefly. Verses 26–40 depict his encounter with an Ethiopian eunuch, a royal official castrated so that he could safely oversee the harem. Again, *Luke's most important point is to show the gospel moving out to groups who were otherwise marginalized by Judaism* (see Deut. 23:1, but cf. Isa. 56:3–8).[95] As an Ethiopian, this man is also almost certainly black.[96] He may well be a God-fearer, a non-Jew who had come to believe in the God of Israel. He is reading the Isaiah scroll and wondering who the suffering servant is. Philip explains that this prophecy has been fulfilled in Jesus. Most Jews in first-century times seem to have understood Isaiah 52–53 as referring to Israel corporately. Though there is a little evidence of pre-Christian interpretation of this text as messianic,[97] that is clearly how early Christianity understood it. A more subordinate point involves the close correlation between belief (presupposed by v. 35) and water baptism. That Philip and the Ethiopian went down into the water and then came up out of it again (vv. 38–39) suggests baptism by immersion, though it is also possible that it was done by effusion (pouring water over a person while standing in a pool or river).[98]

---

[94] Ibid., 58.

[95] Keith H. Reeves, "The Ethiopian Eunuch: A Key Transition from Hellenist to Gentile Mission: Acts 8:26–40," in *Mission in Acts: Ancient Narratives in Contemporary Context,* eds. Robert L. Gallagher and Paul Hertig (Maryknoll, N. Y.: Orbis, 2004), 114–22.

[96] On this identification and on black persons in Scripture more generally, see esp. J. Daniel Hays, *From Every People and Nation: A Biblical Theology of Race* (Leicester and Downers Grove: IVP, 2003).

[97] Martin Hengel, "Zur Wirkungsgeschichte von Jes 53 in vorchristlicher Zeit," in *Der leidende Gottesknecht: Jesaja 53 und seine Wirkungsgeschichte,* eds. Bernd Janowski and Peter Stuhlmacher (Tübingen: Mohr, 1996), 49–91.

[98] Some late manuscripts add at the beginning of verse 37, "Philip said, 'If you believe with all your heart, you may.' The eunuch answered, 'I believe that Jesus Christ is the Son of God'" (reflected in the KJV). But this is clearly an attempt by a later scribe to give a proper confession for the eunuch and not likely to be what Luke originally wrote.

The Conversion of Saul (9:1–31)   The final segment of Luke's second panel spans 9:1–31 and describes the conversion of Saul. Christians know him better as Paul and often assume that he took this new name at his conversion, but Acts does not make the switch until 13:9, when he begins his ministry among Gentiles in earnest. Roman citizens would, in fact, have had three names and, if they were Jews, presumably an additional Jewish name. Thus "Paul" (from a Latin word for "little") was one of this man's three Roman names, but we do not know which one.[99] Saul's family and upbringing made him uniquely equipped to minister to Jews, Greeks, and Romans alike. His tricultural background included *Roman* citizenship by birth, inherited from one or both of his parents (22:28). Brought up in his early years in Tarsus (9:11), he would have been raised in the third largest center of *Greek* culture and university life in the first-century Mediterranean world (after Athens and Alexandria). Finally, his study under Gamaliel in Jerusalem to become a Pharisee and a rabbi (22:3, 6) would have thoroughly inculcated his ancestral Jewish religion in him. This formal study would have occurred somewhere between his twelfth and eighteenth years, although we are unsure if he ever completed it or was formally ordained (see below on 26:10). Saul's persecution of the sect known as "the Way"[100] was not in keeping with Gamaliel's liberal spirit (recall above, p. 33), but students frequently diverge from their teachers in important ways.

Most likely Saul was convinced that this "apostate" group of followers of Jesus was preventing God from blessing the Jews and ushering in the messianic age (which could not have come through Jesus, since as a crucified criminal he would have been cursed by God—Deut. 21:23). Hence, extermination of the sect had to be God's will. In many ways Paul's attitude would have matched those of extremist factions in the Middle East today; not implausibly, N. T. Wright compares him to some modern terrorists.[101] Although his conversion upends his theology entirely, his zeal for his convictions remains unflagging.

One way Luke indicates the significance of Saul's conversion[102] is by including three narratives of it. Not only does he present it here; he has Saul retell his own story twice in chapters 22 and 26. There are minor differences among the three accounts, perhaps most notably on who heard what when,[103] but all attest to the dramatic turnaround caused by this momentous event. It is not much of an exaggeration to say that all the major pillars of Saul's new theology would have appeared as he reflected on this Damascus Road experience. Obviously, his *Christology* was altered as he now recognized Jesus as the Messiah. But that meant that his *soteriology* had to be transformed; salvation must now be through faith in Jesus rather than the works of the law. Similarly, if the Messiah had arrived, then the messianic age had begun, thus changing Saul's *eschatology*. Finally, his *ecclesiology* could no longer claim

---

[99] Fitzmyer (*Acts*, 502) thinks Paul was the *cognomen*; as an extra Jewish name, Saul would be the *supernomen*.

[100] Probably a designation deriving from Jesus' own claim to be "the Way" in John 14:6.

[101] N. T. Wright, *What Saint Paul Really Said* (Oxford: Lion; Grand Rapids: Eerdmans, 1997), 28, 35.

[102] An appropriate label, given Luke's narrative presentation of the changes Saul underwent. See Philip H. Kern, "Paul's Conversion and Luke's Portrayal of Character in Acts 8–10," *TynB* 54.2 (2003): 63–80.

[103] On which, see esp. John B. Polhill, *Acts* (Nashville: Broadman, 1992), 457–62, 498–504.

that the Jews were God's uniquely elect people; this category must instead encompass Christ's followers of whatever ethnic background.[104]

Ever since Martin Luther began the Protestant Reformation in the early 1500s, a popular understanding of the conversion of Saul was that he, like Luther, had long attempted to keep the law to no avail. Thus Saul was psychologically ripe for the dramatic about-face he underwent. Romans 7:14–25 is sometimes claimed as support for this interpretation, but we will see below a more plausible reading of these verses (p. 249). Galatians 1:14 and Philippians 3:4–6 both suggest that Saul saw himself as comparatively blameless and mature in his Judaism, pleasing God and obeying his will better than most in his world. Precisely because of this zeal, God needed to intervene in as dramatic and supernatural way as he did.[105]

Temporarily blinded, Saul follows good Pharisaic practice by praying and fasting (v. 9). He is led to the home of a believer in Damascus by the name of Ananias (not to be confused with the man who was struck dead in chapter 5!). At this point his physical and spiritual healing takes place (vv. 10–19). The Lord reveals to Ananias how Saul will become a pioneer missionary to the Gentiles, but his prominence will bring significant suffering (vv. 15–16). As soon as Saul is adequately instructed, he is baptized (v. 18) and, as at Pentecost, is filled with the Spirit. The baptism is accompanied by the laying on of hands, but it is worth noting that it is neither an apostle nor any other formal church leader who performs the ceremony. Nowhere does Scripture limit who may baptize (or serve the Lord's Supper) to God's people. Pentecostals sometimes make a distinction between Saul's conversion and his later filling by the Spirit, but only three days elapse, and Ananias's teaching was probably vital before Saul could make a full, informed commitment to Christ.[106]

Unlike some throughout church history who have insisted that new converts go through an extensive period of training before they begin to proclaim their convictions to others, Saul starts to preach to his Jewish colleagues almost immediately (vv. 20–22). Indeed, new believers often have some of their greatest opportunities to share their fledgling faith with friends and family right away, before they become so inculturated into the church that they have few non-Christian acquaintances left! In fact, Saul spends "many days" (v. 23) preaching the gospel, a period of time that Galatians 1:18 indicates is three years. But Luke is concerned only to confirm Saul's abrupt change of belief and behavior and to bring Saul back to Jerusalem where we first met him. Now, however, Paul has become the complete antithesis of what he once was. The entire account of 9:1–31 sets the stage for Saul, going by the name of Paul, to become the primary character in Luke's narrative from chapters 13–28.

---

[104] For these and related developments, see Seyoon Kim, *The Origin of Paul's Gospel* (Tübingen: Mohr, 1981; Grand Rapids: Eerdmans, 1982) and Richard N. Longenecker, ed., *The Road from Damascus* (Grand Rapids and Cambridge: Eerdmans, 1997).

[105] See esp. Krister Stendahl, "The Apostle Paul and the Introspective Conscience of the West," *HTR* 56 (1963): 199–215.

[106] For a good catalog of features typical of biblical conversions, see Fernando, *Acts,* 302–4. Biblical conversions can be gradual as well as instantaneous. See esp. Scot McKnight, *Turning to Jesus: The Sociology of Conversion in the Gospels* (Louisville and London: WJKP, 2002).

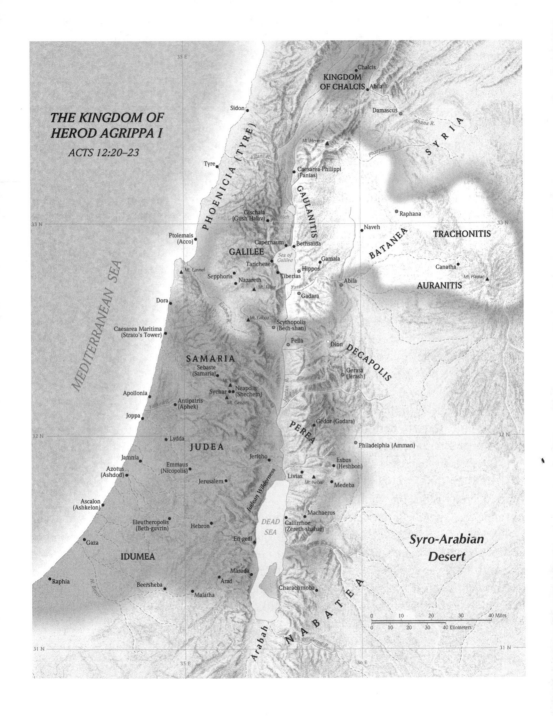

THE KINGDOM OF HEROD AGRIPPA I

ACTS 12:20–23

QUESTIONS FOR REVIEW

1. What were the charges against Stephen, and how does his speech defend him against them?
2. What are the main points of the stories about Philip's ministry in Acts 8? What are more subordinate theological controversies here, and how do you resolve them?
3. What is particularly significant about Saul's background? about his conversion?
4. What can we learn from the immediate aftermath of Saul's conversion?

Advances in Palestine and Syria (9:32–12:24) *Peter's Ministry: Three Vignettes (9:32–11:18)* The third panel of the first half of Acts prepares the way for Saul to take center stage by showing how *Jesus' followers continued to move out from Jerusalem and from the Judaism that it represented.* The first section presents three events in which Peter features centrally. Two short vignettes conclude chapter 9. First, through the power of Jesus Christ, Peter heals a paralytic named Aeneas (vv. 32–35). The passage closely resembles Christ's own healing of a paralytic in Mark 2:1–12 and parallels. It also moves Peter to Lydda (and soon to Joppa), further and further afield from Jerusalem.

Even more miraculously, Peter raises from death a young woman by the name of Dorcas (vv. 36–43). This miracle mirrors Christ's resurrecting the daughter of the synagogue ruler, Jairus, in Mark 5:21–43 and parallels. Even the name of the woman in Aramaic seems significant. Peter would have commanded her, *"Tabitha, koum"* (v. 40), while in the Gospels Jesus' words telling the "young woman" to arise would have been *"Talitha, koum."*[107] The miracle-working power that Christ delegated to the apostles back in Matthew 10 and parallels is having a tremendous effect. We note, moreover, that Peter is staying with a man with a Jewish name (Simon) who is practicing an unclean trade (a tanner) by working with leather (from pig hides). Verse 43 has set the stage for the third episode involving Peter, occupying all of chapter 10, in which he comes to recognize that God is declaring all animals and thus all foods clean.

The length with which Luke narrates the conversion of Cornelius shows its importance for him; like Saul's conversion, it will appear three times in Acts.[108] After taking all of chapter 10 to tell the story, Luke then has Peter recount everything that happens again when he returns to Jerusalem (11:1–18). He will also make brief mention of it at the Apostolic Council (15:7–11). If Acts 8 depicts a Samaritan Pentecost, then chapter 10 portrays a fully Gentile Pentecost.[109]

The story affords a remarkable example of God simultaneously preparing both Peter and Cornelius for the events that will unfold. Verses 1–8 introduce us to the Roman centurion, a commander of one hundred troops, as a God fearer. Like many in

---

[107] Cf. Fernando, *Acts*, 310.

[108] Ronald D. Witherup, "Cornelius Over and Over and Over Again: 'Functional Redundancy' in the Acts of the Apostles," *JSNT* 49 (1993): 45–66.

[109] On which, see esp. J. Julius Scott Jr., "The Cornelius Incident in the Light of Its Jewish Setting," *JETS* 34 (1991): 475–84.

this category, he may have accepted all of the Jewish laws except circumcision—the most difficult command for adult Gentile men to obey in a world without anesthesia! The angel's appearance to him matches the periodic experience of seekers throughout church history. While not the norm, Jesus himself or an angelic messenger can appear directly to a person, even without a human missionary present.

Peter is being prepared, too (vv. 9–23a). He will remember Jesus' teaching about going to the Gentiles in the Great Commission (Matt. 28:18–20), but that mandate never clarified the relationship between the gospel and the law. He likewise heard Jesus explain that nothing that enters the body can make a person unclean (Mark 7:14–19a), but the Jewish kosher laws were so entrenched, mandated as they were in the Hebrew Scriptures themselves (Lev. 11), that he would need even further impetus from God to abandon them. It is true that Mark 7:19b explains that Jesus had proclaimed all foods clean, but that remark appears to be Mark's parenthetical comment when he was writing his Gospel two or three decades after the events of Acts 10. Nothing suggests that such a radical understanding dawned on the disciples immediately.[110]

In this story, however, Peter receives a direct, unambiguous, threefold command from a heavenly voice to eat the meat of a motley collection of animals, both clean and unclean. After initially refusing, perhaps thinking God was testing him in some way, he finally recognizes what is happening. The immediate arrival of Cornelius's friends enables Peter to understand the link between nonkosher food and Gentile people. *If God is declaring all foods to be clean, then he must be proclaiming all people as clean.*[111] Peter may go to Cornelius's house, eat with him, and preach the gospel to him.

Verses 23b–48 bring Peter and Cornelius together. Verse 34 explicitly shows Peter's recognition that "God does not show favoritism but accepts men from every nation who fear him and do what is right."[112] As Peter then tells Cornelius the story of Jesus, the Holy Spirit "interrupts" his preaching, and the commander and his companions begin to speak in tongues (vv. 44–46). This is the second passage in which the Pentecostal package of events seems to be separated in some way. Here the Spirit appears to come upon individuals before they even repent or believe! But when one examines what Peter was proclaiming at the moment the Spirit arrived, one sees that he was explicitly talking about forgiveness of sins through belief in Jesus' name (v. 43). Undoubtedly, Cornelius and his friends were repenting at that very moment, so that the Spirit did indeed descend at the time of their conversion. Once again, water baptism follows as quickly afterwards as is practical (vv. 47–48).

---

[110] "So radical is this notion that its message in the form of the vision is repeated three times, and the heavenly origin of this insight is confirmed by the sheet and its contents returning to 'heaven'" (Kee, *To Every Nation under Heaven,* 137).

[111] Cf. Charles E. Van Engen, "Peter's Conversion: A Culinary Disaster Launches the Gentile Mission: Acts 10:1–11:18," in *Mission in Acts,* eds. Gallagher and Hertig, 133–43. Intriguingly, the very late *Midrash on the Psalms* (146.4) predicts that the Messiah will cleanse all animals, but there is no way of knowing the original source or date of this tradition.

[112] "Luke means that God judges men fairly in accordance with their opportunities. God looks with favour on those who, as far as they know him, fear him and, as far as they know what righteousness is, practise it, and he will make it possible for those who have advanced so far to go further" (Barrett, *Acts,* 154).

The other major interpretive controversy surrounding this passage involves the next example in Acts of speaking in tongues (v. 46). At Pentecost, people heard the apostles speaking in known languages, but here nothing more about these tongues is explained. It is true that Peter observes, "They have received the Holy Spirit just as we have" (v. 47), but that does not mean every aspect of that reception was identical.[113] In 1 Corinthians 12–14, Paul will speak of tongues as a spiritual gift that requires an interpretation (but may not always receive one) and, therefore, cannot be the same phenomenon as at Pentecost. It is impossible to be sure which form of tongues is in view here in Acts 10, but the fact that no message is proclaimed may suggest the latter model. *Glossolalia (the technical term for speaking in tongues) here seems to authenticate the conversions rather than to communicate new information.*[114]

At any rate, it is important to note that this is only the second occurrence of tongues in Acts, even though many people have been saved by this point. The phenomena, therefore, can scarcely be said to be necessary either for salvation or for Christian maturity. But neither does Luke criticize it in any way, so it should not be viewed as aberrant either (for more on tongues, see below, pp. 193–95).

Eventually Peter returns to Jerusalem and tells the story of what has happened. The Christians in Jerusalem remain suspicious at first but finally concede that Peter's testimony is irrefutable. That does not necessarily mean that they like it, however, as renewed hostility to Gentile Christianity will break out again in Acts 21.

The Church in Antioch (11:19–30) Chapter 11 concludes with the one text in Acts that seems to diverge from strict chronological sequence (vv. 19–30). Luke wants to tell the story of how some believers now begin preaching more widely to Gentiles, particularly in Antioch of Syria (vv. 19–22). Antioch was a major urban center, the third largest in the empire after Rome and Alexandria, perhaps with half a million inhabitants.[115] A river port and trade center, it housed the temple of Apollo at the site of the springs of Daphne, a location legendary for its loose morals. Jews accounted for about one-seventh of the population, a sizable percentage for a Greek-speaking city. It would become Paul's home base to which he would return after each of his first two missionary journeys. Antioch is also the city where believers are first called Christians (v. 26b). The suffix was a Latin one, suggesting "followers" (of Christ), and the title appears to have been given to them by outsiders, just as supporters of Herod came to be known as Herodians.[116]

Here Barnabas reappears, this time as an emissary from Jerusalem. He obviously knows about Saul's conversion and brings him from Tarsus to Antioch, where the two minister together (vv. 22–26a). What Saul has been doing since his time in

---

[113] "Peter does not say that Cornelius and company spoke in the same *manner* as at Pentecost, he simply says they received the same Spirit as had happened to the audience at Pentecost" (Witherington, *Acts,* 360).

[114] Gentiles speaking in tongues so as to suggest possession by the Holy Spirit "would have constituted the strongest imaginable inducement for the existing Jewish members of the congregation to abandon their deep-seated aversion to mingling with Gentiles" (Philip F. Esler, "Glossolalia and the Admission of Gentiles into the Early Christian Community," *BTB* 22 [1992]: 142).

[115] Bruce, *Paul,* 130.

[116] Tacitus (*Annals* 15.44) certainly understands *Christianoi* as derogatory in the early second century. The outsiders here may have been Roman leaders viewing the believers as troublemakers and seditious. See Justin Taylor, "Why Were the Disciples First Called 'Christians' at Antioch? (Acts 11,26)," *RB* 101 (1994): 75–94.

Jerusalem in chapter 9 and how much time has elapsed are both impossible to determine.[117] But when we dealt with chronological matters, we saw that his conversion is most likely dated to A.D. 32, his first visit to Jerusalem to 35, and his first missionary journey (beginning in Acts 13) to 48–49. So there is a thirteen- or fourteen-year window of opportunity for this ministry in Antioch to take place.

The famine that verses 27–30 depict was at its height in A.D. 46, at least according to Josephus (*Antiquities* 20.51–53). Thus this paragraph includes events a little later than the death of Herod (A.D. 44, again according to Josephus; see below, p. 47), with which chapter 12 begins. But Luke apparently wanted to keep all of his information about Antioch together, following a topical outline at least at this one point. These verses contain the first of two appearances of a Christian prophet by the name of Agabus, whose prediction enables more well-to-do Christians to help alleviate the poverty of believers in Judea, the part of the empire that was hardest hit. Here also appears the second half of Marx's famous manifesto ("from each according to his ability"—v. 29; recall on 2:45). But this context is an explicitly Christian setting, all the more significant because concern for needy fellow believers is crossing ethnic and national boundaries.[118] This is not the identical model for helping the poor that we saw in chapters 2 and 4 or in chapter 6, but the same concern is exhibited. It is also interesting to note that the gift was sent to the Jerusalem elders, a leadership office already central to each local Jewish synagogue and one that early Christianity presumably took over from Judaism. Perhaps by this time, the apostles were frequently engaged in itinerant mission so that resident local leaders in each congregation were needed.[119]

Herod's Persecution of the Church and His Demise (12:1–24)   Before Luke turns to following exclusively the exploits of Paul, he has one more pair of incidents to narrate, both involving King Herod Agrippa I. The grandson of Herod the Great and nephew of Herod Antipas, Agrippa is friendlier to the Jews than most rulers that Rome appointed in Israel. As a favor to Jewish leaders, he has the apostle James (brother of John and son of Zebedee) martyred (vv. 1–2). Herod plans to do the same with Peter, but God miraculously releases him from prison (vv. 3–11), as he has done before in 5:19. Nothing suggests that Peter was in any way more faithful than James, an important reminder that persecution or other ill fortune is not necessarily tied to Christians' degrees of obedience. It is also quite humorous that, when Peter escapes and goes to the home where believers are praying for him, they do not at first accept that he has truly been released (vv. 12–19).[120] Are we ever too busy praying or preoccupied with our petitions that we fail to observe God's answers? Once Peter convinces them that he is truly alive and well, Luke explains that he leaves for

---

[117] But likely a good portion of this time was occupied in his teaching others. See esp. Martin Hengel and Anna Maria Schwemer, *Paul between Damascus and Antioch* (Louisville: WJKP; London: SCM, 1997).

[118] And disclosing the understanding of the church in Antioch concerning its responsibility to minister to the "mother church." Here is "two-way mission," a key concept for church plants at home and abroad to develop today, including across national boundaries. See González, *Acts,* 142–43.

[119] See further Bauckham, "James and the Jerusalem Church," 437.

[120] J. Albert Harrill ("The Dramatic Function of the Running Slave Rhoda (Acts 12.15–16): A Piece of Greco-Roman Comedy," *NTS* 46 [2000]: 150–57) shows how this scene provides comic relief for the tension surrounding how Peter will be received.

"another place" (v. 17). While a venerable Catholic tradition asserts that the place was Rome, no New Testament text ever tells us where he went.[121] But the fact that he singles out James (obviously not the apostle just martyred but the half brother of Jesus by that same name) fits with the fact that in chapter 15 James appears as the chief elder in the Jerusalem church. Perhaps we find some corroboration here for the idea that the elders have already replaced the apostles as the local authorities in the Jewish capital.

Probably in part as a response to Herod's treachery, verses 20–23 relate how the Lord soon punished him. The more immediate cause was his acceptance of worship as a god during a regal appearance before the inhabitants of Tyre and Sidon. *Josephus* includes an independent report of this same event:

> Here he celebrated spectacles in honor of Caesar, knowing that these had been instituted as a kind of festival on behalf of Caesar's well-being. For this occasion there were gathered a large number of men who held office or had advanced to some rank in the kingdom. On the second day of the spectacles, clad in a garment woven completely of silver so that its texture was indeed wondrous, he entered the theater at daybreak. There the silver, illumined by the touch of the first rays of the sun, was wondrously radiant and by its glitter inspired fear and awe in those who gazed intensely upon it. Straightway his flatterers raised their voices from various directions—though hardly for his good—addressing him as a god. "May you be propitious to us," they added, "and if we have hitherto feared you as a man, yet henceforth we agree that you are more than mortal in your being." The king did not rebuke them nor did he reject their flattery as impious. But shortly thereafter he looked up and saw an owl perched on a rope over his head. At once, recognizing this as a harbinger of woe just as it had once been of good tidings, he felt a stab of pain in his heart. He was also gripped in his stomach by an ache that he felt everywhere at once and that was intense from the start. Leaping up he said to his friends: "I, a god in your eyes, am now bidden to lay down my life, for fate brings immediate refutation of the lying words lately addressed to me. I, who was called immortal by you, am now under sentence of death. But I must accept my lot as God wills it. In fact I have lived in no ordinary fashion but in the grand style that is hailed as true bliss." Even as he was speaking these words, he was overcome by more intense pain. They hastened, therefore, to convey him to the palace; and the word flashed about to everyone that he was on the very verge of death. Straightway the populace, including the women and children, sat in sackcloth in accordance with their ancestral custom and made entreaty to God on behalf of the king. The sound of the wailing and lamentations prevailed everywhere. The king, as he

---

[121] But it is unlikely that he went to Rome prior to the 60s because even as late as about A.D. 57, when Paul writes his letter to the Romans, he betrays no awareness of any apostle having been there earlier.

lay in his lofty bedchamber and looked down on the people as they fell prostrate, was not dry-eyed himself. Exhausted after five straight days by the pain in his abdomen, he departed this life in the fifty-fourth year of his life and the seventh of his reign (*Antiquities* 19.343–50).

Josephus is clearly far more expansive than Luke, and not all of the details of the two accounts match precisely. But it is interesting that the two writers, apparently independently, recognized both a natural and a supernatural cause to Herod's demise, and both also view his death as divine punishment for self-deification. Luke adds, as he finishes the first half of his book, that "the word of God continued to increase and spread" (v. 24).[122]

THE CHRISTIAN MISSION TO THE GENTILES (12:25–28:31)

Paul's First Journey and the Apostolic Council (12:25–16:5) *Commissioning Barnabas and Saul (12:25–13:3)* From here to the end of Acts, we follow the progress of Saul/Paul. This short section provides the second example of an informal ordination ceremony, this time as hands are laid on Barnabas and Saul to commission them for missionary service.[123] The categories remain fluid; the two are also called prophets and teachers. In 14:14, the one text in Acts where Luke diverges from his normal practice, these two are referred to as "apostles" as well. Before they start out, they take a third companion, John Mark, in whose home the Jerusalem prayer group had met (12:12). This reference will foreshadow later, more significant developments involving the disciple better known simply as Mark, who would also author the Gospel that bears his name.

The First Missionary Journey (13:4–14:28) Because Barnabas hailed from Cyprus (4:36), it was natural to set off for that island first (13:4–12). The only event on the island that Luke narrates in any detail involves a rare miracle of destruction (recall Jesus withering the fig tree—Mark 11:20–25 par.). Elymas, a sorcerer, is temporarily blinded. He also has a Jewish name (bar-Jesus), so the condemnation is appropriate inasmuch as Jews knew quite well they should avoid the power of the occult. Furthermore, the miracle had the positive effect of leading the proconsul, Sergius Paulus, to faith in the Lord.[124]

From Cyprus our missionaries proceed north to the mainland of what today is Turkey. But instead of staying along the coast where there were several main cities, they head further north to the high central plateau region of Pisidia. In a different town by the name of Antioch, they find a synagogue and are invited to deliver a sermon on the Sabbath (vv. 13–41). This was one of the communities of the large

---

[122] The most probable original textual reading in this verse has "to Jerusalem" rather than "from Jerusalem." But the text should probably be punctuated so that the translation would read, "Barnabas and Paul returned, having completed their mission to Jerusalem." See Luke T. Johnson, *The Acts of the Apostles* (Collegeville: Liturgical, 1992), 216.

[123] "The message the church received was to release their best for missionary service (13:2), and their earnestness was such that they were willing to do so (13:3)" (Fernando, *Acts,* 377). The significance of Barnabas in early Christian history has often been underestimated. For his rehabilitation and for a plausible reconstruction of his biography, see Bernd Kollmann, *Joseph Barnabas: His Life and Legacy* (Collegeville: Liturgical, 2004).

[124] Note the parallels with Paul's earlier blinding: both men had strongly opposed God's word, both were struck blind, and both had to be led by the hand. See further Johnson, *Acts,* 226–27.

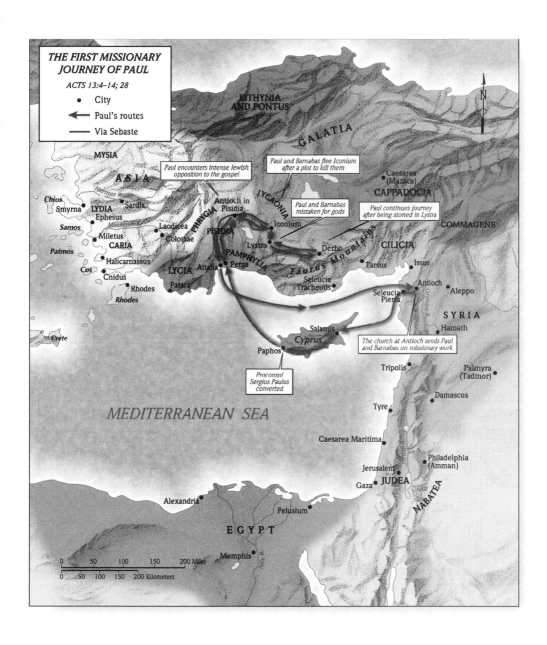

THE FIRST MISSIONARY
JOURNEY OF PAUL

ACTS 13:4–14; 28

• City

← Paul's routes

— Via Sebaste

BITHYNIA
AND PONTUS

GALATIA

MYSIA

ASIA

Paul encounters intense Jewish
opposition to the gospel

Paul and Barnabas flee Iconium
after a plot to kill them

Caesarea
(Mazaca)

CAPPADOCIA

Chios
Smyrna   LYDIA   Sardis
Ephesus

Antioch in
Pisidia

LYCAONIA

Paul and Barnabas
mistaken for gods

Paul continues journey
after being stoned in Lystra

COMMAGENE

Samos

Miletus
Laodicea
Colossae

PISIDIA

Iconium

Patmos   CARIA

PAMPHYLIA

Lystra

Derbe

CILICIA

Halicarnassus

LYCIA   Attalia   Perga

Taurus Mountains

Tarsus

Issus

Cos   Cnidus

Rhodes   Patara

Seleucia
Tracheotis

Antioch   Aleppo

Rhodes

Seleucia
Pieria

SYRIA

Crete

Salamis

Cyprus

Hamath

Paphos

The church at Antioch sends Paul
and Barnabas on missionary work

Proconsul
Sergius Paulus
converted

Tripolis

Palmyra
(Tadmor)

MEDITERRANEAN SEA

Tyre

Damascus

Caesarea Maritima

Jerusalem

Philadelphia
(Amman)

Gaza   JUDEA

Alexandria

NABATEA

Pelusium

EGYPT

0   50   100   150   200 Miles

Memphis

0   50   100   150   200 Kilometers

Roman province of Galatia, to which Paul would later pen his first epistle. Did they head here because of an illness that Paul had contracted (cf. Gal. 4:13)? The low coastal regions were notorious for spawning malaria; sufferers often headed for the higher, drier climate to recover. But it is also interesting that Sergius Paulus had relatives in Pisidian Antioch, so perhaps he had encouraged the group to head there already.[125] Inexplicably, John Mark leaves Paul and Barnabas, returning home rather than accompanying them inland (v. 13). Later Paul will make clear he felt Mark was in the wrong (15:36–41).

In the synagogue in Pisidian Antioch, Paul preaches in detail to the Jews how the key events in their history find their climax in Jesus of Nazareth. Parallels with Peter's and Stephen's earlier sermons lead some critics to see all the speeches in Luke as more redactional than authentic. But we would expect early Christian preachers to use a similar set of texts from Scripture when addressing fellow Jews. C. H. Dodd believed he could even discern a common, primitive *kerygma* in these speeches, which he believed influenced Mark's later composition of his Gospel.[126] Moreover, verses 38–39 contain a very Pauline touch and provide a key link with the epistles, because Acts otherwise discusses the theology of Christ's crucifixion and atonement comparatively sparsely. The aftermath of Paul's preaching offers a precedent for what would happen repeatedly. There is both great interest and growing opposition, and finally Paul turns from his Jewish audience to a Gentile one (vv. 42–52).[127]

From Pisidian Antioch, Paul and Barnabas proceed to the other Galatian communities of Iconium, Lystra, and Derbe and eventually return home to Antioch in Syria (14:1–28). The only major new elements recorded in this chapter involve their ministry in Lystra (vv. 8–18). This time critics complain that Paul's speech (vv. 15–17) is too different from his earlier one to be authentic! But there are no Jews in Lystra; Paul's strategy has to be more creative. The Gentiles in this particular region were especially superstitious,[128] believing, among other things, that the two gods Zeus and Hermes had visited a nearby farm centuries earlier, only to be ignored by most of the people in the area, who were subsequently punished for their disrespect (Ovid, *Metamorphoses* 8:626–724). Was Barnabas linked with Zeus (the head of the Greek pantheon) because he was the larger, better looking of the two? Was Paul associated with Hermes because, like the messenger god, he was the primary speaker? The later apocryphal *Acts of Paul and Thecla* 3 (= *Acts of Paul* 3.3) contains an unflattering enough description of Paul for it to be accurate: "a man small of stature, with a bald head and crooked legs, in a good state of body, with eyebrows meeting and nose somewhat hooked, full of friendliness; for now he appeared like a man, and now he had the face of an angel."[129] The local superstition is also reflected in the wild swings of opinion displayed. A miraculous healing initially triggered their acclamations of

---

[125] See Barrett, *Acts*, 195.

[126] C. H. Dodd, *The Apostolic Preaching and Its Developments* (London: Hodder & Stoughton, 1936), 54–56.

[127] John Kilgallen ("Hostility to Paul in Pisidian Antioch [Acts 13,45]—Why?" *Bib* 84 [2003]: 1–15) argues that the Jewish opponents of Paul here and in neighboring regions reflected the growing Zealotry of the day.

[128] Dean Béchard, "Paul among the Rustics: The Lystran Episode (Acts 14:8–20) and Lucan Apologetic," *CBQ* 63 (2001): 84–101.

[129] Bruce, *Paul*, 468.

divinity (vv. 8–13),[130] but Jews from earlier cities Paul has visited later convince them to stone him (v. 19).

Space prevents us from commenting on all of the significant details in each of the locales in which Paul ministers. *But already during this first journey, several patterns of his missionary activity emerge that are worth highlighting. The more consistent the pattern, the more likely Christians in other times and places are meant to replicate it.*[131]

(1) Wherever there is a Jewish community Paul begins with it first, but he always moves on to the Gentiles as well (cf. Rom. 1:16). Or to generalize in ways that prove cross-cultural, he begins where God's Word was expected to be preached (but possibly absent or deficient in its proclamation) and then moves successively outward to less "reached" people. Hostility in one city never leads Paul to change his approach in the next, so the views that see a particular rejection of the gospel by the Jews somewhere in the book of Acts as a decisive turning point in salvation history, after which the Christian message should no longer be preached to Jewish people, are dangerously wrong.

(2) A consistent pattern throughout Paul's sermons finds him establishing common ground with each audience, leading to an explanation of the gospel in understandable language, with support for his message by either general revelation (e.g., the evidence for God in nature—14:17) or special revelation (e.g., the Hebrew Scriptures—13:16–41).

(3) With few exceptions, Paul concentrates on the major urban centers of the Roman Empire, because from them his message will easily spread into the more rural regions (whereas movement in the reverse direction was by no means as common). (4) Paul repeatedly returns to previously evangelized areas for "follow-up," to disciple new believers. When churches are ready for indigenous leadership, he appoints elders (14:23), recognizing the need for each congregation to have local, self-sustaining government. (5) Finally, Paul does all this despite adversity and opposition, stressing that "we must go through many hardships to enter the kingdom of God" (14:22).[132]

The Apostolic Council (15:1–35) It would be hard to exaggerate the significance of the council in Jerusalem that occupies verses 6–29. To the extent that the divide between Hebrews and Hellenists included theological disagreements with respect to the relationship between the gospel and the law, we may see the tensions of 6:8–8:3 coming to a head here. Some from Judea (presumably the most conservative Hebraic Jewish Christians) come to Syria and Antioch, where Paul is ministering. These Jews are teaching that circumcision is a requirement for salvation (vv. 1–5). They may well have claimed support from the apostles, but verse 24 clarifies that they went out without apostolic authorization. Requiring circumcision in fact amounted

---

[130] Paul's stare and use of a loud voice also may have suggested the presence of deity to the Lystrans. See Rick Strelan, "Recognizing the Gods (Acts 14.8–10)," *NTS* 46 (2000): 488–503.

[131] Cf. Robert C. Tannehill, *The Narrative Unity of Luke-Acts,* vol. 2 (Minneapolis: Fortress, 1990), 182.

[132] On Paul's balanced approach in contextualizing the gospel without falling into syncretism, see Hans-Josef Klauck, "With Paul in Paphos and Lystra: Magic and Paganism in the Acts of the Apostles," *Neot* 28 (1994): 93–108.

to the demand that Gentiles (or even God fearers)[133] must keep all of the law, in essence becoming Jews first en route to becoming Christians, since for many adult men that was the final step in full conversion to Judaism. Had this approach been widely adopted, Christianity might never have been more than another Jewish sect. Not surprisingly, the issue is serious enough that a meeting is convened in Jerusalem to address it.

We now see the apostles and elders together in the Jewish capital (v. 6). Barnabas and Paul are present as well, representing "the accused." Speaking for the apostles, Peter on this occasion gives Paul a ringing endorsement (vv. 6–11). His attitude seems quite different from his confrontation with Paul at Antioch (Gal. 2:11–15), an issue we will deal with when we introduce Galatians below. Here, however, recalling his experience with Cornelius, he sounds certain that God's grace in Christ alone saves a person (vv. 7–11).[134]

Barnabas and Paul speak next (v. 12). Rather than discussing theology, they appeal to the undeniable miracles that God has worked through the Gentiles, as Christian believers apart from obedience to the law. This kind of apologetic can be abused, but it has its place. Satan can counterfeit signs, and humans can manufacture them; but where godly people are preaching the true gospel, serving good ends and only holy living and Christian growth result, the logic of appeal to experience proves compelling.

Finally, James speaks, representing the elders (vv. 13–21). Now Scripture clinches the argument (vv. 16–18; Amos 9:11–12). The problem here is to explain how the passage in Amos supports James's point. The version Luke reproduces is the Septuagint (LXX), which is noticeably different from the Hebrew (MT). The latter speaks of Israel possessing the remnant of Edom rather than the remnant of humanity seeking the Lord. But two documents from the Dead Sea Scrolls (4QFlorilegium and CD 7:16) both contain Hebrew renderings that closely resemble the LXX against the MT,[135] so perhaps James's words *do* reflect the original text of Scripture. Alternately, James's point may be limited to the meaning that is common to both versions, namely, that God will bring Gentiles to Israel in the last days and join them together into one body. An older form of dispensationalism alleged that this was the most important text in Scripture on the *future* of Israel, but almost everyone today recognizes that "after this" in verse 16 is a paraphrase of Amos's words, "in that day," showing at least partial fulfillment beginning already in the first century (recall Peter's use of Joel 2:17 at Pentecost).[136]

At first glance the solution that the council adopts appears surprising. After all parties seemingly agreed that salvation was by God's grace rather than the works of the Law, they now impose four restrictions on Gentiles who are accepting the gospel (vv. 19–21): they must "abstain from food polluted by idols, from sexual im-

---

[133] On which, see esp. Irina Levinskaya, *The Book of Acts in Its Diaspora Setting* (Grand Rapids: Eerdmans; Carlisle: Paternoster, 1996).

[134] John Nolland, "A Fresh Look at Acts 15.10," *NTS* 27 (1980): 105–15.

[135] Jan de Waard, *A Comparative Study of the Old Testament Text in the Dead Sea Scrolls and in the New Testament* (Leiden and New York: Brill, 1965), 24–26.

[136] Robert L. Saucy, *The Case for Progressive Dispensationalism* (Grand Rapids: Zondervan, 1993), 179.

morality, from the meat of strangled animals and from blood." But why these four restrictions? The Western text of Acts deletes the reference to strangled animals, apparently interpreting the remaining three issues as moral ones—idolatry, fornication, and murder. But this seems to be a later attempt to make sense of the decree. If the word for sexual immorality here carries the more restricted sense of forbidden intermarriages, then all the prohibitions might match laws from Leviticus 18:6–18, laws incumbent on the resident alien, as well as the Israelite.[137] Still others think these taboos matched proscriptions from Jewish traditions about laws given to Noah that even Gentiles needed to follow,[138] or that all the forbidden items potentially formed part of idolatrous pagan temple worship.[139]

Whatever their precise origin, the important observation to make is that the council is not imposing on Gentile believers a new law here, however abbreviated. The practices they are to avoid remain particularly offensive for Jews, who had been dispersed throughout most of the Roman Empire (v. 21). When the council writes its letter to believers in Antioch and nearby regions explaining their decision (vv. 22–29), it concludes simply by stating, "You will do well to avoid these things" (v. 29), hardly a way to refer to mandatory legislation. These are merely restrictions that the Christian leaders hope Gentile believers will voluntarily adopt for the sake of not offending Jewish consciences unnecessarily.[140] That the Christians who received this letter were glad and encouraged, sending the letter carriers off with a blessing of peace, suggests they understood the "decree" in the milder sense (vv. 30–35). That Paul later writes about food sacrificed to idols to both the Corinthians (1 Cor. 8–10) and the Romans (Rom. 14:1–15:13), without referring to this decision, likewise suggests its limited scope and audience.

The final section in this panel of Acts describes the preparations for Paul and Barnabas to return to the cities in Galatia where they had planted churches. The two missionaries, however, cannot agree on what to do with Mark, who had deserted them earlier (15:36–41). That Luke is not glossing over the seriousness of the debate is demonstrated by his use of the word *paroxysmos* (cf. the English "paroxysm")! So the two agree to disagree and set out separately with different companions. We hear nothing further of Barnabas in Acts, but we know from the epistles that Paul and Mark are later reconciled (Col. 4:10; 2 Tim. 4:11; Phm. 24).

In 16:1–4, Paul and his new companion, Silas, return to Galatia and invite Timothy, a young believer there, to join them. Because he is half Jewish, he should have been circumcised as a Jew, so Paul takes steps to remedy the situation. But is this not a flagrant contradiction of everything he fought for at the Apostolic Council? No, because there the issue was salvation; here the issue is avoiding unnecessary

---

[137] E.g., Terrance Callan, "The Background of the Apostolic Decree (Acts 15.20, 29; 21:25)," *CBQ* 55 (1993): 284–97.

[138] E.g., Markus Bockmuehl, "The Noachide Commandments and New Testament Ethics, with Special Reference to Acts 15 and Pauline Halakhah," *RB* 102 (1995): 93–95.

[139] E.g., Charles H. Savelle, "A Reexamination of the Prohibitions in Acts 15," *BSac* 161 (2004): 449–68.

[140] On which, see further Craig L. Blomberg, "The Christian and the Law of Moses," in *Witness to the Gospel,* ed. Marshall and Peterson, 407–10. Bruce (*Paul,* 187) observes, "Paul was persuaded that the freedom of the Spirit was a more powerful incentive to the good life than all the ordinances and decrees in the world." Of course, sexual immorality is always wrong, but we learn that from numerous other texts, not this one.

offense while evangelizing Jews. In fact, Paul is adopting the same strategy that the council's "decree" followed and that he himself would enunciate in 1 Corinthians 9:19–23.[141] Again, Luke ends his panel by stressing how God blessed and churches grew (v. 5).

QUESTIONS FOR REVIEW

1. How do the short episodes involving Peter at the end of Acts 9 prepare for what he experiences in chapters 10–11?
2. What is the point of the visions that Peter and Cornelius receive? What is the significance of the latter's conversion? How and why does Luke tell this story three times?
3. What happens in Antioch and why is it important?
4. Compare and contrast the two parts of Acts 12.
5. What are several of the recurring patterns of Paul's missionary activity that Acts 13–14 introduce?
6. Walk through each stage of the Apostolic Council describing the importance of each.
7. How does Paul's subsequent behavior seem to contradict the results of the council, and how can one resolve the apparent contradiction?

Paul's Second and Third Missionary Journeys (16:6–19:20)   *Call to Macedonia (16:6–12)*   After revisiting the cities of Galatia and the neighboring region of Phrygia,[142] Paul and his coworkers travel successively farther to the west. As they seek their next place of ministry, they receive divine guidance both negatively and positively. Luke does not tell us how the Spirit "closed doors" in the regions of Asia, Mysia, and Bithynia; but what is significant is that Paul did not sit back and wait for special instructions from the Lord before probing all the nearby possibilities. Finally, in the coastal town of Troas, he has a vision of a Macedonian begging him to come to minister to that northern half of the country of Greece. *As believers seek God's guidance today, too, they must recognize that he uses a wide variety of ways to communicate with his people. Sometimes it will be by open and closed doors as well, sometimes it will mean more dramatic guidance, and sometimes it will involve simply using sanctified common sense without full assurance that one has made the only possibly correct decision.*[143] After all, 15:28 appears remarkably mild for so momentous a decree—"it seemed good to the Holy Spirit and to us."

Ministry in Philippi (16:13–40)   Luke mentions several stops as our missionaries cross over into Europe but not until they reach Philippi do we read of any of their

---

[141] William O. Walker Jr., "The Timothy-Titus Problem Reconsidered," *ET* 92 (1981): 231–35.

[142] In fact, the text refers to the single region of Phrygia and Galatia, an accurate recognition of how Roman provincial administration had united the two provinces, though only for a comparatively short time in their history. See Colin J. Hemer, "The Adjective Phrygia," *JTS* 27 (1976): 122–26.

[143] And sometimes he communicates through the larger Christian community. Recall 13:1–3 (González, *Acts,* 153–54). See further Gene L. Green, "Finding the Will of God: Historical and Modern Perspectives—Acts 16:1–30," in *Mission in Acts,* eds. Gallagher and Hertig, 209–20.

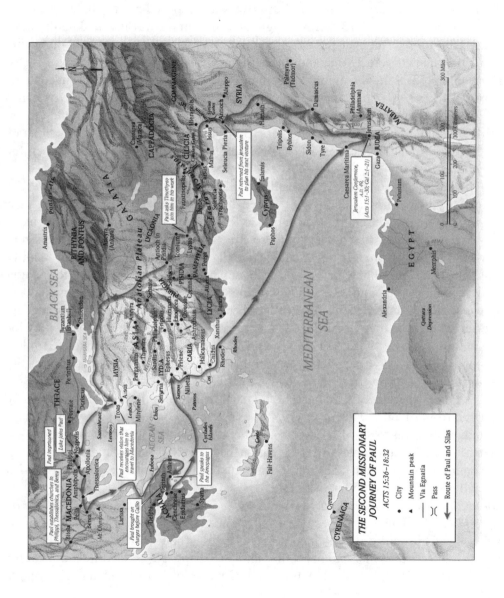

THE SECOND MISSIONARY JOURNEY OF PAUL

ACTS 15:36–18:32

- • City
- ▲ Mountain peak
- —⟋— Via Egnatia
-)(Pass
- ↓ Route of Paul and Silas

Paul establishes churches in Philippi, Thessalonica, and Berea

Paul imprisoned

Luke joins Paul

Paul receives vision that encourages him to travel to Macedonia

Paul brought on charges before Gallio

Paul speaks to the Areopagus

Paul asks Timothy to join him in his work

Paul returned from Jerusalem to plan his next venture

Jerusalem Conference, A.D. 49, (Acts 15:1–30; Gal 2:1–21)

activities.[144] This Roman colony was a popular retirement center for military leaders, but it had almost no Jewish population.[145] Still, Paul is trying to go to the Jews first. To form a synagogue, ten male heads of household were needed; apparently Philippi lacked even this small number. In lieu of an indoor meeting place, Jews were to meet out of doors for prayer, preferably by flowing water. Paul, therefore, goes to the river that ran through town and discovers a group of Jewish women gathered there on the Sabbath (v. 13). Most religious leaders in his world would hardly have bothered with such an inauspicious group, but from this little troupe Paul makes his first European convert, Lydia, and forms the nucleus of a church there (vv. 14–15). Her name perhaps means simply "a woman from the province of Lydia" (in contemporary Turkey); as a businesswoman with no husband mentioned, she may well not be married, although Hellenistic wives at times were more influential and "liberated" than their Jewish counterparts (cf. 13:50; 17:4). That she was "a worshiper of God" may mean that she was a Gentile God fearer, joining the Jewish women for prayers.

The second episode involving Paul in Philippi finds him exorcising a slave girl with a "Pythian spirit" (vv. 16–18). Named after the mythical dragon, Python, such a spirit referred to insanity, ventriloquism, or demon possession. Paul recognizes this girl as suffering from the last of these afflictions. Her message (v. 17) is entirely truthful but unwelcome. In spiritual warfare, knowing someone's name or identity was often a key to gaining mastery over her or him. Just as in the Gospels, the demon or demons inside this girl are actually trying to ward off Paul and his companions, so eventually he has to take action.[146] Her healing, nevertheless, means lost income for her owners, so they seize Paul and Silas and charge them falsely before the local authorities (vv. 19–21). (Timothy and Luke, who were half and full Gentiles, respectively, may have been left alone for that very reason.) The magistrates flog the "criminals" and throw them in prison (vv. 22–24).

As Peter experienced twice earlier, Paul and Silas will now also be miraculously rescued from jail during the night (vv. 25–28). When the jailer realizes what has happened, he prepares to do what was deemed honorable in the Greco-Roman world—to take his own life rather than suffer execution, which was the punishment for allowing prisoners to escape. Paul cries out in time to prevent the suicide, which so amazes the jailer that he asks, "What must I do to be saved?" (vv. 29–30). *Paul's reply forms something like the "John 3:16" of Acts: "Believe in the Lord Jesus, and you will be saved" (v. 31).* This verse goes on to add, "you and your household," suggesting to some that Christianity already incorporated babies as believers at this early date. So, too, in verse 33 the jailer and his entire family are baptized—a favorite prooftext for infant baptism (recall also v. 15). But verse 32 makes plain that Paul and Silas spoke

---

[144] Luke's use of "we" begins and ends at Philippi in this part of the book (16:7, 20:5), suggesting perhaps that Luke was from that city, joining and leading the group there for that reason.

[145] For several options of how Philippi could be called the leading city of that district (v. 12), when Thessalonica was larger, see Witherington, *Acts,* 489–90.

[146] The same phenomenon occurs in the Gospels when demons confess Christ, on which see, e.g., William L. Lane, *The Gospel According to Mark* (Grand Rapids: Eerdmans, 1974; London: Marshall, Morgan & Scott, 1975), 74.

God's word to all the family members, while verse 34 adds that his whole family had come to believe in God. Thus while it is true that ancient families were often large and frequently included babies, there is no evidence from this passage that this family had any.[147] What the story *does* highlight is the importance of reaching heads of household in patriarchal cultures because the chances of influencing the rest of the family for Christ greatly increase to a degree often not true if only a wife or child first believes.[148]

Verses 35–40 depict the aftermath of the aborted jail sentence. The prisoners had actually returned to their quarters for the rest of the night (!), but in the morning the Roman authorities offered to free Paul and Silas privately. Instead of accepting the offer and going away quietly, Paul declares his Roman citizenship and exposes the illegal proceedings of the night before.[149] But why assert his rights now and not on the previous evening? Presumably, he recognized this was the most strategic time to do so, not for his well-being but for the sake of Christianity in Philippi more generally. With a public, Roman declaration that they had done no wrong, the fledgling church would be able to grow free from legal harassment. [150] *Christians in any context trying to decide when to assert their rights and when voluntarily to relinquish them should likewise ask if such action will merely benefit themselves or will actually allow the gospel to flourish more.*[151]

In Thessalonica (17:1–9) The next stop about which Luke narrates any details appears further along a coastal route that traverses eastern Macedonia roughly from the north to the south. The same pattern of Paul's preaching Christ crucified and resurrected, according to the Scriptures, to the Jews first, and eventually being rejected and persecuted unfolds. Luke explicitly refers to ministry in the synagogue for only three Sabbaths (v. 2). Was Paul in town longer? Some think so in light of texts like 1 Thessalonians 2:9 or Philippians 4:16, but we really do not know for sure. Verse 6 is best translated not as "turned the world upside down" (KJV), but moderately derogatorily as "upset" (NASB) or "caused trouble" (NIV).[152] *First Thessalonians confirms how well and quickly the young church here grew, despite the comparatively short time Paul spent in town.* Chapters 1–4 of that epistle form the longest section of sustained praise in all of Paul's letters. A key reason for the successful growth was the Thessalonians' acceptance of the gospel as truly God's word (2:13).

In Berea (17:10–15) The next stop brought our missionaries to a smaller, less important city; but it was the next nearest one of any size. Perhaps the missionaries hoped that it would be their haven, but it was not to be. The identical pattern of

---

[147] Likewise Barrett, *Acts,* 256.

[148] Household evangelism in Acts also fulfills the mandate to the seventy-two in Luke 10:5–7 to evangelize and eat with a receptive household, as their ministry foreshadows the mission to the Gentiles. See David L. Matson, *Household Conversion Narratives in Acts* (Sheffield: SAP, 1996).

[149] Indeed, this passage forms a paradigm for Pauline social ethics in Acts. See esp. David Suazo, "El poder de la verdad para transformar culturas," *Kairós* 37 (2005): 97–110.

[150] Roman citizens who traveled widely often carried with them small clay tablets attesting to their citizenship, much as we might use passports today.

[151] Cf. further González, *Acts,* 196. Weaver (*Plots of Epiphany,* 287) believes, too, that, as elsewhere in Greco-Roman literature, "the opening of the prison is a spatial synecdoche for the opening of the city to the god's cult."

[152] Demonstrating the perception of a subversive element to the Christian faith. See González, *Acts,* 198.

ministry followed by opposition repeats itself, except that the latter comes almost entirely from outsiders pursuing Paul. *The key distinction of the Bereans was their open-mindedness; verse 11 explains that they "examined the Scriptures every day to see if what Paul said was true."* While this description is often used as a prooftext for believers having a daily quiet time or period of Bible study, in context Luke is referring to Jews not yet converted vigorously searching their Bibles and debating with one another to see if they can agree with what Paul has preached.

In Athens (17:16–34) Probably Paul's most famous sermon comes in this next community to be evangelized, the capital and cultural center of Greece. Here appeared statues and temples to the entire Greek pantheon, which "greatly distressed" the apostle (v. 16). Hurrying rapidly past Paul's ministry to Jews, Luke proceeds to describe Paul's interaction with the philosophers in the *agora,* the open-air marketplace (vv. 17–21). As part of the center of an ancient town, the *agora* was the place where people gathered daily to hear the latest news, as well as to shop and visit with one another. The closest modern equivalents would be today's media (newspapers, radio, television, Internet, etc.), not necessarily public or commercial locations (where perhaps the only speakers people expect to encounter are cult members or salespeople). Colleges and universities represent another partially equivalent forum since the stoa (or colonnaded walkways) surrounding the *agora* were where philosophers taught their students. The Areopagus (or Mars Hill) was the original site where the town council met, but the term had come to refer to the council as well as the location, and it is possible that in Paul's day they met in the corner of the *agora* itself.[153]

As elsewhere, Paul begins by establishing common ground with his audience, commenting on their shrine to an unknown god (vv. 22–23) and promising to make that god known.[154] Adopting various beliefs of the philosophers but rejecting others, Paul in essence plays the Stoics and the Epicureans against each other. Paul declares that God is very near to everyone and even quotes a Cretan, Epimenides, from the sixth century B.C. to that effect (vv. 27–28a). But he denies the Stoic belief that everything is a part of god (pantheism). With the Epicureans he believes that God or the gods created people, but against them he denies that the gods have become so far removed from the world as to be uninvolved with it. Once again he quotes a pagan writer, this time Aratus of Cilicia from the third century B.C. (v. 28b).

So Paul reveals God as the one who created and still acts in history, which finally leads him to the story of Jesus and his resurrection, necessitating repentance on the part of all people (vv. 29–31). Likewise today, many cross-cultural missionaries have discovered that they must begin the presentation of the gospel with Genesis 1:1, explaining the nature of the Christian belief in God, before they can go on to

---

[153] The council, in essence, tells Paul, "We possess the legal right to judge what this new teaching is." See Bruce W. Winter, "On Introducing Gods to Athens: An Alternative Reading of Acts 17:18–20," *TynB* 47 (1996), 82.

[154] This introduction would also refute the charge that Paul was promoting foreign deities (v. 18). The word translated in the NIV as "religious" (v. 22) could also mean superstitious. As part of an introduction designed to establish common ground and gain a positive hearing, Paul surely intended his audience to understand it in the positive sense of "God revering," but Luke and his audience might well have heard a double meaning with more negative overtones.

cite John 3:16 and have God's love in Jesus be understood.[155] Despite some dramatic differences between this sermon and Paul's other ones, the general principles adopted dispel the notion that the text is a Lukan creation.[156] *But it is a model for cross-cultural evangelism, particularly for our modern cosmopolitan centers.* Kenneth Gangel's comments a generation ago remain on target: "The intelligentsia of American society today have not been offered by contemporary Christianity as distinctive a witness to truth as that heard by the Greek philosophers in Athens on that day. The 'preaching of the cross' does not have to consist of simplistic verbal meanderings calculated to evoke appropriate emotional responses. The Areopagus sermon offers us a standard of excellence in depth and relevance. Let the modern day Athenians hear again the word of the Risen Christ."[157]

Nevertheless, it is easy to read verses 32–34 and feel some disappointment, especially when we recall the triumphant responses to the gospel at Pentecost. The notion of a resurrected body probably provided the biggest stumbling block for educated Greeks, who generally believed only in the immortality of the soul. A few did believe, two of whom Luke names—Dionysius, one of the council members, and a woman named Damaris, probably an honored guest, because the council itself was made up only of men. Others were at least open to hearing more on a later date. Arguably, this response was and is the more typical paradigm for ministry in major pagan, urban centers.[158] At any rate, Luke provides no support for the notion that Paul adopted a misguided strategy in Athens by not preaching the "simple gospel" of Christ and him crucified, as in Corinth (1 Cor. 2:2), as some have suggested he did. A survey of the entire letter of 1 Corinthians demonstrates that he spoke on a broad array of topics, while Luke's account of Paul's sermon in Athens is obviously drastically abbreviated.[159]

To Corinth and Then Home (18:1–22) Located on a small isthmus, Corinth was an important seaport and trade center. Notorious for its low morals and rampant prostitution, the city bequeathed to the Greek language the slang expression a "Corinthian girl" as a synonym for a harlot. The temple of Aphrodite on the Acrocorinth, a large stone mountain overlooking the city, at least in pre-Christian times, had been said to employ over one thousand sacred priests or priestesses who also doubled as sex partners for worshippers who wanted to achieve union with the goddess.[160] Little wonder that Paul stays in this community the longest thus far trying to establish a viable church—over a year and a half (v. 11).

---

[155] The famous New Tribes Mission has in fact developed an entire curriculum for simply telling the story of the Bible from the very beginning, used with evangelism and discipleship among unreached peoples.

[156] Moreover, Paul has already been preaching to the Athenians (vv. 17–21), so this "sermon" need not declare the *whole* gospel. See further John J. Kilgallen, "Acts 17:22b–31—What Kind of Speech Is This?" *RB* 110 (2003): 417–24.

[157] "Paul's Areopagus Speech," *BSac* 127 (1970): 312. Cf. also J. Daryl Charles, "Engaging the (Neo)Pagan Mind: Paul's Encounter with Athenian Culture as a Model for Cultural Apologists (Acts 17:16–34)," *TrinJ* 16 (1995): 47–62; and Karl O. Sandnes, "Paul and Socrates: The Aim of Paul's Areopagus Speech," *JSNT* 50 (1993): 13–26.

[158] Cf. Patrick Gray, "Implied Audiences in the Areopagus Narrative," *TynB* 55 (2004): 205–18.

[159] On the entire sermon and its consistency with Paul's views in his letters, see Bertil Gärtner, *The Areopagus Speech and Natural Revelation* (Lund: Gleerup, 1955).

[160] For background to Corinth, see Jerome Murphy-O'Connor, *St. Paul's Corinth: Texts and Archaeology* (Wilmington: Glazier, 1983).

Verses 2–4 give us a glimpse of how Paul frequently supported himself during his itinerant ministry—plying a trade that he probably learned as a young man from his father, that of tent-making. In general, Jewish rabbis were forbidden to accept money for their teaching ministry, so they needed another occupation with which to support themselves (see further our discussion at 1 Cor. 9). Paul does on occasion accept gifts from churches outside of where he is currently ministering (see under Philippians), but help from others does not account for most of his needs as he travels.[161] Here he meets up with a husband and wife team of fellow tent-makers, Aquila and Priscilla, who will become significant early Christian leaders in their own right as the narrative progresses.

From this opening paragraph concerning Paul's time in Corinth, we also learn of Claudius's expulsion of the Jews from Rome (v. 2), an event also described by the Roman historian Suetonius, probably occurring in A.D. 49. Suetonius explains that the expulsion was triggered by a riot of Jews in Rome at the instigation of someone named *Chrestus,* which most scholars believe is a garbled reference to *Christus,* the Latin word for Christ, and that what actually happened was a dispute between Christian and non-Christian Jews over the gospel message (*Life of Claudius* 25). Through this it became clear that Christianity was no longer just another Jewish sect; Rome would increasingly no longer privilege it as it did Judaism as a *religio licita* (legal religion) free from the requirement of worshipping the emperor. After Claudius's death in 54, however, many Jews did return to Rome, and there was another decade of relative peace until Nero unleashed his persecution in 64.

Paul's ministry in Corinth follows the by now predictable pattern of preaching to the Jews but eventually receiving enough opposition that he turns to the Gentiles instead (vv. 5–11). It would not be surprising if he experienced considerable discouragement at this point. *At any rate, in a rare "red-letter verse" outside of the Gospels, Jesus speaks directly to Paul encouraging him that he is with him and promising that "I have many people in this city" (v. 10).* Since there is no evidence of Christianity preceding Paul to Corinth, what the Lord must be saying is that he has already ordained that a sizable number of people will respond to the gospel as Paul continues speaking. As throughout Scripture, the doctrine of election is not a hindrance but an incentive to evangelism.[162] Without God's initial activity in a person's life, there would be no hope for anyone ever accepting Christ.

Jewish opposition eventually culminates in Paul's being arraigned before Gallio, the Roman proconsul in Corinth. But Gallio still views the dispute as an intramural one within Judaism and refuses to try Paul. This sets an important precedent for Christianity's legality in Corinth, comparable to Paul's release in Philippi.[163] Curiously, the largely pagan crowd responds by turning on Sosthenes, the synagogue ruler, while Gallio turns a blind eye to the beating, evidence of the depth of

---

[161] On all these practices, see further Blomberg, *Neither Poverty nor Riches,* 185–86.

[162] A wonderful survey of this topic is James I. Packer, *Evangelism and the Sovereignty of God* (London and Downers Grove: IVP, 1961).

[163] More specifically, showing Christianity was still a *religio licita.* See Bruce W. Winter, "Gallio's Ruling on the Legal Status of Early Christianity (Acts 18:14–15)," *TynB* 50 (1999): 222.

anti-Semitism in the Greek world at that time.[164] One wonders if this is the same Sosthenes whose name appears in the opening verse of 1 Corinthians. His predecessor, Crispus, after all had already converted (v. 8).

The final paragraph dealing with Paul's second missionary journey (vv. 18–22) describes Paul cutting his hair at Cenchrea "because of a vow he had taken" (v. 18). This was most likely a Nazirite vow (see Num. 6), which would have culminated in his offering a sacrifice in the temple when he arrived in Jerusalem.[165] Would Paul have actually done this as a Christian, given that Jesus was the once-for-all sacrifice for sins? It is hard to know; Luke makes nothing of the issue and, even if he did, the sacrifice could have been a thanksgiving offering rather than a sin offering.[166] Luke also mentions that Paul makes a brief stop at Ephesus, where he declines the invitation to stay awhile but promises to return (vv. 19–21). Ephesus will in fact form the most prominent stopping-point on Paul's third journey.

Revisiting Cities from the First Journey (18:23) With the last verse of the previous section and this first verse on Paul's newest journey, Luke shows how rapidly he can cover a huge distance and time in Paul's travels. Nevertheless, it is important to observe Paul's ongoing concern for those previously evangelized, the churches he has helped to plant, and the growth of Christianity, particularly in regions where it experienced significant opposition. But Luke is far more interested in what happens in Ephesus, to which he turns next.

Ministry in Ephesus (18:24–19:20) Here Paul will stay nearly three years, and perhaps a little more. Ephesus was another major center of culture and religious life in the Roman world.[167] The first incident Luke narrates (vv. 24–28), beginning before Paul arrives, introduces us to Apollos. Something of the cosmopolitan nature of the first-century empire is disclosed when we recognize that he was a Jew from Egypt taught by Romans in Asia to preach in Greece! He knew his Old Testament, had been instructed in some elements of Christianity, taught accurately about Jesus, but "knew only the baptism of John" (vv. 24–25). Presumably this means that he had not heard of the baptism of the Spirit, or at least not as it was fulfilled at Pentecost, and thus in some sense he was preaching an incomplete message. Priscilla and Aquila fill in for him whatever details he was lacking (v. 26). Interestingly, as in verses 18–19, Luke mentions the wife's name first, an unusual word order for that day. Perhaps we are meant to recognize her as in some way the more prominent member of the pair, but it goes well beyond what the text says to conclude that she is in any sense a formal leader or office holder in the church. On the other hand, it does show the appropriateness of women teaching men in at least some Christian contexts (an important qualification to keep in mind when we wrestle with 1 Tim. 2:12).[168]

---

[164] See also Moyer V. Hubbard, "Urban Uprisings in the Roman World: The Social Setting on the Mobbing of Sosthenes," *NTS* 51 (2005): 416–28.

[165] Luke's reference to "going up" makes one naturally think of Jerusalem, since physically one always went up to reach the hill on which Jerusalem was situated.

[166] On the vow, see esp. Witherington, *Acts,* 557.

[167] For the historical background, cf. esp. Paul Trebilco, *The Early Christians in Ephesus from Paul to Ignatius* (Tübingen: Mohr, 2004).

[168] The Western text adds to verse 27 that the Ephesians had requested Apollos to come and minister to them.

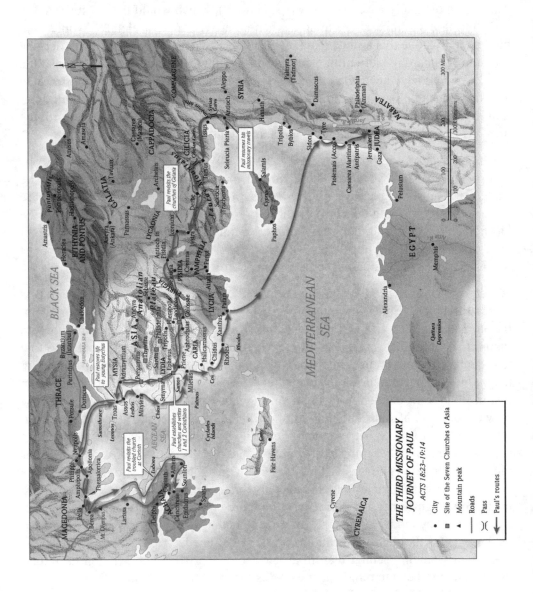

THE THIRD MISSIONARY
JOURNEY OF PAUL

ACTS 18:23–19:14

• City
■ Site of the Seven Churches of Asia
▲ Mountain peak
— Roads
)(Pass
↓ Paul's routes

Acts 19:1–7 presents one of the more curious accounts in this book. When Paul returns to Ephesus, he encounters twelve men whom Luke calls "disciples" (v. 1). By the time we learn everything he has to tell us about these individuals, however, it seems highly likely that he is simply using the term phenomenologically, that is, according to their own self-description. After all, unlike Apollos, who had seemingly not heard only of the *baptism* of the Spirit, these "believers" have not even heard of a *Holy Spirit* (v. 2)! This means that they were not Jews because the Spirit appears all over the Old Testament. But it also means they could not have known much of John the Baptist's message, despite claiming to have received his baptism, because his prediction of one who would come baptizing in the Spirit was central to his message. And they certainly would not have known much of Jesus either, since, particularly in Luke's Gospel, he is regularly said to be empowered by the Spirit.

Thus while, at first glance, this passage appears to be the third and final deviation from the "Pentecostal package" (recall under chaps. 8 and 10) because both Christian baptism and the arrival of the Spirit are separated from initial "belief," in fact it is impossible to imagine these disciples having been Christians from the outset. Only after Paul fills in the massive gaps in their knowledge can they make a true, informed commitment, and then baptism and the coming of the Spirit follow immediately (vv. 4–7). This is also the third and final place in Acts where speaking in tongues appears (v. 6), on which see our comments above (pp. 44–45).[169]

Verses 8–10 show Paul's teaching ministry taking the same pattern as before— first to Jews and then to Greeks. Here is where the Western text of verse 9 adds that Paul taught in Tyrannus's lecture hall "from the fifth to the ninth hour" (i.e., from 11:00 a.m. to 4:00 p.m.). Since this was the hottest time of the day and included a period for an early afternoon siesta, the hall might well have been available, and this additional touch may reflect historical truth. It makes us ask how committed *we* are to teaching or hearing God's word, even if at the least desirable time in our days. Verses 11–12 depict Paul working spectacular miracles reminiscent of Peter's in 5:15, doubtless another deliberate parallel between the portrayals of the two men. God's power in Jesus is demonstrated as genuine. *The quasi-magical nature of these miracles is perhaps appropriate in the city that formed the center of practice for much ancient "magic"—more akin to what today we would call the occult.*[170] But Luke makes sure to stress that *God* performed these extraordinary miracles; it was neither Paul nor the clothing that caused the healings.[171]

Indeed, the very next episode illustrates the power and danger of that magic (vv. 13–19). The seven silly sons of Sceva[172] attempt to manipulate the power of Jesus, just as practitioners of magical incantations tried to manipulate pagan gods, but they

---

[169] Cf. Dunn, *Baptism,* 83–89.

[170] For the "magical" miracles in Ephesus, see Fernando, *Acts,* 520, who also gives a balanced discussion of contemporary application.

[171] Hans-Josef Klauck, *Magic and Paganism in Early Christianity: The World of the Acts of the Apostles* (Edinburgh: T & T Clark, 2000), 98–99.

[172] No high priest by the name of Sceva appears in any of the ancient Jewish records. The name seems to have been a nickname meaning "left-handed." It is possible that he simply made the false claim to be a priest (Kee, *To Every Nation under Heaven,* 231), though many think he was a renegade Jew who became a high priest in some Roman cult.

find themselves overpowered by the demonic instead. A remarkably parallel formula has been preserved in the papyri: "I adjure you by the God of the Hebrews, Jesus." But true divine power requires belief in Christ to appropriate it properly.[173] As word of the debacle spreads, many repent, and the first "book-burning" ceremony in the history of the church takes place.[174] Particularly significant is the amount of wealth lost in the process—the equivalent of fifty thousand days' earnings at minimum wage. Would that Christians today cared about making as much of a dent in, say, the pornography industry! That thousands of these magical papyri from a slightly later date have survived reminds us that the reform was not long lasting. At this point, however, the response was positive enough that Luke refers again to the spread of the Lord's word and brings another panel of his volume to a close (v. 20).

QUESTIONS FOR REVIEW

1. What principles for divine guidance may we deduce from the opening stages of Paul's second missionary journey?
2. How does Paul's ministry in Philippi demonstrate his use of his tricultural background?
3. Compare and contrast Paul's ministry in Thessalonica and Berea.
4. If Paul's approach in Athens was not fundamentally flawed, how do we account for such a poor response there? What timeless principles may we derive from his model of preaching to the Areopagus?
5. How does Paul's ministry in Corinth demonstrate his use of his tricultural background?
6. What is the significance of each of the four episodes involving Apollos and Paul in Ephesus in Acts 18:24–19:19?

Paul's Final Travels to Jerusalem and to Rome (19:21–28:31) *Final Days in Ephesus (19:21–41)* Here is the one place in Luke's outline where the beginning of a new section does not seem to correspond neatly to the beginning or end of a missionary journey, a reminder perhaps that to speak of discrete journeys may be to impose modern precision on Luke's narrative. But verse 21 affords a clear parallel with Luke 9:51, in which Jesus sets his face decisively toward Jerusalem. While Paul will not be crucified there, he will be arrested, tried, and imprisoned just as Jesus was, and he will come near to death on the ill-fated voyage to Rome. It seems likely, then, that Luke sees parallels between the latter stages of the ministries of both men and is deliberately highlighting them.[175] While Paul will still stay in Ephesus a bit longer, from this point on in the narrative he is really looking ahead to Jerusalem, so

---

[173] "Luke is trying to get across the idea that Christianity has nothing to do with magic, and that Jesus' name is no magical-incantation formula" (Fitzmyer, *Acts,* 646). Clinton E. Arnold (*Ephesians: Power and Magic* [Cambridge and New York: CUP, 1989], 19) observes, "In religion one prays and requests from the gods; in magic one commands the gods and therefore expects guaranteed results."

[174] Again, it is important to stress that these were not documents merely *narrating* stories of people involved in the occult. They were *part* of the actual paraphernalia of the diabolical rituals themselves (complete with incantations, formulae, chants, and spells). Cf. Klauck, *Magic and Paganism,* 101–2.

[175] Talbert, *Acts,* 12.

that this is a natural break in the book's outline after all (note how in verse 22 he is sending helpers ahead of him already).

The final event that Luke chooses to record before Paul's departure from town is the riot instigated by the silversmith Demetrius (vv. 23–41). Ephesus contained a temple to the goddess Artemis (in Greek) or Diana (in Latin), patron deity of the hunt but also of fertility. There she was represented by a large statue of a many-breasted woman, allegedly fallen from heaven. The temple was considered one of the seven wonders of the ancient world. Because Christians are making such good inroads into the community, former pagans are abandoning their idol worship so that the economy, based on crafting figurines of the goddess out of silver, is suffering. *Demetrius, roughly comparable to what today would be called the union leader, tries to couch his complaint in religious terms, but it is clear that it is the economic issue that drives his anger (vv. 23–27).*

Whipping the crowd into a frenzy, the silversmiths provoke such disorder that the Roman authorities have to intervene to save Paul's companions. Paul himself would have tried to speak to the crowd had his friends not prevented him (vv. 28–34). The city clerk explains to the mob the danger of having their riot reported to Rome and the availability locally of due legal process, so that he is able to dissipate the crowd (vv. 35–41). Once again, Roman authorities demonstrate that Christians have done nothing illegal.[176]

Beginning to Head Home (20:1–16) Chapter 20 outlines the initial stages of Paul's return journey to Jerusalem (vv. 1–16). Revisiting the churches he planted on his second missionary journey, Paul also gathers delegates from several of them, no doubt in keeping with the stringent accountability mechanisms he sets up to accompany the collection of money he is taking back to Judea (vv. 1–6; cf. 2 Cor. 8–9).[177]

A slightly humorous touch appears in verses 7–12. Stopping in Troas, Paul preaches "on the first day of the week" when the believers "came together to break bread" (v. 7). Here is an important early reference to Christians no longer meeting on the Jewish Sabbath but on Sunday, although in the Roman workweek they would not have had this day off. As would be the case until the fourth century (when Constantine would make Sundays a holiday for the sake of promoting Christianity), believers met either early on Sunday morning, while it was still dark and before going to work or, more commonly, on Sunday evening after work and again after dark. Would we be committed to attend services regularly if we had such restrictions imposed on us? The service included the breaking of bread, which may refer to Communion. At any rate, both because of the stuffy environment and because of Paul's lengthy teaching, a young man by the name of Eutychus grows sleepy, falls out the window he was sitting in, and appears to have died. But Paul throws himself on the young man and declares that he is alive. While it is possible that Eutychus never actually died, it seems more likely that Luke wants us to understand Paul as

---

[176] Cf. further Robert F. Stoops Jr., "Riot and Assembly: The Social Context of Acts 19:23–41," *JBL* 108 (1989): 73–91.

[177] That Paul refers to bringing alms to Jerusalem in 24:17 confirms this suspicion.

being empowered to perform a resurrection, just as both Peter and Jesus have done before him.

Addressing the Ephesian Elders (20:17–38) Paul and his companions stop briefly at various ports of call on their way eastward, but only at Miletus does he stop for any length of time (vv. 13–16). Not wanting to be coaxed to spend a long time in Ephesus itself, he convenes the elders from that community at this nearby port and gives them a farewell charge (vv. 17–35). Tellingly, we find more points of contact in this address with the theology of Paul's letters than in any of his other speeches or sermons in Acts. After all, this is the only message Luke records that Paul delivers to an existing group of Christians rather than as part of an evangelistic outreach.[178] So, too, Paul writes his letters to established churches. A farewell address was a common Jewish oral and/or written genre. The oldest biblical example comes from Jacob in Genesis 49; Jesus himself gives a lengthy one in John 14–16 (and a briefer one in Luke 21). No doubt Luke sees another parallel here between Paul and Christ.

The brunt of Paul's address is his insistence that he has completed his job faithfully among the Ephesians, particularly in preaching the whole counsel of God's word (vv. 20, 27, 31).[179] Paul also anticipates his coming suffering (vv. 22–25), a sign to some that Luke wrote after Paul's death. But just as in the Gospel, if God can reveal future events, then there is no reason to see this as a "prophecy after the fact." Paul charges the elders to faithfulness (vv. 28–31) in a section that equates the "elders" (*presbuteroi*) with "overseers" (*episkopoi*) and "shepherds" (the Greek retains a verbal form of *poimainō*). These three terms come from the root words that in other contexts may be translated as "presbyters," "bishops," and "pastors," respectively. While these six words have come to mean many different things in many different denominations throughout church history, in the New Testament they appear interchangeably to refer to the highest "office" of church leader in a local congregation.[180] Because "the church" in any given community would have been composed of multiple house congregations, once it outgrew the thirty-five to fifty people that a well-to-do home in the ancient Roman Empire could hold, each house probably had one elder assigned to it. Periodically, the entire Christian assembly and given community may have gathered together, presumably out of doors.[181]

Paul's Miletus address contains one verse with particular theological significance. The end of verse 28 refers to "the church of God, which he bought with his own blood." Because Luke does not emphasize the atonement to the extent that the other Gospel writers do or that Paul in his letters does, to read such a claim reassures us that Luke does recognize Jesus' substitutionary sacrifice. If the NIV's translation is correct,

---

[178] Particularly striking are the number and nature of the parallels with 1 Thessalonians, esp. regarding leadership but also concerning suffering, work and money, and Jesus' death. See Steve Walton, *Leadership and Lifestyle: The Portrait of Paul in the Miletus Speech and 1 Thessalonians* (Cambridge and New York: CUP, 2000), 140–85.

[179] "Paul did not fail to proclaim the complete message, regardless of the consequences this carried for him. A second fact is that he touched every place and all the people he possibly could" (Dean S. Gilliland, "For Missionaries and Leaders: Paul's Farewell to the Ephesian Elders—Acts 20:17–38," in *Mission in Acts*, eds. Gallagher and Hertig, 264.

[180] See further Robert L. Saucy, *The Church in God's Program* (Chicago: Moody, 1972), 151–52.

[181] On house churches here and throughout the early Christian world, see Bradley Blue, "Acts and the House Church," in *The Book of Acts in Its Graeco-Roman Setting*, eds. Gill and Gempf, 119–222.

this is also a unique reference not merely to Jesus' blood but also to God's blood, a striking metaphor indeed. But the Greek could equally be translated, "which he bought with the blood of his Own (i.e., his son)," which may be the correct interpretation.

Paul closes his commission with another reminder of his personal modeling of the gospel (vv. 32–35), this time highlighting how he did not covet financial support. In this context Paul cites a saying of Jesus not found in any existing Gospel: "It is more blessed to give than to receive" (v. 35). This is a salutary reminder that not all Jesus taught was by any means included in the written Gospels (cf. John 21:25) and that even before their composition, people were preserving Jesus' teachings by word of mouth.

Overall at least ten Christian principles may be discerned from Paul's servant leadership, especially in these closing stages of his public ministry: (1) a focus on serving Christ; (2) empowering others to serve; (3) mentoring; (4) dealing with the toughest issues personally; (5) a focus on the responsibilities of the churches; (6) leading by persuasion and modeling; (7) leadership training; (8) a person orientation rather than a product orientation; (9) multicultural contextualization; and (10) finishing well.[182]

From Miletus to Jerusalem (21:1–16) This next section reads more like a travel itinerary than a series of discrete episodes. Perhaps the most interesting theological issue emerging from these verses involves the nature of Christian prophecy.[183] In 21:4, believers in Tyre urge Paul "through the Spirit" not to go to Jerusalem. This expression employs the identical Greek (*dia pneumatos*) as in 11:28 when Agabus prophesied. But verse 5 describes Paul and his followers continuing on their way. Then in verses 10–11, Agabus himself appears specifically predicting that Paul will be handed over to the Gentiles in Jerusalem, and his prediction is explicitly attributed to the Holy Spirit. Again a group of Christians pleads with Paul not to go on, but he insists that he must. When the people cannot dissuade him, they declare, "The Lord's will be done" (vv. 12–14)!

What is going on here? Is Paul contravening God's will? Do the people not recognize this? A better explanation is that unlike the prophecy of the Old Testament, which had to be 100 percent accurate if truly from the Lord, New Testament prophets exercise a spiritual gift (see below, p. 190), which must be tested by each congregation in which it appears (1 Cor. 14:29). No other spiritual gift is ever employed flawlessly by Christians, so it would seem inappropriate to insist that the exercise of prophecy as a Christian gift must be inerrant. In this case, probably the Christians in Tyre received the same message that Agabus later announced, and then naturally but incorrectly assumed that, if Paul was to be imprisoned in Jerusalem, it must not be God's will for him to go there. But they made their declaration as if all of it had come directly from the Lord.

---

[182] Grace P. Barnes, "The Art of Finishing Well: Paul as Servant Leader—Acts 18:1–28 and 20:17–38," in *Mission in Acts,* eds. Gallagher and Hertig, 246.

[183] Not to be ignored is verse 9, where Philip's daughters prophesy, in fulfillment of Joel 2:28–29 (recall Acts 2:17–18). "They have therefore taken part in the proclamation of the gospel" (Reimer, *Women in the Acts of the Apostles,* 248).

There is a warning here for contemporary prophets, whether charismatically claiming to speak the very words of God or, in noncharismatic circles, simply proclaiming confidently that "the Lord said to me" or "the Lord says to you," without leaving room for human misinterpretation.[184] In fact, Paul's resolve to proceed remains exemplary, and one quickly recalls the experience of Jesus in Gethsemane (vv. 13–14).

Arrival in Jerusalem (21:17–26)   What begins as a warm reception soon turns tense, as it becomes clear that the problem temporarily resolved at the Apostolic Council still plagues the Jerusalem Christians. Believers have the false impression that Paul is teaching Jews to abandon the Mosaic Law and forbidding circumcision, when in fact all Paul taught was freedom from the law, while clearly believing in practicing it for the sake of Jewish evangelism when no one thought that salvation was at stake (cf. 1 Cor. 9:20). To placate the law-abiding Jewish Christians, the elders suggest that Paul purify himself and pay for the sacrifices for some men who are completing a vow (vv. 17–26). All the same questions reemerge that surrounded Paul's own Nazirite vow earlier (see above, pp. 60–61). Critics charge that Luke's picture here is incompatible with the Paul of the epistles who would never support temple sacrifices. But again Paul may simply be practicing his own strategy of being "all things to all people" so that by all means he might save some (1 Cor. 9:22).[185] On the other hand, perhaps Luke is hinting that this was not the best idea since it actually backfires.[186] In verses 27–32, some Jews from out of town stir up the crowd, falsely reporting that Paul has taken a Gentile into that portion of the temple precincts reserved for Jews. A riot ensues, and Paul has to be arrested by the Roman authorities to be protected from the Jewish crowds![187]

Another odd feature of this passage involves the Jerusalem elders restating the apostolic decree in verse 25 as if no one has heard of it before. Some have assumed that Luke was relying on overlapping sources here, but more likely the point is that, just as the decree was designed to avoid unnecessarily offending Jewish consciences, so too this ploy of Paul helping the men completing their vow was designed to ward off unnecessary suspicion of Paul also. By restating it, the Jerusalem apostles are also reaffirming their commitment to the decree.[188]

Arrest and Address to the Jerusalem Crowd (21:27–22:29)   As Paul is being arrested/rescued, he speaks to the soldiers in Greek (the *lingua franca* or common language that enabled people throughout the empire with different native tongues to speak to one another). Paul then asks permission to address the crowd (21:37–39).

---

[184] Cf. the explanation of Murray J. Harris, "Appendix," in *The New International Dictionary of New Testament Theology*, ed. Colin Brown, vol. 3 (Grand Rapids: Zondervan, 1978), 1183: "Prompted by a prediction of the Spirit they told Paul not to go on to Jerusalem." Cf. also the various works by Wayne Grudem on New Testament prophecy.

[185] So Fitzmyer, *Acts*, 692.

[186] So Barrett, *Acts*, 328.

[187] Unlike other ancient literature impinging on Roman imprisonments, Luke depicts a prisoner (Paul) here and through the end of Acts in key ways actually being helped by incarceration, particularly in spreading the gospel. See Matthew L. Skinner, *Locating Paul: Places of Custody as Narrative Settings in Acts 21–28* (Atlanta: SBL, 2003).

[188] Witherington, *Acts*, 650.

The commander is surprised because he has mistaken Paul for an Egyptian terrorist, perhaps the same revolutionary referred to by Josephus who had escaped Felix's slaughter of thousands of his followers in A.D. 55 (*Jewish War* 2.261–63; *Antiquities* 20.169–72). But when Paul gets the chance to speak to his fellow Jews, he uses Aramaic, now surprising the crowd, given all the rumors flying about Paul having abandoned his Jewish heritage (21:20–22:1).

In fact, Paul goes out of his way to stress his upbringing as an orthodox Jew, his zeal for his religion—even to the point of persecuting Christians—and how it was only the dramatic, supernatural revelation of Jesus himself that turned him in a diametrically opposite direction (22:2–11). He then describes how Ananias ministered to him and how he came to understand his new calling (vv. 12–16). Adding a detail that Luke has not told us about earlier, Paul mentions that in another revelation to him, in the temple in Jerusalem, the Lord prophesied that the Jewish people in general would not accept his testimony (vv. 17–18). When Paul protested that they should know of his past zeal, the Lord replied that his primary commission would be to go "far away to the Gentiles" (vv. 19–21). Tellingly, the crowd listens attentively to all of Paul's testimony until this final statement. Whereas today Christians often find that Jews are unwilling to listen to them talk about Jesus at all, that was not a stumbling block in this context, but *Paul's claim that he was sent to Gentiles was.*[189] Here was the sticking point, understandable when we recall the intense hostility between Jews and Gentiles that often flared up.

Having used his knowledge of *Greek* to speak to the soldiers and his fluency in *Aramaic* to address the crowd, Paul now draws on his *Roman* citizenship to avoid a flogging without a proper trial (vv. 22–29). Once again it appears that he is acting not merely out of self-interest but also to have Christianity publicly vindicated. "Paul's use of his Roman citizenship teaches us that as an expression of God's moral order, and when the laws governing its exercise of power are just, the state may be appealed to for protection of the physical well-being of law-abiding citizens. The Christian's appeal must always be in the interest of the advance of the gospel."[190] After all, Paul submitted five times to the horrible punishment of thirty-nine lashes in Jewish synagogues (2 Cor. 11:24), when he could have renounced his Judaism altogether, been excommunicated and no longer been subject to their jurisdiction. But in the synagogues he was trying to win over his fellow countrymen by remaining part of their community. When the interests of the gospel dictated, Paul was astonishingly ready to submit to personal suffering.

Defense before the Sanhedrin (22:30–23:11)   Because the Romans had "arrested" Paul more to rescue him from the angry mob than because he had demonstrably broken Roman law, the commander arranges for Paul to appear before the *Jewish* court

---

[189] "Those who listen to Paul cannot bear to hear him say that he has been commissioned by heaven to preach a message of salvation to people who would not have to observe the Mosaic Law" (Fitzmyer, *Acts,* 711). For the parallels between this speech and Stephen's, see Clark, *Parallel Lives,* 273–78; Tannehill, *Narrative Unity,* vol. 2, 272–74.

[190] Larkin, *Acts,* 325.

(22:30).[191] Paul begins his defense by claiming a blameless conscience (23:1; cf. Phil. 3:6), which is not the same as saying he has never sinned. Rather, he is insisting that he is not guilty of anything deserving trial. At this point the high priest—yet another Ananias—orders him struck (v. 2), to which Paul replies with perhaps his most vindictive statement anywhere in Acts or his letters (v. 3).[192] The bystanders are shocked that Paul insulted the high priest (v. 4), to which Paul retorts that he did not realize this was the high priest. He appears to apologize, even quoting Scripture (v. 5; cf. Exod. 22:28). Commentators struggle with what to make of this interchange, most thinking that Paul gave a genuine apology, but wondering how he could not have known that Ananias was the high priest. Had he been away from Jerusalem that long (but the high priest wore distinctive robes that would indicate who he was)? Was this less than a formal session of the Sanhedrin so that the priests were not wearing their robes (but it still would have been clear who their leader was by who convened the meeting)?

Perhaps the best suggestion is that Paul's statement in verse 5a reflects bitter irony—Paul could not imagine that a person gratuitously ordering him hit could be the true high priest[193]—and that verse 5b is not part of Paul's reply (recall that the original manuscripts never used signs for quotation marks), but Luke's editorial comment explaining the seriousness of the interchange in verses 4–5a.[194]

In any event, Paul next adopts a strategic ploy to divide the council. Knowing that the Pharisees and Sadducees disagreed as to whether life after death was embodied, *he couches the heart of his message as "hope in the resurrection of the dead" (v. 6).*[195] The Pharisees, however, seem to have been in the minority on the Sanhedrin during most of the first century, so even their support would not be enough to exonerate him. The debate grows violent, so that the Roman troops once again take Paul away (v. 10). At a point when Paul could easily have remained disconsolate, the Lord again directly speaks to him, telling him to take courage and promising that he will be able to testify even in Rome (v. 11). It is important to observe, however, that this promise does not lead Paul to inaction, as if God would orchestrate events for him without his active participation. Indeed, he will later appeal explicitly to the emperor (25:11), which will turn out to be the way God fulfills his promise.

Transfer to Caesarea (23:12–35) The Lord's promise was, however, perfectly timed because the very next day Paul's life is seriously threatened. Providentially, a nephew gains wind of the plot and goes to the prison to warn his uncle (thus also demonstrating that Paul had relatives in Jerusalem). Here again Paul does not sit back and do nothing but sends the boy to the Roman centurion so the guards can

---

[191] On the various arraignments of Paul, see H. W. Tajra, *The Trial of St. Paul: A Juridical Exegesis of the Second Half of the Acts of the Apostles* (Tübingen: Mohr, 1989).

[192] A whitewashed wall suggests one who conceals contamination thinly covered (Fitzmyer, *Acts,* 717). Paul's words could also be taken as prophecy, fulfilled when Ananias was murdered by revolutionaries at the beginning of the Jewish War (Josephus, *Jewish War* 2.441).

[193] Witherington, *Acts,* 689; cf. Johnson, *Acts,* 397.

[194] Craig L. Blomberg, "The Christian and the Law of Moses," in *Witness to the Gospel,* eds. Marshall and Peterson, 415.

[195] More difficult is the interpretation of "neither angels nor spirits" in v. 8. For the various options, see Floyd Parker, "The Terms 'Angel' and 'Spirit' in Acts 23.8," *Bib* 84 (2003): 344–65.

protect him (vv. 12–22). The commander, Lysias, arranges a huge detachment of military personnel to accompany Paul and to whisk him off by night to the garrison on the coast where Felix, the procurator of all Judea, resided (vv. 23–24).[196]

Here is where Luke includes a letter written by the commander to the governor (vv. 26–30), which, as we noted in the introduction (p. 17), would not likely have left Roman hands for Paul or any other Christian to learn about. But perhaps Luke wants us to know that, because in verse 25, innocuously translated in the NIV as "he wrote a letter as follows," the Greek literally reads, "having written a letter having this type." This wording may suggest that, as Thucydides explained, when information was unavailable, a historian could choose language that seemed to him what would have most likely been spoken or written. Even if this is the case, Luke's distinctive introduction shows his concern to be as accurate as possible and not to mislead his audience about what he is doing.[197] Of course, there may have been some way we do not understand that the letter or its contents could have actually gotten into Luke's hands.[198] At any rate, the letter, like the envoy, accomplishes its intended design, and Paul arrives safely in Caesarea (vv. 31–35).

Defense before and Custody under Felix (24:1–27)   Like Pilate two decades earlier, Felix is caught between the proverbial rock and a hard place, needing to please the emperor in Rome without alienating the Jews in Judea, who might revolt and get him in trouble with Rome. Despite the fact that Paul is innocent of any crime Rome should be concerned about, Felix never releases him. At his formal defense, attended by the high priest and some of his colleagues, a lawyer named Tertullus plays the part of prosecutor. His Greek name suggests that Paul's Jewish accusers want to employ someone who is most likely to gain the outcome they desire, even though he is a Gentile. Luke presents enough of Tertullus's opening remarks for us to recognize them as a classic example of ingratiating rhetorical pomposity common in the Greco-Roman world (vv. 2–8), another sign of Luke's verisimilitude in reporting.[199]

When it is his turn to speak, Paul again refuses to admit breaking any law and shifts the focus of discussion to the resurrection (vv. 10–21). When Felix adjourns the proceedings, he promises to render a verdict when the commander, Lysias, arrives. But as Luke's account continues, it becomes clear these are merely stalling tactics. Felix is intrigued enough with Paul to summon him to speak with him on several occasions, but he is also hoping for the customary bribe that would buy Paul his freedom, which the prisoner never provides. Thus Paul languishes in prison for

---

[196] The Western text adds that Lysias feared the accusation of taking money to allow Paul to be killed and the threat of being killed himself.

[197] Cf. Marshall, *Acts,* 370.

[198] For suggestions about how Luke might have had access to this information, see Witherington, *Acts,* 698.

[199] Paul himself attempts to curry the governor's favor with his introduction in verse 10, but it is not nearly as obsequious. On both introductions, see Bruce W. Winter, "The Importance of the *Captatio Benevolentiae* in the Speeches of Tertullus and Paul in Acts 24:1–21," *JTS* 42 (1991): 505–31.

two years,[200] even while having periodic opportunities to preach the gospel to the governor (vv. 22–27).[201]

Custody under and Defense before Festus (25:1–12)   In A.D. 59, Rome deposed Felix, in part because of his ruthlessness, and replaced him with Festus, who had a reputation of being a far more competent administrator (cf. Josephus, *Antiquities,* 20.8.9). There is no indication that Festus thought Paul was guilty of some Roman crime any more than Felix did, but he remained in the same precarious position as other Roman procurators, needing to please both the Jews and Rome. So he attempts to give the Sanhedrin another opportunity to try Paul. Whether Paul knows of the new plot against his life, he certainly remembers the last one and could easily imagine that something else was afoot. Even if he suspected nothing, he knew that he would not get a fair trial before the Jewish council. Despite the various inequities in Roman justice, experience had taught him that he stood a better chance in that system. If a provincial governor was unwilling to hear his case, his remaining option was to appeal to the emperor. Only Roman citizens had this privilege; and once Paul made his appeal, Festus was obligated to honor it.

Paul before Agrippa II (25:13–26:32)   Before Paul can be sent to Rome, he has one more hearing to endure. Agrippa II, son of the Agrippa who was struck dead in 12:23, arrives in Caesarea to see Festus, finds out about the celebrated prisoner, and wants to hear him for himself (vv. 13–22). That Luke takes the time to describe Festus rehearsing the facts of the case for Agrippa shows his ongoing concern to demonstrate Paul's innocence. That Festus acquiesced to Agrippa so readily discloses the delicate relationships between representatives of the two systems that competed in first-century Rome for jurisdiction in Israel. After the ruthless reign of Archelaus, son of Herod the Great, ended in A.D. 6, Rome replaced members of the Herodian family with its own imperial appointees as procurators in Judea and Samaria. From a Christian point of view, the most famous of these was Pontius Pilate, who governed from 26 to 36. Felix and Festus occupied this same office in the late 50s and early 60s. Meanwhile Herod's descendants continued to rule in Galilee and Perea. But for a short three-year period, from 41 to 44, Israel had been united again under Agrippa I, grandson of Herod the Great. Would Rome consider doing that again with Agrippa's son? Festus had no way of knowing and so had to show him some deference.[202]

Particularly scandalous for the Jewish people was the fact that Agrippa II lived with his sister Bernice, and all kinds of rumors flew about their relationship being incestuous (Josephus, *Antiquities* 20.145–47; *Jewish War* 2.217). Yet this Agrippa, like his father, descendant of the original Herod who had professed conversion to

---

[200] The definitive work on prison conditions in ancient Rome is Brian Rapske, *The Book of Acts and Paul in Roman Custody* (Grand Rapids: Eerdmans; Carlisle: Paternoster, 1994).

[201] Felix in fact had an adulterous marriage with Drusilla, herself a Jew, making Paul's topics of "righteousness, self-control, and the judgment to come" all the more appropriate.

[202] Complicating matters further was the fact that it was unclear who had jurisdiction over Paul's case. The Jewish leaders couched a religious issue in political terms to bring Paul before the Roman governors, while Paul insisted the matter was religious yet still appropriate for Roman authorities! Moreover, Claudius had appointed Agrippa curator of the Jerusalem temple with power to appoint the Jewish high priest. Festus, therefore, would view him as a higher *Jewish* authority than anyone on the Sanhedrin. See further Witherington, *Acts,* 724, 727–28.

Judaism, knew plenty about Jewish beliefs and morals, more so than Roman governors typically did, and Paul could exploit this to his advantage in his defense. Luke again records a lengthy introduction to this hearing, further demonstrating Festus's deference to Agrippa and the fact that he has not found Paul guilty of any crime. Perhaps this new hearing will give Festus some charge to send with Paul to the emperor (25:23–27).

Because this is not a formal trial, no charges are levied against Paul; he is simply invited to speak for himself. Because Paul knows that Agrippa is acquainted with Jewish customs, and could even present himself as a Jew in spirit,[203] his strategy closely resembles the tactics he has adopted with various Jewish gatherings. He reasserts his orthodox upbringing, even to the point of living like a Pharisee, persecuting Christians[204] and en route to wreak more havoc when Christ confronted him on the Damascus Road (26:1–14). Not only does Jesus reveal himself as the true Lord, but he appoints Paul to testify to what he has seen and what he will learn and particularly to become an emissary to the Gentiles (vv. 15–18). How could he do anything but obey such a spectacular and persuasive call? Once again he insists that his message is the natural outgrowth of Judaism and the fulfillment of its prophecies, culminating in Jesus' resurrection (vv. 19–23). But when Paul echoes language from Isaiah 9:1–2 about enlightening the Gentiles as well as Israel,[205] Festus interrupts and declares Paul mad (v. 24).

Paul denies the charge but then focuses on Agrippa again. He challenges the client king to acknowledge his sympathies with Judaism by accepting the testimony of the prophets, which Paul believes was fulfilled in Christ (vv. 25–27). Agrippa's reply in verse 28 became famous in the KJV as "almost thou persuadest me to be a Christian." But this translation is almost certainly too positive; rather Agrippa is probably asking a question somewhat sarcastically, "Do you think you can so easily make me a Christian?"[206] Either way, Paul wishes he could, but the king ends the hearing at this point (vv. 29–30). In what would be the height of tragic irony apart from a belief in God's providential guidance, Agrippa and Festus agree that Paul is innocent of any crime and could have been freed on the spot (vv. 31–32). *But Paul, like the reader, knows that God has promised to get him to Rome, and his appeal turns out to be exactly God's mechanism of accomplishing his promise.*

Sea Voyage and Shipwreck (27:1–44) This chapter presents one of the most remarkable, suspense-filled stories in all of Scripture. Luke includes far more detail, about both the various ports of call and the activities on board the ship during the storm, than we would expect given the nature of his narratives thus far. It has often

---

[203] Barrett, *Acts,* 392.

[204] Chapter 26:10 is the verse that leads many to wonder if Paul had actually been on the Sanhedrin. But the expression, "I cast my vote against them," could be a metaphorical way of referring to Paul's agreement rather than a literal reference to being a voting member of the council. After all, Paul would have been considerably younger than the typical age Jewish men were when they were appointed to the high court.

[205] Dennis Hamm ("Paul's Blindness and Its Healing: Clues to Symbolic Intent [Acts 9; 22 and 26]," *Bib* 71 [1990]: 63–72) traces how references to Paul's sight and blindness in his three conversion accounts all symbolize spiritual realities as well—both for himself and for others.

[206] Or, if a statement, it might be a more lighthearted remark such as, "In a short time you think to make me a Christian!" See Marshall, *Acts,* 399–400.

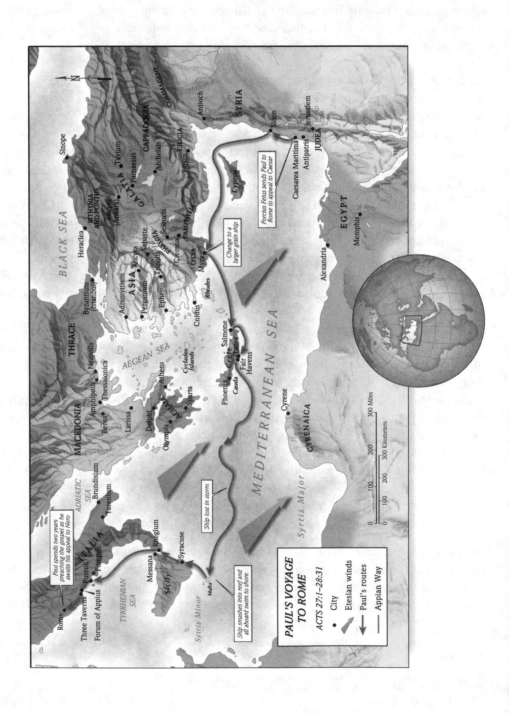

PAUL'S VOYAGE
TO ROME

ACTS 27:1–28:31

• City
Etesian winds
Paul's routes
Appian Way

been alleged that this story is a fictitious creation along the lines of other ancient sea legends, but the supposed parallels really are not close, and Luke's information is so accurate, particularly in nautical detail, that seafaring experts have argued that the story could have been written only by one who had experienced such a voyage. The classic study from this perspective is James Smith's *The Voyage and Shipwreck of St. Paul,* first published in 1856[207] and never effectively refuted (though often ignored). At the same time, Luke writes up his reminiscences according to standard literary forms of the day, with their five elements of travelogue, forecast, storm, speech, and concern for safety.[208]

Paul is handed over to a centurion, Julius, who will be taking a group of prisoners on board a ship headed for Asia Minor, where presumably they will transfer to a boat going to Rome (vv. 1–2). Verses 3–8 outline the itinerary, including one stop where Paul is allowed to go ashore and spend time with, literally, "the friends"—perhaps an early label for fellow Christians. Sidon was a major port for loading cargo bound for points west, while Myra, the largest city in Lycia, was another important port for grain ships. There they found a vessel heading for Italy and made it as far as one of the cities of Crete. Sailing became increasingly dangerous "after the Fast," that is the Day of Atonement. If this is A.D. 59, the date is probably October 5.[209] The period between mid-September and mid-November produced enough bad weather to make it risky to sail the Mediterranean for more than very short trips (Vegetius, *De re militari* 4.39). Afterwards, in the winter, it became almost unnavigable. The whole trip from Jerusalem to Rome during good weather could have been completed in a month; as it turns out, the ship will not even make it to a better port further along the coast of Crete (vv. 9–12).

Deluded by fair skies and gentle winds, and ignoring Paul's advice, the captain of the ship sets sail. Soon, however, a northeaster attacks them (vv. 13–26). This storm, blowing from the northeast, would have hurled the ship in a southwesterly direction into the most dangerous and unprotected parts of the sea. When the storm does not abate after many days and all hope seems lost, Paul can no longer resist the urge, in essence, to say, "I told you so." Still, he goes on to explain how an angel has promised him that he would safely arrive in Rome and save the lives of all the men accompanying him.

A full two weeks after the beginning of the storm, the battered crew finally realizes they are nearing land. This time they are ready to listen to Paul's advice. He insists no one attempt to leave the ship (vv. 27–32), encourages them to take food, and breaks bread and gives thanks to God in front of them all (vv. 33–38). The language of verse 35 has suggested to some a Eucharistic meal. But it is unlikely that Paul would take communion with a group of largely pagan companions, and the wording is standard enough to apply to any Jewish meal. Eventually the ship runs aground on what turns out to be the island of Malta, and the centurion devises a scheme to save

---

[207] Minneapolis: James Family. For a brief update cf. J. M. Gilchrist, "The Historicity of Paul's Shipwreck," *JSNT* 61 (1996): 29–51.

[208] Susan M. Praeder, "Acts 27:1–28:16: Sea Voyages in Ancient Literature and the Theology of Luke-Acts," *CBQ* 46 (1984): 683–706.

[209] Bruce, *Acts,* 481.

Paul's life. God, meanwhile, providentially ensures that none of the prisoners either escapes or perishes (vv. 39–44).

Ashore on Malta (28:1–10) Much like the residents of Lystra in 14:11–19, the Maltese prove both very welcoming and superstitious. They care for the needs of the beleaguered band of storm survivors; but when a viper bites Paul's hand,[210] they conclude he must have been a murderer whom "Justice" (often viewed as a god) is now punishing. Yet when the venom has no ill effect, their opinion swings wildly to the opposite end of the spectrum, as they are ready to deify him (vv. 1–6). One thinks also of the drastic swings of opinion about Jesus during the last week of his life.

The leading official on Malta (literally, "chief man") likewise shows the seafarers great hospitality, in return for which Paul is empowered miraculously to heal this man's father of a serious illness. This leads to a mass healing of other sick people on the island. Interestingly, Luke uses what in the New Testament is the comparatively rare verb *therapeuō*, which was often used for healing via the normal medical practices of the day. Are we supposed to imagine Luke, the physician, assisting here?

At Last to Rome (28:11–31) Verses 11–16 complete Paul's itinerary. Christians meet him along the Appian Way to Rome and help to escort him there. By now he will have written his epistle to the Roman Christians; this letter, combined with the news of his arrival under these extraordinary conditions, will have generated considerable positive, advance interest in his coming. In Rome he is put under house arrest, as he awaits the hearing of his case by the emperor. This form of imprisonment was as mild as possible in the Roman world, though he might have been chained loosely to a soldier who was relieved by a fresh guard every four hours.[211] Paul could summon visitors, receive and send mail, but not leave his domicile, for which he even had to pay rent. Friends probably kept him supplied with food since there was no provision for the state to pay for feeding prisoners under these circumstances.

As in many other communities, Paul summons the synagogue elders (since he can't go and speak in the synagogue) and preaches the gospel to them (vv. 17–28). He again rehearses his testimony, insisting that the gospel is the fulfillment of "the hope of Israel" (v. 20). The elders' response reflects the "hit or miss" character of communication in Paul's day. The Sanhedrin does not exercise jurisdiction over Jews in the Diaspora, and with Paul so far away and under Roman custody, the court apparently feels no need to send letters about Paul to Jewish leaders in Rome. Roman Jews, returned from travels to Judea, report no valid criticisms of Paul, but the rumor mill has provided plenty of grist for slander (vv. 21–23).

As even more return to hear the prisoner on a later occasion, Luke sums up Paul's message as proclaiming the kingdom of God (v. 23), an important reminder that Paul's message still fits in with Jesus' emphases, despite the fact that neither in

---

[210] *Echidna* did not mean only a viper in ancient Greek but was used for a variety of snakes and small reptiles. Thus the complaint that vipers are not found on Malta does not impugn Luke's credibility here. See Kee, *To Every Nation under Heaven,* 337, n. 62.

[211] But Roman citizens were not supposed to be chained, so it is possible that verse 20 is metaphorical (Barrett, *Acts,* 423). The four-hour rotation is affirmed by Witherington, *Acts,* 789 (although his Josephus reference is not correct).

Acts nor in his letters are references to the kingdom nearly as common as in the Gospels.[212] Like Jesus in Luke 24:27, Paul appeals to a wide array of texts from the Law and the Prophets to try to persuade his Jewish audience that Jesus was the promised Messiah (v. 24). Some come to faith, but overall the response is not positive enough for Paul to continue this ministry. Somewhat harshly but understandably in light of the persistent pattern of response he has received throughout his career, Paul cites Isaiah 6:9–10 (the very text Jesus had used to explain his preaching in parables and people's diverse responses to it), seeing it fulfilled again in the obduracy of this group of Jewish leaders (vv. 25–27). As in other cities, Paul will again turn to preaching primarily to the Gentiles, anticipating a more positive response (v. 28).

Marshall explains the intransigence of some: "Once a person deliberately refuses the Word there comes a point where he is deprived of the capacity to receive it."[213] *But even this dramatic conclusion to Paul's time with the Roman Jews does not represent some unalterable rejection by God of all Jewish people, nor even a moment after which it was no longer appropriate for Christians to preach the gospel to Jews (cf. also the positive ending of Isaiah 6). This is simply the last recorded instance in Acts of the pattern of "to the Jew first and also to the Greek."*[214]

Acts closes with two remarkable verses (vv. 30–31). Paul remains under house arrest for two entire years. Imperial cases were supposed to be heard within two years or thrown out (cf. Philo, *Against Flaucus*16.128), leading some scholars to wonder if this is Luke's way of indirectly disclosing that Paul was later released. Given early church tradition, Paul may well have been acquitted, only to be rearrested and executed a few years later (1 Clem. 5:5–7; Eusebius, *Church History,* 2.22),[215] but it seems unlikely Luke is alluding to that here. Courts ancient and modern have regularly fallen behind schedule! What Luke does want to highlight, however, is that even under these most awkward of circumstances (we would normally not refer to imprisonment as "without hindrance"!), the gospel went forward with power and lives were changed.[216] If Philippians is to be dated to this Roman imprisonment (see below, pp. 325–27), then it is fascinating that Paul there declares that the gospel has become clear throughout the whole palace guard (Phil. 1:13). If a large number of soldiers took turns guarding Paul, we can easily see how this happened. Even if a comparatively small number rotated the responsibility, they could just as easily have spread the word to others. God has brought his message through his special apostle to the Gentiles, even in Rome, the heart of the empire. Luke can conclude his volume, even if he does not know the outcome of Paul's appeal.[217]

---

[212] Polhill (*Acts,* 538) reminds us that the book also began with one of Acts' comparatively rare references to the kingdom (1:6). Thus Luke creates an inclusio around his book with this theme.

[213] Marshall, *Acts,* 425.

[214] Tannehill, *Narrative Unity of Luke-Acts,* vol. 2, 328.

[215] For a good survey of the possible course of the last years of Paul's life, after the end of Acts, see Bruce, *Paul,* 441–55.

[216] Winter ("Gallio's Ruling," 223–24) shows that the term could mean that there were no *legal* obstacles to what Paul was doing.

[217] "The open-ended ending of Acts suggests that the message of God's saving work in Jesus Christ would continue in a significant way" (Marion L. Soards, *The Speeches in Acts: Their Content, Context and Concerns* [Louisville: WJKP, 1994], 208).

QUESTIONS FOR REVIEW

1. Highlight the most salient points involving Paul's address to the Ephesian elders.
2. Explain the apparent contradictions between Acts 20:22; 21:4; and 21:11.
3. How could Paul possibly have agreed to support Jewish Christians offering animal sacrifices in the temple?
4. How does Paul use his tricultural background in his arrest and speech to the Jewish crowd in Acts 21:27–22:29?
5. Summarize Paul's main approach in each of his four appearances after his arrest—before the Sanhedrin, Felix, Festus, and Herod Agrippa II. In what ways does his defense remain the same throughout, and in what ways does it change?
6. What theology can we learn from the voyage and shipwreck of Paul?
7. What is the point of each of the episodes of Acts 28, and how does each contribute to the end of Luke's work?

APPLICATION

Numerous specific principles for contemporary Christian living and mission have emerged throughout our treatment of Acts. The bigger picture discloses the church moving ever outward, eager to incorporate more and more people into the community of the redeemed. Throughout much of human history, with its fairly homogeneous groupings of people in local, provincial, and even national clusters, at least as a huge generalization, it has been easier for Christians to witness to people near to home than far away. While this principle continues to hold true for many people in today's world, our global village, with its unprecedented opportunities for transportation and communication, makes the potential for reaching people of every ethnicity, nationality, race, and religion easier than previous generations could have even imagined. In large Western cities one may proclaim the gospel in person to people from dozens of cultures without leaving the metropolitan areas of those cities. Via the Internet, one may reach representatives of every nation and thousands of subcultures around the world, although, the poorer the country, the fewer people in it will have access to such technology.

The model of Acts, however, has not been successfully replicated just when people from many different locales and backgrounds become believers. The next stage is to incorporate them into churches—healthy, growing Christian communities that instruct them in the central truths of the faith, minister to physical and spiritual needs, lead them to love and worship God, guide them in loving and serving their own neighbors (both nearby and far away), uphold them in times of trial and persecution, and reach out to others to expand the impact of God's kingdom even further. Rather than creating a specific cookie-cutter approach to Christian evangelism and discipleship, Acts demonstrates how crucial contextualizing the gospel message is for each new culture and subculture. The basic truths remain the same, but how they are communicated may change dramatically. Holy living requires the identical obedience to the normative commands of Scripture, but how to inculcate those principles can vary widely. Too often throughout its history, the church in one part of the world has brought along at least as much of its national or tribal culture, in its missionary endeavors, as it has actual biblical teaching, no matter how inappropriate its customs may be in another part of the world.

The book of Acts also regularly reminds us that church is not about programs but about people. It is not we who determine the perfect methodology for church growth, but God's Spirit who regularly works in the most unlikely places among the most inauspicious people in the most surprising of ways. True, certain principles of what seems to work well or poorly in various times and places can be discerned, but as soon as believers institutionalize them, depend on them, or take credit for them, the sovereign Spirit is likely to begin to work differently! If there is a timeless method, it is dependence on prayer, the one spiritual discipline many Western churches seem least inclined to prioritize.

Acts is the database for determining much of what a "New Testament church" should look like, but notice the diversity of churches all thinking that they alone have captured the perfect synthesis of the paradigm of Acts. The churches in Jerusalem and Antioch function congregationally, at least to some degree; the elders of the various Ephesian churches resemble a presbytery; and the itinerant apostles and evangelists provide partial precedent for the authority of the later Episcopal model, complete with bishops whose jurisdiction would span large swaths of territory. Charismatic churches regularly appeal to the diverse patterns of the coming of the Spirit and the appearance of glossolalia in Acts; noncharismatic churches equally validly point to the texts on tongues and unusual times for the Spirit's arrival as exceptions that differ from the norm. Egalitarians highlight the numerous women leaders that Acts describes, particularly Lydia, Priscilla, and Philip's daughters. Complementarians rightly observe that women are never described as functioning as elders or overseers in a local congregation. Arminians stress the freedom and necessity of all humans to respond in repentance to the gospel message; Calvinists respond by pointing to God's foreknowledge and election of these free human responses. Baptists emphasize the repeated examples of immersion in water close on the heels of initial belief. Paedobaptists speculate about babies being part of the household baptisms that Luke likewise narrates. These theological debates will simply not be solved on the basis of Acts alone!

On the other hand, there *are* some unalterable principles in Acts, though expressed in various ways from one setting to the next, that many branches of the church today too often ignore—a passionate concern for the poor so that not one needy person remains in the midst of any Christian congregation, a holistic outreach that insists on people's physical and spiritual needs alike being addressed, the commitment by church leaders to work themselves out of their current jobs, so to speak, by discipling and empowering others to use their gifts, and a willingness to speak both boldly and tactfully, even under fire and threat of imprisonment and/or death. Perhaps least imitated of all is the relentless drive in the churches of Acts for a heterogeneity that unites Jew and Gentile (and all different kinds of Jews and all different kinds of Gentiles) into one living, loving organism in a way that demands that a fair-minded observer acknowledge some supernatural force to be at work yet without legislating that which can come about only with people so exhilarated by the gospel's freedom from law and their own personal liberation from the shackles of sin that they live a life of spontaneous gratitude to God with a desire to serve Christ as much as they can. Of course such a lifestyle will make many of the world's powerbrokers jealous, so that persecution of believers becomes commonplace. But that only provokes the sufferers to greater trust in their sovereign God.[218]

SELECT BIBLIOGRAPHY

COMMENTARIES

Advanced

Barrett, C. K. *A Critical and Exegetical Commentary on the Acts of the Apostles.* ICC, rev. 2 vols. Edinburgh: T & T Clark, 1994–98.

Bruce, F. F. *The Acts of the Apostles: The Greek Text with Introduction and Commentary.* Leicester: IVP; Grand Rapids: Eerdmans, rev. 1990.

Conzelmann, Hans. *Acts of the Apostles.* Hermeneia. Philadelphia: Fortress, 1987.

Fitzmyer, Joseph A. *The Acts of the Apostles.* AB. New York and London: Doubleday, 1998.

Haenchen, Ernst. *The Acts of the Apostles.* Oxford: Blackwell; Philadelphia: Westminster, 1971.

Intermediate

Barrett, C. K. *Acts: A Shorter Commentary.* Edinburgh: T & T Clark; New York: Continuum, 2002.

Bruce, F. F. *The Book of the Acts.* NICNT. Grand Rapids: Eerdmans, rev. 1988.

Dunn, James D. G. *The Acts of the Apostles.* London: Epworth, 1996.

González, Justo L. *Acts: The Gospel of the Spirit.* Maryknoll, N.Y.: Orbis, 2001.

Johnson, Luke T. *The Acts of the Apostles.* SP. Collegeville: Liturgical, 1992.

Kee, Howard C. *To Every Nation under Heaven: The Acts of the Apostles.* NTinCont. Harrisburg: Trinity, 1997.

Polhill, John B. *Acts.* NAC. Nashville: Broadman, 1992.

Talbert, Charles H. *Reading Acts.* New York: Crossroad, 1997.

Witherington, Ben, III. *The Acts of the Apostles: A Socio-Rhetorical Commentary.* Grand Rapids: Eerdmans, 1998.

Introductory

Fernando, Ajith. *Acts.* NIVAC. Grand Rapids: Zondervan, 1998.

Gaventa, Beverly. *The Acts of the Apostles.* ANTC. Nashville: Abingdon, 2003.

Larkin, William J. *Acts.* IVPNTC. Downers Grove: IVP, 1995.

---

[218] For outstanding application of Acts, including cross-culturally, see Gallagher and Hertig, eds., *Mission in Acts*; Fernando, *Acts.* More generally, cf. esp. Green, *Thirty Years*; idem, *Evangelism.*

Longenecker, Richard N. "The Acts of the Apostles." In *The Expositor's Bible Commentary,* ed. Frank E. Gaebelein, vol. 9, 207–573. Grand Rapids: Zondervan, 1981.

Marshall, I. Howard. *The Acts of the Apostles.* TNTC, rev. Leicester: IVP; Grand Rapids: Eerdmans, 1980.

Stott, John. *The Message of Acts: The Spirit, the Church and the World.* BST. Leicester and Downers Grove: IVP, rev. 1994.

Williams, David J. *Acts.* NIBC. Peabody: Hendrickson, rev. 1990.

OTHER BOOKS

Cassidy, Richard J. *Society and Politics in the Acts of the Apostles.* Maryknoll, N.Y.: Orbis, 1987.

Clark, Andrew C. *Parallel Lives: The Relation of Paul to the Apostles in the Lucan Perspective.* Carlisle: Paternoster, 2001.

Dibelius, Martin. *The Book of Acts: Form, Style, and Theology,* ed. K. C. Hanson. Minneapolis: Fortress, rev. 2004.

Foakes-Jackson, F. T., and Kirsopp Lake, eds. *The Beginnings of Christianity: The Acts of the Apostles.* 5 vols. London and New York: Macmillan, 1920–33.

Gallagher, Robert L., and Paul Hertig, eds. *Mission in Acts: Ancient Narrative in Contemporary Context.* Maryknoll, N.Y.: Orbis, 2004.

Gasque, W. Ward. *A History of the Criticism of the Acts of the Apostles.* Tübingen: Mohr; Grand Rapids: Eerdmans, 1975.

Green, Michael. *Evangelism in the Early Church.* Grand Rapids and Cambridge: Eerdmans, rev. 2004.

Green, Michael. *Thirty Years That Changed the World: The Book of Acts for Today.* Grand Rapids and Cambridge: Eerdmans, rev. 2002.

Hemer, Colin J. *The Book of Acts in the Setting of Hellenistic History,* ed. Conrad H. Gempf. Tübingen: Mohr, 1989.

Hengel, Martin. *Acts and the History of Earliest Christianity.* London: SCM, 1979.

Jervell, Jacob. *The Theology of the Acts of the Apostles.* Cambridge and New York: CUP, 1996.

Klauck, Hans-Josef. *Magic and Paganism in Early Christianity: The World of the Acts of the Apostles.* Edinburgh: T & T Clark, 2000.

Liefeld, Walter L. *Interpreting the Book of Acts.* Grand Rapids: Baker, 1995.

Marguerat, Daniel. *The First Christian Historian: Writing the "Acts of the Apostles."* Cambridge and New York: CUP, 2002.

Marshall, I. H. *The Acts of the Apostles.* Sheffield: JSOT, 1992.

Marshall, I. Howard, and David Peterson, eds. *Witness to the Gospel: The Theology of Acts.* Grand Rapids and Cambridge: Eerdmans, 1998.

Pervo, Richard I. *Profit with Delight: The Literary Genre of the Acts of the Apostles.* Philadelphia: Fortress, 1987.

Porter, Stanley E. *Paul in Acts.* Tübingen: Mohr, 1999; Peabody: Hendrickson, 2001.

Powell, Mark A. *What Are They Saying about Acts?* New York: Paulist, 1991.

Strelan, Rick. *Strange Acts: Studies in the Cultural World of the Acts of the Apostles*. Berlin and New York: de Gruyter, 2004.

Walaskay, P. W. *"And So We Came to Rome": The Political Perspective of St. Luke*. Cambridge and New York: CUP, 1983.

Winter, Bruce W., ed. *The Book of Acts in Its First Century Setting*, 5 vols. Carlisle: Paternoster; Grand Rapids: Eerdmans, 1993–96.

Witherington, Ben, III, ed. *History, Literature and Society in the Book of Acts*. Cambridge and New York: CUP, 1996.

BIBLIOGRAPHY

Mills, Watson E. *The Acts of the Apostles*. Lewiston and Lampeter: Mellen, 1996.

Penner, Todd. "Madness in the Method? The Acts of the Apostles in Current Study." *CBR* 2 (2004): 223–93.

PART 2

PAUL AND HIS LETTERS

2

Paul: Life and Ministry

F ew dispute that, after Jesus himself, Saul of Tarsus was the most influential Christian leader in the first generation of Christianity. Thirteen New Testament epistles are attributed to him. He became the apostle and missionary without rival to the Gentiles. His understanding of Christian doctrine paved the way for the fledgling religion to become an empire-wide phenomenon, still thoroughly rooted in Judaism but increasingly stripped of the ethnocentric and nationalist restrictions that hampered so many first-century Jew-Gentile relationships. Among skeptical scholars, he has even been called the true founder of Christianity. A brief overview of Saul's life and ministry, beyond what we have learned already from Acts, thus forms an essential backdrop to our study of each of his canonical letters.

AN OVERVIEW OF PAUL'S LIFE

HERITAGE AND UPBRINGING

The term translated "young man" in Acts 7:58 (*neanios*) often referred to someone between the ages of eighteen and twenty-two.[1] If it is being used this precisely, and if Stephen was stoned between A.D. 30 and 32 (see pp. 20–22), then *Saul would have been born around A.D. 10.* From Acts 9:11; 21:39; and 22:3, we learn that he was born in *Tarsus,* where he apparently spent his childhood years. Tarsus was a prosperous, multicultural community with various schools of rhetoric, a major university, a school of Stoic philosophy, and a minority community of Jews. All of these influences on Saul's early life appear in his letters as well.[2] But Jews also tended to live in discrete neighborhoods, even in the diaspora, to preserve their own culture. So in Tarsus, Saul most likely also would have received *the standard Jewish elementary education for boys in the local synagogue, from roughly ages five to twelve,* and been immersed in the memorization and interpretation of the Jewish Scriptures.[3] His coming-of-age at twelve or thirteen may very well have been celebrated with the ancient equivalent of the *bar mitzvah,* the joyous initiation rite in which a young man became a "son of the commandment," owning the Jewish religion for himself and taking upon himself the "yoke of the Torah."

---

[1] John McRay, *Paul: His Life and Teaching* (Grand Rapids: Baker, 2003), 33.

[2] Michael J. Gorman, *Apostle of the Crucified Lord: A Theological Introduction to Paul and His Letters* (Grand Rapids and Cambridge: Eerdmans, 2004), 51. Cf. Bruce Chilton, *Rabbi Paul* (New York and London: Doubleday, 2004), 6–24.

[3] Richard N. Longenecker, *The Ministry and Message of Paul* (Grand Rapids: Zondervan, 1971), 21–22.

Some have inferred from Acts 22:3 that Saul's family moved to Jerusalem very early in his life because he claims to have been "brought up in this city."[4] But the Greek word structure of this verse (one long sentence) can suggest that this nurture refers to his study under Gamaliel, which would have followed the completion of his elementary education. *So his move from Tarsus to Jerusalem probably occurred when he was ready to undergo his more advanced training under the esteemed rabbi (something akin to a personalized seminary education!) during several of the years between ages thirteen and eighteen.*[5]

PAUL'S LIFE BEFORE HIS LETTERS	
A.D. 5–10	Birth in Tarsus
Age 5–12	Elementary Education?
Age 12–14?	Tent-making Apprenticeship
Age 15–18?	Study with Gamaliel in Jerusalem
A.D. 32–35 (age twenty-something)	Conversion/Call/Commission
Until A.D. 47–48	"Hidden Years" but eventually in ministry in Syrian Antioch

Because rabbis normally did not receive remuneration for their ministry, they also had to learn a trade, usually as an apprentice to an established workman of some kind. Often that apprentice was a boy's father, who taught his son the same skills that he had acquired. *If Saul learned tentmaking*[6] *(Acts 18:3) from his father, this most likely occurred during the first two or three years after his initial schooling was complete and before he moved to Jerusalem.* Nuclear and extended families stayed together, even in transit, much more often in the ancient world than today, so that it is very natural to imagine Saul's entire family making the move with him. The fact that Saul's sister is later described as living in Jerusalem, along with her son (Acts 23:16), could suggest that close kin already may have lived there in earlier years, making such a move all the more attractive. But it also means that Saul's parents could have made arrangements for him to move in with whichever other relatives resided there. So we have no way of knowing who, if anyone, actually moved along with Saul.

---

[4] See, classically, W. C. van Unnik, *Tarsus or Jerusalem: The City of Paul's Youth* (London: Epworth, 1962).

[5] For additional arguments for this conclusion after an incisive discussion of both sides of the debate, see Martin Hengel, *The Pre-Christian Paul* (London: SCM; Philadelphia: Trinity, 1991), 18–39.

[6] The word for "tentmaker" in Acts 18:3 (*skēnopoios*) could also be translated "leatherworker," and, in any event, most tents in Paul's day were made out of leather (McRay, *Paul,* 23).

A previous generation of scholarship was often skeptical of Acts' repeated claims that Paul ever had early connections with Jerusalem. How could one who so strongly contended for equality for *Gentile* Christians really call himself "a Pharisee, the son of a Pharisee" (Acts 23:6), using the present tense no less, as if nearly thirty years after his conversion he still aligned with this party that persecuted believers? Paul's theology had few points of contact with what we know from rabbinic literature of Gamaliel's teaching. Surely the firsthand evidence of the letters should be preferred to the secondhand (and therefore less reliable) testimony of Acts, so the argument went. Yet in 2 Corinthians 11:22, Paul refers to himself in the present tense as a Hebrew, an Israelite, and a descendant of Abraham. In Philippians 3:5 he likewise calls himself a "Hebrew of Hebrews" (i.e., not a Hellenistic Jew, despite growing up in the diaspora; recall above, p. 34) and a Pharisee, even though he goes on to clarify that he no longer takes any pride in his Jewish pedigree but has sacrificed it all for Christ's sake (v. 7).

Thus in the polemical context of trying to divide the Sanhedrin against itself by proclaiming Jesus' resurrection, which in principle the Pharisees should not reject, it is understandable why Paul would use the present tense. And *a generation of detailed scrutiny of Paul's letters against the background of first-century Judaism has shown how thoroughly immersed he continued to be in the Hebrew Scriptures, in Jewish forms of reasoning and logic, in the central theological categories of Jewish monotheism, election, eschatology, and the like.* Had he not received the kind of training that could have come in those days only through the formal guidance of an expert rabbi, we are hard pressed to explain where he came by all these skills and convictions.[7]

At the same time, the extent to which Hellenistic customs and culture had pervaded Israel and even the capital city of Jerusalem itself, means that, no matter when he moved from Tarsus to Jerusalem, Paul *would have imbibed numerous dimensions of Greek thought there too.* There is no actual evidence that he ever formally studied Greek literature or rhetoric, but a basic knowledge of popular concepts, key proverbs from famous philosophers or poets, and influential cultural and religious practices would have simply been "in the air" in both cities for residents who frequented the public arena. Still, his mastery of specific rhetorical techniques and the prevalence of Hellenistic schools of oratory in Tarsus could suggest that he spent a year or two after "grade school" and before moving to Jerusalem in a more formal Greek educational context. And his acquaintance throughout his career with the Greek version of the Hebrew Scriptures, the Septuagint, can scarcely be attributed to any period of his life other than when he was still a Jew living outside the land of Israel.[8] All this background, combined with his later ease at moving in the highest circles with

---

[7] Cf. further Hengel, *The Pre-Christian Paul,* 40–62. Though overstated in places, cf. esp. Brad H. Young, *Paul the Jewish Theologian* (Peabody: Hendrickson, 1997).

[8] For all these and related details, see Jerome Murphy-O'Connor, *Paul: A Critical Life* (Oxford: Clarendon, 1996), 32–51. For a full treatment of *Paul and the Popular Philosophers,* see the book so entitled by Abraham J. Malherbe (Minneapolis: Fortress, 1989). More broadly still, cf. Troels Engberg-Pedersen, ed., *Paul in His Hellenistic Context* (Minneapolis: Fortress, 1995); and J. Paul Sampley, *Paul in the Greco-Roman World: A Handbook* (Harrisburg: Trinity, 2003).

political and religious leaders in the provinces he evangelizes, suggests that he came from a fairly high socioeconomic stratum.[9]

Did Saul ever complete his training for the rabbinate? Much depends on the interpretation of Acts 26:10, where he tells Agrippa II that he "cast his vote against" the Christians he had helped to arrest when the Sanhedrin was discussing their possible execution. If this expression is taken literally, then Saul himself must have been part of the Sanhedrin and obviously a distinguished rabbi. But young men in their twenties almost never qualified for this honor, and the expression in Greek can also be used metaphorically to indicate Saul's more informal agreement with the decision. If Saul had been on the Sanhedrin, he almost certainly would have said so in his letters when he was countering the Judaizers.[10] The debate about his religious role ties in directly with the question of his marital status as well. All members of the Sanhedrin had to be married (*b. Sanh.* 36b), and almost all rabbis were. For that matter, only a small percentage of Jewish men in the overall populace ever stayed single their whole lives. Paul's reference to being single in 1 Corinthians 7:8–9 could then imply that by the mid-50s he was either a widower or a divorcee. The former would have been much more likely since few women in Jewish circles were able to divorce their husbands and, in light of Paul's own teaching in this chapter (vv. 10–16), it is highly unlikely he would have ever initiated a divorce, even if his wife had not become a follower of Jesus.[11]

We have already commented on the fierce zeal and loyalty to Yahweh that drove Saul to persecute Christians. As long as he believed Jesus was an impostor and blasphemer, his "theo-logic" remained impeccable. N. T. Wright believes that Saul's activities demonstrate him to have been among the strictest of Shammaite Pharisees, despite his education under the more lenient, Hillelite Gamaliel.[12] This may well be; students sometimes choose ideologies quite different from what their teachers promoted! Numerous writers have attempted psychological analyses of this seemingly volatile personality. Only a few have ever relied in detail on the full breadth of data in Scripture on this intriguing apostle and without reading in numerous assumptions that the text cannot support.[13]

Moreover, we must always keep in mind the sociological background of the ancient Mediterranean world.[14] Like everyone else in his day, Paul would have defined himself much more in terms of the groups to which he was loyal, rather than identifying with individual personality types. We have also observed that there are no signs from either Luke's biographical narrative or Paul's autobiographical information that he was ever a "frustrated Jew," in the sense of being someone who kept

---

[9] Gillian Clark, "The Social Status of Paul," *ET* 96 (1985): 110–11.

[10] John B. Polhill, *Paul and His Letters* (Nashville: Broadman & Holman, 1999), 37.

[11] Murphy-O'Connor, *Paul*, 64–65.

[12] Wright, *What Saint Paul Really Said,* 26. On Paul's zeal, see also Terence L. Donaldson, "Zealot and Convert: The Origin of Paul's Christ-Torah Antithesis," *CBQ* 51 (1989): 655–82.

[13] For about as good an assessment as one can probably produce, see James R. Beck, *The Psychology of Paul* (Grand Rapids: Kregel, 2002).

[14] Recall our introduction in Blomberg, *Jesus and the Gospels,* 64–66. Cf. further Ben Witherington III, *The Paul Quest: The Renewed Search for the Jew of Tarsus* (Leicester and Downers Grove: IVP, 1998), 18–51, and the literature there cited. Particularly helpful is Jerome H. Neyrey, *Paul, in Other Words: A Cultural Reading of His Letters* (Louisville: WJKP, 1990).

trying harder and harder to keep the law while recognizing how far short he fell of God's ideal. *In his eyes, he was doing just fine, and better than most (see above, pp. 40–41)! The dramatic events on the Damascus Road would change all that.*

CONVERSION, CALL, AND COMMISSION

Traditionally, Saul's radical change of alignment from persecuting "the Way" to becoming one of its most active adherents has been labeled his "conversion." But does this mean that Saul saw himself as changing religions, as that term often suggests? Almost certainly not. He had come to understand that Jesus was the *Messiah,* a patently Jewish category. But if the messianic age had indeed arrived, then the time for the fulfillment of the prophecies about God's servant being a light to the *Gentiles* (Isa. 42:6) was at hand. Abraham's seed would finally provide that blessing by which all the nations of the earth were to be blessed (Gen. 12:3). Years later Paul would speak of Christians as the true Jews (e.g., Rom. 2:28–29). The beliefs and practices he came to adopt represented the fulfillment, not the abolition of the Jewish Torah (Gal. 5:14). Perhaps the most profound evidence that Paul still considered himself a Jew was his willingness to submit to the synagogue authorities on no less than five occasions to receive the thirty-nine lashes (2 Cor. 11:24). Had he claimed to have converted to an entirely different religion, the Jewish leaders would have rejected his message but scarcely subjected him to corporeal punishment. They would have simply labeled him an apostate, no longer under their jurisdiction, who had forfeited his covenant standing with God.[15]

Was Saul's Damascus Road experience thus not a conversion? Some have argued that it should be thought of merely as a calling or commissioning to the next stage of his service to God.[16] Surprisingly, Jewish scholars of late have been more willing to grant Paul the label of "convert" than many Christian ones. Alan Segal's definitive work demonstrates that *a change of religious identities and communities is sufficient to produce a "convert," and Saul clearly did change both of these.*[17] A radical reorientation of convictions and belief, of conduct and behavior, of group affiliation and belonging all characterized Saul's shift from Pharisaic to Messianic Judaism.[18] Philippians 3:1–11 encapsulates the dramatic break Paul made from his past, with its ethnocentric, nationalist values. His willingness to mingle intimately and extensively with Gentiles in his missionary outreach could only have provoked additional resentment and hostility from more traditional Jews. Indeed, it would appear that one of his fundamental goals in his itinerant ministry was "to build multicultural communities of Christ-believers consisting of Jews and Gentiles alike."[19]

---

[15] McRay, *Paul,* 49.

[16] See, classically, Stendahl, "The Apostle Paul and the Introspective Conscience of the West."

[17] Alan F. Segal, *Paul the Convert: The Apostolate and Apostasy of Saul the Pharisee* (New Haven and London: Yale University Press, 1990).

[18] Gorman, *Apostle of the Crucified Lord,* 60. Cf. esp. Peter T. O'Brien, "Was Paul Converted?" in *Justification and Variegated Nomism,* eds. D. A. Carson, Peter T. O'Brien, and Mark A. Seifrid, vol. 2 (Tübingen: Mohr; Grand Rapids: Baker, 2004), 361–91.

[19] Gorman, *Apostle of the Crucified Lord,* 63. Terence L. Donaldson (*Paul and the Gentiles: Remapping the Apostle's Convictional World* [Minneapolis: Fortress, 1997]) explores this theme in detail, concluding that Paul was *converted,* but never became a *typical* convert.

Yet it remains accurate to describe Christ's encounter with Saul as a call and a commission, too. In Galatians 1:15, Paul perceives that, as with Jeremiah of old, God had set him apart for this service from before his birth. God then "called me by his grace" and "was pleased to reveal his Son in me so that I might preach him among the Gentiles." Again, in Romans 15:15–16, Paul explains that God's grace caused him to become "a minister of Christ Jesus to the Gentiles with the priestly duty of proclaiming the gospel of God." Although he would never stop evangelizing the Jews and, indeed, would continue to begin the evangelism of each new community he visited by preaching to the Jews, in keeping with his policy of "first for the Jew, then for the Gentile" (Rom. 1:16), the upshot of this pattern would result in his spending most of his time with Greeks and Romans. Thus it is not an exaggeration for him to declare that he "had been entrusted with the task of preaching the gospel to the Gentiles, just as Peter had been to the Jews" (Gal. 2:7). All these autobiographical references confirm what Luke declares secondhand in Acts 22:21 that the Lord had told Paul, "Go; I will send you far away to the Gentiles."[20]

We have already observed how Saul's encounter with the risen Christ would have caused him to begin immediately to rethink fundamental theological tenets (above, p. 40). But changes in derivative doctrines may also have followed as logical corollaries. If God took the initiative to reach down and redirect Saul, he must not only have been "saving" him but *reconciling* him to himself as well. If the messianic age had arrived, then it was also the time for the fulfillment of the promised *new covenant,* complete with its fuller internalization of the law or will of God. It must be the time, too, for the prophesied outpouring of the *Holy Spirit* to come to pass. Because the Spirit empowered and gifted all believers according to his sovereign choice, irrespective of gender, *a less patriarchalist orientation toward gender roles in home and church* would begin to characterize Paul's teaching and practice. Indeed, *freedom tempered with love* would form the centerpiece of the Pauline ethic more generally.[21]

PAULINE MINISTRY BEYOND THE BOOK OF ACTS

Most of what we know of Saul's life as a Christian comes from the relevant sections of the Acts of the Apostles, as surveyed above. These episodes, of course, are filtered through Luke's theological grid. The autobiographical glimpses of this period that Paul discloses in his epistles prove equally subjective. Many corroborate or flesh out what was barred from Luke. But we would not have known of Paul's letters at all just from Acts. What else do the epistles uniquely reveal? What may reasonably be inferred about the course of Paul's ministry from other historical information about that period of time? What may be implicit in Acts and/or the epistles, even if not explicitly stated? And can we make any generalizations about Paul's career that have not already emerged in our text-by-text analysis of Acts?

---

[20] Cf. further John M. G. Barclay, "Paul among Diaspora Jews: Anomaly or Apostate?" *JSNT* 60 (1995): 89–120; James D. G. Dunn, "Who Did Paul Think He Was? A Study of Jewish-Christian Identity," *NTS* 45 (1999): 174–93.

[21] For all of these points, see the relevant articles in Longenecker, ed., *The Road from Damascus.*

The three- and fourteen-year periods between Saul's conversion and his two trips to Jerusalem to meet with the apostles there (Gal. 1:18; 2:1) are shrouded in obscurity. Only after the second of these trips does the bulk of his ministry that Acts describes get underway. Yet Acts 9:20–22 reminds us that Saul began to preach to his contemporaries in Damascus almost immediately after his conversion when his sight and strength were restored. So we should probably imagine his departure into Arabia during those first three years (Gal. 1:17) to be for the purpose of ministry as well. Perhaps he already came to recognize his need to avoid evangelizing those to whom others were already ministering (Rom. 15:20; 2 Cor. 10:16). The Arabs, through Ishmael, were also descendants of Abraham, living relatively nearby (and not that far from Jerusalem where he had most recently been living), and thus were appropriate recipients of his preaching on several counts.[22]

During the longer, fourteen-year period that Acts omits, Saul probably spent considerable time in ministry in and around Tarsus. In Galatians 1:21, he announces that he went to the provinces of Syria and Cilicia during this time. Syria, of course, included Damascus, just as Cilicia contained Tarsus. Acts 9:30 explains that after the first meeting in Jerusalem, the believers sent him off to Tarsus to avoid those who would attack him. The choice of his hometown as a place of refuge proved natural. Then in 11:25, Barnabas went to Tarsus to find Saul to bring him back to (Syrian) Antioch, where they ministered together for one year, apparently just before Paul's second visit to Jerusalem. The references to Cilicia in Acts 15:23, 41 further support an earlier Pauline ministry throughout that region—why else would the apostolic decree be addressed to them as well as to Syrian Antioch and *its* environs? Why else would he travel through *both* regions "strengthening the churches"?[23] Had he not continued in effective ministry during these "hidden" years, it is hard to explain why Barnabas would bring him to Antioch as his helper or why Saul so quickly eclipsed his friend in influence and significance.[24] Paul's time in Antioch brought a new stability into his life and an integration into the body of a local church, which would become his "home base" and launching pad for his later travels.[25]

Paul's three main missionary journeys, at least as they have come to be known, portray him moving ever westward, with the desire eventually to reach the extremity of the known world in Spain (Rom. 15:24). The principle of moving ever further afield continues to apply throughout his whole career, but why head west rather than north, east, or south? Isaiah 66:18–19 prophesies that Yahweh will gather all the nations, in part by sending envoys to the peoples west of Israel, including Greece, Spain, and "the distant islands that have not heard of my fame or seen my glory." If Paul received a special calling to evangelize the Gentiles, he could easily have understood this text as suggesting that his marching orders lay to the west.[26] In Romans

---

[22] Hengel and Schwemer, *Paul between Damascus and Antioch,* 109–18. Cf. also Jerome Murphy-O'Connor, "Paul in Arabia," *CBQ* 55 (1993): 732–37.

[23] Cf. Mark Wilson, "Cilicia: The First Christian Churches in Anatolia," *TynB* 54 (2003): 15–30.

[24] See further Hengel and Schwemer, *Paul between Damascus and Antioch,* 151–77.

[25] Though some of his suggestions seem tenuous, overall Nicholas Taylor (*Paul, Antioch and Jerusalem* [Sheffield: JSOT, 1992]) highlights the central role of this city for Paul better than many studies.

[26] Riesner, *Paul's Early Period,* 245–53. James M. Scott (*Paul and the Nations* [Tübingen: Mohr, 1995]) argues that Paul and Peter, like Jews more generally, would have naturally thought of dividing the world according to the

15:19, he suggests that he has preached "so from Jerusalem all the way around to Illyricum" (in what today is Albania), an arc roughly contiguous with the eastern, Greek-speaking "half" of the empire. This implies considerable additional evangelistic activity than that which Acts explicitly discloses, though doubtless what he refers to is representative mission and church planting in each main region. Not surprisingly, this chapter goes on to describe his desire to tackle the Western, Latin-speaking "half" next—from Rome to Spain (vv. 23–24).

Various other generalizations may aptly characterize this period of Paul's missionary work. Michael Gorman sums up Paul's ministry roles under three main headings: *a traveling preacher, a community builder, and a suffering servant.*[27] We can scarcely overestimate the hardships associated simply with all this travel, often probably on foot. These hardships included the bad weather or terrain, thieves and attackers, and the general wear and tear on the body. Couple all that with the overt persecution and personal harm that stemmed from his preaching Christianity, and he must have been a quite strong and physically resilient person (an observation that rules out certain theories for his "thorn in the flesh" in 2 Cor. 12:7). Several of the sufferings Paul catalogues in 2 Corinthians 11:23b–33 are illustrated in Acts, but many are not. At least while he was "on the road," life was almost constantly a struggle just to survive.

At the same time he did not "go it alone." Throughout all his recorded missionary journeys, he took traveling companions with him, undoubtedly at first as younger colleagues (save perhaps for Barnabas), whom he was training and mentoring. But in the epistles he frequently refers to his companions as coworkers and partners, fellow soldiers, slaves or prisoners, praising them for their strenuous labors and survival of hardships, too. The mission was a collegial affair.[28] Paul's success in using ministry teams can be traced to their fraternal spirit, with no atmosphere of domination, which served outsiders and each other in love.[29] The ecstatic, even mystical experiences, such as his vision of heaven described in 2 Corinthians 12:1–6, may likewise have sustained him during some of his darkest hours.[30]

The metaphors Paul applies in his letters to his own missionary and pastoral ministry also prove telling: *envoy, planter, builder, father/mother/nurse, and priest.* He views his role as a representative of God, charged with the task of initiating ministry in numerous locations, devoted to his people as if they were literal family or close family helpers and interposing himself as an informal mediator between them and God.[31] One who had apprenticed as a tent-maker but trained as a Pharisaic rabbi would probably have come from a family of some means (recall above, pp. 87–88).

Table of Nations in Gen. 10, with Paul focusing on the Japhethites (Europeans) and Peter, the Semites.

[27] Gorman, *Apostle of the Crucified Lord,* 65–71.

[28] For a complete list of the fifty-seven Christians mentioned in the epistles alone, who were involved with Paul's ministry in some way, a number of whom are explicitly labeled coworkers (or something similar), see L. J. Lietaert Peerbolte, *Paul the Missionary* (Leuven: Peeters, 2003), 228–30.

[29] Eddy Paimoen, "The Importance of Paul's Missionary Team," *STJ* 4 (1996): 175–91.

[30] Cf. in detail, Jean Paillard, *In Praise of the Inexpressible: Paul's Experience of the Divine Majesty* (Peabody: Hendrickson, 2003).

[31] Stephen C. Barton, "Paul as Missionary and Pastor," in *The Cambridge Companion to St Paul,* ed. James D. G. Dunn (Cambridge and New York: CUP, 2003), 35–39.

But by relying on manual labor to support himself in most locations and accepting money for ministry only when it came from churches to which he was not presently ministering, he would have been viewed, especially in Greco-Roman status, as foregoing a certain status that could have been his—a practice generally viewed as dishonorable.[32]

Paul was more than disrespected; in some circles he was downright hated, or he would not have received the severity of ongoing opposition that he did. Elizabeth Castelli accuses Paul of the basest of manipulation in wielding his apostolic authority in heavy-handed ways, which would certainly account for some of this opposition.[33] And it is true that when challenged by Judaizers and other false teachers, Paul goes out of his way to stress that his authority matches that of the Jerusalem apostles (see esp. Gal. 1–2; 2 Cor. 10–13; Phil. 3). Moreover, he can threaten individual congregations with severe disciplinary action, trying to shame them into good behavior and, when warnings alone do not work, actually carry out his threats (cf., e.g., 1 Cor. 4:14–21 with 5:1–5). But the little letter to Philemon shows him as the master of tactful persuasion, much preferring not to have to use the authority that is genuinely his. By the standards of his highly patriarchal, imperial society, what would have cut against the grain was not his ability to issue an authoritative decree but his model in many places of servant leadership (e.g., 1 Cor. 3; Phil. 2:5–11), including serving through suffering (e.g., 1 Cor. 4:8–13; 2 Cor. 4:7–12; 6:3–10).[34]

Can we say anything more than we did in studying Acts about the end of Paul's life? In addition to the testimony of Clement and Eusebius that suggests a subsequent release from prison and a later rearrest and execution (see above, p. 77), we may add the following: The mid- to late-second-century Muratorian canon claims that Luke omitted Paul's journey "when he set out from Rome for Spain."[35] From perhaps as early as this same time period, *Acts of Paul* 11:3–5 describes Paul's execution by beheading in Rome during Nero's persecution (between 64 and 68, too late to correspond to the imprisonment of Acts 28:16–31).[36] In the fourth century Jerome echoes Eusebius's claim that Paul was released from his first Roman imprisonment (*De viris illustribus* 5). Numerous local traditions throughout Spain are based on the conviction that the apostle did in fact arrive and evangelize portions of that country. If he also carried through with his plans delineated in the Pastoral Epistles to revisit certain areas to the east of Italy, these could have occurred either before or after a trip to Spain.

But at what stage any or all of these documents cross the boundary from fact to fiction is difficult to determine. Other claims, scattered throughout late Christian

---

[32] Witherington, *Paul Quest,* 128.

[33] See esp. Elizabeth A. Castelli, *Imitating Paul: A Discourse of Power* (Louisville: WJKP, 1991).

[34] Cf. further Witherington, *Paul Quest,* 156–72; Jerry L. Sumney, "Paul's Weakness: An Integral Part of His Conception of Apostleship," *JSNT* 52 (1993): 71–91. Directly countering Castelli, see Trevor J. Burke, *Family Matters: A Socio-Historical Study of Kinship Metaphors in 1 Thessalonians* (London and New York: T & T Clark, 2003).

[35] Bruce, *Paul,* 449.

[36] For a thorough defense of the traditional sequence of the Prison Epistles (Philem./Col./Eph., Phil., 2 Tim.) in the traditional location (Rome), with detailed considerations of conditions of imprisonment, see Richard J. Cassidy, *Paul in Chains: Roman Imprisonment and the Letters of St. Paul* (New York: Crossroad, 2001).

tradition, appear entirely fictitious. For example, Chrysostom claimed that Nero avenged himself against Paul for having converted his favorite concubine. Another story described Paul's head bouncing three times after the executioner severed it from his body and causing springs of water to gush forth at each place where it bounced![37] As a result, many scholars believe that all additional "information" about Paul's life after the end of Acts is simply spurious and that he remained incarcerated from the period of his initial detention to his final execution.

There were, after all, plenty of apocryphal legends that developed about Paul's *ministry* as well, many of them turning him into a preacher and practitioner of asceticism more than his canonical letters support. The most famous of these is a dramatic novel about how the married woman, Thecla, became so enamored not only with the gospel but with Paul's promotion of celibacy that she left her husband to become an itinerant companion and coworker with Paul (*Acts of Paul* 3)! The apocryphal presentations of Paul also portray him as working numerous additional miracles, similar to the healings, exorcisms, and resurrection attributed to him in Acts. These two tendencies converge in one of the strangest legends associated with the apostle. Having baptized a lion who came to him, wanting to become a Christian and an ascetic, he later finds himself in the arena to be killed by a "ferocious" beast who turns out to be none other than the same lion. Taking advantage of a conveniently timed hailstorm, prisoner and animal escape together unharmed. This legend would later help to inspire George Bernard Shaw's famous remake of a partial parallel from ancient Greek lore, *Androcles and the Lion*.[38]

As with the Church of the Holy Sepulchre marking the spot of Jesus' execution in Jerusalem, an elaborate church in Rome has been built to commemorate the spot where Paul was believed to have died and been buried. It is called St. Paul Outside the Walls and is the largest church in Rome after St. Peter's Basilica in the Vatican. No extensive excavation has ever been undertaken there; but again, as with the site memorializing Jesus' death, tradition goes back to Constantine's day that this was the correct location, in this case confirmed by an inscription affirming the martyrdom of the apostle. Three factors make it unlikely that this site was fabricated by later Christians devoted to Paul: (1) it housed a pagan cemetery; (2) it was located in a very narrow space between two roads; and (3) the terrain was swampy, due to it being on the flood plain of the Tiber River.[39]

Whatever surrounding details may be uncertain, Paul's martyrdom culminates a life of imitating Christ after abandoning his youthful quest of his pre-Christian days to turn Jesus' followers into martyrs. But he realized that other Christians would likewise follow his path to persecution and even martyrdom as they too imitated their Lord. Of course, neither Paul nor any other believer atoned for anyone's sins

---

[37] Polhill, *Paul and His Letters*, 439–40.

[38] On the post-Pauline traditions about Paul as ascetic and miracle worker, cf. the survey in Calvin J. Roetzel, *Paul: The Man and the Myth* (Columbia: University of South Carolina Press, 1998), 157–76. More broadly, cf. Dennis R. Macdonald, *The Legend and the Apostle: The Battle for Paul in Story and Canon* (Philadelphia: Westminster, 1983).

[39] Jack Finegan, *The Archaeology of the New Testament: The Mediterranean World of the Early Christian Apostles* (Boulder: Westview, 1981), 30.

through their suffering, but they often demonstrated the genuineness of their faith, their growth in discipleship, and their right to leadership through such hardship.[40]

PAUL AND LETTER WRITING

GENERAL HELLENISTIC EPISTOLOGRAPHY

The Form and Structure of an Epistle Until roughly one hundred years ago, scholars had only the classical works of ancient Greece, including highly literary epistles, with which to compare the letters of Paul. Then, in the decades leading up to World War I, Adolf Deismann translated and analyzed numerous recently discovered nonliterary papyri, especially from Egypt. Deismann championed a sharp disjunction between the flowery rhetoric of the classical letters and the plain, ordinary prose of the papyri, imagining Paul to be far closer in form and style to the latter than to the former.[41] Today scholars place Paul's epistles in between these two ends of the spectrum from formal to informal writing, but their personal and, at times, even casual style still shows greater affinity with their nonliterary counterparts.[42]

The simple structure of short, unadorned Hellenistic letters, even when significantly expanded in form or length, accounts for a sizable majority of the New Testament epistles ascribed to Paul: (1) The letter began with an *introduction,* containing (a) the writer's name, (b) the addressees, and (c) a short greeting. (2) It continued with brief words of *thanksgiving* and/or a wish or prayer for the well-being of the recipients. (3) *The body of the letter came next,* (a) conveying the primary *information* the writer wanted to communicate, followed by (b) a section of requests or *exhortation* of the recipients when needed. The epistle then concluded with (4) *closing greetings.*[43]

The ways in which Paul most differed from this conventional format stemmed from the overtly theological nature of his correspondence. Both introductions and thanksgivings were explicitly Christian, and thanksgivings regularly previewed key themes in the body of the letters themselves.[44] The letter bodies were greatly expanded, carefully constructed; and the amount of exhortation often considerably surpassed the parallels in the papyri. Closing greetings often recapped key themes and added the names of one or more people who sent their best wishes along with Paul's to the audiences addressed.[45] Still, compared to the great poets and playwrights of fourth- to fifth-century B.C. Greece, Paul's style remained comparatively plain.

---

[40] See esp. John S. Pobee, *Persecution and Martyrdom in the Theology of Paul* (Sheffield: JSOT, 1985).

[41] Adolf Deissmann, *Light from the Ancient East* (New York: Harper & Bros.; London: Hodder & Stoghton, rev. 1922), 146–251.

[42] E.g., David E. Aune, *The New Testament in Its Literary Environment* (Philadelphia: Westminster, 1987), 218.

[43] Cf. McRay, *Paul,* 265; Holladay, *A Critical Introduction to the New Testament,* 267–71.

[44] See esp. Peter T. O'Brien, *Introductory Thanksgivings in the Letters of Paul* (Leiden and New York: Brill, 1977). On the form itself, cf. Jeffrey T. Reed, "Are Paul's Thanksgivings 'Epistolary'?" *JSNT* 61 (1996): 87–99.

[45] See esp. Jeffrey A. D. Weima, *Neglected Endings: The Significance of the Pauline Letter Closings* (Sheffield: SAP, 1994).

THE TYPICAL GRECO-ROMAN LETTER

Salutation
- X to Y Greetings

Prayer and/or Thanksgiving

Body
- Main Information
- Exhortation or Request

Concluding Farewell

Uses of Rhetoric Less easy to fit into the nonliterary model of the writing of the day is Paul's rhetoric. Three major rhetorical genres existed in the ancient Mediterranean world: judicial (or forensic), deliberative, and epideictic. *Judicial* rhetoric was used in law courts (or equivalent situations) to render a verdict. *Deliberative* rhetoric predominated in the assembly as speakers argued the pros and cons of various contemplated courses of action. *Epideictic* rhetoric centered on praise or blame, especially in funeral eulogies or oratory contests in various public settings.[46] Some of Paul's letters reflect combinations of two or more of these rhetorical genres, and some are harder to classify than others, but attempts at analysis can be helpful. Galatians appears to be judicial in the condemnatory verdicts Paul pronounces on the Judaizers, 2 Thessalonians employs primarily deliberative rhetoric as Paul commends a certain perspective on eschatology to temper the fervor of some in the Thessalonian congregation, while Ephesians contains large doses of epideictic speech, praising God for what he has done for humanity in Christ.

Potentially even more helpful are the outlines of ancient Hellenistic speeches. As with letters, orations contained a number of designated sections that could be modified or subdivided in various ways, and to which additional subsections could be added or from which they could be deleted. The most common of these outlines included the *exordium* (or introduction), the *narratio* (explaining the nature of the issue to be discussed), the *propositio* (the thesis to be defended), the *probatio* (arguments or proofs), the *refutatio* (refuting the opposition's arguments) and the *peroratio* (summary and final appeal).[47] Below (p. 122) we will present a very influential outline proposed for Galatians along these lines.

Good speech writers gave careful thought to three overall dimensions to their oratory: *ethos, pathos,* and *logos.* Ethos involved "an appeal to the moral character of the speaker;" pathos, "an appeal to the emotions;" and logos, "an appeal to logic."[48] The *probatio* or proof section of the letter body could itself combine all three of these elements. Good writers and speakers recognized that each of the three would appeal to and persuade different kinds of listeners at different times, so that

---

[46] Witherington, *Paul Quest,* 116. For a detailed presentation and discussion, see Stanley E. Porter, ed., *Handbook of Classical Rhetoric in the Hellenistic Period* (Leiden and New York: Brill, 1997).

[47] Witherington, *Paul Quest,* 117–18. Witherington himself has written numerous sociorhetorical commentaries on New Testament books in recent years, highlighting in detail what he believes to be the rhetorical genres and outlines at work in each. Duane Watson has done the same in numerous article-length analyses of the epistles.

[48] Gorman, *Apostle of the Crucified Lord,* 85.

all remained important. Then, as now, emotional appeals could sometimes gain more support for a cause than logic or moral example![49]

Many applications of rhetorical analysis to written letters like Paul's have been rejected on the grounds that letters are not speeches. But because ancient letters were written to be read aloud, there was inevitably some overlap between the two forms. We cannot assume that every letter, whether from Paul or from anyone else, necessarily conformed to a particular rhetorical outline; but proposals that scholars have put forth should be tested for fit on a case-by-case basis rather than rejected or accepted *in toto* simply because a given scholar is convinced that there either was or was not a significant rhetorical dimension to epistles.[50]

Jewish Modifications   Not nearly as many Jewish as Greco-Roman letters have been preserved from antiquity. Those that do still exist sometimes resemble purely Hellenistic letters because of the inroads of non-Jewish cultures into Jewish communities in many places around the empire. Others look more like some of the letter forms we will see in the so-called "general epistles" later on. Not surprisingly, Paul introduces numerous Jewish techniques of argumentation and analysis, especially in his quotations and applications of Old Testament texts. Various forms of *midrashic* interpretation present a broad array of devices of exegetical commentary designed either to explain the meaning and/or significance of opaque texts or to contemporize for the author's era centuries-old laws and texts that at first glance do not appear to be as relevant as they once were.[51] *Pesher* interpretations see the fulfillment in the author's day of ancient prophecy, whether predictive or typological. Numerous other Hebraic interpretive devices appear tucked throughout Paul's letters as well.[52]

Additional Considerations   In a world of unprecedented travel and communication, yet still far removed from the technology of today, letters, especially Paul's, substituted for one's personal presence. The serious matters we would feel we needed to talk with someone about personally could simply not be dealt with that way in the ancient Mediterranean world, with rare exceptions, if the prospective addressees lived very far away.[53] Perhaps the most dramatic example of this in the epistles is Paul's pronouncement of the verdict of excommunication (or death?) on the incestuous offender in Corinth (1 Cor. 5:1–5). More so than with many Hellenistic letters,

---

[49] Cf. esp. Thomas H. Olbricht and Jerry L. Sumney, eds., *Paul and Pathos* (Atlanta: SBL, 2001).

[50] For salutary cautions on using rhetorical analysis with epistles, see Stanley E. Porter, "The Theoretical Justification for Application of Rhetorical Categories to Pauline Epistolary Literature," in *Rhetoric and the New Testament,* eds. Stanley E. Porter and Thomas H. Olbricht (Sheffield: JSOT, 1993), 100–22. For a balanced response, see Janet Fairweather, "The Epistle to the Galatians and Classical Rhetoric," *TynB* 45 (1994): 1–38, 213–43.

[51] Judah Goldin, "Midrash and Aggadah," *The Encyclopedia of Religion,* ed. Mircea Eliade, vol. 9 (New York: Macmillan, 1987), 512.

[52] For a good overview, see Richard N. Longenecker, *Biblical Exegesis in the Apostolic Period* (Grand Rapids and Cambridge: Eerdmans, rev. 1999), 6–35. For Paul's use of the Old Testament more broadly, see esp. Richard B. Hays, *Echoes of Scripture in the Letters of Paul* (New Haven and London: Yale University Press, 1989); Christopher D. Stanley, *Paul and the Language of Scripture* (Cambridge and New York: CUP, 1992); Craig A. Evans and James A. Sanders, *Paul and the Scriptures of Israel* (Sheffield: JSOT, 1993); James W. Aageson, *Written Also for Our Sake: Paul and the Art of Biblical Interpretation* (Louisville: WJKP, 1993; and Francis Watson, *Paul and the Hermeneutics of Faith* (London and New York: T & T Clark, 2004).

[53] Robert W. Funk, "The Apostolic *Parousia*: Form and Significance," in *Christian History and Interpretation,* ed. William R. Farmer, C. F. D. Moule, and R. R. Niebuhr (Cambridge and New York: CUP, 1967), 249–68.

Paul used the epistolary form to address ideological and behavioral controversies that afflicted his readers.[54] More so than with most nonliterary, informal letters, Paul addressed entire communities (i.e., churches or groups of churches) rather than mere individuals. As we shall see, even the four letters addressed to individuals (1 and 2 Timothy, Titus, and Philemon) have congregations that these men are leading to whom Paul is writing as well.

GENRES AND CONSTITUENT FORMS

The Major Epistolary Genres   The anonymous first-century B.C. author who penned a work called *On Style,* in the name of one Demetrius, itemized and gave samples of no less than twenty-one subgenres of a letter. The most common of these subgenres included letters of friendship, family letters, letters of praise and blame, letters of mediation and accusing, accounting, and apologetic letters. So prevalent were letters of exhortation and advice that they could be further subdivided into categories of dissuasion, admonition, consolation, rebuke, reproach, and so on.[55] In our analysis of each of the New Testament epistles, we will suggest plausible classifications according to these and related epistolary genres.

A less thoroughly studied classification of Greco-Roman letters involves more public or official correspondence. Here one may identify three major groups: "reports to a constituted body," "executive or administrative," and "from a private citizen to public officials." These broad categories can in turn generate more specific letter types such as ambassadorial letters, royal edicts, honorific encomia, letters of recommendation, and the like.[56] Several of these types will appear in our analyses of Paul's letters as well. Obviously, the more precisely one can identify a letter's genre, which in turn gives clues to its author's purposes and the ways in which its original audience would have understood it, the better one will be positioned to interpret its meaning for its day and its significance for ours.

Literary Forms Embedded within Letters   Interpreters likewise do well to understand constituent literary forms within a given epistle. While no entire letter matches the ancient genre of *diatribe* (quite different from the current use of the term for an uninterrupted tirade!), several parts of Romans find Paul raising and answering hypothetical objections to his line of reasoning (e.g., Rom. 2:1–4, 17–24; 3:1–9, 27–31; 4:1–3, 9–12; 6:1–4, 15–18; etc.). Whether based on real or imagined opponents, this is precisely what the ancient diatribe regularly did.[57] A number of Paul's letters contain *virtue* or *vice lists.* These comprise extensive lists of key attributes and actions that Christians should either practice or avoid. One thinks, for example, of Romans 1:29–31; 1 Corinthians 6:9–10; and Galatians 5:19–23. Comparisons with

---

[54] See esp. C. K. Barrett, *Paul: An Introduction to His Thought* (London: Geoffrey Chapman; Louisville: WJKP, 1994), 22–54.

[55] For all these categories, with numerous actual samples from the ancient Mediterranean world, see Stanley K. Stowers, *Letter-Writing in Greco-Roman Antiquity* (Philadelphia: Westminster, 1986). Cf. also John L. White, *Light from Ancient Letters* (Philadelphia: Fortress, 1986). For a concise list, with definitions, see deSilva, *An Introduction to the New Testament,* 532–34.

[56] Cf. esp. M. Luther Stirewalt Jr., *Paul the Letter Writer* (Grand Rapids and Cambridge: Eerdmans, 2003), 25–55.

[57] Stanley K. Stowers, *The Diatribe and Paul's Letter to the Romans* (Chico, Calif.: Scholars, 1981).

the prevalent virtue and vice lists in various Jewish, Greek, or Roman documents of the day enable us quickly to assess key similarities to and differences from early Christianity. Humility, for example, was far more prized in Judaism and Christianity than in Greco-Roman philosophy and religion, in which it was often viewed as a weakness.[58] The same remains true today in a variety of non-Christian cultures, suggesting that humility is a character trait believers should meticulously cultivate so that others can clearly see the difference Jesus can make in a person's life.

First Corinthians contains a number of reasonably clear examples, along with several disputed ones, of *slogans* adopted by some in the Corinthian congregation. Thus most commentators agree that Paul himself could not have affirmed that all things are permissible for the Christian (1 Cor. 6:12), even within the context of championing freedom from the Jewish law. As a result, the NIV puts this declaration in quotation marks both times it appears in this verse, understanding the remaining words to reflect Paul's rebutting a perspective that some in the church in Corinth were asserting. But can we use this same method to dispense with the troublesome text in 14:34–35 that seemingly silences all women in church? Probably not. These verses are not slogan-like in brevity or memorability, nor do verses 36–38 read as naturally as a rebuttal.[59]

Also relevant to the debates on gender roles in home and church are the *domestic codes*. These sections of Paul's letters (most extensively found in Eph. 5:22–6:9 and Col. 3:18–4:1) delineate responsibilities of authorities and subordinates in such relationships as government and citizens, masters and slaves, parents and children, husbands and wives, elders and other church members, and the like. Again, a comparison with non-Christian codes of the day makes Paul's counterculturally positive perspectives on women's roles stand out strikingly, even if he at times stops short of the full-fledged "women's liberation" some modern people champion.[60]

Finally, we may call attention to self-contained units of succinct doctrinal writing that affirm numerous key theological (and especially Christological) truths in short compass, often with a poetic structure in the Greek. These have alternately been referred to as *creeds, confessions of faith,* or even *hymns.* Philippians 2:6–11 affords the clearest example of such a "hymn" and alerts us to instances in which Paul is most likely adopting (and sometimes adapting) traditional material that would have been commonly known in the early church. Other highly probable Pauline creeds or hymns include Colossians 1:15–20 and 1 Timothy 3:16.[61] Given that some of these passages contain some of the most exalted affirmations about Jesus and yet must predate Paul's major letters written in the 50s, strong evidence emerges that "high Christology" appeared early in Christian history, not just at some late date, two or

---

[58] Craig A. Evans, "Jesus' Ethic of Humility," *TrinJ* 13 (1992): 127–38.

[59] Cf. further William W. Klein, Craig L. Blomberg, and Robert L. Hubbard Jr., *Introduction to Biblical Interpretation* (Nashville: Nelson, rev. 2004), 436–37.

[60] See esp. William J. Webb, *Slaves, Women and Homosexuals* (Leicester and Downers Grove: IVP, 2001).

[61] For a full treatment, see Robert J. Karris, *A Symphony of New Testament Hymns* (Collegeville: Liturgical, 1996).

three generations and one or more cultures removed from the original time and milieu of Jesus.[62]

Still other segments of Paul's letters, while perhaps focused solely on one Christian doctrine, also seem sufficiently detachable from their context and carefully structured in style that we may think of them as *pre-Pauline tradition.* Occasionally Paul's language of passing on what he had received explicitly confirms such a hypothesis. Probably the most significant of all such instances is the treatment of Christ's death, burial, and resurrection, complete with a list of all the first witnesses to that remarkable event (1 Cor. 15:3–7). Even the noted atheist and skeptic Gerd Lüdemann, who attributes the disciples' experience of the resurrection to subjective visions and wish fulfillment, acknowledges that the testimony Paul recites here would have formed fundamental catechetical instruction for all new Christians. If Paul was converted in A.D. 32, then, in less than two years after Jesus' death, belief in his bodily resurrection was acknowledged as core doctrine. However one chooses to account for this belief, it cannot be explained away as the product of Hellenistic legend decades after the original Jewish context and truth of the matter had been forgotten![63]

The Occasional Nature of the Epistolary Genre   The upshot of all of this discussion about the genre "epistle" is that letters are the most *occasional* of the four major genres that comprise the New Testament (gospels, acts, epistles, apocalypse). That is to say, they are the most tailored to a specific occasion in the lives of the congregations they address. While the other three kinds of writings were also all written to specific groups of believers, the nature of their contents suggests that they were intended to be quickly dispersed much more widely. Some of the contents of Paul's letters are of course much more general than others. Romans is the clearest example of an epistle with large swaths of quickly generalizable material. Yet even here, as throughout the epistles more generally, we must always know the most we possibly can about the specific audience originally addressed. Like letters of many kinds throughout human history, many details may be quite personal, many instructions limited to particular individuals or settings and many understandings of complex issues presupposed because the author already knows his audience well and knows what they already know well, too.[64]

Therefore, one must develop a mechanism for sifting through the instructions in an epistle to determine what will apply unchanged to all Christians in all times and places and what may have to be applied in radically different ways as various contexts dictate. Four principles for recognizing situation-specific material can be phrased as questions: (1) Does the immediate context juxtapose a seemingly contradictory command? (2) Does a given instruction seem to contradict teaching elsewhere in the writings of the same author? (3) Does the rationale for a specific

---

[62] See especially throughout Hurtado, *Lord Jesus Christ.*

[63] Cf. further Gerd Lüdemann with Alf Özen, *What Really Happened to Jesus: A Historical Approach to the Resurrection* (Louisville: WJKP, 1995), 15.

[64] An excellent introduction to interpreting the epistles in light of their occasional nature appears in Gordon D. Fee and Douglas Stuart, *How to Read the Bible for All Its Worth* (Grand Rapids: Zondervan, rev. 2003), 55–87.

command not work at all in a culture different from its original one? (4) Is a unique setting for a particular teaching explicitly introduced into the letter? Complementing these issues are two questions, which, if answered affirmatively, suggest a timeless or normative application: (5) Does a command appeal to the way God first established things in Old Testament times or to the way he is reestablishing them in New Testament times? (6) Does a given teaching reflect a broad cross-cultural principle stated or implied in the text? Elaboration and examples of all these principles may help the novice interpreter make progress on this front.[65]

THE MECHANICS OF LETTER WRITING

In our world of text-messaging, e-mails, and numerous other media for contacting people almost instantly, it is easy to forget how tedious the process in antiquity was of communicating with a person from whom one was separated. Basically, the only two options were to send a friend to speak directly to that person or to send a letter. Often both of these processes came into play at the same time. Material was put in writing so that a courier would not forget or misrepresent the sender's intentions, but, because a letter carrier was needed to deliver the mail, he or she acted as an interpreter of the communiqué, further elaborating on its meaning and its author's intentions.

In a world with high illiteracy rates, many otherwise intelligent and even well-to-do people never learned to write. Therefore, they had to employ professional scribes to turn their thoughts into words in ink written on papyrus. The minority who could write still often found it easier or more effective to pay someone else with expertise at taking dictation to transcribe their words as they spoke them aloud. The technical Greek term for such a scribe was an *amanuensis*. A select number of these amanuenses had also learned a form of shorthand, enabling them to take down someone else's words at their normal rate of speech.

As a rabbinically educated Jew, Paul would have been among the best trained readers and writers in his world. Still, it is clear that he employed an amanuensis at least once, and probably he did so with all of his letters. In Romans 16:22, Tertius identifies himself explicitly as the one who has transcribed the epistle. In 1 Corinthians 16:21; Galatians 6:11; Colossians 4:18; 2 Thessalonians 3:17; and Philemon 19, Paul refers to writing the closing words of the letter "in his own hand," strongly suggesting that all but these conclusions have been penned by an amanuensis. The appearance of comparable postscripts in other letters, combined with the fact that ancient writers typically used scribes either almost all of the time or rarely, suggests that Paul may have composed all of his letters in similar fashion.

But what kind of "dictation" was involved? Four different approaches to taking down a person's thoughts are identified in ancient Greco-Roman literature. *First,* verbatim, word-by-word dictation may occur. *Second,* an amanuensis may take an author's thoughts or words and edit them for stylistic felicity, while leaving the

---

[65] See further Craig L. Blomberg, *Making Sense of the New Testament,* 131–36; Klein, Blomberg and Hubbard, *Introduction to Biblical Interpretation,* 485–98.

content unchanged. *Third,* cosenders could add their input, in terms of either style or content, which the scribe had to take into account. *Finally,* in rare instances (primarily limited to Cicero in the existing literature), an author could give instructions about the form and contents of a letter but leave it up to the amanuensis actually to compose it.[66] These options have a direct bearing on the debate over whether some of the letters attributed to Paul were actually pseudonymous.

Before proceeding to that debate, however, one more word on this topic is in order. We must never lose sight of the fact that Paul lived in an oral culture. Because few Christians would ever be wealthy enough to own a copy of a scroll of one of Paul's letters most had to depend for their familiarity with his teaching entirely on hearing the epistles read out loud in church. No doubt, when a letter first arrived at its congregational destination, the entire church would hear it read from start to finish the next time the people gathered. But as the letters were recognized as authoritative and useful, there would be repeated readings, and eventually, as the Jews did with the Hebrew Scriptures, consecutive selections from Paul's letters would be read along with similar sets of texts from the Gospels, Sunday by Sunday. Eventually this lectionary system became fixed, and later it would become abbreviated to cover only select portions of Old and New Testament texts. But the point here is that the first Christians' acquaintance depended on the epistle writer to craft his message in memorable form so that its hearers (rather than readers) would quickly come to digest, preserve, and pass on its contents. Stylistic devices of numerous kinds in Paul's letters demonstrate that he was indeed concerned with such mnemonic matters.[67]

THE PROBLEM OF PSEUDONYMITY

For a variety of reasons that will be discussed in the introductions to the relevant letters, many scholars during the last two centuries have come to the conviction that as many as six of the New Testament epistles ascribed to Paul were not actually written by him. Second Thessalonians has frequently been suspected to be pseudonymous, though many defenses of its authenticity remain. Colossians has been doubted a little more, Ephesians noticeably more still, and the Pastoral Epistles by a large majority of specialized scholarship on the topic. The most central reasons for these verdicts have related to the distinctive styles and contents of these letters as over against the other seven largely undisputed Pauline writings.[68]

Until recently, most scholars coming to these conclusions also argued that pseudonymity was a recognized literary device (or even genre) in the ancient Jewish and

---

[66] For all of the information thus far on the mechanics of letter writing, see throughout E. Randolph Richards, *The Secretary in the Letters of Paul* (Tübingen: Mohr, 1991). An expansion and popularization of this material is found in idem, *Paul and First-Century Letter Writing: Secretaries, Composition and Collection* (Downers Grove: IVP, 2004), in which Richards clearly opts for a combination of the second and third approaches listed here.

[67] Polhill, *Paul and His Letters,* 121. For extensive detail, see John D. Harvey, *Listening to the Text: Oral Patterning in Paul's Letters* (Grand Rapids: Baker, 1998). For a detailed analysis of one of the most common and elaborate of these mnemonic devices, see Ian H. Thomson, *Chiasmus in the Pauline Letters* (Sheffield: SAP, 1995).

[68] Periodically mathematical models have been employed to try to test these differences to see if they vary enough to qualify for "statistical significance." The results have been mixed; but, more often than not, the answer has been no. For a review of the most important of these studies and for the most ambitious analysis to date, vigorously arguing for the authenticity of all thirteen letters attributed to Paul, see George K. Barr, *Scalometry and the Pauline Epistles* (London and New York: T & T Clark, 2004). Cf. also Kenneth J. Neumann, *The Authenticity of the Pauline Epistles in the Light of Stylostatistical Analysis* (Atlanta: Scholars, 1990).

Greco-Roman worlds, so that to use it reflected no intention to deceive anyone. Nor, they argued, is it likely that anyone *was* fooled by its use. Reasons for attributing a document to an honored person of a past era might include gaining greater authority for the work, the sense that one was simply carrying on in the theological or ideological tradition of that individual (such that credit should be given more to the master than to the student), the possibility (particularly with apocalyptic literature) that one had some kind of ecstatic or visionary experience in which one believed one was temporarily but intimately linked with the named individual in question or simply that it was a standard convention in certain fictitious genres (especially with a person's farewell narrative or last testament). Supporters of this "innocuous" approach to pseudonymity appealed to literature in the Hebrew Scriptures widely believed to be pseudonymous (most notably Daniel), numerous intertestamental writings (particularly in apocalyptic literature) ascribed to patriarchs and heroes from ancient Jewish history, as well as to Greco-Roman letters pseudonymously attributed to such well-known figures as Socrates, Plato, Pythagoras, Apollonius of Tyana, and Diogenes the Cynic.[69]

DISPUTED AND UNDISPUTED LETTERS OF PAUL	
Undisputed • Galatians • Romans • 1 Corinthians • 2 Corinthians • 1 Thessalonians • Philemon • Philippians	**Semi-Disputed** • 2 Thessalonians • Colossians **Heavily Disputed** • Ephesians • 1 Timothy • 2 Timothy • Titus

These supposed analogies, however, must be assessed in light of several observations. *First*, pre-Christian Judaism appears to have believed all the Old Testament attributions of authorship and understood all of its canonical documents as genuinely prophetic in origin. *Second*, there was no difficulty in recognizing that a newly appeared document in the second or first century B.C. ascribed to, say, Enoch could not have come from a character of the antediluvian era. But it is quite different for a second-generation Christian to attribute a document to someone who lived merely one generation before him, as regularly claimed by New Testament scholars. *Third*, the parallels in form and content between the New Testament epistles and the pseudepigraphical letters in the Hellenistic world are fairly few. *Finally*, and most importantly, all the unambiguous evidence that we have of Christian reaction to known pseudepigraphy (i.e., from the mid-second century onward) shows that

---

[69] For an evangelical defense of this perspective, see esp. David G. Meade, *Pseudonymity and Canon* (Grand Rapids: Eerdmans, 1986). For a study of this Greco-Roman genre of literature in its own right, see Charles D. N. Costa, *Greek Fictional Letters* (New York: OUP, 2001).

it was rejected. Indeed, correct ascriptions of authorship, in that they enabled the church to evaluate the apostolicity of a given document (i.e., that it was written by an apostle or a close associate of an apostle), played a greater role than any other single criterion in the acceptance of an early Christian writing as legitimate for use and consideration as Scripture.

But what if first- and early second-century Christianity had a different attitude? Much changed in the mid-second century as this new religion all but lost sight of its Jewish roots and became firmly entrenched in Hellenism. And there are some second-century Christian texts that, depending on how certain disputed details are interpreted, can be taken as limited approval of pseudepigraphy under certain conditions. These include Serapion's comments on the apocryphal *Gospel of Peter*, Tertullian's remarks on the *Acts of Paul* as well as on Mark's dependence on Peter and Luke's on Paul and various comments scattered about the Muratorian fragment on books to be included in the canon. Even a Mishnaic reference to second- or third-century Judaism's perspective suggests that a disciple's words could be treated as though they were his master's. (For the two most suggestive of these Christian and Jewish texts, see below, p. 475.) Thus in principle, students of Scripture should not necessarily object to certain kinds of pseudepigraphic proposals any more than they need to worry about parables as a poetic kind of fiction designed to communicate inspired and authoritative truths.[70]

But the most recent generation of detailed analyses, both of these specific statements about pseudepigraphy and of the documents often cited as analogies, has cast serious doubt on whether Christians on any widespread basis did accept this literary convention or whether such a convention even existed, at least among the authors of the literature most closely parallel to the New Testament letters. What is more, these studies have demonstrated that the concept of literary property was pervasive in the ancient Mediterranean world, so that pseudepigraphy, when it did exist, was most likely intended to have deceived people into believing that certain writings did indeed come from the people to whom they were attributed. Thus if any of the letters ascribed to Paul were in reality written by second-generation disciples of Paul, their authors most likely wanted the Christian world to think that Paul actually wrote them. In addition, all the evidence we have from early Christian discussions of the authorship and/or canonization of Paul's letters suggests that the church *did* believe Paul wrote these letters himself.

This conclusion does not rule out the use of amanuenses, including some who may have been given greater literary freedom to write up Paul's thoughts and instructions in their own style and even with their distinctive emphases. Paul would still have been responsible for approving every word of such works, so that this hypothesis remains quite different from that of someone after his death composing documents in his name.[71] But recent study does call into question the view that

---

[70] Cf. the succinct overview of Terry L. Wilder, "Pseudonymity and the New Testament," in *Interpreting the New Testament*, eds. Black and Dockery, esp. 301–8. Wilder finds this evidence unpersuasive.

[71] For all of the main points in this subsection, cf. esp. Terry L. Wilder, *Pseudonymity, the New Testament, and Deception* (Lanham, Md. and Oxford: UPA, 2004); and Jeremy N. Duff, "A Reconsideration of Pseudepigraphy in Early Christianity" (Oxford: D.Phil thesis, 1998).

early Christians could have written in Paul's name (or any other deceased leader's), following an accepted literary device, with impunity. And the arguments against Pauline authorship are not nearly as watertight as many would lead us to believe.[72]

THE COLLECTION AND CANONIZATION OF PAUL'S EPISTLES

Interestingly, the only seven books of the New Testament that were seriously questioned in the early Christian discussions about canon were all from the last third of the New Testament, after the Gospels, Acts, and Pauline letters. These included Hebrews (because of the uncertainties surrounding who wrote it), James (because of its apparent contradictions with Paul), 2 Peter (because its style was so different from 1 Peter), Jude, and 2 and 3 John (because they were so brief and occasional in nature), and Revelation (because of the controversies surrounding how to interpret it).[73] All of these topics will be taken up again when we treat these individual books.

Paul's letters, on the other hand, quickly began to circulate beyond the communities or individuals to whom they were addressed. Soon it would become natural to gather two or more of them together into small collections, particularly when two letters were written to the same congregation. Romans, 1 and 2 Corinthians, and Galatians were recognized as containing the theological "meat" of Paul and could have formed a natural unit of four letters. So, too, could Galatians, Ephesians, Philippians, and Colossians because of similar length and a number of common topics, especially in Galatians and Philippians and in Ephesians and Colossians. It is also possible that Paul followed the common ancient practice of making copies of his letters for himself, keeping them in a notebook-like codex in Rome and that, after his death, his disciples would have preserved and copied the whole collection.[74] Whether gradual, in sudden bursts or altogether, the emergence of a Pauline canon was necessitated by and played a crucial role in combating second-century heresies, just as many of Paul's letters grappled with first-century counterparts.[75]

The order of the letters initially varied, even when all thirteen epistles began to be collected together. Likewise, as the entire New Testament canon began to take shape, Paul's letters were sometimes put first, at times after the Gospels, often after Acts, and occasionally even after the General Epistles.[76] But eventually they settled in after Acts, which was a chronologically and thematically logical place for them, written after the events described in the Gospels but concurrent with many of the events in Acts, including many in which Paul himself plays a direct role. The order in which Paul's letters were finally codified adopted a common approach to collecting such works in antiquity. They were placed simply in *decreasing order of length, first with*

---

[72] For a defense of the authenticity of all the so-called deutero-Paulines, see Bo Reicke, *Re-examining Paul's Letters: The History of the Pauline Correspondence,* eds. David P. Moessner and Ingalisa Reicke (Harrisburg: Trinity, 2001).

[73] Cf. esp. F. F. Bruce, *The Canon of Scripture* (Leicester and Downers Grove: IVP, 1988), esp. 198–203.

[74] E. Randolph Richards, "The Codex and the Early Collection of Paul's Letters," *BBR* 8 (1998): 151–66.

[75] For an overview and critique of all the major options, see Stanley E. Porter, "When and How Was the Pauline Canon Compiled? An Assessment of Theories," in *The Pauline Canon,* ed. Stanley E. Porter (Leiden and Boston: Brill, 2004), 95–127.

[76] See the tables in McRay, *Paul,* 274–75.

respect to the letters addressed to congregations and then with reference to those addressed to individuals. Only two exceptions break this pattern. Understandably, when two letters were written to the same church or individual, they were kept together. Additionally, Ephesians is slightly longer than Galatians, even while coming after it. It is possible that at some time Galatians was placed at the head of the group of four letters that also included Ephesians, Philippians, and Colossians because of its reference to the *kanōn* (Greek for "rule" or "canon"—the regulating principle for choosing biblical books) in 6:16.[77]

PAULINE THEOLOGY

PAUL ON HIS OWN

The sheer number of books that came from Paul's pen creates unique problems for summarizing his theology. Does one attempt to itemize the main themes of each letter individually and only then create some grand synthesis out of them?[78] Does one use all thirteen letters attributed to Paul or only the seven relatively undisputed ones?[79] Does one arrange the results topically along the lines of most of the systematic theologies composed in the history of the church (so most writers) or on the basis of the stories or narratives presupposed and retold or revised by Paul in the formulation of his doctrine?[80] Does one attempt to identify a "center" of Pauline thought or at least a group of the most central themes and assign them greater importance than more peripheral ones?[81] Does one make room for Paul's understanding of a topic to have "developed" over time? Does it matter if this "development" appears more like the organic evolution from an earlier understanding or more like the radical repudiation of a previous position?[82] What about those who find Paul's positions, even within the undisputed letters, at times hopelessly contradictory?[83] Fortunately the central themes of Paul's teaching remain relatively the same irrespective of the answers to these individual questions, even though numerous secondary issues differ considerably as a result of those answers.

Michael Gorman identifies "a dozen fundamental convictions" of *Paul's theology,* which few would challenge, even as they might rank their importance or analyze

---

[77] Cf. further William R. Farmer with Denis M. Farkasfalvy, *The Formation of the New Testament Canon* (New York: Paulist, 1983), 79–81.

[78] So, e.g., I. Howard Marshall, *New Testament Theology* (Leicester and Downers Grove: IVP, 2004), 209–469.

[79] See esp. Thomas R. Schreiner, *Paul: Apostle of God's Glory in Christ* (Downers Grove and Leicester: IVP, 2001); and James D. G. Dunn, *The Theology of Paul the Apostle* (Grand Rapids and Cambridge: Eerdmans, 1998), respectively.

[80] So, e.g., Ben Witherington III, *Paul's Narrative Thought World: The Tapestry of Tragedy and Triumph* (Louisville: WJKP, 1994). Cf. also Bruce W. Longenecker, ed., *Narrative Dynamics in Paul: A Critical Assessment* (Louisville and London: WJKP, 2002).

[81] See esp. Johan C. Beker, *Paul the Apostle: The Triumph of God in Life and Thought* (Philadelphia: Fortress, 1980).

[82] For the former approach, with respect to Paul's understanding of resurrection and eschatology, a key issue in Paul for which most have adopted the latter hypothesis, see Ben F. Meyer, "Did Paul's View of the Resurrection of the Dead Undergo Development?" *TS* 47 (1986): 363–87; and Paul Woodbridge, "Did Paul Change His Mind?—an Examination of Some Aspects of Pauline Eschatology," *Themelios* 28 (2003): 5–18.

[83] So esp. Heikki Räisänen, *Paul and the Law* (Tübingen: Mohr, 1983; Philadelphia: Fortress, 1986). For a rebuttal, cf. Teunis E. van Spanje, *Inconsistency in Paul?* (Tübingen: Mohr, 1999).

their interrelationships variously: (1) The only true Creator God of the world uniquely elected and covenanted with Israel to be his primary vehicle of divine blessing among the nations of the world. (2) Human sin has separated individuals and groups from that covenant-making God; the Jewish law, despite its many benefits, cannot deliver people from their sin and bring about the righteousness that brings eternal life. (3) God's righteous nature leads him to be faithful to his covenant and exercise saving power over his people, extending mercy to Gentiles on the same basis as he does to Jews. (4) This salvation is brought about by "the revelatory, representative, and reconciling crucifixion of Jesus the Messiah." (5) Jesus' subsequent resurrection and exaltation vindicates his life and teaching and displays him to the cosmos as the Lord of all. (6) Christ thus forms the climax of the covenant, fulfilling all of God's prophecies. But unlike conventional Jewish expectation he does so in two stages, corresponding to what today are called his first and second comings. Meanwhile we live in the "already but not yet," the overlap between the old and new ages of salvation history.

(7) Living in this intermediate period in reconciled relationship with God comes about solely by his justifying activity, which humans appropriate by grace through faith. Obedience to his covenantal obligations follows, as the natural outgrowth of a restored relationship with God, not as a means to accomplishing it. (8) It is appropriate, indeed crucial, to speak about Jesus (and the Holy Spirit who empowered him and now empowers believers) with language once reserved solely for Yahweh, God of Israel. In other words, Paul articulates an incipient trinitarianism. (9) Following Jesus focuses centrally on "cruciformity," the self-denial, love of others, and even suffering that characterized Christ's life and death as well. (10) The Spirit further functions in our life as a sign of those promises of God he has already fulfilled and as a guarantee of the hope that he will similarly act in the future in keeping with his other, still unfulfilled, promises. (11) Christians should gather together for worship, the exercise of their spiritual gifts and mutual encouragement, creating a compelling countercultural community, contrary to the corrupt institutions of the world. (12) Finally, history will culminate in the *parousia* (the return of Christ), the resurrection of all people to eternal life or death, and the final triumph of God against all of his enemies, human or demonic.[84]

Since the Reformation, Protestant interpreters have regularly followed Martin Luther in viewing "justification by faith" as the most central theme in Paul's thought. At the beginning of the twentieth century, Albert Schweitzer's view that being "in Christ" formed the center garnered a considerable following. Rudolf Bultmann's influential existentialism turned attention in the middle decades of the century to humanity's plight (sin) and the decision to live "authentically" before God and others as the solution to that plight. After World War II, W. D. Davies presaged a return to Paul's thoroughly Jewish roots and found belief in Jesus as the Jewish Messiah most theologically central. Not long after this Ernst Käsemann rehabilitated Jewish apocalyptic, believing it to be the fundamental category for interpreting Paul.[85]

---

[84] Gorman, *Apostle of the Crucified Lord*, 131–44.
[85] For additional discussion of all these developments, see Wright, *What Saint Paul Really Said*, 11–18.

Today, however, all of these developments have been overshadowed by *the debate over the so-called "new perspective on Paul,"* which traces its origins primarily to E. P. Sanders's tome, *Paul and Palestinian Judaism,* published in 1977.[86]

Sanders showed in considerable detail that scholarly portraits of pre-A.D. 70 Judaism in Israel contained considerable historical anachronism, as Paul's Jewish contemporaries were being depicted as no different from their rabbinic descendants centuries later. When one focused on demonstrably *pre-Christian* Jewish literature, Sanders argued, one detected the dominance of "covenantal nomism"—an approach to religious life in which Jews saw the works of the law as the way to live out their covenant relationship with Yahweh, not a way to merit inclusion in the community of his people in the first place. After all, birth as a Jew (and for boys, the rite of circumcision) had accomplished that already. Thus Paul and the prevailing Judaism of his day actually agreed that good works were not designed so that a person might "get saved," but that he or she might "stay" saved. The main difference between Paul and his contemporaries was not over the role of the law but over the question of whether the Messiah had already come in Jesus.

James Dunn built on Sanders's ground-breaking work by adding a focus on those works of Torah he dubbed "badges of national righteousness." Circumcision, Sabbath-keeping, and the dietary laws in particular set Jews off from all the surrounding peoples and left them vulnerable to ethnocentric pride. This unwarranted nationalism, rather than classic legalism (trying to save oneself by good works), became for Dunn the best way to understand Paul's complaints with the Jewish leadership of his day.[87] N. T. Wright has teased out several additional key insights from the framework of interpretation established by Sanders and Dunn. Most notably, the "gospel" (or "good news") is far broader than just the announcement of how people become right with God; it is the declaration that Jesus is Lord over the entire cosmos. Not all acknowledged this fact, so "justification," initially at least, was not so much a method for becoming reconciled with God but a criterion of distinguishing, among all those claiming to be part of God's covenant community, who truly were his people. Those who were genuinely "in" would confess, by faith, Jesus as Lord (contrary to Caesar's own claims to be his people's ultimate divine master) and seek to allow that lordship to influence every arena of their lives, individually and corporately.[88]

The "new perspective" has spawned more response in recent years than any other topic in the study of Paul by far. Some accept it uncritically; others uniformly censure it. Both of these extremes usually reflect lack of full understanding of the issues. Most, though, recognize both strengths and weaknesses in the movement.[89] It is right in most of what it affirms about early first-century Judaism but wrong in

---

[86] London: SCM; Philadelphia: Fortress.

[87] James D. G. Dunn (*Jesus, Paul and the Law: Studies in Mark and Galatians* [London: SPCK; Louisville: WJKP, 1990]) includes several of his seminal studies in this area. For a full-orbed presentation of Dunn's approach and how it played out for all of Paul's thought, see his *The Theology of Paul the Apostle.*

[88] Wright, *What Saint Paul Really Said,* 39–150.

[89] Of many helpful, detailed surveys, the most recent (and best?) is Stephen Westerholm, *Perspectives Old and New on Paul: The "Lutheran" Paul and His Critics* (Grand Rapids and Cambridge: Eerdmans, 2004).

much of what it denies about works-righteousness. Three observations in particular prove crucial here. *First,* some "merit theology" (final judgment based on one's good works outweighing one's sins) *does* appear in pre-Christian Jewish sources. While reading later rabbinic thought back into the first century often misleads, Sanders did not recognize the diversity of approaches already present in Paul's day (especially because he ignored the Dead Sea Scrolls).[90] *Second,* "remnant theology" (only a minority of Jews would truly be saved) was much more prevalent in intertestamental Jewish literature than Sanders recognized, and the key criterion for distinguishing who was truly a faithful Jew (out of the much larger group that claimed God's favor based on ethnicity alone) was Torah-obedience.[91] *Third,* in a world that had not yet developed a full-blown notion of "eternal security" (or the "perseverance of the saints," to use later Reformation-era language), works of the law not only flowed from one's faith in Yahweh as its natural outgrowth, but they remained a determining factor on judgment day to prove that one had remained faithful to God.[92]

As a result, the whole landscape of Paul's world was, not surprisingly, much more complex than the Reformers and their heirs recognized. Furthermore, often remembered in the study of Jesus but forgotten in the analysis of Paul is the dominating, oppressive imperialism that Rome promoted. Much of Paul's writing implicitly inverts the political mores of his world as well as the theological ones.[93] At the same time, we do not have to jettison any of the central insights of Reformation theology but merely supplement and nuance them. After all, the more Judaism acknowledged grace and still fell short of God's glory in Paul's eyes, the more the total depravity of humanity is highlighted. The so-called new perspective on Paul and Judaism does not remove but intensifies this element of Paul's theology.[94]

Paul did combat legalism, but he combated covenantal nomism and nationalism or ethnocentrism as well. While many present-day Christian churches largely avoid the first of these heresies, the others have not always been nearly as adequately addressed.

PAUL AND JESUS

To many readers of Paul's letters, it comes as a surprise that he quotes the teachings of Jesus infrequently. Except for Christ's death and resurrection, he refers back to the deeds of Jesus even less. The major themes of the Jesus of the Synoptic Gospels, many of which are usually believed to be about as close as we can get to the historical Jesus, are likewise fairly rare in the epistles, as are Paul's central topics in the Synoptics. The kingdom of God dominates the teaching of Jesus; justification

---

[90] The state-of-the art survey of pre-Christian Judaism, demonstrating this diversity, is now D. A. Carson, Peter T. O'Brien and Mark Seifrid , eds., *Justification and Variegated Nomism,* vol. 1 (Tübingen: Mohr; Grand Rapids: Baker, 2001). Vol. 2 (2004) rethinks key issues in Paul in light of this diversity, showing the Reformers as accurate in many of their understandings of Paul.

[91] See esp. Mark A. Elliott, *The Survivors of Israel* (Grand Rapids and Cambridge: Eerdmans, 2000).

[92] See esp. Simon J. Gathercole, *Where Is Boasting?* (Grand Rapids and Cambridge: Eerdmans, 2002).

[93] See esp. John Dominic Crossan and Jonathan L. Reed, *In Search of Paul* (San Francisco: HarperSanFrancisco, 2004). Cf. Neil Elliott, *Liberating Paul: The Justice of God and the Politics of the Apostle* (Maryknoll: Orbis, 1994); Bruno Blumenfeld, *The Political Paul: Justice, Democracy and Kingship in a Hellenistic Framework* (Sheffield: SAP, 2001).

[94] Dan G. McCartney, "No Grace without Weakness," *WTJ* 61 (1999): 12.

remains crucial for Paul. A Jewish Jesus preaching a message of repentance to his coreligionists primarily within Israel gives way to the apostle to the Gentiles establishing Christ's church with Jew and non-Jew accepted on fully equal terms. The teacher from Nazareth who only rarely gives direct statements about his identity is confidently proclaimed as Messiah, Lord, and Son of God. How are we to explain this state of affairs? Was Paul's understanding of the good news of Christ a radical departure from the actual emphases of the historical Jesus?[95]

In fact, while there are few direct citations of Jesus in the epistles, there are quite a few allusions. Given that none of the Gospels had yet been written, so that Paul's knowledge of Jesus' teachings would have come entirely from oral tradition, lack of verbatim quotation is scarcely surprising. Where Christian "liturgy" probably led to the fixity of certain traditions, we do find direct quotation; observe Paul's rendering of Jesus' words over the bread and wine during the Last Supper in 1 Corinthians 11:23–25 (cf. esp. Luke 22:19–20). Jesus' ethical injunctions are often referred to in ways that suggest Paul knew entire sermons or clusters of teachings on the topic, not just isolated sayings. Thus Romans 12:14 cites the Sermon on the Mount/Plain (Luke 6:28; Matt. 5:44) with its command to bless and not curse those who persecute believers. In verse 17, Paul follows Matthew 5:38 on not repaying evil for evil, while verses 18–19 appear to allude to Luke 6:27, 36 on loving one's enemies. Individual examples of the use of the Jesus tradition to support Paul's ethical injunctions include his command that those who preach the gospel should earn their living from that gospel (1 Cor. 9:14; cf. Luke 10:7), his instructions on divorce (1 Cor. 7:10; cf. Mark 10:2–12 pars.), his injunction for Christians to pay their taxes (Rom. 13:7; cf. Mark 12:17 pars.) and his insistence that Jesus declared all foods clean (Rom. 14:14; cf. Mark 7:18–19 par.).

With respect to theological topics, Paul alludes to Jesus' beliefs most commonly when he is dealing with eschatology. Again we find a cluster of references, this time to the Olivet Discourse (Matt. 24–25 pars.), with such texts as 1 Thessalonians 4:15 on the resurrection of believers at the last trumpet (cf. Mark 13:26 and Matt. 24:31); 5:2, 4 on the thief in the night (cf. Matt. 24:43–44 par.); 5:3 on the "birthpangs" preceding Messiah's arrival (cf. Mark 13:8 par.); and 5:4–6 on being sober and wakeful (cf. Mark 13:33 and related parables). Again, too, the list of examples could be considerably multiplied.[96]

As for Christ's deeds, Stanley Porter provides a secure, if minimalist, catalogue about what we can be sure Paul knew: "He was born as a human (Rom. 9:5) to a woman and under the law, that is, as a Jew (Gal. 4:4), that he was descended from David's line (Rom. 1:3; 15:12) though he was not like Adam (Rom. 5.15), that he had brothers, including one named James (1 Cor. 9:5; Gal. 1:19), that he had a meal

---

[95] The majority of material in this subsection is a drastic abridgment of Blomberg, *Making Sense of the New Testament*, 71–106. The best book-length work on this topic is David Wenham, *Paul: Follower of Jesus or Founder of Christianity?* (Grand Rapids and Cambridge: Eerdmans, 1995).

[96] See esp. the chart of thirty-one items compiled by Seyoon Kim, "Jesus, Sayings of," in *Dictionary of Paul and His Letters*, eds. Gerald F. Hawthorne, Ralph P. Martin, and Daniel G. Reid (Leicester and Downers Grove: IVP, 1993), 481, even if a few of these prove less conclusive than others. The eighteen most ambiguous appear in convenient chart form in Bruce N. Fisk, "Paul: Life and Letters," in *The Face of New Testament Studies*, eds. Scot McKnight and Grant R. Osborne (Grand Rapids: Baker; Leicester: IVP, 2004), 311–12.

on the night he was betrayed (1 Cor. 11:23–25), that he was crucified and died on a cross (Phil. 2:8; 1 Cor. 1:23; 8:11; 15:3; Rom. 4:25; 5:6, 8; 1 Thess. 2:15; 4:14, etc.), was buried (1 Cor. 15:4), and was raised three days later (1 Cor. 15:4; Rom. 4:25; 8:34; 1 Thess. 4:14, etc.), and that afterwards he was seen by Peter, the disciples and others (1 Cor. 15:5–7)."[97]

Additional allusions may well betray knowledge of Jesus' virginal conception (Gal. 4:4), baptism by John (Gal. 4:6), sinless life (2 Cor. 5:21), standard of living and concern for the poor (2 Cor. 8:9), transfiguration (2 Cor. 3:18), servant leadership (2 Cor. 10:1), and so on.

Broader theological comparisons show that the gap between Jesus and Paul again is likewise not nearly as wide as often alleged. "Justification" translates the Greek word *dikaiosunē,* which also means "justice." But Jesus taught his disciples to pray for God's kingdom to come, which included his will being done (Matt. 6:10), and that certainly involves justice for those treated unjustly (cf. Luke 10:25–37; Matt. 25:31–46). Moreover, Paul does refer to the kingdom explicitly on about a dozen occasions, just as Jesus uses the verb *justified* in exactly the same way as Paul at least once, at the end of the parable of the Pharisee and tax collector (Luke 18:14). The comparisons between ministry to Jews and Gentiles simply matches what both Jesus and Paul explicitly recognized was a chronological sequence of priorities (cf. Matt. 10:5–6 with 28:19–20; Rom. 1:16). The shift from more implicit to more explicit Christology, finally, is precisely what one should expect after the resurrection vindicated Christ's earlier ministry and claims. Once more, we could continue with numerous similar comparisons.[98]

With all of this said, however, it still remains striking how little of the contents of the Gospels do reappear, in whatever form, in Paul. At this juncture, several other observations remain important. (1) None of Paul's letters reflects first-time evangelism; he writes to individuals and churches who already know the basics of the gospel story, precisely because they have come to faith. (2) None of the other New Testament epistles has a noticeably larger frequency of references or allusions to the historical Jesus, including the letters of John, which were written by the same individual who penned one of the Gospels! Apparently, quoting Jesus was just not a primary purpose of early Christian letter writing. (3) The first epistle writers, like Christians more generally, quickly realized that Jesus' death and resurrection eclipsed everything else he did or taught in significance and rightly focused on those events in the references to his earthly life that do exist. (4) The frequent tension that Paul felt with those who claimed (rightly or wrongly) to represent the twelve apostles (who had walked with the historical Jesus as his followers) meant that he needed to stress his independence from them. Highlighting his direct encounter with Christ on the Damascus Road would accomplish this much more than frequent citation of words and deeds of Jesus from a time when he was not yet a disciple or eyewitness.

---

[97] Stanley E. Porter, "Images of Christ in Paul's Letters," in *Images of Christ: Ancient and Modern,* eds. Stanley E. Porter, Michael A. Hayes, and David Tombs (Sheffield: SAP, 1997), 98–99.

[98] See also J. P. Arnold, "The Relationship of Paul to Jesus," in *Hillel and Jesus: Comparative Studies of Two Major Religious Leaders,* eds. James H. Charlesworth and Loren L. Johns (Minneapolis: Fortress, 1997), 256–88.

(5) Finally, and as an outgrowth of this last point, the very sense of divine inspiration that guided Paul (1 Cor. 7:12, 25, 40; 1 Thess. 2:13) gave him the freedom to say what he believed the Lord was telling him directly, whether or not it could be expressed in language that echoed what Jesus himself had taught during his ministry on earth.[99]

CONCLUSION

Many would denigrate Paul today, perhaps because of a past overemphasis on his letters to the virtual exclusion of other parts of the canon, perhaps because of a dislike for some of his ethical stances as not sufficiently radical or perhaps because of a preference for narrative over didactic literature. Nevertheless, his writings continue to fascinate countless individuals, by no means all of them Christians, and they always reward those who would carefully study them. *His cruciform perspective on the Christian life still scandalizes those who follow the philosophies of the fallen world, all of which ultimately elevate humanity beyond its rightful place under God.*[100] *But he practiced what he preached, and those who believe in the unique authority of Scripture must give his work a central place in their reflection and obedience.*

QUESTIONS FOR REVIEW

1. What are the most important events in Paul's pre-Christian life for understanding his later experiences, and why are they significant?
2. In what ways was Saul's encounter with Jesus a conversion experience? In what ways was it a call and a commission?
3. What are some of the most important details of Paul's Christian life that only his epistles disclose (i.e., not found in Acts), and why are they important?
4. How does Paul effectively use the major rhetorical genres and smaller literary forms of the Greek-speaking world of his day? Give specific examples.
5. What are some appropriate responses to some scholars' claim that, because pseudonymity was a recognized and accepted device in the ancient Jewish and Greco-Roman world, some of the letters attributed to Paul may be pseudonymous?
6. What are the reasons for the Pauline epistles' placement in the overall New Testament canon? Why are his letters arranged in the order in which they now appear in the Bible?
7. What are the fundamental theological convictions that form the foundation of Paul's thought?
8. Identify specific hermeneutical principles that help a twenty-first century reader of Paul's epistles determine which instructions are prescriptive for all times

---

[99] See esp. Herman Ridderbos, *Paul and Jesus* (Grand Rapids: Baker, 1958). Cf. further F. F. Bruce, *Paul and Jesus* (Grand Rapids: Baker, 1974); Traugott Holtz, "Paul and the Oral Gospel Tradition," in *Jesus and the Oral Gospel Tradition,* ed. Henry Wansbrough (Sheffield: JSOT, 1991), 380–93.

[100] Or conceive of God's role in this age as triumphalistic. See Sylvia Keesmaat, "Crucified Lord or Conquering Savior: Whose Story of Salvation?" *HBT* 26 (2004): 69–93.

and cultures, and which are to be applied differently, depending on contextual circumstances.

9. What can be known with certainty about the end of Paul's life? What are some reliable sources to help construct these details? What principles can be drawn from Paul's martyrdom?

10. What is the relationship between Paul's teachings and the teachings and life of the Jesus portrayed in the Gospels? Identify significant similarities. What are some key observations that help explain the differences in Paul's emphases and the Gospel writers' emphases?

SELECT BIBLIOGRAPHY

Advanced

Boyarin, Daniel. *A Radical Jew: Paul and the Politics of Identity*. Berkeley: University of California Press, 1994.

Crossan, John Dominic, and Jonathan L. Reed. *In Search of Paul*. San Francisco: HarperSanFrancisco, 2004.

Dunn, James D. G. *The Theology of Paul the Apostle*. Grand Rapids and Cambridge, 1998.

Murphy-O'Connor, Jerome. *Paul: A Critical Life*. Oxford: Clarendon, 1996.

Ridderbos, Herman. *Paul: An Outline of His Theology*. Grand Rapids: Eerdmans, 1975.

Roetzel, Calvin J. *Paul: The Man and the Myth*. Columbia: University of South Carolina Press, 1998.

Sanders, E. P. *Paul and Palestinian Judaism*. London: SCM; Philadelphia: Fortress, 1977.

Segal, Alan F. *Paul the Convert: The Apostolate and Apostasy of Saul the Pharisee*. New Haven and London: Yale University Press, 1990.

Intermediate

Bruce, F. F. *Paul: Apostle of the Heart Set Free*. Grand Rapids: Eerdmans, 1977.

Chilton, Bruce. *Rabbi Paul*. New York and London: Doubleday, 2004.

Dunn, James D. G., ed. *The Cambridge Companion to St Paul*. Cambridge and New York: CUP, 2003.

Gorman, Michael J. *Apostle of the Crucified Lord: A Theological Introduction to Paul and His Letters*. Grand Rapids and Cambridge: Eerdmans, 2004.

McRay, John. *Paul: His Life and Teaching*. Grand Rapids: Baker, 2003.

Polhill, John B. *Paul and His Letters*. Nashville: Broadman & Holman, 1999.

Reymond, Robert L. *Paul, Missionary Theologian*. Fearn, Ross-shire, Scotland: Christian Focus Publns., 2000.

Schreiner, Thomas R. *Paul: Apostle of God's Glory in Christ*. Downers Grove and Leicester: IVP, 2001.

Witherington, Ben, III. *The Paul Quest: The Renewed Search for the Jew of Tarsus.* Downers Grove and Leicester: IVP, 1998.

———. *Paul's Narrative Thought World.* Louisville: WJKP, 1994.

Young, Brad H. *Paul the Jewish Theologian.* Peabody: Hendrickson, 1997.

Introductory

Ellis, E. Earle. *Pauline Theology, Ministry and Society.* Grand Rapids: Eerdmans; Exeter: Paternoster, 1989.

Longenecker, Richard N. *The Ministry and Message of Paul.* Grand Rapids: Zondervan, 1971.

Polaski, Sandra H. *A Feminist Introduction to Paul.* St. Louis: Chalice, 2005.

Sanders, E. P. *Paul.* Oxford and New York: OUP, 1991.

Schreiner, Thomas R. *Interpreting the Pauline Epistles.* Grand Rapids: Baker, 1990.

Wiles, Virginia. *Making Sense of Paul: A Basic Introduction to Pauline Theology.* Peabody: Hendrickson, 2000.

Witherup, Ronald D. *101 Questions and Answers on Paul.* New York: Paulist, 2003.

Wright, N. T. *What Saint Paul Really Said.* Oxford: Lion; Grand Rapids: Eerdmans, 1997.

BIBLIOGRAPHY

Seifrid, Mark A., and R. K. J. Tan, *The Pauline Writings: An Annotated Bibliography.* Grand Rapids: Baker, 2002.

The Epistles and Revelation

QUESTIONS FOR EACH BOOK

For each individual book surveyed, be sure you know, to the extent that we can determine them, the circumstances surrounding that book's composition, including the author, date, place of composition, audience addressed, issues affecting the audience, theme (or thesis) sentence or paragraph, literary genre or subgenre, important constituent literary forms, and general sense of the outline with its major divisions and major subdivisions. In addition, note the more specialized questions for review for each book or small group of books as you proceed.

CHRONOLOGY OF PAUL'S LETTERS	
Galatians	48–49
1 and 2 Thessalonians	50–51
1 Corinthians	55
2 Corinthians	56
Romans	57
Philemon/Colossians/Ephesians	60–61
Philippians	61–62
Titus, 1 Timothy	ca. 62
2 Timothy	ca. 68

3

Galatians: The Charter of Christian Liberty

INTRODUCTION

DESTINATION AND DATE

T
wo key problems surround the identification of the circumstances that caused Paul to write the letter we know as the epistle to the Galatians. The first is whether he was addressing churches in the smaller region of what today would be northern and north-central Turkey, which included ethnic Galatians, that is, people who would have used that term to identify themselves, or whether he had in mind the larger Roman province of Galatia, which included a much bigger section of territory in central and south-central Turkey. In 25 B.C. Rome had joined together the regions formerly known as Galatia (in the north) and Phrygia (in the south), and the combination of these terms in Acts 16:6 and 18:23 suggests that at least Luke recognized this provincial reorganization. Locally, however, the ethnic distinctions were generally retained, and people in Phrygia would not naturally have called themselves Galatians.

The resolution of the debate hinges in part on whether Paul's initial ministry to the Galatians (described in Gal. 3:1–5 and 4:12–16) should be matched with any of his missionary journeys described in Acts. In that book there is no record of Paul's preaching in northern or ethnic Galatia, but Acts clearly skips over other portions of Paul's travels disclosed in his letters, so this fact alone is scarcely decisive. On the other hand, Acts 13–14 delineate Paul's ministry in Pisidian Antioch (actually slightly across the border from Pisidia into Phrygia but so designated to distinguish it from yet another Antioch in the heart of Phrygia) and in Iconium, both of which fell into southern or Roman Galatia. Parts of Lycaonia were also incorporated into the larger Roman Galatia, so the cities of Lystra and Derbe may also have been included.[1]

The second key problem, which is intertwined with the first, is whether we understand Paul to have written Galatians before or after the Apostolic Council of approximately A.D. 49 described in Acts 15:1–29. Most liberal scholarship believes that Galatians 2:1–10 contains too many similarities to that council not to be an independent account of the same dispute—Paul and the Jerusalem apostles deciding if circumcision (and thus the keeping of the entire Mosaic Law) was a prerequisite for

---

[1] See esp. F. F. Bruce, *The Epistle to the Galatians* (Exeter: Paternoster; Grand Rapids: Eerdmans, 1982), 3–32. More succinctly, cf. Frank J. Matera, *Galatians* (Collegeville: Liturgical, 1992), 19–24. Of course, just to conclude that the letter was written to south Galatia does not prove these specific cities were in view. Paul may also have evangelized other southern Galatian communities not mentioned in Acts.

Christian salvation. Once this equation is made, however, the remaining discrepancies between Galatians and Acts seem irreconcilable. For example, Paul, Barnabas, and Titus meet privately in Galatians 2:1–2, whereas Paul and Barnabas appear quite publicly in Acts 15. In Galatians 2:6–10 the Jerusalem apostles add nothing to Paul's message; in Acts 15 they add the four restrictions forming the apostolic decree (vv. 19–21).[2] And just enough details included in the one account are absent from the other to make us wonder if these texts really do refer to the same event. On the other hand, if Galatians 2:1–10 is not to be matched with Acts 15, then the question arises how a second disagreement on at least some of the identical topics could have ever resulted, as if no decision had been previously reached.

There are strong reasons, however, for taking the two accounts as referring to separate incidents. If Acts is trusted as a historical source, then we must account for the fact that it describes two visits of Paul to Jerusalem prior to the council of chapter 15. In Acts 9:26–29 we read of Paul's first trip there after his conversion, while in 11:27–30 he and Barnabas go there from Antioch to deliver a gift of aid for the believers impoverished by famine. Galatians likewise refers to Paul's first trip to Jerusalem, in 1:18–24, and the impression we get is that 2:1–10, though fourteen years later, is the next time Paul returns to that city. This would require us to match Acts 9:26–29 with Galatians 1:18–24 and Acts 11:27–30 with Galatians 2:1–10. Acts 15:1, in which "some men came down from Judea to Antioch," and were teaching the Christians, "unless you are circumcised, according to the custom taught by Moses, you cannot be saved," would then fit nicely with the reference in Galatians 2:12 of how "certain men came from James . . . who belonged to the circumcision group" and led Peter and Barnabas into hypocritically dissociating themselves from the Gentiles, with whom they had previously been eating.[3]

This set of correlations also assumes that Paul has omitted no visits to Jerusalem in his autobiographical remarks in Galatians 1–2. This assumption seems highly appropriate because his entire purpose in recounting this history is to show his independence from the Jerusalem apostles. It would have greatly damaged his case if it were discovered that he had omitted mentioning any such visits, so presumably he has included them all.[4]

A weakness of this set of correlations involves the dramatic differences between Acts 11:27–30 and Galatians 2:1–10. Yet no actual contradictions appear, as when we try to match Galatians 2:1–10 with Acts 15. And even while Luke's drastically abbreviated version of this second visit focuses solely on the gift for the impoverished, two interesting details in Galatians 2:1–10 fit much better with Acts 11 than with Acts 15. The first is Galatians 2:2, in which Paul explains how he went to Jerusalem "in response to a revelation"—meshing nicely with Agabus's prophecy in Acts 11:27–28. The second is the concluding reminder that Paul and his companions

---

[2] Cf., e.g., J. Louis Martyn, *Galatians* (New York and London: Doubleday, 1997), 187–211.
[3] See further Colin J. Hemer, "Acts and Galatians Reconsidered," *Themelios* 2 (1977): 81–88. Cf. L. Ann Jervis, *Galatians* (Peabody: Hendrickson, 1999), 7–15.
[4] Robert K. Rapa, *The Meaning of "Works of the Law" in Galatians and Romans* (New York: Peter Lang, 2001), 79–80.

"should continue to remember the poor," the very thing he was eager to do—dovetailing exactly with the gift of Acts 11:29–30.[5]

Peter's backing down from a previously reached agreement is really not that surprising given the volatile nature of the issue. Peter would hardly be the first in human history to have required more than one conversation to firm up his commitment to behave in a new and radical way. It would actually be more surprising if the conflict with Galatians 2:11–15 occurred *after* the more formal council described in Acts 15, complete with written agreements, than if Peter had merely reneged on the more private and informal concord of Galatians 2:1–10.

The problems of destination and date are connected because if one favors a northern Galatian provenance, it is easier to imagine Paul heading north after revisiting the cities of southern Galatia on his *second* missionary journey, when he is admittedly wandering about nearby regions seeking God's guidance as to where to stop next (Acts 16:6–10), than to think of him squeezing in an extra trip on the shorter, faster *first* missionary journey in which he traveled from south of the province to the cities in southern Galatia and back again. Thus most who favor a southern Galatian destination date the letter to *48 or 49, before the Apostolic Council.* Most of those who favor a northern Galatian provenance date the letter to somewhere between 51 and 53 after Paul has moved on from central "Turkey" en route to cities in Greece,[6] though a few would date it even later. Nevertheless there is no necessary correlation between the two issues, and several scholars combine a south Galatian destination with a later date,[7] while, ever so rarely, a few opt for a north Galatian provenance with an early date.[8]

PAUL IN JERUSALEM IN ACTS AND GALATIANS

Acts	Galatians
Conversion (9:1–25)	Conversion (1:15–17)
First Trip (9:26–30)	First Trip (1:18–24)
Second Trip (11:27–30)	Second Trip (2:1–10)
Problems in Antioch (15:1–2)	Problems in Antioch (2:11–14)
	Paul writes this letter
Apostolic Council (15:4–29)	

---

[5] Cf. further Richard N. Longenecker, *Galatians* (Dallas: Word, 1990), 47, 59–60.

[6] Francis Watson (*Paul, Judaism and the Gentiles* [Cambridge and New York: CUP, 1986], 59) observes that Galatians 2:10 shows that this letter must be dated before 1 Corinthians, in which Paul begins to put this agreement into practice by taking up another collection for the poor in Jerusalem.

[7] E.g., Herman N. Ridderbos, *The Epistle of Paul to the Churches of Galatia* (Grand Rapids: Eerdmans, 1953), 22–35.

[8] E.g., Hans Dieter Betz, *Galatians* (Philadelphia: Fortress, 1979), 5, 12.

Among evangelicals, however, the combination of *southern Galatia and an early date* remains the favorite. Interestingly, this was not the view of most of the early church fathers, but that seems to be related to the fact that beginning in A.D. 74 Roman reorganization once again shrunk the territory it designated Galatia, so that later authors simply assumed the geographical divisions that obtained in their day.

An obvious advantage of the southern Galatian hypothesis is that it allows us to correlate the letter with the background information of Acts 13–14. Indeed, a couple of points strike us immediately if we do this. The first is Galatians 3:1, in which Paul asks, "Who has bewitched you?" using a verb that may refer to the ancient belief in certain people being able to cast spells on others by giving them "the evil eye."[9] Only in more "backwater," superstitious places like Lystra, where the inhabitants careen between the extremes of worshipping Paul because they think he is a god and stoning him when they realize he is not, would such language be appropriate. The second is 4:14, which sounds like this first reaction to Paul and Barnabas in Lystra, as Paul describes their being welcomed almost as if they were angels of God or even Jesus himself.

OTHER CIRCUMSTANCES AND PURPOSES

Fortunately, the main thrust of Paul's letter is unaffected by these thorny debates. What is clear on any theory of destination or date is that a group of Jews, professing to be Christians, have come to Galatia after Paul has planted churches there, promoting the belief that circumcision as the sign of initiation into keeping the Mosaic Law is a requirement for salvation. Paul will refer to this practice as "Judaizing" (2:14), so that scholars have come to refer to these people as *Judaizers*. While a few scholars have argued that these are completely non-Christian Jews trying to undo the conversions that God has worked through Paul,[10] 6:12 (on avoiding being persecuted for the cross of Christ) makes this interpretation very difficult. But this same verse also makes it fully understandable why Jews professing Christian faith would have wanted to remain as law-abiding as possible and avoid the charge that they were teaching the Gentiles anything else (recall the problem in Acts 21:20–26).

Indeed, as Jewish frustration with Rome grew throughout the first century and precursors to the Zealot movement developed, the problem of Christians appearing different from Jews became exacerbated because then they could not be counted on to help the cause against Rome.[11] Intriguingly, one of the recently translated fragments from the Dead Sea Scrolls (4QMMT) portrays an attitude toward the Mosaic Law among certain Essene Jews closely similar to what Paul combats in Galatians.[12] So we cannot be entirely sure of the origin or background of Paul's opponents.

In sum, it appears that Paul has learned of Judaizers changing the message he proclaimed to the churches of Pisidian Antioch, Iconium, and perhaps also Lystra

---

[9] On the practice, see Jerome H. Neyrey, "Bewitched in Galatia: Paul and Cultural Anthropology," *CBQ* 50 (1988): 72–100.

[10] Cf. esp. Mark D. Nanos, *The Irony of Galatians: Paul's Letter in First-Century Context* (Minneapolis: Fortress, 2002).

[11] On these developments, see esp. Robert Jewett, "The Agitators and the Galatian Congregation," *NTS* 17 (1970–71): 198–212. For an entire commentary built on this presupposition, see Martyn, *Galatians*.

[12] James D. G. Dunn, "4QMMT and Galatians," *NTS* 43 (1997): 147–53.

and Derbe, in a fashion very akin to the confrontation with Judaizers that he himself had in Syrian Antioch. If the Apostolic Council of Acts 15 has not yet occurred, then Paul must be writing Galatians in the small window of time between the clash with Peter and the Judaizers in Syrian Antioch and the trip to Jerusalem to hash out the problem. The short lag time, coupled with the seriousness of the issue for Paul, explains the urgent and sometimes even harsh tone of the letter.[13]

GENRE AND STRUCTURE

If we are to classify this epistle more precisely, it is perhaps best understood as an *apologetic letter.* That is to say, Paul is giving an *apologia* or defense of his apostolic authority and hence of the correctness of the gospel as he had first preached it to the Galatians. It is possible to outline the letter so that it conforms quite closely to the ancient structure of this form of epistle.[14] Several recent rhetorical analyses of the letter dispute that it uses the judicial rhetoric of formal apologetic, preferring instead to understand it as employing deliberative rhetoric.[15] But the defensiveness of Paul's tone, especially when compared with many of his other letters that clearly do adopt deliberative rhetoric, makes the identification of an apologetic form of speech reasonable. For our purposes, however, it will suffice to note, with the majority of commentators, three basic parts to Paul's argument in between his introduction and conclusion:[16]

I. Greetings (1:1–5)
II. Defending Paul's Divinely Given Apostolic Authority (1:6–2:14)
   A. The Exclusiveness of the Gospel (1:6–10)
   B. Paul's Conversion (1:11–17)
   C. Meeting with the Apostles in Jerusalem (1:18–2:10)
   D. Paul Confronts Peter in Antioch (2:11–14)
III. Defining Justification by Faith Rather Than Law (2:15–4:31)
   A. Thesis Paragraph: Justification by Faith (2:15–21)
   B. Arguments Defending Paul's Thesis (3:1–18)
   C. The Purposes of the Law (3:19–4:7)
      1. To Increase Transgression (3:19–20)
      2. To Deter Sin (3:21–4:7)
   D. More Arguments Defending Paul's Thesis (4:8–31)
IV. Describing Freedom in Christ through the Spirit (5:1–6:10)
   A. Stand Fast in Freedom (5:1)
   B. No Halfway House (5:2–12)
   C. The Law of Christ (5:13–6:10)

---

[13] For broader cultural reasons people in this region may have been attracted by the false teaching Paul has to combat, see Clinton E. Arnold, "'I Am Astonished That You Are So Quickly Turning Away' (Gal. 1:6): Paul and Anatolian Folk Belief," *NTS* 51 (2005): 429–49.

[14] Classically, Betz, *Galatians*, 14–25.

[15] For a full survey of approaches, with appropriate cautions concerning the application of analyses of oral rhetoric to Paul's written letters, see Philip H. Kern, *Rhetoric and Galatians* (Cambridge and New York: CUP, 1998).

[16] Cf. the three major themes in Frank J. Matera, "The Death of Christ and the Cross in Paul's Letter to the Galatians," *LS* 18 (1993): 283–96.

V. Closing (6:11–18)

GALATIANS AS AN APOLOGETIC LETTER

Epistolary Prescript (1:1–5)

Exordium—Statement of Problem (1:6–11)

Narratio—Thesis to be demonstrated and demonstration of facts (1:12–2:14)

Propositio—Summary of points of agreement and what remains contested (2:15–21)

Probatio—Proofs or support (3:1–4:31)

* Types of Arguments

    Logical

    Emotional

    Illustrative

    Figurative

Exhortatio—Parenesis (5:1–6:10)

Epistolary Postscript (6:11–18)

COMMENTARY

GREETINGS (1:1–5)

In at least eight major ways, Paul begins his letter by stressing that he has as much right to tell people the true gospel as anyone else does, even the apostles who were Jesus' companions throughout his ministry. The *first* method affects even Paul's introductory remarks. He writes an unusually detailed and theological greeting, including his identity as apostle, that is, one divinely commissioned for mission, and he stresses the need for rescue from this "present evil age" (v. 3). The *second* of these methods proves even more dramatic. In striking defiance of the conventional custom, he omits any word of thanksgiving or prayer for the Galatians but moves directly to his astonishment at the Galatians' behavior.[17]

DEFENDING PAUL'S DIVINELY GIVEN APOSTOLIC AUTHORITY (1:6–2:14)

The Exclusiveness of the Gospel (1:6–10) The *third* feature appears as Paul begins the body of his letter. He immediately declares that there is no other gospel apart from his message and calls down curses against the legalizing perversion of the gospel that is seducing the Galatians (vv. 6–9). Part of the harshness of this rhetoric can be paralleled in other writings of antiquity, from the curses in Deuteronomy 27 that the people of Israel invoked on themselves were they to disobey the Lord to the

---

[17] Ben Witherington III (*Grace in Galatia: A Commentary on Paul's Letter to the Galatians* [Grand Rapids: Eerdmans; Edinburgh: T & T Clark, 1998], 79–80), observes that the exordium of an epistle could substitute blame for praise or thanksgiving in unusually serious situations. Cf. throughout Robert A. Bryant, *The Risen Crucified Christ in Galatians* (Atlanta: SBL, 2001), esp. 111–42.

punishment that physicians allowed the gods to bring on them were they to violate their Hippocratic oath. It is also significant that Paul does not address these damning words directly to the Judaizers but in warning against them to the church he planted. Thus the severity of Paul's language does not justify us today damning non-Christians with rude language; if our goal is to win them for Christ, this tactic will usually drive them farther away! Nevertheless the seriousness of Paul's concern for those who deny fundamentals of the faith remains clear.[18] To speak so plainly refutes any charges made against him that his attempts in other contexts to be all things to all people (1 Cor. 9:19–23) are simply designed to win human approval (v. 10).[19]

Paul's Conversion (1:11–17)   Paul continues to stress the divine mandate behind his ministry as he shares elements of his autobiography in 1:11–2:14. The *fourth* way he stresses his apostolic authority involves his conversion[20]—something he views as completely God initiated for which his pre-Christian life was in no way preparing him (vv. 11–14).[21] These remarks, coupled with Philippians 3:6, refute the interpretation of Paul, popular since the days of Martin Luther, as someone who (like Luther) was in inner turmoil, wrestling with his inability to keep the law and hence psychologically ripe for conversion. Nothing less than the miraculous revelation of Jesus to Paul on the Damascus Road was needed to bring out this radical change of life (see above, pp. 40–41).[22]

   Fifth, after his conversion Paul did not immediately consult the Jerusalem apostles but spent three years in and around Damascus (vv. 15–17). Some of this time may have involved further preparation for ministry, but more likely he was quickly involved in promoting the Christian gospel (recall Acts 9:20–25; 11:25–26). We must not think of today's desert when we read of him going to Arabia; this would have referred to populated territory not far from Damascus.[23]

Meeting with the Apostles in Jerusalem (1:18–2:10)   *Sixth,* when he finally did meet with the apostles, his contact was minimal, but they praised God for his ministry (1:18–24). Paul speaks of having seen only Peter and James, the Lord's brother, describing them both as apostles (vv. 18–19). This comports with Paul's broader use of "apostle" than that which we noted in Acts, where it normally referred just to one

---

[18] Cf. further Betz, *Galatians,* 50–52.

[19] Longenecker, *Galatians,* 18.

[20] Many would dispute that Paul ever "converted" because that could suggest he was changing religions, whereas Paul seems to have understood his new convictions as the fulfillment of Judaism. But see Segal, *Paul the Convert,* and recall above, pp. 89–90.

[21] These verses do not mean, however, that Paul was not taught considerable additional information about the gospel throughout his Christian life. Elsewhere he will describe what he learned from "tradition" (e.g., 1 Cor. 11:23) or from what he "received" (e.g., 1 Cor. 15:3), probably referring to a fairly fixed body of information that new Christians were taught. See further Knox Chamblin, "Revelation and Tradition in the Pauline *Euangelion,*" *WTJ* 48 (1986): 1–16.

[22] For the possibility that Paul was associated with Zealots as a Jew, see Mark Fairchild, "Paul's Pre-Christian Zealot Associations," *NTS* 45 (1999): 514–32. The Zealots, however, did not become an organized movement until the 60s, so it is better to view them (and perhaps Paul) as "vigilant individuals who took the Law in their own hands when observing cases of gross Torah transgressions." See T. Sealand, "Saul of Tarsus and Early Zealotism: Reading Gal 1,13–14 in Light of Philo's Writings," *Bib* 83 (2002): 471.

[23] For full details of what may be inferred about this period of Paul's life, see Hengel and Schwemer, *Paul between Damascus and Antioch.* But see also N. T. Wright ("Paul, Arabia and Elijah [Galatians 1:17]," *JBL* 115 [1996]: 683–92), who thinks there are deliberate parallels with the life of Elijah.

of the Twelve. It also meshes with Acts 12:17 in which James was already a leader in Jerusalem before Peter moved away. At the same time, while Paul wants to minimize the significance of his contacts with the Jerusalem apostles, this two-week period would have proved crucial for his learning about all manner of details concerning the Christian faith and the historical Jesus.[24]

Galatians 1:22–23 initially poses a problem because Acts 9:26–30 suggests that Paul would have become well-known in and around Jerusalem. On more careful inspection, however, this latter passage never delineates how many apostles Paul saw, and what he did in Jerusalem was to talk and debate with the Hellenistic Jews (v. 29). Apparently he spent the vast majority of his time with his former friends and colleagues, sharing his newfound faith with them, rather than mingling with the Christians in the area.[25] There may be an important lesson here for new Christians today as well. Immediately after conversion is often the best time to talk to others about what has happened to one before one gets resocialized into a church environment and has fewer close non-Christian friends.

The *seventh* way Paul defends his apostolic authority involves his next meeting with the apostles in Jerusalem, a full fourteen years later (2:1–10). This time he met with them more extensively, but they endorsed his ministry of preaching salvation to Gentiles apart from keeping the Mosaic Law. On this occasion he had his coworker Titus, a Greek himself, along with him, and the gathering explicitly decided Titus did not need to be circumcised (v. 3), even though some Jews who professed to be Christians were trying to insist on it (v. 4). Verse 2 could suggest that Paul was uncertain about his take on the gospel, but that would be out of keeping with the spirit of the rest of the letter. More likely, his fear that he might have run in vain means that he was afraid his efforts to keep Christianity free from legalism would fail rather than that he himself was preaching an errant message.[26]

Verses 6 and 9 both refer to what the Jerusalem apostles "seemed to be" or were "reputed to be," which could mean that Paul was slighting them. On the other hand, it need not, and the emphasis in this paragraph is on the agreement that was reached.[27] The division of labor in verse 9 has also puzzled readers, since Paul and Peter alike ministered to both Jews and Gentiles. Probably it refers to their primary target audience, with Paul ministering more extensively to Gentiles than to Jews, while Peter, James, and John would focus primarily on Jews.[28] An easily overlooked verse is verse 10, a reminder that the commitment to the poor, particularly in Christian cir-

---

[24] James D. G. Dunn, *The Epistle to the Galatians* (Peabody: Hendrickson, 1993), 73.

[25] Cf. further Ronald Y. K. Fung, *The Epistle to the Galatians* (Grand Rapids: Eerdmans, 1988), 82.

[26] Had the Jerusalem apostles not endorsed Paul, his ministry could easily have been destroyed and the unity that the church needed to move forward with its mission effectively might never have developed. See further Charles B. Cousar, *Reading Galatians, Philippians, and 1 Thessalonians* (Macon: Smyth & Helwys, 2001), 37.

[27] James M. Boice ("Galatians," in *The Expositor's Bible Commentary,* ed. Frank E. Gaebelein, vol. 10 [Grand Rapids: Zondervan, 1976], 74), observes that Paul has recognized the authority of the Jerusalem apostles without diminishing his own, avoided exaggerated claims about the authority of those leaders, separated the gospel from the policies of the legalizers, and noted the unity between the Twelve and him as over against the legalizers.

[28] Martyn, *Galatians,* 211–12. Recall above, p. 90. On the four major apostolic circles of ministry which emerged in the early church, centered on Paul, James, Peter, and John, see Paul Barnett, *Jesus and the Rise of Early Christianity* (Downers Grove and Leicester: IVP, 1999), 276–327.

cles and most especially among the neediest in Judea, was not merely a concern of Luke in writing Acts but goes back to the earliest stages of Christianity.

Paul Confronts Peter in Antioch (2:11–14)　　The *eighth* and final plank in Paul's defense brings us to a serious conflict in the early church. After Peter agreed that salvation was by grace apart from keeping the law (by endorsing Paul's message in vv. 1–10), and even reasserted that position in Syrian Antioch, more conservative Judaizers arrived from Jerusalem, causing Peter to renege on his commitment (vv. 11–13).[29] That these individuals "came from James" (v. 12) does not necessarily mean that James authorized them (recall Acts 15:24), but they may well have claimed that he did. At any rate, Paul sees Peter's defection as the height of hypocrisy and confronts him directly (v. 14). Presumably, Peter did not back down and admit his error on the spot, or Paul would have recorded it to bolster his argument. Fortunately, by the time of the Apostolic Council, Peter would once again return to his prior convictions (Acts 15:10–11).[30]

DEFINING JUSTIFICATION BY FAITH RATHER THAN LAW (2:15–4:31)

Thesis Paragraph: Justification by Faith (2:15–21)　　Depending on where one puts the close quotation mark (after 2:14 or 2:21), 2:15–21 could be either the continuation of Paul's reply to Peter or Paul's own subsequent commentary on the event.[31] Either way, *2:15–21 forms the thesis paragraph for the entire epistle*. It defines the gospel as Paul understands it and forms the transition to the rest of chapters 3–4, which go on to defend this definition.

PAUL VERSUS THE JUDAIZERS

Judaizers

Faith in Christ + Works of Law → Justification

Paul

Faith in Christ → Justification + Works of Spirit

The key term for Paul in these verses is the verb "justify" (*dikaiō*) and its cognate noun "justification" (*dikaiosunē*). The background of this word group is legal or forensic; justification often referred to acquittal in a court of law. Paul is saying that

---

[29] For a parallel debate in non-Christian Judaism, see Josephus, *Antiquities* 20.2.1–5. Cf. Kang-Yup Na, "The Conversion of Izates and Galatians 2:11–14," *HBT* 27 (2005): 56–78.

[30] Had Peter known what Paul would later write in 1 Corinthians 9:19–23, one can imagine him making appeal to a similar line of reasoning: "I was just being like a Jew to win Jews." After all, the agreement in 2:1–10 did not specifically address the question of eating with Gentiles. On the other hand, the Galatian Gentiles were fellow *Christians,* not unevangelized Jews. Meanwhile, the message of the Judaizers, requiring the law for salvation, so compromised the gospel that it could prove damning. For a more detailed comparison of the two passages, see D. A. Carson, "Pauline Inconsistency: Reflections on 1 Corinthians 9.19–23 and Galatians 2.11–14," *Churchman* 109 (1986): 6–45.

[31] Verses 15–21 do not read like a personal conversation but like the heart of Paul's message to the Galatians (Leon Morris, *Galatians: Paul's Charter of Christian Freedom* [Leicester and Downers Grove: IVP, 1996], 83).

by faith in Christ,[32] rather than the works of the Law, we are declared "not guilty" of the sins we have committed (v. 16). But he also speaks of "Christ . . . in me" (v. 20), enabling him to live the kind of life he previously couldn't. So justification has a moral or relational dimension to it as well.[33] One could compare the concept to a judge who first pays the fine for someone convicted of a misdemeanor (or serves the jail sentence for a felon) but then afterwards invites the freed person to come live with him and his family as an adopted son or daughter (cf. 4:5–6).

But this word group also can mean "righteousness" or "make righteous." A full understanding of justification, therefore, includes both sides in the Reformation-era debate between Protestants and Catholics. When we accept Christ, we have his righteousness "imputed" to us. But through the Spirit who dwells in us we also begin a process by which our lives are increasingly transformed, so that over time we acquire "imparted" righteousness as well.[34] We are not only treated as if we had never sinned; eventually we actually sin less. In various contexts, *dikaiosunē* also carries the sense of "justice" (like the Spanish *justicia,* which does double duty for both "justice" and "righteousness"). As believers grow in righteousness, they should increasingly seek justice for those who have been denied it.[35]

Verse 20 also speaks of crucifixion "with Christ," so that "I no longer live, but Christ lives in me." If one error is to assume that becoming a Christian can take place without any moral transformation whatsoever, the opposite error is to imagine that one can eradicate sin in this life. Various pop psychologies and theologies have at times so stressed the decisive death represented by crucifixion as to suggest that a believer no longer has a sinful nature. But the same "I," who from one perspective no longer lives, clearly still does live because Christ lives in "me." In context, verse 20 is not about death to sin but death to the law (v. 19), or more specifically to attempts to save oneself by the works of the law.[36]

Arguments Defending Paul's Thesis (3:1–18)   Chapter 3 proceeds with a series of four arguments that defend Paul's thesis that justification is by faith and not the

---

[32] Many scholars today argue for taking this expression here and throughout Paul as a subjective genitive, that is, as "the faithfulness of Christ." The most important book-length study supporting this approach and applying it to Galatians is Richard B. Hays, *The Faith of Jesus Christ: The Narrative Structure of Galatians 3:1–4:11* (Grand Rapids and Cambridge: Eerdmans, rev. 2002). Despite what seems to be a growing trend in this direction, convincing arguments remain for taking it as an objective genitive, that is, "(our) faith in Christ." See esp. R. Barry Matlock, "Detheologizing the πίστιν Χριστοῦ Debate: Cautionary Remarks from a Lexical Semantic Perspective," *NovT* 42 (2000): 1–23. Cf. also Roy A. Harrisville III, "Πίστιν Χριστοῦ: Witness of the Fathers," *NovT* 36 (1994): 233–41; Arland J. Hultgren, "The *Pistis Christou* Formulation in Paul," *NovT* 22 (1980): 248–63.

[33] Boice ("Galatians," 450) notes that this is no legal fiction but a real transformation.

[34] E.g., John H. P. Reumann, ed., *"Righteousness" in the New Testament* (Philadelphia: Fortress, 1982); more recently, cf. the 1994 statement, "Evangelicals and Catholics Together," and the 1999 Lutheran-Catholic accord on justification. Cf. Stephen E. Robinson (*Following Christ* [Salt Lake City: Deseret, 1995], 5), reflecting a growing emphasis in at least some circles of the Church of Jesus Christ of Latter-day Saints): "We receive credit for what Christ has done, and it is his infinite merit rather than our own flawed performance that finally secures a 'not guilty' verdict for the new creature we have become in and with Christ" (citing Gal. 2:16). With respect to the adoption motif, cf. p. 18: "I personally find great power and comfort in knowing that as I labor for Christ, I labor as a son, encircled in the arms of his love, from a position of safety in his kingdom. I believe that the gratitude and love I feel in response to that knowledge is a stronger motivation for good than fear and anxiety over some future judgment or possible punishment ever could be."

[35] Elsa Tamez, *The Amnesty of Grace: Justification by Faith from a Latin-American Perspective* (Nashville: Abingdon, 1993).

[36] G. Walter Hansen, *Galatians* (Downers Grove: IVP, 1994), 74–76.

works of the law. *First,* Paul appeals to the Galatians' personal experience—that is how they first heard the gospel and were saved (vv. 1–5). The Holy Spirit came into their lives apart from human effort, and they were even willing to suffer[37] considerably for this faith (but they also saw miracles happen). Examples of both miracles and suffering appeared in Acts 14:1–20. *Second,* Paul develops an argument from the chronology of Jewish history: Abraham, the founder of the nation, so to speak, was justified by faith and not the law as a model for all the Gentiles who would one day be saved in Christ (vv. 6–9). The passages that referred to God's plan for the nations through Abraham's descendants and to his faith (Gen. 12:3 and 15:6, respectively) both appeared before his famous example of obedience to God's command to be willing to sacrifice his only son, Isaac (chap. 22), which most Jews had come to cite as the classic reason for appealing to Abraham as the model of performing good works. Abraham was therefore deemed righteous in God's eyes by his faith; his works merely flowed from that faith.[38]

HISTORY IN ROMANS AND GALATIANS

Promise	(Law)	Fulfillment
Abraham	(Moses)	Jesus

Third, verses 10–14 argue that the law is unable to save anyone anyway, apart from pointing them to Christ. These verses are particularly difficult to follow and have spawned a lot of controversy. But Paul's logic seems to be that the Old Testament itself testifies to right and wrong ways of using the law. Those who think they can obey the law perfectly and thus merit salvation will always fail (vv. 10, 12). Those who follow the law as an outworking of their faith in God and his promises will be saved (v. 11).[39] Before Christ came, faithful Jews offered animal sacrifices for the (temporary) forgiveness of sins in anticipation of a coming age in which sins would be dealt with completely. But now, with Jesus, that age has come. Christ has completely redeemed us from the law's curse on those who failed to keep it (vv. 13–14). Death by crucifixion had already come to be interpreted as close enough to hanging on a tree that the curse of Deuteronomy 21:23 became associated with it as well (11QTemple 64.6–13; 4Q169 1.17–18). But that also meant that one could no longer continue to obey the law, even offering all the right sacrifices, as an adequate expression of faith in God. Faith in the promises of God meant recognizing the law's fulfillment in Christ, trusting in him as the once-for-all sacrifice for sin and ceasing to trust in the law as a means of salvation.[40]

---

[37] The verb (from the Greek *paschō*) could also be translated "experienced." But this is a less common meaning, and the testimony of Acts 13–14 is that believers did suffer in Galatia.

[38] Timothy George, *Galatians* (Nashville: Broadman & Holman, 1994), 221.

[39] Moisés Silva, "Abraham, Faith, and Works: Paul's Use of Scripture in Galatians 3:6–14," *WTJ* 63 (2001): 251–67.

[40] Bruce, *Galatians,* 160–61. For a book-length treatment of how these concepts apply to living out one's Christian life, see Andrew H. Wakefield, *Where to Live: The Hermeneutical Significance of Paul's Citations from Scripture in Galatians 3:1–14* (Leiden and Boston: Brill, 2003), though Wakefield unnecessarily pits this approach against applying the text to how a person gets saved.

Fourth, verses 15–18 round out this section by returning to the historical argument. The Mosaic Law came into effect substantially later than the principle of justification by faith with Abraham and thus does not annul the original principle. Verse 16 has proved difficult because the various Old Testament passages that promise blessings to Abraham's offspring (or "seed") seem to use collective singulars for multiple descendants. But Psalm 72:17, apparently referring back to one of those passages (Gen. 22:17b–18a), clearly understands the fulfillment to come in a single king. The initial fulfillment of the promise also targeted a single individual, Isaac. So Paul's application to the Messiah is not out of keeping with Old Testament interpretive tradition itself.[41] Moreover, his use of the same promise in Galatians 3:29 shows that he understands its collective application as well.

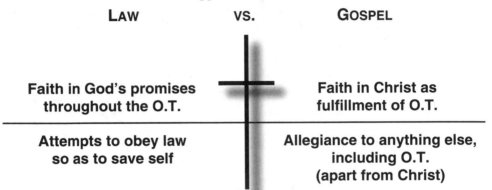

LAW	**VS.**	**GOSPEL**
Faith in God's promises throughout the O.T.		Faith in Christ as fulfillment of O.T.
Attempts to obey law so as to save self		Allegiance to anything else, including O.T. (apart from Christ)

The other problem in this paragraph is the reference to the law coming 430 years after the promise (v. 17). Genesis 15:13 had predicted that the Israelites would be enslaved in Egypt for 400 years, so the additional time from Abraham to Joseph would have been considerably more than another thirty years. The number 430 also appears in Exodus 12:40 as the time of enslavement, perhaps as a more precise number than the rounder number 400, but that only exacerbates the problem. Perhaps Paul had in mind the last time before the end of the patriarchal era that God renewed his promise, at that point with Jacob (Gen. 49:20), which would then leave approximately 430 years until the Exodus and the giving of the law on Mount Sinai.[42]

The Purposes of the Law (3:19–4:7)   Paul interrupts his series of arguments for justification by faith to address *a potential objection* that he probably suspected was already in his listeners' minds. If the law was not given in order to save people, even in Old Testament times, what then was its purpose? Paul will give two answers in this section; a third will appear later in the letter.

To Increase Transgression (3:19–20)   The first answer is discussed only briefly: the law was given "because of transgressions" (v. 19). The Greek preposition is not one of the normal words for "because" but is a comparatively rare word that can also mean "in order to cause" (*charin*). The word for "transgression" (*parabasis*) means "conscious sin." At the very least, giving the Israelites the law increased con-

---

[41] T. Desmond Alexander, "Further Observations of the Term 'Seed' in Genesis," *TynB* 48 (1997): 363–67.

[42] Gleason L. Archer, *Encyclopedia of Bible Difficulties* (Grand Rapids: Zondervan, 1992), 403.

scious sin because when they did something wrong they now knew it was against God's will. But Paul may also mean that *the giving of the law actually provoked some people to disobey it more;* human nature in every culture has demonstrated that "forbidden fruit often seems sweeter."[43] In Romans, Paul comes back to this theme on several occasions (4:15–16; 5:20–21; 7:7–13) and makes plain that, to the extent that the depth of our sin becomes apparent, so too becomes our consciousness of the need of a Savior. Thus the law prepares the way for the preaching of the gospel (cf. also the whole structure of Romans 1:18–3:31).[44]

To Deter Sin (3:21–4:7) If that were the only purpose of the law, however, it would seem a quite circuitous route for reaching God's goals. But Paul goes on to explain *a second purpose* in much greater detail: *the law also has for many people a deterring effect in decreasing the amount of sin in their lives* (3:21–4:7). It has a custodial function—holding us in check—until the coming of Christ. Paul illustrates this function with three metaphors: (1) the jailer who protects society from prisoners (and the prisoners from themselves!)—verses 22–23; (2) the "pedagogue" (*paidogōgos*; NIV "put in charge") or slave in a well-to-do household responsible for seeing that the son made it safely to school and home again—verses 24–25;[45] and (3) guardians and trustees who oversee the estate of a minor—4:1–7. But Paul goes on to stress in each of these illustrations that the custodial period has elapsed; through faith in Christ the prisoner is free, school days are over, and the son has attained his age of majority.[46] This freedom in Christ is visibly symbolized by our baptism (3:26–29).

Tucked into this last-cited paragraph is a verse that many see as one of the most important in all of Paul's thought. Christian freedom unites Jew and Greek, slave and free, male and female (v. 28). This represents a crucial reversal of the standard Jewish prayer in which pious men thanked God that he had created them Jew and not Gentile, free and not slave, male and not female (e.g., *t. Berakoth* 7.18 and *j. Berakoth* 13b). It is important not to claim either too much or too little from this verse. On the one hand, there are other Jewish and Greco-Roman texts that closely parallel Paul's and yet go on to affirm clear role distinctions, for example between men and women. So this verse alone cannot prove whether Paul promoted full-fledged egalitarianism; other texts will have to decide that. On the other hand, this verse suggests more than just some invisible, spiritual equality in Christ. It is set in the context of baptism, an outward ritual that men and women participated in on equal terms, in sharp contrast to its Old Testament counterpart, circumcision, which was reserved for men. *So it does seem that contemporary application of this text should call Christians to look*

---

[43] For both of these options, see Fung, *Galatians,* 159–60.

[44] Verse 20 is notorious for the number of interpretations it has spawned throughout church history. Perhaps the best is that the concept of a mediator itself implies a plurality which stands in contrast to the oneness of God. See further Terrance Callan, "Pauline Midrash: The Exegetical Background of Gal 3:19b," *JBL* 99 (1980): 549–67. More specifically, that a mediator "is not of one" may mean that Moses was not working merely for a simple party (God) but for multiple parties as well (the angels—v. 19b; cf. Deut. 33:2 LXX; Ps. 68:17; Acts 7:38, 53; Heb. 2:2) and thus, mediated an inferior (because more indirect) covenant with God. See Sam K. Williams, *Galatians* (Nashville: Abingdon, 1997), 99.

[45] See esp. Richard N. Longenecker, "The Pedagogical Nature of the Law in Galatians 3:19–4:7," *JETS* 25 (1982): 53–61.

[46] At just the precisely correct, God-ordained time in history (4:4), and enabling a greater intimacy with God, reflected in the Aramaic word *Abba* that Jesus himself used in addressing his heavenly Father (v. 6).

for similarly striking, outward, visible expressions of the equality of all persons in Christ.[47]

More Arguments Defending Paul's Thesis (4:8–31)   Paul can now resume his series of arguments for his conviction that justification comes by faith alone. *First,* in 4:8–11 he appeals to the Galatians' pre-Christian enslavement to "weak and miserable principles" (*stoicheia*—v. 9) and marvels that they would want to return to something similar. The term at least refers to rules and regulations from their pagan lives; it may also hint at demonic powers behind such religion.[48] To apply a term for paganism and demon-worship to the observance of the Jewish law was shocking indeed! *Second,* in verses 12–20 he reminds them of their formerly proper zeal for him and contrasts it with the improperly motivated zeal of the Judaizers. Here is where Paul discloses that he had first come to Galatia because of an illness (v. 13). We do not know what this sickness was. If verse 15 is taken literally, then Paul had some kind of eye problems, but "tearing out one's eyes" may well be metaphorical. The other most common suggestion is malaria because the southern coast of what today is Turkey was notorious for harboring this disease, and sufferers often headed north to the drier, thinner air of the high plateau country to recover. But the important point for Paul is the contrast between the Galatians' original care for him and their current alienation, leading him to agonize like a woman in childbirth (vv. 17–20)! As the mother labors until her child is ready to be delivered fully formed, so Paul earnestly desires the mature spiritual formation of the Galatian Christians (v. 19).[49]

Third, in verses 21–31, Paul appeals to the story of Abraham and his two wives, Hagar and Sarah, to create an allegory that stands on its head the application of the story that the Judaizers were probably making.[50] Following merely physical genealogies, one would observe that Jews were the descendants of Sarah, the free woman; and Gentiles, the offspring of Hagar, the slave woman. Paul, however, points out spiritual parallels that largely reverse these lines of descent: Christians (Jew or Gentile) are the truly free people, while (non-Christian) Jews remain enslaved to the law. Paul is not saying that this allegory is what the story in Genesis originally meant but that this is how it applies in his day. And just as Abraham and Sarah eventually

---

[47] The discussion of this paragraph is heavily indebted to Ben Witherington III ("Rite and Rights for Women—Galatians 3.28," *NTS* 27 [1981]: 593–604), who also gives references to the relevant primary sources. Cf. also his *Grace in Galatia,* 270–81.

[48] Clinton E. Arnold, *The Colossian Syncretism* (Grand Rapids: Baker, 1996), 158–94. The "days and months and seasons and years" of verse 10 will refer primarily to the Jewish celebrations of Sabbaths, new moon festivals, annual feasts, and sabbatical years.

[49] Cf. further Beverly R. Gaventa, "The Maternity of Paul: An Exegetical Study of Galatians 4:19," in *The Conversation Continues: Studies in Paul and John,* ed. Robert T. Fortna and Beverly R. Gaventa (Nashville: Abingdon, 1990), 189–201.

[50] See esp. Longenecker, *Galatians,* 198. The Greek of verse 24a reads literally, "These things *are* being allegorically"—i.e., by the Judaizers; here Paul supplies his "correction" of their allegorical interpretation. For a plausible explanation of the notoriously difficult reference to Hagar as a mountain, and in Arabia no less (v. 5), see Susan Elliott, "Choose Your Mother, Choose Your Master: Galatians 4:21–5:1 in the Shadow of the Anatolian Mother of the Gods," *JBL* 118 (1999): 661–83. The Galatians would have known of mountains in their area personified as mother goddesses and enforcers of law. Once Paul had linked Hagar with those enslaved by the law, her portrayal as a "mountain mother," specifically in connection with Mount Sinai where Moses received the law, would be natural. Arabia was a loose enough designation that it could refer to various desert regions near Israel.

sent Hagar away, so too the Galatians must expel from their midst the teaching that legal works are required for salvation (v. 30).[51]

PAUL'S TYPOLOGY IN GALATIANS 4:21–31

	Physical Descent	**Spiritual Descent**	
Isaac (by Sarah)	Jews (present Jerusalem)	Christians (Jerusalem from above)	**Free**
Ishmael (by Hagar)	Christians (esp. Gentiles)	Non-Christian Jews	**Slaves**
	Judaizers' Views	**Paul's Views**	

DESCRIBING FREEDOM IN CHRIST THROUGH THE SPIRIT (5:1–6:10)

Stand Fast In Freedom (5:1) Thus far Paul's polemic has been entirely one-sided—combating *legalism*. But there is always the danger of the opposite excess—*antinomianism* (living against the law). Christianity does not give its adherents the right to do anything they please. Immoral living really reflects slavery to sin rather than freedom. We do not know if there was an actual antinomian faction in Galatia, along with the Judaizers, or if Paul was just aware of the danger of swinging the pendulum too far in the opposite direction. Either way, he begins this final main section of the body of his letter with a ringing call to stand firmly for freedom.

No Halfway House (5:2–12) Before going on to explain the contents of this freedom, however, the seriousness of the situation leads Paul to an impassioned plea to the Galatians not to think they can mix approaches and have their Christianity as part law and part grace. The strong words against circumcision in verses 2–3 must not be taken out of context. In verse 6a, Paul will clarify that neither circumcision nor uncircumcision has any value for salvation. His point in the beginning of the paragraph, therefore, is that, if one gets circumcised (as the Judaizers would have

---

[51] Or perhaps even the teachers themselves. See G. Walter Hansen, *Abraham in Galatians: Epistolary and Rhetorical Contexts* (Sheffield: JSOT, 1989), 146. John Stott (*Only One Way: The Message of Galatians* [Downers Grove and Leicester: IVP, 1968], 136), adds, "I venture to say that if we were as concerned for God's church and God's Word as Paul was, we too would wish that false teachers might cease from the land."

insisted) because one believes it is a requirement for salvation (v. 4), then one would have to obey all of the rest of the law flawlessly. The expression "fallen away from grace" in verse 4 does not necessarily mean that true Christians have lost their salvation. At the very least, however, it does mean that such people have switched from living the Christian life by grace to trying to live it by the law, and fellowship with Christ has thus been interrupted.[52] But Paul is not against good works (!); verse 6b will stress the need for "faith expressing itself through love."[53]

In verse 7 Paul likens the Galatians' Christian lives to a race.[54] But other runners have cut into their lanes and kept them from running as they should have. That is not what God does (v. 8). Even if there are only a few such Judaizers, their false teaching can quickly infect the entire congregation (v. 9). Paul reasserts his confidence, however, that the Galatians will come around to his perspective and that the Judaizers will be rebutted (v. 10). Once again, Paul reflects on those who might be charging him with having preached a similar Judaizing message in some other contexts in order to try to win Jews (v. 11; recall on 1:10) and clarifies that the scandalous curse associated with Jesus' crucifixion (recall 3:13) would then have been for naught. Finally, as in 1:6–10, Paul reserves his harshest language for those who promote this kind of works-religion (v. 12), because, when followed consistently, it proves damning. If they insist on cutting other men's bodies through circumcision, it would be better for them to cut their own bodies through self-mutilation instead![55]

The Law of Christ (5:13–6:10) Now Paul is ready to return to the theme of freedom in Christ with which he began in 5:1. Such freedom is not lawless; there are ethical demands that flow from the gospel. Here appears *the third use or purpose of the law in Paul's thought—moral guidance for holy living.*[56] But this differs from a literal adherence to the 613 commands of the Mosaic Law, as if Christ's coming had changed nothing. Five segments may be discerned in this section, itemizing the Christian's obligations.[57] (1) Believers must love one another, and in so doing they fulfill the entire law (vv. 13–15; recall v. 6). (2) They must avoid gratifying the "flesh," that is, their sinful natures (vv. 16–21). Verses 19–21 itemize sample sins, highlighting sexual misbehavior and excessive "partying" but focusing even more

---

[52] Cf. Boice, "Galatians," 488.

[53] J. B. Lightfoot (*The Epistle of St. Paul to the Galatians* [Grand Rapids: Zondervan, repr. 1957], 205) calls verse 6 a "bridge over the gulf which seems to separate the language of St. Paul and St. James."

[54] The NIV preserves the Greek play on words with the verb "cut"—as appropriate for racing as it is for circumcision. Galatians familiar with the enslaved, self-castrated *galli,* who served the Anatolian mountains' mother goddess as priests, might well have understood Paul portraying the circumcised as similar slaves to a false god. See Susan Elliott, *Cutting Too Close for Comfort: Paul's Letter to the Galatians in Its Anatolian Cultic Context* (London and New York: T & T Clark, 2003).

[55] Cf. Pheme Perkins, *Abraham's Divided Children: Galatians and the Politics of Faith* (Harrisburg: Trinity, 2001), 98: "The crass proposal that castration would be a suitable punishment for whoever (pl.) is stirring up trouble in Galatia (v. 12) invites the audience to offload the anger and condemnation they may have felt was directed at themselves earlier onto these persons." Paul's wording may in fact refer to the severing of the penis rather than the testicles.

[56] For a detailed unpacking of all three uses, see In-Gyu Hong, *The Law in Galatians* (Sheffield: JSOT, 1993). More generally, cf. Frank Thielman, *From Plight to Salvation: A Jewish Framework for Understanding Paul's View of the Law in Galatians and Romans* (Leiden and New York: Brill, 1989).

[57] See esp. John M. G. Barclay, *Obeying the Truth: A Study of Paul's Ethics in Galatians* (Edinburgh: T&T Clark, 1988; Minneapolis: Fortress Press, 1991).

on interpersonal discord.[58] (3) By way of contrast, Christians will embody the fruit of the Spirit (vv. 22–26). Again Paul enunciates a number of key examples (vv. 22–23a) and then declares, "against such things there is no law" (v. 23b). In other words, virtues such as love, joy, peace, and so on cannot be legislated.[59] Once again, as in 2:19–20, Paul declares the "flesh" to have been crucified, but he immediately goes on to command his readers not to commit the acts of the flesh but to walk by the Spirit (vv. 24–26), demonstrating that Christians always have the possibility of lapsing and serving the old nature that continues to reside in them and compete with their new Christian natures (see further on Rom. 7:14–25).[60]

(4) Christians must bear one another's burdens, when they become too heavy, while not refusing to shoulder their own responsibilities (vv. 1–5). This is the most likely resolution of the apparent contradiction between verses 2 and 5.[61] When they discover fellow believers in sin, they have the double responsibility of confronting them in hopes of bringing them to repentance but doing so in as kind a way as possible—indeed, in precisely the way they would want to be treated if the shoe were on the other foot (v. 1). The humility that comes from recognizing one's vulnerability will also help them not to overestimate their own spiritual maturity (vv. 3–4). (5) Proper financial stewardship, especially in supporting Christian teachers, likewise proves crucial (vv. 6–10). Treating verses 7–10 as a separate paragraph could make Paul appear to have moved on to a different topic from verse 6, but the principles present in them—reaping what one sows, doing good and receiving a harvest—all apply so well to stewardship that Paul probably still has this theme in mind, even if not exclusively.[62] Verse 10 also reminds us that we have a special responsibility to needy fellow Christians, even without excluding the responsibility to help non-Christians when we can.

All of these ethical obligations, and others like them, together form the "law of Christ" (6:2). The language of fulfillment suggests an allusion back to Jesus' teaching in Matthew 5:17 that he came to fulfill all of the Hebrew Scriptures. What Christians call the Old Testament still remains an authority for them but only once they understand how its various laws apply in light of New Testament revelation.[63] But the overriding impression one gets from Paul's discussion in 5:13–6:10 is that Christian ethics, reflecting life in the Spirit, flow from the heart and from a love relationship with God and others much more than from a specific list of do's and don'ts. As Bruce Longenecker phrases it, the law of Christ refers to "the Mosaic law that comes to its fullest proper expression in the relationships of mutual service

---

[58] "Those who live like this" in verse 21 literally reads "those continually practicing such things." People whose lifestyles are consistently characterized by such vices are not true believers, but that does not mean that believers cannot commit grievous sins. Cf. Ernest deW. Burton, *A Critical and Exegetical Commentary on the Epistle to the Galatians* (Edinburgh: T & T Clark, 1921), 312.

[59] Bruce Longenecker, "'Until Christ is Formed in You': Suprahuman Forces and Moral Character in Galatians," *CBQ* 61 (1999): 92–108.

[60] Jon Lambrecht, "The Right Things You Want to Do: A Note on Galatians 5:17d," *Bib* 79 (1998): 515–24.

[61] The Greek, in fact, uses two different words: in verse 2 *barē* can mean a burdensome load, while in verse 5 *phortion* refers to a normal or light pack (Morris, *Galatians*, 180, n. 12).

[62] Max Anders, *Galatians, Ephesians, Philippians & Colossians* (Nashville: Broadman & Holman, 1999), 79–80. Cf. Matera, *Galatians*, 222–23.

[63] Cf. further Klein, Blomberg, and Hubbard Jr., *Introduction to Biblical Interpretation*, 278–83.

within the community of those" whose lives are being transformed by the Spirit in conformity to the character of Christ.[64]

CLOSING (6:11–18)

In verse 11 Paul most likely stops dictating to his amanuensis (recall above, p. 101) and appends his closing greeting in his own hand, writing with large letters probably for emphasis. Verses 12–15 review the major themes of the letter, stressing the cruciform nature of the gospel. Since no one can keep the law perfectly, the law as a whole or any particular commandment can never form a pathway to salvation. Rather, the cross of Christ must drive his followers to faith-based living (making them new creatures), which renounces anything they could be or do as meriting God's favor.[65] The meaning of verse 16 has been hotly disputed, but it seems to imply that either Jewish Christians or all Christians are now the true "Israel of God," that is, his new chosen people.[66] Paul prays for peace and mercy for these believers. He then reminds them of what he has suffered, including physical punishments, for being a follower of Jesus (v. 17) and offers a Christian "good-bye" (v. 18).

APPLICATION

Galatians stands as a clarion call against all forms of legalism in any age. Its most obvious application comes in cases of what has been called "hard legalism"—people, including professing Christians, who allege that certain human works or rituals must be performed in order for one to be saved. But first-century Judaism and Judaizing only rarely proved this blatant; often they practiced what has been called "soft legalism" (or, more technically, "covenantal nomism"—recall above, p. 108)—treating religious life as a set of rules and regulations rather than a relationship with God from which right conduct naturally flows. Such an approach too easily becomes "my efforts by my resources to obey God for my reward." This kind of legalism or nomism has been much more common in the history of Christendom, but Paul's perspective is clear: it is a false approach to religion that can save no one. That does not make the Christian life a lawless one, but Christian ethics are fundamentally inward and attitudinal ("love, joy, peace, patience, kindness, goodness, faithfulness, gentleness and self-control"—5:22–23a). Such character traits cannot be cultivated by enacting laws; they issue from a heart transformed by the indwelling Christ.[67] And to the extent that the "works-righteousness" of first-century Judaism was often

---

[64] Bruce W. Longenecker, *The Triumph of Abraham's God: The Transformation of Identity in Galatians* (Edinburgh: T&T Clark; Nashville: Abingdon, 1998), 86. Michael Winger ("The Law of Christ," *NTS* 46 [2000]: 537–46) similarly conceives of the law of Christ as living by the Spirit under Christ's lordship.

[65] No other letter contains so detailed or specific a review of themes, another indication of the urgency of the problem before the readers (Cousar, *Reading Galatians,* 109).

[66] Most likely the latter. See Andreas J. Köstenberger, "The Identity of the ΙΣΡΑΗΛ ΤΟΥ θΕΟΥ (Israel of God) in Galatians 6:16," *Faith and Mission* 19 (2001): 3–24.

[67] For outstanding expositions and contemporary applications of these themes, see Charles R. Swindoll, *The Grace Awakening* (Dallas: Word, 1990); Chap Clark, *The Performance Illusion* (Colorado Springs: NavPress, 1993); and Philip Yancey, *What's so Amazing about Grace?* (Grand Rapids: Zondervan, 1997). For poignant, cross-cultural and economic insights, see Elsa Tamez, "Hagar and Sarah in Galatians: A Case Study in Freedom," *WW* 20 (2000): 265–71.

a "national righteousness," Galatians stands as a rebuke to all forms of tribalism or ethnocentrism as well.

On the other hand, in many contexts today, the more timely application derives from chapters 4 to 6. In Sam Williams's words, "Only a father can adopt a slave as his son. God does not *compel* people to join the family, but if they choose to do so they must act like members of the family. It does not suffice to *feel* like a family member or to answer correctly a list of questions about what being a member of the family entails. What counts is *conducting* oneself as a son or daughter." Only then is true faith demonstrated, for, as Williams continues, "Faith is not feelings, not even nice feelings about God. Faith is not the mind's assent to certain propositions about Jesus or about one's own sinful state. Faith is the absolute entrustment of the self to God and God alone."[68]

ADDITIONAL QUESTIONS FOR REVIEW

1. Name the different hypotheses offered for the date and destination of the letter to the Galatians. Which date is typically connected to which destination? Why? Which combination of date and provenance has the advantage of correlation with Acts? How?
2. What is distinctive about the structure of Galatians when compared to other Pauline epistles? How does the genre of the letter help explain the structure?
3. What methods does Galatians 1:1–2:10 employ to emphasize Paul's God-given authority to tell people the true gospel? What circumstances in Galatia necessitated such a defense of Paul's apostolic authority?
4. Summarize in your own words the thesis of the letter to the Galatians. What four specific arguments does Paul use in Galatians 3 to support this thesis?
5. How can one respond to the claims that Paul misinterprets Genesis 22:17–18 and that his use of 430 years in Galatians 3:17 is historically inaccurate?
6. What two shocking examples does Paul use to refute the Judaizers in chapter 4? Why was it surprising for Paul to use the term *stoicheia* in relation to Torah obedience?
7. In the "allegory" of Hagar and Sarah, with whom would the Judaizers have associated themselves, and why? How does Paul skillfully turn this allegory on its head?
8. According to Paul, what were the intended purposes of the law before its fulfillment in Christ? How did the law specifically pave the way for the gospel? How did it serve a custodial role?
9. Which of the intended purposes still has application after the coming of Christ? What are a Christian's obligations according to "the law of Christ"?
10. How does one balance Galatians' teaching about freedom from the law and its warnings against ungodly behavior?
11. What are legalism, covenantal nomism, and ethnocentrism? Where do we see contemporary examples of these phenomena in supposedly Christian circles?

[68] Williams, *Galatians*, 161.

SELECT BIBLIOGRAPHY

COMMENTARIES

Advanced

Betz, Hans-Dieter. *Galatians*. Hermeneia. Philadelphia: Fortress, 1979.
Bruce, F. F. *The Epistle to the Galatians*. NIGTC. Exeter: Paternoster; Grand Rapids: Eerdmans, 1982.
Longenecker, Richard N. *Galatians*. WBC. Dallas: Word, 1990.
Martyn, J. Louis. *Galatians*. AB. New York and London: Doubleday, 1997.

Intermediate

Dunn, James D. G. *The Epistle to the Galatians*. BNTC/HNTC. London: Black; Peabody: Hendrickson, 1993.
Fung, Ronald Y. K. *The Epistle to the Galatians,* rev. NICNT. Grand Rapids: Eerdmans, 1998.
George, Timothy. *Galatians*. NAC. Nashville: Broadman & Holman, 1994.
Matera, Frank J. *Galatians*. SP. Collegeville: Liturgical, 1992.
Morris, Leon. *Galatians: Paul's Charter of Christian Freedom*. Leicester and Downers Grove: IVP, 1996.
Witherington, Ben, III. *Grace in Galatia: A Commentary on Paul's Letter to the Galatians*. Grand Rapids: Eerdmans; Edinburgh: T & T Clark, 1998.

Introductory

Hansen, G. Walter. *Galatians*. IVPNTC. Leicester and Downers Grove: IVP, 1994.
Jervis, L. Ann. *Galatians*. NIBC. Peabody: Hendrickson, 1999.
McKnight, Scot. *Galatians*. NIVAC. Grand Rapids: Zondervan, 1995.
Perkins, Pheme. *Abraham's Divided Children: Galatians and the Politics of Faith*. NTinCont. Harrisburg: Trinity, 2001.
Stott, John R. W. *Only One Way: The Message of Galatians*. BST. Leicester and Downers Grove: IVP, 1968.
Williams, Sam K. *Galatians*. ANTC. Nashville: Abingdon, 1997.

OTHER BOOKS

Barclay, John M. G. *Obeying the Truth: A Study of Paul's Ethics in Galatians*. Edinburgh: T & T Clark, 1988; Minneapolis: Fortress, 1991.
Barrett, C. K. *Freedom and Obligation: A Study of the Epistle to the Galatians*. London: SPCK; Philadelphia: Westminster, 1985.
Braxton, Brad R. *No Longer Slaves: Galatians and African American Experience*. Collegeville: Liturgical, 2002.
Bryant, Robert A. *The Risen Crucified Christ in Galatians*. Atlanta: SBL, 2001.
Dunn, James D. G. *The Theology of Paul's Letter to the Galatians*. Cambridge and New York: CUP, 1993.

Elliott, Susan. *Cutting Too Close for Comfort: Paul's Letter to the Galatians in Its Anatolian Cultic Context.* London and New York: T & T Clark, 2003.

Hong, In-Gyu. *The Law in Galatians.* Sheffield: JSOT, 1993.

Longenecker, Bruce W. *The Triumph of Abraham's God: The Transformation of Identity in Galatians.* Edinburgh: T&T Clark; Nashville: Abingdon, 1998.

Nanos, Mark D., ed. *The Galatians Debate: Contemporary Issues in Rhetorical and Historical Interpretation.* Peabody: Hendrickson, 2002.

Silva, Moisés. *Interpreting Galatians: Explorations in Exegetical Method,* rev. Grand Rapids: Baker, 2001.

Tsang, Sam. *From Slaves to Sons: A New Rhetoric on Paul's Slave Metaphors in His Letter to the Galatians.* Bern and New York: Peter Lang, 2005.

BIBLIOGRAPHY

Mills, Watson E. *Galatians.* Lewiston and Lampeter: Mellen, 1999.

4

THE THESSALONIAN CORRESPONDENCE: A BALANCED VIEW OF CHRIST'S RETURN

1 Thessalonians: Christ Is Coming Soon

INTRODUCTION

Thessalonica was the largest city and capital of the province of Macedonia, which occupied roughly the northern half of the modern country of Greece. It was situated on the northeast coast as a major port on the Aegean Sea and a significant stop on the central highway known as the Via Egnatia. Thessalonica was the first Greek city that Acts describes Paul evangelizing on his second missionary journey (Acts 17:1–9). A center of the imperial cult, Thessalonica also housed shrines to many national and local deities and was home to various professional voluntary associations or trade guilds, each of which typically had religious dimensions to it. A homegrown cult to a god named the Cabirus was worshipped by erecting a statue in the shape of a giant phallus![1]

From Acts, we learn that Paul followed his custom of first looking for the opportunity to preach in a local synagogue, and in fact he got to preach in the Thessalonian synagogue on three different Sabbaths. There he pointed out biblical prophecies about Jesus, his suffering and resurrection (Acts 17:2–3). As a result, he was able to plant a small church, comprised of some Jews but a larger number of God fearers (on which, recall above, p. 57) and "not a few prominent women" (v. 4). The only other things Acts tells us involve how Paul's time in Thessalonica ended: some of the Jews who rejected his message started a riot, harassed some of the new Christians, and in essence forced Paul and his companions to leave town (vv. 5–10a).[2]

Scholars debate whether Paul spent a longer period of time in town after leaving the Jewish synagogue. Many find it unlikely that a flourishing church could have been established based solely on what Luke describes in Acts 17:1–4. Philippians 4:16 depicts Paul receiving aid repeatedly while he was in Thessalonica, which

---

[1] On the imperial cult, see J. R. Harrison, "Paul and the Imperial Gospel at Thessaloniki," *JSNT* 25 (2002): 71–96; for other Greco-Roman religions, see Karl P. Donfried, "The Cults of Thessalonica and the Thessalonian Correspondence," *NTS* 31 (1985): 336–56; for the guilds, Richard Ascough, "The Thessalonian Christian Community as a Professional Voluntary Association," *JBL* 119 (2000): 311–28.

[2] For considerable detail on the nature and motivation of this persecution, in light of deviance theory, see Todd D. Still, *Conflict at Thessalonica: A Pauline Church and Its Neighbors* (Sheffield: SAP, 1999).

seems to require more than a three-week stay. First Thessalonians itself seems to presuppose a church comprised primarily of Gentile converts (see, e.g., 1:9), which would have involved additional ministry in town after Paul left the synagogue. Given the numerous gaps in Luke's narrative, there is nothing implausible about this suggestion, but, even if it is accepted, Paul probably spent no more than a few months in Thessalonica on this specific missionary journey.[3]

Acts probably also omits certain details concerning the subsequent travels of Paul's companions for the sake of simplicity. We know that Timothy has been accompanying Paul and Silas on this trip (Acts 16:1–5), though no mention is made of him leaving Thessalonica for Berea with Paul and Silas in 17:10. Yet we must assume he did because in verse 14 Paul moves on from Berea to Athens, leaving Silas and Timothy behind. Not until Paul reaches his next stop, Corinth, do Silas and Timothy rejoin him (18:5). In 1 Thessalonians, however, Paul recalls being left by himself in Athens, when he sent Timothy back to Thessalonica to encourage the believers there (3:1–2) and adds later that Timothy has now just come back to bring him good news about the Thessalonians' spiritual growth (v. 6). Hence, we may assume that Paul is writing this letter *from Corinth* but also that at least Timothy must have come from Berea to Athens, then been sent back to Thessalonica, before finally rejoining Paul in Corinth. Nothing in Acts contradicts this; Luke just leaves this additional material out.[4]

From our chronology of Acts, if Paul is writing from Corinth on his second missionary journey, then 1 Thessalonians must be dated to some time between 50 and 52. Because Paul seems eager for word from Thessalonica, a date closer to the beginning than to the end of this period appears more likely. Most scholars, therefore, date the letter to either *50 or 51.*

The epistle takes the form of a *parenetic or exhortational letter.*[5] The rhetoric is primarily deliberative but with a good dose of epideictic praise.[6] Compared with most of the other churches to which Paul writes, Thessalonica has very little wrong with it and much to commend it. Indeed, the introduction, thanksgiving, and body of the letter (chaps. 1–3) form the single longest uninterrupted stretch of sustained praise for a given congregation in any of Paul's letters. This is all the more striking in light of the comparatively short time that Paul spent in the city and the severity of persecution that this church subsequently experienced (1:6). Chapters 4–5 introduce at least two issues on which some further instruction is needed: working hard and minding one's own business, and questions about eschatology, specifically about what happens when a Christian dies. Both of these issues will reappear in slightly

---

[3] Cf. further Charles A. Wanamaker, *The Epistles to the Thessalonians* (Grand Rapids: Eerdmans; Exeter: Paternoster, 1990), 6–8.

[4] Cf. further D. Michael Martin, *1, 2 Thessalonians* (Nashville: Broadman & Holman, 1995), 25.

[5] Abraham J. Malherbe (*The Letters to the Thessalonians* [New York and London: Doubleday, 2001], 85) thinks it is one of the best examples of this letter form. Closely related is the letter of consolation, the category that Juan Chapa ("Is First Thessalonians a Letter of Consolation?" *NTS* 40 [1994]: 150–60) prefers. Cf. also Abraham Smith, *Comfort One Another: Reconstructing the Rhetoric and Audience of 1 Thessalonians* (Louisville: WJKP, 1995).

[6] Jan Lambrecht, "A Structural Analysis of 1 Thessalonians 4–5" in *The Thessalonians Debate: Methodological Discord or Methodological Synthesis?* eds. Karl P. Donfried and Johannes Beutler (Grand Rapids and Cambridge: Eerdmans, 2000), 177.

different form in 2 Thessalonians. The simplest subdivision of the letter, therefore, appears as follows:

I. Introduction (1:1–10)
   A. Greetings (1:1)
   B. Thanksgiving (1:2–10)
II. Paul's Concerns during and after His Ministry in Thessalonica (2:1–3:13)
   A. Paul's Ministry While Still in Thessalonica (2:1–16)
   B. Paul's Feelings and Actions Since Leaving Thessalonica (2:17–3:13)
III. Exhortations (4:1–5:28)
   A. Moral Living (4:1–12)
   B. Questions about Eschatology (4:13–5:11)
   C. Final Instructions (5:12–22)
   D. Concluding Prayers and Greetings (5:23–28)

COMMENTARY

Introduction (1:1–10)

Greetings (1:1)   The short opening greetings of this letter, with their succinct presentation of coauthors, addressees, and well wishes, more closely approximate standard Greco-Roman form than the beginning of Galatians. That Paul includes the names of Silas and Timothy along with his as the senders could suggest that they were amanuenses, letter carriers, or simply his companions at that time. But most likely he means that they were involved in the composition of the letter in some respect.[7] That the Lord Jesus Christ is linked with God the Father may suggest, if not early trinitarian, then at least binitarian thought. Grace was the conventional Greek greeting, with peace its Jewish counterpart. Paul has combined and Christianized them with his reference to Jesus.

Thanksgiving (1:2–10)   This letter also restores the conventional thanksgiving that Galatians omitted. Indeed, proportionate to the size of the letter, 1 Thessalonians has the longest thanksgiving in any of Paul's epistles. Here Paul lavishes praise on the Thessalonian congregation for its quick growth and relative maturity despite the persecution it has experienced. Paul's thanksgiving prayers typically introduce key themes that he will unpack in the body of his letters.[8] In this case, his gratefulness for the model the church has become and his concern to teach them more about events surrounding Jesus' return are both reflected (vv. 3–9 and 10, respectively). The NIV's rendering of verse 3 is particularly elegant. The Greek offers simply three parallel subjective genitives: work of faith, labor of love, and endurance of

---

[7] I. Howard Marshall, *1 and 2 Thessalonians* (London: Marshall, Morgan & Scott; Grand Rapids: Eerdmans, 1983), 50.

[8] Paul Schubert, *Form and Function of the Pauline Thanksgivings* (Berlin: Töpelmann, 1939); Peter T. O'Brien, *Introductory Thanksgivings in the Letters of Paul* (Leiden and New York: Brill, 1977). On the nature and importance of gratitude throughout Paul's letters more generally, see David W. Pao, *Thanksgiving: An Investigation of a Pauline Theme* (Leicester and Downers Grove: IVP, 2002).

hope, which are turned into the much more fluent "work produced by faith," "labor prompted by love," and "endurance inspired by hope." The triad of faith, love, and hope will recur at the end of the letter as well (5:8) and is made much more famous by its later appearance in 1 Corinthians 13:13 with love as the climax.

Paul is particularly impressed by the effects the gospel message had on these new believers, which he can attribute only to God's supernatural power (vv. 4–5a). Verses 5b–6a introduce a theme prominent in the Thessalonian correspondence and to a certain degree in Paul's letters more generally—that of imitating exemplary models. Philosophers, teachers, and religious leaders in Paul's world did not merely communicate information; would-be followers observed their lives and chose whether to imitate them.[9] In this case the imitation occurred despite severe suffering, which presumably referred to the persecution these believers experienced for their new faith (v. 6b). By the time we read Paul's catalogs of hardships in 2 Corinthians 4; 6; 11; 12, we will understand how particularly suited he was as an example in this respect.[10]

Equally praiseworthy was the fact that the Thessalonian church became a model to believers elsewhere in Greece (vv. 7–10). This statement presupposes at least a few months' lapse in time, if not more, for Paul to establish churches elsewhere in the country, though of course it is always possible that other evangelistic efforts had preceded his that we are simply not told about elsewhere. Even if "everywhere" in verse 8 is a bit hyperbolic, it does suggest that the "they themselves" (v. 9) need not be limited to the other believers. *It may well be that, even as Paul began evangelizing other communities, various Jews or Greeks told him that they already knew something of the gospel from the Thessalonians' activity.*[11] Chapter 1 offers an excellent summary of what was involved in Gentile conversions: turning away from idols and serving the living and true God (v. 9). Paul's prayer closes with an allusion to Christ's second coming (v. 10), as will each of the next three chapters also.

PAUL'S CONCERNS DURING AND AFTER HIS MINISTRY IN THESSALONICA (2:1–3:13)

Paul's Ministry While Still in Thessalonica (2:1–16) The body of Paul's letter falls into two parts. First, Paul describes his ministry when he was with the Thessalonians. The issues he treats and the comments he makes about them suggest that he may have received a little criticism, either inside or outside the church.[12] It would have been easy for some to label Paul's time in Thessalonica a failure, since he was run out of town so quickly, or to allege that his rapid departure from the city implied his lack of care for the new believers. But he stresses that this has hap-

---

[9] On which, see further Abraham J. Malherbe, *Paul and the Thessalonians: The Philosophic Tradition of Pastoral Care* (Philadelphia: Fortress, 1987).

[10] "An effective witness results when the church becomes an example of faithfulness in the midst of suffering by imitating Christ and the apostles" (Gregory K. Beale, *1 and 2 Thessalonians* [Leicester and Downers Grove: IVP, 2003], 55).

[11] Moreover, it appears that the Thessalonians were overtly evangelistic and that Paul expected them to continue to be so. See James Ware, "The Thessalonians as a Missionary Congregation: 1 Thessalonians 1,5–8," *ZNW* 83 (1992): 126–31.

[12] Jeffrey A. D. Weima, "An Apology for the Apologetic Function of 1 Thessalonians 2:1–12," *JSNT* 68 (1997): 73–99.

pened to him elsewhere without failure, while the results for which he thanked God in 1:2–10 certainly reflect considerable success (2:1–2). In the Hellenistic world, many itinerant teachers charged large sums of money for their public speaking, leading some to become cynical about their motives. Such people would often flatter their major patrons to ensure their continued support. Paul denies behaving like such teachers (vv. 3–6).[13]

Turning from what he and his companions did not do in Thessalonica (vv. 1–6a) to their positive model (vv. 6b–12), Paul now employs two parental metaphors to stress his care and concern for these new believers. On the one hand, Paul, Silas, and Timothy were like a mother caring for her children (v. 7); on the other hand, like a father encouraging, comforting, and exhorting his sons and daughters (v. 11). How one reacts to these metaphors depends in large part on the experiences one has had with human parents, but Paul is employing them in an entirely positive sense to stress his deep, affectionate, and ongoing love and commitment to his spiritual children,[14] while still retaining the authority associated with parents, and especially fathers, in his world.[15] The same valid and invalid motives for pastoral ministry remain today. If one is in it primarily for money or praise, one probably will not last long. True success requires the often thankless perseverance exhibited by parents committed to their children in good times and in bad.[16] In this section, Paul also stresses how hard he and his companions worked in order not to burden the Thessalonians (v. 9). By this he means that they plied their trades—in Paul's case, tent-making (recall Acts 18:3)—to provide for their own needs rather than demanding support from the new church they were establishing.[17]

A particularly difficult textual decision is required in verse 7. Many early manuscripts read "babies" instead of "gentle"; the TNIV has in fact reversed the decision of the NIV (which read, "We were gentle among you"), adopting the rendering "We were like young children." The external evidence slightly favors and the internal evidence strongly favors "young children" (i.e., "babies"). "Babies" and "gentle" differ by only one letter in the Greek (*ēpioi* vs. *nēpioi*), and it is more likely that the more jarring metaphor in which Paul describes himself as both the baby and the mother in the same verse would be altered to the concept of being gentle than that the change would have gone in the other direction.[18]

The first half of Paul's letter closes with *a second thanksgiving* (vv. 13–16), a feature not found in most of Paul's letters and another indication of the general health of the Thessalonian congregation. *Verse 13 provides a key clue to why they grew*

---

[13] Bruce W. Winter ("The Entries and Ethics of Orators and Paul [1 Thessalonians 2:1–12]," *TynB* 44 [1993]: 55–74) defends the thesis that Paul is countering comparison with the Sophists.

[14] Beverly R. Gaventa, "Our Mother St. Paul: Toward the Recovery of a Neglected Theme," *PSB* 17 (1996): 33–36, 42.

[15] Trevor J. Burke, "Pauline Paternity in 1 Thessalonians," *TynB* 51 (2000): 59–80.

[16] Cf. esp. Jeffrey A. D. Weima, "Infants, Nursing Mother, and Father: Paul's Portrayal of a Pastor," *TynB* 52 (2001): 1–31; M. Carsoa, "For Now We Live: A Study of Paul's Leadership in 1 Thessalonians," *Themelios* 30 (2005): 23–41.

[17] Ronald F. Hock (*The Social Context of Paul's Ministry* [Philadelphia: Fortress, 1980], 31–37), describes the long hours manual laborers worked and the contempt for their occupation exhibited by the elite.

[18] Jeffrey A. D. Weima, "'But We Became Infants among You,'" *NTS* 46 (2000): 547–61.

so fast and well: they recognized the gospel message as God's very words active in believers to empower them for all God requires. This enabled them to persevere even when persecuted, a feature that linked their experience to that of the Judean church (vv. 14–16).[19] Paul's remarks here have often been mistakenly described as anti-Semitic, though the error is understandable in light of his harsh words. But Paul is not condemning all Jewish people, merely those "who killed the Lord Jesus and the prophets and also drove us out" (v. 15).[20] In other words, those who persecuted God's spokesmen in Old Testament times or Jesus and his followers in the New Testament era will themselves experience God's wrath. This is no stronger a statement than numerous Old Testament judgments pronounced by prophets on those Israelites who were rebelling against God in their day, yet no one accuses the writers of the Hebrew Scriptures of being anti-Semitic![21] Indeed, Paul's criticism of fellow "Christians" in Galatians, Philippians, and 2 Corinthians is even harsher, yet Paul cannot be anti-Christian.[22]

Another interpretive controversy surrounds the final sentence of verse 16. The verb translated "has come" could reflect the prophetic use of the past tense and carry the sense of "will come," referring to judgment day. If it refers to a genuinely past event, then it probably points to the beginning of judgment on the enemies of Christ that the crucifixion and resurrection themselves accomplished. It is of course possible that Paul had some of each of these two perspectives in mind.[23] Equally uncertain is the translation of the last two words of this verse—in Greek, *eis telos.* They could mean "at last" or "to the uttermost," and either could fit the context. Finally, it is interesting that Paul's language in this paragraph parallels many of Jesus' own remarks in his woes to the Pharisees and scribes in Matthew 23, particularly in verses 31–36. Paul may well be relying on oral tradition about Jesus' teaching, since this letter predates the written form of any Gospel.[24] This observation also makes improbable the suggestion that 1 Thessalonians 2:14–16 is a later interpolation by someone other than Paul, a proposal that deals with the alleged anti-Semitism quite differently![25]

---

[19] The specific persecution afflicting the Judean church may be the harassment they received from Jewish zealots in A.D. 48–52 (Gene L. Green, *The Letters to the Thessalonians* [Grand Rapids: Eerdmans, 2002], 143).

[20] The comma after "Jews" therefore misleads and should be removed. See Frank D. Gilliard, "The Problem of the Antisemitic Comma between 1 Thessalonians 2.14 and 15," *NTS* 35 (1989): 481–502.

[21] Particularly intriguing are conceptual and structural parallels between 1 Thessalonians 2:13–16 and Testament of Levi 6:1–11. Verse 11 clearly resembles the end of 1 Thessalonians 2:16. See Jeffrey S. Lamp, "Is Paul Anti-Jewish? *Testament of Levi* 6 in the Interpretation of 1 Thessalonians 2:13–16," *CBQ* 65 (2003): 408–27. For astute reflections on applying verses 13–16 in other times and places, see Michael W. Holmes, *1 and 2 Thessalonians* (Grand Rapids: Zondervan, 1998), 86–92.

[22] Carol J. Schlueter thus identifies Paul's rhetorical style as polemical hyperbole, with notable parallels in the Dead Sea Scrolls, in *Filling up the Measure: Polemical Hyperbole in 1 Thessalonians 2:14–16* (Sheffield: SAP, 1994).

[23] Markus Bockmuehl ("1 Thessalonians 2:14–16 and the Church in Jerusalem," *TynB* 52 [2001]: 1–31) argues that Paul has in mind the recent persecution of the Jerusalem church by Claudius in A.D. 48–49, which was interpreted as unleashing a series of divine judgments against Judaism, including a bloodbath on the Temple Mount during Passover week instigated by Ventidius Cumanus, sporadic famines, and Claudius's edict to expel the Jews from Rome.

[24] Wenham, *Paul,* 319–21.

[25] Jon A. Weatherly, "The Authenticity of 1 Thessalonians 2.13–16: Additional Evidence," *JSNT* 42 (1991): 79–98. An older generation of scholars often posited these verses as a non-Pauline interpolation, a view now increasingly abandoned.

Paul's Feelings and Actions Since Leaving Thessalonica (2:17–3:13)   The second half of the body of the letter turns from Paul's time in Thessalonica to the days and weeks since he left. In 2:17–3:10 Paul discloses his deep concern for the Thessalonians' well-being and then his deep gratitude at hearing how well they were doing spiritually, despite their outward suffering. Initially, Paul wanted to return to Thessalonica himself and made repeated efforts to do so (2:17–18). We are not told in what way "Satan stopped" him, though it would make sense that it had to do with the same kind of harassment that originally drove him out of town (and not only in Thessalonica). Verses 19–20 round out the chapter, explaining the depth of Paul's passion. Unlike those who would glory in earthly or material possessions, Paul recognizes that all he can take with him in the age to come are redeemed relationships.

Chapter 3:1–3 presents his backup plan for revisiting the Thessalonians. He will send Timothy to check up on things and encourage the new believers. Verse 4 seems to confirm our suspicion that the problem that kept Paul himself away involved persecution. A natural temptation in such circumstances is to abandon one's faith, so Paul wants to be sure that the Thessalonians have not reacted this way (v. 5).[26] Fortunately, he learns that they have persevered. Indeed, the church's faith and love remains strong, as does their desire to see Paul (vv. 6–8). In what is *almost a third thanksgiving*, verses 9–10 praise God for the joy their maturity produces and pray that Paul may in fact be able to return and continue to nurture them.[27] Verses 11–13 lapse into a full-fledged doxology, expanding on these themes. Once again, a chapter closes anticipating the completion of the process of Christian growth when Christ comes back. The "holy ones" in verse 13 are almost certainly angels, not previously raptured believers. The language closely echoes Zechariah 14:5, where angels clearly are in view. See also 2 Thessalonians 1:7.

EXHORTATIONS (4:1–5:28)

Moral Living (4:1–12)   The exhortational material of the letter comprises 4:1–5:24. Chapter 5:25–28 forms the letter closing while still including requests and commands. Paul begins by encouraging his friends to continue all the more to live in ways that please God (vv. 1–2). He then defines God's will, as consistently in Scripture, in moral categories—being "sanctified" (v. 3a)—and applies this theme of holiness to a major area of temptation in the ancient (and modern) world—sexual impurity (vv. 3b–8). The word translated "sexual immorality" in verse 3 is *porneia,* the broadest of all terms for sexual sin in the Greek language, encompassing every form of intercourse outside of monogamous heterosexual marriage.[28] A translational crux appears in verse 4, which reads literally "to acquire a vessel" (NIV: "to control his own body"). Because 1 Peter 3:7 (KJV) refers to a wife as a weaker "vessel,"

---

[26] "Part of the basic catechism for new believers was instruction concerning the sufferings they were going to endure" (Green, *Thessalonians,* 161).

[27] Indeed, one can think of 1 Thessalonians 1–3 as almost an overall thanksgiving interrupted by several digressions (Jan Lambrecht, "Thanksgivings in 1 Thessalonians 1–3," in *The Thessalonians Debate,* eds. Donfried and Beutler, 135–62).

[28] Joseph F. Jensen, "Does *Porneia* Mean Fornication? A Critique of Bruce Malina," *NovT* 20 (1978): 161–84.

some have thought that Paul was speaking of how to find a marriage partner. But a majority of scholars today recognize that the expression is probably a euphemism for controlling one's own sexual behavior and reserving it for a lawfully wedded spouse (cf. also v. 5).[29] Some have speculated that verse 6 introduces a new topic, since the word for "matter" can refer to business dealings. But the majority of commentators, probably correctly, understand "this matter" as still referring to sexual purity (cf. vv. 7–8). Once again Paul insists that his instruction is the very word of God. Thus to reject it is to reject God's own Spirit (v. 8).

The ideal instead of lust is true love, so it is natural for Paul to command that next (vv. 9–10). Here he acknowledges that the Thessalonians are doing well and simply encourages them to continue to grow. *The end of verse 10 could be translated, "excel still more," which could also reflect the main theme of the letter.*

Verses 11–12 enjoin the Thessalonians to live a quiet life, mind their own business, and work with their hands.[30] Because Paul has to command some to do their own work and be dependent on no one else, many readers have found here the seeds of the problem of idleness that increases before Paul writes 2 Thessalonians 3:6–15. Both self-sufficiency within the Christian community and respect by outsiders are required. We have problems with both today. Holiness *inside and outside* the church would go a long way toward helping. "If we cannot be holy at our work, it is not worth taking any trouble to be holy at other times."[31]

Questions about Eschatology (4:13–5:11) *Finally, Paul comes to the one apparent doctrinal question that is troubling the Thessalonian Christians.* Perhaps one or more of their members has just died.[32] Quite possibly Paul did not have time to teach in detail all he would have liked to explain about life after death. No doubt he stressed Christ's promises to come back soon, so that some may have been wondering if twenty years after Jesus' death could still be considered "soon." Whatever the precise concerns, Paul provides crucial instruction in this section on the doctrine of eschatology. We may highlight six points in particular.

1. Christians ought not to grieve the loss of Christian loved ones *in an unchristian way* (v. 13). Paul is not forbidding all grief; sorrow forms a natural part of being human. But we ought not to grieve in the way unbelievers do "who have no hope." Epitaphs on Greco-Roman tombstones vividly testify to the despair that many felt as death approached, even though most people believed in some vague form of disembodied life after death.[33]

---

[29] Cf. Robert Yarbrough, "Sexual Gratification in 1 Thess 4:1–8," *TrinJ* 20 (1999): 215–32; Jay E. Smith, "Another Look at 4Q416 2 ii 21, a Critical Parallel to First Thessalonians 4:4," *CBQ* 63 (2001): 499–504; and idem, "1 Thessalonians 4:4: Breaking the Impasse," *BBR* 11 (2001): 65–105.

[30] Minding one's own business was the exact opposite of participating in public or political affairs (Green, *Thessalonians*, 210).

[31] Leon Morris, *The First and Second Epistles to the Thessalonians* (Grand Rapids: Eerdmans, rev. 1991), 132, n. 48, citing James Denney.

[32] See esp. throughout Colin R. Nicholl, *From Hope to Despair in Thessalonica* (Cambridge and New York: CUP, 2004).

[33] "Hopes are for the living, but the ones who die are without hope" (Theocritus, *Idyll*, 4.42, cited in Beale, *Thessalonians*, 130).

2. The reason for Christians' hope is delineated in verse 14. Believers can rejoice that Christian loved ones live with Jesus and will come back with him when he returns. From other passages in Paul, it is clear that no one receives a resurrection body until the second coming (e.g. 1 Cor. 15:23). So Paul here must mean that believers will experience the intermediate state between death and resurrection in disembodied, conscious existence with Christ.[34]

3. Christians living when Jesus returns will have no advantage over those who have already died (v. 15), so they need not worry if they do not live to see the parousia (his coming again). Because Paul writes in the first-person plural in this verse, many commentators have argued that he was sure he would live until Christ returned. This would necessitate that he later changed his mind as he aged and became uncertain if he would live that long (e.g. Phil. 1:22). But the clause, "we who are still alive," need not be that precise. Such an expression can just as easily mean, "whoever is still alive, whether that includes any of you, or me, or not." After all, in 5:10 he again uses "we" but entertains the possibility of being either "awake" or "asleep" at the parousia.[35] Paul also introduces this verse, and perhaps the next two, with the formula, "according to the Lord's own word." While some see this as the word of a Christian prophet, there are enough parallels with Jesus' eschatological discourse (esp. in Matt. 24) to suggest that he knows some form of that tradition.[36]

4. All believers alive on Earth when Christ returns "will be caught up together" with those accompanying him "to meet the Lord in the air" (vv. 16–17). This event has come to be called "the rapture," from the Latin *raptus,* the noun derived from the verb for "caught up." This is the only passage in Scripture that uses this particular imagery of being caught up in the air although the same Greek verb (*harpazō*) appears in 2 Corinthians 12:1–4 when Paul is caught up into the third heaven, either inside or outside the body—he doesn't know. Theologians have extensively debated whether this is a separate event from Christ's visible, bodily, public return at the end of human history. Because Scripture elsewhere seems to teach of a "great tribulation" immediately preceding Christ's return (e.g. Matt. 24:21–28; Rev. 7:14), interpreters have debated the relationship between the tribulation and the rapture, dividing themselves into pretribulational, midtribulational, and posttribulational camps. Most everyone agrees, however, that no text of the Bible ever speaks of both tribulation and rapture at the same time, so theological syntheses of numerous texts are needed to come to conclusions.[37]

It is interesting, however, to observe that the term used in this passage for "meeting" the Lord in the air (Gk. *apantēsis*) is the same word that was often used for a welcome and escort provided for a returning king or visiting dignitary to an ancient Greco-Roman city. The two other appearances of this word in the New Testament match this usage exactly. In Matthew 25:6, the waiting bridesmaids wake up to meet

---

[34] Sleep was a common euphemism for death in both the Jewish and Greco-Roman worlds, so there is no need to resort to a theory of "soul-sleep" here.

[35] A. L. Moore, *The Parousia in the New Testament* (Leiden and New York: Brill, 1966), 78–79.

[36] Seyoon Kim, "The Jesus Tradition in 1 Thess 4.13–5.11," *NTS* 48 (2002): 225–42.

[37] For a helpful guide to the debate, see Richard R. Reiter, Paul D. Feinberg, Gleason L. Archer, and Douglas J. Moo, *The Rapture: Pre-, Mid-, or Post-Tribulational?* (Grand Rapids: Zondervan, 1984).

and escort the bridegroom and his new wife to his parents' home where they will live together. In Acts 28:15, the Christians from Rome leave town to meet Paul on the highway and escort him back to their city. Likewise, here in 1 Thessalonians 4:17, *the imagery suggests the posttribulational understanding of the rapture.* Jesus is descending from heaven to earth at the second coming, and his followers form a welcoming party to meet him part way and then escort him back to the earth in triumph.[38] Interestingly, it is precisely *post*tribulationism here that best supports seeing Paul as *pre*millennial. For why bring Christ back to Earth unless to begin his *earthly* reign, which some Thessalonians feared their deceased fellow Christians would miss?[39]

5. Paul's message is intended to encourage and comfort (4:18; cf. 5:11). Whatever disagreements we have on the details of the rapture dare not divide us or prevent fellowship and cooperative service. Apocalyptic literature in both testaments is regularly intended to console beleaguered Christians, not to divide them into warring camps!

6. The time of the end cannot be predicted, but we can prepare for it (5:1–10). Those who are not expecting Christ to come back will be caught off guard (vv. 1–3), just like the shock of a nighttime burglar or the onset of labor pains in a pregnant woman. To compare Christ's return to a thief is so striking a simile that Paul is almost certainly echoing the Jesus tradition (recall Matt. 24:43). Both Jesus and Paul stressed that it is impossible to predict the time of the parousia, even though over-eager believers throughout church history have frequently tried to do so anyway. If anything, the end will come at a time when no signs lead people to expect it. "Peace and safety" (v. 3) formed an Augustan slogan, indicating the security brought about by the *pax Romana.*[40] But no government can supply the true peace that will permeate the Earth only after Christ's return. What believers can and should do, however, is to remain alert and live godly lives so that whenever the end comes they will be ready (vv. 4–11). Verse 4 "does not mean that the church will know when this day will come but rather clarifies that Christians are those who are prepared for this final event."[41] Paul's triad of faith, love, and hope reappears here, this time using metaphors from a soldier's armor (v. 8), based originally on Isaiah 59:17.

Final Instructions (5:12–22) Paul rounds out his exhortation with more miscellaneous commands, similar in a number of respects to closing lists in other epistles (cf. esp. Rom. 12:9–21). Perhaps these were relatively standard concerns.[42] But certain admonitions tie in with the unique circumstances in Thessalonica, particularly the reminder to work hard (v. 12) and to warn the idle (v. 14).[43] A few other commands

---

[38] Cf. further Robert H. Gundry, "A Brief Note on 'Hellenistic Formal Receptions and Paul's Use of ΑΠΑΝΤΗΣΙΣ,'" *BBR* 6 (1996): 39–41. It is also telling that 4:15–17 and 5:1–11 reflect a continuous set of references from Matthew 24, suggesting that they both, like Jesus' Olivet Discourse, refer to Christ's final, public return. See David Wenham, *The Rediscovery of Jesus' Eschatological Discourse* (Sheffield: JSOT, 1984), 303–14.

[39] Seth Turner, "The Interim, Earthly Messianic Kingdom in Paul," *JSNT* 25 (2003): 323–42, esp. 326–32.

[40] Yeo Khiok-Khng ("A Political Reading of Paul's Eschatology in I and II Thessalonians," *AJT* 12 [1998]: 77–88) shows how large portions of both letters, including the discussions of epiphany, parousia, and apocalypse, would have been heard as counterpoints to the emperor's roles and functions.

[41] Green, *Thessalonians,* 235.

[42] For a comparative chart of the parallels among Romans, 1 Peter, and 1 Thessalonians, see Marshall, *Thessalonians,* 145–46.

[43] Or perhaps the term (*ataktoi*) should be translated "disorderly" (Beale, *Thessalonians,* 163).

merit brief comment since they can easily be misunderstood. "Give thanks in all circumstances" (v. 18) does not mean to give thanks for everything that happens, as if we must be grateful for evil as well as good. Rather, as we will unpack in commenting on Romans 8:28, God is working to bring some kind of good out of all situations, even evil ones, and that is why we can thank him.

Verse 22 has misled many, particularly in the KJV ("abstain from all appearance of evil"), suggesting that even good actions should be avoided if there is some way that others could misconstrue them. But the word for "appearance" in the Greek (*eidos*) does not mean something that looks like that which it is not (as in the English sentence, "the shadow on the road ahead gave the appearance of being a pool of water"), but the actual presence of something (as in, "the actress made her final appearance in town"). Thus the NIV gets it right with its translation, "avoid every kind of evil."[44]

CONCLUDING PRAYERS AND GREETINGS (5:23–28)

Verses 23–24 find Paul closing this epistle with a prayer for the full sanctification of his readers. Spirit, soul, and body must not be thought of as three separate parts of the human being; elsewhere in Scripture "soul" and "spirit" largely overlap in meaning to refer to the immaterial part of a person. Instead, this is a vivid way of referring to the whole person.[45] Otherwise one would have to understand Mark 12:30, which commands us to love God with heart, soul, mind, and strength as dividing the person into four parts, while Hebrews 4:12 would suggest a sixfold division (soul, spirit, joints, marrow, thoughts, and attitudes)!

In Paul's final words (vv. 25–28), two points deserve mention. The holy kiss played a central role in early Christian worship. It was a standard greeting in ancient Mediterranean cultures among close friends and family members, as it still is in various parts of the world, and had no sexual overtones. The charge in verse 27 reminds us that this letter, like presumably all of the books of the New Testament, was originally meant to be read aloud to a congregation of God's people.

THE THESSALONIANS AND CHRIST'S RETURN

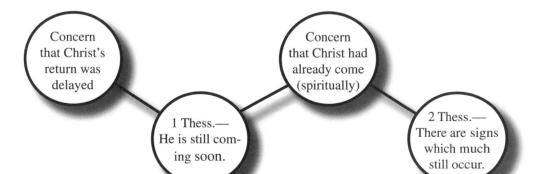

---

[44] Cf. Malherbe, *Thessalonians,* 334.
[45] Earl J. Richard, *First and Second Thessalonians* (Collegeville: Liturgical, 1995), 285–86.

2 Thessalonians: But Not That Soon!

INTRODUCTION

Authorship

While no serious scholarship doubts that Paul wrote Galatians or 1 Thessalonians, *roughly half of the guild of biblical scholars believes that 2 Thessalonians is pseudonymous.* There are seven primary reasons for ascribing authorship to someone other than Paul: (1) First and Second Thessalonians are extremely similar to each other in that they contain two thanksgivings (with a disproportionately long first one and a prayer-wish for the second one), the same general topics throughout the body of the letter, the same elements in the closing in the same order and much of the same vocabulary and style. It is argued that Paul's fertile and creative mind would not likely have penned two epistles to the same community with so few differences. (2) Second Thessalonians does not disclose the same close relationship between the author and his congregation that the first epistle does. (3) The second letter does not contain the same rich array of theological themes as the first, having narrowed the focus almost exclusively to eschatology. (4) Similarly, the ethical concerns of 2 Thessalonians have been reduced to the single issue of idleness or disorderliness. (5) The short interval between the two letters required by the assumption that Paul wrote them both leaves little time for spurious letters written in his name to be composed and circulated (cf. 2 Thess. 2:2, 15). (6) The changed situation also seems to require a greater amount of time to have elapsed. In the first epistle, problems seemed to surround the delay of Christ's return; now some seemed to be claiming that it has already passed! (7) Second Thessalonians appears to rely on previous tradition more than its predecessor, particularly with respect to Jewish and Christian convictions about the Antichrist (2:3–10).[46]

None of these arguments seems particularly strong. Similarities in both style and form would be natural if Paul had to address the same community about several of the same topics. If the situation had deteriorated, it would likewise be natural for Paul to employ a more distant, less personal tone. Likewise, his focus would have to narrow to the most urgent issues at hand. The question about how much time is needed between the two letters depends heavily on the interpretation of 2 Thessalonians 2:2 and 15. If these references speak of apocryphal documents, there may be something to the skeptics' logic. But we will see below that these verses may be interpreted as referring to a misunderstanding of 1 Thessalonians, in which case no extra time is needed other than that which causes persecution of the believers in Thessalonica to intensify. As for the use of preexisting tradition, whether Jewish or Christian, Paul

---

[46] Cf. further Beverly Gaventa, *First and Second Thessalonians* (Louisville: WJKP, 1998), 93–97; Bonnie Thurston, *Reading Colossians, Ephesians and 2 Thessalonians* (New York: Crossroad, 1995), 159–62.

displays no consistent patterns throughout his letters as to when he depends heavily on such material and when he goes his independent way.

So the debate over the internal evidence proves little. External evidence, however, for Paul's authorship of this letter is strong: Polycarp, Ignatius, Justin, and the Didache knew of the letter in the first half of the second century. In the mid-second century Marcion's and the Muratorian canons include it. Irenaeus, toward the end of the second century (*Against Heresies* 26.4), and later church fathers uniformly cite it as Pauline.[47] For those not convinced by these arguments, 2 Thessalonians most likely reflects the response of a writer from the Pauline school of thought in the generation after Paul's life responding to a new problem—that of apocalyptic fervor in Thessalonica.[48] Not surprisingly, though, the most recent, detailed commentary on these letters from a critical perspective not only defends Pauline authorship but concludes that it is unreasonable to call a letter pseudonymous that (1) is concerned about previous communication attributed to the author, (2) refers to what the author taught orally and in a letter, and (3) stresses its own genuineness (2:2, 15; 3:17). This conclusion, which supports Pauline authorship, seems the soundest.[49]

ORDER OF THE LETTERS

Most of church history has assumed that 2 Thessalonians was written after 1 Thessalonians. This is true whether one accepts Paul as author or not. But, as we have seen, the primary reason for the inclusion of these two letters in this sequence in the biblical canon seems to be one of decreasing length rather than chronological order. Thus a handful of scholars from time to time has proposed that the second epistle actually preceded the first.[50] Five primary arguments fuel their case: (1) Various passages in 1 Thessalonians appear to presuppose previous correspondence with Paul. The expression, "now about" (1 Thess. 4:9; 5:1), seems to introduce answers to questions raised earlier by the addressees (cf. 1 Cor. 7:1), while 1 Thessalonians 3:1–2 could refer to Paul sending Timothy with a previous letter. (2) The persecution addressed in 2 Thessalonians still seems to be occurring (1:4–7), while in 1 Thessalonians it appears to be past (2:14). (3) So, too, the problem of disorder in 2 Thessalonians 3:11–15 appears to be a new one, while in 1 Thessalonians 4:10–12 it is treated as a known problem. (4) Second Thessalonians 3:17 is *not* true if 1 Thessalonians precedes it, since in that letter Paul does not highlight a greeting in his own hand at the end. (5) First Thessalonians 5:1 (on the readers needing no instruction about the time of the end) makes best sense if 2 Thessalonians 2:1–12 has preceded it.

Even taken together, these arguments seem fairly weak. Nothing in (1) positively points to 1 Thessalonians as part of any prior correspondence. Concerning (2), most readers have understood the persecution to have gotten worse from the first to the second letter, and nothing reads unnaturally on this assumption. The standard order of the letters makes good sense of the problem of idleness, too (issue 3; that situa-

---

[47] David J. Williams, *1 and 2 Thessalonians* (Peabody: Hendrickson, 1992), 13.

[48] Earl J. Richard, *First and Second Thessalonians* (Collegeville: Liturgical, 1995), 25–29, 32.

[49] Malherbe, *Thessalonians,* 373.

[50] See esp. Wanamaker, *Thessalonians,* 37–45.

tion likewise would have deteriorated from the first epistle to the second). The point relating to (4) is not that Paul calls attention to his closing greeting in every letter, merely that he does take pen in hand to write such a greeting each time. Galatians 6:11 attests to the practice; there is no reason 1 Thessalonians 5:25–28 could not form a second instance without Paul's having specifically labeled it. Certainly in his later letters he does not explicitly "sign off." As for (5), 1 Thessalonians 5:1 cannot be pressed, since Paul is in the midst of giving detailed eschatological instruction anyway.[51]

DATING

What a discussion like this does demonstrate is that there is little conclusive evidence within the two letters to prove either sequence of writing. But in lieu of any strong arguments to the contrary, the approach adopted by the vast majority of commentators, especially in the early church, should not be lightly set aside. We will, therefore, proceed on the assumption that the canonical order of these two epistles is also their chronological one. In this case, 2 Thessalonians would most likely have been written not long after the first letter and thus presumably *while Paul was still in Corinth* (and recall that he stayed there at least a year and half—Acts 18:11). At any rate, Corinth is the only place described in Acts in which Paul and Silas are explicitly said to together from here on (cf. 2 Thess. 1:1). Dates for 2 Thessalonians would thus range from 50 to 52, with *51 or 52* most likely.

CONTEXT AND GENRE

The message that Paul seems to have successfully communicated through 1 Thessalonians about the parousia is that no one needed to doubt Christ's promise to come back soon. But it is quite possible that the Thessalonians overreacted because the essence of the message of his second letter is "but not that soon!" Paul refers to "some prophecy, report or letter supposed to have come from us," saying that the day of the Lord has already come" (2 Thess. 2:2). Such a claim could have emanated from quasi-Gnostic circles that believed in an invisible, spiritual resurrection of all Christians that took place at conversion and left no further need for a later bodily resurrection.[52] But it is also possible that Paul's words refer to a misinterpretation of and overreaction to Paul's first letter. The Greek of this verse literally reads, "a spirit, word or letter, as through us, as if the day of the Lord had come." I. H. Marshall explains that the phrase, "as through us," most likely goes with all three

---

[51] Cf. further Williams, *1 and 2 Thessalonians,* 13–15. On the use of tradition in 2 Thessalonians, see G. S. Holland, *The Tradition That You Received from Us* (Tubingen: Mohr, 1998).

[52] Cf. the following excerpts from the *Treatise on Resurrection,* 46–49: "The thought of those who are saved shall not perish. The mind of those who have known him shall not perish." "But there are some (who) wish to understand, in the inquiry about those things they are looking into, whether he who is saved, if he leaves his body behind, will be saved immediately. Let no one be given cause to doubt concerning this . . . indeed, the visible members which are dead shall not be saved, for (only) the living [members] which exist within them would arise." "Indeed, it is more fitting to say that the resurrection is an illusion, rather than the resurrection which has come into being through our Lord the Savior, Jesus Christ." "Therefore, do not . . . live in conformity with this flesh . . . but flee from the divisions and the fetters, and already you have the resurrection. For if he who will die knows about himself that he will die—even if he spends many years in this life he is brought to this—why not consider yourself as risen and (already) brought to this?"

nouns that precede it, "and that it refers not to whether the sources of teaching were truly Pauline but to whether the message attributed to Paul was a faithful representation of his teaching."[53]

In 3:6, Paul speaks of those who are idle (or disorderly; recall above). These people have often been taken to be believers who stopped working because they thought Christ would return immediately. So whether Paul is addressing those who fear that they have missed the parousia or merely those who think it is close at hand, he uses the body of this epistle to remind them that several things must first occur before Christ can come back. While there are elements of exhortation and consolation as in 1 Thessalonians, the overall genre of this letter falls less clearly into a fixed category from the ancient Mediterranean world. We may think of it, however, as an advisory letter, as Paul advises the Thessalonians not to imagine they have missed the day of the Lord but to keep their distance from the idle.[54] With noticeably less praise, however, the rhetoric is more consistently deliberative.

STRUCTURE

As in 1 Thessalonians, Paul closely follows the standard form of a Greco-Roman letter, with introduction, thanksgiving, letter body (divided into information and exhortation), and closing. For the sake of simplicity, we may combine the introduction and thanksgiving together and tack on the closing to the concluding exhortations. A three-part outline follows, with one main section per chapter.

I.   Introduction (1:1–12)
   A. Greetings (1:1–2)
   B. Thanksgiving (1:3–12)
II. More on the Parousia: There Are Still Signs to Come (2:1–17)
   A. Thesis Statement (2:1–2)
   B. Signs That Must Still Occur (2:3–7)
   C. Judgment on Unbelievers (2:8–12)
   D. Faithfulness for Believers (2:13–17)
III. Conclusion (3:1–18)
   A. Exhortation (3:1–15)
   B. Concluding Prayers and Greetings (3:16–18)

COMMENTARY

INTRODUCTION (1:1–12)

Greetings (1:1–2) As in their previous letter, Paul, Silas, and Timothy indicate that they have collaborated to produce this epistle (on the options for what this involved, see above, p. 141). Overall, this greeting matches the opening of

---

[53] Marshall, *Thessalonians,* 187.
[54] Cf. Wanamaker, *Thessalonians,* 48; Maarten J. J. Menken, *2 Thessalonians* (London and New York: Routledge, 1994), 20.

1 Thessalonians exactly, except that our authors add a second reference to God and Jesus.

Thanksgiving (1:3–12)   Again a theologically rich, personally intense, and comparatively detailed thanksgiving prayer ensues. The parallels with the first epistle continue as Paul and company thank God for the faith, love, and perseverance of these Christians (vv. 3–4). While "hope" does not explicitly appear, the concept of perseverance is surely based on it. The sense we get from the end of verse 4, however, is that the persecutions unleashed on the Thessalonians have been increasing in severity. While mistreatment of believers *per se* does not demonstrate their maturity or faithfulness (people can be harassed simply because they act obnoxiously!), active witnesses for the Christian faith sooner or later will experience some hostility (v. 5).[55] A key to perseverance under such difficulties (and to not lashing back in retaliation) is to recognize the horrible judgments that God's enemies one day will face if they never repent (v. 6).[56] Judgment day will also bring ultimate relief and reward to God's people (v. 7).

Verses 8–9 go on to elaborate the punishment that God's enemies receive. These individuals are defined in two complementary ways. From a relational point of view, they do not know God; from a behavioral perspective, they do not obey the gospel (v. 8). Of course, the fundamental requirement of the gospel that must be followed is not some specific good work but faith in Jesus Christ. Verse 9 affords one of the clearest statements in Scripture on the eternal destiny of the lost. While other texts often refer to unquenchable fire or outer darkness—concepts that if literal could not simultaneously be true[57]—here we have an unambiguously literal description: "everlasting destruction and shut out from the presence of the Lord and from the majesty of his power." Some have argued that "everlasting destruction" suggests the doctrine of annihilation, but the only other use of this expression in biblically related Jewish literature comes in 4 Maccabees 10:15, which clearly refers to unending suffering in the afterlife.[58] On the other hand, verse 9 does teach that all unbelievers will be separated from God and all things good, which should be sufficient to make anyone want to avoid such a fate.[59] Verse 10 reaffirms one more time that this ultimate judgment comes when Christ returns, when believers can look forward to their glorification (on which, see further, p. 252).

---

[55] It is often thought that it is the believers' *endurance* of affliction which points to God's righteous judgment, but it may be simply the affliction itself. See Jouette M. Bassler, "The Enigmatic Sign: 2 Thessalonians 1:5," *CBQ* 46 (1984): 496–510.

[56] "The emphasis on the vengeance of God is calculated to encourage the brothers and sisters in the face of great adversity, supplying them with an eschatological perspective that will enable them to evaluate their present situation rightly" (Green, *Thessalonians,* 287).

[57] So George E. Ladd, *A Theology of the New Testament* (Grand Rapids: Eerdmans, rev. 1993), 196.

[58] Beale, *Thessalonians,* 188.

[59] This verse does not dispute the omnipresence of God, merely that his comfort remains unavailable to people in hell. See Charles L. Quarles, "The 'ΑΠΟ of 2 Thessalonians 1:9 and the Nature of Eternal Punishment," *WTJ* 59 (1997): 201–11.

MORE ON THE PAROUSIA: THERE ARE STILL SIGNS TO COME (2:1–17)

Thesis Statement (2:1–2)   *The first two verses of chapter 2 form the thesis statement of the letter.* Paul must insist that the Thessalonians reject any claim that the day of the Lord's return has already come. The expression "our being gathered to him" (v. 1) naturally suggests the same event as in 1 Thessalonians 4:17, that is, the rapture. Tellingly, what Paul does not say is that his congregation cannot have missed Christ's return because a secret rapture must precede it in which believers are taken from the earth. Yet if Paul believed in a pretribulational rapture, that would be the obvious thing to say: as long as all living Christians still reside in this world, the end cannot have come. But if Paul understood the rapture to occur at the same time as Christ's return (see above, pp. 147–48), and if some of the Thessalonians had mistakenly adopted the notion that Christ might return without everyone seeing him, then their error is understandable.[60] Given that later Gnosticism believed in a spiritual resurrection, in which the new age broke into this world and believers were perfected without a universal, visible, cataclysmic intervention such as the public return of the Lord for all to see, it is possible that the Thessalonians had been misled to adopt similar views here.

Signs That Must Still Occur (2:3–7)   To correct this mistaken eschatology, Paul delineates specific end-time events that must still take place. Two in particular prove noteworthy. *First, the "man of lawlessness" who is "doomed to destruction" must be revealed (vv. 3–4).* The description of this individual links him with the common Jewish expectation of an archenemy of God arising just prior to the messianic age. This person seems to be the same individual to whom John will later refer as the Antichrist (1 John 2:18) and as the "beast coming out of the sea" (Rev. 13:1). This individual will emerge at the time of the "rebellion" (Gk. *apostasia*—a "falling away")—in context probably meaning a revolt against God and the power of law.[61] He will set himself up "in God's temple," a picture reminiscent of the Seleucid ruler Antiochus Epiphanes's desecration of the Jewish temple in 167 B.C. and of the Roman Emperor Caligula's aborted attempt to set up statues of himself in that same building in A.D. 40.

Some have thought that the fulfillment of Paul's prophecy requires the rebuilding of the temple in modern-day Jerusalem. But the sole distinctive of the temple was its role as the place of sacrifice for the forgiveness of sins; weekly worship could and did take place in local synagogues. And it is difficult to square the reestablishment of animal sacrifices with the clear New Testament teaching that Christ has once and for all done away with them (see esp. Heb. 10:18; cf. all of chaps. 7–10). In fact, every other Pauline usage of this word for "temple" (*naos*) is metaphorical, referring to Christians either individually or collectively (1 Cor. 3:16, 17 [2X]; 6:19; 2 Cor.

---

[60] "The present verse brings to grief the popular notion that the rapture of the church will somehow take place before the tribulation" (Green, *Thessalonians*, 301, n. 4). To the objection that Christ's return cannot happen at any time if there are signs yet to take place, Beale (*Thessalonians*, 204–5, n.) observes that the signs may occur so quickly that they simply usher in and form part of Christ's return.

[61] Older dispensationalists often argued that the falling away was the same as the taking away of believers in the rapture, but nowhere else in the New Testament does the word have a meaning even remotely like this. See further F. F. Bruce, *1 and 2 Thessalonians* (Waco: Word, 1982), 166–67.

6:16 [2X]; Eph. 2:21). Perhaps the Antichrist will emerge from within a professing Christian church, initially masquerading as a true believer himself. Or perhaps all of these views are too literal, and Paul is merely stressing this person's complete opposition to all true worship of God.[62]

The second key sign that has yet to appear involves a "restrainer" that must be removed (vv. 5–7). Someone (the word is masculine in v. 7) and/or something (the word is neuter in v. 6) is currently holding back the man of lawlessness, preventing his appearance, and this person or power must be taken out of the way. Pretribulationalists have often understood the restrainer to be the church, but the Greek word for church (*ekklēsia*) is feminine, so that would not fit. Many equate the restrainer with the emperor and imperial government in Paul's day (or any of numerous subsequent world powers). Or else the reference could be to God himself, perhaps through his Holy Spirit.[63]

Judgment on Unbelievers (2:8–12) However we interpret these allusive references, the rest of this chapter gives us two major guarantees. *First,* all the wicked will be judged. When the Antichrist finally appears, his time will be short because Christ will quickly return and destroy him (v. 8). Nevertheless, his counterfeit miracles will have led astray many of those who do not know Christ (vv. 9–10a). Once again Paul describes the lost from complementary perspectives. No less than three separate personal agents play a role in people not coming to faith in Jesus. People themselves are accountable because they refuse to love the truth (v. 10b). But God also confirms them in their rejection of the gospel (vv. 11–12; cf. further on Rom. 1:24, 26, 28), while Satan plays an intermediate role by being the more direct agent of the delusion (v. 9). Verse 12 also presents two complementary descriptors for those who refuse to love the truth: they have not believed, and they have delighted in wickedness. To our fallen, finite minds, we do not understand how all these statements can be simultaneously true. But Scripture regularly holds them together, and therefore so must we.[64]

Faithfulness for Believers (2:13–17) The *second* guarantee is a more positive one. Believers have been chosen and called by God to be saved. We will discuss election or predestination more in conjunction with Romans 8–9 and Ephesians 1, but already here we may observe that God's choices never overrule human freedom or erase human accountability.[65] The means by which people are saved are, from a divine perspective, "the sanctifying work of the Spirit," but from the human perspective, "belief in the truth" (v. 13).[66] Thus Paul can command the Thessalonians to

---

[62] Cf. Bruce, *Thessalonians,* 169: "A graphic way of saying that he plans to usurp the authority of God . . . he demands not only the obedience but also the worship due to God alone." Cf. also Marshall, *Thessalonians,* 191–92: "The culminating manifestation of evil as an anti-theistic power which usurps the place of God in the world."

[63] Or through an angelic delegate. Cf. C. Nicoll, "Michael, the Restrainer Removed (2 Thess. 2:6–7)," *JTS* 51 (2000): 27–53.

[64] Because Satan is subordinate to God and his powers are limited by God, his actions can be used and redirected by God to serve God's own purposes (cf. Williams, *1 and 2 Thessalonians,* 130–31).

[65] William W. Klein ("Paul's Use of *Kalein*: A Proposal," *JETS* 27 [1984]: 53–64) understands calling here, and throughout Paul, as a technical term meaning "to designate" those who are God's own people.

[66] Cf. further Malherbe, *Thessalonians,* 426.

stand firm in their faith (v. 15). As at the end of the letter body in 1 Thessalonians, so also here Paul concludes with a doxology (vv. 16–17).

CONCLUSION (3:1–18)

Exhortations (3:1–15)   Paul requests prayer that his preaching of the gospel will continue to produce fruits and that he will be protected from the opposition (vv. 1–2). Presumably, he is praying for the Thessalonians in return and doing so with confidence because he trusts in God's faithfulness to answer the same two requests on their behalf (vv. 3–4). But an even more important priority is their spirituality—remaining in God's love (v. 5).

The major warning in this exhortational section returns to the problem of the idle or disorderly (vv. 6–15). Paul commands the church to shun such a person if he or she refuses to look for work (v. 15). Typically, these individuals have been understood to be those who thought the parousia was so near that they no longer needed to work. With too much time on their hands, they wound up interfering in the affairs of others, so that in verse 11, in a play on words that is preserved in the NIV, Paul can explain, "They are not busy; they are busybodies." More recently a sociological explanation has commanded greater support: these people formed part of the large number of poor Thessalonians who relied financially on gifts from wealthy "patrons" for whom they provided a variety of intermittent services. Paul would then be trying to woo these people away from dependence on patronage—the closest equivalent to welfare in the Greco-Roman world—and be telling them to find wholesome, full-time work instead.[67] Perhaps elements of each of these approaches were involved.[68]

As he did in 1 Thessalonians 2, Paul again stresses his example of earning his own keep while planting the church so that he did not have to depend on anyone else for financial support (vv. 7–9). Verse 10 is easily misunderstood; it does not mean that all unemployed Christians should starve to death! The Greek does not use the future tense of the verb "work" but employs an entirely separate verb for "will." A less ambiguous translation would be, "Anyone who is not *willing* to work shall not eat." Paul is not opposing charity (or welfare) for the needy who try but are unable to find employment. In fact, there may even be a more specific context to this verse. Robert Jewett cites evidence that the majority of the (mostly poor) Christians in several Greco-Roman communities may have lived in the ancient equivalent of tenement houses and shared communal meals (including Communion) on a regular basis. Irresponsible believers would thus be excluded from these specific meals. After all, it would be hard to see how any Christian community could enforce verse 10 unless it referred to particular meals over which they had direct jurisdiction.[69]

Whatever the precise scenario, Paul insists that all the believers go to work and always do what is right (vv. 11–13). He then repeats his instruction about avoiding

---

[67] See esp. Robert Jewett, *The Thessalonian Correspondence: Pauline Rhetoric and Millenarian Piety* (Philadelphia: Fortress, 1986). Cf. Bruce W. Winter, "'If a Man Does Not Wish to Work . . .': A Cultural and Historical Setting for 2 Thessalonians 3.6–16," *TynB* 40 (1989): 303–15.

[68] M. J. J. Menken, "Paradise Regained or Still Lost? Eschatology and Disorderly Behavior in 2 Thessalonians," *NTS* 38 (1992): 271–89.

[69] Robert Jewett, *Paul: The Apostle to America* (Louisville: WJKP, 1994): 73–86.

those who disobey his commands (vv. 14–15). This does not appear to be full-fledged excommunication, in which flagrantly sinful and unrepentant church members are treated as if they were outside of the faith altogether (as in Matt. 18:15–17). These people are still to be considered fellow believers (v. 15), but Paul hopes that by the church's action of not associating with them they will be ashamed of their behavior and change their ways (v. 14). The disfellowshipping in fact may be limited to their participation in the Lord's Supper. After all, even in the more extreme case of treating someone as a "pagan or a tax collector" (Matt. 18:17), people presumably kept in touch with the sinner just as Jesus called sinners to repentance. Likewise today, studies have shown that the complete withdrawal of fellowship from erring Christians seldom produces the desired repentance, whereas removal of people from leadership positions, church membership, or participation in select activities, while still working with them through accountability teams, probationary periods, and other strategies for restoration, has a much higher success rate.[70]

Concluding Prayers and Greetings (3:16–18) Just as grace and peace combine to form Paul's opening greetings, so now he again prays that God might grant the Thessalonians both of these qualities (vv. 16, 18). He also stresses that this letter is truly from him (v. 17), in light of the confusion that previous communication had caused (2:2, 15).

APPLICATION

First and 2 Thessalonians together provide a crucially needed balance in our modern world concerning the return of Christ. The majority of the church acts as if Christ will *never* literally return, or at least not in the near future. A vocal minority is convinced that he *must* come back within a certain period of time; a few even try to set dates. These letters remind us that we must always be alert for the possibility of the end but never presume to know when it will come. Faithful, moral Christian living, as we share our faith with unbelievers (as churches and individuals) and share our good with needy believers (who are willing to do their part as best they can), remains our central task, however long or short our wait. Trying to read "the signs of the times" in current events or to calculate the interval remaining until Christ's return at best distracts us from our calling and at worst works against our mission since every time believers confidently proclaim the end is at hand, and the world continues unchanged, our overall message loses credibility in many people's eyes.[71]

These principles apply to the timing of one's death as well. We dare not claim that we know we have a certain number of years left to live or be cocksure that we do not. God at times chooses to heal even terminal illnesses miraculously and on other

---

[70] Michael E. Phillips, "Creative Church Discipline," *Leadership* 17.4 (1986): 46–50.

[71] A sane guide in response to date-setters and apocalyptic hysteria (esp. with respect to that which surrounded the end of 1999 and the dawn of 2000) is Robert G. Clouse, Robert N. Hosack, and Richard V. Pierard, *The New Millennium Manual: A Once and Future Guide* (Grand Rapids: Baker, 1999). Cf. also B. J. Oropeza, *99 Reasons Why No One Can Know When Christ Will Return* (Downers Grove: IVP, 1994).

occasions to cut lives short without any advance notice. Faithful living in the present always remains our first priority.

A similar balance is needed in the debates about the rapture. Pretribulationalists sometimes promote a "sinking ship" mentality, whereby they refuse to obey the whole counsel of God's Word in terms of Christian involvement in the world and seek only to "save souls." Posttribulationists sometimes adopt a "siege mentality" similar to secular survivalists, who are convinced that they will suffer the worst and who hoard goods in order to prepare for the onslaught of those who will attack them. Both of these extremes prove highly dangerous. We should never seek suffering for its own sake or claim to know that we will escape the worst of it. Rather, we must pray that God will help us mature and use us for his kingdom work whatever comes our way.

A key piece of that work is the role model. We urgently need large numbers of Christians who will be as transparent and exemplary in their motives and their behavior as Paul was. We do not need new discipleship programs, just mature and honest mentors whom we can watch to understand how believers should live, including what repentance looks like when one sins, as we all repeatedly do. When Christians undergo persecution, these models prove all the more crucial.

ADDITIONAL QUESTIONS FOR REVIEW

1. What is the textual critical issue in 1 Thessalonians 2:7? Which of the variants is most likely the reading from the original manuscript and why?
2. Among the praise Paul lavishes on the recipients of the Thessalonian correspondence, what are the two main exhortations Paul offers? What circumstances within the church necessitated these admonitions?
3. Identify the timeless principles 1 Thessalonians sets forth for constructing a proper doctrine of eschatology.
4. In what ways do internal and external evidence counter the argument for 2 Thessalonians' pseudonymity?
5. If we accept the order of 1 and 2 Thessalonians as presented in the New Testament, what are the key themes addressed in 1 Thessalonians that must be further developed or readdressed in 2 Thessalonians? Compare the theses of each of these letters.
6. How do both 1 and 2 Thessalonians lend credit to a posttribulational view of the rapture?
7. How do 1 and 2 Thessalonians together support a balanced application of Christian eschatology to twenty-first-century end-times watchers?

SELECT BIBLIOGRAPHY

COMMENTARIES

Advanced

Bruce, F. F. *1 and 2 Thessalonians.* WBC. Waco: Word, 1982.

Malherbe, Abraham J. *The Letters to the Thessalonians.* AB. New York and London: Doubleday, 2001.

Wanamaker, Charles A. *The Epistles to the Thessalonians.* NIGTC. Exeter: Paternoster; Grand Rapids: Eerdmans, 1990.

Intermediate

Green, Gene L. *The Letters to the Thessalonians.* PNTC. Grand Rapids and Cambridge: Eerdmans, 2002.

Marshall, I. Howard. *1 and 2 Thessalonians.* NCB. London: Marshall, Morgan & Scott; Grand Rapids: Eerdmans, 1983.

Martin, D. Michael. *1, 2 Thessalonians.* NAC. Nashville: Broadman & Holman, 1995.

Morris, Leon. *The First and Second Epistle to the Thessalonians.* NICNT, rev. Grand Rapids: Eerdmans, 1984.

Richard, Earl J. *First and Second Thessalonians.* SP. Collegeville: Liturgical, 1995.

Introductory

Beale, Gregory K. *1–2 Thessalonians.* IVPNTC. Leicester and Downers Grove: IVP, 2003.

Gaventa, Beverly. *First and Second Thessalonians.* Int. Louisville: WJKP, 1998.

Holmes, Michael W. *1 & 2 Thessalonians.* NIVAC. Grand Rapids: Zondervan, 1998.

Stott, John. *The Gospel and the End of Time: The Message of 1 & 2 Thessalonians.* BST. Leicester and Downers Grove: IVP, 1991.

Williams, David J. *1 and 2 Thessalonians.* NIBC. Peabody: Hendrickson, 1997.

OTHER BOOKS

Burke, Trevor J. *Family Matters: A Socio-Historical Study of Kinship Metaphors in 1 Thessalonians.* London and New York: T & T Clark, 2003.

Collins, Raymond F. *The Birth of the New Testament: The Origin and Development of the First Christian Generation.* New York: Crossroad, 1993.

Collins, Raymond F., ed. *The Thessalonian Correspondence.* Leuven: LUP and Peeters, 1990.

Donfried, Karl P. *Paul, Thessalonica, and Early Christianity* (London: T & T Clark; Grand Rapids: Eerdmans, 2002).

Donfried, Karl P., and Johannes Beutler, eds. *The Thessalonians Debate.* Grand Rapids and Cambridge: Eerdmans, 2000.

Jewett, Robert. *The Thessalonian Correspondence: Pauline Rhetoric and Millenarian Piety.* Philadelphia: Fortress, 1986.

Malherbe, Abraham J. *Paul and the Thessalonians: The Philosophic Tradition of Pastoral Care.* Philadelphia: Fortress, 1987.

Nicholl, Colin R. *From Hope to Despair in Thessalonica.* Cambridge and New York: CUP, 2004.

Still, Todd D. *Conflict at Thessalonica: A Pauline Church and Its Neighbours.* Sheffield: SAP, 1999.

BIBLIOGRAPHY

Weima, Jeffrey A. D., and Stanley E. Porter. *An Annotated Bibliography of 1 and 2 Thessalonians.* Leiden and New York: Brill, 1998.

5

THE CORINTHIAN CORRESPONDENCE: COUNTERING MISGUIDED VIEWS ABOUT CHRISTIAN MATURITY

1 Corinthians: Internal Immaturity and External Hellenizing Threats

INTRODUCTION

THE CITY OF CORINTH

Corinth was a key Greek urban center under Roman rule, already eclipsing Athens in size and importance when Rome destroyed a large portion of it by fire in 146 B.C. Julius Caesar rebuilt the city in 44 B.C. as a Roman colony, with perhaps about 100,000 inhabitants. In Paul's day Corinth had become the wealthiest city in Greece. Tucked between the two port towns of Cenchrea and Lechaeum, it formed a major center of trade. The narrow isthmus, on which Corinth was located, contained a path, the *diolkos*, across which mariners would drag their unloaded boats, between the Adriatic and the Aegean Seas, rather than sail over a hundred miles out of their way around the southern tip of Achaia.

Every other year Corinth hosted the Isthmian games, second only to the Olympics in prominence among athletic competition in Greece. The city housed an eighteen thousand-seat theater, a three thousand-seat concert hall, and a large central market for farmers. A huge stone mountain known as the Acrocorinth, with its temple to Aphrodite perched atop it, towered over the city, and symbolized the dominance of pagan cults. In pre-Christian times it was said to have employed as many as one thousand sacred priests or priestesses who doubled as prostitutes. Still more prostitutes plied their wares at ground level for the many visitors to the town, as well as the local populace. And though their numbers may have been considerably smaller in Paul's day, we are scarcely surprised that Paul has to deal with as many topics of sexual sin in his epistle as he does. Nor is it unusual that the Greek word "to Corinthianize" came to mean "to play the harlot," just as "a Corinthian girl" became a slang term equivalent to our "whore."[1] But the ruins of a small Jewish synagogue in Corinth have been discovered as well, so Paul could appeal to some knowledge of God's law when he arrived in town.[2] Gordon Fee aptly likens the city to the New York, Los Angeles, and Las Vegas of the ancient world all wrapped up into one.[3]

CIRCUMSTANCES LEADING TO THE LETTER

Roughly three to five years have elapsed since Paul penned 2 Thessalonians. He has completed a second missionary journey and spent considerable time in *Ephesus*, his main stopping point during his third journey. In 1 Corinthians 16:8 we learn that he is still there, hoping to come to Corinth again but wanting to wait until after the spring festival of Pentecost. The most likely date for this epistle, then, allowing for Paul's travels and a nearly three-year stay in Ephesus (Acts 19:10; 20:31), is late winter or early spring of *A.D. 55.*

The description of Paul's original evangelistic efforts in Corinth appears in Acts 18:1–17. The first Christians were a mixture of Jew and Gentile, but Gentiles predominated. After preaching first to the Jews, as was his custom, Paul experienced enough hostility from some of them that he shifted his ministry next door to the synagogue to the home of a God fearer, Titius Justus, who had become a believer. Given the proximity of the two buildings and the fact that the synagogue ruler, Crispus, and his entire family had converted and followed Paul as well, tensions between the two communities must have run high. Little wonder that after a year and a half various Jews mounted an attack and arraigned Paul before the proconsul Gallio. As we saw in our discussion of the chronology of Acts, Gallio's short time in Corinth (most likely from summer 51 to summer 52) forms a relatively fixed point, enabling us to date numerous events in Paul's ministry reasonably precisely.

First Corinthians itself discloses that *Paul has received oral reports from the household of a woman named Chloe about the state of the church in Corinth (1:11).* In 16:17, Paul also refers to a trio of believers—Stephanas, Fortunatus, and Achaicus—who have come to Ephesus, presumably from Corinth, and "supplied what was lacking from you," refreshing Paul's spirit (v. 18). It is possible that one or more of these men were the representatives from Chloe's household, but we have no way of being sure. It is assumed that Chloe was a Corinthian Christian, perhaps unmarried or widowed, while members of her household could have included grown children, other relatives, or even slaves. It is possible that the Corinthian letter to Paul was delivered by these three men or by the members of Chloe's household, if they formed a different group, but again this remains speculative. *Chapter 7 further reveals that the Corinthians have written Paul a letter with various questions (v. 1), while 5:9 alludes back to a previous letter that Paul had already sent to the Corinthians.*

---

[1] Aristophanes coined the verb and Plato the noun. See D. Kelly Ogden and Andrew C. Skinner, *New Testament Apostles Testify of Christ: A Guide for Acts through Revelation* (Salt Lake City: Deseret, 1998), 129.

[2] For good introductions to the city of Corinth in Paul's day, see Murphy-O'Connor, *St. Paul's Corinth*; Donald Engels, *Roman Corinth: An Alternative Model for the Classical City* (Chicago: University of Chicago Press, 1990).

[3] Gordon D. Fee, *The First Epistle to the Corinthians* (Grand Rapids: Eerdmans, 1987), 3.

The contents of the letter from the Corinthians to Paul may be discerned from the collection of issues Paul addresses from 7:1 to the end of the letter. The contents of his letter to Corinth remain almost entirely unknown except for what he mentions in 5:9–11. He apparently warned the church against associating with sexually immoral people, which the Corinthians misunderstood as referring to unbelievers, when in fact Paul was talking about professing Christians. Readers throughout church history have posed fascinating but unanswerable questions about this apostolic letter, including why it was not preserved. One may imagine that its contents were so limited or its applications so localized that the church at large recognized it did not have the same abiding value as Paul's later letters, but again we simply do not know. The third-century apocryphal 3 Corinthians is sheer fiction but reflects an early Christian desire, visible in many of the New Testament apocrypha, to fill in gaps left by the canonical record.[4]

STRUCTURE

The overall outline of 1 Corinthians is perhaps clearer than for any other Pauline epistle because Paul simply proceeds through a checklist of the issues plaguing the church in Corinth. A few scholars have tried to pick out certain issues to assign to the oral reports and others to the Corinthians' letter according to various topical or structural parallels. For example, it has been argued that every time Paul says "now concerning" (or "now about"), he is referring to an issue from the Corinthian letter. But the most natural understanding of 7:1a ("now for the matters you wrote about") is that up to this point in the epistle Paul has been dealing strictly with information received from the personal messengers, while from this point on all of the issues he addresses stem from the letter written to him.[5] This enables us to put together an outline that proceeds as follows:

I.   Introduction (1:1–9)
   A. Greeting (1:1–3)
   B. Thanksgiving (1:4–9)
II. Responding to News from Chloe (1:10–6:20)
   A. Divisions in the Church (1:10–4:17)
      1. Outlining the Problem (1:10–17)
      2. The Need to Focus on the Cross of Christ (1:18–2:5)
      3. Christian Wisdom (2:6–16)
      4. Two Kinds of Christians (3:1–23)
      5. True Apostolic Ministry (4:1–21)
   B. Incest in the Church (5:1–13)
   C. Lawsuits among Christians (6:1–11)
   D. The Seriousness of Sexual Immorality in General (6:12–20)
III. Responding to the Corinthians' Letter (7:1–16:4)

---

[4] Wilhelm Schneemelcher, "Acts of Paul," in *New Testament Apocrypha,* ed. Wilhelm Schneemelcher, vol. 2 (London: James Clark; Louisville: WJKP, 1992), 217, 235.

[5] Margaret M. Mitchell ("Concerning *ΠΕΡΙ ΔΕ* in 1 Corinthians," *NovT* 31 [1989]: 229–56) shows that this introductory formula plays no necessary role in distinguishing topics in the Corinthians' letter from other ones.

A. Concerning Marriage (7:1–40)
B. Concerning Food Sacrificed to Idols (8:1–11:1)
  1. Initial Discussion (8:1–13)
  2. A Parallel Example (9:1–18)
  3. The Unifying Principle (9:19–27)
  4. An Absolute Prohibition (10:1–22)
  5. Three Principles Summarized (10:23–11:1)
C. Concerning Worship (11:2–14:40)
  1. Head Coverings on Men and Women (11:2–16)
  2. The Use and Abuse of the Lord's Supper (11:17–34)
  3. The Right and Wrong Use of Spiritual Gifts (12:1–14:40)
D. Concerning the Resurrection (15:1–58)
E. Concerning the Collection for Jerusalem (16:1–4)
IV. Conclusion (16:5–24)
  A. The Travel Plans of Various Christians (16:5–18)
  B. Final Greetings (16:19–24)

This checklist approach to the many problems that beset the Corinthian church, however, does not fit at all closely into any particular epistolary subgenre. Perhaps the most that can be reasonably suggested is that it resembles a Hellenistic *letter of petition* with the unique "request-command-request" structure.[6] The rhetoric for the most part, however, is clear, with deliberative forms dominating.[7]

UNIFYING THEMES

At first glance, 1 Corinthians seems not to have a unifying focus but reads like a laundry list of problems in an immature church. On closer inspection several central themes emerge. Greek philosophy, especially from Plato onwards, was radically *dualist*—that is to say, the material and spiritual worlds were sharply separated. In much thought, and especially in *those strands of philosophy that would generate full-blown Gnosticism* by the end of the first and beginning of the second centuries, it was assumed that matter was inherently evil. Only the spirit could be saved. This dualism led, paradoxically, to two diametrically opposite ethical outworkings. The majority of Gnostics were *ascetics*, that is, trying to deny the (evil) body and its natural appetites in a variety of ways. The minority were *hedonists*, indulging the body since it was hopelessly corrupt anyway. Both strands of thought seem to have been present in Corinth. Those involved in the problems of incest, lawsuits, and promiscuity (chaps. 5–6); the "strong" Christians who ate food sacrificed to idols (chaps. 8–10); the out-of-control women prophets and overindulgent rich at the Lord's table (chap. 11); and those who abused spiritual gifts more generally (chaps. 12–14) all fell into the hedonist camp. Those who were promoting celibacy (chap. 7); the people afraid

---

[6] Linda L. Belleville, "Continuity or Discontinuity: A Fresh Look at 1 Corinthians in the Light of First-Century Epistolary Forms and Conventions," *EQ* 59 (1987): 15–37.

[7] Ben Witherington III, *Conflict and Community in Corinth: A Socio-Rhetorical Commentary on 1 and 2 Corinthians* (Grand Rapids: Eerdmans; Carlisle: Paternoster, 1995), 75.

to eat the idol meat (chaps. 8–10); and church members denying bodily resurrection (chap. 15) were clearly ascetic.[8]

DENYING DESIRES/HUMANITY	INDULGING DESIRES/HUMANITY
False sense of maturity Claims to special wisdom Advocating celibacy Forbidding certain food and drink Believing in only spiritual 　resurrection	Sexual sin Lawsuits Eating food without concern for 　others Requiring pay for Christian work Drunkeness at the Lord's table Disrespect for appearance of sexual 　propriety Worship chaotic
ASCETICISM	**HEDONISM**

The results of too sharp a division between body and spirit

Numerous scholars have attempted to identify more precisely certain ideological opponents of Paul and the philosophical challenges that were leading various members of the Corinthian church astray. *Hellenistic Jewish wisdom* may well have contributed to the mix of ideas,[9] and various *local cults* could easily have exacerbated the sexual sin or produced models for such divisive practices as prophecy and speaking in tongues.[10] But the most convincing proposal concerning the historical background finds the school of philosophy and rhetoric known as *sophistry* as particularly influential, especially with its strong emphasis on polished, elegant speech, often stressing form over substance.[11]

Compounding these ideological problems was the sheer *factionalism* of the Corinthian church. Chapters 1–4 make plain the problem of divisions (see esp. 1:10–12). We will note below that theological explanations for these divisions have largely given way to sociological ones, with the possibility of different house churches reflecting competing allegiances to different Christian leaders. On top of that, Paul's rebukes suggest that the church was permeated with a kind of *triumphalism*—believers' misguided sense of their own maturity (see esp. 4:8). Anthony Thiselton has plausibly attributed this to an *overly realized eschatology,* that is to say, to a faulty

---

[8] Cf. further Robert McL. Wilson, "Gnosis at Corinth," in *Paul and Paulinism,* eds. Morna D. Hooker and Stephen G. Wilson (London: SPCK, 1982), 102–14; and John Painter, "Paul and the πνευματικοί, at Corinth," in ibid., 237–50.

[9] See esp. James A. Davis, *Wisdom and Spirit: An Investigation of 1 Corinthians 1.18–3.20 against the Background of Jewish Sapiential Traditions in the Greco-Roman Period* (Lanham: UPA, 1984).

[10] See esp. Christopher Forbes, *Prophecy and Inspired Speech in Early Christianity and Its Hellenistic Environment* (Tübingen: Mohr, 1994; Peabody: Hendrickson, 1997).

[11] See esp. Bruce W. Winter, *Philo and Paul among the Sophists* (Grand Rapids and Cambridge: Eerdmans, rev. 2002).

sense of how much spiritual growth and freedom from sin the Christian can achieve in this life.[12]

An outgrowth of the sociological analysis of the letter further indicates that a large percentage of the problems can be attributed to the *divisions between rich and poor*.[13] Chapter 1:26–29 discloses that not many of the Corinthian Christians were wise, influential, or wellborn, according to the standards of their society. But that, of course, means that a few were. Any well-to-do believers coming out of the Greco-Roman context would have most likely been patrons, that is, responsible for a number of "clients" under their patronage. The system of patronage was the closest ancient equivalent to welfare, in that the rich were expected to surround themselves with a group of poorer people whose material needs they would look after, in return for which the clients provided seasonal work, waited on their superiors in their homes, gave them pubic acclaim in the marketplaces and forums, and provided political support. Countless hints throughout the New Testament suggest that numerous problems in early Christianity stemmed from believers, rich or poor, still trying to function under the system of patronage and the tit-for-tat reciprocity that was endemic to it.[14]

In 1 Corinthians alone the factionalism of the opening chapters may have resembled the competition between rival patrons and their supporters. About the only conceivable reason the church would not have disciplined the incestuous man in chapter 5 was if he had been a powerful patron.[15] Lawsuits, for the most part, were initiated only by the rich, usually against other rich people, more to acquire greater honor in the public eye than to amass more wealth.[16] Well-to-do Roman young men regularly looked forward to coming-of-age parties, complete with courtesans or "high-class" prostitutes.[17] The poor people in town often ate meat only at festivals in local temples with overtly pagan dimensions to them.[18] Accepting money for ministry regularly implied that one's patrons could "call the shots."[19] Only wealthy women had enough leisure time to become sufficiently educated religiously and emancipated socially to have caused the kinds of disruptions described in chapters 11 and 14.[20] The abuse of the Lord's Supper, we will see, clearly reflects discrimination by the rich against the poor.[21] Even the tendency to flaunt one's spiritual gifts likely afflicted the wealthy more than other socioeconomic groups.[22]

---

[12] Anthony C. Thiselton, "Realized Eschatology at Corinth," *NTS* 24 (1977–78): 510–26.

[13] Andrew D. Clarke, *Serve the Community of the Church: Christians as Leaders and Ministers* (Grand Rapids and Cambridge: Eerdmans, 2000), 174–85.

[14] See esp. Andrew D. Clarke, *Secular and Christian Leadership in Corinth* (Leiden and New York: Brill, 1993); John K. Chow, *Patronage and Power: A Study of Social Networks in Corinth* (Sheffield: JSOT, 1992).

[15] Bruce W. Winter, *After Paul Left Corinth* (Grand Rapids and Cambridge: Eerdmans, 2001), 44–57.

[16] Ibid., 58–75.

[17] Ibid., 76–109.

[18] The most helpful background information and exegetical discussion appears in Wendell L. Willis, *Idol Meat in Corinth* (Chico: Scholars, 1985), 14.

[19] Hock, *The Social Context of Paul's Ministry,* esp. 59–62.

[20] Antoinette C. Wire, *The Corinthian Women Prophets* (Minneapolis: Fortress, 1990).

[21] Gerd Theissen, *The Social Setting of Pauline Christianity* (Philadelphia: Fortress, 1982), 145–74.

[22] Dale Martin, "Tongues of Angels and Other Status Indicators," *JAAR* 59 (1991): 547–50.

COMMENTARY

INTRODUCTION (1:1–9)

Greeting (1:1–3)   In this letter Paul introduces Sosthenes as his cosender (for the options for what this role might mean, see above, p. 141). While we cannot be sure, it is natural to connect this Sosthenes with the synagogue ruler beaten in front of the Roman magistrate in Acts 18:17 (again, see above, p. 60), who may well have become a Christian after that. This is the only letter in which Paul addresses all Christians everywhere in addition to a specific local church. Perhaps he realized that the array of problems besetting the Corinthians included issues that almost every congregation would face at one time or another.

Thanksgiving (1:4–9)   Again Paul introduces key themes in his thanksgiving prayer that will recur throughout the letter. What is most striking is how positive he can be, thanking God for the way he has gifted the Corinthians in the areas that have proved most troublesome (vv. 4–7; cf. chaps. 12–14). Verses 8–9 explain his enthusiasm; he has confidence in God's power to bring them to maturity.[23]

RESPONDING TO NEWS FROM CHLOE (1:10–6:20)

Divisions in the Church (1:10–4:17)   *Outlining the Problem (1:10–17)*   As the body of the letter begins, Paul sets out one of the main problems afflicting the church in Corinth—factionalism—and appeals for a restoration of unity. The divisions follow party lines. Various groups pledge allegiance to Paul, Apollos, Peter, and Christ, respectively (v. 12). Traditionally, it has been assumed that these were theological divisions—perhaps the Paul and Peter factions mirrored the debate at Antioch (Gal. 2:11–14), while Apollos stressed the "wisdom" of the gospel (cf. Acts 18:28 on his rhetorical skills). The "Christ party" might then have included those who refused to align themselves with any human leader, though that does not necessarily mean they were any less sectarian in doing so.[24]

More recent scholarship has focused on possible sociological divisions instead. The church at Corinth was probably a loose collection of "house congregations," each no more than thirty to fifty in number. The handful of wealthy members (1:26)[25] may have hosted the various congregations since no one else would have had a place large enough to accommodate such gatherings. As we saw in the introduction, they may still have relied on their pre-Christian positions of power as patrons to produce rival parties rather than the unity that the gospel was intended to foster. Verses 14–17 give an additional clue to the nature of the factions. Here Paul plays down the value of baptism, not because it was unimportant but because it was not significant enough to be a matter causing division. *Perhaps members of the various groups were simply*

---

[23] Richard B. Hays, *First Corinthians* (Louisville: WJKP, 1997), 18.

[24] For a rare, recent attempt to defend largely theological differences among the factions, see Michael D. Goulder, *Paul and the Competing Mission in Corinth* (Peabody: Hendrickson, 2001).

[25] There may also have been a small middle-class, as argued by Dirk Jongkind, "Corinth in the First Century A.D.: The Search for Another Class," *TynB* 52 (2001): 139–48.

aligning themselves with the human leaders who first led them to Christ and under whose ministry they were thus baptized.[26]

The Need to Focus on the Cross of Christ (1:18–2:5)   If the exact nature of the problem is unclear, the solution is not. In 1:18–2:5, Paul calls the Corinthians to return to concentrating on what Christ did for them in the crucifixion (see esp. 2:2). The ground is indeed level at the foot of the cross; it is difficult to exalt oneself over against other believers while meditating on the utter abasement Christ suffered on our behalf. The world considers the message of a crucified Messiah foolish (1:18–25), among Jews because it demonstrates God's curse (Deut. 21:23) and among Gentiles because it highlights Christ's weakness rather than his strength. Moreover, Jews looked for utterly unambiguous signs, which even Christ's miracles did not provide, while Greeks looked for the kind of sophisticated philosophical wisdom that Christ's straightforward message did not match. The "wise" of both cultures therefore rejected the gospel. But Paul points out that *God has chosen to save people by what many of the intellectuals of his day considered foolish.*[27]

The fact that the majority of the Christians in Corinth did not come from the rich, powerful, or well-educated minority of ancient society demonstrates the point (1:26–31). And the way in which Paul first preached to them offers further corroboration; by the standards of the philosophers of the day, most notably the Sophists, Paul's rhetoric was very plain (2:1–5; cf. 2 Cor. 10:10). Nothing in these paragraphs implies that believers should despise education, forgo careful sermon preparation, or preach about nothing but the crucifixion. Paul's own model disproves all of these notions. He regularly draws on his insights of both Jewish and Greco-Roman backgrounds and culture, 2 Corinthians 10–13 displays shrewd and well-thought-out use of rhetoric and 1 Corinthians discusses far more than the cross of Christ. But any attempt to rely on one's own resources apart from the Spirit's empowerment for cruciform living and teaching is what Paul eschews.[28]

Christian Wisdom (2:6–16)   Indeed, Christians must strive to become as wise as they can, not by mimicking the "wisdom" of the godless society around them but by adopting God's wisdom (recall 1:24) by the Spirit's power (recall 2:4). Chapter 2:6–16, therefore, expands on the proper kind of wisdom believers should acquire and encourages the Corinthians to mature so that they will put aside their current factionalism. Here Paul speaks of a "secret wisdom" (v. 7a), which could sound like some form of elitism. But what was once secret and hidden, and what remains hidden to

---

[26] Lyle D. Vander Broek (*Breaking Barriers: The Possibilities of Christian Community in a Lonely World* [Grand Rapids: Brazos, 2002], 40) observes that Paul's strong reaction to a dangerous situation was based on the Corinthians' improper attachments to certain leaders, accompanied by a faulty understanding of preaching—which valued the display of human wisdom through logic, persuasion, and the beauty of fine rhetoric.

[27] Paul's playing the role of fool may also have been in part derived from the world of theater. Cf. further L. L. Welborn, *Paul the Fool of Christ: A Study of 1 Corinthians 1–4 in the Cynic Philosophic Tradition* (London and New York: T & T Clark, 2005); and Duane Litfin, *St. Paul's Theology of Proclamation: 1 Corinthians 1–4 and Greco-Roman Rhetoric* (Cambridge and New York: CUP, 1994).

[28] The scandal of the cross remains central, however, for all of Paul's ethics, as unpacked in H. H. D. Williams, "Living as Christ Crucified: The Cross as a Foundation for Christian Ethics in 1 Corinthians," *EQ* 75 (2003): 117–31. For its role in the letter more generally, see Raymond Pickett, *The Cross in Corinth: The Social Significance of the Death of Jesus* (Sheffield: SAP, 1997).

the non-Christian powers in Paul's day (vv. 7b–9), is now revealed to believers (v. 10). In fact, it is likely that some of the Corinthians were boasting in their wisdom and setting themselves above others in the church as the truly "mature" (Gk. *teleioi*). In the mystery religions, this term often referred to initiates into a particular cult who had come to understand secret spiritual truths that the rest of the group did not know. Paul stands this approach on its head, using the same term to refer to all believers over against unbelievers rather than to create two categories of Christians.[29]

Thus in verses 11–16, Paul distinguishes between the "natural" (*psychikos*) person and the "spiritual" (*pneumatikos*) person, to use the translations made famous by the KJV. The NIV rightly recognizes these as equivalent to "the man without the Spirit" (v. 14) and "the man with the Spirit" (v. 15), respectively. Only those who are Christians, and therefore have the Spirit indwelling them, can discern things from God's perspective. These verses do not mean that non-Christians cannot cognitively understand or accurately represent Christian claims or biblical truths, merely that they do not *accept* them as actually from God (v. 14). After all, the only ultimately legitimate form of "understanding" from a biblical perspective is that which accepts the gospel.[30]

Two Kinds of Christians (3:1–23) In chapter 3, however, Paul makes a different kind of comparison. Now he uses the term "spiritual" to refer to *mature* believers, which he thinks the Corinthians should have become by now, as over against "worldly" (NIV) or "carnal" (KJV) Christians (*sarkinos/sarkikos*) who are still *immature*. We must carefully observe what signs of immaturity Paul has in mind. The Corinthians are not nominal believers who have only marginal affiliation with the church. Rather, they remain active but active in divisive ways. Thus Paul alludes to their fighting and factionalism again (vv. 1–4) as what makes them worldly. Throughout church history some Christians have used the category of worldly or carnal Christian to justify their belief that a person can make a superficial profession of faith at some point in life, show no signs of spiritual vitality, even for years on end, die in this state, and still be saved. That is scarcely what Paul has in view in this context![31] Instead, the Corinthians are gifted believers (recall 1:7), but they are employing their gifts for self-centered purposes rather than building up the body of Christ.

The rest of chapter 3 illustrates the fundamental equality of all persons in Christ that should quash the Corinthians' factionalism. First, Paul compares the church to God's field in which all believers are coworkers (vv. 5–9a). The different Christian leaders whom the Corinthians are pitting against one another are simply farmers, utterly dependent on God to produce a crop. They may play different roles, but this does not legitimate the elevation of one role above another.

---

[29] And, to the extent that the Spirit gifts believers for the building up of the church, one may speak of Christians collectively as well as individually having "the mind of Christ" (v. 16). See Allen R. Hunt, *The Inspired Body: Paul, the Corinthians, and Divine Inspiration* (Macon: Mercer, 1996).

[30] Peter Stuhlmacher, "The Hermeneutical Significance of 1 Cor 2:6–16," in *Tradition and Interpretation in the New Testament,* eds. Gerald F. Hawthorne and Otto Betz (Grand Rapids: Eerdmans, 1987), 328–47.

[31] Fee, *First Corinthians,* 121–28.

Second, the church resembles stones in a building, laid on top of the foundation, which is Christ (vv. 9b–17). Although judgment day will bring to light the varying qualities of different Christians' works (vv. 12–15), the main contrast in this section is between those who are at least building in some way and those who are only trying to destroy the building (vv. 16–17).[32] Verses 12–15 are often cited as support for the idea that Christians may experience differing degrees of reward in heaven. Without a doubt, here and elsewhere Scripture describes believers having entirely unique experiences before God on judgment day as their lives are reviewed. But neither this text nor any other teaches that we will have different statuses or varying privileges that last throughout eternity. After all, if the life to come is perfect, it is logically contradictory to speak of degrees of perfection. The parable of the laborers in the vineyard (Matt. 20:1–16) portrays all of Jesus' followers receiving the same recompense for greatly varying degrees of work, precisely what we should expect if salvation is by grace through faith alone and not good works.[33] Interestingly, the doctrine of eternal degrees of reward in heaven was a Reformation-era carryover from the Catholic notion of purgatory.[34] Martin Luther, however, warned sharply against it (see, e.g., *Works* 51.282–83).

A major danger associated with this doctrine resembles the problem with applying the category of carnal Christian to nominal practitioners of the faith. It is too easy to give oneself or others false hope that one is truly "in," even if just barely, when in fact the lack of ongoing commitment suggests that one was never "in" to begin with. That seems to be precisely the problem with those Paul mentions in verses 16–17. The most divisive of the Corinthians may in fact not be contributing to God's work at all, and, in attempting to destroy that work, they demonstrate that they are not saved but on their way to eternal destruction. In these verses, too, Paul shifts from describing an unspecified building to depicting the holiest of buildings in his world—a temple. Later he will refer to individual Christians as temples of the Holy Spirit (6:19), but here he is speaking of the church collectively. Those who destroy the unity of so sacred an entity are flirting with the eternal wrath of a just and holy God![35]

Verses 18–23 summarize the chapter by reminding us that all believers have equal access to all spiritual privileges. Therefore, there is no need to boast about one leader over another or to exalt oneself. Indeed, the Lord knows the thoughts of a person, so he can recognize prideful attitudes even before they turn into actions.

True Apostolic Ministry (4:1–21)   Chapter 4 concludes the response to the factions in Corinth by focusing on the right attitude to have toward Paul and his fellow apostles. *First,* verses 1–5 describe them as faithful stewards. The term used for "servant" (*hyperetēs*) in verse 1 denotes a person who is put in charge over an estate

---

[32] Hays, *First Corinthians,* 58.

[33] See further Craig L. Blomberg, "Degrees of Reward in the Kingdom of Heaven?" *JETS* 35 (1992): 159–72.

[34] Emma Disley, "Degrees of Glory: Protestant Doctrine and the Concept of Rewards Hereafter," *JTS* 42 (1991): 77–105.

[35] Anthony C. Thiselton, *The First Epistle to the Corinthians* (Grand Rapids: Eerdmans; Carlisle: Paternoster, 2000), 318.

and/or other servants but is still subordinate to his master.[36] Likewise, Paul, while given great authority and responsibility as an apostle and missionary, nevertheless remains merely a servant of Christ. Thus when Paul disavows concern about how the Corinthians judge him or even how his own conscience judges him, he is not slighting the church but simply stressing that only God's evaluation of a person ultimately matters (vv. 2–5).

Second, verses 6–7 point out that proper assessments should be scripturally based. Verse 6 contains a notorious crux: where does the saying come from and what does it mean not to go beyond what is written? The quotation is not an excerpt from Scripture. Some have wondered if it refers to how Greco-Roman children were taught to write, by tracing the letters of the alphabet and not going outside of the lines. Others speculate that it refers to following rules of arbitration in the workplace. But the most probable suggestion is that it means that all one's actions should be biblically based.[37] This will eliminate the pride that is promoting the factions. After all, all believers' gifting comes wholly from God rather than from anything they have done. The verb translated "applied" in verse 6 is more literally rendered "transformed." It is possible, therefore, that Paul is indicating that the real problem resides among the Corinthian leaders, not between Apollos and him: but he is writing more allusively so as to avoid so direct a confrontation.[38]

Third, true apostolic ministry often involves suffering, including suffering unjustly (vv. 8–13). The poignant catalog of persecutions and hardships that Paul presents contrasts starkly with the triumphalism of some in the Corinthian church. Verse 8a must be understood as bitter irony. The Corinthians have not really become rich or begun to reign, as the second half of the verse makes clear. Paradoxically, if they had matured in a true spiritual sense, they would be suffering along with Paul.[39] But their conception of the Christian life does not allow for them to be treated as "the scum of the earth, the refuse of the world" (v. 13). The words translated here as "scum" and "refuse" are fairly vulgar in the original Greek;[40] their closest English equivalents would offend so many people that modern translations use euphemistic language like this instead!

Finally, and more positively, the apostles are specially related to the Corinthians (vv. 14–21). Paul in particular is the spiritual father to many in the church, giving him the right to speak in both tough and tender tones (vv. 14–15).[41] As with the Thessalonians, Paul urges them to imitate him (v. 16),[42] and since he cannot be with them at the moment he will send his letter with Timothy, who will also spend some time providing them with additional instruction and modeling Paul's Christlike

---

[36] Paul Ellingworth and Howard Hatton, *A Translator's Handbook on Paul's First Letter to the Corinthians* (New York: UBS, 1985), 75.

[37] David E. Garland, *1 Corinthians* (Grand Rapids: Baker, 2003), 135.

[38] David R. Hall, "A Disguise for the Wise: μετασχημάτισα in 1 Corinthians 4.6," *NTS* 40 (1994): 143–49.

[39] Cf. esp. K. A. Plank, *Paul and the Irony of Affliction* (Atlanta: Scholars, 1987).

[40] Thiselton, *First Corinthians,* 365: "the lowest, strongest, most earthy language."

[41] Cf. Eva M. Lassen, "The Use of the Father Image in Imperial Propaganda and 1 Corinthians 4:14–21," *TynB* 42 (1991): 127–36.

[42] Tellingly, only three verses removed from the elaborate description of his suffering. On the *mimesis* theme in Paul more generally, see esp. Andrew D. Clarke, "'Be Imitators of Me': Paul's Model of Leadership," *TynB* 49 (1998): 329–60.

behavior for them (v. 17). But if this gentle approach fails, Paul will come back to Corinth himself and intervene in a harsher fashion to punish those who have not abandoned their arrogance (vv. 18–21).[43]

Incest in the Church (5:1–13) From the broad problem of factionalism, Paul turns to a series of specific issues in which certain Corinthians appear to be flaunting (and misunderstanding) their freedoms (chaps. 5–6). The first issue is that of a man who is having sexual relations with his stepmother. Because Paul refers to the woman as the man's "father's wife" (v. 1), he almost certainly does not mean a biological mother. Because second wives were often considerably younger than their husbands, this woman may have been closer in age to the son than to the father, thus explaining the son's attraction to her. Yet incest was the one sexual offense on which even the profligate Greco-Roman world seriously frowned (Cicero, *Pro Cluentio* 15), and here the church acts as if it is proud of its "freedom" in Christ to tolerate such behavior (vv. 2)! Paul does not hesitate to use his authority in this situation to command excommunication of the unrepentant offender (vv. 3–5) in order to preserve the purity of the church (vv. 6–8). At least that is how the NIV understands verse 5. But the word translated "sinful nature" is *sarx* (literally, "flesh"), which could also refer to the man's physical body.

Some commentators, therefore, understand Paul's command to involve the death of the man in some way. Perhaps he has a sexually transmitted disease, and Paul is saying in essence, "Let him die." Or perhaps Paul imagines that God will strike him dead in a more supernatural fashion. But whether we take Paul's injunction as referring to death or to excommunication, his purpose is clearly remedial: so that the man's "spirit [might be] saved on the day of the Lord." Given that 2 Corinthians 2 and 7 both refer to a flagrant sinner in Corinth whom the church has punished, who has repented, and whom Paul encourages the church to welcome back, it seems more likely that excommunication is involved here and that the disciplinary action has its intended, restorative effect.[44]

It is in this context we learn that Paul has written a previous letter to the Corinthians (vv. 9–13; cf. above, p. 164). Thus he points out that the church has completely reversed the intention of that communication. They are separating from sinful unbelievers while tolerating gross immorality in their midst, whereas they should be purifying themselves while staying close enough to unbelievers to have a positive effect on them. It is striking how often the conservative Christian church has reversed these priorities in subsequent centuries!

Lawsuits among Christians (6:1–11) Equally shameful is the practice of Christians taking each other to secular courts over legal disputes (v. 1).[45] The most

---

[43] For outstanding exposition and application of chaps. 1–4, see D. A. Carson, *The Cross and Christian Ministry* (Grand Rapids: Baker, 1993).

[44] Garland, *1 Corinthians*, 181: "The church walks a tight rope between being a welcoming community that accepts confessed sinners and helps the lapsed get back on their feet and being a morally lax community where any thing [*sic*] goes."

[45] This topic is linked with chapter 5 because the church has again failed to act as a community and take responsibility for one another (Hays, *First Corinthians*, 93).

common kind of lawsuit in Paul's world involved quarrels over property. Wealthy "patrons" in the Greco-Roman world often initiated legal action to enhance their status and shame their opponents.[46] Christians, however, at the very least should follow the Jewish precedent of settling their own disputes "in-house" (vv. 2–6). In most cases, rabbinic legislation prohibited Jews from using Greco-Roman courts, while synagogues did "double duty" by functioning as sites where they could try their own cases. If verse 4 is translated and punctuated as in the NIV, then "men of little account" must refer to the way outsiders would have labeled believers. More likely, the NIV margin is to be preferred: Paul is asking, "Do you ask a ruling from those whose way of life is scorned in the church?" that is to say, from Gentile magistrates.[47]

Verses 7–8 prove even more challenging. While Paul recognizes that fallen people must have mechanisms for settling their disputes, the Christian ideal would be never to seek redress merely for oneself. This does not mean that believers cannot fight for justice for others who have been oppressed or disenfranchised. Neither does it mean that they may not have to resort to secular courts for issues that involve non-Christians. But the question Christians must ask themselves with any contemplated legal action is if the publicity will bring the gospel into disrepute or enhance the way outsiders perceive it.[48] Given the increasing proliferation of Christian mediation ministries, at least in the U.S., there is little excuse for "in-house" complaints ever to move outside the church.

Paul underlines the seriousness of this issue by linking it to the continual practice of various forms of sexual immorality, idolatry, theft, covetousness, drunkenness, slander, and embezzlement (vv. 9–10). The fact that Paul uses noun forms to characterize the people who commit these sins ("idolaters," "adulterers," etc.) suggests that he is not speaking of an occasional lapse but a regular lifestyle. Such people have no place in God's kingdom. But of course, one can repent, follow Christ, change one's ways, and be saved (v. 11). The terms translated "male prostitutes" (*malakoi*) and "homosexual offenders" (*arsenokoitai*) refer to the more passive and more active partners in male homosexual intercourse, respectively.[49] We will comment on homosexual practice in more detail in conjunction with Romans 1, but for now it is important to stress that these words, when used in combination, cannot be limited just to certain forms of homosexual behavior such as prostitution or pederasty.

The Seriousness of Sexual Immorality in General (6:12–20)   Paul returns to the theme of sexual offense but broadens it to warn against any kind of promiscuity, especially prostitution. In verses 12–13, he introduces a form of argumentation, which he will employ repeatedly throughout the rest of the epistle, that has been called his *"yes, but . . . " logic.* In each case he seems to quote a Corinthian "slogan"—a

---

[46] D. Neufeld, "Acts of Admonition and Rebuke: A Speech Act Approach to 1 Corinthians 6:1–11," *BI* 8 (2000): 375–99.

[47] Reginald H. Fuller, "First Corinthians 6:1–11: An Exegetical Paper," *Ex Auditu* 2 (1986): 100.

[48] Cf. Fee, *First Corinthians*, 238.

[49] David F. Wright, "Translating *ΑΡΣΕΝΟΚΟΙΤΑΙ* (1 Cor. 6:9; 1 Tim. 1:10)," *VC* 41 (1987): 396–98; David E. Malick, "The Condemnation of Homosexuality in 1 Corinthians 6:9," *BSac* 150 (1993): 479–92. On the other hand, the terms represent those who commit actual acts of homosexual intercourse, not those who may feel homosexual desires or longings but remain celibate, refusing to act on their urges. See William L. Petersen, "Can *arsenokoitai* be translated by 'Homosexuals'? (1 Cor. 6:9; 1 Tim. 1.10)," *VC* (1986): 187–91.

perspective that some in the church had adopted, that Paul can affirm up to a point, but that he also must significantly qualify. Here the NIV puts the slogans in quotation marks. It is true that in a law-free gospel, from one point of view, everything is permissible, but that does not make everything good or acceptable (v. 12). The Corinthians were apparently also reasoning from the destruction of the body that, just as eating is a morally neutral matter, so also is having sex in any way one desires (v. 13a).[50] Here Paul takes explicit objection. Sexual intercourse is the most intimate form of bodily self-communication and reflects an interpersonal unity that is to be reserved for one to whom one is ultimately committed (vv. 13b–18).[51] Paul again appeals to the fact that Christians' bodies are temples of the Holy Spirit because of our redemption in Christ (vv. 19–20), but this time he is thinking more individually than collectively (recall on 3:16–17). "We are bought with a price, a painful price—Christ's atoning blood." Christians thus "ought to reflect their gratitude for that infinite payment in their attitudes and behavior."[52]

RESPONDING TO THE CORINTHIANS' LETTER (7:1–16:4)

Concerning Marriage (7:1–40)   Now Paul addresses the ascetic wing of the church. The key to understanding chapter 7 is to recognize, as in the NIV margin, that *verse 1b forms a Corinthian slogan.* The church father Origen affirmed this in his commentary as early as approximately A.D. 200. The Greek literally reads, "It is good for a man not to touch a woman." But "touch" was a euphemism for sexual relations. Some in Corinth were advocating celibacy—complete sexual abstinence—as the norm for all Christians. Paul affirms that celibacy can be good but refuses to absolutize it—his "yes, but . . ." logic again.[53]

He begins by considering *those already married.* The pro-celibacy faction would promote abstinence even between husband and wife. Verse 2 does not mean that each person should acquire a spouse but that each married person should continue to have sexual relations with his or her spouse (likewise vv. 3–4). It is important to note how here and throughout this chapter Paul issues exactly parallel commands to both husband and wives, treating them as fully equal to each other.[54] Paul does grant his opponents one concession, allowing a married couple to abstain from sex for a short time by common consent for the sake of spiritual discipline. But he recognizes that

---

[50] The quotation marks should perhaps extend to the end of the sentence, "God will destroy them both." The next clause begins with a "but," which the NIV leaves untranslated.

[51] See esp. Brendan Byrne, "Sinning against One's Own Body: Paul's Understanding of the Sexual Relationship in 1 Corinthians 6:18," *CBQ* 45 (1983): 613. Bruce N. Fisk ("*ΠΟΡΝΕΥΕΙΝ* as Body Violation: The Unique Nature of Sexual Sin in 1 Corinthians 6:18," *NTS* 42 [1996]: 558) concludes that "other sins may be physically destructive (e.g., suicide, gluttony) corporately destructive (e.g., gossip, divisiveness) or spiritually defiling (e.g., idolatry) but for Paul, because sexual sin is uniquely body-joining, it is uniquely body-defiling."

[52] Ogden and Skinner, *Acts through Revelation,* 134.

[53] The exposition of this chapter is heavily indebted to Fee, *First Corinthians,* 266–357. It is possible that the pro-celibacy faction claimed leadership roles based on claims of inspiration or revelation derived from their asceticism, as was often the case in the surrounding pagan culture. See Judith M. Gundry-Volf, "Celibate Pneumatics and Social Power: On the Motivations for Sexual Asceticism in Corinth," *USQR* 48 (1994): 105–26. For the view that Stoic and Cynic influences prevailed in the pro-celibacy faction, see Will Deming, *Paul on Marriage and Celibacy* (Cambridge and New York: CUP, 1995).

[54] Unlike all the surrounding cultures and religions. Cf. G. W. Peterman, "Marriage and Sexual Fidelity in the Papyri, Plutarch and Paul," *TynB* 50 (1999): 163–72.

prolonged enforcement of such a regimen might simply lead one or both partners to seek sexual fulfillment elsewhere; and, therefore, he cannot support it except as a brief change in routine for special spiritual purposes (vv. 5–6). Here is where we may infer that Paul was unmarried, at least at the time of writing this letter (v. 7a). But even in expressing his preference for the single life, he recognizes that only those so gifted by God should pursue it (cf. Matt. 19:10–12).

In verses 8–9, Paul turns to *widowers* (probably a better translation here than "unmarried") *and widows*. In this case, he can consider celibacy much more favorably because he, too, is single, and possibly even a widower. But marriage is preferable to lust and promiscuity. The verb for "can" does not appear in the Greek of verse 9a; an accurate translation would read, "But if they *are* not controlling themselves, they should marry." In verse 9b, the Greek reads merely, "It is better to marry than burn," but the NIV correctly adds "with passion." Greek romantic novels regularly made similar claims in contexts of celebrating sexual pleasure in marriage, so this would not have sounded to the Corinthians like the grudging concession it often seems to us.[55]

Verses 10–16 consider the married again, but this time *those who might be contemplating divorce* as the way to get out of having sex. This section contains what has come to be called the Pauline privilege, the second of two biblical exceptions to the general prohibition against divorce. Jesus had allowed for it in the case of sexual unfaithfulness (Matt. 5:32; 19:9); Paul now permits it when an unbelieving spouse wishes to leave (vv. 15–16). In other situations, however, if the separation or divorce has already occurred without any remarriage taking place, the estranged parties should either reconcile and get back together or remain unmarried (vv. 10–11). Two key exegetical questions divide commentators at this point. First, is it the abandonment or the mixed marriage (or both) that triggers Paul's exception? Many have assumed it was the mismatched relationship, but it is interesting that, if one focuses on the abandonment, then Jesus and Paul have each put their finger on one of the two fundamental constituent elements of marriage—leaving and cleaving (vs. abandonment) and becoming one flesh (vs. sexual infidelity), as defined in Genesis 2:24. So perhaps the mixed marriage is simply the more situation-specific element.

Second, do Jesus' and Paul's teachings cover every conceivable situation in which divorce could reflect God's (permissive) will? Obviously, Jesus' teaching was not exhaustive or Paul could not have added to it. Similarly, Paul betrays no awareness of Jesus' exception, so his list of (one) exceptional situation cannot be comprehensive either. Various interpreters, therefore, have suggested additional extreme situations in which divorce may be the least evil of several options. It is probably best not to add to the biblical list, however, but simply to treat other cases one at a time, asking if the marriage has in reality been as fundamentally destroyed as if sexual unfaithfulness or irrevocable abandonment had occurred.[56]

---

[55] See J. Edward Ellis, "Controlled Burn: The Romantic Note in 1 Corinthians 7," *PRS* 29 (2002): 89–98.

[56] See further Craig L. Blomberg, "Marriage, Divorce, Remarriage, and Celibacy," *TrinJ* 11 (1990): 161–96, esp. 186–94. The best recent book-length treatments of the topic are Craig S. Keener, . . . *And Marries Another: Divorce and Remarriage in the Teaching of the New Testament* (Peabody: Hendrickson, 1991); and David Instone-Brewer, *Divorce and Remarriage in the Bible* (Grand Rapids and Cambridge: Eerdmans, 2002). Paul may also be countering

The contrast between verses 10 and 12 has also puzzled many readers. Is Paul saying that he is inspired in the first context but not in the second? Not likely, in view of verse 40! Rather, in verse 10 he is referring back to a word of the historical Jesus, whereas in verse 12 he does not know of any specific teaching from Christ that he can cite.[57] So, too, in verse 25, Paul is not denying inspiration; he believes his judgment has come from the Lord's trustworthy mercy.[58] And in verse 40, he is most likely tingeing his remarks with irony, not disclosing doubt concerning divine guidance. After all, the elitists in Corinth would have argued that they alone had the Spirit, so Paul adds that he believes he has the Spirit as well.

MARRIAGE AND DIVORCE IN MATTHEW 19 AND 1 CORINTHIANS 7

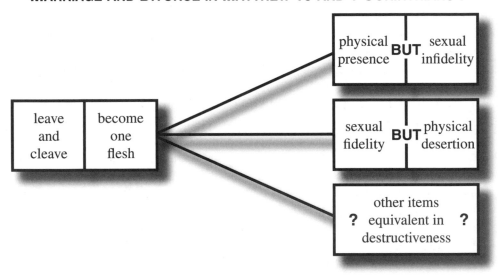

FORMING A MARRIAGE   **RUPTURING A MARRIAGE**

Yet one more verse in this section has proved troubling. At first blush verse 14 would seem to teach that, if one parent in a family accepts Christ, all the family members will be saved! This misreading comes about because Paul regularly uses the verb "sanctify" to refer to believers. But its root meaning is merely to "set apart" or "place in an environment of holiness." Since Paul will stress in the next two verses that a believing partner cannot count on leading his or her spouse to the Lord, he cannot be referring to salvation in verse 14. Rather, he must mean that one Christian parent will bring an aura of holiness to the family and create greater opportunities for the other members to trust in Christ.[59]

---

those who feared such mixed marriages rendered the Christian partner unclean. See Yonder M. Gillihan, "Jewish Laws on Illicit Marriage, The Defilement of Offspring and the Holiness of the Temple: A New Halakic Interpretation of 1 Corinthians 7:14," *JBL* 121 (2002): 730.

[57] Fee, *1 Corinthians,* 291.

[58] Indeed, *gnōmē* could be translated maxim, befitting the form of this verse, suggesting that Paul is countering the slogan of verse 1 with proverbial wisdom he *can* endorse. See Rollin A. Ramsaran, "More Than an Opinion: Paul's Rhetorical Maxim in First Corinthians 7:25–26," *CBQ* 57 (1995): 531–41.

[59] Nigel Watson, *The First Epistle to the Corinthians* (London: Epworth, 1992), 71.

Verses 17–24 offer a preliminary conclusion that might be paraphrased, *bloom where you're planted.* Applied to the advocates of celibacy, Paul would be saying not to do anything radical just to get out of having sex, but he applies the principle more widely to other issues as well. Verse 21b has been translated in two diametrically opposite ways throughout the history of the church, often based on one's preconceived attitudes toward slavery. The Greek literally reads that if a slave can gain his or her freedom, "much more, use [it]." Does this mean, "be that much more eager to use the opportunity for freedom" or "rather stay in your present situation"? Scott Bartchy's detailed historical and grammatical study has convinced the vast majority of commentators that the former is correct.[60] After all, in most cases if an owner chose to manumit a slave, the slave did not have the right to refuse!

In verses 25–35, Paul turns to *those who have never been married.* With the pro-celibacy proponents, he encourages them to remain single, but unlike them refuses to mandate this state of affairs. Moreover, his rationale for his encouragement is totally different from theirs. Paul is concerned about "the present crisis" (v. 26). But what is this crisis? Some think it has to do with vestiges of the famine in the late 40s, but the immediate context suggests the more convincing answer. In verse 29, Paul explains, "What I mean . . . is that the time is short." Paul does not know how quickly Christ will return and bring about an end to this world as we know it (v. 31), and he therefore wants believers to be as free as possible to devote all their energies to kingdom work (vv. 32–35). Yet, as in each of the other sections of this chapter, Paul recognizes that God prepares only certain believers for this particular lifestyle. So, against his opponents, he stresses that those who do marry have not sinned (v. 28).[61] How often do Christians contemplating getting married ask the question of whether a prospective partner will enable them to serve the Lord better? If they cannot realistically imagine ways in which this could happen, they are probably not ready to "tie the knot."

Verses 36–38 present the translator with another difficult decision. As the NIV footnote points out, Paul could be addressing a father trying to decide whether to give away his daughter in marriage. But recent lexical research has demonstrated fairly convincingly that this is *an engaged couple* trying to decide whether to proceed with marriage.[62] Paul agrees with the proponents of celibacy that such a couple is not required to consummate their marriage, but he cannot insist on their remaining single. His appreciation of his singleness leads him to prefer that option, but he stresses again that the alternative is scarcely sinful.

The chapter concludes with a reminder that *marriage is intended to last for life* (vv. 39–40). But when a spouse dies, a Christian is free to remarry—as long as the new spouse is a believer as well—though for one last time Paul reminds his audience

---

[60] Scott Bartchy, *ΜΑλλΟΝ ΧΡΗΣΑΙ: First-Century Slavery and 1 Corinthians 7:21* (Missoula: Scholars, 1973). For the view that Paul's text is inherently ambiguous, see Brad R. Braxton, *The Tyranny of Resolution: 1 Corinthians 7:17–24* (Atlanta: SBL, 2000).

[61] The balance Paul repeatedly seeks to achieve on these issues led Vincent L. Wimbush to entitle his book, *Paul: The Worldly Ascetic* (Macon: Mercer, 1987).

[62] Bruce W. Winter, "Puberty or Passion? The Referent of ὑπερακμος in 1 Corinthians 7:36," *TynB* 49 (1998): 71–89.

of his preference for the single life. The word for "bound" in verse 39 is not identical in the Greek as the one in verse 15, but the two words are largely synonymous. Because the chapter does not explicitly address the question of remarriage after a biblically permissible divorce, the most relevant observation we can make is that, if not being "bound" in the one verse means freedom to remarry, then it most likely means that in the other verse as well. Additionally, the right to remarry after a legitimate divorce was universally accepted among Jews, Greeks, and Romans, so if Paul were deviating from this assumption, he would have had to state it explicitly.[63]

Concerning Food Sacrificed to Idols (8:1–11:1) *Initial Discussion (8:1–13)* In the next three chapters both the ascetic and the hedonistic wings of the church come into play. The first group is refusing to eat meat sacrificed to idols. Many of these people may have been among the poorer Christians who were not able to afford meat on a regular basis and who associated eating it with the rituals in the pagan temple in Corinth. The second group has come to realize there is nothing inherently immoral in eating such meat, but they are not taking those Paul calls their "weaker brothers" into account. They ignore *the problem that Christian liberty can become license.* Paul's "yes, but . . ." logic comes to the fore again, as 8:1–3 sets out the problem— Christian liberty can become license. Those who have the correct knowledge about the morally neutral nature of idol meat must temper that knowledge with love. As in the NIV margin, "We all possess knowledge" is probably another Corinthian slogan to which Paul's reply is, "Knowledge puffs up, but love builds up" (v. 1).[64]

The *main application of Paul's principle* comes in 8:4–13. Although there is nothing inherently wrong with eating food sacrificed to idols (vv. 4–6, 8), Christians should avoid it if it causes their fellow believer to fall into sin (vv. 7, 9–13). The way these Corinthians might have sinned would probably have been in their inability to distinguish eating meat bought in the marketplace and previously blessed by a pagan priest (cf. 10:25) from eating in the context of pagan worship or in their inability to distinguish between other events held in the temple precincts that involved eating idol meat (weddings, parties, guilds) and overtly religious rituals with similar food (cf. v. 10a). Or it may have been simply that the weaker Christian ate meat in a non-religious context but did not have a clear conscience in doing so (vv. 10, 12).[65]

It is important to observe whom Paul does not include in this context as a "weaker brother [or sister]." Paul is *not* thinking of the fellow Christian who is simply of-

---

[63] David Instone-Brewer, "1 Corinthians 7 in the Light of the Graeco-Roman Marriage and Divorce Papyri," *TynB* 52 (2001): 101–16, 225–43. On chaps. 5–7 together, cf. esp. Brian S. Rosner, *Paul, Scripture and Ethics: A Study of 1 Corinthians 5–7* (Leiden and New York: Brill, 1994; Grand Rapids, Baker, 1999).

[64] The most detailed and helpful background information and exegetical discussion appear in Willis, *Idol Meat in Corinth.* Even more thorough background but less convincing exegesis is found in Derek Newton, *Deity and Diet: The Dilemma of Sacrificial Food at Corinth* (Sheffield: SAP, 1998).

[65] The reconstruction of events adopted here closely follows Bruce N. Fisk, "Eating Meat Offered to Idols: Corinthian Behavior and Pauline Response in 1 Corinthians 8–10," *TrinJ* 10 (1989): 49–70; Cf. also E. C. Still, "The Meaning and Uses of *EIΔOΛOΘYTONO* in First Century Non-Pauline Literature and 1 Cor 8:1–11:1: Toward Resolution of the Debate," *TrinJ* 23 (2002): 225–34. Several recent studies have argued that Paul, in fact, forbids the eating of all idol meat anywhere except in a private home where no one calls attention to the meat's origin, but they do not adequately deal with the more nuanced arguments in works like these two. Still's argument that Paul then commends those with knowledge to forego completely their right to eat idol meat does not necessarily follow; however, nor does it square with the closing emphases in 10:23–11:1.

fended or upset that another believer would participate in a morally neutral practice that the person who takes offense thinks is wrong. In these situations, there is almost no chance at all that the offended person would ever imitate the debated practice; that is precisely why he or she is upset that someone else *is* involved in it! Of course, we should not go out of our way to offend anyone, but there are times when the greater good of the gospel may require it. Curiously, it is often some of the most creative, novel, and effective evangelistic methods with which other tradition-bound Christians disagree. In such instances, it is far more important to bend over backward to reach the unbeliever than to worry about never offending a single traditional believer (9:19–23). Numerous other illustrations could be suggested as well.[66]

Tucked into verses 4–6 is important theology that dare not be overlooked. Paul's main point obviously is to endorse monotheism; the polytheistic gods and goddesses of the Greco-Roman world have no objective existence. Verse 6 must not be interpreted as suggesting that everything is subjective, that is, that Christians believe there is only one God, others disagree, and there is no way of adjudicating between them. Rather, what Paul means by "for us" is "we know" (whereas others do not) that only one true God exists in the universe. But even more striking are Paul's words in the second part of verse 6, in which he makes virtually the identical statements about Jesus as he did about God. There is "but one God, the Father, from whom all things came and for whom we live; and there is but one Lord, Jesus Christ, through whom all things came and through whom we live." Just as we saw in Acts, the first generation of Christianity did not shrink from making the same affirmations about Jesus as they did about Yahweh, the God of Israel, yet without believing in two separate gods! Because Jesus was somehow God himself, he too is Creator and Sustainer of the universe. If this is not yet trinitarian thought, it is at least binitarian.[67]

A Parallel Example (9:1–18)   In 9:1–18, Paul gives *a different example of restraining Christian liberty.* At first glance it appears he has simply moved on to a new topic. But chapter 10 will make clear that he has not. Instead, he is discussing another controversial issue in Corinth that requires the application of the same principles that eating idol meat mandated. While Christian ministers have a right to earn their living by the gospel (vv. 1–12a, 13–14), they dare never demand this right. Indeed, if it causes a potential scandal—for example, the accusation of preaching for the wrong motive—they should minister free of charge and provide for their material needs in other ways, as Paul himself often did (vv. 12b, 15–18). The fact that itinerant philosophers and religious teachers in the Greco-Roman world often charged (and, at times charged exorbitantly) for their services easily called into question their motives, and Paul wants nothing to do with this kind of misperception of his ministry. Furthermore, as we have seen, wealthy patrons of another person's ministry often

---

[66] For further application, see Garry Friesen with Robin Maxson, *Decision-Making and the Will of God* (Portland: Multnomah, 1980), 382–83; and Joseph C. Aldrich, *Life-Style Evangelism* (Portland: Multnomah, 1981), 39–76.

[67] A feature surprisingly pervasive even in earliest Christian thought and writing. See esp. Hurtado, *Lord Jesus Christ*. Taking Paul's teachings about God, Jesus, and the Spirit together *does* permit us to speak of trinitarianism at this time, too. See Ulrich Mauser, "One God and Trinitarian Language in the Letters of Paul," *HBT* 20 (1998): 99–108. See esp. 1 Corinthians 12:4–6.

felt that they had the right to "call the shots," whereas Paul will not obligate himself to anyone who thinks they can tell him what to say or what not to say.[68] Several less central points in this section merit brief comment. Verses 1–2 link Paul's apostleship to his witness of the resurrected Jesus, suggesting that Paul saw himself as an apostle not merely by having the spiritual gift of apostleship but in the stronger sense being an eyewitnesses to the resurrection (like the Twelve). Verses 3–6 raise the question of whether Paul was married at some point, though he may have been mentioning the issue simply for Barnabas's sake. One of the stranger uses of the Old Testament in the New appears in verses 9–10. Paul applies the Mosaic command not to muzzle an ox while it is treading out grain (Deut. 25:4) to the responsibility of believers not to hinder the work of their "full-time" ministers by not paying them (or by not paying them enough)! One can understand how the situations are analogous, and New Testament writers regularly applied Old Testament texts to their contemporary situations without claiming that they were elucidating their original meaning. But what proves particularly puzzling here is that Paul seems to say that this scriptural text was "entirely" (*pantōs*) written for our sake (cf. NASB: "or is he speaking altogether for our sake?"). But the word can also mean "surely" (as in the NIV) or even "certainly," in the sense that the application of the text cannot be limited to animals, which is undoubtedly what Paul had in mind.[69]

Why does Paul insist so strongly on the right to receive money for ministry, if he ultimately stresses that he regularly relinquishes this right? Presumably, he does so for the sake of others in his situation. Verse 14 even alludes to a saying of Jesus (cf. Luke 10:7, cited again in 1 Tim. 5:18) that underlies the obligation of people to support those ministering to them. When Paul senses no potential conflict of interest, he in fact is grateful for such help himself (Phil. 4:10–20), but he refuses to demand it. Bivocational ministry does have its advantages, not least in that one has a "secular" platform from which to share the gospel regularly, just as Paul did as he made and sold tents.[70]

The Unifying Principle (9:19–27)   Paul's motive behind his approaches to both the debate over food sacrificed to idols and the issue of accepting money for ministry is *to remove as many unnecessary obstacles as possible that might prevent people from coming to Christ* (vv. 19–23). Of course, in becoming all things to all people, Paul did not commit actual acts of sin (as if he became a drunkard to win drunkards, etc.). But in any morally neutral arena, even if his practices seemed to contradict what he did on other occasions (recall his circumcision of Timothy in Acts 16:3), he bent over backwards to bring unbelievers to the Lord. Do we have the same passion in our world today?[71]

---

[68] For a detailed reconstruction of the possible charges against Paul, see Peter Marshall, *Enmity in Corinth: Social Conditions in Paul's Relations with the Corinthians* (Tübingen: Mohr, 1987), 282–340.

[69] Garland, *1 Corinthians*, 410: *pantōs* can mean "surely," "doubtless," "assuredly," "especially," or "simply."

[70] For a book-length treatment of asking for money in the New Testament, see Jouette M. Bassler, *God and Mammon* (Nashville: Abingdon, 1991).

[71] Cf. Michael Prior, *The Message of 1 Corinthians* (Leicester and Downers Grove: IVP, 1985), 162: "Paul's versatility in seeking to win men of all backgrounds to Christ challenges us to cross the culture gap between the Christian sub-culture of cozy meetings and holy talk and the pagan culture of our local community. The task of identification with and incarnation into our contemporary paganism, of all kinds, is one of the biggest tasks confronting the church."

In this context Paul appropriates metaphors from the racetrack and boxing ring, highlighting in each case the strenuous preparation required for competition (vv. 24–27).[72] Failure to follow the demanding Christian lifestyle of verses 19–23 leaves a person in danger of being "disqualified" (v. 27). It is always easier to declare that questionable practices are completely wrong or completely right than to treat specific situations sensitively on a case-by-case basis. But that is not the biblical model. Nor may we water down the concept of disqualification for the prize and make it mean simply a loss of reward in heaven. The adjective "disqualified" (*adokimos*) comes from the same root as "test" (*dokimazō*) in 3:13, which referred to judgment day. Paul wants to ensure that his lifestyle demonstrates the fruit befitting repentance all the way to the end, lest God tell him that he was never "the real thing" in the first place![73]

An Absolute Prohibition (10:1–22) Not every ethical issue, however, falls into a gray area. The Bible does teach that certain things are inherently wrong, and in these areas a Christian does not have freedom to indulge. Thus Paul turns in verses 1–13 to the tragic chapter in Israel's history when her idolatry and the immorality that resulted from it led to severe judgment from God. Despite her "baptism" into Moses (v. 2)—that is, her identification with Moses when the nation was guided by God and miraculously enabled to cross the sea—many of the Israelites rebelled (vv. 7, 8a, 9a, 10a) and were killed by God (vv. 8b, 9b, 10b). These people likewise experienced the miraculous provision of manna and water from a rock in the wilderness, which Paul sees as a typological foreshadowing of Christ (v. 4),[74] yet still they forgot God's provision, defied his commands and died as a result (v. 5). As with narrative material throughout the Old Testament, Paul recognizes an exemplary function. In this case, the Israelites' behavior was meant to warn later generations against acting similarly (v. 6), particularly when the messianic age would arrive (vv. 11–12).[75] Even though Paul takes twelve verses in this passage to issue his warning, he does end on a note of encouragement. God's people can always resist temptation if they yield themselves to his Spirit; he will never give them more than they can handle with his help (v. 13).

Paul introduced the example of the Israelites' idolatry to prepare the way for warning the Corinthians against similar false worship. Here is his *one absolute prohibition: they must not participate in an actual temple service dedicated to worshiping the gods* of Greece or Rome (vv. 14–22). While those gods themselves have no objective

---

[72] On which, see Victor C. Pfitzner, *Paul and the Agōn Motif* (Leiden and New York: Brill, 1967), 82–98.

[73] Cf. further Judith M. Gundry-Volf, *Paul and Perseverance: Staying in and Falling Away* (Louisville: WJKP, 1991), 233–47.

[74] Because God provided water from the rock both near the beginning and near the end of the Israelites' wanderings, Jewish traditions developed that streams of water or a well filled with water actually followed God's people during their travels. It is a short jump from this belief to the concept of a traveling rock that can provide streams of water. (F. F. Bruce, *1 and 2 Corinthians* [London: Marshall, Morgan & Scott, 1971; Grand Rapids: Eerdmans, 1980], 91). "Local mythology also attributed Corinth's chief spring to a struck rock" (Craig S. Keener, *1–2 Corinthians* [Cambridge: CUP, 2005], 85, n. 181).

[75] On the use of the Old Testament in this section, see Wayne A. Meeks, "'And Rose Up to Play': Midrash and Paraenesis in 1 Corinthians 10:1–22," *JSNT* 16 (1982): 64–78. The view of Meeks and others that this section (or at least 10:1–13) formed a preexisting midrash, however, seems unlikely. See B. J. Oropeza, "Laying to Rest the Midrash: Paul's Message on Meat Sacrificed to Idols in Light of the Deuteronomic Tradition," *Bib* 79 (1998): 57–68.

existence (recall 8:4–6), demonic powers do lurk behind all false forms of religion (vv. 19–22). Central to pagan worship was a sacrificial meal in which celebrants believed they were uniting themselves with the gods. The similarity with the Christian Eucharist leads Paul to point out the mutual exclusivity of the two rites (vv. 14–17).

It is important to recognize, against many, that freedom remains the more fundamental principle, not curtailment. "Paul's concern in 1 Cor 10:23–31 is to affirm the use of individual rights when an understanding of community sensitivity is firmly in place." Again, "The freedom of the individual must not be enslaved by the scruples of the weak because the very identity of believers is as those who, having been freed in Christ's death are now graced by God with all things to be used for God's glory."[76]

Three Principles Summarized (10:23–11:1)   As Paul rounds out his discussion, he repeats *three key principles that have united chapters 8–10*. First, Christianity implies freedom from legalism in relation to everything that is not inherently evil (vv. 23a, 25–27, 29b–30). Second, one must voluntarily curtail one's freedom in various situations for the sake of those who might otherwise be led into sin (vv. 23b–24, 28–29a, 32–33). Third, in both cases, glorifying God remains the highest motivation (v. 31). The way these principles play out with the issue of food sacrificed to idols is that believers have full freedom to eat any meat sold in the marketplace, even if it was blessed by pagan priests and/or sacrificed to the gods in an earlier temple ceremony. Believers may eat this food on their own or even when they are served it by pagan friends. The only restriction is if someone calls attention to the nature of the food in a context in which someone's conscience could be hurt—that is, in which they might join in the eating without believing they really had the freedom to do so.

Eating idol meat does not represent one of the top one hundred moral dilemmas for most Western Christians, though it remains a sensitive issue in various other parts of the world. These same three principles, however, apply to countless issues that do affect Westerners and others—the drinking of alcohol, various fashions and hairstyles, recreational practices, forms of entertainment, certain kinds of meditation, therapies and self-improvement techniques in the business world, and so on. In identifying "weaker" brothers or sisters, we must again remember that Paul is not talking about people who might be offended at a given activity without ever being inclined to participate in it themselves. Rather he is referring to those who would actually be led to engage in the morally neutral behavior without a clear conscience about doing so, or to those who would go beyond the debatable practice into something that was clearly sinful. If we capture this balance, then we will truly be imitating Paul, even as he imitated Jesus (11:1).[77]

Concerning Worship (11:2–14:40)   *Head Coverings on Men and Women (11:2–16)*   The next four chapters deal with three problems afflicting the Corinthians at worship.[78] Paul employs his characteristic "yes, but . . ." logic again in verses 2–3.

---

[76] Ramsaran, *Paul's Use of Liberating Rhetorical Maxims in 1 Corinthians 1–10*, 71.

[77] Cf. R. L. Plummer, "Imitation of Paul and the Church's Missionary Role in 1 Corinthians," *JETS* 44 (2001): 225: "the restatement of Paul's exhortation to evangelistically-motivated self-denial."

[78] "The Corinthians' tendency to see themselves as virtuoso spiritual soloists is nowhere more evident than in their behavior at worship." Thus Hays, *First Corinthians*, 182.

The church seems to have captured Paul's basic teaching on this topic, but there still are some problems he needs to correct. Quite possibly they recognized the privileges of Christian liberty, so they understood that outward dress or hairstyles were inherently amoral. But they failed to realize that certain practices could send the wrong signals to a watching world. It is even possible that, like some in the pagan world of Greco-Roman worship, they may have been trying to "transcend" their sexuality and recreate the supposed original androgynous human being. So Paul reminds them that the husband is "head" of the wife[79] as Christ is for the man and God for Christ. Whether one translates *kephalē* (head) as "authority" or "source,"[80] the meaning in context is "one who should be honored."

Husbands and wives then reflect their respective roles through the use or non-use of head coverings in worship (vv. 4–16). What kind of covering did Paul have in mind? Many have assumed that it was a veil, but that word never appears in the Greek except in a few late manuscripts at verse 10 (which influenced the KJV). Some Jewish and a few Greco-Roman women still wore face veils (or other external head coverings) in the first century, but the practice was dying out. In verses 13–15, the head covering in view is clearly hair, and this fits well with the contrast with the shaven head in verses 5–6 too. A good case can in fact be made for something along the lines of the NIV margin as best explaining verses 4–7. Then the question of long or short hair would be the issue at stake throughout the passage.[81]

Whether an external head covering or just long hair, why should women have it, and men not, when Christians gathered for worship? In the Greek world, married women who wore shawls on their heads often did so to show that they were no longer "available." Pagan prophetesses, however, bared their heads and loosed their hair during the ecstatic frenzy that accompanied their worship. For men, a head covering may have resembled the Roman priests' togas pulled over their heads while they were worshipping their gods. If long or short hair is the issue, then it is noteworthy that overly short hair or shaven heads on women could be a sign in the Greek world of being the more "masculine" partner in a lesbian relationship, while overly long hair on some Greek men indicated homosexuality. Whichever historical-cultural background one follows, Paul's point almost certainly is that head coverings in Corinth symbolized either *sexual or religious faithfulness versus infidelity.*[82]

A few Christians would still take this entire passage as normative, but they miss the changed significance of most hairstyles or head coverings today. Even in Paul's world there were honorable men who never cut their hair (e.g., the Jewish Nazirites). Many Christians, therefore, wonder whether any of this passage remains normative, yet Paul teaches elsewhere that all Scripture is authoritative and relevant in some

---

[79] The Greek terms can mean either man and woman or husband and wife. Given that unmarried women no longer living in their father's home had no one particular man as their "head," the latter translation seems better.

[80] Despite sweeping claims by some that one or the other of these meanings is wholly unattested in ancient Greek, reasonably clear examples of both have been presented, though each is rare. The vast majority of uses of the term refer to the actual part of a person's or animal's anatomy.

[81] See esp. David E. Blattenberger, *Rethinking 1 Corinthians 11:2–16 through Archaeological and Moral-Rhetorical Analysis* (Lewiston and Lampeter: Mellen, 1997).

[82] For a fuller range of options, see Craig L. Blomberg, *1 Corinthians* (Grand Rapids: Zondervan, 1994), 210–11.

way at all times (2 Tim. 3:16). It is probably best to see the issue of head coverings as culture specific but the principle of honoring one's spiritual head, including by means of appropriate fashion and outward demeanor, as the timeless mandate. Verses 8–9, after all, do ground Paul's injunctions in the way God created man and woman before the fall. But these verses come immediately after Paul's contrast between the man as the glory of God and the wife as the glory of the husband (v. 7), relationships that are clearly related to the roles described in verse 3.[83] They do not directly qualify the commands regarding head coverings in verses 4–6. Paul's supporting arguments in verses 13–16 do deal directly with long and short hair, but each of these relies on culture-bound rationales. What is "proper" (v. 13), "disgraceful" (v. 14) or "glorious" (v. 15) varies from one culture to the next, at least with respect to personal appearance. While Paul regularly uses "nature" (v. 14) to refer to God's created order, the counterexample of the Nazirites demonstrates that it must mean "custom" in this context. Verse 16, at first blush, seems more sweeping, but all it need mean is that the *first*-century church had no different practice.[84]

1 CORINTHIANS 11:2–16			
	Hair?	**Head Coverings?**	
Greco-Roman Background	Long hair = homosexuality	Roman priest: toga pulled over head for worship	**Men**
	Short hair = "masculine" partner in lesbian relationship	"Bun" / veil sign of marriage vs. Greek priestesses in ecstatic frenzy	**Women**
Jewish Background	? But recall Nazirites	? Reverse of later use of yamulke	**Men**
	Changed penalty for convicted adulteress	"Veil" sign of marriage?	**Women**

---

[83] The parallelism is, however, deliberately partial. The man is the image and glory of God but the woman is not the *image* and glory of man. Both genders equally reflect the image of *God*. Cf. Garland, *1 Corinthians,* 523.

[84] The rationale expressed in verse 10 is notoriously opaque. But perhaps the best suggestion is that Paul echoes the Jewish belief that angels functioned in part as guardians of worship and therefore would not have wanted to observe a lack of decorum in the Corinthian congregation. The NIV gratuitously adds "a sign of," which is not in the Greek. A better translation would be, "The woman ought to have control over her head"—i.e., have the culturally appropriate head covering on. See ibid., 524–25.

It is also important to observe the balance between verses 8–9 and 11–12. There are culture-transcending differences between men and women, but among Christians mutual interdependence should most characterize interpersonal relationships. Even more revolutionary are the implications of verse 5. Prophecy in the ancient Mediterranean world involved highly diverse phenomena, ranging all the way from prepared addresses to spontaneous utterances, unified by the conviction that the speaker was delivering a message given to him by God or the gods. While not limited to delivering sermons, prophecy seems to have included at least *Spirit-filled* preaching (see below, p. 190), and therefore Paul presumably made room for women to preach, so long as they did so in a way that demonstrated their subordination to the authorities over them. This can easily be implemented today when married women preach with their husbands' blessing and when any woman preaches while under the authority of the male eldership of a given church (see further below, pp. 363–65).[85]

The Use and Abuse of the Lord's Supper (11:17–34)   On this topic Paul demonstrates the seriousness of the problem by departing from his "yes, but . . ." approach and offering no praise at all (v. 17). Verses 17–22 describe the problem—the more well-to-do Christians are bringing more food and drink than the other participants, and they are overeating and getting drunk at the expense of poorer Christians in the communal meals that the early church shared (what Jude 12 calls "love feasts"). Paul reminds them, therefore, of the tradition of Jesus' teaching about this meal (vv. 23–26). This is the longest quotation of the Jesus tradition anywhere in the epistles, and its contents most closely approximate the form of "the words of institution" found in Luke's Gospel (Luke 22:17–20). Given that 1 Corinthians predates Luke by at least seven years, we have important confirmation here that even the distinctive forms in the later Gospels of paralleled sayings of Jesus were not creations of the Gospel writers but dependent on earlier tradition. And, of course, the earlier the tradition, the more likely its reliability.[86]

Throughout church history, countless debates have centered on the meaning of Christ's words, when he broke the bread and called it his body and took the cup and referred to it as his blood. It is scarcely likely, however, that any of his followers, seeing him hold these elements and declare, "This is . . ." would have imagined that he meant that the bread and wine had actually become extensions of his arms or hands. When we realize that Jesus would almost certainly have been speaking in Aramaic, and that Aramaic often omitted a form of the verb "to be" when a statement was clear enough without it, it becomes all the more improbable that he was affirming that the elements literally turned into his body and blood.[87] Like the prophets in the

---

[85] For further detail on all of the points about this passage, see Craig L. Blomberg, "Women in Ministry: A Complementarian View," in *Two Views on Women in Ministry,* ed. James R. Beck (Grand Rapids: Zondervan, rev. 2005), 155–61. For an argument that prophecy and teaching are to be sharply distinguished and that New Testament prophecy "is always reporting something God spontaneously brings to mind," see Wayne Grudem, *Evangelical Feminism and Biblical Truth* (Sisters, Ore.: Multnomah, 2004), 228–32. Grudem argues that "women could prophesy but not teach in the church" (p. 230).

[86] For both the meaning and tradition history of the Lord's Supper, see esp. I. Howard Marshall, *Last Supper and Lord's Supper* (Grand Rapids: Eerdmans; Exeter: Paternoster, 1980).

[87] Hays (*First Corinthians,* 199) notes that the Lord's Supper expresses precisely the opposite of a real presence by acknowledging the absence of the Lord, recalling his death and awaiting his coming again.

Old Testament, Jesus is acting out a visual parable to portray graphically the symbolism of the meal.[88] Those who eat and drink with him should remember his atoning death for the sins of humanity and look forward to the days when he will come again and celebrate his messianic banquet with all his followers. In between, he is spiritually present with believers and particularly so during this special ordinance.

Verses 27–34, therefore, warn the Corinthians not to eat or drink in a selfish fashion, lest God should judge them, even with sickness or death. "In an unworthy manner" in verse 27 translates the Greek adverb "unworthily" (*anaxiōs*). It does not imply that those who are or who feel "unworthy" (an adjective) must refrain from the Lord's table. Communion is precisely for sinners! It does mean that *those who are unwilling to share their material goods with needier Christians in their midst should not partake.* "Without recognizing the body of the Lord" (v. 29) in this context most probably means "not being adequately concerned for the rest of the church." "The body of the Lord" is, on this view, just a synonym for Paul's favorite expression, "the body of Christ."[89] Derivatively, it is possible that Paul also means that those who partake should understand the significance of the death of Christ.[90]

Either way, only true believers can fulfill these criteria, and only they should be permitted to celebrate the Eucharist. But there is no justification for withholding the elements from people simply because they come from a different Christian denomination. And, as with baptism (see p. 41), there is no Scripture that ever indicates that Communion must be administered by some particular kind of Christian holding a certain office. More cultural and traditional overlay seems to have shrouded the original practice of these two ordinances in virtually all Christian denominations than with any other aspect of church life, so that they impose restrictions that go far beyond biblical mandates!

The Right and Wrong Use of Spiritual Gifts (12:1–14:40)   The last of the three problems involving the Corinthian worship services requires the most detailed correction.[91] We may subdivide these chapters into at least six major sections:

1. *The recognition of the gifts* (12:1–3). Various Greco-Roman cults exhibited characteristics similar to those represented by Christian counterparts, most notably with respect to prophecy and tongues. All apparent manifestations of spiritual gifts, therefore, must be evaluated. The foundational test is whether those practicing them truly acknowledge Jesus as Lord (v. 3).

2. *The distribution of the gifts* (12:4–11). In short, God wants to create diversity within unity. To do this he gives different people different gifts, even though they all come from the same triune God (vv. 4–6). Verses 4–6 reflect further incipient trinitarianism, on the assumption that "Lord" refers to Christ. Every Christian receives at least one spiritual gift (v. 7a), and each is to be used for mutual edification (v. 7b). Paul then gives samples of some of these gifts (vv. 8–10). Other lists appear in Romans 12:3–8 and Ephesians 4:11. There is no evidence that any of the lists or all

---

[88] David Wenham, "How Jesus Understood the Last Supper: A Parable in Action," *Themelios* 20 (1995): 11–16.

[89] Thiselton, *First Corinthians,* 890.

[90] Fee, *First Corinthians,* 559, 563.

[91] On these three chapters, see esp. D. A. Carson, *Showing the Spirit* (Grand Rapids: Baker, 1987).

of them put together were intended to be comprehensive.[92] One helpful classification divides the gifts into those that merely magnify traits expected of all believers, those that reflect distinctive leadership roles and the more "supernatural" phenomena that God works through some Christians periodically but do not reflect abilities they can call upon at will.[93] Verse 11 underlines the fact that God's Spirit determines which believers receive which gifts; they are not something we manufacture according to our desires.

Nevertheless, spiritual gifts range from abilities given to Christians totally different from anything they could do as unbelievers all the way to talents they clearly already had, now sanctified and used for God's kingdom purposes.[94] Thus some gifts can clearly be cultivated, as our skills improve with practice. But it is misleading to suggest that we can have any gift we want if we simply follow a certain prescribed formula.

3. *The importance of all the gifts* (12:12–26). Like the physical body, the church is made up of mutually interdependent parts, every one of which is necessary, even if all are not equally prominent. Our common baptism reminds us that the same Holy Spirit indwells all of us (v. 13). Given that Paul can affirm that every Corinthian Christian has the Spirit, in spite of the rampant immaturity present in that congregation, this is one of the strongest texts in the New Testament in support of the conviction that every believer has been baptized in the Spirit (recall above, pp. 23–24). If there is a hierarchy of gifts, it is not those that empower leaders or public speakers that prove most valuable. Just as we cover our private parts because of the great value we assign to them, so too believers whose gifts did not necessarily put them in the limelight may at times be the most needed (vv. 22–24). One thinks, for example, of those empowered to exercise special measures of faith or giving.

4. *The ranking of the gifts* (12:27–31a). Even though Paul has just compared the more hidden gifts with the more public ones and suggested that in some sense the former prove more valuable, he really was not expressing a preference for one gift over another. The whole thrust of verses 12–26 was the importance of all the gifts. But, in light of the Corinthian leaders overestimating their own importance, Paul wanted to level the playing field. Now he again appears to contradict himself, if verses 27–31 establish a different kind of hierarchy. This would be a more fundamental contradiction because here he seems to reinstate leadership gifts like apostleship, prophecy, and teaching as the most significant (v. 28). More probably, the ranking

---

[92] For more detail on the various gifts, see esp. Kenneth Hemphill, *Spiritual Gifts* (Nashville: Broadman, 1988).

[93] A classification arrived at by combining the best insights of Michael Green, *I Believe in the Holy Spirit* (Grand Rapids: Eerdmans, rev. 2004), 210–59; and Donald Bridge and David Phypers, *Spiritual Gifts and the Church* (London: IVP, 1973), 18–89. Numerous inventories exist for helping believers to identify their spiritual gifts; one of the simplest, yet still helpful, is found in Eddie Gibbs, *I Believe in Church Growth* (Grand Rapids: Eerdmans; London: Hodder and Stoughton, 1981), 452–53.

[94] Cf. Ralph P. Martin, *The Spirit and the Congregation* (Grand Rapids: Eerdmans, 1984), 37: "Any condition of life may *become* a person's *charisma* from God 'only when I recognize that the Lord has given it to me and that I am to accept this gift as his calling and command to me.'" Again, "no 'gift' is inherently charismatic, but it has the possibility of becoming so if it is claimed and utilized under the domain of Christ. Thus the natural order is 'sacralized' by being owned for Christ." Cf. also Prior, *1 Corinthians,* 198: "It would seem wrong either, on the one hand, to *confine* the gifts of the Spirit to natural abilities harnessed and released by God or, on the other hand, to assert that the *real* gifts of the Spirit are only those which are manifestly supra-natural."

implied by "first," "second," and "third" is that of the chronological priority of certain gifts. In order even to have a church there must be a missionary or church planter (the root meaning of "apostle"), one who proclaims God's Word (the function of a "prophet"),[95] and one who teaches the body of Christian doctrine to new disciples. Then, and only then, can all the rest of the gifts come into play.

CLASSIFICATION OF SPIRITUAL GIFTS ROM. 12, 1 COR. 12, EPH. 4		
Virtues commanded of all Christians	**Special roles for leadership**	**"Supernatural" charisms**
• Wisdom • Knowledge • Faith • Service • Exhortation • Giving • Sharing • Mercy	• Apostles • Evangelists • Pastors • Teachers • Administrators	• Healing • Miracles • Prophecy • Distinguishing spirits • Tongues • Interpretation of tongues

The order of these remaining gifts seems largely random, except for the last. While not demeaning tongues *per se,* Paul recognizes that the Corinthians have been overexalting this specific gift and so demotes it to last on his list. The rhetorical questions of verses 29–30 all employ the negative adverb in the Greek that indicates the implied answer to each is no. Christians who claim that all believers should receive or even seek after a particular spiritual gift flatly contradict God's Word at this point. What then does Paul mean by ending this section with the command to "eagerly desire the greater gifts" (v. 31a)? In this context, he probably implies that one should aspire to the more hidden, behind-the-scenes roles that too few of the Corinthians are playing. It is entirely proper to pray for certain gifts so long as one leaves room for the Spirit to answer those prayers however he chooses. God always encourages us to pour out our hearts' desires to him, but we must always allow him to be sovereign and not presume to tell him what to do or claim to know how he will respond.

5. *The role of love* (12:31b–13:13). Many people scarcely familiar with the Bible in any detail have nevertheless heard or read chapter 13. It is a perennially favorite text at weddings, especially in Christian circles. But few seem aware that this passage does not form an independent poem or rhapsody in praise of love but falls squarely in the middle of Paul's discussion of spiritual gifts. Verses 1–3 itemize

---

[95] "Prophets perform speech-acts of announcement, proclamation, judgment, challenge, comfort, support, or encouragement, whereas teachers perform speech-acts of transmission, communicative explanation, interpretation of texts, establishment of creeds, exposition of meaning and implication, and, more cognitive, less temporally applied communicative acts" (Thiselton, *First Corinthians,* 1017). More simply, prophecy can be defined as "the declaration of God's will to the people" (Garland, *1 Corinthians,* 582) or "pastoral preaching" (David Hill, *New Testament Prophecy* [London: Marshall, Morgan & Scott; Atlanta: John Knox, 1979], 123.

several gifts as examples to make the point that, without love, even the greatest of gifts remains worthless.[96] Verses 4–7 list positive and negative qualities of love that the Corinthians especially needed to practice or avoid. It has often been pointed out that these character traits perfectly match the life Jesus modeled, so that as we grow in these attributes we become more Christlike. An excellent encapsulation of the portrait of love painted here is "the unsolicited giving of the very best you have on behalf of another regardless of response."[97] Moreover, "love becomes a way of battling a world still filled with sin; it is something we do for others *in spite* of who they are and *in spite* of our feelings about them."[98]

In verses 8–13, Paul again selects sample gifts, stressing their transience as compared with the permanence of love (and later of faith and hope—v. 13). In the light of 1:7 ("therefore you do not lack any spiritual gift as you eagerly wait for our Lord Jesus Christ to be revealed"), "the perfect" in verse 10 almost certainly refers to Christ's return. This imagery fits the immediate context as well. While some have tried to argue that Paul is speaking of the end of the apostolic era or the close of the canon, believers did not know everything or grow to perfect maturity in the first century (vv. 9–10). Nor did they see God "face-to-face," as we all will when Jesus personally comes back (v. 12). The argument that only certain gifts—that is, the more supernatural ones—ceased at the end of the first century fails to note that in fact they continued with some frequency well into the third century of the Christian era and continued to reemerge (though comparatively rarely) here and there throughout church history.[99] This position often further alleges that tongues will cease by themselves (i.e., earlier than the less supernatural gifts) because the verb for "be stilled" in verse 8 is in the middle voice. But this Greek verb (*pauomai*) had become a virtual deponent in first-century Greek, so that there is no difference between this form and an active one, which affirms merely that, at some point in the future, the gift will no longer continue.[100]

When the Christian era comes to a close, therefore, tongues (like every other gift) will no longer be needed because we will not be building the church any more. But faith, hope, and love will remain (v. 13a). This suggests that all three of these virtues will endure throughout eternity, which makes sense "if faith is taken as belief in Jesus and faithful service to him, and if hope refers to the expectant anticipation

---

[96] There is an important textual variant in verse 3, as the NIV margin points out ("that I may boast" rather than "to the flames"). Given the unlikelihood of a scribe changing the more vivid reading of the NIV text to the marginal alternative, it seems likely that we should accept the marginal reading as the more original one.

[97] Richard Walker, AMOR Ministries' motto (Murray, Ky.). Walker is a longtime Baptist pastor and missionary to the upper Amazon basin in Brazil.

[98] Vander Broek, *Breaking Barriers,* 146.

[99] A good history of speaking in tongues appears in Morton Kelsey, *Tongues Speaking: The History and Meaning of Charismatic Experience* (New York: Crossroad, 1981). A good study of prophecy in an influential part of the third-century church is Cecil M. Robeck Jr., *Prophecy in Carthage: Perpetua, Tertullian, Cyprian* (Cleveland: Pilgrim, 1992). More briefly but more generally, cf. the catalog of references to the ongoing presence of the more supernatural gifts in the early centuries of the church's history in C. H. Talbert, *Reading Corinthians* (New York: Crossroad, 1987), 82–83, 88–90. Moreover, nothing in any of Paul's writings betrays any awareness of a coming end of an "apostolic age" or the "close of a canon." The church fathers consistently equated the "perfect" with the parousia; see Gary S. Shogren, "How Did They Suppose the Perfect Would Come? 1 Corinthians 13.8–12 in Patristic Exegesis," *JPT* 15 (1999): 99–129. As Hays (*First Corinthians,* 229) puts it, Paul's language is "patently eschatological" and the interpretation of the "perfect" as the end of the first century "is simply nonsense."

[100] Cf. Carson, *Showing the Spirit,* 66–67.

of the good things God has in the future for us."[101] But love remains the greatest, probably because it is the most foundational and most central to the Christian ethic.

6. *Comparing prophecy and tongues* (14:1–40). Paul now singles out the two gifts that are most dividing the Corinthians. The "big idea" of this chapter is to *prefer prophecy to tongues*. Verses 1–25 explain why prophecy (the intelligible proclamation of God's Word, whether prepared or spontaneous) is superior: it is immediately understandable (vv. 1–19) and is not as likely as tongues to make the uninitiated think Christians are mad (vv. 20–25). Like prophecy, speaking in tongues took various forms in the ancient Mediterranean world. Common to these forms was the sound of an unknown language, but formal linguistic structure need not have been present.[102] Tongues, of course, can function like prophecy, once they are interpreted (v. 5).[103] But there is no guarantee that an interpreter will be present in any context in which a tongues speaker exercises his or her gift, so Paul cannot get as excited about the deployment of this particular charism. Verses 6–12 offer several analogies to combinations of sounds that remain potentially ambiguous. Since the glossolalia in Corinth was not automatically heard by the audience in understandable languages, we know this is a different phenomenon from that which accompanied the descent of the Spirit at Pentecost (Acts 2).

In light of the problems tongues were causing, it would have been tempting for Paul simply to forbid the practice altogether. But verses 13–19 make clear that Paul resists this temptation. Those who have the gift should pray for an interpreter or that God would give them the interpretation. Otherwise, they should exercise their gift in private (probably similar to what contemporary charismatics call a "prayer language") and employ more cognitive skills in public. Somewhat surprisingly, Paul admits that he speaks in tongues more than all of the Corinthians (v. 19), but they may well have not even known this since he does so almost entirely outside "the church."

Paul continues to elaborate on his theme of what is most intelligible and least misleading (vv. 20–25). Quoting Isaiah 28:11–12 (v. 21), he deduces that tongues "are a sign, not for believers but for unbelievers; prophecy, however, is for believers, not for unbelievers" (v. 22).[104] But this seems to be entirely backwards! As Paul goes on immediately to explain, he is concerned when unbelievers visit the Christian worship service that they not be "turned off" by the strangeness and potential unintelligibility of tongues (v. 23). So how can tongues be a sign for unbelievers? The answer emerges from considering the Isaiah quotation in its original context. There the prophet was predicting the Assyrian invasion of Israel as part of God's judgment against his rebellious people. So, too, tongues can function as a sign of judgment when unbelievers react negatively and thus fail to come to Christ. Prophecy, on the

---

[101] Blomberg, *1 Corinthians*, 260.

[102] Carson, *Showing the Spirit*, 77–88. Dale B. Martin ("Tongues of Angels and Other Status Indicators," *JAAR* 59 [1991]: 547) has shown that tongues were often thought of as angelic languages in Paul's day, which may well account for 13:1 as well.

[103] Garland, *1 Corinthians*, 635.

[104] On the contrasts between the communities of those "in Adam" and those "in Christ" seen as ontological realities, Sang-Won (Aaron) Son, *Corporate Elements in Pauline Anthropology* (Rome: PIB, 2001).

other hand, primarily involves preaching to believers. But the convicting power of the Holy Spirit can use it to bring outsiders to the Lord as well (vv. 24–25).[105]

The second half of chapter 14 generalizes from Paul's main point (about preferring prophecy) to the necessary order in the exercise of spiritual gifts more generally. Verse 26 depicts a typical worship service, in which each person who has a gift of utterance can have a chance to use it. Contemporary worship services would do well to create opportunities at least periodically for similar spontaneity; it is hard to understand how we allow the Spirit to be sovereign when nothing occurs in church that was not planned at least several days in advance! But the purpose of such opportunities is for the upbuilding of the church, not for individual believers to parade their piety in public! Paul then returns to specific provisions for the two particularly controversial gifts—tongues and prophecy (vv. 27–33a). In both instances, he limits the number of people allowed to participate and insists that no one interrupt another. For tongues, there must be an interpretation. If none emerges, that speaker should remain silent until there is reason to believe an interpreter is present. For prophecy, the congregation should assess the credibility of what they hear.[106]

Simply because people say, "The Lord declares to us today . . .", does not necessarily mean that God is speaking through them. Even if they have received a message from the Lord, believers never exercise any spiritual gift perfectly, so they may add some of their own interpretive conclusions to the message, which may or may not be what God intends (recall on Acts 21:4). Hence, the need for testing Paul's instructions likewise implies that even those endowed with the more supernatural gifts can control their exercise of them (vv. 28, 32). This is not "ecstasy," in the technical sense of an inability to stop certain behaviors, as at times occurred in pagan religious practices.

Verses 33b–38 present the modern reader with the second perplexing passage in this epistle about gender roles.[107] Taken out of context, they appear to forbid all women from opening their mouths in church! But in light of 11:5, this is the one thing the passage cannot mean. What then do we do with the text? We will list five main approaches in what we think is an increasing order of probability.[108]

---

[105] See further David E. Lanier, "With Stammering Lips and Another Tongue: 1 Cor 14:20–22 and Isa 28:11–12," *CTR* 5 (1991): 259–85. Cf. Karl O. Sandnes, "Prophecy—a Sign for Believers (1 Cor 14, 20–25)," *Bib* 77 (1996): 1–15.

[106] The evaluation of prophecy must be distinguished from the spiritual gift of discerning spirits (12:10). The latter involves deciding whether a spiritual phenomenon even comes from the Lord at all. See Wayne A. Grudem, *The Gift of Prophecy in 1 Corinthians* (Lanham: UPA, 1982), 263–88. The "others" in verse 29 (who should carefully weigh alleged prophecy) more likely refer to the entire congregation than to the rest of the prophets, given the specific word that Paul uses (*hoi alloi* rather than *hoi loipoi*)—Carson, *Showing the Spirit*, 120. We are not told the specific criteria that would have been used to judge prophetic claims, but Michael Green (*To Corinth with Love* [London: Hodder and Stoughton, 1982], 77–78) combines numerous Scriptures together to make seven suggestions: (1) Does it glorify God rather than the speaker, church, or denomination? (2) Does it accord with Scripture? (3) Does it build up the church? (4) Is it spoken in love? (5) Does the speaker submit himself or herself to the judgment and consensus of others in spiritual humility? (6) Is the speaker in control of him- or herself? (7) Is there a reasonable amount of instruction, or does the message seem excessive in detail?

[107] Again, for more detail, see Blomberg, "Women in Ministry," 161–65.

[108] Philip B. Payne ("Fuldensis, Sigla for Variants in Vaticanus, and 1 Cor 14.34–5," *NTS* 41 [1995]: 240–62) has argued that certain markings in various manuscripts do in fact indicate that these verses were at times omitted, but he has been refuted by Curt Niccum ("The Voice of the Manuscripts on the Silence of Women: The External Evidence for 1 Cor 14.34–5," *NTS* 43 [1997]: 242–55). For further arguments on each side of the debate, see Philip B. Payne, "MS. 88 as Evidence for a Text without 1 Cor 14.34–5," *NTS* 44 (1998): 152–58; and J. Edward Miller, "Some

1. In a few late manuscripts, verses 34–35 appear after verse 40. Could this be because they were a later textual addition and not what Paul wrote at all? This is most unlikely because no manuscripts omit them altogether, and the change in location is natural since they seem intrusive where they are. An explanation for their appearance in this context, however, appears below.

2. Are verses 34–35 another Corinthian slogan that Paul refutes in verses 36–38?[109] Probably not, since all the other slogans in 1 Corinthians represent the more libertine wing of the church, are phrased in short and proverbial form, and receive at least qualified endorsement by Paul. None of these features fits verses 34–35.

3. Were the women, particularly those of Jewish background, used to being segregated in worship and chattering or gossiping with little actual involvement in the service?[110] Perhaps some were, but nothing in the text indicates this is the problem here, so at best this solution is entirely speculative. And the evidence for segregating women in Jewish worship comes from centuries later and does not seem to have applied in Paul's day.

4. Given the general lack of access to education for women in antiquity, were they asking disruptive questions that were better dealt with by husbands or fathers outside the worship service?[111] This would fit verse 35a particularly well, but for Paul to have silenced all women and no men (when at least a few women were well educated and many men were not) would seem hopelessly sexist.

5. Perhaps the best view is that which limits the type of speech that Paul forbids here to some specific form of speaking in the context of the use of spiritual gifts. The immediately preceding passage has discussed criteria for tongues, their interpretation, prophecy, and its evaluation, in that order, and all but one of the twenty-three other uses of the verb "speak" in this chapter are similarly restricted. Yet of the four specific forms of speech cited, only the evaluation of prophecy is not a spiritual gift given by the Spirit as he determines. Although all are called to evaluate an alleged prophecy (v. 29), the ultimate responsibility; for passing judgment would have fallen on the church leaders (elders or overseers); and, at least in Paul's day, it seems that all of these were men (see on 1 Tim. 2:8–15 below). So it is probably speaking in this limited context of *the authoritative evaluation of prophecy* that Paul forbids to women; this would also account for why this passage appears where it does, precisely on the heels of the regulation of prophecy in verses 29–33a.[112] It is even possible to combine this view with 4. *Some wives may have been asking embarrassing questions or challenging their husbands' prophecy during the worship service.* This

Observations on the Text-Critical Function of the Umlauts in Vaticanus with Special Attention to 1 Corinthians 14.34–35," *JSNT* 26 (2003): 217–36.

[109] See esp. David W. Odell-Scott, "Let the Women Speak in Church: An Egalitarian Interpretation of 1 Cor 14:33b–36," *BTB* 13 (1983): 90–93; idem, "In Defense of an Egalitarian Interpretation of 1 Cor 14:34–36," *BTB* 17 (1987): 100–3.

[110] E.g. J. Keir Howard, "Neither Male nor Female: An Examination of the Status of Women in the New Testament," *EQ* 55(1983): 31–42.

[111] See esp. Craig S. Keener, "Women in Ministry: An Egalitarian View" (pp. 205–53) and Linda L. Belleville, "Women in Ministry: An Egalitarian View" (pp. 21–103), both in *Two Views on Women in Ministry,* ed. Beck.

[112] E.g. D. A. Carson, "'Silence in the Churches': On the Role of Women in 1 Corinthians 14:33b–38," in *Rediscovering Biblical Manhood and Womanhood,* eds. John Piper and Wayne Grudem (Wheaton: Crossway, 1991), 140–53.

would account for verse 35a, which otherwise remains a bit puzzling on interpretation (5).[113]

---

1 CORINTHIANS 14:26–40

General Commands Re: Worship (v. 26)

- Tongues (v. 27)

- Interpretation of Tongues (v. 28)

- Prophets and Evaluation (vv. 29–33a)

Silencing the Women (vv. 33b–38)

- Conclusion Re: Prophecy and Tongues (vv. 39–40)

Whether similar restrictions ever apply today will depend on one's interpretation of the 1 Timothy passage. As in 1 Corinthians 11:2–16, the timeless principle might not involve more than appropriate submission of wives to husbands (v. 34). After all, that is the broad principle reflected throughout the Old Testament to which Paul appeals in verse 34.

Chapter 14 closes with two excellent summary commands that, if observed, would have gone a long way toward alleviating the Corinthians' disunity. They remain crucial for contemporary contexts in which these gifts still prove divisive or controversial. On the one hand, believers should be eager to exercise their gifts, particularly those that are the most immediately intelligible; but *no gift, not even tongues, should ever be forbidden* (v. 39). On the other hand, *the exercise of the gifts must never be allowed to get out of control* (v. 40). Of course, what is considered "out of control" itself remains culturally determined. Noncharismatic African worship services are often "wilder" than some charismatic British worship! Control in this context is largely defined by the criteria of verses 26–33a. And "those of us who insist that all things in the church be done 'decently and in order' need to be reminded that order is defined by the Spirit's control of us, not our control of the Spirit."[114]

Concerning the Resurrection (15:1–58) Hellenistic dualism led many Greeks and Romans to believe merely in the immortality of the soul rather than also in the resurrection of the body. In response, Paul affirms *the certainty of the resurrection* (vv. 1–34) and then replies to a potential objection by discussing *the nature of the resurrection* (vv. 35–58). The first of these two sections can be subdivided into Paul's reminder about the fact of Christ's bodily resurrection (vv. 1–11) and the guarantee that his resurrection produces for the general resurrection of all believers one day (vv. 12–34).

Paul begins by stressing the centrality of this doctrine (vv. 1–2). Christians may debate other issues; but without a belief that Jesus bodily rose from the dead, one

---

[113] Thiselton, *First Corinthians*, 1150–61.
[114] Vander Broek, *Breaking Barriers*, 150.

cannot be saved (Rom. 10:9). The verbs "received" and "passed on" are technical terms in both Greek and Hebrew for the oral transmission of basic religious teaching. What Paul goes on to describe was probably taught to him shortly after his conversion in A.D. 32. In other words, the list of witnesses to Christ's resurrection from the dead is not the legendary invention of a generation or two after the foundation of Christianity but a fundamental conviction of Jesus' first followers within two years or less after his death. One may argue that they were deceived or that they had some kind of subjective vision of Christ, but resurrection faith *was* integral to Christian belief from its earliest days onward.[115]

Because of its quasi-poetic structure, many scholars think that part or all of verses 3b–7 represent an early creed or preformed unit of tradition that antedated Paul's writing. If accurate, the suggestion could provide early *written* testimony to belief in this doctrine alongside the oral tradition. The list of witnesses is impressive; not merely the apostles but a group of five hundred followers of Jesus saw him raised from the dead. The fact that most were still alive means that skeptics could question them and decide for themselves how credible they were.[116] Paul too had his "audience" with Christ on the Damascus Road, but it took place after Jesus' ascension into heaven, not during the forty-day period he was appearing to other people. Thus Paul speaks of himself as "one abnormally born" (v. 8). The word usually means a "miscarriage," but that would be a premature birth, whereas here Paul's experience of the risen Christ came significantly later than everyone else's. Either way, Paul recognizes his utter unworthiness to have had Christ single him out for such special attention, which totally revolutionized his life (vv. 9–11).[117]

Other portions of Scripture highlight the significance of the resurrection as vindicating Christ's previous claims about his person and work or as representing one key step en route to his return to the right hand of the Father. But here the implications Paul wishes to underline involve the resurrection of all people at the end of the age. If Jesus' body remained in the tomb (or was never buried at all and left to be eaten by birds of prey and scavenger dogs, as some modern revisionists claim[118]), then Christian faith is futile (vv. 12–19). No one has any hope for resurrection life if Christ is not raised.[119]

---

[115] Thus even Lüdemann with Özen, *What Really Happened to Jesus,* 15. Lüdemann began his scholarly career as a liberal Christian but eventually abandoned all belief in God. He adopts the subjective vision hypothesis but recognizes it emerged at a very early date, even before Paul's conversion.

[116] By far and away the most magisterial study of the resurrection, with respect to both its reality and its meaning, is now N. T. Wright, *The Resurrection of the Son of God* (London: SPCK; Minneapolis: Fortress, 2003).

[117] Undoubtedly one reason Paul does not discuss this event in his letters more than he does, compared with Luke's particular emphasis on it in Acts (recall above, p. 11). Cf. further Gaye Strathearn, "'Jesus Christ, and Him Crucified': Paul's Testimony of Christ," in *Jesus Christ: Son of God, Savior,* ed. Paul H. Peterson, Gary L. Hatch, and Laura D. Card (Provo: Religious Studies Center, 2002), 338–40.

[118] John Dominic Crossan, *Who Killed Jesus?* (San Francisco: HarperSanFrancisco, 1995), 160–88.

[119] "Resurrection means endless hope, but no resurrection means a hopeless end" (Garland, *1 Corinthians,* 721). "If there is no resurrection, this self-denying style of life makes no sense; those who follow the example of Jesus and Paul are chumps missing out on their fair share of life's rewards" (Hays, *First Corinthians,* 262). "If Jesus did not have the power to rise from the tomb, power to save the body—as he said he did—then he did not have power to forgive sins, to save the soul" (Robert L. Millet, *Jesus Christ: The Only Sure Foundation* [Salt Lake City: Bookcraft, 1999], 80).

But if the resurrection truly took place, as Paul knows it did, then his new life becomes one of the "firstfruits" guaranteeing many more resurrections to come (vv. 20–28). Adam's sin led to death for the entire human race; "in Christ all will be made alive" (v. 22). This cannot mean that all people will be saved; Paul too frequently talks about the eternal punishment of the lost for that to be the case. Rather, as verse 23 makes clear, he is speaking of all believers. First, Christ is raised; then when he returns, all his followers will be raised. "Then the end will come" (v. 24). The pair of words used for "then" in verses 23–24 often appeared in contexts where some interval of time ensued between the events linked. This has led a few commentators to wonder if Paul is envisioning a significant gap between the parousia and the final dissolution of the universe and re-creation of heavens and earth (as in Rev. 20–21). If so, it is the only place in Paul's writing where any millennial period is implied. What more interests Paul here is that after Christ has completed his cosmic work, he takes his rightfully subordinate position beneath his heavenly Father (v. 28).[120]

Paul next musters additional arguments for the resurrection (vv. 29–32) to try to convince those whose belief had been corrupted by skeptics (vv. 33–34). All three of his arguments are *ad hoc*; that is to say, they reason from events that have actually occurred without necessarily commending those events. No one thinks that Paul believed the persecution and harassment he experienced (vv. 30–32) was something good to be sought.[121] But unless Paul had hope for a better life after this one, he was a fool to put up with what he did for his Christian commitment. Likewise, verse 29 proves equally *ad hoc*. Mid-second-century evidence suggests that some Greek Christians were in fact baptizing living believers on behalf of dead, unbaptized believers (see esp. Chrysostom, *Homily on 1 Cor. 40:1*), and it is quite possible that something similar afflicted first-century Corinth as well.[122] But that scarcely means that Paul was endorsing much less mandating the practice, as contemporary Mormon thought usually alleges.

Paul now turns to address the question of the nature of the resurrection body.[123] While some may have exhibited genuine curiosity, most asking this question probably meant to ridicule the whole notion of a physical body in the afterlife. By way of reply, Paul points to a variety of analogies in creation that illustrate physical continuity and discontinuity with a previous form of existence (vv. 35–49). If God can bring a fruit-bearing plant out of a tiny seed that looks almost wholly different, he can transform our bodies in magnificent ways as well (vv. 36–38). There are different kinds of flesh in the world, just as there are both earthly and heavenly bodies; God's endlessly diverse creativity should inspire confidence that he can create yet one more kind of life form in the world to come (vv. 39–49). We now have physical

---

[120] Cf. further Craig S. Keener, "Is Subordinationism within the Trinity Really Heresy? A Study of John 5:18 in Context," *TrinJ* 20 (1999): esp. 47–49.

[121] Because Roman citizens were exempt from having to fight animals in the gladiators' ring (*Digest* xxviii. 1.8.4), most commentators take the "wild beasts" of verse 32 to be a metaphor for Paul's human opponents.

[122] For a full discussion, see Thiselton, *First Corinthians,* 1242–49. Recipients of this rite were probably being baptized as proxy only for deceased believers who had never been baptized. Cf. N. H. Taylor, "Baptism for the Dead (1 Cor 15:29)?" *Neot* 36 (2002): 111–20.

[123] S. Hultgren, "The Origin of Paul's Doctrine of the Two Adams in 1 Corinthians 15.45–49," *JSNT* 25 (2003): 343.

(or natural) bodies; when Christ returns we will receive spiritual (or supernatural) bodies. What these are like we cannot tell, except by whatever legitimate inferences we might make from the nature of Christ's resurrection body. But what his followers saw was a transitional form as he was in between earth and heaven (it still had scars), so even this may not be a wholly reliable strategy.

Nevertheless, the transformation of our bodies is necessary because "flesh and blood" (a Jewish idiom for frail, mortal, fallen humanity) cannot coexist with an infinite and completely holy God until it is perfectly glorified and rid of all sin and imperfection (vv. 50–58).[124] The details of this paragraph comport well with our understanding of 1 Thessalonians 4–5. Some believers will be alive when Christ returns, others will have already died, but all will be resurrected at that time, never to die again. Again, apocalyptic promises are meant to encourage (v. 58).

Concerning the Collection for Jerusalem (16:1–4)   The last item about which the Corinthians wrote that Paul addresses in the body of his letter involves a collection he had been organizing for believers in Jerusalem. Paul will have much more to say about this in 2 Corinthians 8–9 and Romans 15:26–27. From these latter verses, we learn of two primary motivations for the offering: to alleviate the needs of the poor Christians there and to offer a kind of tribute for the "mother church" from which all early Christian communities were ultimately derived. These correspond very roughly to the two major purposes of Christian giving throughout church history: helping the physical and spiritual needs of people and remunerating ecclesiastical authorities. Here Paul establishes two principles: setting aside a sum of money weekly and giving in proportion to one's means (v. 2).[125] That Paul refers to "the first day of every week" may suggest a Sunday worship service, in which case this is the first recorded example of a weekly offering in church.

CONCLUSION (16:5–24)

The Travel Plans of Various Christians (16:5–18)   Paul begins his conclusion by explaining his eagerness to see the Corinthians but only when the timing is right (vv. 5–9). Verses 8–9 disclose a profound understanding of when to stay and when to move on in ministry. Of course, Paul would be encouraged by the great door for effective work, but he also has to combat significant opposition. Successful ministry regularly catches Satan's attention! Had Paul experienced nothing but opposition, he might well have moved on, but this combination of victory and struggle convinces him he is strategically placed and must remain for a while. The comments about Timothy and Apollos reflect some of the tensions in Corinth (vv. 10–12), but Paul hopes the worst has passed.[126] Unlike typical Hellenistic letters, 1 Corinthians has

---

[124] Alan Padgett, "The Body in Resurrection: Science and Scripture on the 'Spiritual Body' (1 Cor 15:35–58)," *WW* 22 (2002): 162.

[125] "Apostolic teaching on possessions is in fact much more demanding than a title; the Gospels demand complete sacrifice, arguing that Jesus' followers should live like people matter more than possessions" (Keeneer, *1–2 Corinthians*, 139).

[126] A key function of the references to other Christians in chap. 16 is to remind the Corinthians they belong to a wider network of communities to which life in Christ requires them to be linked (Hays, *First Corinthians*, 283).

not saved up the exhortational material for a sizable, discrete section after the informational body of the epistle, but vestiges of this form remain in verses 13–14.

The final short paragraph of this section commends the visitors from Corinth (vv. 15–18). The apparent contradiction created by calling these men "the first converts in Achaia" (v. 15), despite the fact that Paul evangelized Athens before Corinth (Acts 17–18), is probably best resolved by recognizing that Achaia sometimes referred to a smaller region in the south of Greece that included Corinth but not Athens.[127]

Final Greetings (16:19–24)   Conventional greetings ensue. The "holy kiss" (v. 20) was not erotic but displayed the unity and love, even across background, rank, or gender.[128] As in Galatians and 2 Thessalonians, Paul explicitly takes pen in hand to write a personal greeting (v. 21). The jarring juxtaposition of Paul's curse on unbelievers with the bestowal of grace on believers (vv. 22–23) reflects his passion and conviction that people really do fall into one of only two categories—the saved and the lost.

APPLICATION[129]

The problem of factions in Corinth seems miniscule compared with the thousands of denominations and subdivisions into which the Christian church has split over the centuries. As at Corinth, there have often been philosophical-theological and/or socioeconomic reasons for these divisions, but alignment with unnecessarily rival human leaders continues to dominate the rationale behind church splits. Cross-centered, selfless Christian living and leading, which renounces one's rights, may be even harder to practice today than in first-century Corinth. Asceticism and hedonism continue to plague our world as well. The more the latter rages out of control among our sex-crazed media, and in countless other arenas that promote instant gratification of personal desires, the more those properly horrified by the excess may succumb to the temptation to absolutize injunctions in morally gray areas that demand mature, informed Christian consciences to enable decision-making on a case-by-case basis. The harmonious exercise of all the gifts God grants believers in each local congregation and worldwide, in anticipation of the coming resurrection fellowship guaranteed by Christ's bodily resurrection, could go a long way to rectifying these problems.

Today the divide between rich and poor, especially in the church worldwide, often overshadows other divisions. Because of so much homogeneous church groupings, many believers are not as vividly or as regularly reminded of the divide as they should be. Conservatively, 200,000,000 evangelical *Christians* live below the U.N. poverty line, while we in the West and the North struggle in record numbers with obesity, "gas (petrol) guzzling," personal and corporate debt, and other forms of wanton consumption of shrinking supplies of resources to our own detriment.

---

[127] Fee, *First Corinthians*, 829, n. 19.

[128] See William Klassen, "The Sacred Kiss in the New Testament," *NTS* 39 (1993): 135.

[129] Cf. also Craig L. Blomberg, "Applying 1 Corinthians in the Early Twenty-First Century," *SWJT* 45 (2002): 19–38.

Restraint, coupled with generous giving to others, can slowly begin a process of reversing these trends.

ADDITIONAL QUESTIONS FOR REVIEW

1. What were the competing ideologies of ancient Corinth that Paul combats in his first letter to the Corinthians? In addition to these outside philosophies, what were several internal problems in the Corinthian church?

2. How does Paul's definition in 1 Corinthians 3 of a worldly or carnal (*sarkinos/ sarkikos*) Christian compare to the way Christians sometimes use the term today? What is the danger of applying the category of carnal Christian to nominal practitioners of the faith? How does a closer look at Paul's intended meaning of this term enlighten the doctrines of soteriology and eternal security?

3. Does 1 Corinthians 3:17–19 confirm or deny eternal degrees of reward in heaven? What would be the most logical conclusions regarding eternal reward based on this passage and Matthew 20:1–16, the parable of the laborers in the vineyard?

4. According to 1 Corinthians 4–6, what are some attitudes the Corinthians should adopt toward the words of Paul and his companions, those who are true apostles? How does such an attitude quell factional problems such as lawsuits in the church? To what types of sin does Paul link lawsuits among believers in order to shame the Corinthians in their factional behavior?

5. What would be an appropriate summary of 1 Corinthians 7, Paul's discussion of marriage, celibacy, and divorce? Is Paul mainly concerned with marital status, or is he addressing something deeper? If so, what issue does this discussion address?

6. How would one best respond to an interpretation of 1 Corinthians 7:14 that espouses the view that if a parent accepts Christ, then the entire family will be saved on account of the believing parent's decision?

7. Since food sacrificed to idols is not an issue with which twenty-first-century Western Christianity typically grapples, what is the overarching principle offered in chapters 8–10 here that can be applied to relationships within today's church? How does the issue of accepting money for ministry tie into this principle?

8. What are the three principles Paul offers for maintaining the appropriate use of Christian liberty? Name some specific issues in modern Christianity to which these three principles remain particularly relevant.

9. What ancient cultural practices need to be remembered when interpreting both of the passages in 1 Corinthians on gender roles? In both of these passages, what is normative and what is culture bound? What is the only restriction placed on women in both of these contexts? What phenomenon in the church seems to have prompted Paul's exposition on this subject?

10. What were the Corinthians doing wrong in celebrating the Lord's Supper? What would contemporary application of Paul's response to this problem look like?

11. What was going wrong with the Corinthians' use of their spiritual gifts? How does Paul reply? How is his reply structured—i.e., what are his main points, and what are the subordinate ones under those main points?
12. What does Paul believe about resurrection? of Christ? of believers? Why is this such a crucial topic for him?

SELECT BIBLIOGRAPHY

COMMENTARIES

Advanced

Collins, Raymond F. *First Corinthians.* SP. Collegeville: Liturgical, 1999.
Conzelmann, Hans. *1 Corinthians.* Hermeneia. Philadelphia: Fortress, 1975.
Garland, David E. *1 Corinthians.* BECNT. Grand Rapids: Baker, 2003.
Thiselton, Anthony C. *The First Epistle to the Corinthians.* NIGTC. Carlisle: Paternoster; Grand Rapids: Eerdmans, 2000.

Intermediate

Fee, Gordon D. *The First Epistle to the Corinthians,* rev. NICNT. Grand Rapids: Eerdmans, 1987.
Keener, Craig S. *1–2 Corinthians.* NCBC. Cambridge: CUP, 2005.
Kistemaker, Simon J. *Exposition of the First Epistle to the Corinthians.* NTC. Grand Rapids: Baker, 1993.
Talbert, Charles H. *Reading Corinthians.* New York: Crossroad, 1987.
Watson, Nigel. *The First Epistle to the Corinthians.* London: Epworth, 1992.
Witherington, Ben, III. *Conflict and Community in Corinth: A Socio-Rhetorical Commentary on 1 and 2 Corinthians.* Grand Rapids: Eerdmans; Carlisle: Paternoster, 1995.

Introductory

Blomberg, Craig L. *1 Corinthians.* NIVAC. Grand Rapids: Zondervan, 1994.
Hays, Richard B. *First Corinthians.* Int. Louisville: WJKP, 1997.
Johnson, Alan F. *1 Corinthians.* IVPNTC. Leicester and Downers Grove: IVP, 2004.
Morris, Leon. *The First Epistle of Paul to the Corinthians,* rev. TNTC. Leicester: IVP; Grand Rapids: Eerdmans, 1985.
Prior, David. *The Message of 1 Corinthians: Life in the Local Church.* BST. Leicester and Downers Grove: IVP, 1985.

OTHER BOOKS

Adams, Edward, and David G. Horrell, eds. *Christianity at Corinth: The Quest for the Pauline Church.* Louisville and London: WJKP, 2004.

Brown, Alexandra R. *The Cross and Human Transformation: Paul's Apocalyptic Word in 1 Corinthians.* Minneapolis: Fortress, 1995.

Chow, John K. *Patronage and Power: A Study of Social Networks in Corinth.* Sheffield: JSOT, 1992.

Clarke, Andrew D. *Secular and Christian Leadership in Corinth.* Leiden and New York: Brill, 1993.

Dutch, Robert S. *The Educated Elite in 1 Corinthians: Education and Community Conflict in Gaeco-Roman Context.* London and New York: T & T Clark, 2005.

Furnish, Victor P. *The Theology of the First Letter to the Corinthians.* Cambridge and New York: CUP, 1999.

Grant, Robert M. *Paul in the Roman World: The Conflict at Corinth.* Louisville and London: WJKP, 2001.

Horrell, David G. *The Social Ethos of the Corinthian Correspondence.* Edinburgh: T & T Clark, 1996.

Marshall, Peter. *Enmity in Corinth: Social Conventions in Paul's Relations with the Corinthians.* Tübingen: Mohr, 1987.

Martin, Dale B. *The Corinthian Body.* New Haven and London: Yale University Press, 1995.

Mitchell, Margaret M. *Paul and the Rhetoric of Reconciliation: An Exegetical Investigation of the Language and Composition of 1 Corinthians.* Tübingen: Mohr, 1991.

Pickett, Raymond. *The Cross in Corinth: The Social Significance of the Death of Jesus.* Sheffield: SAP, 1997.

Winter, Bruce W. *After Paul Left Corinth.* Grand Rapids and Cambridge: Eerdmans, 2002.

BIBLIOGRAPHY

Mills, Watson E. *1 Corinthians.* Lewiston and Lampeter: Mellen, 1996.

2 Corinthians: Increasing Maturity but Infiltrating Judaizing Threats

INTRODUCTION

The situation in between 1 and 2 Corinthians proves extremely difficult to reconstruct. The beginning and end of a complex sequence of events seem relatively secure, but the intermediate stages lead to numerous competing proposals. We will highlight the most important of these without attempting a comprehensive coverage of all the alternatives proposed.

Paul originally hoped to visit Corinth soon after his time in Ephesus was up, probably shortly after Pentecost in A.D. 55 (1 Cor. 16:8). He originally hoped to sail directly across the Aegean Sea from Ephesus, stopping in Corinth en route to Macedonia further north, and then planned to return the way he came (2 Cor. 1:15–16). After receiving 1 Corinthians, however, the church in Corinth did not react as positively as Paul had hoped. So he was compelled to make *an abbreviated visit to and from Corinth while he was still ministering in Ephesus* (presumably via a direct boat trip back and forth across the Aegean). In 12:14 Paul says, "Now I am ready to visit you for the third time."

Thus 2 Corinthians 13:1 specifies that "this will be my third visit to you," even though Acts narrates only two trips—the visit during Paul's second missionary journey when he founded the church in Corinth (Acts 18:1–18) and another stop on his third missionary journey (presumably as part of his three-month stay in Greece in Acts 20:2–3). Second Corinthians 2:1 most likely refers to this intervening visit between the two itemized in Acts since Paul explains that he made up his mind not to "make another painful visit" to the Corinthians. The period of time during his establishing the church there could scarcely have been so characterized, and the other visit that Acts narrates does not take place until after 2 Corinthians has been written.

It also appears likely that Paul penned *an additional letter in between the two we know of as 1 and 2 Corinthians.* In 2 Corinthians 2:3–4, Paul insists that, "I wrote you out of great distress and anguish of heart and with many tears." Traditionally, this reference has been taken as describing the letter we call 1 Corinthians. But despite the potpourri of problems Paul has to address in that epistle, its overall tone seems scarcely anguished enough to merit this description. Modern scholars across the whole theological spectrum, therefore, almost unanimously understand this verse to describe a letter Paul wrote to Corinth in between the two preserved in the canon. We have already seen an unambiguous reference in 1 Corinthians 5:9 to another piece of Pauline correspondence with Corinth that has not been preserved, so the proposal of a second such letter can scarcely cause objections in principle. On this reconstruction, 2 Corinthians 7:8 and 12 refer to this same lost "painful letter," since verses 8–13 describe the repentance of the offending man in response to that letter, a response that seems not to have occurred immediately after Paul's intermediate visit (1:23–2:2). We may, therefore, conclude that *the intermediate visit preceded the intermediate letter, and only after the latter did the situation in Corinth begin to resolve itself.* [130]

THE CORINTHIAN CORRESPONDENCE	
Paul to Corinth A	1 Corinthians 5:9
Corinth to Paul A	1 Corinthians 7:1
Paul to Corinth B	1 Corinthians
Paul to Corinth C[#]	2 Corinthians 2:4, 7:8
Paul to Corinth D	2 Corinthians 1–9
Paul to Corinth E[##]	2 Corinthians 10–13

[#] or C = B
[##] or D and E were one letter interrupted by fresh news
or D and E were planned as they are from the outset

All this is made somewhat more complicated by the specific contents of 2:5–11 and 7:8–13, which call the Corinthians to forgive a church member whom they had disciplined and welcome him back into their fellowship. After reading about the incestuous offender in 1 Corinthians 5:1, it is natural to assume that this same man is in view. That, of course, depends on understanding "the destruction of the flesh" in 1 Corinthians 5:5 to refer to the man's sinful nature (or characteristically sinful lifestyle) rather than to his physical death. Obviously if the man had died, he could not later be restored to fellowship! Because 1 Corinthians 5:1–5 makes good sense on either interpretation, we cannot be too dogmatic about which one is correct. Even more relevant in the minds of many commentators is the fact that 2 Corinthians 2:5 and 10 read as if this man had personally offended Paul in some way, leading to the conclusion that he was a different individual from the incestuous offender altogether. Yet while 1 Corinthians 5 discloses nothing to suggest such a personal encounter and offense, it makes good sense to imagine *Paul confronting the man himself during his intermediate visit so that his initial sin became compounded by his defiance of the apostle's call to repentance.* [131]

---

[130] For this sequence of events, cf. also Frank J. Matera, *II Corinthians: A Commentary* (Louisville and London: WJKP, 2003), 15–20; Paul Barnett, *The Second Epistle to the Corinthians* (Grand Rapids and Cambridge: Eerdmans, 1997), 9–15.

[131] See esp. Colin G. Kruse, "The Relationship between the Opposition to Paul Reflected in 2 Corinthians 1–7 and 10–13," *EQ* 61 (1989): 195–202. Cf. David Garland, *2 Corinthians* (Nashville: Broadman & Holman, 1999), 121–23.

COMPOSITION

Chapters 10–13   Further complicating matters is the observation that 2 Corinthians 10–13 breaks sharply from the largely relieved and congratulatory tone of the first nine chapters of the epistle and turns harsh enough in tone that it could qualify for the label of a painful, sorrowful, or even severe letter. *Some have suggested, therefore, that chapters 10–13 are out of place chronologically and contain the heart of what originally was the intermediate letter written before 2 Corinthians 1–9.*[132] There is, however, no ancient manuscript support for this theory nor any convincing explanation for why these chapters, if they were written earlier, would be tacked onto the end of a later letter rather than put at the beginning of it. And while the tone is certainly severe, the problems seem to be largely different ones. No solitary offender appears anywhere in 2 Corinthians 10–13. Rather, an apparently new group of itinerant teachers akin to the Judaizers that troubled the Galatians have recently arrived from outside of Corinth and are leading some astray within that church.

THE BUILDING BLOCKS OF 2 CORINTHIANS

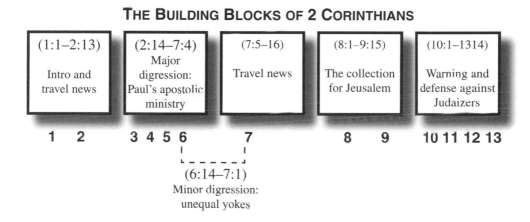

Other arguments for equating 2 Corinthians 10–13 with the painful letter prove equally weak. It is alleged that in 12:16–18, the Corinthians suspect a lack of integrity in Paul's handling of finances, whereas in 8:11; 9:2; and 9:12–15 Paul praises the Corinthian attitudes toward the collection. But those are two different issues; the one deals with Paul's motives, the other with the Corinthians' attitudes. And a careful look at the latter three references reveals that Paul is referring to the Corinthians' exemplary attitudes in the past and the benefits of good stewardship in the future. It actually says nothing to contradict the rest of chapters 8–9 that make plain his dissatisfaction with their contributions to the collection in the present. Others have argued that chapters 10–13 should precede 1–7 because Paul faces harsh opposition in the former but has been reconciled to his opponents in the latter. But if 10–13 represent a new group of opponents, this argument breaks down entirely. Finally, some consider the references in 2 Corinthians 3:1 and 5:12 to Paul's self-commendation to be describing key parts

---

[132] E.g., Talbert, *Reading Corinthians*, xviii–xxi. In detail, see Brian K. Peterson, *Eloquence and the Proclamation of the Gospel in Corinth* (Atlanta: Scholars, 1998).

of chapters 10–13. But, more generally, misunderstanding of Paul's motives seems to have prevailed throughout his years of ministry and interaction with the Corinthians. Recall his scathing rebukes already in 1 Corinthians 4:8–21.[133] Paul's reference to "the brother" with Titus in 12:18 sounds like it refers back to the equally anonymous "brother" of 8:18 and 22, which argues for chapters 10–13 being written after 1–9 (with both sections ultimately unified in the same letter.)[134]

If 2 Corinthians 10–13 did not originally precede chapters 1–9, then how do we explain the abrupt change in tone at this juncture in the letter? Three major answers compete for acceptance. First, *Paul could have known all along that he would have to include some pointed words for those Corinthians tempted to follow the false teachers.* But he adopts good psychology and praises them first for their appropriate handling of the disfellowshipped offender and for a generally good response to his other instructions in his first letter to them (chaps. 1–7). Then Paul broaches the topic of the collection, which appears to be the one issue of "old business" to which they have not adequately responded (chaps. 8–9), while saving his sternest words for the end, addressing the most recent problem of these new false teachers from outside (chaps. 10–13). Until recently, few commentators at any point on the theological spectrum argued strongly for this position, but several recent commentaries and other more specialized studies may be turning the tide.[135]

One can also view the letter as a unity by conceiving of it in an a-b-a structure where Paul begins by focusing on his apostolic ministry using comparatively tender tones (chaps. 1–7), moves to the outstanding problem of the collection (chaps. 8–9), and then returns to the theme of Paul's apostolic ministry, this time adopting tougher tones (chaps. 10–13).[136] Still others suggest structures based on Greco-Roman forms of rhetoric or oratory, though their outlines do seem a bit contrived in places.[137]

---

2 Corinthians

Paul's Apostolic Ministry (Tender Tones)
Chapters 1–7; A

The Offering for Jerusalem
Chapters 8–9; B

Paul's Apostolic Ministry (Tough Tones)
Chapters 10–13; A'

---

[133] For a thorough survey of arguments for and against, see Margaret E. Thrall, *A Critical and Exegetical Commentary on the Second Epistle to the Corinthians,* vol. 1 (Edinburgh: T & T Clark, 1994), 13–20.

[134] Cf. Keener, *1–2 Corinthians,* 243.

[135] See esp. David R. Hall, *The Unity of the Corinthian Correspondence* (London and New York: T & T Clark, 2003). Cf. Witherington, *Conflict and Community in Corinth,* 327–36; David A. deSilva, "Measuring Penultimate against Ultimate Reality: An Investigation of the Integrity and Argumentation of 2 Corinthians," *JSNT* 52 (1993): 41–70.

[136] Cf. Frances M. Young and David F. Ford, *Meaning and Truth in 2 Corinthians* (London: SPCK, 1987; Grand Rapids: Eerdmans, 1988), 16–40.

[137] E.g., J. D. H. Amador, "Revisiting 2 Corinthians: Rhetoric and the Case for Unity," *NTS* 46 (2000): 92–111; David A. Hester, "The Unity of 2 Corinthians: A Test Case for a Re-discovered and Re-invented Rhetoric," *Neot* 33 (1999): 411–32. DeSilva (*An Introduction to the New Testament,* 584) finds the shift in tone accounted for adequately by Paul's choice to use the literary device of *sunkrisis* ("comparison"—in this case, with other teachers) in chaps.10–13, and cites examples of equally abrupt shifts in Demosthenes's Second Epistle.

A *second option treats chapters 10–13 as the body of a letter that Paul wrote* after *chapters 1–9.* In other words, the Judaizers had not yet made their way to Corinth when Paul wrote the material that now comprises the first nine chapters of 2 Corinthians; but when he learned of this fresh trouble, he dashed off another shorter but sharper rejoinder. This theory makes sense, at least of the sequence of chapters, unlike the one postulating that chapters 10–13 chronologically preceded 1–9.[138] But again there is no manuscript evidence to suggest that more than one letter was ever combined by some later scribe, nor any early church testimony to that effect. Indeed, all of the theories of multiple letters in 2 Corinthians that we will discuss have been entirely the product of scholarly hypotheses over roughly the last two hundred years. On the other hand, in four instances ancient compilers of Cicero's letters created multiple-letter collections on a single manuscript, in the chronological order of the letters, with the first letter comprising the substantial majority of the document. So there is no reason in principle to object to the suggestion that a redactor did the same thing with two of Paul's epistles.[139]

The third main possibility is that Paul was dictating this epistle over a period of time, as often occurred in ancient letter writing. When he began it, he had not yet heard of the Judaizers' arrival in Corinth. But at some point along the way, fresh reports alerted him to the problem so that he shifted gears and moved in an unanticipated direction in chapters 10–13, resorting to severer rebukes than he had expected to have to use when he began his dictating. The entire letter would still have been written and sent exactly as we have it, but the jarring clash between chapters 1–9 and 10–13 is successfully accounted for. Arguments against this option usually play down the Jewishness of the false teachers (but see 11:22) and stress their predilection for elitist spiritual experiences (which would account well for 12:11–13) and triumphalism (contrast 11:16–21). One might then imagine these teachers being akin to those Paul apparently rebuffs already in 1 Corinthians 2:6–16 and 4:8–21.

But the fact that almost nothing in 1 Corinthians can be viewed as a response to teachers boasting in their Jewish credentials, and almost everything makes sense as a response to problems triggered by Christians from Gentile backgrounds in Corinth (see our introduction to 1 Corinthians), makes this approach more suspect. Other possible premonitions of unresolved problems (2 Cor. 3:1; 4:1–6; 5:11, 13) remain theologically vague enough that there is no reason to tie them directly to the false teachers Paul blisteringly refers to as "super-apostles" in 12:11.[140]

Other theological and conceptual parallels between the two sections of 2 Corinthians seem genuine enough but do not demonstrate that Paul intended them from the start. Even if Paul had to add to what he originally planned to write when news of fresh problems in Corinth arrived, it would be natural for him to rely on the

---

[138] E.g., Victor P. Furnish, *II Corinthians* (Garden City: Doubleday, 1984), 35–41; Thrall, *Second Corinthians,* vol. 1, 5–13.

[139] Thomas Schmeller, "Die Cicerobriefe und die Frage nach der Einheitlichkeit des 2. Korintherbriefs," *ZNW* 95 (2004): 181–208.

[140] Nor should the "super-apostles" be equated with the Jerusalem apostles or even viewed as endorsed by them (recall our discussion of the parallel problem in Galatians), as is done in C. K. Barrett, *The Second Epistle to the Corinthians* (London: Black; New York: Harper & Row, 1973), 28–32.

same theological foundation and conceptual framework that he had been using all along. It is hard to choose between the second and third alternatives presented here, but *perhaps the overall evidence slightly favors this third option.*[141]

Chapters 8–9   There are still other theories, though none of them is widely held, about the composite nature of 2 Corinthians. Chapter 8, beginning the discussion of the collection for Jerusalem, has seemed to some as if it were unrelated to the rest of the letter and therefore has been treated as a separate epistle. Chapter 8:1–5 seems to present an entirely positive portrait of the Macedonians, unlike the portrait of the harassment Paul outlines in 7:6, while rhetorical analyses have suggested ways of seeing chapters 8–9 as the body of a self-contained letter on its own.[142] On the other hand, the psychology of saving the problem of the collection until after Paul has praised the Corinthians as much as he can makes good sense of the existing structure. Chapter 7:5 more likely reflects non-Christian persecution of Paul, unrelated to his positive testimony about the Christians in northern Greece, while rhetorical analyses seem somewhat strained and require the omission of all of the introductory and concluding parts of the Hellenistic letter.

Still other scholars have tried to subdivide chapters 8 and 9 into separate letters or to leave chapter 8 with chapters 1–7 and then treat chapter 9 on its own. Particularly problematic for them is 9:1 ("There is no need for me to write to you about this service to the saints"), which appears to start all over again on the same topic as chapter 8. They thus argue that chapter 9 would be superfluous had Paul already written chapter 8 in the same letter.[143] On the other hand, the NIV leaves untranslated the first three Greek words of 9:1 (*peri men gar*—"For on the one hand concerning . . ."), which read far more naturally as a continuation of the topic of the previous chapter than the beginning of an independent letter. And despite Paul's claim that he need not address the topic, it is obvious even from chapter 9 alone that the Corinthians leave much to be desired in their understanding of stewardship. It is better, therefore, to take 9:1 as implying, "I shouldn't have to keep saying these things to you, [but I will . . .]." And the actual contents of chapter 9, for the most part, differ from those of chapter 8.[144]

Major and Minor Digressions?   Two other puzzling structural phenomena lead to still further theories of partition. Chapter *2:14–7:4* seems to function like a long digression about Paul's apostolic ministry, interrupting his discussion of his travels and his concern for how the Corinthians were progressing. More strikingly, if one passed over these chapters and moved directly from 2:13 to 7:5, the text would read completely smoothly ("I still had no peace of mind, because I did not find my brother Titus there. So I said good-bye to them and went on to Macedonia. So when we

---

[141] Cf. Ralph P. Martin, *2 Corinthians* (Waco: Word, 1986), xlvii–li; Carson and Moo, *An Introduction to the New Testament,* 434–36.

[142] See esp. Kieran J. O'Mahony, *Pauline Persuasion: A Sounding in 2 Corinthians 8–9* (Sheffield: SAP, 2000).

[143] For the fullest presentation of all the options concerning chapters 8 and 9, see Hans Dieter Betz (*2 Corinthians 8 and 9* [Philadelphia: Fortress, 1985]), who argues that each chapter was a separate letter.

[144] Cf. further Stanley K. Stowers, "Peri Men Gar and the Integrity of 2 Cor 8 and 9," *NovT* 32 (1990): 340–48.

came into Macedonia, this body of ours had no rest, but we were harassed at every turn—conflicts on the outside, fears within.").[145]

The same is true of *6:14–7:1.* This short paragraph on not being yoked together with unbelievers seems to digress entirely from Paul's appeal to the Corinthians to resume their earlier affection for him. And if one reads 6:13 and 7:2 back to back, it is clear that the two verses continue the identical theme ("As a fair exchange—I speak as to my children—open wide your hearts also. Make room for us in your hearts. We have wronged no one, we have corrupted no one, we have exploited no one."). Thus some scholars attribute one or both of these "digressions" to originally separate letters, and similarities between 6:14–7:1 and various Qumran writings lead a few commentators to suggest that Paul was borrowing from an Essene Jewish source similar to some found among the Dead Sea sect or that the paragraph is a fragment of an entirely non-Pauline source interpolated into what we now call 2 Corinthians.[146]

On the other hand, it is clear even from the framing sections of chapters 1–7 (1:1–2:13 and 7:5–15) that Paul's apostolic integrity has been called into question, so a long digression on this topic should cause no surprise. But "digression" seems scarcely the correct term for a section that is longer and more foundational to the letter than the framing material. A better case can be made for 2:14–7:4 forming *the most central section of the epistle.* As for the sutures between 2:13, 14 and between 7:4, 5, the commentary below will suggest rationales for the sequence of paragraphs as they stand.

The same will be the case with the location 6:14–7:1 itself. In addition, it is worth pointing out that the real unit of thought is 6:11–7:4 as a whole, that there are close thematic links between 7:5–6 on joy and comfort, that opening one's heart to Paul would naturally involve closing it to idolatry (thus accounting for the insertion of 6:14–7:1 into 6:11–7:4) and that the juxtaposition of 6:13 and 7:2 is not quite as smooth as most allege since it involves the conceptual repetition of opening/making room in the Corinthians' hearts. While numerous outlines of 2 Corinthians have been suggested and less consensus as to structural detail appears here than with any of Paul's other letters, a chiastic proposal for chapters 1–7 appears to point the way forward, accounting for some of the odd breaks in the second half of the outline (Paul is simply resuming the next topic required by proceeding through the first half of his outline in inverse fashion),[147] though other proposed structures can make sense of the text as it stands as well.[148]

---

[145] See esp. Günther Bornkamm, "The History of the Origin of the So-Called Second Letter to the Corinthians," *NTS* 8 (1962): 258–64.

[146] A recent study reviewing these hypotheses and building on them is Stephen J. Hultgren, "2 Cor 6.14–7.1 and Rev 21.3–8: Evidence for the Ephesian Redaction of 2 Corinthians," *NTS* 49 (2003): 39–56.

[147] Craig L. Blomberg, "The Structure of 2 Corinthians 1–7," *CTR* 4 (1989): 3–20. The first three matched sections of this chiasm are also identified by Laurence L. Welborn ("Like Broken Pieces of a Ring: 2 Cor 1.1–2.13; 7.5–16 and Ancient Theories of Literacy Unity," *NTS* 42 [1996]: 559–83), but he views them as two halves of an original letter, with 2:14–7:4 originally separate.

[148] See esp. David A. deSilva, "Meeting the Exigency of a Complex Rhetorical Situation: Paul's Strategy in 2 Corinthians 1 through 7," *AUSS* 34 (1996): 5–22.

SUMMARY AND OVERALL STRUCTURE

At any rate, Paul is now writing at least the majority, if not all, of what we call his second epistle probably in *A.D. 56, as he has left Ephesus and traveled overland to Troas and Macedonia and will soon be arriving in Corinth (2:12–13, 13:1).* He had dispatched Titus to prepare the way for his visit and has been eager to get his report as to how things were going in the church (2:13, 7:5). When he finally meets up with him, he is greatly relieved to learn of the generally positive response of the Corinthians thus far (7:6–7). Shortly thereafter he begins to write this epistle. It may be described (at least in the first seven chapters) as *a letter of apologetic self-commendation,* as Paul waxes eloquent about the nature of, and in defense of, his apostolic ministry.[149] A possible overall outline follows:

I.   Introduction and Thanksgiving (1:1–11)
    A. Greetings (1:1–2)
    B. Blessing (1:3–11)
II. Paul's Ministry with the Corinthians (1:12–7:16)
    A. Paul's Confidence in His Motives (1:12–22)
    B. Paul's Sorrow (1:23–2:11)
    C. Paul's Travels to Macedonia (2:12–13)
    D. A Series of Contrasts: Those Saved versus Those Perishing (2:14–4:6)
    E. Present Afflictions versus Coming Glory (4:7–5:10)
    F. The Core of Ministry: Reconciliation (5:11–21)
    G. Present Afflictions versus Present Glory (6:1–10)
    H. Christ versus Belial/Believers versus Unbelievers (6:11–7:4)
    I. Paul's Travel Report Resumed (7:5–7)
    J. The Corinthians' Sorrow (7:8–13a)
    K. Paul's Confidence in the Corinthians (7:13b–16)
III. The Collection for Jerusalem (8:1–9:15)
IV. "From Triumphalism to Maturity" (10:1–13:14)
    A. Paul versus the False or "Super" Apostles (10:1–12:13)
    B. Final Warnings and Greetings (12:14–13:14)
        1. Final Warnings (12:14–13:10)
        2. Final Greetings (13:11–14)

More so than in many of Paul's letters, one may therefore identify discrete sections in which each of the three kinds of Greco-Roman rhetoric dominate: forensic in the apologetic material (2:14–7:4), deliberative in the chapters on the collection (8–9), and epideictic—blame and censure—in the tirade against the false teachers (chaps. 10–13).[150]

---

[149] Linda L. Belleville, "A Letter of Apologetic Self-Commendation: 2 Cor. 1:8–7:16," *NovT* 31 (1989): 142–63.
[150] Cf. Witherington, *Conflict and Community in Corinth,* 46.

---

2 CORINTHIANS 1–7
PAUL'S MINISTRY WITH THE CORINTHIAN CHURCH

A   Confidence in His
　　Motives (1:12–22)

　　B   Sorrow for Those
　　　　Punished (1:23–2:11)

　　　　C   Upcoming Travel
　　　　　　Plans (2:12–13)

　　　　　　D   The Spirit vs. the Letter
　　　　　　　　(2:14–4:6) (New vs.
　　　　　　　　Old Covenant)

　　　　　　　　E   Present Afflictions
　　　　　　　　　　vs. Coming Glory
　　　　　　　　　　(4:7 5:10)

Confidence in the   **A**
Corinthians (7:13b–16)

Sorrow Among the   **B**
Corinthians (7:8–13a)

Travel Plans   **C**
(Resumed) (7:5–7)

Christ vs. Belial   **D**
(6:11–7:4)
(Belief vs. Unbelief)

Present Afflictions   **E**
vs. Present Glory
(6:1–10)

F   Core of Ministry –
Reconciliation
(5:11–21)

COMMENTARY

INTRODUCTION AND THANKSGIVING (1:1–11)

Greetings (1:1–2)   The introductory greetings in 2 Corinthians are less expansive than in Paul's previous letter to Corinth. Only Paul and Timothy write as coauthors, and they address only the church in and around Corinth in southern Greece. The form, however, closely follows the Hellenistic letter opening.

Blessing (1:3–11)   Paul departs from his characteristic thanksgiving form of prayer and composes a classic Jewish *berakah* or blessing. He still thanks or praises God but not so much for the Corinthians themselves as for God's comforting him in all his sufferings, which can overflow into the Corinthians' lives to encourage them also.[151] Despite the slightly different form, Paul still introduces key themes here that

---

[151] More specifically, Paul does not yet have as much to thank God for concerning the Corinthians, and he needs them to give thanks for him and what God is doing in and through him (Garland, *2 Corinthians*, 55–56).

will permeate his letter, most notably concerning affliction and consolation.[152] The noun and verb from the Greek root *parakal-* appear eight times in verses 3–7. The terms combine the ideas of comfort, consolation, encouragement, and exhortation. The barrage of these words in this short space makes Paul's "big idea" clear: God can pull us through even the hardest of times! *But God's comfort should not merely alleviate our affliction; in turn, we should be better equipped to comfort others who are afflicted. This is the first main principle on suffering that Paul presents in this letter.* Even in the secular arena, it is obvious that people who have endured specific illnesses or injuries (and matured from them) are often best poised to encourage and empathize with others having the identical problems. How much more in the spiritual realm, when God's supernatural power is available and at work!

Verses 8–11 refer to the particular hardships Paul has most immediately in mind. Undoubtedly, the Corinthians knew the details, but we do not, and Paul does not supply enough information for us to be sure what precise peril made him think he would not survive. The reference to Asia (Minor) naturally suggests circumstances in Ephesus. There is an ancient Christian tradition of Paul being imprisoned for a short time in that city (the Marcionite Prologue to Colossians), but we do not know how reliable it is.[153] First Corinthians 15:32 spoke of him fighting wild beasts there, and we noted in that context that the expression most likely referred to human opponents, since Roman citizens were exempt from literally being thrown to the animals. The actual opposition described in Acts 19 never becomes life threatening, so we must ultimately admit that every suggestion will remain somewhat speculative. What Paul wants us to go away with is not the scenario of his sufferings but God's remarkable deliverance of him from them, not least in response to the Corinthians' prayers.

PAUL'S MINISTRY WITH THE CORINTHIANS (1:12–7:16)

Paul's Confidence in His Motives (1:12–22)   Paul begins the body of his letter with a defense of his change in travel plans. Verses 12–14 insist that his motives were pure all along. No doubt some in Corinth saw his vacillation as a sign of weakness. If some of the spiritual elitists he had to confront in his first letter were still thinking that the apostles and not they were the worldly people, then Paul's defensiveness proves understandable, as he reverses those labels. And he is still sufficiently optimistic to hope that they will come around to understand things from his perspective. While not as clearly as in some of his letters, this opening paragraph of the body of the epistle can still be seen as announcing its overall theme. The boasting in which Paul engages, here and throughout the letter, does not refer to self-glorification but to "confidence" or "justifiable pride."[154]

Verses 15–17 specify the changed itinerary. By this time Paul had hoped to see the Corinthians in person twice more, but the unpleasant events that intervened in between his letters (see above) have kept him from coming. His new travel plans,

---

[152] Sze-Kar Wan, *Power in Weakness: The Second Letter of Paul to the Corinthians* (Harrisburg: Trinity, 2000), 34.

[153] Bruce, *Paul,* 298.

[154] Barnett, *Second Epistle to the Corinthians,* 94.

which would lead him to visit Macedonia twice and Corinth only once (rather than the other way around as previously hoped), could easily have been viewed as a snub by his critics.[155] His critics might even have quoted the Jesus tradition; after all, Christ himself had commanded his followers to let their yes be yes and their no be no—that is, to be people whose word could be trusted (Matt. 5:37).[156] Again, Paul turns the tables on his critics and points to Jesus' perfect model of integrity to defend his change in plans (vv. 19–20). What is more, God's Spirit dwelling within us has "sealed" (from *sphragizō*) us, functioning as a deposit or down payment (*arrabōn*) of his future maturing ministry in our lives (v. 22). Both terms are semitechnical ones in Paul's theology and provide a strong guarantee that "he who began a good work in [us] will carry it on to completion until the day of Christ Jesus" (Phil. 1:6).[157]

Paul's Sorrow (1:23–2:11)   Chapter 1:23–2:4 can be taken as the end of the section begun above because Paul explains that his decision not to visit Corinth at once was intended to spare them another unpleasant encounter. Apparently there still was too much conflict afoot (1:23–2:1). But 2:2–4 introduces the emotional language of grief and joy, distress and gladness, which ties the section in with 2:5–11. Paul wants the Corinthians to make him rejoice rather than anguish over their behavior, so he is giving them more time to mend their ways. The experience of writing the "painful letter" (see above, pp. 203–4) caused him enough grief; he would prefer not to repeat that experience in person.[158]

A significant portion of the conflict has involved a specific individual who appears to have opposed Paul, who in turn wrote to the Corinthians that they should discipline the man (2:5–11). It is tempting to equate this person with the incestuous offender of 1 Corinthians 5, in which case the letter alluded to in 2 Corinthians 2:9 could be 1 Corinthians, rather than the painful letter (unless those two are one and the same). But there are other possibilities (recall above, pp. 205–8). Whoever the man is and whatever he has done, the church has responded appropriately, and the offender has repented (cf. 7:8–13). So now Paul is concerned that they forgive him and welcome him back into their fellowship, lest prolonged alienation prove counterproductive (precisely what Satan would prefer). If the man has personally offended Paul, the apostle assures all the Corinthians that he extends his forgiveness as well.[159]

Paul's Travels to Macedonia (2:12–13)   Despite the delay and the new, more circuitous travel route, Paul is now at last coming, and he does not stop elsewhere, even for worthwhile ministry. "No good purpose is served, we learn, in any Christian's attempting a piece of service when his or her real interests lie elsewhere."[160] Paul's

---

[155] Victor P. Furnish, *II Corinthians* (Garden City: Doubleday, 1984), 144–45.

[156] Wenham, *Paul*, 271–74.

[157] A. J. Kerr ("*APPABΩN*," *JTS* 39 [1988]: 92–97) prefers the translation, "a first installment."

[158] On the role of pity, anger, and zeal in the framing material of chaps. 1–7, see Laurence L. Welborn, "Paul's Appeal to the Emotions in 2 Corinthians 1.1–2.13; 7.5–16," *JSNT* 82 (2001): 31–60.

[159] Cf. further Colin G. Kruse, "The Offender and the Offense in 2 Corinthians 2:5 and 7:12," *EQ* 60 (1988): 129–39.

[160] Martin, *2 Corinthians*, 42.

top priority is to meet up with Titus returning from Corinth and find out the news from that church. We expect Paul to continue with the description of his travels, but instead he breaks into a long "digression" from this topic (2:14–7:4). This section, however, should actually be seen as the heart of the body of the letter, describing in detail the nature of genuine apostolic ministry.

A Series of Contrasts: The Saved versus Those Perishing (2:14–4:6) Paul's literal travels lead him to reflect on another kind of travel procession—a victorious army returning from battle with prisoners of war in its train.[161] This is the imagery that lies behind the verb translated "leads us in triumphal procession" in 2:14. One and the same parade proves glorious for the army and ignominious for the POWs. So, too, Paul's apostolic travels, filled with so many hardships, seem to discredit him in the eyes of those who judge by worldly standards but remain a sign of legitimate ministry among those in the process of being saved.[162] Similarly, his ministry resembles an elixir of life for some but a deadly poison for others (vv. 15–16). The rabbis taught much the same thing about Torah.[163] Verse 17 represents how other itinerant Greco-Roman teachers often traveled—seeking money for ministry as they went. They also typically advertised themselves by letters of recommendation from people who knew them (3:1). Such practice leads Paul to contrast their written letters with the Corinthians, whom he calls living letters of recommendation for himself (3:2–6). *This contrast between two kinds of letters* parallels the differences between two kinds of tablets, one made of stone and the other of human hearts (v. 3). But speaking of these letters *also calls to mind the contrast between the "letter" of the Law and the Spirit* (v. 6), a comparison that will be developed in verses 7–18.[164]

The Mosaic covenant, of course, inaugurated the age of the law (or Old Testament period, as Christians subsequently called it), while the Spirit permanently indwells God's people in the age of the new covenant. In the Old Testament, Jeremiah had explicitly prophesied about this coming age (Jer. 31:31–34). *So it is natural for Paul to compare the glories of the two covenants.* The reference to tablets may also have made him think of the law since the Ten Commandments were given to Moses on tablets of stone on Mount Sinai. The specific contrast between the two kinds of glory (vv. 7–18) has puzzled many readers, especially because many English translations do not reflect the Greek accurately enough. The event to which verse 7 alludes appears in Exodus 34:29–30. There Moses descended from the mountain with the tablets, unaware that his face was radiant from having spoken with God. The people were afraid to approach him because of the supernatural glow. The text says nothing about the glory fading, though obviously it had to disappear some time. This pro-

---

[161] On this section and its narrative flow, see esp. Scott J. Hafemann, *Suffering and Ministry in the Spirit: Paul's Defense of His Ministry in II Corinthians 2:14–3:3* (Grand Rapids: Eerdmans, 1990).

[162] Cf. further Paul B. Duff, "Metaphor, Motif, and Meaning: the Rhetorical Strategy behind the Image 'Led in Triumph' in 2 Corinthians 2:14," *CBQ* 53 (1991): 79–92. For Paul, the procession may have resembled an epiphany parade of Roman dignitaries.

[163] Philip E. Hughes, *The Second Epistle to the Corinthians* (Grand Rapids: Eerdmans, 1962), 81.

[164] It is not sufficient to argue that Paul merely contrasts a legalistic use of the law with a spiritual one; rather, he contrasts an old age, which has now passed, with a new age and its new arrangements for putting people in right relationship with God. See Sigurd Grindheim, "The Law Kills but the Gospel Gives Life: The Letter-Spirit Dualism in 2 Corinthians 3.5–18," *JSNT* 84 (2001): 97–115.

cess was repeated whenever Moses entered and exited the Lord's presence (Exod. 34:33–35).

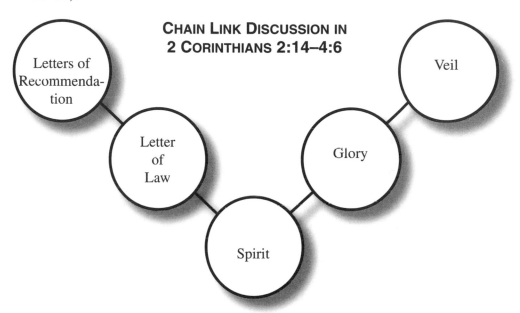

**CHAIN LINK DISCUSSION IN
2 CORINTHIANS 2:14–4:6**

Letters of Recommendation

Letter of Law

Veil

Glory

Spirit

Paul reasons that the ministry of the Spirit must be more glorious since it brings righteousness rather than the condemnation associated with the law. As in Galatians 3, he anticipates his fuller discussions in Romans 7 of the law's inability to save and in Romans 8 of the freedom the Spirit brings. Logically, then, the law must only condemn. He does not dispute that the law contained within itself provisions for forgiveness—animal sacrifice—but after the once-for-all sacrifice of Christ this approach no longer works. The only salvific function of the law is to point people to Christ (recall above, pp. 128–29).[165]

The comparison continues in verses 12–18. Verse 13 contains the sentence that is often mistranslated. The Old Testament does not indicate that Moses veiled his face to keep people from watching the glory fade. Quite the opposite, it was to keep them from being overwhelmed by its brightness! But a more literal translation of verse 13b reads, "So that the children of Israel might not attend to *the end of that which was being abolished.*" In view of the same participle ("being abolished" or "fading away") being employed of the covenant in verse 11, it is probably best to see Paul's use in verse 13 as likewise referring to the end or goal of the covenant and not to the fading radiance on Moses' face (as in v. 7). Of course, this too goes beyond the Old Testament text, but it does not contradict it. It also requires the 20-20 hindsight of living in the New Testament age, after it became clear that the Mosaic covenant was not permanent.[166]

---

[165] Cf. further Thrall, *Second Epistle to the Corinthians*, vol. 1, 235, 244.
[166] See further Linda L. Belleville, *Reflections of Glory: Paul's Polemical Use of the Moses-Doxa Tradition in 2 Corinthians 3* (Sheffield: JSOT, 1991), esp. p. 295. Cf. Carol K. Stockhausen, *Moses' Veil and the Glory of the New Covenant: The Exegetical Structure of II Cor. 3,1–4,6* (Rome: PIB, 1989).

The final play on words in this section involves the term "veil." If Moses placed a literal veil over his face, unbelievers who read the Old Testament in the Christian era but do not find Christ in it have a metaphorical veil covering their hearts, preventing a proper response (vv. 14–15). When they come to the Lord, however, then they can understand the Hebrew Scriptures completely (v. 16). And for Christians, the Lord is no longer simply God, nor even merely God in Christ, but the trinitarian God that includes the Holy Spirit. This Spirit brings freedom, not least from the law's inability to save, and also begins the process of transforming believers into increasing Christlikeness (vv. 17–18). This does not mean that we become gods ourselves, but we are more and more re-created in God's image, which we were originally intended to reflect without sin (Gen. 1:26–27). The word rendered "likeness" in the NIV is actually the word that the Septuagint uses (*eikōn*) to translate the Hebrew term for "image" in Genesis 1:26.[167]

Chapter 4:1–6 repeats and summarizes the main themes of this section: Paul's renunciation of deceptive forms of self-commendation, his straightforward presentation of the gospel, the twofold response of acceptance and rejection with which it meets, and the rationale for both kinds of response. The "god of this age" (v. 4) is, of course, Satan. But to include law-abiding Jews among those Satan has blinded created about as shocking a juxtaposition of concepts as Paul could have produced.[168]

Present Afflictions versus Coming Glory (4:7–5:10)   Despite the glories of the new covenant, they remain hidden all too often in the fragile, mortal, sinful, and persecuted human bodies of believers.[169] But Paul sees a positive side to this otherwise depressing state of affairs. *When Christians live above their grievous circumstances, it becomes more apparent to others that God's supernatural power sustains them (4:7–12). Here is a second principle on suffering and a reminder of how to cope* (recall p. 212, for the first reason). Verses 8–10 present the first of 2 Corinthians' three catalogs of hardships that Paul has experienced (cf. 6:4–10; 11:23b–27).[170] What proves particularly striking is how close to the "edge" God can allow his followers to come, yet he never permits them to fall off it, as long as they rely on his power.[171] Paul never displays a Stoic indifference to suffering. Hardships are real, they hurt, they discourage, and they are not a cause for celebration. They are not to be sought, though they can be endured, but only "with superhuman confidence and tenacity."[172]

---

[167] On the interpersonal attributes associated with this transformation, see R. Ward Wilson and Craig L. Blomberg, "The Image of God in Humanity: A Biblical-Psychological Perspective," *Themelios* 18.3 (1993): 8–15.

[168] Compare further Mohan Uddin, "Paul, a Devil and 'Unbelief' in Israel (with Particular Reference to 2 Corinthians 3–4 and Romans 9–11)," *TynB* 50 (1999): 265–80.

[169] Had Paul stopped at 4:6, he could have been accused of preaching the same message of power and strength as his opponents, but he immediately adds a section on his ministry of hardship—a more appropriate symbol for a message about Jesus' death (Wan, *Power in Weakness,* 77–78).

[170] On the imagery in these passages, see esp. Jack T. Fitzgerald, *Cracks in Earthen Vessels* (Atlanta: Scholars, 1988).

[171] There is a play on words in the Greek at the end of verse 8 that could be reflected in English with the translation "stressed, but not stressed out" (Garland, *2 Corinthians,* 229).

[172] William R. Baker, *2 Corinthians* (Joplin: College Press, 1999), 185.

The gospel requires a form to match its content, whether in preaching or in the preacher; thus God's treasure *must* remain in fragile, earthen vessels.[173]

A third principle on suffering is to recognize the eternal glory that one day will far more than compensate for the worst of hardships in this life (4:13–18). Even though Paul's bold witness for Christ leads to physical torture, he can look forward to his perfected, glorified, and resurrected body in the life to come (vv. 13–14). Meanwhile, people are coming to Christ through his ministry, which makes even present suffering worthwhile (v. 15). Thus Paul experiences spiritual renewal even as his body deteriorates (v. 16).[174] Verse 17 comprises one of the most remarkable statements in Scripture and demonstrates the drastically changed perspective that dwelling on eternal realities produces. Compared to an eternity of perfect bliss, even the worst and most prolonged of human agony pales into insignificance! The famous epithet that certain Christians "are so heavenly minded that they are no earthly good" must originally have been based in real personality traits of various individuals, even if somewhat caricatured. But today, by far the greater problem involves believers who are so earthly minded that they are no heavenly good! In striking contrast, Paul models a focus on invisible, eternal verities (v. 18).

Chapter 5:1–10 elaborates on eternal glory. Here Paul expands on the hope of a resurrected body. He refers to one's present physical body as an "earthly tent" that will be replaced by a "building from God, an eternal house in heaven" (v. 1). Because Paul uses the present tense, "we have," with his promise of a new body, some have imagined that he thought believers received it immediately upon death.[175] But this is hard to square with the teaching of 1 Thessalonians 4–5 and 1 Corinthians 15, which we have already surveyed. Much more likely, the verb employs the futurist use of the present tense to emphasize the certainty of resurrection, even if it occurs after some interval following one's death.

The metaphors of verses 2–4 present further exegetical riddles. Now Paul imagines putting on the new body, not as if one were undressing and changing clothes but as if one were putting on another garment on top of what one was already wearing (the verb *ependuomai* literally means "to overclothe"). Does this suggest that there will be no interval between death and receipt of one's resurrected body after all? This appears unlikely. More probably the imagery reflects Paul's preference for living until the parousia rather than experiencing the disembodied intermediate state between death and resurrection.[176] Either way, though, our new life is guaranteed,

---

[173] Stephen J. Kraftchick, "Death in Us, Life in You: The Apostolic Medium," in *Pauline Theology*, vol. 2, ed. David M. Hay (Minneapolis: Fortress, 1993), 172.

[174] Cf. esp. A. E. Harvey, *Renewal through Suffering: A Study of 2 Corinthians* (Edinburgh: T & T Clark, 1996). Harvey notes how unparalleled this perspective is in the history of religion, though it is not as clear how many of Paul's convictions developed only after 1 Corinthians.

[175] E.g., Murray J. Harris, *Raised Immortal* (London: Marshall, Morgan & Scott; Grand Rapids: Eerdmans, 1985), 219–26. Harris has now adopted a mediating position, in which he sees the "future acqusition of the spiritual body at death as an ideal possession actualized at the parousia" (idem, *The Second Epistle to the Corinthians* [Milton Keynes: Paternoster; Grand Rapids: Eerdmans, 2005], 378–80).

[176] Others argue for the concept of "soul sleep," in which people simply cease conscious existence at death, so that the next moment they experience is at the resurrection, however much later that turns out to be. But by far and away the most common understanding throughout church history is that Paul speaks of a conscious, disembodied intermediate state in which a believer's spirit experiences the presence of God. See esp. Joseph Osei-Bonsu, "Does

again by the Spirit's role in our lives (v. 5; the word for "deposit" is the same as in 1:22).

Verses 6–8 further support the doctrine of an intermediate state. As long as Christians remain in their physical bodies on earth, they do not experience the immediate presence of God as they will in the afterlife (v. 6). Indeed, they must exercise faith that an unseen realm, which God inhabits, exists in the first place (v. 7). Their preference would be to experience God more directly in the intermediate state, even if it meant being without a body for a time (v. 8).[177] But the time of their death is not theirs to choose, so that in whatever state they find themselves they still aim to please the Lord (v. 9) because when Christ does return and initiate the resurrection of all believers they will face him in judgment to give account for how they spent their lives (v. 10). This judgment, already depicted in 1 Corinthians 3:13–15, will provide a public demonstration of God's justice and mercy, not a first-time determination of the fate of the dead.

The Core of Ministry: Reconciliation (5:11–21) *This half chapter forms the theological heart of the epistle.* Ralph Martin has argued that its theme of reconciliation represents the center of all of Paul's thought.[178] If chapters 1–7 are chiastically structured (see above, p. 211), then this text also forms the center and climax of the chiasm. Reconciliation involves the reestablishment of a loving relationship between previously estranged parties. Like justification (recall on Gal. 2), it begins at conversion but is not complete until the eschaton.[179]

If we will be judged for how we live as believers, then we must share the gospel whenever we can (v. 11), not so that we can boast about it but so that others can take a rightful pride in our behavior (v. 12). Verse 13 could mean simply that some people will think this lifestyle insane, but Paul could be referring to his more ecstatic experiences (see on 12:1–6) or even to complaints against his style of rhetoric.[180] But he will put up with whatever reactions come his way for the sake of his ministry of the gospel (vv. 14–21). This tightly worded passage contains numerous items of crucial Christology: Christ's unlimited atonement (vv. 14–15), as one who was more than an ordinary man (v. 16), bringing about in the salvation of believers the foretaste of the promised re-creation of the cosmos (v. 17), offering himself as our substitute, and experiencing the wrath and judgment of God we deserved (vv. 18–19, 21). On the basis of Christ's sacrificial ministry, reconciling God and believers, we are called to be "ambassadors" of that reconciliation, including peace-making among believers (v. 20).

---

2 Cor 5.1–10 Teach the Reception of the Resurrection Body at the Moment at Death?" *JSNT* 28 (1986): 81–101; idem, "The Intermediate State in the New Testament," *SJT* 40 (1987): 571–90.

[177] On these verses, see esp. William L. Craig, "Paul's Dilemma in 2 Corinthians 5.1–10: A 'Catch-22'?" *NTS* 34 (1988): 145–47.

[178] Ralph P. Martin, *Reconciliation: A Study of Paul's Theology* (London: Marshall, Morgan & Scott; Atlanta: John Knox, 1981). For profound reflection on how reconciliation, not merely justice, must be the ultimate goal of all human, societal and spiritual relationships, which alone can then produce true justice, and with special reference to Paul's writings, see Miroslav Volf, "The Social Meanings of Reconciliation," *Int* 54 (2000): 158–72.

[179] For the fullest recent study of this word, see Stanley E. Porter, Καταλάσσω *in Ancient Greek Literature, with Reference to the Pauline Writings* (Córdoba: Ediciones el Almendro, 1994).

[180] Moyer Hubbard, "Was Paul out of His Mind? Re-reading 2 Corinthians 5.13," *JSNT* 70 (1998): 39–64.

Several specific items in verses 14–21 merit further attention. Verse 16b has often been used to allege that Christians need not understand the Jesus of history; what alone matters is that they believe in the risen Christ by faith. But that is to rip the verse entirely out of context; in context, it means that believers may no longer assess people, including Jesus, as if they had never been saved.[181] The full significance of verse 17 is also often missed. The Greek literally reads, "If anyone [is] in Christ, new creation"! In other words, if the messianic age has arrived enabling people to be united to the Messiah, then the beginning of the re-creation of the cosmos is underway. More than just personal renewal is involved (cf. Rom. 8:19–22). Finally, the literal wording of verse 21a proves significant. Here Paul writes, "[God] made him who had no sin [to be] sin on our behalf." As Murray Harris explains, "it seems Paul's intent [is] to say more than that Christ was made a sin offering and yet less than that Christ became a sinner. So complete was the identification of the sinless Christ with the sin of the sinner, including its dire guilt and its dread consequences of separation from God, that Paul could say profoundly, 'God made him . . . to be sin for us.'"[182]

Present Afflictions versus Present Glory (6:1–10) To the extent that chapters 1–9 follow the typical Greco-Roman letter structure, *here begins the more direct exhortational material.* Paul urges the Corinthians to continue returning to a true understanding of the gospel that is not embarrassed by the style of his apostolic ministry and his afflictions (vv. 1–3). His appeal that they not receive the grace of God in vain implies that they be reconciled to him since he is Christ's ambassador.[183] Paul also seems to retrace his steps through the topics discussed in the first five sections of 2:14–7:16, but this time in reverse order. Verses 4–10 present another poignant catalog of his sufferings comparable to 4:7–12, but here he contrasts them with the present blessings that help to offset them. The structure drives this point home in striking fashion. First he rehearses his severe afflictions (vv. 4–5), then abruptly in mid-sentence he shifts to the virtues by which the Spirit enables him to live above his circumstances (vv. 6–7), and finally to a series of contrasts between diametrically opposite interpretations of his ministry (vv. 8–10).

Christ versus Belial (Satan) / Believers versus Unbelievers (6:11–7:4) The second exhortation appeals to the church in Corinth to restore its original affection for Paul (6:11–14; 7:2–4). Into these framing paragraphs, Paul inserts his command not to be unequally yoked with unbelievers because of the vast gulf that separates belief and unbelief (6:14–7:1; recall the contrasts of 2:14–4:6).[184] The verb for "unequally

---

[181] See, e.g., James M. Scott, *2 Corinthians* (Peabody: Hendrickson; Carlisle: Paternoster, 1998), 134.

[182] Murray J. Harris, "2 Corinthians," in *The Expositor's Bible Commentary,* ed. Frank E. Gaebelein, vol. 10 (Grand Rapids: Zondervan, 1976), 354. Or, with N. T. Wright ("On Becoming the Righteousness of God: 2 Corinthians 5:21," in *Pauline Theology,* vol. 2, ed. David M. Hay [Minneapolis: Fortress, 1993], 206), "the covenant ambassador . . . represents the one for whom he speaks in such a full and thorough way that he actually *becomes* the living embodiment of this sovereign [as well as] the *dying* embodiment."

[183] Matera, *II Corinthians,* 150.

[184] Cf. also William J. Webb (*Returning Home: New Covenant: Second Exodus as the Context for 2 Corinthians 6.14–7.1* [Sheffield: JSOT, 1993]) for other connections between 6:14–7:1 and its context, based especially on the Old Testament traditions used within this segment.

yoked" (*heterozugeō*) is not the same one that is used elsewhere for marriage,[185] and in this context the only kind of "mismatch" that appears is between Christianity and idolatry. Given the specific mention of temples in verse 16, the kinds of problems involved in continuing to attend pagan religious services (recall 1 Cor. 8–10 and esp. 10:14–22) may be foremost in view.[186] For the minority of Christians in Corinth from a Jewish background, there may also be application to the law. Jewish boys, when they came of age, accepted upon themselves the "yoke of the Torah," by which they committed to obey the commandments of Moses. Christians, on the other hand, were under the "law of Christ" (Gal. 6:2; 1 Cor. 9:21). In the Old Testament, people separated from false religion geographically (vv. 17–18, quoting Isa. 52:11; Ezek. 20:34, 41), but Paul has already rejected that approach (1 Cor. 5:10), so presumably he is thinking here of moral separation from sin, not physical separation from sinners.

Paul's Travel Report Resumed (7:5–7)   At last Paul picks up where he left off in 2:13 and describes his elation at the arrival of Titus and the good news of the Corinthians' concern for Paul and their sorrow over their sin. Internal and external conflicts seemed the worst just before God comforted him through his coworker. The sky often appears the darkest just before the dawn.

The Corinthians' Sorrow (7:8–13a)   This section corresponds to 1:23–2:11 and especially to 2:5–11 in describing further the Corinthians' appropriate response to Paul's painful letter and his call to deal with the offending party in the church. Paul was afraid he had done more harm than good, but now rescinds any apologies he might have made because his severity produced godly sorrow leading to repentance. He reiterates that he was more concerned that the entire church react properly than merely that the offender change his ways. This forms a natural sequel to Paul's outrage in 1 Corinthians 5:2 that the congregation had boasted rather than grieving over the man living with his father's wife. Again, this does not prove the two passages are referring to the same individual, but they do fit nicely together.

Paul's Confidence in the Corinthians (7:13b–16)   Just as Paul began this large first section of the body of his epistle by speaking of the confidence he had in his own motives, he now ends by affirming his confidence in the Corinthians after the good report from Titus. This confidence encourages him to move on to the one remaining ethical topic of great importance to him, the collection for the believers in Jerusalem. Just as he had boasted to Titus that the Corinthians would finally come around and see things his way on the other matters he had addressed in previous letters and visits, so also he must enjoin them to carry through on their commitment to the collection (recall 1 Cor. 16:1–4).

---

[185]Other Hebrew, Greek, and Latin expressions meaning "yoke," however, *were* used for marriage, so it is difficult to know if Paul is deliberately avoiding them because he does *not* have marriage in view or if he is using a synonym, expecting the Corinthians to apply a similar metaphorical use here.

[186] Matera, *II Corinthians,* 162, including n. 62.

THE COLLECTION FOR JERUSALEM (8:1–9:15)

These two chapters form the longest uninterrupted teaching passage in the New Testament on stewardship. On the one hand, we must keep in mind the historical situation. Paul is organizing a collection for the impoverished, primarily Jewish Christians in Judea, still suffering in the aftermath of the famine of the late 40s. Scholars have often speculated that Paul placed a special importance on this offering because he hoped to show the more conservative Jewish churches in Israel that the Gentile believers in the Diaspora recognized the debt they owed to the "mother church." Undoubtedly, he wanted to bridge the gap between the two diverse groups and bring greater unity to the empire-wide Christian movement.

More speculatively, he may have hoped that unbelieving Jews in and around Jerusalem would come to faith in Christ when they saw how generously the Gentile Christians shared with their Jewish brothers and sisters. We have already seen the hints in Acts (20:4; 21:24) which suggest that Luke knew about the collection, but his refusal to describe it explicitly may well suggest that it failed to accomplish Paul's objective. On the other hand, the principles Paul outlines here in 2 Corinthians prove remarkably applicable to Christian giving in just about any context.[187] Throughout, words deriving from the *char-* stem for "grace" in Greek predominate, reminding us that even the desire and ability to give is a gift from God.

We may enumerate *four overarching principles in 8:1–15. First,* sacrificial giving proves most praiseworthy (vv. 1–4). The poorer Macedonian Christians surprised Paul by contributing far beyond what he thought they were able to offer. Indeed, he seems not to have planned on asking them to help out at all, but they pled for the opportunity, which they viewed as a privilege. In this light, surely the richer Corinthians could do much, much better![188]

Second, fully Christian giving emerges as part of the larger surrender of one's entire self to Christ (vv. 5–7). Again following the Macedonians' lead, Paul urges that the project form part of the Corinthians' overall service to the Lord and submission to his will. Derivatively, it will reflect their submission to Paul's apostolic authority as well.[189] Verse 7 suggests that this issue remains the one area introduced in Paul's first epistle on which the Corinthians have made no progress.

Third, believers should demonstrate their sincerity by following through on their financial commitments (vv. 8–11). In this setting, it is not so much the size of the gift that matters as the fact that the Corinthians had originally taken the lead in the collection and made promises of further generous giving. Now they were in danger of reneging on those promises and making themselves and the apostle look foolish in the eyes of their poorer Macedonian counterparts. If Jesus could give up the eternal splendors of heaven to become incarnate as a man and be born and die in ignominy, surely the richer Corinthians could sit a little more loosely to their wealth.

---

[187] The two most important book-length studies of this collection are Dieter Georgi, *Remembering the Poor: The History of Paul's Collection in Jerusalem* (Nashville: Abingdon, 1992); and Keith F. Nickle, *The Collection* (London: SCM; Naperville: Allenson, 1966).

[188] Betz (*2 Corinthians 8 and 9,* 48) notes the additional dynamic of an ethnic and political rivalry between Corinth and Macedonia, which would have made Paul's comparisons between the two motivate even more.

[189] Martin, *2 Corinthians,* 255.

Fourth, giving should be proportional to one's income (vv. 12–15). Occasionally, when Christian leaders appeal for sacrificial donations, listeners wonder if they are asking them to trade places with the poor. Paul explicitly refutes this notion (v. 13). He is requesting merely that they give from their surplus but that they be ruthlessly honest about how much *is* surplus![190] Applying the Golden Rule (Matt. 7:12), they should contribute as much as they would want to receive if in another context they turned out to be the ones in dire straits (v. 14). God's provision of manna in the wilderness (Exod. 16:18) provided an apt parallel. Different Israelites had different needs and varying abilities to gather the flaky bread-like substance. Thus the "equality" was hardly ever absolute. But God saw to it both that no one starved and that no one had more than they could reasonably eat (v. 15). God's people today should voluntarily work toward creating similar equity.[191]

Tellingly, nothing appears here or anywhere else in the New Testament after the death and resurrection of Christ (i.e., when the age of the law gave way to the era of the gospel) about giving a tithe. Christians who support a tithe often do not realize that the Old Testament commanded three separate offerings, which came to be understood as requiring faithful Jews to give 23 1/3 percent of all their annual earnings to the Lord's work in various arenas. Plus they had their temple tax (and under Rome hefty additional tribute to pay to the occupying empire).[192] Even if someone today were prepared to imitate ancient Judaism in these respects, the point of this passage would be missed. For most millionaires, even giving away 20 percent of their earnings scarcely seems sacrificial. For someone below the poverty line, even a tithe may reflect irresponsible giving of money desperately needed for basic necessities. What fairly qualifies as sacrificial or generous cannot be tied to a percentage but must be decided on a person-by-person, situation-by-situation basis.[193] Freedom in giving "runs the risk of some people giving less than ten percent," but "it also opens the doors for unlimited generosity well beyond ten percent."[194]

In 8:16–9:5, Paul turns to *the protection of giving.* He gives elaborate instructions about how various people will accompany the gift to Jerusalem so that all goes where it is earmarked and there can be little chance of financial mismanagement. The list of Paul's travel companions in Acts 20:4 suggests that he was concerned to have representatives from as many of the regions involved in the collection as possible. Some have wondered if the "brother who is praised by all the churches for his service to the gospel" in 8:18 was Luke. He certainly would have qualified for this label, but only if "the gospel" is taken to mean the written book that bears his name is there any reason for selecting Luke out of numerous first-generation Christians who could be described by this expression. And that is not how Paul uses the word for "gospel" anywhere else in his writings.

---

[190] Cf. further Wan, *Power in Weakness,* 110.

[191] Indeed, "equity" or "that which is equitable" is probably a better translation in this context than "equality." See Linda L. Belleville, *2 Corinthians* (Leicester and Downers Grove: IVP, 1996), 223.

[192] Cf. further Blomberg, *Neither Poverty nor Riches,* 46–49.

[193] Cf. Garland, *2 Corinthians,* 381: "Some can give far more than the tithe and have more than enough to provide all the necessities of life. Others barely have two mites for their daily needs."

[194] Baker, *2 Corinthians,* 329.

Interestingly, Acts makes no mention of any representative from Corinth or anywhere else in Achaia. Perhaps this reflects the Corinthians' reluctance to participate, although Romans 15:26–27a suggests that they eventually came around, at least to some degree. But the representatives served a second purpose as well, helping to hold the Corinthians accountable to their original promises (9:3–5). While a number of individuals accompany the delivery of the collection to Judea, it appears that only Titus and two unnamed individuals go to Corinth to retrieve their donations. This trio creates the interesting dynamic of combining one man chosen by Paul (8:17–18), one chosen by the other churches (8:19), and one in whom both Paul and the churches have confidence (8:22–23). Thus if any dispute should ensue between Paul and the churches involved in the collection, each side will have someone to represent them and a third party who is trusted by both. One could hardly imagine greater parity.[195]

Chapter 9:6–15, finally, specifies *the rewards of giving*. God's blessings are proportionate to the generosity of any person's particular gift (v. 6). Giving should be voluntary, not coerced; but once one understands the principle of verse 6, one will want to give generously (v. 7). These blessings cannot be limited to material resources as verses 8–11 clarify: Paul is referring to all forms of grace that enable believers to do good, reap righteousness, and become rich in every way that God knows will contribute to that person's spiritual growth.[196] Obviously, many faithful Christians throughout history have suffered impoverishment through no fault of their own. But we should not forget 8:13–15 as God's desired mechanism of alleviating such poverty: meeting the financial needs of his people through the generosity of the church. Given the juxtaposition of 9:8 and 9 here, part of the "good work" that God's gifts enable us to "abound in" must involve passing on some of those gifts to the poor.[197]

When the church shares in this fashion, obviously many people will praise and thank God for the help they receive (vv. 12–15). But verse 13 makes it difficult to limit this thanksgiving just to the believers directly helped. Even if "everyone else" hyperbolically generalizes somewhat, Paul surely would not have included these two words unless he imagined a wider group of people, including unbelievers who will come to the Lord in part because they see the exemplary sharing of the Christian community. Nor can believers imagine that their responsibilities lie only with needy Christians locally. After all, this entire collection involved people from throughout the empire, demonstrating practical concern for believers in a quite distant part of their world.[198]

---

[195] Betz, *2 Corinthians 8 and 9*, 78.

[196] "There is no hint here of a 'prosperity theology.' Enrichment, like 'overflowing' (v. 8), is metaphorical, and is not at all motivated by self-interest. This 'ministry' is for the purpose of generosity, and that with a view to thanksgiving to God" (Barnett, *Second Epistle to the Corinthians*, 443).

[197] Wan (*Power in Weakness*, 120) thus labels the "self-sufficiency" of v. 8 "nothing more than a middle-term between grace and good work."

[198] Paul believes "in a worldwide covenant fraternity, for which the constituent members had obligations of reciprocity. Paul is not narrowly congregationalist nor individualistic in his outlook" (Barnett, *Second Corinthians*, 447).

"FROM TRIUMPHALISM TO MATURITY" (10:1–13:14)[199]

Paul versus the False or "Super Apostles" (10:1–12:13) Suddenly Paul unleashes a torrent of sarcasm against new intruders into the Corinthian church who are promoting a Judaizing and triumphalist form of Christianity.[200] He refers to these individuals alternately as "false apostles" (e.g., 11:13) and, ironically, reflecting their self-estimation, as "super-apostles" (e.g., 11:5). He probably does not have any of the Twelve in view but interlopers who are falsely claiming to reflect the Jewish-Christian perspective (as in Galatia). They are boasting in their ethnic and ministerial credentials in ways that forced Paul to "return the favor." But Paul will boast primarily in his weakness, in spiritual attributes that the worldly criteria of these Judaizers demean.[201] We may itemize six of these attributes, one for each of the major subsections of 10:1–12:10. These criteria remain as valid today as they were in the first century.

First, we must rely on spiritual rather than fleshly authority (10:1–11). Paul is accused of being weak when personally present with the Corinthians but then threatening them more forcefully from a distance (v. 1). So he makes clear that he could take decisive action when he arrives (v. 2). But he prefers not to use his apostolic authority in a heavy-handed fashion, both because that is not consistent with servant leadership and because of his affection for the churches he has personally planted (see 1 Cor. 4). What seems weak by worldly standards may actually reflect divine power (vv. 3–4; recall 1 Cor. 1:18–2:5). This power will ultimately destroy all of the non-Christian forces that appear so much stronger in this age (vv. 5–6). In modern discussions of spiritual warfare, verse 4 is often cited out of context, with "strongholds" referring to overtly demonic activity, so that the Christian is promised to be able to repel Satan in various supernatural encounters with his evil horde. Such a promise may be implied in other texts (e.g. 1 John 4:4), but not here. In this context, Paul is declaring the gospel's superiority to non-Christian philosophical ideologies, which have enthralled his Corinthian opponents (v. 5). As Paul abundantly demonstrates throughout his letters, these are combated by rigorous, logical refutation combined with the Holy Spirit's guidance. Ironically, it is often the more anti-intellectual wing of the church that appeals to this passage as if the Spirit and the mind remained opposed to one another. But in fact, each is indispensable (recall 1 Cor. 2:6–16).

Alister McGrath has alleged that "the future of Evangelicalism lies in the forging of rigorous theological foundations and intellectual credibility." But "for this to

---

[199] Borrowing the title of the excellent exposition of these four chapters by D. A. Carson (Grand Rapids: Baker, 1984).

[200] "Meekness and gentleness" are the pejorative terms for the manifestations of what Paul's opponents believe to be his weaknesses. The NIV could just as easily have put them in quotation marks as they did "timid" and "bold" later in v. 1. See Carson, *From Triumphalism to Maturity*, 101. Alternatively, perhaps Paul is using only "mild irony," and his words should be translated, "by the leniency and clemency of Christ." See Donald D. Walker, *Paul's Offer of Leniency (2 Cor 10:1)* (Tübingen: Mohr, 2002).

[201] These charges, in particular, point to Paul's redefinitions of "masculinity" *vis-à-vis* his culture (Jennifer Larson, "Paul's Masculinity," *JBL* 123 [2004]: 85–97) and his boasting in beatings, rather than war wounds, another cultural sign of ignominy (Jennifer A. Glancy, "Boasting of Beatings" [2 Corinthians 11:23–25], ibid., 99–135.

happen, Christ must reign supreme in our minds."[202] Thus when Paul's detractors look only at his lack of formal, rhetorical training and at his plainness of oratory, they misjudge him and fail to appreciate both the cogency of his reasoning and the Spirit's power resident within him (vv. 7–11).

Second, we should limit our work to territories that have not been allotted to others (10:12–18). Not all of the factionalism behind 1 Corinthians has disappeared, and the newly arrived false teachers are simply making matters worse. Although Paul planted the Corinthian church, others, whether local house-group leaders or the outside interlopers, are trying to take credit, redirect attention to themselves, and insist that they are outperforming Paul. Two lines of reasoning comprise a proper reply. To begin with, such comparisons and self-commendation prove unwise, most notably because they often do not reflect the Lord's assessment of individuals (vv. 12, 18). Even more importantly, such competition for the allegiance of a specific congregation diverts attention from the more fundamental task of outreach to those who have not yet heard the gospel (vv. 13–16).

As we saw in Acts, Paul consistently aimed to plant churches, disciple fledgling believers, appoint indigenous leadership, and move on to a new area as quickly as possible. Today, a disproportionately large amount of Christian ministry occurs in already well-evangelized parts of the world, while unreached people and people groups receive comparatively scant attention. Undoubtedly, the Lord today wishes that many more believers would implement the "regions beyond" (v. 16) priorities of this passage.[203] Of course, that would often mean far less outward church growth, which makes ministries look more anemic to those judging by worldly standards, but the only kind of boasting that counts for anything is boasting in what God does, not in what we do (v. 17).

Third, we should reject every kind of "knowledge" that turns one away from Christ to Satan, regardless of any masquerade that may attempt to confuse the two (11:1–6, 13–15). Having just denounced those who are elevating themselves at Paul's expense by appealing to worldly standards of success, Paul now recognizes that he must make some comparisons between the false teachers and him to correct the misunderstandings afoot in Corinth. Admitting the incongruity, he speaks of what he is about to write as a little "foolishness" (v. 1). But he recognizes that the competing perversions of the Christian message so seriously misrepresent it that people's eternal destinies are at stake. So he must defend his apostolic authority as in no way inferior to his opponents' alleged links with the apostles in Jerusalem (vv. 2–6). Whether because of the opposition's Judaizing or due to its triumphalism (or both), he must label its spokesmen as false apostles who are unwittingly being used by the devil. Such duplicity should not surprise since evil often appears superficially

---

[202] Belleville, *2 Corinthians*, 256; summarizing Alister McGrath, "Why Evangelicalism Is the Future of Protestantism," *CT* 39 (1995): 18.

[203] Even in ministries with objectives other than frontline evangelism, the question must be asked if a given venture merely duplicates what other evangelical Christians are already doing well nearby (in which case cooperation rather than competition proves essential) or if it truly addresses an unmet need.

attractive (vv. 13–15).[204] The language in verse 4 about "a different spirit" or "a different gospel" and in verse 14 about deceitful angels so closely resembles the warnings of Galatians 1:6–9 that Paul probably recognizes the same kind of Judaizers in Corinth as those who previously afflicted Antioch and Galatia.[205]

Fourth, we should not accept money for ministry whenever it might call the integrity of our message into question (11:7–12). As we saw in conjunction with 1 Corinthians 9, itinerant philosophers and orators in ancient Greece and Rome often charged large sums for public declamations, while Paul preached his message free of charge. The Judaizers probably requested support, too. The mind-set among Paul's detractors stemmed from the notion, still prevalent today, that "you get what you pay for." So Paul must explain his rationale. He did accept financial support from other churches (v. 8),[206] most notably Philippi, but even then he has to ensure that the gift comes with no strings attached (see under Phil. 4:10–20). Wealthy patrons who often funded rhetorical enterprises expected, to some degree, to be able to control the contents of the oratory, whereas Paul will tolerate no interference with words he believes come from God himself. Additionally, he recognizes that to solicit funds from a church already reluctant to give generously to a collection for needier Christians would unnecessarily burden them even more. Out of love for them, he therefore refrains from asking for any support for himself (v. 11).[207]

Fifth, we may expect persecution even when we have full authority to be ministering as we are (11:16–33). In Paul's case his impeccable Jewish pedigree by itself qualified him to understand the role of Torah in the age of the gospel. To the extent that the Judaizers were boasting in their Jewish credentials, Paul can match them point for point (v. 22). But he recognizes it is still foolishness to make these kinds of comparisons (vv. 16–19).[208] If he has to defend the legitimacy of his apostolicity, he will do so by challenging them to match his sufferings. If true Christian authority appears in servant leadership, often seeming weak to those employing worldly criteria of strength and power, then it is his persecutions and hardships that help demonstrate the Spirit's role in his life (vv. 23b–29). This catalog of sufferings combines experiences caused directly by his ministry (most notably, his imprisonments, floggings,[209] and stoning) and events common to those who traveled widely throughout the em-

---

[204] Paul Barnett (*The Message of 2 Corinthians: Power in Weakness* [Leicester and Downers Grove: IVP, 1988], 170) observes that this letter has thus revealed a threefold role for Satan: he seeks to divide the church by bitterness and unforgiveness (2:10–11), to maintain sinners in spiritual blindness (4:4), and to sever the believer from Christ via false doctrine (11:3, 14).

[205] Wan, *Power in Weakness,* 139.

[206] Paul's claim to have "robbed other churches" is entirely sarcastic and, in fact, underlines his appreciation for his supporters (Baker, *2 Corinthians,* 384).

[207] At the same time, by having to rely on manual labor to support himself, Paul would have endured the scorn of the upper classes who despised such work (see Cicero, *De officiis* 150–51) and could have been perceived as rejecting an offer of friendship and declaring himself an enemy of the would-be patrons (Keener, *1–2 Corinthians,* 229).

[208] The references to violence in vv. 20–21 are probably metaphorical, just as the slavery and exploitation are in v. 20. Both refer to the authoritarian ways of the false teachers, including their demands for support.

[209] The thirty-nine lashes were administered by Jewish synagogue leaders. Paul could have avoided these punishments altogether by simply renouncing his Judaism and making a clean break from its institutions. His refusal to do so demonstrates not only his theological understanding of Christianity as the fulfillment of Judaism, but his incredible desire to win his coreligionists to his newly found faith so that he would stay within the orbit of their discipline.

pire (e.g., shipwreck, robbery, hunger, and the like). After a list that would discourage anyone (vv. 23b–27), Paul appears to conclude anticlimactically with the daily pressure of his "concern for all the churches" (vv. 28–29). But this last hardship is the only one on the list that never went away, so it forms an appropriate climax after all. Pastoral ministry in every age, when practiced wholeheartedly, will generate the same pressure and concern.[210]

Verses 30–33 then depict the ultimate ignominy—being snuck out of town in a basket lowered over the city walls of Damascus—the exact antithesis of the highest military honor of the day, which was given to the soldier who was first to *scale* enemy walls. Truly Paul was boasting in his weaknesses to the nth degree![211] At the same time, it is important to realize that certain Greco-Roman philosophy had acknowledged that boasting in one's weakness was acceptable and in fact the noblest kind of self-commendation possible. So even as Paul denounces the overemphasis on rhetorical sophistication that placed form above substance and focused attention entirely on the individual orator, he knows enough philosophy and rhetoric to use to his own advantage an oratorical device that undergirded the message of the gospel.[212]

Sixth, and finally, we must endure our "thorns in the flesh," in spite of any wonderful spiritual experiences God may have granted us (12:1–13). The juxtaposition of verses 1–6 and 7–10 produces a jarring dissonance. In the first paragraph, Paul describes "visions and revelations from the Lord," much as the false teachers may have been claiming (v. 1). He then depicts perhaps the most dramatic example of these that he has experienced (vv. 2–5). At first it seems that he is speaking about someone else because he writes in the third-person, but by verse 7 he reverts to the first-person form. At that point it becomes clear that he has been speaking of himself all along, but because he wants to distance himself from this kind of elitist spiritual experience, he describes it as if it happened to another person. The details of his visit to heaven remain vague.[213] He does not even know if he had a genuine out-of-the-body experience or a more subjective vision of some kind (vv. 2–3). God did not allow him to tell others what he heard during this time (v. 4), so we really have no way of knowing what went on. Moreover, Paul recognizes that to brag about the

---

[210] The depth of a good pastor's daily concern for his or her "flock" is a hardship that few people not in such a position appreciate. Cf. Matera, *II Corinthians*, 220.

[211] Second Corinthians 10:3–6 presents the most extensive use of military imagery anywhere in Paul's epistles, yet by 11:32, his self-portrayal as a kind of military figure becomes the soldier who escapes down the wall, defeated and humiliated from a worldly perspective but spiritually empowered from God's vantage point (Brian Peterson, "Conquest, Control, and Cross: Paul's Self-Portrayal in 2 Corinthians 10–13," *Int* 52 [1998]: 258–70).

[212] Christopher Forbes, "Comparison, Self-Praise and Irony: Paul's Boasting in the Conventions of Hellenistic Rhetoric," *NTS* 32 (1986): 1–30.

[213] Jewish apocalyptic thinking often spoke of three or even seven heavens, the last one being the place where Yahweh himself dwelt. In the case of three heavens, the first represented the visible sky with sun, moon, and stars. The second referred to the invisible realm where angels and demons often did battle. The third contained the very throne room of God. The word "paradise" in v. 4 derived from a Persian loan-word referring to a beautiful park and came to be used by Jews and Christians alike for the delightful afterlife that God's people would experience. For a thorough study of 12:2–4, with the conviction that Paul's glimpses of the highest heaven enabled him to write in this letter and elsewhere, so positively and assuredly about the coming glory that far outweighs present suffering, see James D. Tabor, *Things Unutterable: Paul's Ascent to Paradise in its Greco-Roman, Judaic, and Early Christian Contexts* (Lanham and London: UPA, 1986).

awesomeness of his heavenly journey would simply be to exalt himself over the false apostles using their carnal criteria (vv. 5–6).[214]

To drive this point home, Paul immediately narrates an opposite experience that has kept him humble in spite of the remarkable spiritual privileges God has granted him. This famous "thorn in the flesh" (v. 7) has puzzled readers throughout church history. The main categories of interpretations have included a recurring physical ailment, a personal opponent, and spiritual warfare more generally. The latter two options stem from the fact that Paul also identifies the problem as "a messenger of Satan," but the literal meaning of "thorn" (*skolops*) is "stake," and the only natural way to interpret a stake in one's "flesh" is as some bodily affliction.[215] Here the two most common suggestions have been eye problems and malaria (recall above, p. 92), but we must honestly admit we cannot know the specifics. No doubt the Corinthians knew what was troubling Paul, and it may be providential that he does not tell us. After all, our natural inclination would be to argue that Paul's teaching applied only to people who suffered an identical malady.

THIRD HEAVEN	God's throne
SECOND HEAVEN	Angelic and demonic realm
FIRST HEAVEN	Atmosphere

As it stands, the Lord's answer to Paul's repeated fervent prayer for relief can apply to virtually any form of suffering that Christians experience through no fault of their own: *"My grace is sufficient for you, for my power is made perfect in weakness." This is the climax of this epistle's teaching about how to understand and respond to suffering, and it is the epitome of a perspective flatly contrary to the standard approaches of this fallen world.*[216] Not surprisingly, Christ speaks directly to Paul to underline this principle; verse 9 is the only "red-letter" verse in 2 Corinthians.

---

[214] This approach in fact provides a model for how believers should treat many of their most personal spiritual experiences with God, whether "charismatic" or not. It is probably wise to "keep them private as much as possible and not use them as barometers to compare spiritual depth or maturity" (Baker, *2 Corinthians,* 427).

[215] Cf. the thorough discussion of options and conclusions in Thrall, *Second Corinthians,* vol. 2, 814–18. The most vociferous opponents of this view are often those who refuse to accept the idea that God may not want a person physically healed. This idea tends to appear more commonly in certain charismatic circles, but see John Christopher Thomas, "'An Angel from Satan': Paul's Thorn in the Flesh (2 Corinthians 12.7–10)," *JPT* 9 (1996): 39–52. Thomas argues as a charismatic scholar that a physical ailment nevertheless represents the most likely meaning of Paul's thorn here.

[216] Baker (*2 Corinthians,* 433) rightly calls this verse the "signature motto" for the whole letter and for Paul's entire apostolic life. For a profound exploration of this theme throughout the epistle, see Timothy B. Savage, *Power through Weakness: Paul's Understanding of the Christian Ministry in 2 Corinthians* (Cambridge and New York: CUP, 1997).

Verses 11–13 transition to the final main section of this letter. Paul reiterates once more that his boasting has been foolish. But the danger posed by the competition has driven him to it. If the Judaizers impress the Corinthians with their miracle-working ability, God used Paul in similar ways on previous occasions (v. 12). The only arena in which Paul's ministry does not measure up is in the amount he charged—nothing (v. 13)! This entire section, indeed the whole epistle, represents the most sustained theological rebuttal to the so-called "health-wealth gospel" found anywhere in Scripture. Christians must always remember that God can often use them in their weaknesses, including illness and poverty, better than he can in other situations because we remain more visibly dependent on him.

Final Warnings and Greetings (12:14–13:14) *Final Warnings (12:14–13:10)* Paul's closing comments prepare his readers for his impending visit. He desperately wants to be able to display his love for the Corinthians, like parents showering their affection on their children. In fact, this analogy offers one more reason for not charging the church for his ministry—parents support their children as they are growing up, not vice versa (vv. 14–18). But if the congregation has not substantially changed its ways by the time he arrives, Paul will instigate whatever discipline is necessary (vv. 19–21). Because this will be his third visit to Corinth, Paul thinks of the Deuteronomic command that requires two or three witnesses to establish various legal matters (Deut. 19:15). Metaphorically, each of his visits functions as a witness to the condition of the church in Corinth. By this time, their response to his commands will be completely clear and, if they have not obeyed, Paul will be fully justified in punishing the recalcitrant as severely as necessary. The centrality of Christ's crucifixion regularly requires living in ways the world considers weak, but Jesus' resurrection gives believers great power as well, including the authority and responsibility to discipline the wayward in their midst (13:1–4).

Chapter 13:5–10 proceeds with a call to the Corinthians to examine themselves to see if they really are Christians. People who buy into so diametrically opposite a message from the cross-centered gospel of power through weakness must make sure they really have the Spirit of Jesus living in them. If they do, they will also admit that Paul preaches the truth and the intruders represent a lie. Then he will not have to treat them harshly when he arrives, and he can use his authority to edify them instead.

Final Greetings (13:11–14) A final call to live in the peace that produces restored community[217] gives way to the standard command to exchange the holy kiss. All the believers with Paul send greetings. The most distinctive feature of this letter closing is the trinitarian benediction in verse 14. "May the grace of the Lord Jesus Christ, and the love of God, and the fellowship of the Holy Spirit be with you all," remains a cherished prayer to end worship services in many parts of the world to this day.

---

[217] The verb *katartizō* essentially means to mend, restore, or set right more than to "aim for perfection" (NIV). See Garland, *2 Corinthians*, 552–53.

APPLICATION

In a word, the theological problem of the Corinthians throughout both epistles has been triumphalism or, as we have suggested in our titles to these last two chapters, a vastly overrated sense of their own maturity in Christ. Triumphalism remains an insidious danger in modern Western evangelicalism in the twenty-first century. In the mid-1970s, American evangelicals traded places with more liberal expressions of Christianity by becoming the more affluent wing of the church in the United States, and their riches have multiplied ever since. In some charismatic circles, we have watched the emergence of the "name it and claim it" heresy; other less explicitly heretical fellowships nevertheless remain enthralled with the miraculous, at times bordering on the bizarre, rather than reveling in the cross-centered gospel of power in weakness. As successful missionary and evangelistic ventures in various parts of the Third World explode with growth, a resurgence of postmillennialism sweeps certain circles. Some set dates or at least confidently proclaim that within one generation we will fulfill the Great Commission and usher in Christ's return. Meanwhile, our theologies of suffering remain anemic, and we threaten to give up our commitments to God and one another at the slightest signs of hardship.

Other examples of a misguided triumphalism include church growth schemes that virtually guarantee success if precise formulas are followed; self-help literature, recordings, and seminars on countless topics that promise good results if one simply does what the instructions outline; and the assumption of many college and seminary graduates that their education entitles them to "successful" careers by the worldly criteria of income, size, and influence. The list could be extended at length, and the next generation will undoubtedly create new manifestations of this ancient temptation. Second Corinthians 8–9 alone should challenge most Western Christians to reorder their personal and corporate spending practices in dramatic ways. And chapters 10–13 remind us, just as 1 Corinthians 5 and 9 did, not to kowtow to the legalistic believer while ignoring the lost outside our churches. Precisely the opposite is required: sharp rebukes and, if necessary, discipline for the overly narrow religious insider who should know better, accompanied by imaginative forms of outreach to the outsider that bend over backwards to place no unnecessary obstacle in the path of anyone coming to Christ.[218]

ADDITIONAL QUESTIONS FOR REVIEW

1. Based on the available evidence, reconstruct the most likely order of the communication between Paul and the Corinthians, including both written letters and personal visits by Paul and both written letters and personal emissaries bringing news from Corinth to Paul.

2. How is the difficulty of the seemingly disjointed chapters 10–13 of 2 Corinthians best resolved? What are the other competing options?

---

[218] Cf. further Craig L. Blomberg, "The New Testament Definition of Heresy (or When Do Jesus and the Apostles Really Get Mad?)," *JETS* 45 (2002): 59–72.

3. What are the main principles on suffering that Paul presents in 2 Corinthians?
4. How does the situation with the man in the incestuous relationship, which was first presented in 1 Corinthians, become resolved in 2 Corinthians? What principles does this offer us for following up on situations where church discipline has been exercised?
5. Taken together with other Pauline texts on the hope of a resurrected body (esp. 1 Thess. 4–5 and 1 Cor. 15), what does 2 Corinthians 5:1–10 suggest about the interval between death and receiving an eternal, resurrected body? Why does Paul prefer the disembodied state to life here on earth?
6. What is the theological heart of 2 Corinthians? What clues in terms of both content and structure does the text give us to alert us to Paul's central emphasis?
7. In his two-chapter excursus on appropriate stewardship (2 Cor. 8:1–9:15), what overarching principles does Paul offer? What does this passage, along with all other post-Pentecost passages about stewardship in the Bible, teach on the issue of tithing?
8. Several timeless truths about the characteristics of true Christian ministry emerge in Paul's defense of his own apostolic authority in chapters 10–13. What are these principles that realistically portray the pressures and concerns of those who have been called to lead God's people?
9. How many contemporary "Christian" examples of triumphalism can you identify? How would each of these best be modified?

SELECT BIBLIOGRAPHY

COMMENTARIES

Advanced

Furnish, Victor P. *2 Corinthians*. AB. Garden City: Doubleday, 1984.
Harris, Murray J. *The Second Epistle to the Corinthians*. NIGTC. Carlisle: Paternoster; Grand Rapids: Eerdmans, 2005.
Martin, Ralph P. *2 Corinthians*. WBC. Waco: Word, 1986.
Thrall, Margaret E. *A Critical and Exegetical Commentary on the Second Epistle to the Corinthians*. 2 vols. ICC, rev. Edinburgh: T & T Clark, 1994, 2000.

Intermediate

Baker, William R. *2 Corinthians*. CollegePressNIV. Joplin: College Press, 1999.
Barnett, Paul. *The Second Epistle to the Corinthians*. NICNT, rev. Grand Rapids and Cambridge: Eerdmans, 1997.
Garland, David E. *2 Corinthians*. NAC. Nashville: Broadman & Holman, 1999.
Hafemann, Scott J. *2 Corinthians*. NIVAC. Grand Rapids: Zondervan, 2000.
Kistemaker, Simon J. *Exposition of the Second Epistle to the Corinthians*. NTC. Grand Rapids: Baker, 1997.
Matera, Frank J. *II Corinthians*. NTL. Louisville and London: WJKP, 2003.

Witherington, Ben III. *Conflict and Community in Corinth: A Socio-Rhetorical Commentary on 1 and 2 Corinthians.* Grand Rapids and Cambridge: Eerdmans, 1995.

Introductory

Barnett, Paul. *The Message of 2 Corinthians: Power in Weakness.* BST. Leicester and Downers Grove: IVP, 1988.

Belleville, Linda L. *2 Corinthians.* IVPNTC. Leicester and Downers Grove: IVP, 1996.

Kruse, Colin. *The Second Epistle of Paul to the Corinthians,* rev. TNTC. Leicester: IVP; Grand Rapids: Eerdmans, 1987.

Scott, James M. *2 Corinthians.* NIBC. Peabody: Hendrickson; Carlisle: Paternoster, 1999.

Wan, Sze-Kar. *Power in Weakness: The Second Letter of Paul to the Corinthians.* NTinCont. Harrisburg: Trinity, 2000.

OTHER BOOKS

Becker, Eve-Marie. *Letter Hermeneutics in 2 Corinthians.* London and New York: T & T Clark, 2004.

Crafton, Jeffrey A. *The Agency of the Apostle.* Sheffield: JSOT, 1991.

Fitzgerald, John T. *Cracks in an Earthen Vessel: An Examination of the Catalogues of Hardships in the Corinthian Correspondence.* Atlanta: Scholars, 1988.

Harvey, Anthony E. *Renewed through Suffering: A Study of 2 Corinthians.* Edinburgh: T & T Clark, 1996.

Murphy-O'Connor, Jerome. *The Theology of the Second Letter to the Corinthians.* Cambridge and New York: CUP, 1991.

Peterson, Brian K. *Eloquence and the Proclamation of the Gospel in Corinth.* Atlanta: Scholars, 1998.

Savage, Timothy B. *Power through Weakness: Paul's Understanding of the Christian Ministry in 2 Corinthians.* Cambridge and New York: CUP, 1996.

Stegman, Thomas D. *The Character of Jesus: the Linchpin to Paul's Argument in 2 Corinthians.* Rome: PIB, 2005.

Sumney, Jerry L. *Identifying Paul's Opponents: The Question of Method in 2 Corinthians.* Sheffield: JSOT, 1990.

Young, Frances M., and David F. Ford. *Meaning and Truth in 2 Corinthians.* London: SPCK, 1987; Grand Rapids: Eerdmans, 1988.

BIBLIOGRAPHY

Mills, Watson E. *2 Corinthians.* Lewiston and Lampeter: Mellen, 1997.

6

Romans: The Most Systematic Exposition of Paul's Gospel

INTRODUCTION

CIRCUMSTANCES

Romans 15:23–33 provides most of the necessary background for introducing this epistle. Already in verse 19 Paul asserts that "from Jerusalem all the way around to Illyricum, I have fully proclaimed the gospel of Christ." Illyricum was a territory on the eastern shore of the Adriatic Sea that overlapped parts of what today would be Albania and Macedonia. From Illyricum to Jerusalem marks out roughly the eastern, Greek-speaking half of the Roman Empire in Paul's day, or at least its most densely populated parts. Thus when verses 23–24 speak of no more place for Paul to work "in these regions" and of his hopes to visit the Romans and eventually even the Spaniards, he is in essence announcing a transition in his ministry to the western, more Latin-speaking half of the empire.[1]

Of course, there were still plenty of unreached individuals in the east but, given Paul's priority of establishing viable churches with indigenous leadership and then moving on as quickly as possible to entirely unevangelized areas (recall 2 Cor. 10:13–16), his announcements make sense. Romans 15:20 reiterates this principle: "It has always been my ambition to preach the gospel where Christ was not known, so that I would not be building on someone else's foundation." Where a sustainable local congregation has been established as a bridgehead, Paul is content to leave evangelism of that area to the newly formed Christian community.[2]

Of course, Paul does not yet know about his upcoming arrest in Jerusalem and the fact that he will not visit Rome as a free man. Whether he was ever released from his Roman imprisonment to complete his mission to Spain remains disputed (see above on the end of Acts, p. 77). At this time, however, he projects what we might call a fourth missionary journey that will send him ultimately to the westernmost part of the empire. Even though he has not founded the Roman church, he recognizes its strategic location and wants to minister to them, be encouraged by them and perhaps receive some material assistance for the arduous journey ahead (cf. also 1:10–13). The verb for "assist" in 15:24 often refers specifically to financial assistance.[3]

---

[1] Douglas J. Moo, *The Epistle to the Romans* (Grand Rapids: Eerdmans, 1996), 3.
[2] David G. Peterson, "Maturity: The Goal of Mission," in *The Gospel to the Nations: Perspectives on Paul's Mission*, eds. Peter Bolt and Mark Thompson (Leicester and Downers Grove: IVP, 2000), 187–88.
[3] James D. G. Dunn, *Romans 9–16* (Dallas: Word, 1988), 872.

Meanwhile, he is embarking for Jerusalem with the collection for the impoverished Jewish Christians there (15:25–27), and then he hopes to be able to return westward (vv. 28–29). Yet even before Agabus's predictions of hostilities in the Jewish capital (Acts 21:11), he realizes that the situation may prove dangerous and that even the Christian Jews may not readily be reconciled to his law-free, Gentile-oriented ministry. Hence, he asks for their prayers in verses 30–33.

All of this information enables us to date this epistle precisely to the end of Paul's three-month stay in Greece at the close of his third missionary journey, just as he was getting ready to set sail for Syria (Acts 20:2–3). The reference to the greetings sent by Erastus, the director of public works of the city from which Paul was writing (Rom. 16:23), would seem to point specifically to *Corinth* because an inscription has been discovered there bearing the name of precisely such an individual in that kind of position. Second Timothy 4:20 also refers to a certain Erastus who "stayed in Corinth." At the same time, Paul's commendation of Phoebe, who was perhaps carrying the letter to Rome and who came from the church in Cenchrea (16:1), could suggest that Paul has already made his way to that port city nearby Corinth. Because he is imprisoned shortly after his arrival in Jerusalem (Acts 21:33) and remains there for two years until Governor Felix is succeeded by Festus (Acts 24:27) and because that change of leadership most probably occurred in A.D. 59, we should therefore date Romans to about *A.D. 57,* roughly a year after Paul wrote 2 Corinthians.[4]

Romans, therefore, marks a turning point in Paul's career from numerous perspectives. He thinks he is getting ready to move from east to west. In fact, he will soon be imprisoned, appear in a series of hearings before Jewish and Roman authorities, and finally appeal to the emperor. En route to Rome, he suffers the ill-fated sea voyage on the Mediterranean and ends up finding himself under house arrest for another two years in the imperial capital (where the book of Acts ends). *Romans is also the first letter we know of that Paul has written to a church that he did not personally found.* No one knows who did. Its roots may go all the way back to Pentecostal pilgrims returning from Jerusalem to Rome after A.D. 30 (or 33)—see Acts 2:10. Prevailing Catholic tradition, of course, makes Peter the founder and places him there soon after he departs from Jerusalem in about A.D. 42–44 (see above on Acts 12, p. 46). But there is no conclusive evidence inside or outside the Bible of Peter's presence in Rome prior to the 60s.[5]

A crucial event in the recent history of the Roman church that enables us to understand large swaths of the contents of this epistle was *the expulsion of Jews from Rome under the emperor Claudius in 49* (recall Acts 18:2). As we saw there, according to the Roman historian Suetonius, this was due to the instigation of a riot led by someone named *Chrestus* (*Life of Claudius,* 25). Because the Latin for Christ is only one letter different from this (*Christus*), most historians think that Suetonius's state-

---

[4] Joseph A. Fitzmyer, *Romans* (New York and London: Doubleday, 1993), 85–87.

[5] For survey of the evidence that does exist and for a vigorous argument by a conservative evangelical in favor of Peter's earlier arrival in Rome in about 42–44, see John Wenham, *Redating Matthew, Mark and Luke* (Leicester and Downers Grove: IVP, 1992), 146–72.

ment reflects a garbled reference to Christian and non-Christian Jews squabbling over the truth of the gospel. But in 54 after Claudius's death, the edict was rescinded, and Jews would have begun to return to Rome.[6]

In other words, *for a full five years the church would have been almost exclusively Gentile.* Suddenly, significant numbers of Jewish believers, many of whom preceded the Gentiles in coming to faith and helped to build up the Roman congregation, would have returned. It is only natural to imagine that many of these people might have wanted their leadership roles back. Even if not, the assimilation of a sudden influx of new people from a rival ethnic group is never an easy task for any church. No doubt some of the tensions between Jewish and Gentile Christians were not entirely resolved three years later in 57, and *a large part of Paul's purpose in writing would be to try to unify these different factions.*[7]

GENRE AND STRUCTURE

At the same time, Paul also introduces himself and his message by giving *the fullest and most systematic exposition of the gospel in any of his letters.* This fits a church that had not yet heard him personally articulate his understanding of the good news of Jesus Christ. As for the genre of the epistle, it is perhaps best understood as an *ambassadorial letter* written to pave the way for Paul's hope for a visit to Rome.[8] More so than in his other epistles, Paul also uses the diatribe form of answering potential objections of imaginary interlocutors, though this genre cannot account for the letter as a whole.[9] It does, however, make the deliberative form of rhetoric as clear as anywhere in Paul's corpus of writings.[10]

The structure of the epistle falls as neatly into the Hellenistic letter paradigm as any of Paul's writings. Given his lack of first-hand knowledge of the church, and without denying the unifying emphases just discussed, this letter is his least "occasional" or situation-specific, and he has no need to deviate from the standard structure because of unique circumstances in the church he addresses. Thus he proceeds from greetings (1:1–7), to thanksgiving (1:8–15), to the letter body. A clear thesis initiates this largest of sections in his outline, describing the availability of God's righteousness by faith for Jew and Gentile alike (1:16–17). Subdivisions of this section logically proceed through the main theological elements of the gospel message—from the universal sin of humanity, to the justification by faith in Christ

---

[6] The date of the expulsion, along with its extent, have been debated in recent years. But these traditional conclusions remain the most probable. See Ben Witherington III with Darlene Hyatt, *Paul's Letter to the Romans: A Socio-Rhetorical Commentary* (Grand Rapids and Cambridge: Eerdmans, 2004), 11–16.

[7] Thomas R. Schreiner, *Romans* (Grand Rapids: Baker, 1998), 15–23. Schreiner surveys other subordinate purposes as well. For a book-length treatment, cf. Philip F. Esler, *Conflict and Identity in Romans* (Minneapolis: Fortress, rev. 2003).

[8] Robert Jewett, "Romans as an Ambassadorial Letter," *Int* 36 (1982): 5–20. James D. Hester ("The Rhetoric of *Persona* in Romans: Re-reading Romans 1:1–12," in *Celebrating Romans: Template for Pauline Theology,* ed. Sheila E. McGinn [Grand Rapids and Cambridge: Eerdmans, 2004], 104) similarly speaks of Romans as a *diplomatic* letter.

[9] See esp. Stanley K. Stowers, *The Diatribe and Paul's Letter to the Romans* (Chico: Scholars, 1981).

[10] Cf. Witherington with Hyatt, *Romans,* 19. Anthony Guerra (*Romans and the Apologetic Tradition* [Cambridge and New York: CUP, 1995]), however, argues for a "protreptic" genre and apologetic purpose that combine elements of all three species of rhetoric and seek to commend Paul's ministry and gospel.

that the good news offers, to the lifelong process of sanctification through the Spirit (1:18–8:39).

What some have viewed as a digression, on the status of Israel in 9:1–11:36, in fact plays a central role in the letter, given the need to reunify Jew and Gentile in the church. Then the informational part of the letter body comes to an end, and the ethical implications of the gospel follow immediately (12:1–15:13). This section corresponds to the exhortational material often but not always found at the end of the body of a Hellenistic letter. Finally, Paul explains his travel plans and appends the lengthiest collection of closing greetings in any of his letters (15:14–16:27). Questions of the authenticity of chapter 16 and the textual variants that disagree on where the letter originally ended will be taken up in our commentary when we reach the relevant verses.

Perhaps the only significant disagreement among commentators on this broad outline involves chapter 5. Traditionally, it has often been viewed as presenting the results of justification and thus belonging with 3:21–4:25.[11] Among recent commentators, the trend has been to prefer to see it as introducing the process of moving through sanctification to glorification that characterizes chapters 6–8.[12] Undoubtedly the chapter is transitional, and it is even possible to make the division between the two main subsections after 5:11,[13] but the traditional division still seems somewhat preferable.[14] The outline we will follow for Romans thus unfolds as follows:

I. Introduction (1:1–15)
   A. Greetings (1:1–7)
   B. Thanksgiving (1:8–15)
II. The Theological Exposition of the Gospel (1:16–11:36)
   A. The Thesis of the Letter: Righteousness by Faith for Jew and Gentile (1:16–17)
   B. The Universal Sin of Humanity (1:18–3:20)
      1. The Characteristic Sins of the Gentiles (1:18–32)
      2. Avoiding Jewish Smugness (2:1–3:8)
      3. Scriptural Support for the Unrighteousness of All Humanity (3:9–20)
   C. Justification by Faith (3:21–5:21)
      1. The Thesis Elaborated (3:21–31)
      2. The Example of Abraham (4:1–25)
      3. The Results of Justification (5:1–21)
   D. Sanctification through the Spirit (6:1–8:39)
      1. Freedom from Sin (6:1–23)
      2. Freedom from the Law (7:1–25)
      3. Freedom from Death (8:1–39)

---

[11] As still reflected, e.g., in Robert H. Mounce, *Romans* (Nashville: Broadman & Holman, 1995), 57.

[12] Esp. in light of C. E. B. Cranfield, *A Critical and Exegetical Commentary on the Epistle to the Romans,* vol. 1 (Edinburgh: T & T Clark, 1975), 28.

[13] Charles H. Talbert, *Romans* (Macon: Smyth & Helwys, 2002), 16.

[14] See Dunn, *Romans 1–8,* 242–44, 271.

COMMENTARY

INTRODUCTION (1:1–15)

Greetings (1:1–7)   Appropriately for the most detailed and theological of the epistles, Paul pens an unusually full and rich greeting. In his salutation he includes important information about his Master (Jesus as both human and divine—vv. 3–4), his mission (the apostle to the Gentile world, of which Rome is the heart—v. 5a) and his message ("the obedience that comes from faith"—v. 5b, a key statement for understanding his later teaching about good works).[15] He also anticipates his fuller instruction about the relationship between law and gospel (the former predicted the latter—v. 2) and the significance of the resurrection. Jesus did not become divine only after he was raised from the dead (the view known as adoptionism); rather he was declared to be "Son of God in power" (the literal Greek word order in v. 4) by the resurrection. His victory over the grave demonstrated his powerful divine sonship in ways his incarnation never could. The entire picture of this opening paragraph, depicting a divine Son announcing the good news of salvation ("the gospel of God"), who was also a king ("a son of David"), would have clearly established Jesus as a rival to the emperor, who made almost identical claims.[16]

Thanksgiving (1:8–15)   Paul's customary thanksgiving preserves the form of a prayer only briefly (vv. 8, 10b). His gratitude that the Romans' faith is becoming known empire-wide quickly leads him to explain his own commissioning to preach throughout the Gentile world and his hopes to come to Rome to further that end (vv. 9–15). He also anticipates that the church and he can mutually encourage each other (vv. 11–12), encouragement that may include financial support for his proposed travels further westward (15:24). We cannot be sure what has prevented Paul from

---

[15] Cf. esp. Don B. Garlington, *"The Obedience of Faith": A Pauline Phrase in Historical Context* (Tübingen: Mohr, 1991). Neither legalism, nor covenantal nomism, nor ethnocentrism remains appropriate but rather *Christian* works which flow from salvation (along with the concluding material in 15:14–16:27).

[16] Witherington with Hyatt, (*Romans*, 31–32) describe this opening paragraph as reflecting anti-imperial rhetoric.

coming to Rome sooner (1:13–14)—perhaps merely the needs of the churches he has previously planted further east. With Rome as the heart and soul of the Gentile world, however, he cannot rest content until he has had a chance to preach there, too (v. 15). Verse 14 reminds us, though, that he does not overlook his Jewish compatriots in his evangelistic mission. The references to "wise" and "foolish" remind us of the labels in 1 Corinthians 1:20–25. Different from most of his letters, this "prayer"/ transition to the body of the letter does not introduce key themes of the epistle so much as establish a warm relationship with a congregation Paul has not yet met.[17]

THE THEOLOGICAL EXPOSITION OF THE GOSPEL (1:16–11:36)

The Thesis of the Letter: Righteousness by Faith for Jew and Gentile (1:16–17)   In two succinct verses, Paul sets forward his gospel in a nutshell. Contra the typical Jewish nationalism of the day, his message addresses all ethnic groups, but with the Jews as God's originally chosen people always having the first chance to respond (v. 16). Contra the typical Jewish focus on the works of the law, Paul defines righteousness as conferred by God and received entirely by faith (v. 17). Martin Luther's breakthrough at the time of the Protestant Reformation included the recognition that "the righteousness of God" referred not merely to an attribute God possessed but also to a gift he granted to those who believed (cf. 3:22). Still, "faith" in the quotation from Habakkuk (v. 17b; cf. Hab. 2:4) also involved "faithfulness," so Paul's words do not rule out good works as an appropriate response to God's gift (recall 1:5).[18]

The Universal Sin of Humanity (1:18–3:20)   Before one can appreciate a message of salvation, one needs to recognize a need for a Savior. So, although Paul has much more to say to unpack the concepts of verses 16–17 (see esp. 3:21–31), he must first establish the fact that all humans remain spiritually dead in their sins without Jesus. The wonderful promise that God's righteousness is being revealed must be balanced by its sobering counterpart that his wrath is likewise being revealed against all sin, and therefore against all people who have refused to acknowledge the true God of the universe and have their sins forgiven (v. 18).

The Characteristic Sins of the Gentiles (1:18–32)   Paul first demonstrates this point with the Gentile world. The catalog of sins scattered throughout this section closely matches typical Jewish perceptions of the most heinous transgressions in Greco-Roman culture[19] (which, of course, Jews who did not value their distinctive traditions occasionally imitated[20]). Verses 18–20 argue that even those without the Jewish law remain accountable for their sins because they know God's truth through what theologians have come to call general revelation.[21] They can know that God exists

---

[17] Grant R. Osborne, *Romans* (Leicester and Downers Grove: IVP, 2004), 35. The combined effect of the greetings and thanksgiving also establishes why Paul believes his apostolic authority extends to this church that he has not personally founded. See L. Ann Jervis, *The Purpose of Romans* (Sheffield: JSOT, 1991).

[18] Dunn, *Romans 1–8*, 48–49.

[19] Paradigmatically expressed in Israelite traditions about Sodom and Gomorrah centuries earlier (Philip F. Esler, "The Sodom Tradition in Romans 1:18–32," *BTB* 34 [2004]: 4–16).

[20] See esp. Wisdom of Solomon 13–19 and *Life of Adam and Eve*.

[21] On which, see esp. Bruce A. Demarest, *General Revelation* (Grand Rapids: Zondervan, 1982).

from the order and design of creation (what philosophers today call the teleological argument for God's existence). This does not mean that everyone acknowledges God because humanity in its wickedness has suppressed this truth. But the logic proves cogent even among the unredeemed, so that God's judgment remains fair.[22]

Verses 21–23 characterize the essence of human rebellion as *idolatry*. Throughout history, not all idolaters have worshipped literal replicas of animals or people (as in v. 23). But all idolatry does involve worshipping created things rather than the Creator (v. 25). Three times Paul depicts God's response as giving these people over to their sinful desires (vv. 24, 26, 28), a crucial elaboration of what the revelation of God's wrath means. As C. S. Lewis memorably phrased it, "There are only two kinds of people in the end: those who say to God, 'Thy will be done,' and those to whom God says . . . 'Thy will be done.'"[23] God's wrath is not the spiteful vindictiveness so often associated with human anger but the just expression of his love in not overruling human free choice but eventually confirming people in their evil choices if they do not repent of them.

Idolatry regularly leads to *immorality,* not least in the sexual arena. Not surprisingly, then, Paul presents *sexual sin as "exhibit A"* of human rebellion (vv. 24–27). Interestingly, *heterosexual and homosexual sins are paired here* (vv. 24, 26–27), with neither described as any worse or any better than the other. Because of the contemporary climate that portrays homosexual intercourse as acceptable, verses 26–27 have received intense scrutiny. Numerous writers have argued that only certain forms of homosexual practice are in view—for example, "sacred prostitution" in various Greco-Roman temples or pederasty (the common Greco-Roman relationship of adult men with young adolescent boys). But while some biblical passages at times employ terms that in other contexts can be so narrowed, the language here is too general to allow that. Paul speaks simply of dishonorable desires (NIV: "shameful lusts"), natural use (or relations) and that which is shameful (NIV: "indecent acts").

Some have argued that, for the homosexual, "natural relations" would involve same-sex partners; for them heterosexual behavior would be unnatural. But this imports modern orientations into ancient vocabulary that cannot sustain them. Most male homosexual behavior in Paul's world would better be labeled bisexual since men who had relationships with boys usually did so only for a short time preceding heterosexual marriage, while temple prostitutes likewise typically made themselves available to the preferences of "worshippers" of both genders. Moreover, the term for "natural" here (Gk. *phusis*) almost without exception in Paul means "the way God created things," according to his Jewish background, while Old Testament and intertestamental Jewish literature uniformly agreed that homosexuality violated the

---

[22] Robert Coles (*Spiritual Life of Children* [Boston: Houghton Mifflin, 1990]) has done psychiatric fieldwork worldwide across numerous cultures and argues that all children have a sense of God, though some later suppress it.

[23] C. S. Lewis, *The Great Divorce* (London: Geoffrey Bles, 1948), 66–67. Cf. also Beverly R. Gaventa, "God Handed Them Over: Reading Romans 1.18–32 Apocalyptically," *ABR* 53 (2005): 42–53.

created order. Responsible exegesis has no choice but to conclude that gay and lesbian sex always contravenes God's will.[24]

Yet we must not lose sight of the forest for the trees. The larger point of this subsection is to demonstrate that *all* have sinned, not to rank sins according to some hierarchy of wickedness. Verses 29–31 cover the waterfront of human evil, including such "mild" transgressions as greed, gossip, and arrogance! No one reading this "vice list" need point the finger at anyone else; there is plenty in each person's life to work on without attacking others. In the contemporary Western world in which combating the gay lifestyle seems to dominate many evangelicals' political agendas, Christians need to expend far more energy showing Christ's love to those who often feel personally hated. Jesus modeled the compassion for sinners without condoning their behavior, which should characterize our relationships as well.

Verse 32 rounds out this subsection with an additional argument for why sinners remain accountable before God: all people have an inherent sense of morality and know that they transgress it. Philosophers have come to call this the moral argument for God's existence. Or as Mark Twain put it, humans are the only animals who blush or need to! Anthropologists, of course, have shown that not every culture acknowledges the identical list of behaviors as wicked. But that is not Paul's point. Rather, it is that every people group that has ever lived believes that *some* actions are evil (thus the generalizing "such things" in this verse). But atheistic ideologies have no satisfying explanation for how amoral creatures evolved into beings with a profound sense of right and wrong. Only a Creator, who instilled such values in the one form of life stamped in his image, adequately accounts for this incongruity.[25]

Avoiding Jewish Smugness (2:1–3:8)   The Jewish Christians in Rome could well have been agreeing wholeheartedly with all that Paul had written thus far. *Yes, many Gentiles behave exactly as Paul just described,* they might have been thinking. Suddenly, he turns the tables on them. In this subsection he establishes that Jews are equally guilty of breaking the law God had given them and hence equally sinful and accountable to God. It is not entirely clear if Paul begins thinking explicitly about Jews in verse 1, since he addresses just those who pass judgment on someone else. But it is obvious by verse 17 that he is contrasting Jewish attitudes and behavior with their Gentile counterparts. Either way, his point throughout is that those who have greater access to God's revealed will are no more privileged than anyone else as soon as they violate that will. And in 3:9–20, he firmly establishes the point that sooner or later all people fail to live up to whatever portion of divine law they do understand. All human judgmentalism, therefore, ultimately rebounds on the judge meting it out (2:1–4)![26]

---

[24] Outstanding treatments of the relevant biblical texts, ancient historical and cultural backgrounds, and modern sociological analysis appear in Thomas E. Schmidt, *Straight and Narrow? Compassion and Clarity in the Homosexuality Debate* (Downers Grove: IVP, 1995); James B. de Young, *Homosexuality* (Grand Rapids: Kregel, 2000); and Robert A. J. Gagnon, *The Bible and Homosexual Practice* (Nashville: Abingdon, 2001). On just this passage, see esp. John Nolland, "Romans 1:26–27 and the Homosexuality Debate," *HBT* 22 (2000): 32–57.

[25] For all these points, cf. John Stott, *Romans: God's Good News for the World* (Leicester and Downers Grove: IVP, 1994), 74.

[26] Cf. further Jouette M. Bassler, *Divine Impartiality: Paul and a Theological Axiom* (Chico: SBL, 1982).

Chapter 2:5–16 at first seems out of sync with this logic. The central point remains the same as in 1:18–32—all sin and deserve condemnation (v. 12). But in verses 6–11 and 13–16, Paul seems to believe that some people can attain eternal life by doing good, even while others experience God's rejection because of their wicked ways. The same tension reappears in verses 17–29. Verses 17–24 reiterate the hypocrisy of condemning other lawbreakers while violating the law oneself. But then verses 25–29 again seem to envision two categories of people—those who do and do not keep the law. How do we account for this apparent anomaly?

Three approaches have competed for acceptance throughout the history of the church. (1) Paul is speaking merely hypothetically; in fact no one ever does keep the law, so no one ever achieves salvation by the works of the law (so, e.g., Martin Luther). (2) Those "who by persistence in doing good seek glory, honor and immortality" (v. 7) receive eternal life are Christians whose good works demonstrate their faith in Jesus (so, e.g., St. Augustine). (3) These people are pre-Christian Jews following the Mosaic covenant but not trusting in their deeds to make them right with God. Instead, they recognize their sinfulness and offer the prescribed sacrifices to receive God's forgiveness, which they trust he will grant them (so, e.g., John Wesley).

The first of these options forms a central Christian truth, but it seems unlikely that is what Paul means here. After all, in verses 27 and 29 he explicitly refers to those who are obeying the law, though not circumcised, as inward Jews empowered by the Spirit. This hardly sounds like an impossible hypothetical. The second option makes excellent sense of verses 25–29 but not of 2:14, in which "Gentiles, who do not have the Law, do by nature things required by the Law."[27] Christians do not obey the Law because of some inborn propensity; and once they become believers, they *do* have the law in their possession. The third option fits the overall context best since 1:18–3:20 is demonstrating that all have sinned prior to the coming of Christ (cf. the transition from 3:20 to 3:21). No other verses in this subsection suggest that Paul has already begun to refer to those who have accepted the salvation available in Jesus. And already in the Old Testament times, there were true Jews and false ones, depending on whether God's Spirit had truly worked in their lives.

But what then of the uncircumcised mentioned in verses 26–27? And what of the Gentiles who do not have the law in verse 14? At the very least, these would have included non-Jewish people in pre-Christian times who worshipped the God of Israel apart from knowledge of his revelation to Abraham and his descendants. One thinks, for example, of Melchizedek, Job, and Naaman.

The fate of the unevangelized is a theological conundrum that has puzzled believers throughout church history. No one orthodox position has ever established itself among evangelical Christians.[28] Some have argued that since all have sinned and the penalty for sin is eternal punishment, those who never hear the gospel are automatically lost; others, that God can manifest himself more directly to certain seekers; and

---

[27] Proponents of this view retranslate the verse as "Gentiles, who do not have the law by nature, do the things required by the Law." But this is not as natural a rendering of the verse; see Fitzmyer, *Romans*, 310.
[28] See the excellent survey in Sanders, *No Other Name*.

still others, that God will judge people according to the light they have received. The text most frequently cited by those in this last group is Romans 2:14–16. Sir Norman Anderson, for years evangelicalism's premier scholar of world religions, wrote:

> May this not provide us with a guideline to the solution of the burning problem of those in other religions who have never heard—or never heard with understanding—of the Saviour? It is not, of course, that they can earn salvation through their religious devotion or moral achievements, great though these sometimes are—for the New Testament is emphatic that no man can ever earn salvation. But what if the Spirit of God convicts them, as he alone can, of something of their sin and need; and what if he enables them, in the darkness or twilight, somehow to cast themselves on the mercy of God and cry out, as it were, for his forgiveness and salvation? Will they not then be accepted and forgiven in the one and only Saviour?[29]

At the same time, even if Anderson is correct, study of the major non-Christian ideologies of the world does not hold out much hope that many people will follow this path, and there is no way for us to know if any actually do, so the missionary mandate remains as urgent as ever. In fact, it is precisely the cause of evangelism (given the number of people who reject Christianity because they think it requires them to believe the seemingly unfair teaching that God will damn individuals for not accepting a message they have never heard) that makes it crucial for all believers to study this issue carefully and be able to articulate their reasons for adopting the position they take.[30]

Having stressed the guilt of Jews as much as the guilt of Gentiles, Paul now addresses an anticipated objection. Are there no longer any advantages to being Jewish (3:1)? Of course there are. The Jewish heritage, centered on the Hebrew Scriptures, gives many a head start in coming to faith (vv. 2–4). Those who do not exhibit faith nevertheless unwittingly magnify God's graciousness in saving those who do, though that hardly justifies deliberate sinning (vv. 5–9). Paul will unpack this logic in 5:20–6:4; perhaps he realized that some were actually adopting such reasoning.

Scriptural Support for the Unrighteousness of All Humanity (3:9–20) By citing a barrage of Old Testament texts to prove his point, the apostle wraps up his case that Gentile and Jew alike have sinned and thus remain separated from God. Again, as we discussed under Galatians 3, this does not mean that no one was saved in pre-Christian Judaism. The entire sacrificial system was created to generate temporary forgiveness of sins. But it does mean that even before Jesus' lifetime, God's people knew their plight apart from his provisions for reconciling them to himself. No one ever obeyed his law perfectly, and therefore no one ever was saved by the works of

---

[29] Sir Norman Anderson, ed., *The World's Religions* (London: IVP, rev. 1975; Grand Rapids: Eerdmans, 1976), 234.

[30] On the exegesis of the relevant parts of Romans 2, see further Glenn N. Davies, *Faith and Obedience in Romans* (Sheffield: JSOT, 1990), 53–71; Klyne R. Snodgrass, "Justification by Grace—to the Doers: An Analysis of the Place of Romans 2 in the Theology of Paul," *NTS* 32 (1986): 72–93.

the law (v. 20). Salvation, even in Old Testament times, came through faith in God's promises (recall Gal. 3:6–7).[31]

Justification by Faith (3:21–5:21) *The Thesis Elaborated (3:21–31)* With the coming of Christ, however, God has provided a decisive and permanent solution to the problem of the universal sinfulness of humanity. Again as in Galatians, Paul summarizes this solution as justification by faith. Chapter 3:21–31 enunciates this core principle in tightly packed prose. God's righteousness, imputed to believers, is now fully and solely available through the atonement of Christ. One appropriates it through faith in Jesus,[32] not legal works, though Christians do not jettison the Hebrew Scriptures because they testify and point forward to these theological truths and because living by faith fulfills the meaning of the law in the Christian dispensation (vv. 21–22, 27–31). The essential problem with sin is that it falls short of God's glory and, therefore, disqualifies us from abiding in his presence (v. 23). We thus need God to make salvation possible in a way that does not require us to earn it. Mercifully, he has done precisely that in sending Jesus and, at the same time, has demonstrated his justice by not continuing to forgive people's sins without providing a full and final sacrifice for them (vv. 24–26).

We have already seen that "justification" as a metaphor for our salvation comes from the legal arena, referring to a "not guilty" declaration pronounced over one who had in fact been guilty. Here Paul introduces two additional metaphors to explain other dimensions of the process. "Redemption" (v. 24) was a commercial metaphor, most commonly used to describe the price paid to buy a slave's freedom. "Propitiation" (v. 25 KJV; "sacrifice of atonement" NIV) was a religious metaphor, common to the temple sacrifices in both Judaism and Greco-Roman religion that were offered to appease God's wrath. Some have attempted to limit this term (Gk. *hilasterion*) merely to the forgiveness of sins and translated it as "expiation," but this captures only half of its meaning. The NIV margin nicely expresses both halves, despite the number of words needed: "as the one who would turn aside his wrath, taking away sin." Our transgressions do not just separate us from God; they leave him angry at our behavior![33] The *hilasterion* also conjures up memories of the lid of the ark of the covenant in ancient Israel's worship, which became the "mercy seat" when blood from the sacrifices was sprinkled on it, symbolizing the atonement for sin.[34]

The Example of Abraham (4:1–25) Chapter 4 introduces a major objection many Jews would have had to Paul's line of argument thus far (again, recall Gal. 3): but

---

[31] Recall our discussion of Paul and covenantal nomism above, pp.108–9. Against the tendency of the "new look on Paul" to narrow the focus in 3:20 to Jewish works or even to the "badges of national righteousness," see Moo, *Romans,* 206–17; and Schreiner, *Romans,* 162–73.

[32] As in Galatians 2:16, indeed as in several key texts in Paul, the expression rendered "faith in Christ" is translated by some as "the faithfulness of Christ." But as we saw above (p. 125), this seems less likely. However, *pistis* still suggests believers' *faithfulness* (or faith more as "trust" than as mere "assent"). In popular religious thought, too many evangelicals have defined faith solely in terms of belief, leading, among other things, to Latter-day Saint rejection of *sola fide.* But see the balanced presentation in Robinson, *Following Christ,* 78–90.

[33] The classic demonstration of this meaning for "propitiation" appears in Leon Morris, *The Apostolic Preaching of the Cross* (Grand Rapids: Eerdmans, 1955), 125–85.

[34] Moo, *Romans,* 231–36.

what about Abraham? Wasn't the man who was considered the founding father of Israel saved by his good works, culminating in his willingness to offer his only son Isaac on the altar (Gen. 22:15–18)? After all, the Mishnah would later opine that "Abraham our father had performed the whole law before it was given" (*Kidd.* 4:14). And 1 Maccabees 2:52 had already queried, "Was not Abraham found faithful when tested, and it was reckoned to him as righteousness?" Paul's reply points his audience further back in the life of Abraham when God declared him righteous because of his faith (Rom. 4:3, quoting Gen. 15:6). Whereas "justified" came from a forensic background, "reckoned" or "credited" reflects a commercial background—the language of bookkeeping that credits a particular sum of money to an individual's account.[35] *Abraham's faith, rather than his works, was what was written in his spiritual ledger, so to speak.* Indeed, his willingness to offer Isaac must have reflected enormous faith (cf. Heb. 11:17–19), but here Paul points to another crucial incident—believing the divine promise that he and Sarah, despite their advanced age, would bear a son in the first place (Rom. 4:18–22; cf. Gen. 18:1–15).[36] Moreover, Abraham was also justified by faith before his circumcision (Rom. 4:1–12; cf. Gen. 17), so that he forms a model for how the circumcised and uncircumcised alike can be saved today (Rom. 4:13–25).[37]

As a result, neither Abraham nor any other person of faith has anything to boast about in God's presence (v. 2).[38] While most Pauline texts describing the impotence of good works in providing salvation have the commandments of the Mosaic Law primarily in view, here a more general principle emerges: when individuals work, their "wages are not credited to" them "as a gift, but as an obligation." But to those who do not work but trust "God to justify the wicked," their "faith is credited as righteousness" (v. 4). In other times and places, humans attempt to please God through good behavior not necessarily related to the Law of Moses. But no matter, these attempts likewise fail.[39] It is true that those who receive God's special revelation in the Scripture become even more accountable when they disobey it than those who do not directly know it. "Transgressions" refers to conscious violations of a known standard, so that when verse 15 avers, "Where there is no law there is no transgression," Paul means simply that those without the Torah sin without consciously rebelling against it. But their knowledge of general revelation (recall 1:18–20) still holds them liable to be punished (cf. 5:14).

The Results of Justification (5:1–21) Those who emulate Abraham, however, and become right with God by grace through faith, can experience *peace, joy, and hope* (vv. 1–5). These attributes must not be defined as merely subjective emotions but as objective characteristics of our new status as people who have been reconciled

---

[35] Witherington with Hyatt, *Romans,* 121.

[36] The initial laughter of the elderly couple is thoroughly understandable. But "from that time on Abraham exhibited an incredible trust in God" (Osborne, *Romans,* 119).

[37] Cf. further Michael Cranford, "Abraham in Romans 4: The Father of All Who Believe," *NTS* 41 (1995): 71–88.

[38] On this theme, see esp. Simon J. Gathercole, *Where Is Boasting? Early Jewish Soteriology and Paul's Response in Romans 1–5* (Grand Rapids and Cambridge: Eerdmans, 2002).

[39] Cf. further Moisés Silva, "The Law and Christianity: Dunn's New Synthesis," *WTJ* 53 (1991): 339–53.

to God through Christ (v. 2). We still experience afflictions in this life; but when we recognize their maturing character, we can see them as part of God's loving plan for us (vv. 3–5). The amazing nature of Christ's sacrificial death for us becomes apparent when we consider how rarely human beings voluntarily die on behalf of others and almost never for those who are their enemies (vv. 6–8, 10a). But if Jesus underwent the agony of crucifixion for us when we instead deserved only his wrath, how much more will life with him, now and in the age to come, surpass all expectation (vv. 9, 10b–11)![40] Robert Millet concisely captures the sequence and personal applications of the core concepts at work here: "Grace represents God's acceptance of me. Faith represents my acceptance of God's acceptance of me. Peace is my acceptance of me."[41]

This peace, objective and subjective that comes from salvation is available for all humanity because just as Adam's sin led to the threat of spiritual death for all people, so Christ's death makes spiritual life available for all (vv. 12–21). Verse 12 has spawned numerous debates over the nature of "original sin"—how the transgression of the first human couple affected the rest of the race and continues to affect humanity even to this day.[42] The Latin Vulgate, for over a millennium the translation of the Bible that was used in Roman Catholic services, rendered the Greek *eph' hō*, at the beginning of the last clause in this verse, with an expression that meant "in whom." This led to debates about Christ's "federal" or representative headship (by which God simply determined that he would treat all people on the basis of how Adam behaved) versus a more "realistic" transmission of sin (in which all of Adam's descendants were believed somehow to be actually present in his body—cf. Heb. 7:10). But the Greek expression most likely just means "because" (as in the NIV).[43]

Thus, this verse affirms two complementary truths: sin spread to all people because of Adam's initial disobedience, and all individuals voluntarily choose to sin as well. The relationship between these truths remains unexplained, though with our modern understanding of genetics, it is easier to conceive of behavioral tendencies being passed on to the entire human race by its progenitor.[44] At the same time, verses 13–14 could suggest that those who for whatever reason (age, mental incompetence, etc.) do not consciously choose to reject God and his commandments will not be judged for their sins in the same way. They still die physically, but it may be that they will not experience spiritual death in hell. Here is where the concept of an "age of accountability" arises—the idea that human beings who never reach the intellectual maturity to consciously rebel against God will be saved. But we must admit that this

---

[40] Some modern theologians argue that God's sacrifice of his Son is repugnant and akin to divine child abuse. But this reflects a faulty understanding of the Trinity; Father and Son are so intertwined that Jesus is the incarnation of God himself and his sacrifice represents God's willingness to lay down his own life, as it were. For further response, see esp. Charles H. Talbert, *Romans* (Macon: Smyth and Helwys, 2002), 140–44.

[41] Robert L. Millet, *Are We There Yet?* (Salt Lake City: Deseret, 2005), 141.

[42] For details, see G. C. Berkouwer, *Sin* (Grand Rapids: Eerdmans, 1971), 424–65.

[43] Luke T. Johnson, *Reading Romans* (New York: Crossroad, 1997), 88–89.

[44] Indeed, 4 Ezra 3:7–22 already propounded a belief in the seminal transmission of sin at the end of the first century.

is not a doctrine explicitly taught anywhere in Scripture; at best it seems to be a logical inference from texts like this one.[45]

Paul's larger interest, however, in verses 12–21 is not the explication of the nature of sin but the elaboration of the wonder of salvation. Thus verses 15–21 compare and contrast the sin of Adam with the salvation made available in Christ. In both cases, the actions of individual men began the process, their actions affected the entire human race, and one specific action provided the impetus for everything that would follow it. On the other hand, Adam's transgression brought sin and death, while Christ's crucifixion brings salvation and life. With Adam, one sin created the entire problem, whereas Christ's provision for salvation was a response to the many sins accumulated by humanity up to his day. Finally, the original sin led to the definite condemnation of those who imitated it, whereas Christ's cross work merely opens up the opportunity of salvation for all humanity. People must still appropriate it by faith in Jesus.

This last point is sometimes challenged because of the wording of verse 18. The Greek literally reads, "Consequently therefore, just as through one man [came] transgression unto all people leading to judgment, so also through one man [came] a righteous act unto all people leading to justification of life." But verse 17 has just made clear that one inherits life by receiving "God's abundant provision of grace" and "the gift of righteousness," not simply by being born into the human race. So the sense of verse 18 must be that Christ's atonement brings the *possibility* of life to all people. Verse 19 seems to confirm this interpretation by shifting from the use of "all" to "many." While it is true that all became sinners, and the number involved were certainly "many," not all will be made righteous though "many" (i.e., all *believers*) will.[46]

Chapter 5:20–21 prepares the reader for the topic of sanctification that will span chapters 6 through 8. As in Galatians 3:19–20, Paul explains that the giving of the Mosaic Law increased the amount of trespasses (conscious, deliberate violations of God's standard), but this simply pointed out humanity's need of a Savior even more clearly. As in Romans 3:5–8, this result could lead some people to imagine that they should deliberately sin a lot in order to magnify God's grace (6:1). But such logic entirely misses the fact that believers have died to sin. They have been given a new nature that makes them want to please God rather than grieve him (v. 2). But at this point, we have moved on to Paul's next topic.

Sanctification through the Spirit (6:1–8:39) *Freedom from Sin (6:1–23)* As a result of our right legal standing before God (justification), we should grow in holiness throughout our Christian lives (sanctification).[47] Paul unpacks this thought in

---

[45] For an overview of the various Christian solutions to this problem, see Ronald H. Nash, *When a Baby Dies* (Grand Rapids: Zondervan, 1999).

[46] For all these points, cf. Peter Stuhlmacher, *Paul's Letter to the Romans* (Louisville: WJKP, 1994), 87–88.

[47] "To be justified is to be free from sin, to be legally right before God. To be sanctified is to be free from the *effects* of sin, to have had sinfulness and the enticements of sin rooted out of our hearts and desires" (Millet, *Jesus Christ: The Only Sure Foundation*, 123).

three stages, one per chapter, which we may label "freedom from sin" (chap. 6), "freedom from the law" (chap. 7), and "freedom from death" (chap. 8).[48]

As we have just seen, chapter 6 begins with a transition from previous material by a potential objection to Paul's argument followed by his answer. Increased disobedience may magnify God's grace, but his grace was never intended to give us permission to sin (vv. 1–2). Christians have been freed from sin, first through union with Christ as symbolized by baptism (vv. 2–11) and second through allegiance to a new Lord (vv. 12–23). Verses 2–11 do not teach baptismal regeneration (salvation through baptism) because 1 Corinthians 10:1–12 showed that a "baptism" does not guarantee a right relationship with God. What Romans 6:3–11 does demonstrate is the close link between a profession of belief and baptism in New Testament times. The references to baptism in this passage may well reflect the figure of speech known as a "metonymy"—the use of one concept to stand for a separate but closely related concept (e.g., a flag for its country).[49]

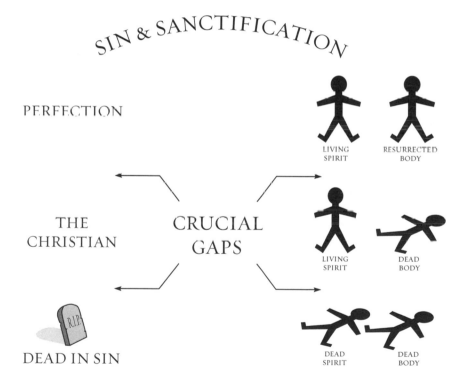

[48] F. F. Bruce, *The Epistle of Paul to the Romans* (Leicester: IVP; Grand Rapids: Eerdmans, rev. 1985), 65.
[49] The emphasis in verse 3 is on "the spiritual reality which water baptism depicts" (Witherington with Hyatt, *Romans,* 157). On the other hand, we may not reduce this passage to speaking merely of the baptism of the Spirit. "Baptism" without further qualification by the time of Romans almost always meant water baptism (Moo, *Romans,* 359).

C. E. B. Cranfield helpfully itemizes four senses in which believers have died to sin: the juridical sense (God no longer looks upon them as sinners), the baptismal sense (they ratify their acceptance of God's decision on their behalf), the moral sense (they are called and progressively given the ability to stop sinning in this life), and the eschatological sense (they will never sin again at all in the life to come).[50]

Against those who overemphasize the first half of Romans 6 and claim that believers no longer have an old, sinful nature in this life, the second half of the chapter commands Christians continually to die to sin (vv. 12–23). These commands would be pointless if there were no possibility of believers disobeying them! Paul even needs to warn against becoming enslaved once more to sin. What then does it mean that our old selves have been "crucified with" Christ (v. 6) or that we have been "set free from sin" (v. 18)? Simply this: once we had no choice but to serve sin as our master. Now we have a choice, and we are called to choose rightly.[51] This relates closely to the relationship between theology and ethics in Paul's writing, which has often been described as the indicative leading to the imperative. *Precisely because our sin nature is never eradicated even as Christians, we must continually "become what we are" already in God's eyes.* Likewise, just as we have a new master in Christ, so also we must keep on making him our master on a daily basis (vv. 12–14, 17–18, 22).[52]

Freedom from the Law (7:1–25)   Romans 7 describes the freedom from the law that Christians enjoy. Apart from its current role as fulfilled in Christ (recall under Gal. 5–6), the law works only to serve sin. This chapter falls into three parts. *First,* being under the law is like a marriage vow—it remains in force only until one party dies (vv. 1–6). The period of time during which the Mosaic covenant was in force ended with the death and resurrection of Jesus. Now, the Holy Spirit permanently indwells all of God's people, giving them new power over their sinful natures and guiding their growth in holy living apart from literal obedience to the 613 commandments of the Torah (vv. 4–6).

Second, there was a time prior to the giving of the law when there was no explicit knowledge of sin as lawbreaking, but that time has long since passed (vv. 7–11). "Once I was alive apart from law, but when the commandment came, sin sprang to life and I died" (v. 9). Commentators debate whether Paul is speaking as a representative Jew and thinking of Moses receiving the law on Mount Sinai or if he is referring to Adam and Eve in the garden and their transgression of the first law that God ever gave humanity. He might even be recalling the occasion at age twelve or thirteen when, in the predecessor to today's *bar mitzvah* ceremony, he agreed to take upon himself the "yoke of the Torah."[53] On all of these interpretations, however, once

---

[50] Cranfield, *Romans,* vol. 1, 300–1.

[51] Talbert, *Romans,* 166.

[52] For grammatical detail, see David Mathewson, "Verbal Aspect in Imperatival Constructions in Pauline Ethical Injunctions," *FN* 9 (1996): 21–35.

[53] Or any two or all three of these. Osborne (*Romans,* 174) labels Paul's writing here both autobiographical and typical of all humanity. L. Ann Jervis ("The Commandment Which Is for Life [Romans 7.10]: Sin's Use of the Obedience of Faith," *JSNT* 27 [2004]: 193–216) can even make a plausible case for seeing life apart from the law as Christian life, with the commandment referring to Christian obligation.

humans become aware that certain behaviors transgress God's perfectly righteous and holy standards, they often desire all the more to do that which offends him. Thus while law itself is not evil, Paul can speak of sin personified as the power that abuses the law and makes it produce death rather than life (vv. 10–12).

Third, after the age of the law has ended, substantial freedom in Christ becomes available, but even then the old and new natures in a believer frequently war against each other (vv. 14–25). This last section is by far the most controversial in the chapter, perhaps in the entire epistle. Commentators are relatively evenly split between seeing this as Paul's Christian reinterpretation of his life under the law or as his ongoing Christian experience, and in either case he would be speaking as a representative of others in the same situation. Scholars who view this as the pre-Christian Paul, in turn, subdivide themselves into those who see Paul speaking from a distinctively Jewish perspective and those who think he is representing fallen humanity more generally. The biggest weakness with the last of these views is that it is difficult to imagine the average non-Jewish unbeliever agonizing over disobedience to the Law of Moses (v. 22). The most serious charge leveled against taking this as the Christian Paul is the claim that, while believers wrestle with sin, they do not remain slaves to their sinful natures (vv. 14, 25b). But we have already seen in 6:12–23 that we do have a choice, even as Christians, whom or what we will serve. We also rejected (above, p. 248) the claim that believers no longer have a sinful nature, which rebuttal also tips the scales in favor of understanding this section as describing the Christian Paul.[54]

In fact, *several arguments favor taking these verses as depicting a struggle that all Christians at one time or another face.* (1) The verb tenses in verses 7–13 and 14–25 shift from past to present. (2) The sequence of the two parts of verse 25 suggests the tension persists after salvation. First, Paul praises God for his rescue in Christ, and then he describes the tension between serving the law and serving sin. (3) It is often only when people are filled with the Spirit and fully understand the unsurpassable holiness of God and the extent of their own depravity that the tension between what they should do and what they actually do becomes the greatest.[55] (4) Galatians 5:17 likewise describes the desires of the sinful nature as in conflict with the Spirit in a context where Paul is clearly speaking of believers. (5) Chapter 8:10 may sum up matters best: "But if Christ is in you, your body is dead because of sin, yet your spirit is alive because of righteousness."[56]

The pastoral implications of adopting this position on verses 14–25 are profound. Often individuals who appear to all outsiders as Christians, and who clearly exhibit the fruit of the Spirit, doubt their own salvation due to particularly sensitive consciences aware of how far short of fully pleasing God they still fall. Fellow Christians

---

[54] Other arguments include the shift to triumph over sin in the believer's life in chapter 8 and the alleged parallel in Gal. 5:17. But see our treatment of both of these texts below.

[55] "The Christian will be made more aware of the depth and seriousness of life's antagonisms." Thus Hans D. Betz, "The Concept of 'Inner Human Being' (ὁ ἔσω ἄνθρωπος) in the Anthropology of Paul," *NTS* 46 (2000): 341.

[56] For this position, cf. further Cranfield, *Romans,* vol. 1, 344–47. Schreiner (*Romans,* 372–92) argues that believer and unbeliever alike are in view.

can often help them by pointing out that the disparities between desires and behavior that torment them would not likely cause such agony in unbelievers uncommitted to following God's ways. The tension they experience testifies to the genuineness of their Christian faith![57]

Freedom from Death (8:1–39) Chapter 8 concludes the first half of this epistle by unpacking the freedom from condemnation and thus from spiritual death that the believer enjoys. Paul makes five main points, one for each main subdivision.

First, although Christians experience warfare between sin and righteousness, through the Spirit substantial victory over sin can be obtained (vv. 1–11). Just as we dare not overestimate our progress in sanctification, neither may we rest content with a lack of continual, visible growth in holiness. Christ's atoning work on the cross was not designed merely to give us new life in a world to come but to provide a new freedom to live in the ways God knows are ultimately best for us even in this world.

To accomplish that, God sent his own Son "in the likeness of sinful man to be a sin offering. And so he condemned sin in sinful man" (v. 3b). This half verse is probably the most difficult to translate in this chapter; literally, it reads "in the likeness of sinful flesh and concerning sin he condemned sin in the flesh." Some have mused that Paul believed that Jesus actually had a sinful nature; he just never acted upon it and, therefore, never committed specific sinful deeds. But it is probably significant that Paul does not use the term "image" here, merely "likeness." While these words can be synonyms, the latter is more readily understood in this context as pointing to resemblance rather than complete identity. After all, the likeness or appearance of Adam and Eve remained the same before and after the fall. Thus a sinless human could still be described as retaining the likeness of a sinful human and vice versa. It is harder, though, to accept the position that Christ was "impeccable"—that there was no possibility for him ever to have sinned. That would appear to make his temptations a charade. A mediating view seems best: like Adam and Eve before the fall, Christ had no sinful nature but had the real possibility of sinning had he chosen to do so. But unlike the original human pair, Christ never gave in to temptation by sinning and therefore never acquired a sinful nature.[58]

Second, the Spirit not only works righteousness in us but makes us adopted sons of God with all the accompanying inheritance rights (vv. 12–17). As in Galatians 4:5–7, our adoption places us into an intimate relationship with our heavenly Father, allowing us to address him as Aramaic speakers did with a familiar term (*Abba*) almost equivalent to our English "Daddy." And this too is a work of the Spirit.

Third, unity with Christ produces sufferings, but these pale in comparison with the coming glorification of all creation (vv. 18–25). Verse 18 ranks with 2 Corinthians 4:17 as one of the most remarkable perspectives on human suffering to be found

---

[57] Cf. Michael P. Middendorf, *The "I" in the Storm: A Study of Romans 7* (St. Louis: Concordia, 1997), 224.

[58] Augustine phrased it nicely centuries ago: "What does sinful flesh have? Death and sin. What does the likeness of sinful flesh have? Death without sin. If it had sin it would be sinful flesh; if it did not have death it would not be the likeness of sinful flesh. As such he came—he came as Savior. He died but he vanquished death" (*Sermons for Easter Season,* Homily 233.3).

anywhere. Paul's own afflictions scarcely permit him to minimize the extent of such evil but, compared to the grandeur and permanence of the new heavens and earth and their glorified inhabitants, he can anticipate looking back one day on the horrors of this life as a passing shadow. Verses 19–22 remind us that, metaphorically speaking, the whole universe groans under its corruption and longs for its re-creation. Human sin brought discord to the entire cosmos, and the enmity between "nature" and humanity will continue until the final redemption of all things. These observations are important in constructing a theodicy—a response to the problem of evil. "Natural" disasters are just as much a result of the fall as human sin, so that we should not expect God to prevent Christians from being hurt by them in this life any more than we imagine we can attain a state of sinless perfection in the here and now.[59]

Fourth, the Spirit helps us in our weakness, even when we are unable to pray cognitively (vv. 26–27). Just as creation groans figuratively as it awaits its redemption (v. 26), believers likewise long (and sometimes literally groan) for the day when all their suffering will cease (v. 27). The extent of our fallenness often leaves us baffled as to how to pray, precisely because we do not know God's will in various situations. So Paul assures us that the Spirit, who perfectly knows God's mind, intercedes for us on these occasions. A few commentators have argued that the word "groans" points to speaking in tongues, another form of divinely given utterance that bypasses human cognition (recall above, p. 192), but it is doubtful that we can pinpoint any manifestation of this ministry that specifically.[60]

Fifth, believers can rest secure that nothing in all creation can separate them from God's love in Christ because the process of salvation God has set in motion is guaranteed to continue through to its completion (vv. 28–39). This subsection begins with one of the most famous promises in the Bible, yet it is often mistranslated. The NIV has it right: "*In all things* God works for the good of those who love him." All things do *not* work together for good (*contra* the KJV)! Some things are wicked and contrary to God's purposes, but he remains at work *in* them nevertheless, creating good even where evil holds sway.[61]

Verses 29–30 contain Paul's famous *ordo salutis* ("order of salvation"), beginning with God's foreknowledge and ending with the believer's glorification. Most Arminians see this foreknowledge as the explanation of and basis for the predestination that follows, yet this seems to make salvation a human rather than a divine accomplishment—God merely knows in advance how we are going to respond freely. Most Calvinists argue that foreknowledge here carries the Old Testament sense frequently attached to the Hebrew verb *yada'* (to know) of election or choice, yet the *Greek* word actually used (*proginōskō*) does not normally convey this sense, even in

---

[59] For an excellent introduction to the topic more generally, see D. A. Carson, *How Long O Lord? Reflections on Suffering and Evil* (Grand Rapids: Baker, 1990).

[60] Cf. further Emmanuel A. Obeng, "The Origins of the Spirit Intercession Motif in Romans 8:26," *NTS* 32 (1986): 621–32; idem, "The Reconciliation of Rom. 8.26f. to New Testament Writings and Themes," *STJ* (1986): 165–74; idem, "Abba, Father: The Prayer of the Sons of God," *ET* 99 (1988): 363–66.

[61] See esp. Carroll D. Osburn, "The Interpretation of Romans 8:28," *WTJ* 44 (1982): 99–109.

the Septuagint. A mediating view seems necessary: God initiated plans for conforming those who would come to him in sonship.[62]

So God knows in advance how all possibly created people would freely respond to the gospel (foreknowledge). He chooses a particular collection of those people to create and in that sense determines that their destinies will correspond to their choices (predestination).[63] The Holy Spirit then begins to work on the hearts of those God knows will respond in faith, and they freely choose Christ as a result (calling). When they accept him, they are declared righteous in God's eyes (justification). Finally, God promises to see them through to their coming bodily resurrection (glorification). Because this future is guaranteed, Paul can write of it using the aorist or past tense. The set of all people God foreknows contains the identical members as the set of those he predestines, the set of those he calls, the set of those he justifies, and the set of those he glorifies. Hence, we can be certain that nothing can thwart the salvific purposes of God (vv. 31–39). Verses 38–39 contain perhaps the strongest statement in all of Scripture of the believer's security in Christ.[64] The fact that the individuals in the chain from foreknowledge to glorification remain the same throughout refutes the claim that believers can voluntarily opt out of the process. Indeed, no true believer would ever want to do so.[65]

ROMANS 8:29–39		
Calvinism	"Calminianism" (incl. middle knowledge)	Arminianism
God's Sovereignty Prior	God's Sovereignty and Human Freedom in Balance	Human Freedom Prior

The Status of Israel (9:1–11:36) *The Frequent Disobedience of Israel and Its Consequences (9:1–29)* Paul's doctrinal survey is complete; he has taken humanity from sin, to justification, to sanctification and glorification. Now he must address an almost certain objection in the minds of some in his audience, whether Jew or Gentile. If this gospel really is the fulfillment of the hopes of Israel, why have so many Jews rejected it? Paul gives three basic answers: *(1) This is consistent with the frequent disobedience of the Israelites throughout Old Testament times (9:1–29);*

---

[62] Millard J. Erickson, *Christian Theology,* vol. 1 (Grand Rapids: Baker, 1983), 356–62.

[63] Cf. further the treatment of this "middle knowledge" in William L. Craig, *The Only Wise God* (Grand Rapids: Baker, 1987): 127–51. Craig defends the popular medieval view that God knew all possible free choices of all possibly created beings and chose to create the best possible combination of such creatures, while still recognizing that the freedom he insisted on giving them would lead to enormous amounts of sin and evil.

[64] "Ultimate failure is out of the question for the disciple of Jesus Christ. No person or circumstance will thwart him or her in the end" (Ogden and Skinner, *Acts through Revelation,* 179).

[65] Perhaps the most balanced and biblical reflections on these difficult themes appear in Thomas R. Schreiner and Ardel B. Canaday, *The Race Set Before Us: A Biblical Theology of Perseverance and Assurance* (Downers Grove and Leicester: IVP, 2001).

(2) They have treated the law as a means of works righteousness rather than living by faith (9:30–10:21); (3) This is only a temporary rejection preparing the way for the widespread outpouring of faith among the Jews (11:1–36).

Paul begins the first of these answers by affirming his anguish and the extent of his identification with his fellow Jews (9:1–5). He would even be willing to be damned for their sake if it were possible (v. 3)! This sentiment is the polar opposite of the anti-Semitism that has so often characterized the largely Gentile church. Paul also lists the legacy of advantages to being Jewish (recall 3:1–4), which includes birthing the Messiah. Here appears one of the comparatively rare explicit equations of Jesus with God in the New Testament (v. 5).[66]

Paul proceeds to highlight how only a remnant of Abraham's seed chosen by grace represented the true people of God throughout Old Testament times (vv. 6–29, see esp. vv. 27–29). To this end he points out how the line of promise passed through only one of Abraham's two children, Isaac, and through only one of Isaac's two children, Jacob (vv. 6–13). Here he is probably not talking about election to eternal salvation or damnation, but about the way God's plan for human history would work itself out in *this* life. After all, Esau's reconciliation with Jacob (Gen. 33) suggests that Esau ended his life right with God. But his offspring still did not form part of the chosen nation of Israel. We may speak of this as corporate, temporal election.[67]

CORPORATE ELECTION IN THE TORAH
(ROMANS 9:6–21)

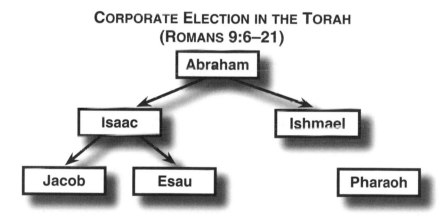

Verses 14–29 raise the potential objection, "Is this fair?" Paul in essence offers four replies.

First, it was fair in the context of Moses and Pharaoh (vv. 14–18). Again Paul is not talking about election to eternal destinies; Exodus never tells us how Pharaoh reacted to the final tragedy of the loss of his army after numerous, previous "faked" acts of repentance. Rather, Paul talks about how God hardened Pharaoh's heart in

---

[66] This has been challenged by punctuating the text so that the sentence ends after "Christ," and the rest of the verse is translated "God who is over all be forever praised, Amen." But this is not nearly as natural an interpretation of the specific syntax. See esp. Murray J. Harris, *Jesus as God: The New Testament Use of* Theos *in Reference to Jesus* (Grand Rapids: Baker, 1992), 143–72.

[67] See further Craig L. Blomberg, "Elijah, Election, and the Use of Malachi in the New Testament," *CTR* 2 (1987): 111–16; William W. Klein, *The New Chosen People* (Grand Rapids: Zondervan, 1990), 173–75, 197–98. Even the language of love and hate in v. 13 in Hebrew and Semitized Greek can mean "choose" and "not choose," respectively.

response to Pharaoh's hardening his own heart (recall the sequence of events in Rom. 1:18–32) for temporal and even merciful purposes, namely, the salvation of Israel.[68]

God's choices are fair, *second,* because God is Creator and can make vessels for noble or menial use (vv. 19–21). But these are not irrevocable categories because 2 Timothy 2:20–21 can use the identical imagery and yet speak of those who cleanse themselves from ignoble purposes (by faith in Christ) and are saved. Once again, it appears Paul is speaking of election to various roles played during certain stages in one's temporal life.

Third, when God does predestine to salvation, it is what theologians call single rather than double predestination (vv. 22–23). In this section we have clearly reached the New Testament age, and Paul is talking about those called to form the Christian church, so presumably more than temporal purposes are in view. But the asymmetry between verses 22 and 23 is striking: (a) *God* prepares the vessels of mercy, but the vessels of wrath are simply "prepared" (the Greek could even be translated "have prepared themselves") for destruction; and (b) the vessels of mercy are prepared *"in advance,"* whereas no such qualifier attaches itself to the vessels of wrath.[69]

To those who object that the only logically coherent positions are either double predestination (both to salvation and to damnation) or no predestination (in the traditional sense of God's electing individuals to their eternal destinies), we may reply: (1) Our finite, fallen minds cannot always be expected to understand the entire logic of God's ways, but there is nothing demonstrably self-contradictory about single predestination. (2) This seems to be the consistent teaching of Scripture, inasmuch as the Bible regularly attributes a person's salvation entirely to the grace of God, whereas those who are damned are judged according to their works and have only themselves to blame. (3) This rings true to human experience: those who have become believers uniformly encountered circumstances outside their control that helped to make them open to faith in Christ, while unbelievers do not report any coercive powers that prevent them, against their will, from believing.[70]

Fourth, God's election is fair because it enables Gentiles to be saved as well as Jews (vv. 24–29). What would have been unfair is preserving the Jewish people as God's uniquely elect nation, especially since they had only seldom intentionally spread his word to other ethnic groups throughout their long history (despite Gen. 12:3, which called them to bless all the earth's people groups).[71]

What Went Wrong and How to Make It Right (9:30–10:21)   What then led the unbelieving Israelites astray? In a nutshell, it was their misuse or misunderstanding of Old

---

[68] "God's hardening is an act directed against human beings who are already in rebellion against God's righteous rule. God's hardening does not, then, *cause* spiritual insensitivity to the things of God; it maintains people in the state of sin that already characterizes them" (Moo, *Romans,* 599).

[69] Cf. esp. Cranfield, *Romans,* vol. 2 (1979), 495–96.

[70] For an excellent comparison of the three views on predestination, see Fred H. Klooster, "Predestination: A Calvinistic Note;" Wilber T. Dayton, "A Wesleyan Note on Election;" and David P. Scaer, "The Doctrine of Election: A Lutheran Note," in *Perspectives on Evangelical Theology,* eds. Kenneth S. Kantzer and Stanley N. Gundry (Grand Rapids: Baker, 1979), 81–94, 95–103, and 105–15, respectively.

[71] On the "ardent desire for keeping the Law *whether Gentiles were in view or not,*" see Vincent M. Smiles, "The Concept of 'Zeal' in Second-Temple Judaism and Paul's Critique of It in Romans 10:2," *CBQ* 64 (2002): 282–99 (quotation from p. 285).

Testament revelation (9:30–10:13). They did not recognize that even within the law, righteousness came by faith rather than obedience to Torah (9:30–33). Recall Paul's programmatic use of Habakkuk 2:4 already in Romans 1:17. Neither did they recognize that the goal and termination of the law was Christ (10:1–4).[72] As in Galatians 3:10–14, Paul quotes the Old Testament "against itself" to show the right and wrong ways of responding to it (10:5–8).[73] Now, with the coming of Christ, the right way of reading the Hebrew Scriptures leads to the confession of Jesus as Lord—both God and master—as confirmed by his resurrection (vv. 9–10). *Here appears perhaps the earliest and certainly the most fundamental expression of the basic essentials of the Christian faith.* And it is made available on identical terms to Jews and Gentiles alike (vv. 11–13).

Still the question of fairness lurks in the background. Even with the energetic missionary effort of the first generation of Christianity, can it truly be said that all have had a fair chance to respond to God's revelation? The next four verses stress the need for Christians to continue to spread the word so that more can believe (vv. 14–17). But then Paul queries, "Did they not hear?" and answers his own question by declaring, "Of course they did," and by citing Psalm 19:4, which describes the general revelation of God to all humanity in the handiwork of his creation (v. 18). Just as in Romans 1:19–20, all humanity remains accountable before God because everyone can see the "intelligent design" in the universe.[74] It may be that Paul also applies this psalm to the spread of the gospel in a representative sense throughout the known world of his day (more or less contiguous with the Roman Empire), in light of his claim in 15:19 and his knowledge of the work of other evangelists. But many who have heard have remained obstinate, especially among the Jews, while many Gentiles unexpectedly are responding in the right way (vv. 19–21).

The Future of Israel (11:1–36)   Must the future for Israel remain so bleak? By no means. First, Paul articulates a present hope. Many Jews *have* become believers in Christ (11:1–10). If Paul could become one, anyone can (v. 1)! The Roman Christians dare not underestimate the numbers even in their day like Elijah did in his (vv. 2–6; cf. 1 Kings 19:10–18). But there is also a greater future hope. Even more Jews will one day become believers, provoked by the jealousy of seeing Gentiles coming to faith in the present age (11:11–24). Here Paul develops his famous olive tree metaphor, likening the Jewish people to the natural branches and Gentiles to ingrafted

---

[72] The Greek word for "end" in v. 4 is *telos*, which, as in English, can mean either goal or termination. Despite many scholars who opt for one against the other, it is probable that Paul had both meanings in view. For a detailed survey of all the major positions and combinations of positions, see Robert Badenas, *Christ the End of the Law: Romans 10.4 in Pauline Perspective* (Sheffield: JSOT, 1985).

[73] Paul sees Deuteronomy 30 fulfilled typologically in Christ, given the larger narrative of blessings and curses in chaps. 27–29 that suggests the right and wrong uses of the law (Osborne, *Romans*, 269).

[74] The intelligent design movement among scientists, by no means limited to Christians, has more than adequately corroborated this. For a popular-level introduction, see Lee Strobel, *The Case for the Creator* (Grand Rapids: Zondervan, 2004). For more technical treatments, see the works cited therein, esp. by Michael Behe and William Dembski.

branches.[75] Verses 20–22 make clear that nothing is automatically promised to all Jews simply by virtue of their ancestry if unbelief persists. But verses 23–24 make the possibility of reingrafting equally plain. When "the full number of the Gentiles has come in," that is, when all non-Jews foreknown and predestined to believe have become Christians, then "all Israel will be saved" (v. 26). In other words, when we reach the end of the church age, as the "deliverer" (the Messiah) comes from Zion (v. 26b; Christ's second coming), a large number of Jewish people will put their trust in Jesus.[76]

Countless questions about this event remain unanswered. When exactly does this happen? Is it in response to Christian preaching or something more directly supernatural? Just how many people comprise the "all"? We simply do not know. But the following deductions seem probable. "All" need not mean every single Jew alive at that time; the Talmud contains a similar saying in which "all Israelites inherit the kingdom," but the immediate context disqualifies numerous categories of flagrant, unrepentant sinners (b. Sanh. 10). Nothing in Romans (or elsewhere in the New Testament) requires the restoration of the Jews to the land of Israel for this widespread outpouring of faith to occur. The Old Testament texts that promise a return to the land (esp. Ezek. 37) and a rebuilt temple (chaps. 40–48) prove notoriously difficult to interpret from a New Testament perspective. Some believe the widespread Jewish rejection of Jesus made the people forfeit this promise. Others entirely spiritualize the passage and take it to refer to heaven. More probably, it will be fulfilled either literally in the millennium or metaphorically in the new heavens and new earth (or both).[77]

But even if one takes this promise as requiring a repatriation of Jewish people to Israel prior to Christ's return, the biblical texts are clear that this occurs only when these people once again follow God devoutly. Thus, while it is intriguing that Jewish people have again lived in an independent nation of Israel for nearly the past sixty years, this state of affairs need not reflect the fulfillment of any biblical prophecy. A majority of Jews in Israel today are secularized; orthodox Judaism accounts for a small percentage of the country's inhabitants. At most, the current state of Israel might be the prelude to the fulfillment of prophecy; on the other hand it might be utterly irrelevant to it. Even on a literal interpretation of Ezekiel 37, Jews might be again evicted from the land one or more times before finally resettling it in fulfillment of Scripture. So it is dangerous for Christians to support the political policies of the current state of Israel uncritically, especially when it violates the principles of justice laid down in the Hebrew Scriptures. The problem of providing justice for

---

[75] Some have argued that Paul imagines a form of horticulture unknown in his day, but see Columella, *De re rustica* 5.9.16, on grafting a wild olive branch onto an old olive tree. For the view that Paul is deliberately subverting standard Greek forms of agriculture to stress the Jews' ongoing privileged position in salvation history, see Philip F. Esler, "Ancient Oleiculture and Ethnic Differentiation: The Meaning of the Olive-Tree Image in Romans 11," *JSNT* 26 (2003): 103–24.

[76] See esp. Richard H. Bell, *Provoked to Jealousy* (Tübingen: Mohr, 1994). Cf. Jennifer Glancy, "Israel vs. Israel in Romans 11:25–32," *USQR* 45 (1991): 191–203.

[77] For a concise presentation of the major options, see John B. Taylor, *Ezekiel* (London: Tyndale; Grand Rapids: Eerdmans, 1969), 250–54.

Palestinians and Jews alike in Israel seems almost intractable, but Christian ethics demand that we work for a solution that treats both fairly.[78]

An alternative interpretation takes the *houtōs* at the beginning of verse 26 as logical rather than chronological. Instead of understanding the salvation of "all Israel" to occur *after* the complete number of Gentiles has come to faith, this approach would translate the clause, "And *in this way* all Israel will be saved." "All Israel" is then taken to mean the sum total of God's people throughout history, just as "the Israel of God" in Galatians 6:16 can mean all believers. In other words, Jewish believers past and present will combine together with Gentiles who become Christians to form the complete people of God.[79] On the other hand, *houtōs* can mean "then," and in Romans 9–11 every other reference to Jews refers to literal Jewish people, so that without clear contextual clues to support it this second perspective seems less likely.[80]

THE DESTINIES OF THE JEWS

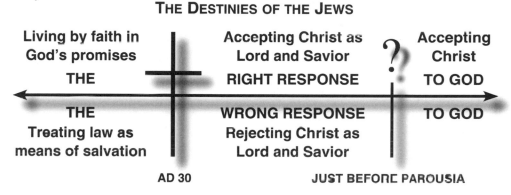

On either reading, however, no support emerges here for the "two covenants theory," which claims that modern-day Jews can be saved apart from belief in Jesus as their Messiah, if they simply follow the Mosaic covenant faithfully. Paul's whole point back in 1:18–3:20 was that no one ever did that anyway. And the sacrificial system that provided a measure of forgiveness under the old covenant has now been superseded by Christ's once-for-all sacrifice under the new covenant.[81] Not surprisingly, Paul completes this long theological portion of his letter body with a resounding doxology of praise to God for his inscrutable ways (vv. 33–36).

THE ETHICAL IMPLICATIONS OF THE GOSPEL (12:1–15:13)

The Basic Principle (12:1–2)   Just as Paul's doctrinal section followed a highly systematic structure, so his exhortational material adopts a similarly logical sequence. What is God's will for how believers should live in light of this marvelous plan of salvation? First, the basic principle applicable to all Christians is transforma-

---

[78] Cf. esp. Gary M. Burge, *Whose Land? Whose Promise? What Christians Are Not Being Told about Israel and the Palestinians* (Cleveland: Pilgrim, 2003).

[79] See esp. N. T. Wright, *The Climax of the Covenant: Christ and the Law in Pauline Theology* (Edinburgh: T & T Clark, 1991; Minneapolis: Fortress, 1992), 231–57.

[80] P. W. van der Horst, "'Only Then Will All Israel Be Saved': A Short Note on the Meaning of καὶ οὕτω in Romans 11:26," *JBL* 119 (2000): 521–25.

[81] Cf. further Talbert, *Romans,* 267.

tion of body and mind. When we think about determining God's will for our lives, we often jump immediately to specific issues like whom to marry, where to live, what to do for work, etc. Yet, as we noted in conjunction with 1 Thessalonians 4:3–8, in Scripture the most fundamental element of God's will always involves moral living. Once we have rejected the ungodly desires and behaviors of fallen humanity and committed ourselves to allowing the Spirit to transform our lives, then we are in a position to ask more specific guidance from God. When this transformation affects both our bodies (v. 1) and our minds (v. 2), then our entire selves are yielded to God's will,[82] and we please God with our worship. The adjective in verse 2 that is translated "spiritual act" (*logikos*) combines the meanings of logical, rational, spiritual, and worshipful, but the heart of the meaning appears to be "reasonable."[83]

Using One's Gifts (12:3–8) The next step is for each individual to discover his or her own unique mix of spiritual gifts and exercise them wholeheartedly for the growth of the body of Christ. On spiritual gifts more generally, see above under 1 Corinthians 12. Here the emphasis is on a proper assessment of how God has gifted us, neither overestimating nor underestimating our abilities and calling. Once again, Paul stresses the diversity of gifts and the importance of all believers to be true to what God has done and is doing in their lives, rather than trying to be like someone they are not (or insisting that others try to mimic their gift mix).

Exercising the Gifts in Love (12:9–13:14) This next collection of commands has often been viewed as more miscellaneous in nature. But it begins by referring to love (12:9a), and its final subsection urges love in light of the nearness of the end (13:8–14). In between, blessing and doing good to one's enemies clearly expresses love to them (12:14–21), while 13:1–7 balances the previous material by stressing the occasional responsibility of governments to exercise force. So it seems reasonable to imagine that Paul saw love as the unifying theme of this entire section.[84] When one recalls that 1 Corinthians 13 offered up a beautiful rhapsody to love immediately after the discussion of spiritual gifts in chapter 12, it becomes all the more probable that Paul is again reminding his readers that their gifts must be exercised lovingly.[85]

Chapter 12:9–13 suggests that love needs to be worked at; notice the expressions "cling," "be devoted," "never be lacking in zeal," and "keep your spiritual fervor." Verses 14–21 then extend that love to one's enemies. Almost certainly Paul alludes to the teaching of Jesus here (see esp. Luke 6:35).[86] He does not deny the due process of law; 13:1–7 will insist on the role of government to punish wrongdoers. So

---

[82] In a day in which rampant sexual immorality shipwrecks many Christians' ministries, the temptation might be to stress only the transformation of our bodies. But Cranfield (*Romans*, vol. 2, 633) reminds us as well that "in lives which are truly being transformed by the renewing of the mind there is no room for slackness or sloth, for that attitude which seeks to get by with as little work and inconvenience as possible, which shrinks from dust and heat and resents the necessity for any exertion as a burden and imposition."

[83] Osborne, *Romans*, 320–21, n. on 12:1.

[84] See, in detail, Walter T. Wilson, *Love without Pretense: Romans 12.9–21 and Hellenistic-Jewish Wisdom Literature* (Tübingen: Mohr, 1991).

[85] Talbert, *Romans*, 287.

[86] On this and other possible uses of the Jesus tradition in the exhortational material of Romans, see Michael Thompson, *Clothed with Christ: The Example and Teaching of Jesus in Romans 12.1–15.13* (Sheffield: JSOT, 1991).

he must be prohibiting private revenge for wrongs committed and encouraging the church, as a countercultural community, to create positive models of peacemaking.[87] Heaping burning coals (v. 20) reflects an Egyptian rite of carrying charcoal and ashes in a dish on one's head as a public act of penance and thus probably refers to the pangs of shame that can come upon an enemy when the offended person does good in return rather than retaliating for some wrong done.[88]

Here is one area where New Testament instruction contrasts sharply with the Old Testament. Although Paul can quote Proverbs 25:21–22 to support his commands, this passage differs from almost all of the rest of the teaching of the Hebrew Scriptures on dealing with enemies.[89] Indeed, it was not until the intertestamental period "that the prohibition against personal retribution was first grounded in God's prerogative to avenge."[90] Even then, applications were largely limited to disputes within the Jewish community. Whatever side one comes down on in the debates on government-sanctioned war and capital punishment (see below), Christians ought to agree that the world should be able to see the church as an institution promoting reconciliation, relief efforts, and humanitarian aid in all situations of human violence. Sadly, at least among more conservative Christians, the separation between church and state on these issues seems at times invisible.

Chapter 13:1–7 turns to the role of the governing authorities. Taken on its own, this passage seems puzzlingly unqualified. Does Paul really mean that Christians must obey any command, however immoral or idolatrous, that the emperor or some local magistrate issues? As a well-educated Jew, he obviously knew about the divinely sanctioned examples of civil disobedience in the Old Testament (e.g., the Israelites' midwives disobeying Pharaoh's order to kill all the Israelites' male babies or Daniel's refusal to worship Nebuchadnezzar's statue). So, too, he almost certainly learned about Peter's insistence on obeying God rather than the merely human authorities in the Sanhedrin (see above, p. 31). Later in the New Testament (Rev. 13), the end-times government of the Antichrist will be described as demonically rather than divinely inspired. One even wonders if Paul would have written in exactly the same way seven years later in A.D. 64, when Nero began the first imperial persecution of Christians.

Several exegetical observations help us make progress in solving these conundra. *First,* to submit to someone does not always require obedience to that person. One may choose to disobey the order of a human authority if it violates God's laws, but one can do so in a peaceful and kind spirit and thus exhibit a certain respect for the office of the superior.[91] *Second,* it is just possible that the expression "governing authorities" in verse 1 (literally, "the authorities surpassing you") could be interpreted as referring to those who are morally superior and thus not suggest submission to

---

[87] On which, see esp. Glen Stassen, *Just Peacemaking: Transforming Initiatives for Justice and Peace* (Louisville: WJKP, 1992); and Walter Wink, *The Powers That Be* (New York and London: Doubleday, 1998).

[88] Cf. Dunn, *Romans 9–16* (1988), 751.

[89] See Craig L. Blomberg, *Contagious Holiness: Jesus' Meals with Sinners* (Leicester and Downers Grove: IVP, 2005), 32–64.

[90] Kent L. Yinger, "Romans 12:14–21 and Non-Retaliation in Second Temple Judaism: Addressing Persecution within the Community," *CBQ* 60 (1998): 78.

[91] Cf. further Cranfield, *Romans,* vol. 2 (1979), 660–63.

evil rulers at all.[92] *Third,* the two occurrences of the verb "rebel" in verse 2 translate a present participle and a perfect indicative, both of which suggest ongoing action. Paul may not be precluding brief protests against injustice, but ruling out "determined and persistent rebellion."[93]

Fourth, verses 3–4 reflect the two main roles of government in the Roman Empire: rewarding (or giving public acclaim to) benefactors and punishing criminals. The expression to "do (what is) right" in verse 3 may well have this more limited sense of doing good with one's money or material possessions.[94] Thus it could be that Paul is arguing simply for submission to governments to the extent that they properly perform these two tasks. (While verse 4 has often been used as support for capital punishment, the Romans did not use the sword to execute individuals, so this passage may prove irrelevant to that debate.[95]) *Fifth,* this entire passage plays a subversive role when one realizes that the emperors would not have believed they were serving Yahweh, the God of Jews and Christians. *Finally,* the special mention of paying taxes (vv. 6–7) may be a response to the recent social unrest that would lead to a Roman tax revolt in A.D. 58 and may disclose Paul's desire that Christians not be perceived as similar "rabble rousers."[96] The reference to conscience in verse 5 reminds us that ultimately all believers must obey what they believe God is telling them to do in a situation in which authorities require them to compromise Christian convictions in some way, but they can still take the action they do in a manner that will minimize a negative impact on the spread of the gospel and that will accept the consequences that follow.[97]

Chapter 13:8–10 returns explicitly to the theme of love. Verse 8 "does not forbid a Christian from ever incurring a debt; it rather demands that Christians repay any debts they do incur promptly and in accordance with the terms of the contract."[98] As in Galatians 5:14, acting in a loving way in every context fulfills the law (vv. 9–10). Such behavior does not lead to the famous "situation ethics" of the 1960s that denied all biblical absolutes because it was believed that there was always some situation in

---

[92] Stanley E. Porter, "Romans 13:1–7 as Pauline Political Rhetoric," *FN* 3 (1990): 115–39. For two diametrically opposite applications of this passage, in light of this ambiguity, to a corrupt African regime today, see Lovemore Togarasei, "'Let Everyone Be Subject to Governing Authorities': The Interpretation of New Testament Political Ethics Towards Authorities after Zimbabwe's 2002 Presidential Elections," *Scriptura* 85 (2004): 73–80.

[93] Witherington with Hyatt, *Romans,* 313.

[94] Bruce W. Winter, *Seek the Welfare of the City: Christians As Benefactors and Citizens* (Carlisle: Paternoster; Grand Rapids: Eerdmans, 1994), 19–20; on this specific text, cf. pp. 25–40. For a broader understanding of doing good in society, see Philip H. Towner, "Romans 13:1–7 and Paul's Missiological Perspective: A Call to Political Quietism or Transformation?" in *Romans and the People of God,* eds. Sven K. Soderlund and N. T. Wright (Grand Rapids and Cambridge: Eerdmans, 1999), 149–69.

[95] Glen H. Stassen and David P. Gushee, *Kingdom Ethics: Following Jesus in Contemporary Context* (Downers Grove: IVP, 2003), 206–10. The use of this text to justify certain wars is more complicated. The attractive aspect of the "just peacemaking" position is that it is compatible with both just war theory and pacifism. On either of those two views, the Bible still requires Christians to do all that they can proactively and retrospectively to produce peace and reconciliation among individuals and peoples. See esp. Glen H. Stassen, *Just Peacemaking: Ten Practices for Abolishing War* (Cleveland: Pilgrim, 1998).

[96] Osborne, *Romans,* 346.

[97] Augustine captured another necessary balance: "If anyone thinks that because he is a Christian he does not have to pay taxes or tribute nor show the proper respect to the authorities . . . he is in very great error. Likewise, if anyone thinks that he ought to submit to the point where he accepts that someone who is his superior in temporal affairs should have authority even over his faith, he falls into an even greater error" (*On Romans,* 72).

[98] Moo, *Romans,* 812.

which love demanded the breaking of a scriptural command.[99] Rather, it recognizes that fundamental principles, such as the commandments cited, embody what in fact *is* loving in every situation (v. 9). And the demonstration of this love becomes all the more urgent as the end of this age draws ever nearer (vv. 11–14).

Christian Tolerance (14:1–15:13) The final section in Paul's exhortational material completes the sequence of steps to understanding God's will. Love leads naturally to Christian tolerance. Here Paul addresses issues similar to those in 1 Corinthians 8–10, though perhaps more along the lines of the divisions between Jewish Christians who still kept a kosher table and Gentile believers who felt free to eat everything. Both groups are given the freedom to follow their own scruples, but neither has the right to disparage the other.[100]

That the situation is slightly different from that in Corinth is also indicated in the opening paragraph of this subsection (14:1–4). Some in the Roman church "eat only vegetables;" others partake of "everything" (vv. 2–3). Neither of these expressions is entirely literal. These verses contrast the vegetarian, who avoids all meat because kosher fare was hard to find, with the person who observed no dietary restrictions.[101] Neither group may judge the other because in Christ neither eating nor abstaining from certain foods remains a moral issue and because God is everyone's ultimate judge anyway (cf. also vv. 9–12; recall Mark 7:19b). The same is true for holy days. In Judaism, these would have included the weekly Sabbaths, the monthly new moon festivals and the annual feasts in Jerusalem. As long as one follows one's conscience and dedicates one's behavior to the Lord, either celebrating or refraining from participation in these days is acceptable (vv. 5–8).

At the same time, Christians must temper their freedom with the love that exhibits concern lest fellow believers be led into sin or into practicing something morally neutral that nevertheless violates their consciences (vv. 13b, 14b–15). Once again, the words for "stumbling block" and "obstacle" most likely refer to behaviors that would actually "trip up" someone else rather than merely offending them.[102] And even in this section on voluntary restraint, Paul returns to his previous emphasis in verses 13a, 14a, and 16–17. "No food is unclean in itself" (v. 14a) more literally reads, "Nothing is unclean in itself." Since Paul has already spoken of both food and holy days, he is probably generalizing to all morally neutral practices. But, of course, we must not so generalize that we imagine him to be commending that which is inherently sinful! In verse 17, he includes drink along with food as morally indifferent (and in v. 21 specifies wine in particular), contrasting those who are

---

[99] Made particularly famous by Joseph Fletcher, *Situation Ethics: The New Morality* (Philadelphia: Westminster, 1966).

[100] On this section, see esp. Robert Jewett, *Christian Tolerance: Paul's Message to the Modern Church* (Philadelphia: Westminster, 1982).

[101] Moo, *Romans*, 837. Some scholars play down the Jewish connection, since Greco-Roman sects at times practiced vegetarianism and celebrated their own holy days. Mark Reasoner (*The Strong and the Weak: Romans 14.1–15.13 in Context* (Cambridge and New York: CUP, 1997) includes both Jew and Gentile among the weak and views the "strong" as people of high status, mostly Roman citizens. Recently, Mark Nanos (*The Mystery of Romans* [Minneapolis: Fortress, 1996]) has argued that the weak were non-Christian Jews, but Witherington with Hyatt (*Romans*, 331) point out that this group abstains unto the Lord (vv. 5–8), and in v. 9 the Lord is clearly Jesus. So Moo's approach still reflects a fair consensus.

[102] Osborne, *Romans*, 366.

preoccupied with what they or others do or do not eat or drink with those who please God by focusing on "righteousness, peace and joy in the Holy Spirit."

Verses 19–23 basically just repeat these same themes for emphasis. The Roman believers must practice what builds up one another rather than causing one another either to sin in reality or to sin against their consciences ("everything that does not come from faith"—v. 23b). Chapter 15:1–6 reiterates these concepts once more, this time appealing also to Christ's model of serving others above self (v. 3a) and to glorifying God the Father (v. 6). Specifically, Paul cites Psalm 69:9 and applies it typologically to Jesus. As in 1 Corinthians 10:6, his justification for this procedure is his conviction that all of the Old Testament "was written to teach us" (v. 4), that is, we who live in the New Testament age in which all the outstanding patterns and promises of God begin to reach their fulfillment.

Paul's final word on the topic, however, brings the discussion full circle to his emphasis on freedom and mutual acceptance. Only in this way will unnecessary obstacles be removed from Gentiles coming to faith, which represents Paul's commission and passion (vv. 7–9a). So he quotes no less than four scriptural texts to remind the "weaker" Jewish Christians, who were still concerned to obey the law and impose it on others, of the importance of reaching non-Jews with the gospel (vv. 9b–12).[103] The body of the letter then concludes, appropriately, with a prayer for the Romans to experience the various signs of God's kingdom in their midst that were itemized in 14:17 (v. 13). Thus the discussion of 14:1–15:3 falls into an ABA structure: *14:1–12 stresses freedom and acceptance; 14:13–15:6 highlights the importance of not causing others to sin; and 15:7–13 stresses freedom and acceptance again.*[104] Just as in 1 Corinthians 8–10, Paul is more concerned about winning the outsider to Christ than about kowtowing to the scruples of the legalistic insider.

Modern applications should consider ways in which we wrongfully mandate distinctions such as those that separated Jews and Gentiles in the first century. Some, for the sake of Jewish or Muslim evangelism today, insist that those who have become Christians out of these backgrounds (or even those who minister to them not from these backgrounds) observe those religions' dietary laws. In so doing, they make exactly the same mistake that these Romans were making. Voluntary restraint for the sake of winning others is commendable, but mandatory restrictions compromise the very liberation that the gospel promises. Recalling our application of Galatians, we need to expand our horizons to think about how Paul's principles in this section can help curtail racism, nationalism, and ethnocentricity in the church of Jesus Christ as well. Homogeneous groupings of believers may prove helpful in winning the lost to Christ, but they dare not characterize all subsequent Christian living![105]

---

[103] Indeed, the success of the worldwide mission depends to a significant degree on the mutual acceptance of Jews and Gentiles in Christ. See further Scott Hafemann, "Eschatology and Ethics: The Future of Israel and the Nations in Romans 15:1–13," *TynB* 51 (2000): 161–92.

[104] Cf. further James C. Miller, *The Obedience of Faith, the Eschatological People of God, and the Purpose of Romans* (Atlanta: SBL, 2000).

[105] While not as directly parallel, it is probably also legitimate to apply these principles to doctrinal issues on which the Bible does not give unambiguous guidance and on which godly, Bible-believing Christians have never agreed. Osborne (*Romans,* 361) plausibly suggests as illustrations the debates over the timing of the rapture, charismatic gifts, gender roles, and Calvinism versus Arminianism.

CONCLUSION (15:14–16:27)

Travel Plans (15:14–33)   Before Paul brings his more formal closing greetings, he discusses his recent and coming travels. Just as 1:8–15, the second short subsection of the letter, introduced Paul's desire to come to Rome, so also 15:14–33 returns to this topic as the second-to-the-last subsection of the letter. As noted in our introduction (pp. 233–34), here is where we learn much of our background information on this epistle. In addition to the observations made there, we may note the following. Although Paul does not know the Roman church nearly as well as those congregations he personally founded, he in essence speaks optimistically of them. If some find his wording bold, it is only because of his unique commitment to spreading the gospel among the Gentile world, of which Rome forms the heart (vv. 14–16). He reiterates his "regions beyond" principle, by which he seeks to expand the circles of his preaching to virgin territory whenever viable churches exist in places closer to home (vv. 17–22). Now the Roman church appears next on his itinerary, once he has returned to Jerusalem with the collection for the poorer Jewish Christians there, a collection that has finally generated sufficient funds for Paul to accompany it.

Paul does not yet know of his coming imprisonment in Jerusalem, which will bring him to Rome under unexpected circumstances and, temporarily at least, thwart his intentions of heading even further west to Spain (vv. 23–29). Yet he does not expect smooth sailing in the Jewish capital, aware that non-Christian Jews may receive him with hostility and that Jewish Christians may not be sufficiently placated by his collection. So he requests prayers for both those situations to turn out positively enough that he can indeed move on to Rome (vv. 30–33).

Closing Greetings (16:1–27)   Chapter 16 comprises Paul's more formal closing. What is striking about it is how many people Paul greets, far more than in any other New Testament epistle, and yet this is the one church to date that he has never visited! This anomaly has led some scholars to propose that this chapter is misplaced and belonged as the ending to Ephesians, the letter to the church with which Paul had spent the longest period of time. After all, Ephesians concludes without Paul naming a single individual to whom he sends greetings. But there is no manuscript support anywhere for such a displacement, and there is a much better explanation for the long list of names at the end of Romans. *Precisely because Paul had not visited the Roman church, he wanted to build as many bridges to the congregation through these greetings as possible.* If these were individuals he had met in his various travels outside of Rome, it would be natural to mention them here in hopes that they would still think well of him and commend him and his message to the rest of the congregation. We know that this is exactly the case with the first people on his list, Priscilla and Aquila (see Acts 18:2). And it was not just a proverb in the ancient empire that all roads led to Rome. Many people were consistently migrating from elsewhere to the imperial capital. So it makes sense that the others Paul greets might have been in the identical situation as the couple mentioned in verse 3.

Complicating matters somewhat are a series of textual variants that affect the end of this letter. The mid-second-century heretic Marcion had a copy of Romans that lacked chapters 15 and 16 altogether. But Marcion was known for deleting those portions of the New Testament he disliked, so this truncated document proves little about the original text of Paul's letter. Intriguingly, however, a number of manuscripts put the doxology of verses 25–27 after chapter 14, while a few put it both after chapter 14 and at the end of the letter, making scholars wonder if some scribes knew of other texts that lacked the rest of these last two chapters.[106] But even if they did, such texts need not have been independent of Marcion's. One early manuscript places the doxology after chapter 15, and one extremely late manuscript lacks 16:1–24 entirely. While tantalizing, this evidence hardly overthrows the overwhelming manuscript support for the original text of Romans matching the sequence of chapters and passages in our modern translations.

Verses 1–2 introduce Paul's final chapter by commending to the Romans a woman by the name of Phoebe. She probably was delivering this epistle from Corinth to Rome, and she is described as a *diakonos* of the church in Cenchrea and a *prostatis* of many, including Paul. Although translations often render the first of these terms simply as a "servant," this was the standard word for "deacon," and a distinctively feminine form of the noun had not yet developed in Greek usage. Given that Phoebe is called a *diakonos* of a specific church, the term is more likely a label for an office in this context. On the origin of the diaconate, see above under Acts 6:1–7. The second Greek term most likely means "patron," indicating that the kind of help she has provided for many is largely financial. Like the wealthy women who provided for Jesus and the Twelve (Luke 8:1–3), Phoebe generously helped to support Paul and supplement what he earned from his tentmaking and occasionally received by way of gifts from other churches.[107]

In verses 3–16, Paul greets twenty-six people and three house churches (five of the households in vv. 10–11 are also churches). Most of the names are Gentile names, seemingly confirming the consensus view that the church was more Gentile than Jewish in makeup, though of course some of these individuals may have been God fearers before becoming Christians. Most of the names also are those that proliferated primarily or exclusively among the lower classes, including slaves, freedpersons, and craftspeople.[108] Sixteen of the individuals are singled out in some special way. "This is no ordinary greeting card. It is more like an honor roll."[109] *Nine of the twenty-six persons are women, several described as having worked with Paul "in the Lord," demonstrating how valuable they were in Paul's ministry.*

Most of those whom Paul greets appear only here in ancient Christian literature, and we know nothing more about them. But two individuals merit further brief comment. Verse 7 refers to two of Paul's relatives who had been imprisoned with him. They are described as "outstanding among the apostles," an expression that has been

---

[106] Or the evidence could suggest that the doxology itself was a later creation inserted at various places in the manuscripts. Defending its authenticity and integrity in its current location, however, is I. Howard Marshall, "Romans 16:25–27—an Apt Conclusion," in *Romans and the People of God,* eds. Sodelund and Wright, 170–84.

[107] On both terms, see R. A. Kearsley, "Women in Public Life in the Roman East: Iunia Theodora, Claudia Metrodora and Phoebe, Benefactress of Paul," *TynB* 50 (1999): 189–211. Cf. also Caroline F. Whelan, "Amica Pauli: The Role of Phoebe in the Early Church," *JSNT* 49 (1993): 67–85.

[108] Osborne, *Romans,* 403–4.

[109] Witherington with Hyatt, *Romans,* 380.

unsuccessfully explained as meaning "outstanding in the eyes of the apostles" when in fact it attributes apostleship to these two themselves.[110] Older translations often render the individuals' names as Andronicus and Junias, but the second name in Greek is almost certainly a woman's name and is better rendered in English as Junia. The two may well have been husband and wife.[111] Clearly they were not part of the Twelve, but we must remember that Paul uses "apostle" to refer to a spiritual gift as well, similar to our modern use of "missionary" or "church planter" (see above, p. 190).[112]

While the Roman church does not seem to have been beset by anything remotely approaching the factionalism of Corinth, Paul knows all too well how easily it could begin. Whatever tensions existed between Jews and Gentiles in the congregation could readily be exploited by anyone so inclined. So in verses 17–19, he warns his listeners to beware of such threats. Verse 20 offers the Romans God's grace and peace, though for those implacably opposed to Christ this peace will be established only through their destruction. Verses 21–23 bring greetings to the church from several individuals who may well be present with Paul as he writes. We know Timothy already from Acts 16 and elsewhere. Some have wondered if Lucius is the same person as Luke; more likely they are separate individuals. Jason could be the Thessalonian Christian of Acts 17:5–9, though the name seems to have been common. So(si)pater and Gaius are probably the delegates mentioned in Acts 20:4 who accompanied the collection for Judea. And Erastus is almost certainly the person named on an inscription uncovered by archeologists in Corinth (recall p. 234). The name of Tertius is important not because we know him from elsewhere but because he offers the one utterly unambiguous example of Paul using an amanuensis or scribe, as was the Hellenistic custom, to whom he dictated his letters (recall above, p. 101). Verses 25–27 round out the epistle with another uplifting doxology that also summarizes a number of the book's key themes.

APPLICATION

The epistle to the Romans led Martin Luther to reconsider the medieval Catholicism that he had been taught and to recover a biblical theology of justification by faith rather than works. Thus no other portion of Scripture was more instrumental in spawning the Protestant Reformation beginning in the early 1500s. Similarly, it was Romans that led John Wesley two centuries later to recover the need for a personal conversion experience within a significant portion of the Church of England that had often lost sight of this. As a result, a new branch of Protestantism

---

[110] Richard Bauckham, *Gospel Women: Studies of the Named Women in the Gospels* (Grand Rapids and Cambridge: Eerdmans, 2002), 172–80. Cf. Linda L. Belleville, "A Re-examination of Romans 16.7 in Light of Primary Source Materials," *NTS* 51 (2005): 231–49; Eldon J. Epp, *Junia: The First Woman Apostle* (Minneapolis: Fortress, 2005)..

[111] Schreiner, *Romans*, 795–96.

[112] The significance of this observation for the debate about gender roles in ministry is disputed. Clearly such a person exercised authority over both men and women, but she does not seem to have played the same role as the elders of a local church. Unlike many missionaries throughout church history, the New Testament ideal seems to have been for them to "work themselves out of a job" and turn over responsibility to local leadership as soon as it was viable, so that they could move on to places where Christian churches did not yet exist.

was born that came to be known as the Methodist Church, which in turn would later produce various other holiness churches (e.g., the Nazarenes) and ultimately the twentieth-century Pentecostal and charismatic movements. Also in the twentieth century, Romans would transform the young German liberal, Karl Barth, who went on to become perhaps the most influential theologian of the century anywhere in the world, establishing what came to be called neo-orthodoxy.

These developments should cause no surprise. This epistle of Paul provides the most systematic answer anywhere in Scripture to the question of how to become right with God, which is the fundamental question of human existence on the assumption that God exists at all. More comprehensively, incorporating both the theological and ethical material of the epistle, Romans sums up the Christian answer to the question of how to know God's will for one's life. *This letter is the "Gospel of John" of the epistles—the fullest and most organized presentation of the heart of the gospel.*[113] All human beings have sinned and thus have become alienated from God. Restoring a desirable relationship with their Maker required the atonement wrought by Jesus Christ. Actualizing this relationship—what Christianity calls salvation—necessitates faith in Christ, which combines belief in his deity and bodily resurrection with submission to his lordship (making him ultimate Master of one's life). No form of works righteousness can ever bring about this salvation.

Still, those who have truly been justified will by definition have living within them the Spirit, who guarantees their transformation into increasingly godly people, though undoubtedly in as many different ways as there are individual believers and not without plenty of lapses and fresh starts. This "progressive sanctification" culminates in the ultimate glorification of the believer when Christ returns, which combines a resurrected body free from the decay that leads to death with a morally perfected spirit that never again sins. Because moral change begins already in this age, believers are commanded to yield themselves increasingly to the Spirit, who will empower them to obey the commands of the gospel. At the most general level, these commands involve physical and mental purity in the dedication of one's entire self to the Lord. They then proceed to the level of discovering one's individual spiritual gifts and exercising them faithfully and in love. And they point out that Christian maturity exhibits itself in the joyful tolerance and even encouragement of other believers to live as God has shaped them and as he guides their consciences on all issues other than the small handful of biblical absolutes that remain nonnegotiable.

If we begin acting on all of these precious truths that we can know clearly represent God's will for our lives, then we will be poised to understand his guidance on the often more difficult questions about our personal callings, including where to work, where to live, whom to marry (or whether to stay single), whether to have children, when to move, and so on. At times, this guidance may lead us to understand

---

[113] These generalizations remain true even after full allowance is made for the specific historical and sociological content of the letter. The full range of proposals is well represented in Karl P. Donfried, ed., *The Romans Debate* (Peabody: Hendrickson, rev. 1991). As Jeffrey A. D. Weima ("The Reason for Romans: The Evidence of Its Epistolary Framework [1:1–15, 15:14–15, 27]," *RevExp* 100 [2003]: 17–33) shows, the material surrounding the body of the letter all reinforces the conviction that Paul's primary purpose in Romans remains the preaching of the gospel to them as he understands it.

that God is giving us the freedom to rely on what can be called "sanctified common sense." In other words, as we saw in Acts, God frequently does not disclose his will through unambiguous signs but through a process of our exploration of numerous possibilities, all of which could reflect acceptable ways to serve him, but only one of which actually materializes. Or, in other cases, we simply have to choose among God-honoring activities, since we can do only so many things in so many places in this finite, fallen existence of ours.

ADDITIONAL QUESTIONS FOR REVIEW

1. What is the date and provenance of Paul's letter to the Romans? What information helps us to date and locate this letter so precisely? Why does the time at which Paul pens this letter constitute a turning point in his evangelistic career? What significant event in Rome helps enables a reader to understand a large amount of the content of Romans, and how did this event affect the church in Rome?

2. How is the letter body of Romans best divided? What is a good thesis statement for each of the main sections? How do the subdivisions of the first section aid our understanding and presentation of the gospel? What is a good summary statement for each of the subdivided sections?

3. What is Paul's main point in Romans 1 about all sin, including homosexuality? How has his list of sins been taken out of context and used abusively, especially in recent evangelicalism? How could a sound exegetical approach to this text work to remedy the imbalanced accusations leveled at homosexuals?

4. What does Romans 3–5 assert about one's worthiness to be justified through faith? Did association with and obedience to Jewish laws provide an upper hand in being justified? What does the application of Paul's teaching mean for today for those who would seek justification?

5. Based on Romans 5, what is a good conclusion about how "original sin" affects all of humanity? What is the larger point of Romans 5?

6. According to Romans, what is the relationship between justification and sanctification? What happens to a person's sin nature after he or she is justified by faith in Christ? How do the various interpretations of Romans 7:14–25 affect Paul's theology of sanctification? What are the pastoral and personal implications of each of the interpretations of Romans 7:14–25?

7. According to Romans 8, what gifts are bestowed on those who are justified by faith in Jesus? What is the process of the order of salvation?

8. What principles can be drawn from Romans 9–11 about the fairness of God's election and predestination? How should the discussion of Israel's election inform and direct our political affiliations?

9. What exegetical observations inform Paul's discussion of submission to governing authorities in Romans 13?

10. What does the structure of Romans 14 highlight as most important in this chapter? What is the practical application of this principle to daily Christian living?

11. What is unique about the closing to Romans when compared to all of the other epistles attributed to Paul? What might account for this difference?

SELECT BIBLIOGRAPHY

Commentaries

Advanced

Cranfield, C. E. B. *A Critical and Exegetical Commentary on the Epistle to the Romans,* 2 vols. ICC, rev. Edinburgh: T & T Clark, 1976–79.
Dunn, James D. G. *Romans,* 2 vols. WBC. Dallas: Word, 1988.
Fitzmyer, Joseph A. *Romans.* AB. New York and London: Doubleday, 1993.
Käsemann, Ernst. *Commentary on Romans.* Grand Rapids: Eerdmans, 1980.
Schreiner, Thomas R. *Romans.* BECNT. Grand Rapids: Baker, 1998.

Intermediate

Johnson, Luke T. *Reading Romans.* New York: Crossroad, 1997.
Moo, Douglas J. *The Epistle to the Romans,* rev. NICNT. Grand Rapids and Cambridge: Eerdmans, 1996.
Morris, Leon. *The Epistle to the Romans.* PNTC. Leicester: IVP; Grand Rapids: Eerdmans, 1988.
Mounce, Robert H. *Romans.* NAC. Nashville: Broadman & Holman, 1995.
Stuhlmacher, Peter. *Paul's Letter to the Romans.* Louisville: WJKP, 1994.
Talbert, Charles H. *Romans.* SHBC. Macon: Smyth & Helwys, 2002.
Witherington, Ben, III, with Darlene Hyatt. *Paul's Letter to the Romans: A Socio-Rhetorical Commentary.* Grand Rapids and Cambridge: Eerdmans, 2004.

Introductory

Bruce, F. F. *The Epistle of Paul to the Romans.* TNTC. Leicester: IVP; Grand Rapids: Eerdmans, 1963.
Moo, Douglas J. *Romans.* NIVAC. Grand Rapids: Zondervan, 2000.
Osborne, Grant R. *Romans.* IVPNTC. Leicester and Downers Grove: IVP, 2004.
Stott, John. *Romans: God's Good News for the World.* Leicester and Downers Grove: IVP, 1994.

Other Books

Bryan, Christopher. *A Preface to Romans.* Oxford and New York: OUP, 2000.
Davies, Glenn N. *Faith and Obedience in Romans.* Sheffield: JSOT, 1990.
Donfried, Karl P., ed. *The Romans Debate.* Peabody: Hendrickson, rev. 1991.
Elliott, Neal. *The Rhetoric of Romans.* Sheffield: JSOT, 1990.
Esler, Philip F. *Conflict and Identity in Romans.* Minneapolis: Fortress, rev. 2003.
Guerra, Anthon J. *Romans and the Apologetic Tradition: The Purpose, Genre and Audience of Paul's Letter.* Cambridge and New York: CUP, 1995.

Haacker, Klaus. *The Theology of Paul's Letter to the Romans.* Cambridge and New York: CUP, 2003.

Hay, David M., and Elizabeth Johnson, eds. *Pauline Theology,* vol. 3: *Romans.* Minneapolis: Fortress, 1995.

Jervis, L. Ann. *The Purpose of Romans.* Sheffield: JSOT, 1991.

McGinn, Sheila E., ed. *Celebrating Romans: Template for Pauline Theology.* Grand Rapids and Cambridge: Eerdmans, 2004.

Soderlund, Sven, and N. T. Wright, eds. *Romans and the People of God.* Grand Rapids and Cambridge: Eerdmans, 1999.

Stowers, Stanley K. *The Diatribe and Paul's Letter to the Romans.* Chico: Scholars, 1981.

Stowers, Stanley K. *A Rereading of Romans: Justice, Jews, and Gentiles.* New Haven and London: Yale, 1994.

Tobin, Thomas H. *Paul's Rhetoric in Its Contexts: The Argument of Romans.* Peabody: Hendrickson, 2004.

Wedderburn, A. J. M. *The Reasons for Romans.* Edinburgh: T & T Clark, 1988.

Westerholm, Stephen. *Preface to the Study of Paul.* Grand Rapids and Cambridge: Eerdmans, 1997.

Yeo, Khiok-khng. *Navigating Romans through Cultures.* London and New York: T & T Clark, 2004.

BIBLIOGRAPHY

Mills, Watson E. *Romans.* Lewiston and Lampeter: Mellen, 1996.

7

The Prison Epistles: General Introduction

our of Paul's letters have traditionally been viewed as coming from his Roman imprisonment described at the end of the book of Acts. If this tradition is accurate, then they must be dated to approximately A.D. 60–62. The four letters in question are Philemon, Colossians, Ephesians and Philippians. All four contain references to Paul in jail (Philem. 1; Col. 4:3; Eph. 6:20; Phil. 1:14); thus they have come to be known as the Prison Epistles. A fifth letter attributed to Paul, 2 Timothy, also places him in jail (2 Tim. 1:16–17), but there are reasons for treating this as a separate, later imprisonment (see below, p. 375). What is more, in terms of style and content, 2 Timothy belongs with 1 Timothy and Titus, as one of the three "Pastoral Epistles," and so it is excluded from consideration here.

Traditionally, too, Philemon, Colossians, and Ephesians have been assumed to come from one period of Paul's imprisonment and Philippians from another. We will say more about Philippians under the introduction to that letter; we want to focus on the other three epistles here. In both Ephesians 6:21–22 and Colossians 4:7–8, Paul names Tychicus as the "mailman" or letter carrier. In both Colossians 4:10–14 and Philemon 23, Paul lists the same five companions who send greetings—Epaphras, Mark, Aristarchus, Demas, and Luke. This suggests that Paul sent all three letters at the same time. *Philemon was apparently a member of the Colossian church.* Philemon 2 and Colossians 4:17 both send greetings to Archippus, a member of Philemon's household, which makes sense if that family lives in Colossae. Ephesus was the nearest major urban center to Colossae, a little over one hundred miles to the west on the Aegean coastline, so it would have been natural for all three of these epistles to be sent by means of one courier from Rome, stopping first at Ephesus after probably traveling by boat and then proceeding on by land to Colossae in the Lycus valley. Perhaps during Paul's Ephesian ministry he had met up with or even shared the gospel for the first time with Epaphras, the native of Colossae he credits with founding the church there (Col. 1:7, 4:12).

Scripture itself, however, never specifies the location or time of the imprisonment (or imprisonments) referred to in these four letters. As a result, two other important suggestions about the time and place of Paul's penning these epistles have garnered periodic support throughout church history. We know from Acts 23:23–24:27 that Paul spent two years in jail in *Caesarea* on the Palestinian coast (A.D. 57–59), so perhaps he wrote one or more of the Prison Epistles from this venue.[1] But Caesarea is over four hundred and fifty miles from Ephesus, which would have been quite a distance to expect a letter carrier to traverse. What is more, in Philemon 22, Paul

---

[1] See, e.g., Robinson, *Redating the New Testament,* 61–67.

CHARACTER LINKS BETWEEN THE PRISON EPISTLES

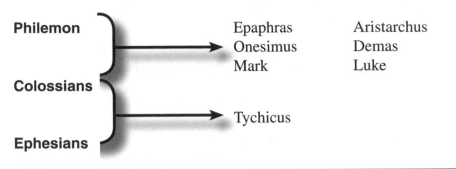

Philemon	Epaphras	Aristarchus
	Onesimus	Demas
	Mark	Luke
Colossians		
	Tychicus	
Ephesians		

Philippians

remains hopeful for his release from prison in the near future, an optimism not apparent in Paul's attitude or circumstances as described in Acts 23–24.

What is probably the earliest post-New Testament tradition about the setting of Colossians (the anti-Marcionite prologue to this letter) cites *Ephesus* as the place of Paul's incarceration, which would then date the letter to between 52 and 55. This would have made Paul's correspondence with the Ephesians and Colossians comparatively easy. Tychicus would only have had to travel across town to deliver the one letter and less than one hundred miles with the other. This hypothesis would explain how Onesimus, Philemon's runaway slave, could have reached Paul without great difficulty, though one wonders if a runaway would have stayed so comparatively close to his home.[2] As we will see in the introduction to Philemon, however, there are other explanations of Onesimus meeting up with Paul.

At the same time, there is no explicit reference to an Ephesian imprisonment in the New Testament. The hardships Paul suffered in Asia (Minor), alluded to in 1 Corinthians 15:32 and 2 Corinthians 1:8, could support such an imprisonment but could just as easily refer to other forms of life-threatening harassment or persecution. Perhaps more tellingly, the account in Acts 19 of Paul's Ephesian ministry is not one of those portions of Acts in which Luke uses the first-person plural (the so-called "we" passages). Yet, as we have observed, he is present with Paul for the writing of Philemon and Colossians, with Paul sending greetings on Luke's behalf. For those who find Colossians pseudonymous (see below, pp. 287–88), this proves less of a problem. But given the virtual unanimity of opinion that Philemon is genuinely Pauline, Luke's presence with Paul for the penning of this short letter still remains a problem.

The strongest argument against the tradition of a Roman imprisonment is that Philemon 22 declares Paul's intention to visit Colossae when he is released, while in Romans 15:24 Paul explains his plan to proceed from Rome in the opposite direction—westward to Spain. But Romans was written before Paul knew he would be arrested in Jerusalem and come to Rome as a prisoner rather than a free man. His two

---

[2] See, e.g., N. T. Wright, *Colossians and Philemon* (Leicester: IVP; Grand Rapids: Eerdmans, 1986), 34–39.

years under house arrest could easily have changed his plans, as could circumstances in the communities addressed in the Prison Epistles. A second problem involves the distance between Rome and the cities to which these letters were sent. The distance from Rome to Colossae, as the crow flies, was nearly nine hundred miles, well over twice as far as from Colossae to Caesarea! How could Onesimus have made that trip unaided, at least on his westward journey, and how could Paul expect a letter carrier to safely navigate the return trip, even if accompanied by Onesimus?

On the other hand, if Onesimus was not a fugitive, he may not have set off without help, and the Roman mail service, outstanding by ancient standards, in fact regularly sent well-guarded couriers across its comparatively excellent roads even greater distances. If he were a fugitive, Rome was a natural slave haven and large enough that Onesimus could easily get lost in the population of a million or so inhabitants with little risk of being caught and returned to Asia Minor. The fact that the dominant early church tradition, including statements by Jerome, John Chrysostom, and Theodoret, supports Rome (in spite of the objections and notwithstanding other alternatives known in the early church) still makes this location the most likely site for Paul's imprisonment. Indeed, modern scholars who have supported an Ephesian provenance for one particular Prison Epistle have most often chosen Philippians rather than any of the other three, for reasons to be discussed below. *At least Philemon, Colossians, and Ephesians, then, seem most probably to stem from Rome in about A.D. 61.*[3]

QUESTIONS FOR REVIEW

1. What New Testament letters are alleged to be written by Paul from prison? What three letters were sent at the same time, and what evidence in the text supports this conclusion?

2. What are the options for the place of imprisonment from which Paul writes these letters, and how do these locations interact with evidence of imprisonment in Acts?

---

[3] Cf. further Markus Barth and Helmut Blanke, *Colossians* (New York and London: Doubleday, 1994), 126–34.

Philemon: A Christian Response to Slavery

INTRODUCTION

Philemon is clearly the shortest, most personal, and most occasional of all Paul's letters. Still, it is addressed to an entire house congregation (v. 2), and its inclusion in the canon demonstrates the early church's belief in its abiding applicability. Ignatius, bishop of Antioch, in the early second century, reported that Onesimus was bishop of Ephesus at that time (*Ign. Eph.* 1:3; 2:1; 6:2). If accurate, this claim could also account for the letter's preservation (though there is always the outside chance that he was referring to a different person by the same name). *The setting for this brief epistle is Paul's request for Philemon, the slave owner and apparent leader of this individual congregation within the larger church in Colossae, to welcome home one of his slaves, Onesimus, who has now become "useful" (exactly what his name meant), as a new believer in Christ (vv. 10–11), with Paul's promise of financial redress (v. 18).*

The most common assumption throughout church history has been that Onesimus was a runaway slave who had perhaps stolen some of Philemon's property, as runaways in the ancient Roman empire were often known to do. How he came to run into Paul becomes far more uncertain, but believers in providential guidance need not answer this question definitively to find the account plausible.[4]

On the other hand, *three interesting alternative explanations of Onesimus's departure from Colossae* and encounter with Paul merit some attention. *First,* perhaps Onesimus had not run away at all. He could, in fact, have been sent to Paul in prison as a representative of the Colossian church, perhaps to bring Paul material aid of some kind. Nothing in the letter ever explicitly refers to Onesimus as a runaway or states that he had committed any crime. Verse 13, speaking of Onesimus providing help Philemon could have wanted to offer himself, fits the suggestion that he was commissioned to come to Paul, while verses 18–19 could be hypothetical or could refer to the monetary worth of lost man-hours during Onesimus's time away.[5] On the other hand, Onesimus was not a believer prior to meeting Paul (v. 10) and apparently was regarded as useless (v. 11), so it seems unlikely that he would have been chosen as the emissary for this task. And the reference to the possibility that Onesimus has wronged Philemon (v. 18a) seems to be a random remark, unless the slave had at least been accused of some crime.

A *second* alternative option, popularized by abolitionists in the nineteenth century, takes the reference to Onesimus as Philemon's brother in verse 16 entirely literally. The term "slave" in this same verse must then be understood metaphorically as someone who had been estranged from his biological sibling. This hypothesis

---

[4] For a good, recent defense of this traditional perspective, see John G. Nordling, "Onesimus Fugitivus: A Defense of the Runaway Slave Hypothesis in Philemon," *JSNT* 41 (1991): 97–119.

[5] See esp. Sara C. Winter, "Paul's Letter to Philemon," *NTS* 33 (1987): 1–15.

exactly inverts the traditional understanding concerning which of these two terms should be understood literally and which metaphorically. Onesimus could have come to Rome, knowing Paul's relationship with Philemon, in hopes that Paul would intercede and bring reconciliation between the two family members. This would also explain Paul's language in verse 16b that Onesimus is even more beloved to Philemon than to Paul, a statement which, on the traditional reading, must be understood at best as what Paul hopes will become a future reality.[6]

This scenario, nevertheless, flies in the face of the highly consistent uses of the terms for "brother" and "slave" in the New Testament. *Adelphos* ("brother") occasionally refers to a biological sibling, but contextual information always makes that clear. Far more common, however, is the unqualified use of the term to refer to spiritual kin, either among fellow Jews, fellow disciples of Jesus, or fellow believers in the early church. On the other hand, the word for slave (*doulos*) in the New Testament consistently refers to a literal indentured servant (unless otherwise qualified such as in the common expression "a slave of Jesus Christ"), and nothing in Philemon suggests that *doulos* should be taken in any fashion other than literal.[7]

A *third* alternative option proves the most promising. This approach builds on the common Roman practice of seeking an *amicus domini* ("friend of the master") to mediate in serious disputes that have otherwise reached an impasse. It is clear that Onesimus has wronged Philemon in some respect, even if not by theft. Perhaps Onesimus fled (or was sent) with the intention of meeting up with Paul from the outset, in hopes that he would intervene and help settle whatever issue had put Onesimus and Philemon at odds. This would explain his lengthier journey, his encounter with Paul, and the language of verses 16 and 18. On this reading, the only unexpected turn of events was Onesimus's conversion to Christianity while in Rome, which simply made Paul's conviction all the more settled that reconciliation should occur. A majority of recent studies and commentaries on Philemon have adopted this perspective, with varying degrees of confidence, and it appears to merit serious consideration.[8] Its biggest weakness is the distance it requires Onesimus to have traveled just to seek out mediation.[9]

Whether one takes the traditional approach to Onesimus as a runaway slave or the more recent understanding of him appealing to an *amicus domini,* the letter to Philemon provides an excellent illustration of a *letter of recommendation* (also called a letter of introduction or an intercessory letter).[10] This kind of letter was common among the papyri, designed to introduce the bearer of the letter to its recipient and then to request a certain favor. Often the writer of the letter was a close friend or relative of the recipient and was promising to return the favor in some way. Of course in this instance, Onesimus is already known to Philemon but not as the new

---

[6] In recent years, this view has become particularly associated with Allen D. Callahan. See esp. his *Embassy of Onesimus: The Letter to Philemon* (Valley Forge: Trinity, 1997).

[7] Cf. Murray J. Harris, *Slave of Christ* (Leicester and Downers Grove: IVP, 1999), 57–59.

[8] See esp. Chris Frilingos, "'For My Child, Onesimus': Paul and Domestic Power in Philemon," *JBL* 119 (2000): 91–104. Cf. also Brian M. Rapske, "The Prisoner Paul in the Eyes of Onesimus," *NTS* 37 (1991): 187–203.

[9] Carson and Moo, *An Introduction to the New Testament*, 591–92.

[10] David E. Aune, *The New Testament in Its Literary Environment* (Philadelphia: Westminster, 1987), 211–12; Stowers, *Letter-Writing,* 155.

Christian he now is. The letter of recommendation naturally takes the form of deliberative rhetoric.[11] While brief, the epistle conforms to the standard Hellenistic letter structure, too, which may be outlined as follows:

I. Greeting (1–3)
II. Thanksgiving (4–7)
III. Letter Body: The Actual Request (8–22)
   A. Preparation for the Appeal (8–16)
   B. The Actual Appeal (17–22)
IV. Closing Greetings (23–25)

COMMENTARY

GREETING (VV. 1–3)

Even though this letter is by far the shortest of all those attributed to Paul, it still contains a standard-length greeting. Unlike those letters in which Paul writes as a free man, this brief letter introduces its author as a prisoner on account of his Christian commitment (v. 1). In this lowly condition the apostle resembles the slave for whom he intercedes more than we might suspect.[12] As in 1 and 2 Corinthians, Timothy appears at least as a cosender, perhaps even as a coauthor. Paul addresses Philemon as a beloved fellow worker, suggesting the two had ministered together at some previous point in their careers. Two additional addressees include Apphia and Archippus, described merely as "our sister" and "our fellow-soldier," respectively (v. 2).

Commentators have often wondered if these were Philemon's wife and grown son; otherwise the most we can say about them is that they are fellow Christians and that Archippus also had labored for the gospel in some way. Yet this letter is sent not merely to a private family but to a house church, which gives it a more public nature and application and undoubtedly helps explain why it was preserved and ultimately canonized. The greeting of grace and peace matches what we have come to expect of Paul in his previous letters (v. 3).

THANKSGIVING (VV. 4–7)

The opening thanksgiving is understandably briefer than elsewhere but still more substantive than many prayers in Hellenistic letters. As elsewhere, key words introduce important concepts that the letter body will take up: love, prayers, partner(ship), good, heart, refresh, and brother.[13] Just as Paul often praises God for the progress of entire congregations, here he is grateful for Philemon's personal faith and love. The Greek of verse 5 reads literally, "Hearing [about] your love and faith, which you have for the Lord Jesus and for all the saints [i.e., believers]." Because it seems

---

[11] Joseph A. Fitzmyer, *The Letter to Philemon* (New York and London: Doubleday, 2000), 41.
[12] Markus Barth and Helmut Blanke, *The Letter to Philemon* (Grand Rapids and Cambridge: Eerdmans, 2000), 244.
[13] David E. Garland, *Colossians/Philemon* (Grand Rapids: Zondervan, 1998), 319.

inappropriate to speak of someone having faith directed toward other Christians, at least in the same way one has faith in Jesus, it has been suggested that this verse forms a chiasm. Thus, Philemon's love would be directed toward the saints, while his faith would find its object in the Lord Jesus.[14] The NIV adopts precisely this interpretation and rearranges the word order in English to make it clear.

On the other hand, the translation in the NIV of verse 6 proves altogether misleading. The ambiguous Greek expression here is *hē koinōnia tēs pisteōs sou*—"the fellowship of your faith." Taking the case ending of the word for "faith" as an objective genitive yields the idea of "sharing your faith" and suggests that Paul wants Philemon to become an active evangelist. In some circles today this verse has become a favorite prooftext for encouraging personal witnessing. But nothing in the context of this letter has anything to do with Philemon proclaiming the gospel to others, while in fact the epistle is all about him demonstrating his love to his slave who has become a new believer. Moreover, other pairs of nouns in Paul's letters that reflect a similar construction of abstract virtues, with the second noun in the genitive case, most often reflect subjective genitives (e.g., Gal. 5:19; 1 Thess. 1:3, 5:8; Rom. 1:5, etc.). This grammatical category fits this context perfectly. *Paul wants Philemon's normally warm interpersonal relationships to extend even to Onesimus, so he prays for "the fellowship produced by your faith"* (cf. TNIV).[15]

The second half of verse 6 is also susceptible to several possible translations. A word-for-word rendering would read, "Might become active in the knowledge of every good thing which is in us [some manuscripts, 'you'] in Christ." It would appear that Paul's prayer for Philemon includes the hope that he will recognize that welcoming rather than punishing Onesimus flows from his Christian convictions. This meaning, too, is obscured more in the NIV than in the TNIV. With verse 7, however, the NIV gets back on track, as it acknowledges Philemon's history of loving behavior with both Paul and many other believers. These very characteristics give the apostle hope that Philemon will treat his slave kindly as well.[16]

LETTER BODY: THE ACTUAL REQUEST (VV. 8–22)

Preparation for the Appeal (vv. 8–16) Although information and exhortation are woven throughout the short body of this epistle, one may divide it into two main subsections: verses 8–16 and 17–22. As Paul prepares in the first of these sections for the request he will make more explicitly in the second, he appeals to Philemon to act out of his friendship for Paul and not merely as submitting to an apostolic mandate. These verses provide a masterful model of pastoral tact and psychology.[17] Paul in no

---

[14] Eduard Lohse, *Colossians and Philemon* (Philadelphia: Fortress, 1971), 193.

[15] So most recent commentators. See, e.g., James D. G. Dunn, *The Epistles to the Colossians and to Philemon* (Carlisle: Paternoster; Grand Rapids: Eerdmans, 1996), 318–20. The TNIV corrects the NIV with the much more probable rendering, "I pray that your partnership with us in the faith may be effective in deepening your understanding."

[16] "Paul's letter circles around the central theme of the Christian community bound together by mutual love and commitment" (Marianne M. Thompson, *Colossians and Philemon* [Grand Rapids & Cambridge: Eerdmans, 2005], 214).

[17] On which, see esp. Andrew Wilson, "The Pragmatics of Politeness and Pauline Epistolography: A Case Study of the Letter to Philemon," *JSNT* 48 (1992): 107–19. Holladay (*A Critical Introduction to the New Testament*, 383) terms it "a diplomatic masterpiece because of its sensitive handling of a delicate situation."

way wants to coerce, and yet he also wants to ensure that Philemon complies! *The clear portion of his request is that he wants Philemon to welcome Onesimus back home and thus not punish him as slave owners were free to do under Roman law, even including as extreme a reprisal as execution.* What else Paul may mean is less clear.

Verses 8–9 contrast the two approaches Paul could take. Because of his authority, he could simply tell Philemon the right thing to do, but he would prefer that Philemon owned for himself the Christian response in this situation. Thus the apostle appeals to the principle of love and generates some pathos for his own situation by alluding to his age and imprisonment. The word for "old man" (*presbutēs*) differs by only one letter from the word for "ambassador" (*presbeutēs*), and barely if at all in pronunciation, leading some to suggest the latter as what Paul originally wrote or meant. But that would weaken the pathos; "old man" fits better with "prisoner" as a second reason Philemon should empathize with Paul's situation and take his advice.[18]

In verse 10, we learn that Paul considers Onesimus his "son," a probable reference to the fact that the apostle had led the slave to the Lord when they met up in Rome ("while I was in chains"). Verse 11 forms a pun or play on words based on the meaning of Onesimus ("useful"). Only since he has come to Christ has the slave truly lived up to his name.[19] Paul had no legal right to keep Onesimus with him, since he still belonged to Philemon, so he is sending him back to his master (v. 12). But the apostle refers to the converted slave as "my very heart" (from the same Greek word that the KJV often translated as "bowels of mercy"—the center of one's emotions and passions).[20] He then adds that he wished he could keep the newly reborn Onesimus with him to help him in some combination of practical and spiritual assistance during his house arrest. He even refers to this role as replacing what he apparently thinks Philemon himself would have wanted to do had he had the opportunity (v. 13).

But again Paul stresses that he prefers full, voluntary agreement on Philemon's part (v. 14). He recognizes that God's purposes for Onesimus may be to keep him with his master, but now in a new relationship (vv. 15–16).[21] Exactly what that relationship involves, however, remains ambiguous. At the very least, Philemon must recognize that Onesimus's conversion makes him a fellow believer equal in every respect to his master in God's eyes. This alone should make Philemon love and value Onesimus even more than Paul does because Philemon better appreciates the drastic transformation that has occurred. But the expression "no longer as a slave" hints at

---

[18] The word for "old man" often referred to someone between the ages of 50 and 56, which also fits within the parameters of Paul's life that are known (see above, p. 86), although these are not so specific that this information enables us to exclude any of the three main possible dates for the letter (see above). See further Dunn, *Colossians and Philemon*, 327.

[19] There may be a second pun, too, with the word for "useless" (*achrestos*), which differs only by one letter from the word for non-Christian (*achristos*) (Garland, *Colossians/Philemon*, 330).

[20] By calling Onesimus his "very own heart," it is as if Paul himself were coming to Philemon in the person of Onesimus (Fitzmyer, *Philemon*, 109).

[21] "For good" translates the Greek for "forever," as in our English expression, "she finally came home for good." While Onesimus may well have been more "good" in an ethical sense after his return, the Greek does not allow for that meaning here.

the possibility that Paul is requesting full-fledged manumission,[22] a possibility that becomes a probability when one recognizes the unusually emphatic grammatical form used for "no longer."[23]

The Explicit Appeal (vv. 17–22)   Although this second half of the letter body finally comes around to Paul's actual request, we still remain unsure of just what he is asking. Nevertheless, several features suggest that he would prefer Philemon to free Onesimus.[24] First, he asks his "partner" (a term that could refer to their previous cooperation either in business or in ministry) to "welcome him as you would welcome me" (v. 17), and Paul is obviously not a slave. Second, in recognizing that this would deprive Philemon of recouping past losses or gaining any future material benefits from Onesimus, Paul promises to pay them himself (vv. 18–19a).[25] In prison, he probably did not have the resources to do this at that moment, thus his language of charging it to his account. But such a sum could one day prove exorbitant, so that Paul could be promising something he could never deliver. He apparently counts on Philemon not "cashing in" on this offer. Just in case he is tempted to try to do so, Paul adds, "not to mention that you owe me your very self" (v. 19b), probably implying that Paul led Philemon to the Lord as well.[26]

In verse 20, the apostle returns to the play on words with Onesimus's name, now desiring that Philemon, too, show himself useful (Greek *onaimēn*; NIV "have some benefit"). Finally, confident of Philemon's cooperation, Paul specifies that he is sure his friend "will do even more" than he has asked. But the only thing he has not come out and explicitly requested is Onesimus's freedom. So verse 21 provides the strongest argument for seeing this slave's liberty as Paul's ultimate burden in this brief letter. Some even suspect that, if Paul has hinted at manumission earlier, this comment implies he wants Philemon to send Onesimus back to him.[27]

At first glance, verse 22 would appear to begin the letter closing as it turns to a more incidental request—to prepare a guest room for Paul since he hopes soon to be freed and to travel to Colossae. But we must realize this as a further mechanism of holding Philemon accountable to respond properly to Paul's appeal. If the apostle comes in person, he can take further action if Onesimus has not been treated well enough.[28] Indeed, the very dynamic of addressing this letter not merely to one in-

---

[22] Fitzmyer, *Philemon*, 114–15. The expression, "Both as a man and as a brother in the Lord," translates the Greek *kai en sarki kai en kuriō* (literally, "Both in the flesh and in the Lord"). Barth and Blanke (*Philemon*, 454) observe that "a brother and a neighbor has the right to be loved in his own right, as a specific and unique person."

[23] Barth and Blanke, *Philemon*, 416–17. The Greek is *ouketi*, but because the clause this word introduces is dependent on a *hina*-clause, which takes the subjunctive mood, one would have expected *mēketi*. "Paul intended to speak of facts, not of a mere possibility, desirability, or faint expectation. What has actually happened to Onesimus, and what has become of him—this is the ground of the apostle's intervention and hope for the future status and treatment of Onesimus."

[24] Cf. Robert W. Wall, *Colossians and Philemon* (Leicester and Downers Grove: IVP, 1993), 213–18.

[25] The alternative is to view Paul as promising to pay for Onesimus's manumission—a more manageable task. See Laura L. Sanders, "Equality and a Request for the Manumission of Onesimus," *RestQ* 46 (2004): 113–14.

[26] This point is emphasized all the more as the apostle now takes pen in hand himself. See our earlier comments about his appended autographs at the ends of his letters.

[27] Barth and Blanke, *Philemon*, 492.

[28] Lohse, *Colossians and Philemon*, 206–7.

dividual or a private family but to a house church places not too subtle pressure on Philemon to comply.

CLOSING GREETINGS (VV. 23–25)

Epaphras apparently planted the church in Colossae (see below, p. 290). Mark is most likely the John Mark of Acts 12:12, 25; 13:13; and 15:37, 39. That he is with Paul suggests that they have been reconciled. Aristarchus may well be the representative of the churches in Macedonia who accompanied Paul's collection to Judea (Acts 19:29; 20:4; 27:2). Demas may be the same person who later abandoned Paul (2 Tim. 4:10), while Luke is surely the beloved physician of Colossians 4:14 who alone remained with Paul in 2 Timothy 4:11. As elsewhere, the apostle closes this precious letter with another prayer wish for grace.

APPLICATION

The main issue for contemporary readers that this letter raises is the problem of slavery. Throughout significant portions of church history, the epistle was not interpreted as a request for manumission. Even today, when it is widely acknowledged that Paul probably at least hints at his hopes for Onesimus's freedom, the question remains why he does not challenge the institution of slavery directly. At least seven factors need to be kept in mind by way of reply.[29]

1. We must not envision slavery in ancient Rome as if it closely resembled the institution that bought and enslaved Africans in the American South (and elsewhere) until after the Civil War of 1861–65. Slaves held almost every kind of job in the ancient workplace. These included senators, doctors, teachers, all kinds of craftsmen and manual laborers, as well as the more despised trades like rowers or mine workers. This is not to say that Roman slaves were not at times severely mistreated. Female slaves, in particular, were often subject to the sexual whims of their masters. But it is to point out that slaves with good positions and reasonable masters often lived better than many freed persons.

2. Again, unlike the American experience, slavery in the Greco-Roman world was not based on racism but on the subjugation of conquered territories. Thus no visual clues set slaves apart from their free counterparts; people of all the existing races and ethnic groups could become enslaved or freed. Individuals at times even voluntarily sold themselves into slavery in order to pay off debts.

3. There was little ideological precedent for the abolition of slavery. Among Jews, only the Essenes and the Egyptian Therapeutae publicly renounced the use of slaves, and in Greco-Roman philosophy only the sophists opposed it in any consistent fashion. While various slave revolts punctuated pre-Christian history, all without exception failed and most led to ruthless massacres of the insurgents.

---

[29] For good overviews of slavery in Paul's world, see K. R. Bradley, *Slavery and Society at Rome* (Cambridge and New York: CUP, 1994); Peter Garnsey, *Ideas of Slavery from Aristotle to Augustine* (Cambridge and New York: CUP, 1996). For a survey of recent research, see John Byron, "Paul and the Background of Slavery: The *Status Quaestionis* in New Testament Scholarship," *CBR* 3 (2004):116–39.

4. Closely related to this last point, in a culture that had never experienced any alternatives and in which Christianity had no significant power base, attempts at the emancipation of slaves in general, who comprised perhaps as much as one-third of the Roman population, would almost certainly have failed and perhaps led to the destruction of Christianity in the process.

5. The eventual manumission of slaves in the Roman Empire was normal, with most domestic servants set free by age thirty.

6. Even after manumission, slaves often remained in relationship with their previous masters, at times still owing them financial obligations of various kinds. But the measure of freedom they received required them to provide for their own "room and board," which was often more difficult and at a lower standard than when they worked as slaves, especially when their masters were reasonably prosperous.

7. Perhaps most importantly of all, the main concern of apostolic Christianity involved the inward, spiritual transformation that occurred when human beings were reconciled to God and that enabled them to look forward to a glorious eternity with him, whether they ever experienced the outward, physical liberation from unpleasant circumstances in this world (recall 1 Cor. 7:17–24).[30]

Nevertheless, Paul had taught in 1 Corinthians 7:21b that slaves who could acquire their freedom should do so (see above, p. 179). And by focusing on equality in Christ, irrespective of social or economic status, Paul certainly planted the seeds for the more explicit abolition movements in later centuries, instigated primarily by people with Christian convictions.[31] As F. F. Bruce phrases it, "What this letter does is to bring us into an atmosphere in which the institution [of slavery] could only wilt and die."[32] Who knows how much bloodshed in subsequent centuries could have been avoided if revolutions and liberation movements had progressed more slowly and "spiritually." Yet, in the face of unrelenting evil oppression, even the Bible at times condones violence. So perhaps we must tolerate it, in a fallen world, as a last resort.[33]

ADDITIONAL QUESTIONS FOR REVIEW

1. Aside from the traditional option that has assumed Onesimus is a runaway slave, what are the other explanations for Onesimus's departure from Philemon's household? What textual evidence supports or denies each of these options. Based on cultural context, which option is most likely?

2. What are the translation issues that have often led to proof-texting in both halves of Philemon 6? How are these issues best translated and understood?

---

[30] Craig S. de Vos ("Once a Slave, Always a Slave? Slavery, Manumission and Relational Patterns in Paul's Letter to Philemon," *JSNT* 82 [2001]: 89–105) thinks Paul was requesting something even harder than manumission—that Onesimus would treat Philemon as an equal, a friend, and an honored guest, even while still a slave.

[31] For early Christian practices, cf. J. Albert Harrill, *The Manumission of Slaves in Early Christianity* (Tübingen: Mohr, 1995); with Jennifer A. Glancy, *Slavery in Early Christianity* (Oxford and New York: OUP, 2002).

[32] Bruce, *Paul*, 401.

[33] Cf. further the contrasting perspectives of Mikeal Parsons, "Slavery and the New Testament: Equality and Submissiveness," *Vox Evangelica* 18 (1988): 89–96; and Lloyd G. Lewis, "An African American Appraisal of the Philemon-Paul-Onesimus Triangle," in *Stony the Road We Trod*, ed. Cain H. Felder (Minneapolis: Fortress, 1991), 232–46.

3. In what specific ways does the entire letter of Philemon serve as a model of pastoral tact and psychology? What exactly is Paul asking Philemon to do in this letter? What features of the second half of the epistle suggest Paul's intention in writing Philemon?

4. What appropriate responses can be issued when Paul (and by extension, Christianity) is accused of supporting slavery because he does not challenge the institution of slavery directly? By focusing on Christian transformation, how was Paul subtly subverting the institution of slavery, and what other Pauline texts contribute to this subversion?

SELECT BIBLIOGRAPHY

COMMENTARIES

Advanced

Barth, Markus, and Helmut Blanke. *The Letter to Philemon.* ECC. Grand Rapids and Cambridge: Eerdmans, 2000.

Dunn, James D. G. *The Epistles to the Colossians and to Philemon.* NIGTC. Carlisle: Paternoster; Grand Rapids: Eerdmans, 1996.

Lohse, Eduard. *Colossians and Philemon.* Hermeneia. Philadelphia: Fortress, 1971.

O'Brien, Peter T. *Colossians, Philemon.* WBC. Waco: Word, 1982.

Wilson, Robert McL. *Colossians and Philemon: A Critical and Exegetical Commentary.* New York and London: T & T Clark, 2005.

Intermediate

Bruce, F. F. *The Epistles to the Colossians, to Philemon, and to the Ephesians*, rev. NICNT. Grand Rapids: Eerdmans, 1984.

Fitzmyer, Joseph A. *The Letter to Philemon.* AB. New York and London: Doubleday, 2000.

Melick, Richard R., Jr. *Philippians, Colossians, Philemon.* NAC. Nashville: Broadman, 1991.

Thompson, Marianne M. *Colossians & Philemon.* THNTC. Grand Rapids and Cambridge: Eerdmans, 2005.

Thurston, Bonnie B., and Judith M. Ryan. *Philippians and Philemon.* SP. Collegeville: Liturgical, 2005.

Introductory

Garland, David E. *Colossians/Philemon.* NIVAC. Grand Rapids: Zondervan, 1998.

Lucas, Richard C. *The Message of Colossians and Philemon.* BST. Leicester and Downers Grove: IVP, 1980.

Wall, Robert W. *Colossians and Philemon.* IVPNTC. Leicester and Downers Grove: IVP, 1993.

Wright, N. T. *Colossians and Philemon*, rev. TNTC. Leicester: IVP; Grand Rapids: Eerdmans, 1986.

OTHER BOOKS

Petersen, Norman R. *Rediscovering Paul: Philemon and the Sociology of Paul's Narrative World.* Philadelphia: Fortress, 1985.

BIBLIOGRAPHY

Byron, John. "Paul and the Background of Slavery: The *Status Quaestionis* in New Testament Scholarship." *CBR* 3 (2004): 116–39.

Mills, Watson E. *Philemon.* Lewiston and Lampeter: Mellen, 1993.

Colossians: Christ as Lord of the Cosmos and the Church

INTRODUCTION

C olossians is the second letter Paul wrote to a church he did not personally found. The immediate occasion for the correspondence is the problem of false teaching in Colossae, described as an example of "hollow and deceptive philosophy, which depends on human tradition and the basic principles of this world rather than on Christ" (2:8). If our conclusions about the setting of the Prison Epistles in general are accurate (see above, pp. 271–73), then we already know that Paul is addressing this church in a comparatively small Gentile community in the Lycus valley, though with a significant minority of Jews, in about A.D. 61 during his Roman imprisonment and sending the letter with Tychicus and Onesimus (see esp. 4:7–9). Even making allowance for hyperbolic language, the statements in 1:6 and 23 about the spread of the gospel throughout the empire best fit this later date and imprisonment and echo the tone of Acts 28:31, in which the message of the kingdom continues to spread without hindrance. *Whereas Philemon's household represented simply one home congregation within the church in Colossae, this epistle is addressed to the entire Christian community there.*

THE COLOSSIAN HERESY

Huge amounts of ink have been spilled trying to pin down more precisely the nature of the false teachings that Paul was afraid might be infecting the Colossians. Chapter 2:8–3:17 most directly addresses this "philosophy." A cautious application of "mirror reading" would suggest the following heretical elements: denial of Christ's full deity (2:8–10); requiring circumcision (2:11–15); insisting on certain dietary restrictions (v. 16a); participation in weekly, monthly, and annual religious festivals (v. 16b); "the worship of angels" (vv. 18–19); and other legalistic ordinances (vv. 20–22), particularly of an ascetic nature (v. 23). The false philosophy seems to have driven a sharp wedge as well between the spirit and the body, perhaps engaging in mystical exercises (3:1–4), without paying adequate attention to basic morality (vv. 5–17).

Several scholars have proposed that this heresy can be explained entirely in Jewish (or more probably Jewish-Christian) categories.[34] Clearly, circumcision, kosher laws, Sabbath, new moon and seasonal festivals would fit well into a Jewish background. At first glance, "the worship of angels" would not fit at all since the Jews remained far more strongly monotheistic than the largely polytheistic Greco-Roman religions. But this presupposes that the expression reflects an objective genitive (worship directed toward angels) rather than a subjective genitive (the worship

---

[34] Referring to mainstream Jewish practices, see Allan R. Bevere, *Sharing in the Inheritance: Identity and the Moral Life in Colossians* (London and N.Y.: SAP, 2003). An orientation to asceticism and mysticism in Jewish apocalyptic is discerned by Thomas J. Sappington, *Revelation and Redemption at Colossae* (Sheffield: JSOT, 1991).

that angels themselves offer). In the latter case, various forms of Jewish mysticism and/or apocalypticism could qualify. Still, Judaism in general, including these more esoteric branches, was not primarily characterized by an ascetic lifestyle. And while later Jewish Christians (the Ebionites of the second century) did deny Christ's full deity, they scarcely disputed the bodily form of his humanity (as in 2:9). And Colossians 2:10 reads much more like a response to some Greco-Roman form of thought in which an overly realized eschatology (present entirely in this life) has replaced Judeo-Christian belief in a future bodily resurrection.

Other commentators at times have swung the pendulum to the opposite extreme, thinking they could account for the false philosophy entirely with Greek categories.[35] Various cults and mystery religions at times practiced dietary restrictions. The Greco-Roman world had its annual and monthly festivals, too. Making angels the objects of worship and various ascetic practices mesh well with this hypothesis, but circumcision does not fit at all, and no forms of Greco-Roman religion had anything corresponding to a Sabbath—one day of rest each week.

THE COLOSSIAN HERESY

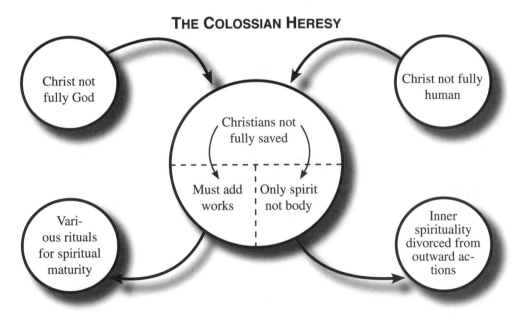

Thus the majority of scholars, ancient and contemporary, agree that *the Colossian heresy combined in "syncretistic" fashion both Judaizing and Hellenizing elements.*[36] The latter have often been linked more specifically to incipient forms of Gnosticism, particularly in light of the prominent role of the term *plēroma* ("fullness")—as in 2:9–10—which defined the Gnostic godhead. But Clinton Arnold's detailed study

---

[35] Eduard Schweizer (*The Letter to the Colossians* [Minneapolis: Augsburg, 1982], 132–33), for example, finds substantial parallels between the Colossian heresy and the Greek cult of Pythagoreanism. Troy W. Martin (*By Philosophy and Empty Deceit: Colossians as Response to a Cynic Critique* [Sheffield: SAP, 1996]) sees a purely Cynic background to the opponents.

[36] For a good summary, see Petr Pokorný, *Colossians: A Commentary* (Peabody: Hendrickson, 1991), 113–20. For a detailed outworking that finds the Colossian heresy to blend Jewish and Greek (esp. Middle Platonic) influences with Christian elements in the pursuit of wisdom, see Richard E. DeMaris, *The Colossian Controversy: Wisdom in Dispute at Colossae* (Sheffield: JSOT, 1994).

suggests that the distinctive twists to the philosophy can be accounted for by local folk superstitions, Phrygian religion, and various mystery cults, so that a uniquely Gnostic perspective need not be presupposed.[37]

Combining the elements of the philosophy disclosed by the epistle suggests that the heresy affected three major doctrines—*Christology, soteriology, and anthropology*. The more Judaizing element could have denied Christ's full deity (an inadequate Christology), leading to an incomplete atonement (an inadequate soteriology) that had to be supplemented by human works (an inadequate anthropology). The more Hellenizing elements could have denied Christ's full humanity (another inadequate Christology), leading to salvation only for the human spirit (another inadequate soteriology) and to a radical separation of inward spirituality from outward morality (another inadequate anthropology). Paul's thought can in fact be understood as addressing all three of these doctrines exactly in this sequence (2:9–15, 16–23; 3:1–17)[38] though see an alternate analysis in our commentary below. As for the morality or ethical behavior enjoined by the errorists, it would appear that it centered on "rites and physical markers associated with an ascetic response to the world."[39]

Authorship

The other major introductory debate surrounding the letter to the Colossians involves the question of who wrote the letter. Pauline authorship is often denied, somewhat more frequently than with 2 Thessalonians (see above, p. 151), though not as commonly as with Ephesians and the Pastoral Epistles (see below, pp. 303–6, 343–46).[40] The language and style of the letter differ considerably from Paul's undisputed epistles, with frequent paragraph-length sentences and sectarian vocabulary. But the specific diction clearly reflects Paul's need to reply to the Colossian heresy, and the different style can be explained by Paul's extensive use of traditional materials,[41] and/or a different amanuensis (scribe) given freedom to write Paul's thoughts in his style (recall above, p. 102). Particularly because Timothy is named with Paul in the opening verse (1:1), several scholars have suggested that he participated more extensively in the actual composition of this letter than in others in which his name appears as a cosender.[42]

The theology of Colossians seems to differ as well, particularly in the arenas of Christology, ecclesiology, and eschatology. Chapters 1:15–20 and 2:9 make some of the strongest affirmations of Christ's deity in the entire New Testament. In 1:18, Christ appears as the head of his body, the church, rather than believers themselves making up all of the body (as in 1 Cor. 12 and Rom. 12). Finally, the eschatology of the epistles seems more "realized" and less future oriented (3:1–3). At the same time, one can point to indisputably Pauline texts like Romans 9:5 and Philippians

---

[37] Clinton E. Arnold, *The Colossian Syncretism* (Grand Rapids: Baker, 1996).

[38] For a reasonably similar analysis, with expansion, see Barth and Blanke, *Colossians,* 25.

[39] Margaret Y. MacDonald, *Colossians and Ephesians* (Collegeville: Liturgical, 2000), 12.

[40] The arguments are set out in detail in Lohse, *Colossians and Philemon,* 84–91 and 177–83.

[41] On which, see esp. George E. Cannon, *The Use of Traditional Materials in Colossians* (Macon: Mercer, 1983).

[42] E.g., Schweizer (*Colossians,* 23–24) suggests that Timothy wrote the letter and Paul approved sending it in his own name. Cf. also Dunn, *Colossians and Philemon,* 38.

2:5–11 for equally exalted language about Christ. Paul's metaphors are notoriously fluid (recall 1 Cor. 3:9), and 3:4 at least partially balances the author's present hope with a reminder of what yet remains to come in the future.[43] One may also point to the silence of the author of Colossians with respect to financial matters present in all of the undisputed Paulines,[44] but all of those discussions surround apocalyptic enthusiasm, patron-client relationships persisting among young Christians or the collection for Judea, all of which would have receded into the background by the early 60s.[45]

Colossians and Ephesians turn out to be remarkably similar in style and content. Each resembles the other more than any other letter attributed to Paul. Thus just as with similarities between 1 and 2 Thessalonians, these parallels have afforded further rationale for some to dispute the authenticity of one or both of these letters. But this argument alone typically leads people to doubt Pauline authorship of Ephesians (see below, pp. 303–4), not Colossians, and if a pseudepigrapher were overly slavishly following a model of a previous letter in attempts to pass his composition off as the work of another individual, he would presumably choose an authentic letter of that individual to mimic. Thus the similarities between Colossians and Ephesians actually speak in favor of the authenticity of Colossians, even on the assumption of Ephesians' pseudonymity.

It is also worth asking if the pseudepigraphic writer would choose a church Paul did not found to address in attempting to pass off his letter as Pauline, and particularly one in a town that was smaller and more insignificant than any of the others addressed by the letters ascribed to Paul. A final argument against pseudonymity observes that a devastating earthquake in approximately A.D. 61 or 62 destroyed the town of Colossae, and no ancient documents point to it ever being rebuilt. This strongly suggests that the letter was written no later than early 61. Pseudepigraphy, on the other hand, was a device by which later generations attempted to contemporize the thought of a revered master for new situations and audiences, so that almost everyone who denies Pauline authorship of Colossians also dates the letter to some time during the last three decades of the first century. But unless the references to Colossae are equally fictitious (and, again, why would such a comparatively obscure place be picked for this kind of fiction?), then we must assign the date of the letter's composition to well within the period of Paul's life and ministry. We will thus proceed on the assumption that Paul wrote Colossians.[46]

STRUCTURE AND GENRE

Fewer proposals for the genre of Colossians (beyond merely an epistle) have been made than for any other New Testament letter. The structure approximates the

---

[43] For a detailed defense of Pauline authorship, see Barth and Blanke, *Colossians,* 114–26. On the issue of eschatology in particular, which for many scholars seems to be the most decisive theological distinctive, see Todd D. Still, "Eschatology in Colossians: How Realized Is It?" *NTS* 50 (2004): 125–38.

[44] Mark Kiley, *Colossians as Pseudepigraphy* (Sheffield: JSOT, 1986), 46–51.

[45] "Colossians gives us a taste of Paul's gospel precisely when it is *not* being formulated in terms of justification by faith, in direct relationship to Torah and Judaism, or in the categories seen in Galatians and Romans" (Thompson, *Colossians & Philemon,* 9).

[46] Cf. further Garland, *Colossians/Philemon,* 17–22.

Hellenistic letter form, which we have now seen several times, although a syntactical break between the thanksgiving and the body of the letter seems lacking. This may be accounted for by the use of a pre-Pauline creed or confession in 1:15–20 (see below), just as the distinctive form of a "domestic code" in 3:18–4:1 appears in the middle of the exhortational material. Andrew Lincoln helpfully labels the letter as "Pauline thought in wisdom mode,"[47] but this is not quite an identification of a specific letter genre. Walter Wilson finds parenesis dominating throughout, not just in 3:1–4:6, and divides what he identifies as the body into three parts—1:3–2:7 as the theological affirmations foundational to the exhortation; 2:8–23 as the necessary correctives to the false philosophy prior to the exhortation; and 3:1–4:6 as the actual exhortation itself.[48] A more conventional outline does not necessarily conflict with the purposes identified in Wilson's tripartite structure.

  I. Introduction (1:1–14)
      A. Greeting (1:1–2)
      B. Thanksgiving (1:3–14)
  II. Letter Body (1:15–4:6)
      A. Theological Exposition (1:15–2:23)
          1. The Christ Hymn (1:15–20)
          2. The Application of the Christ Hymn (1:21–2:23)
      B. Ethical Implications (3:1–4:6)
          1. Defining Holiness (3:1–17)
          2. The Domestic Code (3:18–4:1)
          3. Proper Prayer and Speech (4:2–6)
III. Closing Greetings (4:7–18)

To the extent that the first half of this letter praises God in Christ for his cosmic salvation, the rhetoric remains epideictic, though the response to the heresy introduces deliberative rhetoric. The second half naturally transitions more fully into the deliberative rhetoric characteristic of Pauline exhortations. This two-part pattern will reemerge even more clearly in Ephesians (see below p. 307).

COMMENTARY

INTRODUCTION (1:1–14)

Greeting (1:1–2) After referring to himself as a prisoner in the opening verse of Philemon, Paul reverts back to his more typical practice of identifying himself as an apostle in this more general letter sent to the Colossian church. Somewhat distinctively, he addresses these Christians not as a "church" per se but as "holy and faithful brothers," that is, spiritual kin. But his conventional pronouncement of grace

---

[47] Andrew T. Lincoln, "The Household Code and Wisdom Mode of Colossians," *JSNT* 74 (1999): 112.
[48] Walter T. Wilson, *The Hope of Glory: Education and Exhortation in the Epistle to the Colossians* (Leiden and New York: Brill, 1997), 229–52.

and peace reappear, even though the textual evidence makes it doubtful whether he originally included a reference to Jesus alongside God.

Thanksgiving (1:3–14)   As is his custom when he can do so in good conscience, Paul begins his prayer of thanksgiving by praising God because of the growth of the church to which he is writing (vv. 3–8).[49] As in Philemon, he speaks of both faith and love, but here he clearly delineates that their love is for fellow believers and their faith is in Christ (vv. 4–5), perhaps confirming the suggestion of a chiasm in Philemon 5 (above, pp. 277–78). By adding a reference to hope in Colossians 1:5, he completes his favorite triad of attributes (recall above, p. 142). This hope, of course, stems only from the gospel message, which has been spreading all around the known world, that is, the Roman Empire (v. 6). Paul highlights that this proclamation has reached even Colossae, no doubt because he knew he did not personally found the church there. The man who did was Epaphras, whom Paul likewise commends and names as the source for his information about this congregation (vv. 7–8).

The second portion of Paul's prayer turns from praise to intercession, as the apostle petitions God for the further growth of the Colossians (vv. 9–14). Verse 9 seems overloaded with words dealing with intellectual maturity, but in light of the philosophy that is afflicting this church, right thinking is obviously crucial. And true Christian wisdom and understanding are never merely cognitive; they always issues in godly living (v. 10).[50] Both of these dimensions come about only through God's power, given the obstacles in this life constantly being thrown at us (vv. 11–12). But this power is precisely what our redemption in Christ provides for us, so that we may triumph even now over Satan's realm (vv. 13–14).[51]

LETTER BODY (1:15–4:6)

Theological Exposition (1:15–2:23)   *The Christ Hymn (1:15–20)*   The Greek of Colossians 1:15 does not even begin a new sentence, yet no further signs of Paul's prayer reappear, and we are clearly into the heart of the theological information he wishes to convey. The relative pronoun "who," which ties verse 15 back to verse 14 (the NIV starts a new paragraph by changing this to "he") often indicates the insertion of traditional material, and this may well account for the unusual grammar here. *Verses 15–20 are poetic in structure and form a coherent unity, divisible almost exactly in half, into verses 15–17 and 18–20, with part one proclaiming Christ's sovereignty over creation and the second declaring his supremacy over the church.* This "poem" may well have been already used in the early church as a confession of faith or even a hymn before Paul incorporated it into this epistle, in which case it reminds

---

[49] In fact, this thanksgiving is entirely commendatory, perhaps to help Paul secure a favorable hearing for his message with this new audience. See Thurston, *Colossians, Ephesians, and 2 Thessalonians*, 14.

[50] J. Goetzmann, "σύνεσιν," in *The New International Dictionary of New Testament Theology*, ed. Colin Brown, vol. 3 (Grand Rapids: Zondervan, 1978), 130–33.

[51] Terence Y. Mullins ("The Thanksgivings of Philemon and Colossians," *NTS* 30 [1984]: 288–93) plausibly posits that if Colossians were pseudepigraphic, its thanksgiving would parallel Philemon's as closely as the greetings in the two letters do but without the same correspondence between themes introduced in the thanksgiving and those elaborated in the letter body. In fact, Colossians has fewer similar themes to Philemon's than dissimilar ones and its themes *are* largely unpacked in the rest of Colossians.

us that high Christology did not merely "evolve" at a late date in the development of the Christian faith.[52]

Be that as it may, verses 15–20 clearly present tightly packed doctrine about the person and work of Christ, which no doubt begins *to combat the inadequate Christology of the Colossian heresy,* even before Paul formally introduces the problem of its intrusion into the church in 2:8.[53] Jesus is (1) "the image of the invisible God"—the exact replica in bodily form of the non-embodied Father (v. 15a, probably drawing on both Gen. 1 and Prov. 8:22–36); (2) "the firstborn over all creation"— the Greek word *prototōkos* can mean not only a first-created being, which would contradict 2:9, but also first in *rank* or *prominence* (v. 15b);[54] (3) God's agent in creation—see also John 1:3–4 and Genesis 1:3 (v. 16); (4) preexistent before all creation (v. 17a); (5) providentially sustaining the world (v. 17b); (6) the "head" of the church—in light of verse 18c, clearly implying his authority or lordship (v. 18a); (7) the first of those to be resurrected—thereby guaranteeing our resurrection (v. 18b);[55] (8) fully God—the word for "fullness" (*plēroma*) later being used by Gnostics for their godhead of multiple "aeons" or emanations from the one unknowable, original God (v. 19); and (9) making possible universal reconciliation through his crucifixion to all who repent—not to be confused with "universalism," in which all creatures are automatically saved no matter their response to the gospel (v. 20).[56]

The Application of the Christ Hymn (1:21–2:23)   From these lofty doctrinal heights, Paul turns to the practical application of Christ's work to the church, though still thinking primarily in theological rather than ethical categories. Here he *combats the Colossians' inadequate soteriology. First, reconciliation with God is guaranteed granted the Colossians' perseverance (1:21–23).* Verse 23a is a first-class condition and does not introduce any doubts into the "if-clause."[57]

Second, in keeping with Paul's distinctive labor as apostle to the non-Jewish world, reconciliation between Gentiles and Jews in Christ is revealed (1:24–2:7). For Paul, this means agonizingly hard work (1:24–29). With a vivid metaphor, Paul speaks of filling up in his flesh what is still lacking in Christ's afflictions (v. 24). This expression is often taken as a reference to the common Jewish belief in a period of messianic woes—an intense but fixed amount of tribulation for God's people prior to the full arrival of the messianic age—in which case the more Paul suffered, the more

---

[52] On the poetry in the passage, see Steven M. Baugh, "The Poetic Form of Col 1:15–20," *WTJ* 47 (1985): 227–44. On both structure and message, see esp. N. T. Wright, "Poetry and Theology in Colossians 1.15–20," *NTS* 36 (1990): 444–68. More recently, cf. L. Carlos Reyes, "The Structure and Rhetoric of Colossians 1:15–20," *FN* 12 (1999): 139–54.

[53] Jarl Fossum, "Colossians 1.15–18a in the Light of Jewish Mysticism and Gnosticism," *NTS* 35 (1989): 183–201.

[54] See Garland (*Colossians/Philemon*, 87), who also notes that the expression appears as a title of sovereignty in Ps. 89:27.

[55] The term "firstborn" here clearly means both preeminent and chronologically first. See Dunn, *Colossians and Philemon*, 97–98.

[56] But those who are not saved will nevertheless find themselves "submitting against their wills to a power which they cannot resist" (Peter T. O'Brien, *Colossians, Philemon* [Waco: Word, 1982], 56; cf. F. F. Bruce and E. K. Simpson, *Commentary on the Epistles to the Ephesians and the Colossians* (Grand Rapids: Eerdmans, 1957), 210.

[57] "From God's point of view, genuine faith is assured of continuing to the end. From the human point of view, Christians discover whether their faith is of the genuine sort only by patient perseverance" (Wright, *Colossians and Philemon*, 83).

he would be reducing the need for other Christians to suffer.[58] Alternately, he may be modeling his ministry after Christ's and claiming that he has not yet suffered to the extent Jesus did, namely in laying down his life.[59]

Either way, Paul is not promoting an incomplete atonement, but merely showing that Jesus' suffering did not eliminate the need for his followers to suffer. Indeed, union with him requires it. Paul recognizes he is teaching a fuller revelation from God than previous generations have received (v. 25), which can thus be thought of as the revelation of a mystery—something that once was secret and even now remains somewhat ineffable (v. 26),[60] namely that the Messiah's work would place Jews and Gentiles on an equal footing (v. 27; cf. Eph. 3:6). That as many people as possible can have their lives transformed by these truths remains Paul's abiding passion (vv. 28–29).

For the Colossians, the significance of these principles is that they should allow Christ to lead them into greater unity in love, maturity, and understanding (2:1–7). This desire sets the stage for Paul's discussion of the heresy, while this growth prepares the church to withstand the false teaching (v. 4). Here Paul inserts the information that he is also "struggling" for "those at Laodicea" and others he has not personally met (v. 1). Laodicea was one of the two nearest towns to Colossae (along with Hierapolis), and 4:16 discloses that Paul has written to the Laodiceans as well and that he wants the two churches to exchange letters after they have read the ones initially sent to them. As we will see later, some scholars suggest that the letter Paul wrote to the Laodiceans is the same as his epistle to the Ephesians (below, pp. 305–6). If it is not, then it has been lost (just like the additional Corinthian correspondence) and is not to be equated with the much later apocryphal epistle to the Laodiceans.[61]

Beginning in 2:8, Paul confronts the Colossian heresy head-on. This verse should not be taken to mean that Christians should never study non-Christian philosophy (if we do not study it, we can never intelligently interact with it), much less that there is no such thing as Christian philosophy! What it warns against is adopting any ideology that has a merely human origin or that conflicts with Christian principles. The word for "basic principles" is *stoicheia,* which we saw in Galatians 4:9 probably included demonic forces as well. As discussed in the introduction to Colossians (above, p. 287), there are Christological, soteriological, and anthropological dimensions to the specific false teaching. Verses 9–10 insist that Christ is fully God in fully human form, enabling him to conquer and to empower us to gain victory over all opposing powers, even diabolical ones (the frequent meaning of "power[s]" and "authorit[ies]").

Verses 11–15 imply that literal circumcision is no longer necessary for believers, having been replaced by the metaphorical or spiritual circumcision not performed by human hands of the "putting off of the sinful nature" (*sarx*; "flesh"—v. 11). This

---

[58] E.g., F. F. Bruce, *The Epistles to the Colossians, to Philemon, and to the Ephesians* (Grand Rapids: Eerdmans, 1984), 83–84.

[59] Andrew Perriman, "The Pattern of Christ's Sufferings," *TynB* 42 (1991): 62–79.

[60] Chrys C. Caragounis, *The Ephesian Mysterion* (Lund: Gleerup, 1977).

[61] The text comprises twenty short verses, many of them derived from Philippians, and has been dated as early as the late second century and as late as the fourth century. See Wilhelm Schneemelcher, "The Epistle to the Laodiceans," in *New Testament Apocrypha,* ed. Schneemelcher, vol. 2, 44–45.

wording demonstrates that Paul does not consider baptism in the new covenant as the exact equivalent to circumcision in the old.[62] It is faith and repentance that save a person, not an outward ritual. Otherwise Paul would be reverting to the very regulations of the written code, which verse 14 declares Christ has abolished. For the same reason, neither can these verses prove that infants must be baptized simply because Jews circumcised babies; after all, they did *not* circumcise girls whereas Christians *do* baptize women. Not everything in the two rituals is parallel. Verse 12 must therefore be understood exactly like Romans 6:3–4. Baptism is a metonymy for salvation because it regularly followed closely on the heels of saving faith.[63]

Verses 13–15 reinforce this interpretation by contrasting the spiritual circumcision of conversion with the spiritual uncircumcision of the unconverted life. Christ's cross work rescued us from the demonic powers that previously enslaved us, whether we recognized it or not, and began a new era in salvation history in which we do not literally have to obey all of the Mosaic commands. People were never able to follow the law perfectly anyway, and thus it only pointed out their need for a savior (recall our unpacking of these themes in Galatians and Romans). The "written code" could refer to the Mosaic Law or to an IOU or (most likely) to both.[64] The entire expression, "the written code, with its regulations, that was against us" probably carries the sense of the law "which stood against us *on the basis of the demands.*"[65] The word for "triumphing" in verse 15 employs the same root that we saw in 2 Corinthians 2:14 for a Roman triumphal procession with prisoners of war in tow. "To treat the cross as a moment of triumph was about as huge a reversal of normal values as could be imagined."[66]

In verses 16–17, Paul turns to other aspects of the Mosaic Law (but also of various Greco-Roman religions) that the false teachers were insisting be followed, responding much as in 1 Corinthians 8–10 and Romans 14–15: believers should not judge each other on these morally neutral matters. These two verses present some of the clearest teaching in all of the New Testament against Sabbatarianism—the conviction that Christians must keep a Sabbath (whether on Saturday or Sunday) as a mandatory day of rest.[67] All of the ritual or ceremonial laws of the Old Testament have been fulfilled in Jesus (v. 18) and need not be adopted by Christians, even though there are spiritual principles we can learn from each one of them. But only the moral law remains fully in force (recall above, pp. 132–34).

Some have imagined that, because it was found even in the Ten Commandments, the Sabbath legislation persists as a requirement today. But nothing in either testament ever sets off these ten laws as noticeably more binding than others. And the early church, prior to Constantine's legalizing of Christianity in the fourth

---

[62] See, e.g., John P. T. Hunt, "Colossians 2:11–12, The Circumcision/Baptism Analogy, and Infant Baptism," *TynB* 41 (1990): 227–44. Hunt also shows how the analogy between circumcision and salvation, not circumcision and baptism, corresponds to the earliest Patristic writers' perspectives. Only *after* infant baptism developed was Colossians 2:11–12 enlisted as supposed biblical support.

[63] See further Barth and Blanke, *Colossians,* 368.

[64] Wright, *Colossians and Philemon,* 111–12.

[65] Barth and Blanke, *Colossians,* 329–30.

[66] Dunn, *Colossians and Philemon,* 170.

[67] Cf. esp. D. A. Carson, ed., *From Sabbath to Lord's Day* (Grand Rapids: Zondervan, 1982).

century, uniformly rejected those who would require Sabbath-keeping, calling them Judaizers![68] Christians began worshipping on Sunday because that was the day of the Lord's resurrection, not because they were creating a different day of rest. On the other hand, too many Christians today do not even worship on a weekly basis, which creates an entirely different set of problems!

As we saw above (pp. 285–86), "the worship of angels" in verse 18 is ambiguous; but given the expectation of a direct object following verbs for worship, the objective genitive (worship directed toward angels) seems most likely.[69] The expression "disqualify you for the prize" may in fact mean "condemn," "injure," or "take advantage of."[70] The word translated "go into great detail" more likely should be rendered "enter into," referring to a pagan worshipper's initiation into a series of visionary experiences in a Greco-Roman temple.[71] Too much fascination with any spiritual beings other than God himself can quickly lead one astray, in this case apparently to ascetic as well as visionary experiences (vv. 20–23). Since angels do not procreate, they presumably do not have sex and thus could suggest to those who value them too highly other unnecessary restrictions on Christian behavior. Worse still, such persons often delude themselves into thinking that their practices actually make them spiritually superior to others, even though outwardly they may present themselves to others as quite humble (v. 18). But Christian maturity seeks the growth of the whole church, an objective that an elitist mentality never promotes (v. 19).

Indeed, ascetic practices often "lack any value in restraining sensual indulgence" (v. 23). One who fasts, for example, often eats so much when the fast is complete that the benefits of the fast are entirely lost. Even when this is not the case, refraining from satisfying normal bodily appetites has spiritual value only when accompanied by religious disciplines or exercises that help a person to mature. Otherwise, one's heart easily lusts for whatever has been given up, at which point the asceticism actually leads a person into sin (cf. Matt. 5:28).[72]

Ethical Implications (3:1–4:6) *Defining Holiness (3:1–17)* As Paul turns to his exhortational material and, as in Romans, uses a "therefore" (*oun*) to shift from theology to ethics, he proceeds *to counter the inadequate anthropology of the Colossian heresy.*[73] He begins by encouraging his listeners to concentrate on heavenly things (3:1–4). Taken on their own, these verses could suggest a kind of mysticism, perhaps precisely what the heresy was promoting. But verses 5–17 go on immediately to explain that *setting one's mind on things above (v. 2) implies holy living.* Paul refuses to bifurcate between the spirit and the body or between heaven and earth. The extent

---

[68] William Barclay, *The Plain Man's Guide to Ethics: Thoughts on the Ten Commandments* (Glasgow and London: Collins, 1973), 26–48.

[69] Arnold, *Colossian Syncretism,* 92–95. Arnold also notes that he can find no example in existing Greek literature of the word used here for "worship" in the context of worshipping with someone, which the subjective genitive (worshipping along with the angels) would require.

[70] Kent L. Yinger, "Translating καταβραβευέτω ('Disqualify' NRSV) in Colossians 2.18," *BT* 54 (2003): 138–45.

[71] Arnold, *Colossian Syncretism,* 104–57.

[72] Thurston (*Colossians, Ephesians, and 2 Thessalonians,* 47) observes that 2:6–23 combats any "imposed spirituality" that judges others who do not practice spiritual disciplines in exactly our preferred fashions.

[73] Chapter 2 concludes with the Colossians having been set free *from* the powers of evil; chapter 3 begins with them having been set free *for* living a life above moral reproach (Garland, *Colossians/Philemon,* 200).

to which believers can claim to experience the resurrection life already in this present age depends on their willingness to live in godly, moral ways in all the humdrum activities of ordinary human existence.[74]

This transformation can be likened to taking off old, filthy clothes and putting on new clean ones (contrast vv. 5 and 12). That Paul must give these commands to those who already profess Christian faith offers a further reminder that the sinful nature does not disappear at conversion (recall above, p. 249). At the same time, believers now have the power to resist sin, so that the behaviors proscribed in verses 5–9 should become largely a thing of the past (v. 7). Then one can speak, in a relative sense at least, of having put off the old person and having put on the new (vv. 9–10a). But Paul immediately reminds us that he is still thinking about a process, as he describes our dressing ourselves in new, spiritual clothing as "being renewed" (i.e., over a period of time) in the knowledge of God's image. Here is one of the clearest texts in the entire Bible to help us understand what it meant for humans to be created in the image of God. Whatever else this concept may mean (cf. Gen. 1:26–28), it obviously includes the fact that humans alone are moral beings among the creatures in the universe, uniquely created with the capacity for relationship with God.[75]

When redemption in Christ restores this relationship to a person, "there is no Greek or Jew, circumcised or uncircumcised, barbarian, Scythian, slave or free, but Christ is all, and is in all" (v. 11). The last part of this verse suggests that Paul is still refuting the Gnostic-like notion that there are many emanations from God, each responsible for different parts of the universe. Instead, the omnipresent Christ is sovereign over it all. The first part of the verse has proved more controversial. Clearly Paul is choosing some of the major barriers between categories of people in his world and announcing their abolition. Yet, as we saw with Galatians 3:28, one cannot prove the full-fledged obliteration of all distinctions simply from generalized statements of this nature.[76] What should be visible to a fallen world, however, is a heterogeneous Christian fellowship that demonstrates people getting along with one another who have no human reason for doing so.[77]

Contemporary counterparts could include blacks and whites in some parts of America, Koreans and Japanese in many parts of the world, Jews and Arabs in Israel, warring tribal factions in black Africa, previously warring factions in the Balkans, and so on. When churches organize themselves strictly along racial or ethnic lines and then rarely, if ever, interact with one another, this astonishing unity

---

[74] In other words, setting their minds on things above means that their moral vision is controlled by the coming divine reality (ibid., 214). Cf. further John R. Levison, "2 Apoc. Bar. 48:42–52:7 and the Apocalyptic Dimension of Colossians 3:1–6," *JBL* 108 (1989): 93–108.

[75] See esp. G. C. Berkouwer, *Man: The Image of God* (Grand Rapids: Eerdmans, 1962).

[76] The distinctions do not cease to exist, but they become irrelevant for the love, honor, and respect to be shown to these individuals and groups (Wright, *Colossians and Philemon,* 140).

[77] The puzzling part in the list of enemies is "barbarian, Scythian," since both of these would have been enemies of Jews, Greeks, and Romans but not of each other. Most commentators assume that Paul's point is simply that the Scythians were particularly brutish and savage among the outsiders to these three cultures (which is all that "barbarian" necessarily meant in antiquity). Troy Martin ("The Scythian Perspective in Col 3:11," *NovT* 37 [1995]: 249–61) argues that Scythian here resembles "Cynic" as one who protested against the rest of humanity, thus creating a contrast even with "barbarian." Douglas A. Campbell ("Unravelling Colossians 3.11b," *NTS* 42 [1996]: 120–32) thinks this half verse creates two chiasms—Greek, Jew, circumcised, uncircumcised (clear enough); and barbarian, Scythian, slave, free (arguing from evidence that equated Scythians with slaves).

in Christ cannot be perceived by the non-Christian world that most desperately needs to see it.

Of course, loving those different from ourselves can be hard. But if we practice the virtues itemized in verses 12–17, God will give us the power to overcome our carnal factionalism. Forgiveness plays a central role; but love, as throughout Paul's ethic, proves even more crucial (vv. 13–14). Christian love leads naturally to peace, unity, and thankfulness (v. 15) and is nurtured by teaching God's Word with wise exhortation and hymnic praise (v. 16). Consciously dedicating all one's speech and service to the Lord Jesus can keep one's focus on these crucial practices (v. 17).[78]

THE DOMESTIC CODE (3:18–4:1)   Martin Luther labeled this section on wives and husbands, children and parents, and slaves and masters a *Haustafel,* a German expression roughly translated as a "household" or "domestic" code. Many such sets of instructions about relationships within extended households existed in antiquity, including ones in Ephesians 5–6, 1 Peter 2–3, Josephus, Philo, ben Sira, and the Stoics.[79] The ancient world, with considerably fewer choices about jobs, spouses, places of living or classes in society, was more preoccupied with the virtuous life within whatever circumstances one found oneself. The greatest distinctive of the Christian *Haustafeln* (the *n* makes the word plural) was the reciprocal nature of the responsibilities commanded. Husbands, fathers, and masters were not accustomed to having anyone restrict them in the way Paul does![80] To those who argue that the Paul who wrote Galatians 3:28 could not have commanded the submission of any category of believers to any other, it is important to point out that *whoever* wrote Colossians 3:18, 20 and 22–24 also wrote verse 25, which reaffirms the essential equality of all human beings by stressing that there is no favoritism with God. And unless one argues that the author of Colossians borrowed a preexisting household code and failed to eliminate material in it contradictory to his own views, one has to assume that 3:11 can also be harmonized with commands to submit and obey.[81] Finally, if Paul's original sequence of thought did indeed move from 3:17 to 18, then he appears to imply that the morality of the new covenant just outlined begins at home.[82]

Most of the commands in the Colossian code are repeated and expanded in Ephesians, so we will reserve extended comment for our discussion of that letter (below, pp. 317–19). Here we may comment briefly on the qualifiers and rationales Paul includes for his various injunctions. Wives' submission must model what "is fitting in the Lord" (3:18). This phrase implies "that only that degree of subjection to the husbands which is 'fitting in the Lord' is to be countenanced."[83] In other words, if husbands want their wives to do something that would violate God's will, then wives

---

[78] Thompson (*Colossians and Philemon,* 80) stresses how the virtue and vice lists here concentrate on traits that promote unity versus divisiveness.

[79] See esp. David L. Balch, *Let Wives Be Submissive: The Domestic Code in 1 Peter* (Chico: Scholars, 1981).

[80] Cf. Andrew T. Lincoln, *Ephesians* (Dallas: Word, 1990), 374.

[81] For both of these points, see Stephen Motyer, "The Relationship between Paul's Gospel of 'All One in Christ Jesus' (Gal. 3:28) and the 'Household Codes,'" *Vox Evangelica* 19 (1989): 37, 44.

[82] Wright, *Colossians and Philemon,* 145.

[83] Dunn, *Colossians and Philemon,* 248.

must refuse. Husbands' love precludes harshness (v. 19), despite the long-standing tradition of the Roman *paterfamilias*, or head of household, having the freedom to behave however severely he desired.

Verse 20 is perhaps better translated, "Obey your parents in every circumstance," rather than "in everything," since again obeying a command that transgressed God's law would never "please the Lord."[84] Verse 21 demonstrates shrewd psychology not always understood in the ancient world. Verse 25 explains how slaves could work heartily even when serving unkind masters. Not only are they doing it for Christ rather than any human authority (v. 23), but they recognize that God's judgment of unsaved masters will one day unleash far harsher punishment for all their sins than anything human retribution could inflict. Chapter 4:1 indirectly reminds masters of this same truth.

THE "DOMESTIC CODE"
(HAUSTAFEL) IN THE EPISTLES

Colossians/Ephesians		1 Peter	
Husbands	**Parents**	**Government**	**Parents**
Wives	**Children**	**Citizens**	**Children**
Masters		**Masters**	**Elders**
Slaves		**Slaves**	**Rest of Church**
Must be consistent with 3:11		2:11–3:7	5:1–5a

To be consistent, those who argue that this household code is simply socially conditioned would have to insist that Christians today follow all of the norms of family living in non-Christian society around them, too. Objections to the abiding applicability of this material usually fail to observe that in Christ "there is no striving for equality in the sense of equal plenitude of power, but rather an equality based on loving and serving one another."[85] To those who object that, since we have rightly abolished slavery, we should abolish submission in marriage, it is important to stress that the institutional equivalent to slavery would be marriage itself, which presumably we would not wish to abolish! Nor do most egalitarians insist on deleting submission and obedience from the commands to children. The point is simply that while there are parallels among the three parts to the household code, there are unique features in each of the institutions as well. And the injunctions to slaves and

---

[84] Peter T. O'Brien, *The Letter to the Ephesians* (Grand Rapids and Cambridge: Eerdmans; Leicester: IVP, 1999), 417. O'Brien is commenting on the parallel expression in Ephesians 5:24.
[85] Barth and Blanke, *Colossians*, 438.

masters can profitably be employed by other categories of people responsible for working "above" and "under" others.[86]

Proper Prayer and Speech (4:2–6) This paragraph closes the body of the letter and its exhortational subsection with more loosely linked instructions, as we have frequently seen at these junctures in Paul's epistles. The Colossians must pray for themselves, both to guard themselves against spiritual danger and to thank God for all the instances of his goodness they have already experienced, as well as to pray for Paul that the ministry of the gospel would progress despite his imprisonment (vv. 2–4). Praying for clear speech to non-Christians leads naturally to more general injunctions about wise behavior toward "outsiders" and to grace-filled conversation (vv. 5–6). Here C. F. D. Moule proves particularly insightful: "This verse is a plea to Christians not to confuse loyal godliness with a dull, graceless insipidity. If a Christian is ever difficult company, it ought to be because he demands too much, not too little, from his fellows' responsiveness and wit."[87]

CLOSING GREETINGS (4:7–18)

In Romans, Paul greeted large numbers of Christians he had met elsewhere who had migrated to Rome, in order to build as many bridges as possible with a church he had not founded.[88] In the far smaller Colossae, addressing the second church that he did not establish, Paul would not necessarily have known very many at all. So instead of greeting numerous people by name, he sends his greetings from everyone who is with him. These companions include Tychicus, who will carry the letter and explain anything in it that he needs to (vv. 7–8); Onesimus, the returning slave (v. 9); a series of Jewish-Christian coworkers (vv. 10–11), two of whom we discussed under Philemon (Aristarchus and Mark) and one about whom we know nothing else (Jesus Justus); Epaphras, the Colossian church planter who may also have established congregations in Laodicea and Hierapolis (vv. 12–13); and Luke, the beloved Gentile physician, along with Demas (v. 14; cf. on Philem. 24).

Because Laodicea was so nearby and because the Christian communities in both Colossae and Laodicea would undoubtedly have been small and in need of encouragement, Paul asks the Colossians to send his greetings to the believers in that neighboring city as well. It seems he knows at least one woman from Laodicea, Nympha, who hosts a house church there (v. 15). He also expects the Laodicean and Colossian churches to exchange letters (v. 16, on which see above). He does know Archippus from Philemon's home and encourages him to complete some unspecified work (v. 17). Finally, he takes the pen from his scribe and writes a final greeting himself, as he is accustomed to do (v. 18).

---

[86] For a full analysis of similarities and differences (and bringing the vexed issue of homosexual behavior into purview as well), see Webb, *Slaves, Women and Homosexuals.* Thompson *(Colossians and Philemon,* 96) captures the exact balance reflected here when she explains, "Paul stands the typical injunctions to husbands, fathers, and masters on their needs by making it very clear that those who are in power may not set the rules according to their own whims and preferences . . . [or] . . . use their power for their own ends, but most exercise it on the side of the disadvantaged."

[87] C. F. D. Moule, *The Epistle of Paul to the Colossians and to Philemon* (Cambridge: University Press, 1962), 135.

[88] Thurston, *Colossians, Ephesians, and 2 Thessalonians,* 65.

APPLICATION

Aberrant versions of each of the three major doctrines that Colossians addresses continue to require correction. With respect to Christology, most non-Christians, many liberal "Christians," and numerous members of cults or sects deny Christ's deity. A few descendants of ancient Gnosticism, particularly within the New Age movement, still deny his full humanity. Concerning soteriology, traditional Catholicism and certain forms of cultic religion deny the completeness of his atonement. Legalism and nomism, as noted under Galatians, run rampant throughout our church and world. Focusing on anthropology leads to perhaps the most pointed applications for today's evangelical church. Paul's insistence on the inseparability of doctrine and ethics, worship and obedience, or the inward life and outward practice, calls into serious question the claims of individuals and groups professing faith in Christ who refuse to allow him to transform major areas of their personal or corporate ethics—whether in the bedroom or in the boardroom.

As has often been observed, Christianity in the West has become increasingly privatized, withdrawing from the public square (or focusing on a narrow range of social issues when it does speak out), and marginalized or misrepresented by the media. In the United States the separation of church and state was originally intended to preserve freedom *for* religion, whereas today the concept has been perverted into the notion of freedom *from* religion! In countries with state churches, an important original motive was that Christianity would positively affect society better with an established church. Ironically, a majority of leaders in the state churches in these countries have abdicated this responsibility (at least as judged by biblical ethics), so that their cultures today are *less* influenced by authentic Christianity than in America with its "wall of separation"! In a postmodern age, it becomes far too easy for Christians themselves to believe that their religion should not encompass the whole of life or affect every daily decision and relationship.

The good news is that the ancient Roman Empire was far more pluralistic than even the contemporary Western world (despite the serious decline in overt Christian influence in recent decades), and yet "sold-out" Christians in the first three centuries made huge differences not only in people's personal lives but eventually in the public arena as well. The same spiritual power that ennobled them remains available today for those who will embrace it. As Margaret MacDonald summarizes, "The central aspect of the religious significance of Colossians is that it offers a vision of human victory in the face of an evil that can reach cosmic proportions."[89]

ADDITIONAL QUESTIONS FOR REVIEW

1. What is the occasion for Paul's letter to the Colossians, and how is Paul's relationship with the Colossians different from his relationship with the majority of the churches to which he writes?

---

[89] MacDonald, *Colossians and Ephesians,* 15. For a powerful reading and provocative application of Colossians (and Philemon) against the backdrop of empries, ancient and modern, see Brian J. Walsh and Sylvia C. Keesmaat, *Colossians Remixed: Subverting the Empire* (Downers Grove: IVP, 2004).

2. What are some of the key elements of the heresy that has infected the Colossian community, and what Christian doctrines could the heresy potentially affect?
3. Identify some elements in Colossians that differ from the undisputed Pauline letters, causing some to doubt Pauline authorship. What arguments can be made to lend credit to traditional claims of authorship by Paul?
4. What does Paul's response to Sabbatarianism in Colossians 2 suggest about the application of Old Testament law to the newly formed Christian community? Which laws are still binding?
5. How can affirmations of the equality of all persons and the command to submission in the domestic codes be harmonized? How should the domestic codes be applied today? What are the implications of relegating the domestic codes to ancient first-century society? of not doing so?
6. Summarize a concise statement based on Colossians about each of the doctrines of Christology, soteriology, and anthropology. What are some examples of modern philosophies that subvert some or all of these doctrines? In what ways do they prove subversive?

SELECT BIBLIOGRAPHY

In addition to the works listed under the bibliography for Philemon, see:

COMMENTARIES

Advanced

Barth, Markus, and Helmut Blanke. *Colossians.* AB. New York and London: Doubleday, 1994.

Intermediate

MacDonald, Margaret Y. *Colossians and Ephesians.* SP. Collegeville: Liturgical, 2000.
Pokorný, Petr. *Colossians: A Commentary.* Peabody: Hendrickson, 1991.
Schweizer, Eduard. *The Letter to the Colossians.* Minneapolis: Augsburg, 1982.

Introductory

Hay, David M. *Colossians.* ANTC. Nashville: Abingdon, 2000.

OTHER BOOKS

Arnold, Clinton E. *The Colossian Syncretism.* Tübingen: Mohr, 1995; Grand Rapids: Baker, 1996.
Bevere, Allan R. *Sharing in the Inheritance: Identity and the Moral Life in Colossians.* Sheffield: SAP, 2003.
Cannon, George E. *The Use of Traditional Materials in Colossians.* Macon: Mercer, 1983.

de Maris, Richard E. *The Colossians Controversy: Wisdom in Dispute at Colossae.* Sheffield: JSOT, 1994.

Martin, Troy W. *By Philosophy and Empty Deceit: Colossians as Response to a Cynic Critique.* Sheffield: SAP, 1996.

Sappington, Thomas J. *Revelation and Redemption at Colossae.* Sheffield: JSOT, 1991.

Walsh, Brian J., and Sylvia C. Keesmaat. *Colossians Remixed: Subverting the Empire.* Downers Grove: IVP, 2004.

Wilson, Walter T. *The Hope of Glory: Education and Exhortation in the Epistles to the Colossians.* Leiden and New York: Brill, 1997.

BIBLIOGRAPHY

Mills, Watson E. *Colossians.* Lewiston and Lampeter: Mellen, 1993.

Ephesians: Unity in Diversity as a Witness to the "Powers"

INTRODUCTION

There are three key problems or distinctives in the letter to the Ephesians that set it off from all of the other writings attributed to Paul. *First, a variety of features seem unusual in an epistle addressed to a church Paul knew so well.* From Acts 19–20, we learned that he ministered in Ephesus for approximately three years during his third missionary journey, a longer stay than in any other place Acts describes. Yet Ephesians reads more like Romans, which was written to a church of which Paul had no firsthand knowledge, in that it sets out a very systematic summary of his theology with seemingly little reference to any explicit problems or circumstances of the addressees. Two verses in particular stand out. In 3:2, the author writes, "Surely you have heard about the administration of God's grace that was given to me for you," as if he did not know his audience personally but trusted that they had learned of his distinctive commission. Again in 4:21, we read, "Surely you heard of him [Christ] and were taught in him in accordance with the truth that is in Jesus." Here the author seems not even to be entirely certain if his congregation all know the Lord, or at least if they all know the orthodox gospel.

Second, Ephesians and Colossians prove more similar in content, in outline, and at times even in exact wording than any other pair of letters ascribed to Paul. For example, both contain similar household codes (Eph. 5:22–6:9; Col. 3:18–4:1) and pairs of sentences in which up to thirty-two consecutive words in the Greek are identical (Eph. 6:21–22; Col. 4:7–8; cf. also Col. 1:14 with Eph. 1:7). Over one-third of the words in Ephesians reappear in Colossians.[90] More generally, both writings proceed from a detailed exposition of the person and work of Christ, to the reconciliation and unity of Jew and Gentile in the church, to exhortational material that addresses a number of the same themes in both letters.[91] Both epistles reflect the same distinctive style, with long, convoluted sentences (e.g., Eph. 1:3–14; Col. 1:9–17). Both works contain the same high Christology (e.g., Eph. 1:5–10; Col. 1:15–20); the same universal ecclesiology (the church as the worldwide body of believing Jews and Gentiles now united together in Christ); and the same realized eschatology (with heavenly blessings available in the present rather than the future; Ephesians does not even mention the second coming of Jesus).

In these and other respects, Ephesians also differs from the seven undisputed letters of Paul. For example, whereas in an undisputed letter like 1 Corinthians Jesus is the only foundation of the church (3:11), in Ephesians the foundation is formed by

---

[90] C. Leslie Mitton, *Ephesians* (London: Marshall, Morgan & Scott, 1976; Grand Rapids: Eerdmans, 1981), 11.

[91] For a detailed chart of the parallels, see Andrew T. Lincoln, *Ephesians* (Dallas: Word, 1990), xlix.

the apostles and prophets (2:20). Whereas elsewhere in the unchallenged epistles, Paul exclusively uses the term *Satan* to refer to the head of the fallen angels (eight times), in Ephesians only the word *devil* appears (twice, in 4:26 and 6:11). Overall, forty-one words in Ephesians appear nowhere else in the New Testament, while another eighty-four do not appear elsewhere in Paul's writings, though they do occur in other New Testament books.[92]

Third, in the three earliest and most reliable manuscripts of this epistle (p[46], a, B), the words "in Ephesus" in 1:1 do not appear. A handful of later texts and church fathers also lack this address, even though the vast majority of witnesses contain it. Marcion alleged that this letter was originally written to the Laodiceans, which would also explain the reference in Colossians 4:16 to an epistle to that congregation.

Five major explanations of these three distinctives of Ephesians have competed for acceptance. *The most common theory among scholars today is that a disciple of Paul, perhaps up to a generation after his life, wrote a pseudonymous letter in his name.* This hypothesis is usually explained as based on the Jewish tradition, believed by some to be represented in the Old Testament and recognized by all to be used in the intertestamental period, in which contemporary works were written in the names of ancient authors to enhance their authority and at times to contextualize their work for a new age.[93] These works are not viewed as literary forgeries but as a kind of substitute for our modern use of footnotes—to give credit where credit was due for use of various concepts, styles, or genres.[94] Except for the Pastoral Epistles, no letter ascribed to Paul has been more commonly attributed, at least in the modern era, to some other author than Ephesians. The hypothesis of pseudonymity would account for the distinctive style and form of this letter, as well as for its similarities to Colossians. While not able to imitate Paul in every respect, the author did what he could to make his writing look like an authentically Pauline document. For those who also find Colossians pseudonymous, Ephesians is then usually attributed to a separate pseudepigrapher.

But would the early church have accepted a letter as canonical if they knew it was pseudonymous? The only clear evidence we have, admittedly from no earlier than the mid-second century, suggests not.[95] But then that leaves only the option that the church was fooled into accepting something as authentic that was not, which raises crucial questions for the canonicity and authority of the letter today (see further above, p. 104).[96]

---

[92] Harold W. Hoehner, *Ephesians: An Exegetical Commentary* (Grand Rapids: Baker, 2002), 24–25.

[93] So even the otherwise excellent evangelical commentary by Lincoln (*Ephesians*). In the standard critical commentary on this letter, Ernest Best (*A Critical and Exegetical Commentary on Ephesians* [Edinburgh: T & T Clark, 1998], 13) explains that the author "does not write with the intention to deceive, but only to instruct Christians in the new situations in which they were finding themselves in the way Paul would have done had he still been alive."

[94] See esp. David G. Meade, *Pseudonymity and Canon* (Tübingen: Mohr, 1986; Grand Rapids: Eerdmans, 1987).

[95] From two different theological perspectives, observe the agreement on this point between Donald Guthrie (*New Testament Introduction* [Leicester and Downers Grove: IVP, 1990], 1011–28) and Lewis R. Donelson (*Pseudepigraphy and Ethical Argument in the Pastoral Epistles* [Tübingen: Mohr, 1986]).

[96] Stanley E. Porter and Kent D. Clarke, "Canonical-Critical Perspective and the Relationship of Colossians and Ephesians," *Bib* 78 (1997): 57–86.

The second option stems from the mid-twentieth century. *E. J. Goodspeed proposed an influential hypothesis in which Ephesians was viewed as pseudonymous but also written as a cover letter for a collection of previously disparate and somewhat neglected authentic Pauline epistles.*[97] This theory would account for the general nature of the epistle and the lack of reference to any original addressees, at least by location. It would also explain why Acts never refers to any letters of Paul, even though it covers precisely those portions of his ministry during which most of them were written. But if Ephesians served as an introduction to all or most of the other letters of Paul, why was its position not retained in the early canonical sequences? And all of the problems attaching to pseudonymity still remain for this hypothesis as well.

Third, a number of writers have suggested that Paul gave a different amanuensis greater freedom in literary composition. Such a scribe would certainly have tried to copy Paul's style closely, and if Paul wanted his letter to Ephesus to treat the same basic range of topics as Colossians, the scribe would naturally have modeled his writing on that letter. Yet at the same time, his different style would clearly have shone through. The style and diction of Ephesians is in some ways closer to Luke's than to Paul's undisputed letters, and Luke stayed with Paul during his Roman imprisonment, so perhaps we should think of him.[98] But this view still fails to explain the missing city name from the earliest manuscripts.

Fourth, it is possible that one should think of an authentically Pauline core of Ephesians supplemented by a later redactor's work. After all, more traditional scholarship has often pointed out that cross-references to genuine Pauline theology appear in a sizable majority of the verses of this letter, so much so that it has been called "the quintessence of Paulinism."[99] Plus, 3:1–13 reflects so personal a prayer of Paul for the Ephesians that it may be the hardest portion of the letter to ascribe to a pseudepigrapher who was not simply trying to fool or to forge. On the other hand, this view accounts for the distinctive elements of Ephesians that have led many to consider it pseudonymous. But attempted reconstructions of a Pauline original require there to have been considerable expansions at a later date, and the criteria for separating tradition from redaction prove notoriously slippery to apply.[100] Here, too, close parallels in ancient epistolography are harder to find even than for entirely pseudonymous letters, so it is not surprising that this is the least commonly suggested alternative to full-fledged Pauline authorship.

Finally, it has often been suggested that Paul composed this letter as an encyclical or circular letter, much like Revelation (see Rev. 2–3), intended for both Ephesus and nearby churches (just as with Revelation itself). The intriguing reference in Colossians 4:16 to the epistle to the Laodiceans and Paul's request that Laodicea and Colossae exchange letters after each congregation had read the ones addressed to them could support Marcion's view. Perhaps the letter we know as the

---

[97] E. J. Goodspeed, *The Key to Ephesians* (Chicago: University of Chicago Press, 1956).

[98] E.g., Martin, *New Testament Foundations*, vol. 2, 227–33.

[99] See throughout Bruce, *Colossians, Philemon, and Ephesians*.

[100] See throughout John Muddiman (*The Epistle to the Ephesians* [London and New York: Continuum, 2001]), who nevertheless endorses this hypothesis.

Ephesians was originally addressed to several churches, including at least Ephesus and Laodicea, which would explain the omission of the city name from the original manuscripts. Each church might then have chosen to insert its own name in the copy of the manuscript that it kept.[101] This option seems best to account for the textual evidence and for the general nature of the contents, but not as well for the distinctive style or the similarities with Colossians, although it has been observed that Paul's most cumbersome sentences seem to occur in his doxologies, prayers, doctrinal sections, and parenthetical material, which proliferate far more in Colossians and Ephesians than elsewhere.[102] Paul's unique contents may therefore have dictated a significant portion of the unique style of this letter.

But it is not clear that a majority of the distinctives can be accounted for in this fashion.[103] *Perhaps a combination of the third and fifth views is therefore required: Paul gave an amanuensis greater literary freedom in his composition while clearly guiding him in the topics he wanted addressed, and he intended the letter as a circular communiqué to two or more of the churches in Asia Minor.*[104] As for the supposed theological differences from the undisputed letters of Paul, recall our discussion of the same problem in Colossians (pp. 287–88).

We have already briefly introduced the city of Ephesus above (pp. 61–65). A booming city and a key coastal port in Asia Minor, it was the home of Dionysiac cults, Artemis worship, a major library, indoor and outdoor theaters, marble streets in the city center complete with outdoor lamplighting, state-of-the-art Roman bathhouses, spas, a gymnasium, and an athletic stadium. Ephesus had an unusually large percentage of Roman citizens and a considerable number of temples of the imperial cult and civic courts staffed by local magistrates.[105]

ADDITIONAL CONTEXT AND CIRCUMSTANCES

In several recent works, Clinton Arnold has demonstrated the significant role that *the theme of Christ's victory over oppressive, occultic, and even demonic powers* plays in this letter. Precisely this theme *matches much of what we read in Acts about Paul's time in Ephesus.*[106] The extraordinary miracles he performed there included casting out evil spirits, and the other seemingly more superstitious signs (Acts 19:11–12) may have been necessary because of the extent of spiritual warfare in that region (recall above). Verses 13–16 describe the dangers of attempting to appropriate the Spirit's power magically without knowing the Lord, while verses 17–20 depict the burning of the magical papyri that proliferated in that area. So

---

[101] Michael D. Goulder ("The Visionaries of Laodicea," *JSNT* 43 [1991]: 15–39) supports Pauline authorship of Ephesians but thinks it was originally intended *primarily* for Laodicea.

[102] A. van Roon, *The Authenticity of Ephesians* (Leiden and New York: Brill, 1974), 105–11. Markus Barth ("Traditions in Ephesians," *NTS* 30 [1984]: 3–25) likewise explains a large portion of the distinctive style and contents as due to Paul's use of traditional material.

[103] Though see the valiant attempts in Hoehner, *Ephesians,* 2–61.

[104] van Roon, *Authenticity* (which is the most detailed defense of Pauline authorship available); cf. esp. O'Brien, *Ephesians,* 4–47.

[105] See further G. H. R. Horsley, "The Inscriptions of Ephesus and the New Testament," *NovT* 34 (1992): 105–68.

[106] See esp. Arnold, *Ephesians.* Cf. also idem, "Ephesians, Letter to the," in *Dictionary of Paul and His Letters,* eds. Gerald F. Hawthorne, Ralph P. Martin, and Daniel G. Reid (Leicester and Downers Grove: IVP, 1993), 238–49.

while many writers still refer either to our inability to determine a life-situation to which Ephesians was addressed, or to rather vague parallels to turn-of-the-century Gnosticism and its use of terms like "fullness" and "mystery," and such concepts as a descending and ascending redeemer or a building as a metaphor for people,[107] a direct tie-in with Ephesus and its environs in the 60s is not nearly as improbable as many have imagined.

This then allows for us to reinsert the other information that applied to the date and circumstances of Philemon and Colossians. Ephesians would have been written and sent out at the same time with Tychicus and Onesimus as those other two Prison Epistles, in 60 or 61, by Paul from Rome while he remained under house arrest there. After delivering the letter intended for Ephesus and other nearby communities, the duo would have proceeded to Colossae with their other two letters for the church there.

GENRE AND STRUCTURE

Most commentators have puzzled over the question of what specific kind of letter Ephesians represents. The most common suggestions have included a tractate (or theological essay), liturgical writing, meditation, speech, and homily or sermon.[108] H. Hendrix, however, has observed the common pattern of praising benefactors in ancient inscriptions via a sustained prayer or *encomium,* which could account for all of Ephesians 1–3. Extolling patrons' virtues then often led to the resolutions or commitments that flowed from those often lavish words of thanksgiving, which could account for chapters 4–6.[109] Further subdividing each "half" of the epistle leads to an outline as follows:[110]

I. Opening Greetings (1:1–2)
II. Theological Exposition: The Spiritual Privileges of the Church—Making Unity among Believers Possible (1:3–3:21)
   A. Praising the Triune God (1:3–14)
   B. Praying for the Ephesians (1:15–23)
   C. The Blessings Believers Share (2:1–10)
   D. Unity in Christ (2:11–22)
   E. Further Prayer for Empowerment (3:1–19)
   F. Doxology (3:20–21)
III. Ethical Implications: The Spiritual Responsibilities of the Church—Making Unity among Believers Actual (4:1–6:20)
   A. Achieving Maturity through Spiritual Gifts Used in Love (4:1–16)
   B. Putting Off the Old and Putting On the New (4:17–5:21)
   C. The Domestic Code (5:22–6:9)
   D. Arming Oneself for Spiritual Warfare (6:10–20)
IV. Closing Greetings (6:21–24)

---

[107] Best, *Ephesians*, 88.
[108] Ibid., 61.
[109] Holland Hendrix, "On the Form and Ethos of Ephesians," *USQR* 42 (1988): 3–15.
[110] Cf. esp. William W. Klein, "Ephesians," in *EBC*, vol. 12 (Grand Rapids: Zondervan, forthcoming). On the unity of the two main sections, see Peter W. Gosnell, "Honor and Shame Rhetoric as a Unifying Motif in Ephesians," *BBR* 16 (2006): 105–28.

Even more so than in Colossians, the first half of the letter reflects primarily the epideictic rhetoric appropriate for praising benefactors, while the second half elaborates the believers' appropriate response with deliberative rhetoric.[111]

COMMENTARY

OPENING GREETINGS (1:1–2)

The most intriguing feature about these opening two verses is the omission of "in Ephesus" in the three oldest and most reliable manuscripts (see discussion above, p. 304). The grammatical detail that leads some to suspect this omission to be a later corruption of the text is the wording that remains when this phrase is left out—literally, "To the saints, the ones being and to the faithful in Christ Jesus." Only when a preposition and a place name are added after "being" does the statement make any sense.[112] Many have speculated that a gap was left in the original manuscript for precisely such phrases to be added as the letter circulated to the various cities that Paul hoped it would reach, but the existing manuscripts that lack these words disclose no gaps. On the other hand, later scribes unaware of the purpose of the gaps could easily have deleted them, thinking they were merely the product of some careless copyist. Otherwise, Paul's form adheres closely to his standard conventions.

THEOLOGICAL EXPOSITION: THE SPIRITUAL PRIVILEGES OF THE CHURCH— MAKING UNITY AMONG BELIEVERS POSSIBLE (1:3–3:21)

Praising the Triune God (1:3–14)   As in 2 Corinthians (1:3), Paul begins with the more Jewish form of prayer known as a *berakah,* or blessing, rather than a thanksgiving *per se.* He thus opens by addressing God rather than by either describing or desiring the Ephesians' growth. This passage is clearly the most detailed and theologically rich of all of Paul's recorded prayers.[113] It is punctuated by the threefold use of the phrase "to the praise of his glory/glorious grace" (vv. 6, 12, 14). In the Greek, these twelve verses actually form one long, uninterrupted sentence. Each segment deals with one person of the Trinity. *In short, Paul gives thanks for God the Father's role in predestining believers (vv. 3–6), for Christ's role in redeeming them through his blood (vv. 7–12), and for the Holy Spirit's role as the guarantor of their salvation (vv. 13–14).*

The topic of predestination is, of course, fraught with theological controversy (recall above, pp. 251–54).[114] Verse 3 introduces the first segment of Paul's blessing with one of five references in this letter to "the heavenly realms" (1:3, 20; 2:6; 3:10; 6:12), an expression not found anywhere else in the Bible. It appears to refer

---

[111] Lincoln, *Ephesians,* lxxv.

[112] E.g., Hoehner, *Ephesians,* 144–48. Hoehner nevertheless recognizes that the letter could have been circular even if this verse does not provide evidence for it (p. 141).

[113] On which, see esp. D. A. Carson, *A Call to Spiritual Reformation: Priorities from Paul and His Prayers* (Grand Rapids: Baker, 1992).

[114] For the major, competing perspectives, see David Basinger and Randall Basinger, eds., *Predestination and Free Will: Four Views of Divine Sovereignty and Human Freedom* (Downers Grove: IVP, 1986).

to the unseen world where angels and demons do battle (see below on 2:2), and the combined effect of all of its uses in Ephesians assures us of triumph in Christ over all cosmic forces.[115] Verse 4 employs the language of election; "chose" translates a form of the Greek verb *eklegomai,* from which the English "elect" derives. God's choosing, however, is not arbitrary; it is "in him," that is, in Christ. God freely chose all who would accept Christ (v. 13) to become his adopted children,[116] a loving choice he made even before he began to create anything (vv. 4–5). Here this appears to be corporate election.[117] At any rate, Paul does not even mention God's plans for unbelievers in this context. As in Romans 9:22–23, this also seems to be single predestination.[118]

The second segment of the prayer turns to Christ's specific role. As in Romans 3:24, redemption alludes to the price paid to buy a slave's freedom. Spiritually, it was Jesus' shed blood on the cross that enabled this purchase (v. 7). As in Colossians 1:26 and 2:2, the details of God's plan of salvation for humanity may be depicted as a "mystery" that he has been successively revealing over time, culminating in its full disclosure in the messianic age (vv. 8–10a). Verse 10b refers to God's ultimate goal—to restore the entire fallen, corrupt universe to its rightful submission under the lordship of Christ Jesus (recall our comments under Col. 1:20). The age of this restoration has begun with the first believers in Jesus, demonstrating that God's sovereign choices are being worked out in history (vv. 11–12).[119]

Finally, Paul illustrates the Spirit's role by means of two metaphors. Believers are "sealed" (v. 13; from Gk. *sphragizo*), just like an official scroll was kept rolled up by wax insignia joining its two ends together. The Spirit similarly functions as a "deposit" or "down payment" (v. 14; Gk. *arrabōn*), just as individuals who buy something expensive may pay only a portion of its cost "up front" as a pledge that they will supply the rest at a later date.[120] Both metaphors guarantee that when God's Spirit indwells a person at conversion, he promises to continue to work in that individual all the way to the stage of glorification (recall Rom. 8:30). Then believers will receive their full spiritual inheritance.

Praying for the Ephesians (1:15–23)   After this opening prayer, one would expect Paul to begin the body of his letter. But he has not yet thanked God for the Ephesians' faith and love, nor has he prayed for their further spiritual growth. So this next paragraph undertakes both of these tasks (vv. 15–19). Exactly as in Colossians, Paul then transitions mid-sentence to start his theological exposition, introducing

---

[115] See esp. Andrew T. Lincoln, *Paradise Now and Not Yet* (Cambridge and New York: CUP, 1981).

[116] William W. Klein, *The New Chosen People* (Grand Rapids: Zondervan, 1990), esp. 179–81, 186–87.

[117] See esp. Markus Barth, *Ephesians 1–3* (Garden City: Doubleday, 1974), 105–9.

[118] In other words, no reference is made to the lost, only to the saved. "Those who come to believe in Christ find themselves participating in God's eternal plan" (Pheme Perkins, *Ephesians* [Nashville: Abingdon, 1997], 38).

[119] The Greek for "to bring all things together" means "to sum up." Best (*Ephesians,* 142) finds an architectural analogy here: Christ sums up the universe just as "an architect's plan sums up what is built; the shape of what comes into existence is both summarised in the plan and determined by it."

[120] In modern Greek the word can refer to an engagement ring. Or, preserving the ancient metaphor, "the Spirit of God operating in our lives is like the Lord's 'earnest money' on us—His sweet certification that He seriously intends to save us with an everlasting salvation" (Robert Millet, "The Process of Salvation," in *Salvation in Christ: Comparative Christian Views,* ed. Roger R. Keller and Robert L. Millet [Provo: Religious Studies Center, 2005], 164).

his remarks with a relative pronoun. The subordinate clause with which verse 20 begins makes an already long Greek sentence even longer, so that all of verses 15–23 remain a single syntactical unit. Thus it is almost impossible to break up this giant sentence midstream to mark out the beginning of the body of the epistle, yet the form of a prayer has clearly given way to doctrinal instruction by the end of verse 19. The main thrust of verses 20–23 is to explain how believers can become confident that a great inheritance awaits them. It is by the incomparable power of God that raised Christ from the dead, leading to his reenthronement in that exalted heavenly position next to God himself, with every created entity subordinate to him (vv. 20–22a). By definition this includes believers, yet verses 22b–23 make the extraordinary claim that Christ's headship over the cosmos (which in this context must refer to his "authority") is designed to *benefit* God's people (v. 22b), who form his "body" (v. 23a; recall 1 Cor. 12:12–27).

The last part of verse 23 proves notoriously difficult to translate and interpret but seems to suggest a distinction somewhat analogous to Jesus' teaching on church versus kingdom. While God's regal power particularly resides in the community of Christ's followers (here described as his "fullness"), it remains at work omnipresently throughout the universe as well.[121]

The Blessings Believers Share (2:1–10)   Again, it is possible to view this section as the grammatical continuation of the previous one, so that the sentence begun in 1:15 would not end until 2:7! But it is perhaps more likely, despite the *kai* ("and") with which 2:1 begins, to see this passage as starting a new sentence, from which Paul digresses in 2:2, so that he has to repeat himself in verse 5 and then move on from there. The unifying theme of this paragraph is the abundant blessing believers share because of Christ's victory over the grave. We, too, can triumph over every ungodly power as we are spiritually coresurrected and coexalted along with Christ (v. 6). Even though we have not yet been physically resurrected and exalted, Paul can use the past tense because in the spiritual realm we may be described as joining in heavenly blessings already in the present.[122] Once we were dead in our sins, as we wittingly or unwittingly served "the ruler of the kingdom of the air," a reference to Satan (vv. 1–3). As in 2 Corinthians 12:2, the Jewish concept of three heavens may be in view here (see above, p. 227). The second or middle "heaven" in between the atmosphere and God's throne room, which could also be called the "air," represented the invisible domain of spiritual warfare, from which the devil still ruled in the lives of unbelievers.[123]

But God has graciously saved us from all that, not by any meritorious works that we could perform but solely by his undeserved favor, which we appropriate through faith (vv. 4–9). Verses 8–9, of course, have been memorized and treasured by countless believers over the centuries. In both verses 5 and 8, Paul employs a periphrastic perfect participle to stress the ongoing nature of spiritual liberation as God's free

---

[121] The participle *plēromenou* is more naturally taken as a passive than a middle voice, in which case the church is being filled by Christ, just as Christ is being filled by God (Best, *Ephesians,* 188–89).

[122] Bruce, *Colossians, Philemon, and Ephesians,* 286.

[123] Cf. Lincoln, *Ephesians,* 95–97.

gift. *Paul's emphasis on salvation by grace through faith sets Christianity off from all other major religions and enables one to distinguish genuine from corrupt forms of Christianity itself.*[124] *Yet these verses must never be isolated from verse 10, which stresses equally emphatically that God has designed believers from before their creation to do good deeds and please him. But these deeds never save anyone; rather, they inexorably flow from true saving faith.*[125]

Unity in Christ (2:11–22)   Not only does salvation make us right with God; it enables reconciliation among even the worst of human enemies. If Jesus' death has conquered Satan's domain, it can certainly handle any earthly alienation. If an ancient Near Eastern sovereign was expected to provide peace among the peoples he conquered, how much more could Christ be counted on to reconcile warring factions.[126] In Paul's world, Jew versus Gentile epitomized such enmity, outwardly signified by the rite of circumcision that marked Jewish men off as different from all their pagan contemporaries. The uncircumcised were thus excluded from Israel and from all of God's promises to that nation. As Jews and Gentiles become Christians, however, that alienation is abolished (vv. 11–13). Christ's death replaces hostility with peace among those who turn to him.

The controlling metaphor in verses 14–18 is the destruction of the barrier described as "the dividing wall of hostility" (v. 14). Paul may have in mind the balustrade that separated the outer court of the Gentiles from the inner court of the Jews in the Jerusalem temple, which Gentiles crossed on penalty of death. But he applies this word picture to the law, "with its commandments and regulations" (v. 15), presumably to be interpreted much as in Colossians 2:14.[127] If there is any difference, it is that here Paul is addressing reconciliation between warring peoples, not just the estrangement of humans from God. Thus he can speak of the creation of one new person "out of the two" (Jew and Gentile), much as Scripture repeatedly refers to a husband and wife as "one flesh." Gentiles were far away from God, while Jews were much closer (v. 17). But now both have identical access to God through Christ's cross-work,[128] thereby establishing peace between the two races by God's Spirit (vv. 16, 18).

Nor dare we limit this reconciliation to relationships between individuals. Verses 19–22 reflect corporate imagery for the unity that results in the church. Believers, no matter what their background, are no longer spiritual aliens but citizens with all the accompanying rights and privileges (v. 19a). Even more intimately, they can be described as forming God's family (v. 19b). From the concept of a "household," it is

---

[124] See esp. Sir Norman Anderson, *Christianity and World Religions: The Challenge of Pluralism* (Leicester and Downers Grove: IVP, rev. 1984).

[125] "Since salvation is seen as a creation in Christ for good works, such works cannot be the cause of [people's] salvation" (Lincoln, *Ephesians,* 113).

[126] Timothy G. Gombis, "Ephesians 2 as a Narrative of Divine Warfare," *JSNT* 26 (2004): 403–18.

[127] Peter Balla, "Is the Law Abolished according to Eph. 2:15?" *EJT* 3 (1994): 9–16. Cf. Klein, "Ephesians": "Again Paul compounds synonyms, perhaps to capture the Gentiles' distaste for the detailed minutiae of the numerous Jewish ceremonies and regulations that effectively walled the Gentiles out."

[128] "Access to a monarchy in virtue of the full rights of citizenship may be part of what is meant." But primarily we have a "cultic reference," as all ethnic barriers to one's "approach into the presence of God through worship" are removed (Muddiman, *Ephesians,* 138).

a small step to the idea of a house or a building with Christ as the chief cornerstone (v. 20b).[129] Large buildings in antiquity required the largest, squarest, and most solid rock to be laid first, at one of the four corners of the edifice about to be erected. Then the rest of the first layer of stones forming the foundation of the building could be added, with additional layers fitted above.

This picture does not contradict 1 Corinthians 3:10–15, even though there Paul calls Jesus the only foundation that can be laid (v. 11). In that passage he is not trying to rank Christian leaders but overcome rivalries in the church, so of course Jesus must be the only foundation of the whole building. But here the point is that church planters and preachers form the foundation for further human activity in church building (recall 1 Cor. 12:28).[130] Whichever metaphor we examine, Paul's point remains that one must start with Christ, so that Christians' works can build only on him and on what he has already done (here, see Eph. 2:21–22).[131] The holiest and most beautiful of ancient buildings were the temples, so it is natural for Paul in verses 21–22 to close this section by thinking of the church in this light.

Further Prayer for Empowerment (3:1–19)   Now Paul begins a third prayer. We can understand why some think almost the entire first half of this letter can be viewed as an extended prayer. But we do not realize this yet in verse 1 because Paul breaks off his sentence midstream and so digresses that he has to begin again in verse 14. At that point his reference to kneeling before his father clarifies that he is praying. In between, in verses 2–13, he describes his unique commission for those who might not previously have heard of it.[132] As in Colossians, he refers to *the mystery of Christ,* here even more explicitly specified as *the unity of Jew and Gentile in Christian faith* (v. 6). Verse 5 contains an ambiguity: does "as" mean "whereas" or "to the same extent as"? In other words, is Paul saying that this entire secret has now been revealed for the first time in the Christian era? More likely, in light of all of the Old Testament texts that Christians understood as predicting a messianic age, the apostle is implying that God's plan of salvation for the future was not as clear in previous eras as in his day, even though prophetic writers had glimpses of what was to come.[133]

In describing his commission, Paul once more highlights God's powerful grace that was able to break through to him even when he was strongly (if unwittingly) resisting God's will by persecuting believers (v. 8). He again refers to the mystery, now explaining that this unity of Jew and Gentile in Christ must be demonstrated in the church (v. 10a). In other words, *it is not enough for individual Christians of*

---

[129] Some scholars argue for the translation "capstone" or "keystone," but this seems less likely. For explanation, see Rudolf Schnackenburg, *Ephesians: A Commentary* (Edinburgh: T & T Clark, 1991), 123–24.

[130] Both the order of the terms "apostles and prophets" and the context of 3:5 demonstrate that Paul is speaking of New Testament prophets, not Old Testament ones. Against the view that this foundation requires the cessation of the so-called charismatic gifts at the end of the apostolic age, see Jon Ruthven, "The 'Foundational Gifts' of Ephesians 2:20," *JPT* 10 (2002): 28–43.

[131] Indeed, it is only when the translation "capstone" is used that any real tension is introduced. See Hoehner, *Ephesians,* 406.

[132] Although these verses form a grammatical digression, they further the theme of spiritual warfare that permeates the epistle. Even imprisonment (v. 1) has not hindered God's working through Paul against demonic powers (v. 10). Cf. Timothy Gombis, "Ephesians 3:2–13: Pointless Digression, or Epitome of the Triumph of God in Christ?" *WTJ* 66 (2004): 313–23.

[133] Caragounis, *Ephesian Mysterion,* 102–3 (*contra* many).

warring racial or ethnic backgrounds to be reconciled to one another. The gathered community of God's people must exhibit a loving heterogeneity to a watching world.[134] Indeed, even the most hostile cosmic powers will then sit up and take notice (v. 10b). While some have argued that "the rulers and authorities in the heavenly realms" refer in exaggerated language just to the most powerful of human leaders, the consistent usage of these expressions throughout Paul and various other writers outside Scripture suggests that angels and demons are primarily in mind.[135]

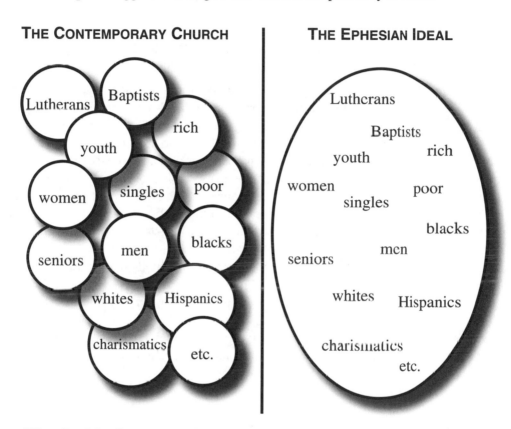

| THE CONTEMPORARY CHURCH | THE EPHESIAN IDEAL |

When Paul finally returns to his prayer, he acknowledges that all humanity owes its origin to God (v. 15), an insight that no doubt encouraged him in his ministry to the Gentiles.[136] He proceeds to pray for the Ephesians' spiritual growth, particularly with respect to the centerpiece of Christian ethics—love (vv. 17–19). His petition that the Ephesian believers may find Christ dwelling in their hearts (v. 17) does not mean that Jesus through his Spirit has not already come to live in them. The word

---

[134] See esp. Bruce W. Fong, "Addressing the Issue of Racial Reconciliation according to the Principles of Eph 2:11–22," *JETS* 38 (1995): 565–80.

[135] O'Brien, *Ephesians,* 246–47. At the same time, while Walter Wink's equation of these powers with religious, governmental, and even multinational institutions (*The Powers That Be* [New York: Doubleday, 1998]) probably "demythologizes" this concept, there is no question that demonic forces can work through human institutions so that the total of their evil is more than the sum of their individual parts. In this respect, Christians must confront structural evil in society.

[136] Cf. Best, *Ephesians,* 338–39. Since the universal scope of God's creation is in view, "social group" rather than "family" might better render the Greek *patria* here.

he uses (from *katoikeō*) "connotes a settled dwelling"[137] parallel to the metaphor of being "rooted and established" that immediately follows. Today we might speak of someone who was "well grounded in the faith."

Doxology (3:20–21) At last Paul brings the doctrinal section of his letter to a close. He offers up a resounding word of praise to the incomparable God who can and does perform far more than we could ever dream of. He alone deserves all glory forever and ever! Little wonder that Paul ends with an Amen, which means, "This is most certainly true."[138]

ETHICAL IMPLICATIONS: THE SPIRITUAL RESPONSIBILITIES OF THE CHURCH— MAKING UNITY AMONG BELIEVERS ACTUAL (4:1–6:20)

Achieving Maturity through Spiritual Gifts Used in Love (4:1–16) The theme of unity forms a bridge between the doctrinal and ethical halves of Paul's letter. As Paul turns to describe the appropriate lifestyle that should issue from the salvation so gloriously depicted above (v. 1), he continues to expound such qualities as love, unity, and peace (vv. 2–3). To reinforce the need for unity, he stresses how there is only one body (i.e., the church universal), one Holy Spirit, one Lord (Jesus Christ), one God (thus creating another clear reference to the Trinity) and one Christian hope, faith, and baptism (vv. 4–6). As in 1 Corinthians 8:4–6 and 12:4–6, Paul can use unswervingly monotheistic language and yet express trinitarian arithmetic: $1 + 1 + 1 = 1$![139]

As in Romans 12, immediately after enumerating fundamental principles required of all believers, Paul inserts a discussion of spiritual gifts. Ephesians differs from Paul's teaching on this topic elsewhere by prefacing a list of sample gifts with the depiction of how Christ made the distribution of the gifts possible (vv. 7–10). Verse 8 presents one of the most puzzling uses of the Old Testament in the New, in that the text cited (Ps. 68:18) in both the MT and LXX refers to God receiving gifts *from* people rather than giving them to anyone. But the Syriac Peshitta and a targumic tradition each make the same change as Ephesians, so at least Paul parallels a preexisting Jewish tradition. That tradition (or at least Paul) may have understood the purpose of God's receiving gifts as a triumphant conqueror to be their redistribution among his people.[140] After Pentecost, it is natural for Paul to interpret the Lord's ascension as a reference to Jesus' return to the Father, which was followed by the outpouring of the Holy Spirit and gifting of believers (recall Acts 2).

The interpretation in verses 9–10 (along with 1 Pet. 3:18–22) led many in the history of the church to imagine a descent of Christ into hell, especially since verse

---

[137] Hoehner, *Ephesians,* 480.

[138] Cf. Best, *Ephesians,* 351–52.

[139] Cf. esp. Richard Bauckham, *God Crucified: Monotheism and Christology in the New Testament* (Carlisle: Paternoster, 1998; Grand Rapids and Cambridge: Eerdmans, 1999).

[140] Richard A. Taylor, "The Use of Psalm 68:18 in Ephesians 4:8 in Light of the Ancient Versions," *BSac* 148 (1991): 319–36. Alternately, Paul may have understood Ps. 68:18 to have been informed by Num. 8:19, in which Levites were called "gifts" like the Christian leaders here in v. 11, and 18:8, in which various offerings presented to the Lord are then given to the Levites. This too would support the logic of "receiving in order to redistribute" (Gary V. Smith, "Paul's Use of Psalm 68:18 in Ephesians 4:8," *JETS* 18 [1975]: 181–89), or else Paul has simply "offered his own midrash," recognizing Jewish precedent for his logic (Klein, "Ephesians").

9b reads more literally, "the lower parts of the earth." But the word "parts" does not occur in a number of important, early manuscripts, while "of the earth" probably reflects an appositional genitive—"the lower [parts], namely, the earth."[141] After all, since the ascension in verse 10 describes Christ's return from earth to heaven, his previous descent most likely refers to the incarnation, when he came from heaven to earth.[142]

At any rate, all commentators are agreed as to what Paul means by Christ's ascension, so that a reference to the gifting of his people follows naturally. Verse 11 differs from Paul's other lists of gifts by naming the people so gifted rather than just the abstract qualities or roles given to them, but this does not appear to create a significant variation.[143] We have seen those with gifts of apostleship, prophecy, and teaching before. New here are evangelists and pastors (though recall Acts 20:28). Particularly telling is the combination of "pastors and teachers" in a Greek construction that suggests a close overlap between the two.[144] All pastors should incorporate a significant element of teaching into their ministry, while all teachers should care enough for their students to exercise some shepherding role with them. Verses 12–13 likewise supplement Paul's earlier teaching about spiritual gifts by stressing their purpose in building up the church and its people to full maturity.[145] It is the task not merely of a church's leadership but of the entire congregation to exercise their gifts and make the church everything God intends it to be.[146] Verses 14–16 explain why this task is crucial; without it, believers are easily led astray in doctrinal matters and/or fail to display the unity of the body in love. "Speaking the truth in love" (v. 15) succinctly encapsulates two essential dimensions of Christian living. Without truth, all the love in the world can save no one. Without love, few people are likely to listen to the truth!

Putting Off the Old and Putting On the New (4:17–5:21) Parallel to the discussion in Colossians 3:5–17, Paul next enunciates the fundamental vices to avoid and virtues to embrace as the Ephesians continue the process of being transformed from their old to their new selves. Verses 17–19 describe the ignorance of God's ways that characterized the Gentiles who had not been given God's law. This lack of knowledge led to futile thinking and impure behavior, which should not characterize Christians'

---

[141] Schnackenburg, *Ephesians,* 178.

[142] W. Hall Harris (*The Descent of Christ: Ephesians 4:7–11 and Traditional Hebrew Imagery* [Grand Rapids: Baker, 1998],) argues for the descent by the Spirit at Pentecost, but this seems less likely since it came after rather than before Christ's ascension into heaven.

[143] Markus Barth, *Ephesians 4–6* (Garden City: Doubleday, 1974), 435 (*contra* many). After all, v. 8 has just referred to "gifts," not merely to "gifted individuals."

[144] Because the nouns are plural, Granville Sharp's rule does not strictly apply. Still, constructions such as this one usually refer to united, overlapping, or subset groupings when they do not represent identical ones. See Stanley E. Porter, *Idioms of the Greek New Testament* (Sheffield: JSOT, 1992), 111.

[145] "The ability to hold diversity within a harmonious unity is the mark of maturity" (Mitton, *Ephesians,* 154).

[146] Despite passionate debate on each side, it is grammatically impossible to determine whether the three clauses in vv. 12a, 12b, and 12c run parallel to each other or build on one another. But given Paul's dependence on the Pentecost account, in which the Spirit poured out gifts on all God's people (Acts 2:17–18), he is surely stressing the need for leadership to equip all the people to play their God-given roles. Even if this is not Paul, one cannot drive a wedge between the theology of this passage and Paul's teaching on spiritual gifts in the undisputed letters. See further O'Brien, *Ephesians,* 303; and Peter W. Gosnell, "Networks and Exchanges: Ephesians 4:7–16: and the Community Function of Teachers," *BTB* 30 (2000): 135–43.

lives (vv. 20–22). Instead, their new lives should disclose progressive growth in righteous attitudes and practices (vv. 23–24). The parallels between Ephesians 4:24 and Colossians 3:10 are close enough that, even without an explicit reference to God's likeness, it is clear that becoming "like God" here refers not to deification but to re-creation in the image of God.[147]

Paul next stresses the implications of this process for Christians' speech, highlighting the need for truth and forgiveness rather than lies, hurtful words,[148] and anger (vv. 25–27, 29–32). Verse 26a clearly distinguishes between anger and sin; there is such a thing as righteous indignation. But the second half of this verse reminds us that Paul's anger should remain short-lived. Tucked in between these two sections is an important principle for combating theft (and various other criminal behaviors). Restitution rather than retribution leads to rehabilitation (v. 28).[149] Chapter 5:1–2 probably belongs as the conclusion to this discussion. Imitating God, whom we cannot see, by imitating Christ's earthly life, which was visible, will produce in us the qualities that God desires in the new age. These can be summarized in the concept of self-giving, sacrificial love.

Instruction in basic Christian morality continues in 5:3–7. The lists of fundamental sins to avoid are revealing: sexual immorality and greed or covetousness are regularly placed side by side. The early church understood the relationship between the two since both kinds of sins refuse to delay the gratification of material or fleshly desires.[150] Tragically, today we often elevate the former to the worst possible kind of offense and relegate the latter to a trivial peccadillo. A literal rendering of verse 3 would read, "Let not [these sins] be named among you." But of course Paul has just named them! So the NIV captures the correct sense: "There must not be even a hint" of these vices. The three words translated "obscenity," "foolish talk," and "coarse joking" in verse 4 appear only here in the New Testament and all refer to highly vulgar language, not just ordinary humor.[151] Verse 5 should be understood along the lines of 1 Corinthians 6:9–10: those whose lifestyles are characterized by these sins cannot be true believers.

But genuine Christians have put these traits of spiritual "darkness" in their past and therefore should have nothing further to do with them (vv. 8a, 11–12). Instead, they must practice godly living (spiritual "light") and expose corruption just as light illuminates darkness (vv. 8b–10, 13–14). All this obviously requires wisdom and care (v. 15), accompanied by constant vigilance, because of the pervasive wickedness in the world (v. 16). The NIV's "making the most of every opportunity" more literally reads "redeeming the time." Unless people consciously seek to serve the

---

[147] Bruce, *Colossians, Philemon and Ephesians,* 358–59.

[148] The adjective in the expression "unwholesome talk" in v. 29 is *sapros,* which is elsewhere used for "rotten wood, withered flowers, and rancid fish." It goes beyond merely foul language to anything that tears down rather than building up other people. See Hoehner, *Ephesians,* 628–29.

[149] Lincoln (*Ephesians,* 304) adds, "The motive for work is not individual profit but rather communal well-being."

[150] See esp. Augustine's *Confessions.*

[151] O'Brien, *Ephesians,* 360–61. Paul may have used these terms because of the words and actions of participants in local mystery religions. See Larry J. Kreitzer, "'Crude Language' and 'Shameful Things Done in Secret' (Ephesians 5:4, 12): Allusions to the Cult of Demeter/Cybele in Hierapolis?" *JSNT* 71 (1998): 51–77.

Lord with every moment granted them, at best they will fritter away their time; at worst they will practice evil.

To distinguish good from bad requires a knowledge of God's will (v. 17). In this context Paul focuses on God's desire that Christians be *repeatedly*[152] filled with the Holy Spirit, as opposed to a prevailing temptation in Ephesus, with its cults worshipping the god of wine, Dionysius, whose members were filled with other kinds of spirits (v. 18)! As we saw in Acts (above, p. 23), Christians are permanently indwelt by the Spirit from conversion onwards but are repeatedly filled by the Spirit as they yield to him and his will in specific situations. Luke regularly stressed the filling as the occasion for bold acts of witness and service; Paul here highlights aspects of worship, again no doubt because of the competition from the other religions in town. Subordinate to the main command to be filled are three modal or instrumental participial clauses unpacking what is involved in that filling.[153] *First,* believers speak or sing to one another with poems and with songs of praise and encouragement (v. 19). *Second,* they give thanks on behalf of everything (*huper pantōn*)—again a reference to seeing God in all circumstances, not an affirmation of every event as somehow a disguised good (v. 20). *Third,* they submit to one another in Christian reverence (v. 21).

This verse forms a transition between Paul's instruction on the filling of the Spirit and his household code, which spans 5:22–6:9. On the one hand, the submission enjoined of wives, children, and slaves in the Ephesian *Haustafel* must be tempered by the mutual submission commanded here. There are appropriate times for all authority figures to defer to those under them. Particularly between free adults (in this case, husbands and wives), relationships should resemble a partnership more than a chain of command.[154] On the other hand, it is logically impossible for every Christian to submit to every other Christian in the same way at the same time. Verse 21 by itself cannot prove egalitarianism; it may in fact be a headline introducing the three examples of submission to follow.[155]

The Domestic Code (5:22–6:9) Many of the same points enunciated in the Colossian code are repeated here, though often in expanded form. In addition to the comments already made above (pp. 296–97), we may add the following. Verse 22 does not even contain a verb, so the command "submit yourselves" from verse 21 must be supplied. Grammatically, the sentence begun in verse 18 may not end until after verse 24! The combination of "submit" (from *hypotassō*) and "head" (*kephalē*) makes it difficult not to infer that some kind of authority structure is

---

[152] This is the force of the Greek present-tense imperative in this context.

[153] Timothy G. Gombis, "Being the Fullness of God in Christ by the Spirit: Ephesians 5:18 in Its Epistolary Setting," *TynB* 53 (2002): 259–71. Gombis also takes 5:18–21 as strictly corporate in application, an important corrective to the purely individualistic application but one which need not rule out the latter as a corollary.

[154] Sarah Sumner (*Men and Women in the Church* [Downers Grove: IVP, 2003], 202) observes that roughly 90 percent of evangelical marriages in the U.S. take on this appearance, whether the couples are complementarian or egalitarian in outlook.

[155] James B. Hurley, *Man and Woman in Biblical Perspective* (Grand Rapids: Zondervan; Leicester: IVP, 1981), 139–41.

in view (vv. 22–23), despite numerous recent attempts to avoid this conclusion.[156] Nevertheless, Paul does not envision unqualified submission by any means. Unlike his commands to children and slaves (6:1, 5), he never tells wives to "obey" their husbands but uses a term for "respect" or "honor" instead (v. 33). "As to the Lord" in verse 22 should probably be explained along the lines of the parallel expression in Colossians 3:18—"as is fitting in the Lord" (see above, p. 296). What is fitting is always to put Christ first. If there is a conflict between authorities, God must be honored above human leaders (recall Moses' mother, Daniel, and Peter before the Sanhedrin). "In everything" (v. 24) should again be rendered "in all circumstances," to avoid the false impression that Paul means, "Do everything you're told"![157]

With his commands to husbands (vv. 25–28), Paul radically redefines marital hierarchy in terms of sacrificial, self-giving love—the equivalent to Jesus' teaching on servant leadership (e.g., Luke 22:24–30). If husbands retain any unique authority, it is that of *responsibility rather than privilege.*[158] This kind of "complementarian" marriage will not look dramatically different from an egalitarian marriage, except that, in the case of an impasse in decision-making, loving one's wife as Christ loved the church means taking the lead to put her interests *above* the husband's (giving "himself up for her"—v. 25)! Verses 28–30 further compare loving one's wife to the care one normally lavishes on one's own body. Paul does not have pathological exceptions in view here!

Verses 31–33 complete the passage by drawing the analogy more generally between the relationship of husband and wife and the intimacy of Christ and the church. Both were designed at creation to be undissolved unions exhibiting unswerving loyalty and love.[159] Thus, on the one hand, Paul preserves the husband's authority by grounding it in the "new creation" model of Christ's love for the church. On the other hand, he gives it a substantially new look by presenting it as a self-sacrifice for one's wife by means of that very same model.[160]

The commands to children and parents (6:1–4) only partially parallel the previous passage. Here Paul does not merely enjoin submission but commands outright obedience (v. 1). This fulfills the fourth commandment to "honor" father and mother, which is followed by the promise of long life (vv. 2–3). In both Old and New Testaments, this promise must be interpreted corporately. As Israel or the church

---

[156] Just as in the extrabiblical literature, in Ephesians and Colossians, *kephalē* can stress more the sense of "authority" (Eph. 1:22; Col. 1:18; 2:10) or more the idea of "source" (Eph. 4:15; Col. 2:19), but one does not find "source" without any sense of "authority" at all. Cf. Stephen Bedale, "The Meaning of *Kephalē* in the Pauline Epistles," *JTS* 5 (1954): 214, *contra* the impression one gets from many egalitarians who cite Bedale's article.

[157] On this material, see esp. Gregory W. Dawes, *The Body in Question: Metaphor and Meaning in the Interpretation of Ephesians 5:21–33* (Leiden and New York: Brill, 1998).

[158] See further Blomberg, "Women in Ministry: a Complementarian Perspective," 173–75.

[159] The progression of thought in these three verses can easily be misunderstood. Verse 31 cites Gen. 2:24 on the union of husband and wife. Paul recognizes a "profound mystery" even in this most special of human relationships but quickly explains that he has just applied this passage, by analogy, to Jesus and his "bride"—the church (vv. 29b–30). In v. 33, however, he returns to the primary theme of the paragraph and sums up his commands for husbands and wives. Cf. Andreas J. Köstenberger, "The Mystery of Christ and the Church: Head and Body, 'One Flesh,'" *TrinJ* 12 (1991): 79–94.

[160] See esp. Stephen F. Miletic, *"One Flesh": Eph. 5.22–24, 5:31: Marriage and the New Creation* (Rome: PIB, 1988). Cf. Timothy G. Gombis, "A Radically New Humanity: The Function of the *Haustafel* in Ephesians," *JETS* 48 (2005): 317–30.

promoted "family values," the quality and quantity of life was enhanced. But there never was any direct correlation between every individual's faithfulness and his or her personal longevity.[161] Parents, in turn, must not provoke their children, while nevertheless giving them appropriate discipline and guidance (v. 4). There is no evidence that these commands cease at any age for either children or parents, but the form in which they are applied certainly changes as one progresses through life's developmental stages, particularly if one gets married (recall 5:31). And they must be balanced with Christ's clear teaching to serve him above even the closest of human allegiances (cf. esp. Luke 14:26).[162]

The third part of this household code addresses slaves and masters (6:5–9). Slaves (or voluntary subordinates in other work settings) must labor diligently at all times and give their best because God watches them even when others do not. Masters/authorities must treat their slaves/subordinates impartially. Verse 9 may thus contain a hint that Paul would like masters to give slaves equal status with them and, therefore, free them. But for all the reasons enumerated in our application of the letter to Philemon (above, pp. 281–82), he does not explicitly call for the abolition of slavery even while arguably setting the stage for that development at a later date. Meanwhile, the relationship between slaves and masters should become at least "mutually helpful."[163]

Arming Oneself for Spiritual Warfare (6:10–20) This section brings the body of the letter to a close with a climactic discussion of the evil powers of the universe and the believer's victory over them. Our triumph does not come without a battle, but God gives us the spiritual armor to resist. The various pieces of protection described match a typical Roman soldier's array of armor, but parts of the imagery were no doubt inspired by Isaiah (cf. 11:5; 52:7; 59:17). There is no necessary correlation between one specific piece of armor and its spiritual counterpart, especially since Isaiah often matches them in different ways from Paul's. Rather, it is the overall effect of the picture that matters; truth, righteousness, peace, faith, and salvation are the weapons that will defeat the devil and his minions. But it is interesting that belts, breastplates, shoes, shields, and helmets all represent defensive protection, while the sword (v. 17b) represents the one offensive weapon in the soldier's armor. Whether or not Paul explicitly intended it, it is certainly true that God's Word must play a central role in our combating the false teaching with which Satan attacks us through all of the anti-Christian ideologies of our world.[164]

A further intriguing feature about this collection of defensive and offensive weaponry is that it contains no unusual or exotic elements. Unlike the proponents of magic and the occult so pervasive in Ephesus, Paul commands no sensationalistic, formulaic, manipulative, or superstitious form of spiritual warfare. Instead, he

---

[161] Mitton, *Ephesians,* 212. On the problem of calling this the first commandment with a promise, see Hoehner, *Ephesians,* 791. We should probably see Paul's meaning as referring to either the first *important* commandment or the first *specific* promise.

[162] Best, *Ephesians,* 563, 565. Care for elderly parents was an important obligation of adult children in the ancient world, for example.

[163] Bruce, *Colossians, Philemon and Ephesians,* 401–2.

[164] Cf. Schnackenburg, *Ephesians,* 279–80.

calls believers simply to stand fast in the theological and moral basics of the faith as reflected in Scripture. Undergirding this armor is consistent Spirit-filled prayer (v. 18). This picture differs dramatically from certain popular, modern approaches to spiritual warfare, replete with territorial exorcisms, "naming and claiming" spiritual authority, identifying modern-day apostles to whom demons and believers alike must submit without qualification, and the like.[165]

CLOSING GREETINGS (6:21–24)

Surprisingly, the only person Paul mentions in his letter closing is Tychicus, the "mailman" who is also delivering Colossians (Col. 4:7–8) and accompanying Onesimus (v. 9). The two men are therefore probably also bringing the letter to Philemon with them (Philem. 12). If Ephesians, however, is a circular letter (see above, pp. 305–6), then the lack of greetings to members of individual churches is more explicable. Plus, Tychicus is clearly being sent with instructions to communicate more information by word of mouth (Eph. 6:21–22). As at the end of many of his letters, Paul concludes with a benediction offering his audience such character traits as peace, love, faith, and grace. He also combines his references to God and Jesus together in a way that reflects no material difference between them (vv. 23–24).

APPLICATION

The spiritual unity of believers, which transcends all humanly erected boundaries, remains a preeminent aspect of God's will for his people. Some early Christians, when required in a court of law to declare their citizenship, affirmed only that they were Christians. Christianity thus came to be labeled "the third race," that is, neither Jew nor Gentile. The enmity in antiquity of these first two "races" is paralleled in the twenty-first-century world by the intense hostility, racism, and national or religious hatred found among fanatical Muslims for "infidels," some Jews and Arabs (or Palestinians) in the Middle East, warring tribes in a number of sub-Saharan African countries and rebel groups versus governmental forces in such disparate locations as Indonesia, the Philippines, Sri Lanka, Chechnya, and the Yucatán. Not too many years ago, one would have added Serbs versus Albanians, Protestants versus Catholics in Northern Ireland, or blacks versus whites in America, even though these conflicts have somewhat subsided more recently. But just because people groups live in an uneasy truce with each other does not mean that personal animosity or prejudice has vanished.

Against all these divisions, Ephesians calls upon Christians to take substantial steps toward reconciliation, both as outsiders functioning as peacemakers in hostile contexts and even more when they themselves represent one of the people groups involved. It causes no surprise that some of the most successful Christian outreach in

---

[165] Cf. Thomas R. Yoder Neufeld, *"Put on the Armour of God": The Divine Warrior from Isaiah to Ephesians* (Sheffield: SAP, 1997), 151: "The armour is made up of largely ethically identifiable virtues." Moreover, the focus remains corporate first, then individual. Believers together in local churches, and as the church worldwide resist the devil; here is no call for individual Christians to fight the battle alone.

contemporary Israel occurs when Palestinian and Jewish believers gather and work together, displaying a love for each other that one rarely sees in other settings. But as long as Christians around the world insist on remaining hermetically sealed from one another in entirely homogeneously grouped fellowships, the enormous evangelistic potential of such unity in diversity will never be tapped. Indeed, the visible unity of individuals in Christ who have little human reason for associating with one another may be God's most powerful tool for reaching a lost world today. Massive implications for the importance of networking among diverse churches follow, including institutional cooperation and even church mergers, where the fundamentals of the gospel are not compromised.

Two additional key themes in Ephesians contribute to this unity in diversity. First, households adopting Paul's domestic code will encourage a broken world that not all relationships need be dysfunctional and that families can be safe havens, extending love to their diverse members and reaching out to those around them who are not experiencing similar security and acceptance. Second, every-member ministry, in which all church members use their spiritual gifts for kingdom purposes, will maximize Christianity's efforts for good in the world more generally. This good must extend to society as well as to individuals. As Markus Barth phrased it over thirty years ago, "The church would unduly limit her task if she cared only for the souls of men or for an increase in membership. Rather she has to be a sign and proof of a change that affects the institutions and structures, patterns and spans of the bodily, spiritual, social and individual existence of all men."[166] Still, any group of people can function as a catalyst for change in the world only as each member of the group is individually transformed, particularly by the ethics highlighted in Ephesians 4:32–5:2.[167]

A balanced view of spiritual warfare proves equally crucial. Most secular people and not a few professing Christians implicitly or explicitly deny the reality of the devil and demonization. A few overly zealous believers revert to exotic techniques of spiritual warfare or, doubtless in overreaction to the first group, cower in fear at the thought that demons could oppress them anywhere. Paul is clearly aware of the existence and power of the demonic realm, but he stresses Christ's and, therefore, Christians' victory over it, simply through the power of godly living. No Christian need fear demonic oppression unless he or she willfully and repeatedly rebels against God's standards and dabbles in the overtly evil or occult.[168]

ADDITIONAL QUESTIONS FOR REVIEW

1. What are the key distinctives that set Ephesians off from all other letters by Paul? What theories attempt to explain these differences, and which explanation is the most satisfactory?

---

[166] Barth, *Ephesians 1–3*, 365.

[167] Unpacked with remarkable clarity, in list form, in deSilva, *Introduction*, 731–32.

[168] Particularly balanced in this respect is Clinton E. Arnold, *Powers of Darkness: Principalities & Powers in Paul's Letters* (Leicester and Downers Grove: IVP, 1992), esp. 167–209 on contemporary application.

2. How can the addition of the words "in Ephesus" in the greeting be justified when the three oldest and most reliable Greek manuscripts omit the prepositional phrase? How can the omission be explained?

3. What specific actions does Paul attribute to each member of the Trinity in his theologically rich opening prayer? How does this interact with and supplement theological statements and ideas in the letter to the Romans?

4. How does Ephesians 2 explain the balance between faith and good works? How are these two related with regard to salvation? How does the role of grace in Christianity set it off from every other world religion and even from divergent "Christian" heresies?

5. What are the implications of salvation for our relationships with other people? What metaphors does Paul employ to demonstrate the reconciliation that should occur between warring individuals and people groups? In the context of this discussion, how does Paul define "the mystery of Christ"?

6. What is the intended purpose of reconciliation within the body of Christ? What tools have been given to believers to ensure church unity and maturity? How and by whom are these gifts to be exercised?

7. How do the household codes fit into Paul's larger theme of unity within the body of Christ? Are these commands culturally bound, or do they remain relevant today? What specific feature in the text helps us answer these questions? How are Paul's views noticeably "progressive" when compared to his society, especially with regard to husbands and wives and to masters and slaves?

8. How does understanding the historical context in Ephesus further illumine our understanding of the significance of spiritual armor in Ephesians 6? What valuable insight does the metaphor provide in helping believers understand how to stand against Satan and his army?

SELECT BIBLIOGRAPHY

In addition to the work by MacDonald listed under the bibliography for Colossians and the work by Bruce listed under the bibliography for Philemon, see:

COMMENTARIES

Advanced

Barth, Markus. *Ephesians,* 2 vols. AB. Garden City: Doubleday, 1974.

Best, Ernest. *A Critical and Exegetical Commentary on Ephesians.* ICC, rev. Edinburgh: T & T Clark, 1998.

Hoehner, Harold W. *Ephesians: An Exegetical Commentary.* Grand Rapids: Baker, 2002.

Lincoln, Andrew T. *Ephesians.* WBC. Dallas: Word, 1990.

Intermediate

Best, Ernest. *Ephesians: A Shorter Commentary.* Edinburgh: T & T Clark, 2003.

Mitton, C. Leslie. *Ephesians.* NCB. London: Marshall, Morgan & Scott, 1976; Grand Rapids: Eerdmans, 1981.

Muddiman, John. *The Epistle to the Ephesians.* BNTC. London and New York: Continuum, 2001.

O'Brien, Peter T. *The Letter to the Ephesians.* PNTC. Leicester: Apollos; Grand Rapids and Cambridge: Eerdmans, 1999.

Schnackenburg, Rudolf. *Ephesians: A Commentary.* Edinburgh: T & T Clark, 1991.

Introductory

Klein, William W. *Ephesians,* rev. The Expositor's Bible Commentary. (Grand Rapids: Zondervan, forthcoming).

Liefeld, Walter L. *Ephesians.* IVPNTC. Leicester and Downers Grove: IVP, 1997.

Perkins, Pheme. *Ephesians.* ANTC. Nashville: Abingdon, 1997.

Snodgrass, Klyne. *Ephesians.* NIVAC. Grand Rapids: Zondervan, 1996.

Stott, John R. W. *The Message of Ephesians: God's New Society.* BST. Leicester and Downers Grove: IVP, 1979.

OTHER BOOKS

Arnold, Clinton E. *Ephesians: Power and Magic.* Cambridge and New York: CUP, 1989.

Best, Ernest. *Essays on Ephesians.* Edinburgh: T & T Clark, 1997.

Caragounis, Chrys C. *The Ephesian Mysterion.* Lund: Gleerup, 1977.

Dahl, Nils A. *Studies in Ephesians.* Tübingen: Mohr 2000.

Jeal, Roy R. *Integrating Theology and Ethics in Ephesians: The Ethos of Communication.* Lewiston and Lampeter: Mellen, 2000.

Lincoln, Andrew T. *Paradise Now and Not Yet.* Cambridge and New York: CUP, 1981.

Strelan, Rick. *Paul, Artemis, and the Jews in Ephesus.* Berlin: de Gruyter, 1996.

van Roon, A. *The Authenticity of Ephesians.* Leiden and New York: Brill, 1974.

BIBLIOGRAPHY

Klein, William W. *The Book of Ephesians: An Annotated Bibliography.* New York and London: Garland, 1996.

Philippians: Rejoice in All Circumstances

INTRODUCTION

RELATIONSHIP WITH THE OTHER PRISON EPISTLES AND PLACE OF PAUL'S IMPRISONMENT

Paul evangelized Philippi on his third missionary journey (Acts 16:12–40). A stable, thriving, medium-sized Macedonian town and largely Roman colony, it was home to numerous retired soldiers (recall above, p. 54). Many, no doubt, could readily envision Paul's imprisonment and supervision by the Roman guard.[169] But it is unlikely that many in the church were Romans, veterans, or very prosperous, given Paul's remarks about the poverty of the Macedonian Christians (2 Cor. 8:2) and the suffering that the Philippian letter itself reflects.[170] Positioned on the Via Egnatia, a major east-west "highway" crossing northern Greece, Philippi welcomed many travelers from out of town, who would lodge there, learn of local news, and bring reports of goings-on elsewhere in the empire. If not as big as Thessalonica, Athens, or Corinth, Philippi nevertheless remained a strategic Greek city for the dissemination of any new ideology.

This is the fourth of Paul's so-called "Prison Epistles." It is often studied separately from Ephesians, Colossians, and Philemon, however, because what it discloses about Paul's circumstances suggests he is in more serious trouble than when he wrote the other three letters. Here Paul seems to have seriously contemplated the fact that he might soon die (1:21–25; 2:17). This could make the case for an Ephesian imprisonment stronger here than elsewhere. Recall how in 2 Corinthians 1:8–9 Paul reported that he had despaired even of life itself for a time while in Asia (Minor). If this refers to the severe opposition he metaphorically described as fighting wild beasts in 1 Corinthians 15:32, then we know that the peril took place in Ephesus. But as with Ephesians, Colossians, and Philemon, we must consider the evidence for and against three possible sites for Paul's imprisonment.

Ephesus? The most significant factor favoring an Ephesian imprisonment is the comparatively short distance that would have been required for Timothy and Epaphroditus to travel back and forth between Paul and Philippi (2:19–30), including with the recent financial gift for Paul (4:18). The more somber setting of Paul's imprisonment could also fit Ephesus better than Rome since nothing in Acts suggests Paul ever feared for his life in the latter location. His nearly three-year stay in Ephesus in 52–55 (or 53–56) allows plenty of time for a lengthy enough imprisonment to accommodate the comings and goings of his subordinates that this letter describes. And he would not have had to change his mind about heading westward, as he would have if he were in Rome (recall above, pp. 272–73). Interestingly, just

---

[169] For a fuller introduction to Philippi in antiquity, see Charalambos Bakirtzis and Helmut Koester, eds., *Philippi at the Time of Paul and after His Death* (Harrisburg: Trinity, 1978).

[170] Cf. Peter Oakes, *Philippians: From People to Letter* (Cambridge and New York: CUP, 2001).

as in Philemon he expressed a desire to come to Colossae, here too he strongly hopes he can return to Philippi (1:26–27).[171]

On the other hand, there is no evidence from the ancient Roman world for the existence of a praetorian guard (1:13; Gk. *praitōrion*) in Ephesus.[172] Nor is it likely that Paul, the Roman citizen, who was willing to use his citizenship to the advantage of the gospel (see above, p. 57), would have been detained long without just cause in a city without high-level Roman leadership with enough clout to flaunt the law. Even in Philippi, a Roman colony, his citizenship procured his freedom from jail after only one night (Acts 16:22–40), and Ephesus was noticeably less Roman in makeup than Philippi. And while we saw one ancient witness that did describe the writing of Colossians to Ephesus (above, p. 272), no known testimony from antiquity attributes the writing of Philippians to that city.

Caesarea?   A small number of scholars have favored a Caesarean imprisonment as the setting for the writing of Philippians. At least we know Paul was imprisoned there, from 57 to 59, and that there were plots against his life (Acts 23–26). His two years in jail would have provided ample time for the events presupposed by this epistle. His hearings before Felix, Festus, and Herod Agrippa II could easily have been referred to as defenses (cf. 1:7, 16–17). The Roman garrison headquartered in Caesarea was at times called a praetorian guard. And we do not have to imagine Paul changing his plans after his release and heading for Greece and the east rather than for Spain, as in the hypothesis of a Roman imprisonment.[173]

At the same time, if the distance from Caesarea to Colossae and Ephesus seemed prohibitive, it was even farther to Philippi. Would Paul's emissaries really have come and gone so easily and so often over such a long distance? While it is true that there was a praetorium in Caesarea, it was tiny in comparison with Rome's so that Paul's boast that the gospel had spread throughout the whole guard (1:13) might have seemed rather presumptuous to the Philippians, a community housing many retired Roman officers, for such a "small" accomplishment. Moreover, Paul's language about defending and confirming the gospel (1:7) scarcely suggests any formal, legal hearing like he had in Caesarea. Finally, Acts never indicates that Paul thought seriously that he would be released from Caesarea, as Philippians 1:25 suggests about the imprisonment during which he wrote this letter.

Rome?   All the ancient testimony agrees that Philippians was penned from Rome (the oldest being found in Marcion's writings and in numerous subscripts on manuscripts of the letter itself). Despite a fair distance between Rome and Philippi, Paul's two years of house arrest there do leave sufficient time for the events presupposed in this epistle.[174] We have already noted how Paul's changed circumstances could eas-

---

[171] See, e.g., Carson and Moo, *An Introduction to the New Testament*, 503–6 (very tentatively) or Holladay, *A Critical Introduction to the New Testament*, 372–73 (somewhat more confidently).

[172] I. Howard Marshall, *Philippians* (London: Epworth, 1991), xix–xx.

[173] Among the major commentaries, see esp. Gerald F. Hawthorne, *Philippians* (Waco: Word, 1983), xxxvii–xliv.

[174] For a detailed outworking of one possible scenario, see Stephen Llewelyn, "Sending Letters in the Ancient World: Paul and the Philippians," *TynB* 46 (1995): 337–56.

ily have led to a change in travel plans (above, pp. 272–73). "Caesar's household" (4:22) is most naturally understood as referring to a portion of the emperor's retinue in Rome itself. The problem of life-threatening circumstances can be explained if Paul's situation degenerated just after the time during which Luke wrote Acts. It is easy to imagine Paul temporarily giving up hope for release, especially if the two-year time limit for examining imperial cases elapsed without any action taken. *On balance, a Roman imprisonment for Philippians should be preferred, with this letter dated after the other three Prison Epistles, in late 61 or some time in 62.*[175]

OTHER CIRCUMSTANCES

Yet despite this potentially bleak setting, *the overall theme of Philippians involves joy in the midst of suffering.* It has been said that "the letter to Philippi may be the happiest, most positive and most personal of all Paul's writings."[176] It certainly ranks with 1 Thessalonians as a letter to a church on whom Paul lavishes significant praise. *Paul's general attitude to the Philippians seems to be one of gratefulness and encouragement.*[177] *Indeed, the most immediate occasion for the letter may be to express thanks, however circumspectly, for a recently received gift of financial support from the church (4:10–20).*

At the same time, Paul does have to warn against some opposition to the Philippian congregation, from both within and without. Chapter 3:2–6 depicts a group of Judaizers who threaten the church, perhaps from inside. Nothing suggests they have come to town from elsewhere, as was the case in Galatians and 2 Corinthians 10–13. In a Roman colony that would have required emperor worship, including the affirmation of Caesar as Lord and Savior, it would have been natural for Jewish Christians to retreat to the safety of purely Jewish belief in the umbrella of a *religio licita* that exempted them from making this confession. Perhaps they envisaged a way in which the entire church could similarly be viewed as Jewish.[178] Chapter 1:27–30 describes the threat from outside the Philippian congregation, hostility severe enough that Paul's coworker, Epaphroditus, almost died from it (2:30). Roman officials attempting to impose the imperial cult on Christians no longer perceived to be Jews form the natural candidates for this harassment.[179]

Two other groups that give Paul grief are the rival teachers in 1:15–18 and the "enemies of the cross of Christ," whose "god is their stomach" and whose "glory is in their shame" (3:18–19). The latter group may or may not be the same as the Judaizers. We will discuss both groups in more detail in our commentary on the relevant passages.[180]

---

[175] Cf. further Markus Bockmuehl, *The Epistle to the Philippians* (London: Black; Peabody: Hendrickson, 1998), 25–32.

[176] Ogden and Skinner, *Acts through Revelation,* 187.

[177] It is true that Paul's various appeals for unity could suggest something less than a fully harmonious congregation, but finding disunity as a major problem in Philippi (as in Davorin Peterlin, *Paul's Letter to the Philippians in the Light of Disunity in the Church* [Leiden and New York: Brill, 1995]) considerably outstrips the evidence.

[178] Gordon D. Fee, *Paul's Letter to the Philippians* (Grand Rapids: Eerdmans, 1995), 33.

[179] Mikael Tellbe, "The Sociological Factors behind Philippians 3.1–11 and the Conflict at Philippi," *JSNT* 55 (1994): 97–121.

[180] On all the main groups of opponents of Paul in Philippi, cf. Jerry L. Sumney, *"Servants of Satan," "False Brothers" and Other Opponents of Paul* (Sheffield: SAP, 1999), 160–87.

GENRE AND STRUCTURE

As with 2 Corinthians, modern scholars have often doubted the unity of Philippians as we now have it. Chapter 3:1 appears to refer to a previous letter and seems to announce the beginning of the end of this letter, but Paul is only half done, and 4:8 will repeat the "finally"! Chapter 3:2 suddenly interrupts the train of thought begun in the previous verse as Paul unleashes his tirade on the Judaizers, and he never gets back to the topic of rejoicing in the Lord (3:1) until 4:1. Chapter 4:2–3, commanding Euodia and Syntyche to get along with each other, though a shorter digression, seems equally intrusive, especially when Paul returns yet again to the theme of rejoicing in verse 4. Finally, 4:10–20 introduces the issue of the Philippians' gift, for which nothing else in the letter clearly prepares the reader. Various theories of multiple-letter composition have thus been developed, usually involving two or three originally separate documents,[181] but none has garnered consensus support. Polycarp's second-century letter to the Philippians (3:2) refers to Paul's *letters* to that same community, but Paul could easily have written other communiqués now lost.

More recently, numerous literary and rhetorical studies from scholars across the theological spectrum have made plausible cases for the unity of the epistle as it stands. Ben Witherington itemizes six points in favor of this conclusion: (1) No ancient textual evidence supports any other theory of composition, not even to the extent that we saw with Romans. (2) Chapter 3:20–21, while appearing in the larger "digression," develops themes from 2:6–11. (3) Chapter 4:10–20 has indeed been prepared for by 1:4–5 and 2:25. (4) Paul's epistles frequently contain "sudden shifts of tone and direction," so that appearances of digression fail to prove theories of interpolation. (5) The theme of the unity of the church spans all subsections of the letter. Finally, (6) those who support composite authorship fail to explain the haphazard fashion in which the various letters or letter fragments would have had to be combined together.[182] (As for the problems of 3:1, see below, pp. 335–36.)

On the other hand, a suggestive hypothesis by Loveday Alexander can account for the sequence of topics in Philippians. Alexander identifies this epistle as a *family letter,* which regularly included reassurances about the well-being of the author, requested reassurances about the well-being of the recipients, and provided information about the movement of intermediaries between author and recipients. All three of these features appear in sequence in the body of Philippians (see the outline below), whereas no other letters of Paul developed any of these items into sustained, discrete sections. Alexander concludes that Paul has elaborated this letter form by the addition of sections representing the specific circumstances that triggered the sending of this epistle at this particular time—the presence of false teachers, the problem of the two quarreling women, and the need to acknowledge the arrival of the Philippians' gift. This unique situation, rather than any composite letter hypothesis, can account

---

[181] For a succinct list of the main proposals, all of which originated in German scholarship, see Udo Schnelle, *The History and Theology of the New Testament Writings* (Minneapolis: Fortress, 1998), 135. For a recent American variation on the theme of composite origin, see Philip Sellew, "*Laodiceans* and the Philippians Fragments Hypothesis," *HTR* 87 (1994): 17–28.

[182] Ben Witherington III, *Friendship and Finances in Philippi: The Letter of Paul to the Philippians* (Valley Forge: Trinity, 1994), 27–28.

for the seeming digressions.[183] Without adopting her outline in its entirety, Gordon Fee substantially follows Alexander, while identifying the document via the related category of a "letter of friendship."[184]

One plausible outline, therefore, proceeds as follows:

I. Greetings and Thanksgiving (1:1–11)
   A. Greetings (1:1–2)
   B. Thanksgiving (1:3–11)
II. Reassurance about the Sender: Description of Paul's Imprisonment (1:12–26)
III. Request for Reassurance about the Recipients: Call to Christlike Living (1:27–2:18)
   A. Living in a Fashion Worthy of the Gospel (1:27–30)
   B. Imitating Christ's Selfless Sacrifice (2:1–11)
   C. Working Out Salvation (2:12–18)
IV. Information about Movement of Intermediaries: Concerning Timothy and Epaphroditus (2:19–30)
V. Special Concern: Warnings about the False Teachers (3:1–4:1)
VI. Final Instructions, Thank-Yous, and Greetings (4:2–23)
   A. A Plea to Two Quarreling Women (4:2–3)
   B. Commands to Rejoice, Pray, and Dwell on the Good (4:4–9)
   C. A Thankless Thank You (4:10–20)
   D. Closing Greetings (4:21–23)

Epideictic rhetoric dominates the sections of praise, a bit of forensic rhetoric intrudes into Paul's defense against the Judaizers, and the rest of the letter comprises mostly deliberative rhetoric.[185]

COMMENTARY

GREETINGS AND THANKSGIVING (1:1–11)

Greetings (1:1–2) As with 2 Corinthians and Colossians, Philippians begins by naming both Paul and Timothy as cosenders. Otherwise, the only distinctive in this very short opening greeting is the specific mention of "overseers and deacons" in

---

[183] Loveday Alexander, "Hellenistic Letter-Forms and the Structure of Philippians," *JSNT* 37 (1989): 87–101. For a different kind of outline based on Greco-Roman rhetoric but equally plausibly demonstrating the unity of the letter, see Duane F. Watson, "A Rhetorical Analysis of Philippians and Its Implications for the Unity Question," *NovT* 30 (1988): 57–88. Other important recent studies arguing for the literary integrity of the letter include David E. Garland, "The Composition and Unity of Philippians," *NovT* 27 (1985): 141–73; A. Boyd Luter and Michelle V. Lee, "Philippians as Chiasmus: Key to the Structure, Unity and Theme Questions," *NTS* 41 (1995): 89–101; and Jeffrey T. Reed, *A Discourse Analysis of Philippians* (Sheffield: SAP, 1997). On the limitations of these kinds of studies, see esp. Stanley E. Porter and Jeffrey T. Reed, "Philippians as a Macro-Chiasm and Its Exegetical Significance," *NTS* 44 (1998): 213–31.

[184] Fee, *Philippians*, 2–14. For the less plausible view that this epistle is a letter of consolation, see Paul A. Holloway, *Consolation in Philippians: Philosophical Sources and Rhetorical Strategy* (Cambridge and New York: CUP, 2001). This approach requires that the Philippians' distress over Paul's imprisonment be viewed as the main stimulus for the letter, nor their financial gift, nor Paul's gratitude for their overall maturity, nor his concern for the Judaizers and/or other opponents. But all of these later themes appear more central.

[185] Cf. Witherington, *Philippians*, 16–17.

addition to the church in general. Whatever the reason for Paul's singling out the leadership in this way, this is an important reference. The same two categories of leaders will reappear in 1 Timothy 3, where many scholars argue for a level of institutionalization in the church that had not yet developed during Paul's lifetime. Philippians, however, demonstrates that these two groups existed in one of the churches addressed by an indisputably Pauline epistle, even if we are told nothing further about their roles here.[186]

Thanksgiving (1:3–11)   Paul returns in Philippians to his most common form of introductory prayer, in which he first thanks God for the church to which he is writing and its growth (vv. 3–8) and then petitions his Lord that it might grow even more (vv. 9–11). Distinctive here are the references to his joy (v. 4), their (financial) partnership with him in the ministry (v. 5), and his imprisonment (v. 7). Additionally, verse 6 reveals Paul's confidence that God will complete the work begun in this congregation and spiritually preserve its members until judgment day.[187] Indeed, Paul displays a deep affection for this group of believers, which verse 8 reinforces. At the same time, the love of which he speaks must grow in knowledge and moral behavior. It is, thus, far more than a feeling; it becomes "an established disposition within us," or "a habit."[188]

REASSURANCE ABOUT THE SENDER: DESCRIPTION OF PAUL'S IMPRISONMENT (1:12–26)

Paul has special reason to include this section of a "family" letter because he is in prison. Nevertheless, this imprisonment has actually helped to spread the gospel among the praetorian troops who have learned of Paul's message (vv. 12–14). If he is referring to the Roman "palace guard," then he could have been thinking of the more than nine thousand soldiers among the *praetoriani*! We have no idea how many soldiers rotated through the four-hour shifts over at least a two-year period. But either Paul had an opportunity to witness personally to a large number of the guard, or else the smaller group that took turns watching him found his message so fascinating that they told many of their cohorts.[189] This effective evangelism encouraged other Christians in town to testify more boldly as well.

Some of these "preachers" even seemed to be trying to outdo the apostle by testifying in the spirit "of envy and rivalry" (vv. 15–17). But this does not bother Paul because Christ is preached and more people are having the chance to accept the salvation he offers (v. 18). Apparently, the rival teachers' message is sufficiently accurate that Paul remains confident people are hearing the true gospel, and so he rejoices. It is only these teachers' motives (vv. 17–18a) that are misguided.[190] How

---

[186] Cf. Ibid., 32–33.

[187] Hawthorne (*Philippians*, 21–22) argues that the "good work" begun in the Philippians is only their ministry of the gospel to others, but it seems difficult to limit so broad a term in this fashion, especially when Paul regularly thanks God and prays for the spiritual preservation and growth of his congregations more generally in his epistolary thanksgivings.

[188] Stephen E. Fowl, *Philippians* (Grand Rapids and Cambridge: Eerdmans, 2005), 33.

[189] The praetorium could also refer to the building (or barracks) that housed the guard, in which case the latter of these two options would be the only possibility.

[190] Cf. further Fee, *Philippians*, 125–26.

often do we exactly invert this pattern today by quarreling with people who minister the true gospel in an unnecessarily competitive spirit, while not becoming upset with those who err in fundamental doctrine, however sincere they might be?

Paul does admit an internal struggle in his imprisonment, in which he did not immediately know how to pray (vv. 18b–26). His life had been long and hard, even by ancient standards; incarceration, even if only by house arrest, remained grueling; and he had no guarantee of release rather than execution. He recognizes that he can glorify God by staying alive and continuing his ministry or by entering more directly into his presence in the life to come (vv. 20–22a). So he discloses his dilemma: "Yet what shall I choose? I do not know! I am torn between the two" (vv. 22b–23a). This question in no way implics that Paul is contemplating suicide, as a few scholars have suggested.[191] The word for "choose" here is probably better translated "prefer" in this particular context.[192] Paul does have the choice as to what he prays for, and it is this deliberation to which he refers. Clearly the impression he received of how God was answering that prayer reassured him that his work was not finished, including among the Philippians, and that he would therefore remain alive.

At the same time, he recognized how much better off he himself would be if he departed this life and went to be with Christ (vv. 23b–24). Thus by the time he writes this epistle, he rejoices with the confidence that the Spirit will eventually deliver him from prison and enable him to minister further among the Philippians (vv. 18b–19, 25–26). The very fact that he contemplated the possibility of being alive with Christ after his death and before the final resurrection does, however, again disclose his belief in an intermediate state of conscious, disembodied bliss in the presence of the triune God (recall on 2 Cor. 5:1–10).[193]

REQUEST FOR REASSURANCE ABOUT THE RECIPIENTS: CALL TO CHRISTLIKE LIVING (1:27–2:18)

Living in a Fashion Worthy of the Gospel (1:27–30) Here appears the theological heart of the epistle, but it comes as the next standard section of a family letter. The apostle now wants to be as confident about the Philippians' conduct as he has become about his own. Then he will not be concerned if either he or they come under increasing persecution (1:27–30). His interpretation of this opposition, which is afflicting the Philippians as it had Paul when he first came to Philippi, resembles 2 Corinthians 2:15–16—a sign of salvation for believers and of damnation for the persecutors (v. 28). Since Paul was briefly imprisoned by a Roman jailer in Philippi after the local Greeks dragged him to the authorities (Acts 16:19–28), it is natural to assume that he is referring to local Gentile hostility against the Philippian church as

---

[191] E.g., Arthur J. Droge, "*Mori Lucrum*: Paul and Ancient Theories of Suicide," *NovT* 30 (1988): 263–86; James L. Jaquette, "A Not-So-Noble Death: Figured Speech, Friendship and Suicide in Philippians 1:21–26," *Neot* 28 (1994): 177–92.

[192] Peter T. O'Brien, *The Epistle to the Philippians* (Carlisle: Paternoster; Grand Rapids: Eerdmans, 1991), 126. Moreover, N. Clayton Croy ("'To Die Is Gain' [Philippians 1:19–26]: Does Paul Contemplate Suicide?" *JBL* 122 [2003]: 517–31) points out the close parallels to Paul's language in Isocrates, *On the Peace,* 38–39, and other Greco-Roman examples of the rhetorical and literary device of "feigned perplexity" to dramatize an argument, the conclusion to which was nevertheless clearly in view (esp. p. 525).

[193] Cf. further Moisés Silva, *Philippians* (Grand Rapids: Baker, rev. 2005), 80–82.

well (see also above, p. 327).[194] It is also striking how Paul views suffering as a gift granted by God to believers; it is a privilege because of the sanctification and ultimate glorification to which it leads.[195] Stephen Fowl sees all of Philippians summed up in the choice presented the Philippians here, whether to glory in the possibilities of Roman citizens or in their common life worthy of the gospel and heavenly citizenship (cf. 3:20).[196]

Imitating Christ's Selfless Sacrifice (2:1–11) The unity with Christ that leads to maturity and the ability to withstand suffering imitates Jesus in another way as well—by putting others' interests above one's own. Chapter 2:1–4 highlights Christian humility, which itself is made possible only by the Spirit's empowerment (v. 1). This kind of behavior in Philippi will give Paul even greater joy (v. 2). By definition it is inconsistent with selfish attempts to "look out for number one" (v. 3). Verse 4 is so radically phrased that many translations (including the NIV) tone it down, but the TNIV captures the literal sense: "Not looking to your own interests but each of you to the interests of the others."[197]

With 2:5–11, we come to the most famous portion of the entire letter. The humility Paul hopes for from the Philippians imitates Christ's behavior both in his incarnation and, preeminently, in his crucifixion (v. 5).[198] Verses 6–11 comprise what is often called the Philippian hymn. This passage is highly poetic in the original Greek, symmetrically structured, filled with tightly packed fundamental Christological teaching, and separable from its current context once the introductory relative pronoun is replaced with its antecedent, "Christ Jesus." All of these details match features frequently found in early Christian hymnody and creedal affirmations.[199] Of course, it is possible that Paul composed such a passage himself,[200] but it is interesting that the text as we have it contains two stanzas of almost identical length, balancing Christ's humiliation (vv. 6–8) with his vindication (vv. 9–11). Each of the stanzas, in turn, contains three strophes of three lines each, each with three stressed syllables. Each line breaks at a natural place in the progression of thought, and each strophe presents a discrete stage in the experience of Christ: incarnation, condescension, and suffering; resurrection, exaltation, and universal glorification. But one additional phrase, at the end of verse 9, breaks this otherwise perfect pattern—"even death on a cross."

---

[194] Cf. further Fee, *Philippians,* 167, 172. Some commentators, however, equate this opposition with the Judaizers, in which case they could not have emerged from within the church but must be interlopers from outside (contrast above, p. 327).

[195] We dare not separate explicit suffering for one's faith from other kinds of afflictions. As Silva (*Philippians,* 97–98) explains, "for the person whose life is committed in its totality to the service of Christ, every affliction and every frustration becomes an obstacle to fulfilling the goal of serving Christ. It surely would be impossible to think that believers who enjoy freedom of religion and so suffer no physical persecution or religious discrimination are thereby deprived of an essential element in their sanctification."

[196] Fowl, *Philippians,* 62 *et passim.*

[197] See also Bockmuehl, *Philippians,* 113–14.

[198] The text is actually more elliptical, reading, "Think this among yourselves that which also in Christ Jesus." Are we meant to supply "was" before "in Christ" or "you are"? The ambiguity may be deliberate; Paul may wish to affirm both that we should imitate Christ and that we can do this only when we are united with him. See Silva, *Philippians,* 109–10.

[199] For a full catalogue of criteria for identifying creeds or hymns, see Barth, *Ephesians 1–3,* 7–8.

[200] See esp. Gordon D. Fee, "Philippians 2:5–11: Hymn or Exalted Pauline Prose?" *BBR* 2 (1992): 29–46.

Given that "Jesus Christ and him crucified" formed the heart of Paul's message (1 Cor. 2:2), it would make excellent sense if Paul adopted a well-known, early Christian confession and then adapted it to his particular interests by the insertion of this one extra line of two stressed syllables.[201] If this hypothesis is correct, then we have one more example of how some of the loftiest beliefs about the person and work of Christ developed at an astonishingly early date, well before the completion of Paul's undisputed letters, rather than at some time late in the second generation of Christianity, as evolutionary hypotheses of the development of early Christian thought typically allege.[202]

The Christological affirmations of this passage include: *(1) Jesus was fully God (v. 6a).* Although the word *morphē* can mean "form" in the sense of "outward appearance only," it reappears in verse 7, in which Paul stresses Jesus' true humanity and servanthood. So the NIV is almost certainly correct to translate the word as "very nature" in both verses.[203] *(2) Jesus existed before his incarnation (v. 6b).* Only on this assumption could he consciously choose not to retain his heavenly position but come to earth.[204] The expression "something to be grasped" (*harpagmos*) has generated substantial controversy, but it is best understood as an exalted status to which Jesus refused to cling. It does not mean that there was a time when he was not equal with God.[205] *(3) Jesus emptied himself of the independent exercise of his divine attributes during his incarnation (v. 7a).* The verb translated "made himself nothing" (from *kenoō*), from which is derived the cognate *kenosis* (the term used in many theological discussions of what Christ gave up in the incarnation), in this context probably refers to his pouring himself out in total service for others.[206] But when one asks what Jesus could or could not do during his earthly life as reported in the Gospels, it is clear that he retained his divine miracle-working powers but used them only when it was God's will. In the context of his entire ministry, these were the exceptional situations rather than the norm.

(4) Jesus was fully human (v. 7b). The word *likeness* can again in certain contexts mean "in appearance only," but, paralleling "the very nature" in this verse, it must mean "the real thing"! *(5) Jesus so demeaned himself that he submitted to the most degrading and excruciating of human deaths—crucifixion—*otherwise reserved only for slaves and the worst of criminals (v. 8). *(6) As a result, God exalted him, literally, to a higher place than he had been before* (v. 9; from *huperupsoō*). Once more, this does not mean that he once was not God but that he had not been as clearly

---

[201] See originally Ernst Lohmeyer, *Kyrios Jesus* (Heidelberg: Winter, 1928); endorsed and elaborated by Ralph P. Martin, *A Hymn of Christ* (Downers Grove: IVP, 1997). Martin also provides a full history of research and detailed exegesis of this passage overall.

[202] See further Hurtado, *Lord Jesus Christ*, 146–49.

[203] For this and various other exegetical details in this list of items, see esp. Paul D. Feinberg, "The Kenosis and Christology: An Exegetical-Theological Analysis of Philippians 2:6–11," *TrinJ* 1 (1980): 21–46. Markus Bockmuehl ("'The Form of God' [Phil. 2:6]: Variations on a Theme of Jewish Mysticism," *JTS* 48 [1997]: 1–23) proposes the intriguing hypothesis that *morphē* here may also refer to the visible divine form disclosed in Old Testament theophanies and Christ's incarnation.

[204] Against those who see only Adamic Christology—the true man coming into the world—see Lawrence D. Hurst, "Re-enter the Pre-existent Christ in Philippians 2.5–11?" *NTS* 32 (1986): 449–57; and Charles A. Wanamaker, "Philippians 2.6–11: Son of God or Adamic Christology?" *NTS* 33 (1987): 179–93.

[205] See esp. Roy W. Hoover, "The HARPAGMOS Enigma: A Philological Solution," *HTR* 64 (1971): 95–119.

[206] Hawthorne, *Philippians*, 86.

recognized as God until after his resurrection. *(7) One day Christ will receive universal allegiance from every sentient power in the universe (vv. 10–11).* The expression, "in heaven and on earth and under the earth," is a comprehensive way of referring not only to all humanity but also to angelic and demonic beings. Paul does not imply that everyone will one day be saved because he is quoting Isaiah 45:23–24, which adds that God's opponents will be shamed. Therefore, his point must be that all will be forced by the reality of Christ's visible return to acknowledge that he is Lord, even if they have not voluntarily made him their Lord and thereby received salvation.[207]

THE PHILIPPIAN HYMN (2:6–11)

Stanza 1: The Condescension of Christ

Who being in very nature God Did not consider equality with God Something to be grasped	The Attitude
But made himself nothing Taking the very nature of a servant Being made in human likeness	The Abandonment
And being found in appearance as a man He humbled himself And became obedient to death—	The Humiliation
even death on a cross!	**Paul's Addition?**

Stanza 2: The Exaltation of Christ

Therefore God exalted him to the highest place And gave him the name That is above every name	The Restoration
That at the name of Jesus Every knee should bow In heaven and on earth and under the earth	The Adoration
And every tongue confess That Jesus Christ is Lord To the glory of God the Father	The Confession

---

[207] O'Brien, *Philippians,* 243. For a wide-ranging anthology of significant perspectives on Philippians 2:5–11, see Ralph P. Martin and Brian J. Dodd, eds., *Where Christology Began: Essays on Philippians 2* (Louisville: WJKP, 1998). And, as with Rom. 10:9–10, if Jesus is Lord, then Caesar and Rome are not.

Working Out Salvation (2:12–18) This marvelous hymn should greatly encourage the Philippian believers (vv. 12–18). They should "work out" their "salvation with fear and trembling" (v. 12), committing themselves afresh to Christian discipleship despite its hardships because they recognize what Christ has done for them and the joy that awaits them in the long term. Verses 12 and 13 illustrate the consistent biblical balance between God's sovereignty and human responsibility. No one can ever work *for* their salvation, but, once saved, every believer can work it *out,* exhibiting the fruits that demonstrate genuine repentance (Matt. 3:8). Yet even that activity proves impossible apart from God's working in a person's life according to his will.[208] In this context God's will calls for believers to stand out from the sinful world around them by refusing to complain or argue and showing themselves to be pure and faultless,[209] not least for the sake of evangelism (vv. 14–16). Then both Paul and the Philippians can continue to rejoice, even if his imprisonment should lead to death (or even if it feels at the moment like he is dying—vv. 17–18).

INFORMATION ABOUT MOVEMENT OF INTERMEDIARIES: CONCERNING TIMOTHY AND EPAPHRODITUS (2:19–30)

From the most theological portion of this letter, we turn to the most personal. The next section of the family letter provides information about people coming and going between the writer(s) and the addressee(s). In this case the principal intermediaries between Paul and the Philippians are Timothy and Epaphroditus. Both have proved exceptionally faithful servants of Paul and of God, so the Philippians should welcome them, and Paul in turn will be cheered. Timothy exemplifies the selfless priorities of 2:1–4 so that he can model godly conduct until the apostle can come in person (vv. 19–24). Epaphroditus apparently came to Paul as a representative from the Philippians, both with their monetary gift and to support him in prison in whatever other ways he could. Epaphroditus became deathly ill but now has recovered, so Paul is eager to send him home since his return has been delayed and people are understandably worried about him (vv. 25–29).[210]

SPECIAL CONCERN: WARNINGS ABOUT THE FALSE TEACHERS (3:1–4:1)

Paul now inserts the first of the extra sections into his family letter, reflecting the immediate circumstances of the church in Philippi. Judaizers are troubling them; as in Galatians and 2 Corinthians, Paul reserves his strongest condemnation for the legalizing or nationalizing wing of Jewish Christianity that threatens to destroy the very basis of salvation—by grace through faith alone. The words for "finally" (*to loipon*) do not necessarily indicate that the author is close to finishing; they may

---

[208] See D. A. Carson, *Divine Sovereignty and Human Responsibility* (London: Marshall, Morgan & Scott; Atlanta: John Knox, 1981).

[209] The terms here do not refer to a sinless perfection but to a maturity in moral living free from justifiable external criticism. The same kind of language recurs in 3:6 with Paul's reference to his pre-Christian life. Cf. O'Brien, *Philippians,* 380–81.

[210] "There may be a charming word play in v. 30. The participle *paraboleusamenos,* which means 'staked,' 'gambled,' or 'risked,' may have been coined by Paul. The name Epaphroditus means 'favorite of Aphrodite,' the goddess of gambling (among other vices), whose name one would invoke for luck when rolling the dice. Thus Paul may be saying that Epaphroditus rolled the dice, but in the work of the Lord he staked his very life in order to fill up the lack of service the Philippians would not have been able to give otherwise" (Witherington, *Philippians,* 81).

simply introduce the last main theological topic of the letter.[211] The "same things" (v. 1) need not refer to a previous Pauline epistle because Paul has been repeatedly commanding the Philippians to rejoice, even just in this letter. And the transition from verse 1 to verse 2 may not be as abrupt as it first seems because the reference to a "safeguard" prepares the way for a warning in the next section.[212]

Paul employs the standard Jewish slur for Gentiles ("dogs") and turns it on the Judaizers instead (v. 2). Because they are requiring circumcision for salvation (recall Acts 15:1), Paul can also label them "mutilators of the flesh." He reminds his readers that Christians are now the true, spiritual circumcision (v. 3; recall Col. 2:11–12). He understands that Jewish credentials no longer count for anything in God's sight; however, because the Judaizers are boasting in their pedigree, he points out his impeccable lineage as well (v. 4; recall 2 Corinthians 11:22). This includes not only circumcision as a Jew but also descent from an honored tribe, identity as a Hebraic rather than a Hellenistic Jew, affiliation with the elite sect of the Pharisees, and, before his conversion, zeal for the law and for persecuting Christians, whom he believed were standing in the way of God's blessings for Israel (vv. 5–6).[213]

As a Christian, however, Paul recognizes the worthlessness of this resumé. All that matters is that he has made Christ his Lord and no longer attempts to establish his right standing with God through the works of Torah (vv. 7–11). The religious efforts on which he no longer relies he now identifies as "rubbish" (v. 8; *skubala*), at least as strong an expression as those he used in 1 Corinthians 4:13 (see above, p. 173).[214] Conversely, with equal passion, he now desires solely to grow in Christ, understanding the power of both Jesus' death and resurrection, so that he might respond properly to his sufferings and then enjoy his heavenly reward (vv. 10–11). Verse 11 does not imply that Paul doubts he will receive it; he is admitting merely that he does not fully understand the process.[215]

At the same time, Paul never presumes on God by thinking that he has arrived at full maturity or that he can "coast" through life because his salvation is secure. "Eternal security," better labeled with the Reformers "the perseverance of the saints," means that those who are true believers will persevere. But the only way we can know who those people are is by watching and seeing who remains in the faith. Too complacent an attitude toward the Christian life could indicate that a person was not truly saved. Paul takes quite the opposite tack by continuing to press on and work hard for the heavenly prize that awaits him in the life to come (vv. 12–14). Indeed, he hopes that all Christians will adopt a similar attitude, while recognizing that it is

---

[211] Jeffrey T. Reed, "Philippians 3:1 and the Epistolary Hesitation Formulas: The Literary Integrity of Philippians, Again," *JBL* 115 (1996): 82–83.

[212] Demetrius K. Williams, *Enemies of the Cross of Christ: The Terminology of the Cross and Conflict in Philippians* (London: SAP, 2002), 149–53.

[213] The NIV's "legalistic righteousness" in v. 6 overtranslates the Greek, which refers just to the "works of the Law." But *amemptos* ("blameless" or "faultless") does not mean sinless. Paul asserts simply that he was as devoted to Torah as any in his world (recall on Gal. 1:11–14). See further Alan J. Thompson, "Blameless before God?" *Themelios* 28: (2002): 5–12.

[214] "Rubbish, trash, or yet stronger words to that effect, including excrement: everything that is thrown out in a living situation without plumbing" (Carolyn Osiek, *Philippians, Philemon* [Nashville: Abingdon: 2000], 91).

[215] Ralph P. Martin, *Philippians* (London: Marshall, Morgan & Scott, 1976; Grand Rapids: Eerdmans, 1980), 135–36.

ultimately God who guides believers into how they live out their faith (v. 15). But everyone in the church should be able to agree at least not to "backslide" and to maintain the level of maturity they have already reached (v. 16).[216]

As throughout his epistles, Paul does not merely command others how to live but commends himself and like-minded believers as models to imitate (v. 17). Such models prove particularly crucial when dramatically different ones compete for Christians' loyalty. Verses 18–19 could refer to a hedonistic element among the Gentile unbelievers in Philippi, but nothing in the letter thus far has prepared the reader for such a reference. Instead, we may be meant to understand these verses as another allusion to the Judaizers of 3:2–6, including a pointed attack on their insistence on keeping the dietary laws ("their god is their stomach"—v. 19).[217] Moreover, the Greek word *koilia* did not just refer to the stomach; it was sometimes used as a euphemism "for the sexual organ, so that Paul may be saying that they regard their circumcision as an idol."[218]

Of course, Paul has already clarified that eating or not eating kosher food is a matter of moral indifference in the age of the new covenant (Rom. 14–15). But just like circumcision or any other individual work of the law, when individuals insist on it as a requirement for salvation, then it flies in the face of justification by faith. Those who promote such legalism or nomism, whether or not they realize it, have become "enemies of the cross of Christ" because if salvation can be achieved through Torah-obedience then there was no need for the crucifixion.

Focusing on food, however, represents "earthly things," whereas Christians should be focusing on heavenly realities. While many of the Romans in Philippi gloried in the privileges their earthly citizenship procured, Paul wants the Philippian Christians not to think of themselves as either Jew or Gentile but as citizens of a new form of existence that will not fully appear until after Christ's return (vv. 20–21).[219] At the same time, "the already but not yet" nature of God's kingdom means that his people form a colony or outpost (other possible translations of *politeuma* or "citizenship") of heaven already in this world.[220] It becomes our responsibility to model to the lost what godly living in society can accomplish. This is how we "stand firm in the Lord" (4:1).[221]

FINAL INSTRUCTIONS, THANK-YOUS, AND GREETINGS (4:2–23)

A Plea to Two Quarreling Women (4:2–3) As is obvious from what we have already surveyed, family or friendship letters did not neatly divide into theological and exhortational sections. Exhortation has been scattered throughout this epistle, but now it takes center stage as Paul begins to close. Euodia and Syntyche are two

---

[216] Cf. further Fee, *Philippians*, 355–62.

[217] For the full range of options, see Hawthorne, *Philippians*, 163. Williams (*Enemies of the Cross of Christ*, 221–22) notes that "enemies of the cross of Christ" (v. 18) most naturally refers back to the various descriptions of the Judaizers earlier in the chapter, even though he leaves the door open for seeing the opponents as libertines.

[218] Marshall, *Philippians*, xxiv.

[219] Our "lowly bodies" probably refers to the discipline they experience from the kind of humility advocated in 2:2–5 and exemplified in 2:6–11. This is not a disparagement of our physical bodies as such. See Peter Doble, "'Vile Bodies' or Transformed Persons? Philippians 3.21 in Context," *JSNT* 86 (2002): 3–27.

[220] Cf. Silva, *Philippians*, 214.

[221] Cf. Witherington, *Philippians*, 98.

women in the Philippian church about whom we know nothing other than what we can infer from these verses. Some kind of disagreement between them has become serious enough that Paul asks an unnamed close friend to intervene and help settle matters.[222] That he should single them out by name in the first place could suggest they played some prominent role in the congregation.[223]

Commands to Rejoice, Pray, and Dwell on the Good (4:4–9)   Just as Paul has referred to his joy repeatedly throughout the letter, now he commands the Philippians to rejoice (v. 4). But rejoicing need not imply boisterous exuberance; people can be gentle and happy, too (v. 5). Instead of letting anxiety consume them, they should bring all their concerns to God in prayer, who can provide for them a supernatural peace irrespective of the specifics of his answers (v. 6). Focusing on all that is true, beautiful, and excellent also helps to keep a person in the right frame of mind (vv. 7–8). And once again, Paul generalizes by referring not merely to his teachings but to his behavior as an overall model to emulate (v. 9).

A Thankless Thank-You (4:10–20)   For a second time Paul inserts an extra section into the standard family-letter outline. If the most immediate occasion for the Philippians' contact with him was their gifts sent by Epaphroditus, then Paul must acknowledge and express appreciation for these funds. At the same time, in the "tit-for-tat" world of reciprocal obligations between patrons and clients (recall above, p. 168), if Paul declared his explicit gratitude in a formal thank-you, he would have been implying his intention to pay the Philippians back in some way. So he comes as close as he can to thanking them without actually doing so! As a result, this entire section oscillates between Paul approving of their concern for him (vv. 10–11, 14–16) and insisting that he could have gotten along without it (vv. 12–13, 17–18). If the Philippians need a payback, God can provide it directly (vv. 19–20).[224] Specific verses in this passage must not be removed from this context. Verses 11–12 by themselves could sound like Stoic resignation; here they reflect admirable trust in God's all-sufficiency.[225]

Verse 13 clearly does not mean that Christians can count on performing physical or mental feats that would otherwise have been impossible for their bodies or minds or that God will enable them supernaturally to perform works of service for which he has not gifted or called them. The "everything" that Paul can do is defined by the previous two verses—he has learned to be content in every economic setting in which he finds himself.[226] At the same time, he is appreciative of the Philippians'

---

[222] "True companion" translates the Greek γνήσιε σύζυγε, which could also be rendered "loyal Syzygus," with the second word a proper name. But it was not a common name and its meaning (literally, "yokefellow") fits very well here. Recall how Paul did not identify the "brothers" in 2 Cor. 8:23 either.

[223] As did women in the Philippian church more generally. See A. Boyd Luter, "Partnership in the Gospel: The Role of Women in the Church at Philippi," *JETS* 39 (1996): 411–20.

[224] See esp. Gerald W. Peterman, "'Thankless Thanks': The Epistolary Social Convention in Philippians 4:10–20," *TynB* 42 (1991): 261–70; idem, *Paul's Gift from Philippi* (Cambridge and New York: CUP, 1997), 121–61.

[225] Abraham J. Malherbe, "Paul's Self-Sufficiency (Philippians 4:11)," in *Friendship, Flattery and Frankness of Speech,* ed. John T. Fitzgerald (Leiden and New York: Brill, 1996), 125–39.

[226] Cf. Fee, *Philippians,* 436: "Those in 'want' learn patience and trust in suffering; those in 'wealth' learn humility and dependence in prospering, not to mention the joy of giving without strings attached!"

support, not only with their financial gifts but with their faithfulness to the gospel more generally.[227]

Closing Greetings (4:21–23) No specific individuals are named either as greeters or those to be greeted, though there are obviously a number of people in both categories. Paul does, however, allude once more to his praetorian imprisonment by sending greetings from those in "Caesar's household"[228] who have become Christians. He then closes with a characteristic grace wish.

APPLICATION

We may derive at least one application for ministry from each main section of the letter. (1) Thank God for the growth of the people among whom you minister, no matter how erratic it is, and keep on fervently praying for God to bring them further along the path toward maturity. (2) Challenge your people to put others above self, which will produce a unity that remains impossible when they always want their way first. Model the behavior yourself, so they can see how it is possible. (3) Commend faithful believers publicly, especially those who have worked hard and made significant sacrifices for the sake of following Jesus and advancing his kingdom. (4) Warn against heresy forthrightly when people's salvation is at stake. But be sure you "pick your battles" carefully. The issue must be an absolutely fundamental one, lest you destroy the unity of the body over peripheral or nonsalvific doctrines. If it is merely a matter of rivalry or impure motives on the part of those ministering the true gospel, rejoice anyway! (5) Thank people for their support and be content, however little or great it is.

Overshadowing all five of these points, however, is Paul's remarkable joy in the midst of imprisonment by the Romans, competition from fellow Christians, and attacks by outsiders against his spiritual children. Only a strong trust in God's sovereign care and love could make this possible. Only a strong commitment to following Jesus' journey to the cross could make it actual. Contemporary Western Christian life and ministry, so caught up in its cultural captivity to "inalienable rights," "self-actualization," and rigid, protective boundaries around both property and psyche, stands little chance of fathoming much less experiencing this kind of suffering or this kind of joy. Indeed, we will need to concentrate on imitating others who, like Paul, have already taken further steps down this path of countercultural discipleship.[229]

---

[227] See esp. John Reumann, "Contributions of the Philippian Community to Paul and to Earliest Christianity," *NTS* 39 (1993): 438–57. Cf. also Craig S. Wansink, *"Chained in Christ": The Experience and Rhetoric of Paul's Imprisonments* (Sheffield: SAP, 1996), 146.

[228] Either civil servants or imperial slaves, and not to be confused with the praetorian guard. See Witherington, *Philippians,* 135–36.

[229] Fowl (*Philippians,* 220) elaborates: "If churches . . . are not calling and enabling Christians to form and sustain such friendships with God and each other, the state has nothing to fear from us and no reason to be hostile toward us." Cf. also p. 1671: "The only arrogance surrounding the language of imitation would be the arrogance of those so formed by the ethos of individualism that they think they can walk [this] path . . . without observing, learning from, and imitating [such people]."

ADDITIONAL QUESTIONS FOR REVIEW

1. Why is Philippians studied separately from the other three Prison Epistles? What are the three possible sites for Paul's imprisonment when he penned Philippians? What is the evidence for and against each site?
2. What is the occasion for the letter to the Philippians? How is this letter best characterized, and what are its main themes? How can this letter be defended as a single, literary whole?
3. Summarize the theological heart of Philippians. What does the Christ hymn assert about the Christology of early Christianity? What specific truths does the hymn assert about the person of Jesus Christ?
4. What is Paul's first major digression from the form of family letter and the theme of joyfully enduring persecution? How does Paul use his former position as a quintessential Jew and his present position as a Christian in his argument against the Judaizers? What agenda are the Judiazers pushing? Are there any contemporary parallels to such an agenda?
5. What is the topic of Paul's second extra insertion in this family letter? How does historical context enlighten understanding of this section of Philippians?
6. What is a good summary of Philippians 4:13, and how has it often been misquoted by well-intentioned Christians?
7. Identify a contemporary application for each major section of Philippians. What are a few features of contemporary Western society that must be relinquished in order for a Christian to enjoy the type of joy Paul exhibits despite his difficult circumstances?

SELECT BIBLIOGRAPHY

COMMENTARIES

Advanced

Hawthorne, Gerald F. *Philippians.* WBC. Waco: Word, 1983.
O'Brien, Peter T. *The Epistle to the Philippians.* NIGTC. Exeter: Paternoster; Grand Rapids: Eerdmans, 1991.
Silva, Moisés. *Philippians.* BECNT. Grand Rapids: Baker, rev. 2005.

Intermediate

Bockmuehl, Markus. *The Epistle to the Philippians.* BNTC. London: Black; Peabody: Hendrickson, 1998.
Fee, Gordon D. *Paul's Letter to the Philippians.* NICNT. Grand Rapids and Cambridge: Eerdmans, 1995.
Fowl, Stephen E. *Philippians.* THNTC. Grand Rapids and Cambridge: Eerdmans, 2005.
Marshall, I. Howard. *The Epistle to the Philippians.* London: Epworth, 1993.

Thurston, Bonnie B., and Judith M. Ryan. *Philippians and Philemon.* SP. Collegeville: Liturgical, 2005.

Witherington, Ben, III. *Friendship and Finances in Philippi: The Letter of Paul to the Philippians.* NTinCont. Valley Forge: Trinity, 1994.

Introductory

Carson, D. A. *Basics for Believers: An Exposition of Philippians.* Grand Rapids: Baker, 1996.

Fee, Gordon D. *Philippians.* IVPNTC. Leicester and Downers Grove: IVP, 1999.

Motyer, Alec. *The Message of Philippians: Jesus Our Joy.* BST. Leicester and Downers Grove: IVP, 1984.

Thielman, Frank. *Philippians.* NIVAC. Grand Rapids: Zondervan, 1995.

OTHER BOOKS

Bloomquist, L. Gregory. *The Function of Suffering in Philippians.* Sheffield: JSOT, 1993.

Davis, Casey W. *Oral Biblical Criticism: The Influence of the Principle of Orality on the Literary Structure of Paul's Epistle to the Philippians.* Sheffield: SAP, 1999.

Hellerman, Joseph H. *Reconstructing Honor in Roman Philippi: Carmen Christi* as *Cursus Pudoram.* Cambridge and New York: CUP, 2005.

Holloway, Paul A. *Consolation in Philippians.* Cambridge and New York: CUP, 2001.

Oakes, Peter. *Philippians: From People to Letter.* Cambridge and New York: CUP, 2001.

Peterlin, Davorin. *Paul's Letter to the Philippians in the Light of Disunity in the Church.* Leiden and New York: Brill, 1995.

Ware, James P. *The Mission of the Church in Paul's Letter to the Philippians in the Context of Ancient Judaism.* Leiden and Boston: Brill, 2005.

Williams, Demetrius K. *Enemies of the Cross of Christ: The Terminology of the Cross and Conflict in Philippians.* London: JSOT, 2002.

BIBLIOGRAPHY

Mills, Watson E. *Philippians.* Lewiston and Lampeter: Mellen, 1999.

8

The Pastoral Epistles: General Introduction

F irst and 2 Timothy and Titus are all addressed to pastors, and they are the only New Testament letters so addressed. Timothy was pastoring the church in Ephesus; Titus, in Crete. Or at least that is what these three epistles claim. As a result, modern scholars regularly refer to these letters as the "Pastoral Epistles." Timothy is well-known to us for accompanying Paul on his second and third missionary journeys (recall Acts 16–19). Paul has also included his name as a cosender with five of his undisputed epistles. We know Titus only from Paul's other letters, but he played a prominent role in the Jerusalem visit of Galatians 2:1–10 and in functioning as an emissary to, and overseeing the collection in, Corinth (2 Cor. 7–8).[1] The contents of these three letters overlap considerably, particularly in 1 Timothy and Titus. The linguistic style is also extremely similar as one compares the three. So there are a number of good reasons for discussing these documents together before introducing each separately.

In fact, there are three major problems that the Pastoral Epistles have in common relating directly to the question of their historical setting. *First, the linguistic and literary style is not only relatively homogeneous among these three letters; it also differs markedly from the styles of all the other Pauline epistles.* As many as 175 words appear here that are used nowhere else in the New Testament and another 130 that are never found elsewhere in Paul.[2] Many involve terms from Greek philosophy, such as "religion," "godliness," "piety," and "modesty." Five proverbial texts are identified as "trustworthy sayings" (1 Tim. 1:15; 3:1; 4:9; 2 Tim. 2:11–13; Titus 3:4–7), a label Paul uses nowhere else.[3] Other words found in Paul are used in non-Pauline ways, most notably the expressions "the faith" and "sound doctrine," to refer to the fixed deposit of Christian teaching. Additionally, key Pauline terms are entirely absent from these three letters—for example, "evangelize," "give thanks," "spiritual," "wisdom," "body," and "soul."

Second, the doctrinal focus of these epistles seems different from the undisputed writings of Paul. A high Christology (esp. Titus 2:13) more resembles that of Ephesians and Colossians. The heresy intruding into the churches addressed appears to represent a Jewish form of Gnosticism similar to that which developed only in the late first century and beyond. And "early catholic" ecclesiology, similar to the insti-

---

[1] Because of the more widespread ministries of these two individuals, Luke T. Johnson prefers to entitle these three epistles, and his commentary on them, *Letters to Paul's Delegates* (Valley Forge: Trinity, 1996).

[2] Donald Guthrie, *New Testament Introduction* (Leicester and Downers Grove: IVP, 1990), 619, n. 4.

[3] On which, see esp. George W. Knight III, *The Faithful Sayings in the Pastoral Letters* (Grand Rapids: Baker, 1979). Cf. also R. Alastair Campbell, "Identifying the Faithful Sayings in the Pastoral Epistles," *JSNT* 54 (1994): 73–86.

tutionalized church of the early second century with its various orders of bishops and deacons, seems to be present (contrast the "charismatic" freedom and undeveloped church structure in 1 Cor. 12–14). First Timothy 5:3–16 even discusses in detail the criteria for enrolling a widow on the church rolls for financial support; an office of widow looks more like later Catholic monasticism than anything elsewhere in the New Testament (or first century). The ethics of these epistles have often been called "bourgeois" because they appear to promote conventional Hellenistic morality with little of the sharp, cutting edge of distinctively Christian lifestyle requirements.[4] Meanwhile, major doctrinal emphases in the rest of Paul's letters remain absent: the centrality of the cross, the conflict between flesh and spirit, the Holy Spirit filling believers, union with Christ, and so on.[5]

Third, there is no obvious historical setting within the events narrated in the book of Acts into which the composition of these letters fits. First Timothy is apparently written from Macedonia after Paul's three-year stay in Ephesus (1:3; 3:14); Titus, after the evangelization of Crete (1:5). Yet in Acts 27:7–12, early in Paul's ill-fated sea voyage, Luke mentions no Christians on the island as he does on other occasions when Paul's travels by ship lead him to dock briefly at various ports (e.g., 21:1–9 and even 27:3 on the current voyage). Yet this trip culminates in Paul's house arrest in Rome so that he never again appears in Acts as a free man to do the type of traveling 1 Timothy describes.

There have been four major proposals to deal with these anomalies. *The most common among modern scholars is the theory that the Pastoral Epistles are pseudonymous.* Even some who accept 2 Thessalonians, Colossians, and Ephesians as authentic find the arguments against Pauline authorship of the Pastorals compelling. On this view an anonymous Christian wrote in Paul's name a generation or more after his life, applying his gospel to changed circumstances. According to A. T. Hanson, 1 Timothy provided a handbook for church leaders, Titus issued a specific warning to fight heresy, while 2 Timothy strove to strengthen the Pauline tradition more generally.[6] Dates for the publication of these epistles then range from the 80s all the way into the mid-second century, although apparent allusions to the letters in the writings of Ignatius in the 110s[7] make most scholars more reluctant today than they once were to suggest a date much later than the beginning of the second century.

Yet, as we noted with Ephesians, it is not at all clear that the early church would have accepted letters with false attributions of authorship as canonical. The clear examples of early Christian pseudonymity were actually intended to deceive (recall above, p. 104). Nor is it easy to explain the numerous personal references scattered throughout these letters, particularly in 2 Timothy, if Paul or any of the other people mentioned were no longer alive or active in ministry. Moreover, why would an early

---

[4] For further detail on several of these, see A. T. Hanson, *The Pastoral Epistles* (London: Marshall, Morgan & Scott; Grand Rapids: Eerdmans, 1982), 3–5, 13, 31–42.

[5] J. N. D. Kelly, *A Commentary on the Pastoral Epistles: I Timothy, II Timothy, Titus* (London: Black, 1963), 18.

[6] Hanson, *Pastoral Epistles*, 23.

[7] I. Howard Marshall with Philip H. Towner, *A Critical and Exegetical Commentary on the Pastoral Epistles* (Edinburgh: T & T Clark, 1999), 5.

Christian wanting to gain authority and credibility for his writings, for whatever motives, not select readily recognizable settings in Paul's life to make his pseudepigraphy more plausible?[8] And why did he write to individual pastors or delegates rather than directly to entire churches, as with all of the previously known Pauline letters?[9]

The second option is the fragment hypothesis. On this theory, portions of genuinely Pauline letters were combined with post-Pauline additions to address new issues in the decades after Paul's day. The classic exponent of this perspective was P. N. Harrison, in a book written not quite a century ago,[10] but shorter studies have occasionally revived the hypothesis in the years since.[11] This approach would account for the personal references and other information that seem too situation specific for the more general purposes that a pseudepigrapher would have had. If this theory involved just the light editing of documents essentially Pauline in origin, there would be ample ancient precedent and no objections in principle. But exponents of this view normally find only a minority of the data in these letters as stemming from Paul. And because the fragments would have had to be strewn throughout the documents in a jigsaw-puzzle type of way, the proposal becomes less plausible. Now no true parallels remain among documents from Paul's world, Christian or otherwise.[12]

The third possibility, adopted by most evangelicals but by no means limited to them,[13] is to continue to defend Pauline authorship. As with Colossians and/or Ephesians, Paul may have employed a different amanuensis and given him the literary freedom to write up Paul's thoughts in his own style. An even better case can be made for Luke playing this role here than with Ephesians, in light of even greater linguistic and syntactical similarities with his Gospel and the Acts.[14] Alternately, the differences in vocabulary and style may reflect the different content, purposes, and genre of these letters (esp. given that the author is initially addressing individual persons rather than entire congregations). Other variables include his older age[15] throughout these letters and his use of preformed traditions (in addition to the "faithful sayings," various creedal elements appear).

It is also intriguing that the most non-Pauline features appear clustered in discrete sections, which could support the fragment hypothesis but could also fit Paul

---

[8] Likewise Kelly, *Pastoral Epistles,* 9.

[9] Philemon, of course, was an indivdual, but a house church met in his home.

[10] P. N. Harrison, *The Problem of the Pastoral Epistles* (London: Oxford, 1921).

[11] Among recent works, see esp. James D. Miller, *The Pastoral Letters as Composite Documents* (Cambridge and New York: CUP, 1997).

[12] Kelly, *Pastoral Epistles,* 29.

[13] Outside evangelicalism, see esp. Luke T. Johnson, *The First and Second Letters to Timothy* (New York and London: Doubleday, 2001), 55–99; more briefly, cf. Kelly, *Pastoral Epistles,* 27–34. Outside of English-speaking circles, particularly significant are the commentaries by Joachim Jeremias, *Die Briefe an Timotheus und Titus* (Göttingen: Vandenhoeck und Ruprecht, rev. 1975); and Ceslaus Spicq, *Les Épîtres Pastorales,* 2 vols. (Paris: Gabalda, rev. 1969).

[14] See esp. Stephen G. Wilson, *Luke and the Pastoral Epistles* (London: SPCK, 1979; Minneapolis: Fortress, 1995). Wilson, however, dates these letters to after Paul's death so that Luke is the full-fledged author. For the hypothesis as we have stated it, see George W. Knight III, *The Pastoral Epistles* (Carlisle: Paternoster; Grand Rapids: Eerdmans, 1992), 48–51.

[15] For the full array of data in these letters that point to an "old Paul" as author, see Abraham J. Malherbe, *"Paulus Senex," RestQ* 36 (1994): 197–207.

himself as author, especially since they appear in those places where the Pastorals deal with subjects not considered in the undisputed letters.[16] Further, it is by no means certain that the Pastorals provide a large enough database from which to draw statistically significant conclusions about differences in vocabulary or style from the larger Pauline corpus.[17] Finally, the testimony of the church fathers, beginning with Irenaeus in the late second century, uniformly attributes these epistles to Paul.

The differences in theology between the Pastorals and the other Pauline epistles are seldom hard and fast, being a matter of how much emphasis is given a certain doctrine instead. We have already seen the high Christology of Romans 9:5 and Philippians 2:6–11. Philippians 1:1 refers to overseers and deacons as the two leadership groups in the church, while Acts 6:1–7 and 14:23 present even earlier precedents for both offices. Acts 6:1–7 also displays early Christian measures to care for widows and avoid abuse of the system in the process. Parallels to the combination of Judaizing and Hellenizing (or proto-Gnosticizing) that the Pastorals combat have already appeared in 1 Corinthians and Colossians.[18] The author may have in part contextualized his message in the language of Hellenistic ethics; there was plenty of overlap between Christianity and Greco-Roman philosophy with respect to basic principles of right and wrong.[19] But the basis for the Pastorals' ethics is thoroughly Christian, and the differences even at the level of content can easily be exaggerated.[20] Against the argument that hope for the parousia has receded into the background, a case for the balanced "already but not yet" eschatology of the other Pauline epistles can still be made (cf. 1 Tim. 4:1; 6:13–14; Titus 2:13; 2 Tim. 3:1; 4:1).[21]

As for the historical setting, two possibilities exist. The most commonly defended one is that all three of these letters should be dated to the final period of Paul's life, after the years described in the book of Acts. We have already noted the early Christian support for Paul's release from house arrest in Rome in about 62. That would have given him the freedom for the writing and traveling implied by 1 Timothy and Titus. Second Timothy would then stem from a second, later imprisonment, during the persecution Nero unleashed against Christians in and around Rome (64–68). For further details on the circumstances, see below in our introductions to each individual letter. The biggest obstacle to this reconstruction is Paul's declaration in Acts 20:25 that the Ephesian Christian leaders would never see Paul again, whereas 1 Timothy 1:3 reads as if Paul had been in Ephesus before moving on to Macedonia and he is now

---

[16] Johnson, *1 Timothy, 2 Timothy, Titus,* 12.

[17] T. A. Robinson, "Grayston and Herdan's 'C' Quantity Formula and the Authorship of the Pastoral Epistles," *NTS* 30 (1984): 282–88.

[18] Gordon D. Fee, *1 and 2 Timothy, Titus* (San Francisco: Harper and Row, 1984), xxii.

[19] John J. Wainwright, "*Eusebeia*: Syncretism or Conservative Contextualization?" *EQ* 65 (1993): 211–24.

[20] See esp. Philip H. Towner, *The Goal of Our Instruction: The Structure of Theology and Ethics in the Pastoral Epistles* (Sheffield: JSOT, 1989). Cf. idem, "Pauline Theology or Pauline Tradition in the Pastoral Epistles: The Question of Method," *TynB* 46 (1995): 287–314. For a succinct comparison of the theology of the Pastorals more generally with the rest of Paul, coming to similar conclusions, cf. Marshall with Towner, *Pastoral Epistles,* 92–108.

[21] See further Philip H. Towner, "The Present Age in the Eschatology of the Pastoral Epistles," *NTS* 32 (1986): 427–48. For an attempt to fit even 2 Timothy into a time frame of a supposed Ephesian imprisonment between Acts 20:3 and 4, see Terrence Y. Mullins, "A Comparison between 2 Timothy and the Book of Acts," *AUSS* 31 (1993): 199–203.

commanding Timothy to remain behind. But perhaps he had been elsewhere instead, or Acts 20:25 may be based on what God had revealed to Paul prior to his imprisonment in Jerusalem without yet taking into account the changed plans that would result from his ordeal and its aftermath.

The less well-known alternative is to place Paul's writing of 1 Timothy and Titus into his three-year stay in Ephesus during the third missionary journey. One can easily imagine a gap of at least a number of months between Acts 19:20 and 21. Perhaps this is the time when Paul made his additional trip to Corinth and back (see above, p. 203). Now both 1 Timothy 1:3 and 3:14 (in which Paul hopes to come to Ephesus soon) make perfect sense, and there is no tension with Acts 20:25 because that pronouncement takes place at a later date. The writing of 1 Timothy and Titus could also fit the period described in Acts 20:1–6. There, too, Paul has been in Macedonia after his lengthy time in Ephesus, and he presumably knows he wants to touch base with at least the Ephesian church leaders one more time (even if he subsequently chooses to call them together at nearby Miletus—vv. 16 17).

As for Titus, nothing says that *Paul* must have evangelized the island, while the argument from the silence of Acts 27 seems precarious in view of the fact that, if Paul knew no one on Crete, there would be no reason for the centurion to have given him leave and no need for Luke to have mentioned any Christian community there. Second Timothy could then come from Paul's house arrest in Rome in 60–62 (cf. 2 Tim. 1:16–18).[22]

The final option is a cross between the first and the third. I. Howard Marshall's detailed, recent commentary has meticulously analyzed all of the arguments for the various positions thus far surveyed (and others) and decided that the linguistic differences are just not adequately explained by the traditional evangelical approaches. But he finds nothing theologically untrue to Paul or that could not have been written very close to Paul's lifetime. Neither does he detect any ancient evidence to support the idea that Christianity, even in the first century, would ever knowingly have accepted a pseudonymous writing as authoritative. Pseudonymity in other circles, he concludes, did intend to deceive people concerning authorship, however benignly, in order to enhance the authority of the document in question.[23] Thus the concept put forward by some supporters of the Pastorals as pseudepigraphic—that these were transparent fictions, never intended to fool anyone and that, in fact, they never actually fooled anyone—is without true parallel in the ancient Mediterranean world.

Yet that is precisely what Marshall is convinced the Pastorals reflect, so he coins an entirely new word for the process. *Instead of pseudonymity, he speaks of "allonymity,"* coining a term created from the Greek word *allos,* meaning "other," rather than from *pseudos,* meaning "a lie." Yet he concedes that he can point to no ancient parallels to this process so that the author of these letters must have been inventing

---

[22] Cf. variously, Philip H. Towner, *The Letters to Timothy and Titus* (Grand Rapids and Cambridge: Eerdmans, 2006), 12–15; and Robinson, *Redating the New Testament,* 81–84. For an attempt to fit even 2 Timothy into a time frame of a supposed Ephesian imprisonment between 20:3 and 4, see Terrence Y. Mullins, "A Comparison between 2 Timothy and the Book of Acts," *AUSS* 31 (1993): 199–203.

[23] Cf. also Stanley E. Porter, "Pauline Authorship and the Pastoral Epistles: Implications for Canon," *BBR* 5 (1995): 105–23.

something new. And he never really explains why the more traditional notion of Paul giving an amanuensis greater literary freedom could not adequately account for the linguistic differences that he finds so telling.[24]

We will therefore adopt the third approach and continue to speak of the author of these works as Paul. As for the date and historical setting, we see no reason to reject the dominant view throughout church history, including the testimony of early Christian writers, which supports the "release and second imprisonment" approach. *This leaves roughly the years 63–67, depending on the exact year Paul died, in which to locate these three letters.* But we acknowledge that an earlier date during or just after Paul's time in Ephesus (55–56) could also work exegetically.

QUESTIONS FOR REVIEW

1. What are three major problems the Pastoral Epistles have in common with regard to historical setting? What are the major responses to these difficulties, and which one of these responses proves most convincing and why?
2. What specific circumstances help explain the differences in theology between the undisputed letters of Paul and the Pastoral Epistles? What appears to be the best setting and date for the Pastoral Epistles?

SELECT BIBLIOGRAPHY

Works that treat all three Pastoral Epistles appear here; books on only one or two of the three appear after our comments on the individual books.

COMMENTARIES

Advanced

Knight, George W., III. *The Pastoral Epistles*. NIGTC. Carlisle: Paternoster; Grand Rapids: Eerdmans, 1992.

Marshall, I. Howard, with Philip H. Towner. *A Critical and Exegetical Commentary on the Pastoral Epistles*, rev. ICC. Edinburgh: T & T Clark, 1999.

Mounce, William D. *Pastoral Epistles*. WBC. Nashville: Nelson, 2000.

Intermediate

Collins, Raymond F. *I & II Timothy and Titus*. NTL. Louisville and London: WJKP, 2002.

Fee, Gordon D. *1 and 2 Timothy, Titus*. NIBC. Peabody: Hendrickson, 1988.

Johnson, Luke T. *Letters to Paul's Delegates: 1 Timothy, 2 Timothy, Titus*. NTinCont. Valley Forge: Trinity, 1996.

Kelly, J. N. D. *A Commentary on the Pastoral Epistles: I Timothy, II Timothy, Titus*. BNTC. London: Black, 1963.

---

[24] For the entire discussion of authorship, see Marshall with Towner, *Pastoral Epistles*, 57–92. On allonymity, specifically, see 83–92. It must be stressed that this approach is strictly Marshall's and not Towner's. Cf. Towner (*Letters to Timothy and Titus*, 9–36), who favors the third approach discussed above.

Lea, Tommy D., and Hayne P. Griffin. *1, 2 Timothy, Titus*. NAC. Nashville: Broadman, 1992.

Towner, Philip H. *The Letters to Timothy and Titus*. NICNT. Grand Rapids and Cambridge: Eerdmans, 2006.

Introductory

Bassler, Jouette M. *1 Timothy, 2 Timothy, Titus*. ANTC. Nashville: Abingdon, 1996.

Guthrie, Donald. *The Pastoral Epistles*. TNTC, rev. Leicester: IVP; Grand Rapids: Eerdmans, 1990.

Liefeld, Walter L. *1 and 2 Timothy, Titus*. NIVAC. Grand Rapids: Zondervan, 1999.

Stott, John R. W. *Guard the Truth: The Message of 1 Timothy and Titus*. BST. Leicester and Downers Grove: IVP, 1997.

Towner, Philip H. *1–2 Timothy & Titus*. IVPNTC. Leicester and Downers Grove: IVP, 1994.

OTHER BOOKS

Fiore, Benjamin. *The Function of Personal Example in the Socratic and Pastoral Epistles*. Rome: BIP, 1986; New York: Paulist, 2001.

Harding, Mark. *What Are They Saying about the Pastoral Epistles?* New York: Paulist, 2001.

Kidd, Reggie M. *Wealth and Beneficence in the Pastoral Epistles*. Atlanta: Scholars, 1990.

Knight, George W., III. *The Faithful Sayings in the Pastoral Epistles*. Grand Rapids: Baker, 1979.

Lau, Andrew Y. *Manifest in Flesh: The Epiphany Christology of the Pastoral Epistles*. Tübingen: Mohr, 1996.

Stepp, Perry L. *Leadership Sucession in the World of the Pauline Circle*. Sheffield: Sheffield Phoenix, 2005.

Towner, Philip H. *The Goal of Our Instruction: The Structure of Theology and Ethics in the Pastoral Epistles*. Sheffield: JSOT, 1989.

Van Neste, Ray. *Cohesion and Stucture in the Pastoral Epistles*. London and New York: T & T Clark, 2004.

Verner, David C. *The Household of God: The Social World of the Pastoral Epistles*. Chico: Scholars, 1983.

Young, Frances. *The Theology of the Pastoral Letters*. Cambridge and New York: CUP, 1994.

BIBLIOGRAPHY

Mills, Watson, ed. *Pastoral Epistles*. Lewiston and Lampeter, 2000.

Titus: A Manual on Church Order

INTRODUCTION

Having been freed from Roman imprisonment, Paul writes to Titus whom he has appointed to pastor the church on the island of Crete (1:5). Most likely, Paul intended for Titus to read the letter himself and then ensure that his congregation or congregations heard it as well. That we know little else about Titus's ministry apart from the time he spent with Paul, or about the Cretan church in general, makes both author and addressees unlikely candidates for a would-be pseudepigrapher to choose in trying to convince others of his letter's authenticity. We are not told where Paul is when he writes, but he hopes to winter in Nicopolis in southwestern Macedonia and would like Titus to join him there (3:12). Meanwhile, *he gives instructions for dealing with a similar, though apparently less severe form of the Ephesian heresy in Crete* (see the introduction to 1 Timothy). *There are clearly Jewish elements to the false teaching and possibly Gnostic-like features* (see below on 1:10–16), but the Gnostic or Hellenistic dimensions prove slighter than in Ephesus.[25] Luke Johnson, in fact, believes that the letter to the Galatians looks most like Titus in the undisputed Pauline corpus.[26] And in Galatia, of course, the false teachers were strictly Judaizers. Given the sizable Jewish community on Crete,[27] we should not be surprised by the resemblances.

The similarities between the circumstances and contents of Titus and 1 Timothy indicate that these two letters may have been sent out virtually simultaneously, but we really have no way of knowing for sure. *It is just possible that the lengthier and more formal introduction in Titus, arguably abbreviated in 1 Timothy, suggests that it was written first.*[28] The less-developed nature of the church on the island, along with what appears to some to be a more primitive ecclesiology, has been said to support this perspective, but this argument would work only if the churches in Ephesus and Crete began at exactly the same time and progressed in exactly the same ways! Besides, the household code or commands to various categories of people in the church are somewhat more elaborate in Titus than in 1 Timothy.

In terms of genre, Titus and 1 Timothy may both be thought of as *mandate letters,* analogous to epistles from Greco-Roman rulers to newly appointed delegates in districts or provinces. Formally addressed to individuals, they nevertheless were more public in character and were intended to be read widely. This genre may account for a number of the stylistic differences from the other Pauline epistles, along with their differing outlines.[29] For Titus, the structure may be displayed as follows:

---

[25] Sumney (*"Servants of Satan,"* 290–301) accounts for Titus's opponents entirely by recourse to Jewish Christians advocating "interpretations and observances of the Law" (300), which Titus rejects.

[26] Johnson, *Letters to Paul's Delegates,* 214.

[27] Raymond F. Collins, *I & II Timothy and Titus* (Louisville and London: WJKP, 2002), 298.

[28] Jerome D. Quinn, *The Letter to Titus* (New York: Doubleday, 1990), 19–20.

[29] Johnson, *Letters to Paul's Delegates,* 32, 106–8, 214. For an analysis of the sequence of thought in the light of six typical stages of "revitalization" movements, see Kenneth D. Tollefson, "Titus: Epistle of Religious Revitalization,"

  I. Greetings (1:1–4)
  II. Instructions for Various Groups in the Church (1:5–2:15)
     A. Concerning Elders (1:5–9)
     B. Concerning False Teachers (1:10–16)
     C. Concerning Men and Women of Various Ages (2:1–8)
     D. Concerning Slaves (2:9–10)
     E. Concluding Rationale (2:11–15)
  III. Concluding Exhortations: Do What Is Good (3:1–11)
  IV. Closing (3:12–15)

The rhetoric of all three of the Pastoral Epistles, like that of the moral exhortation they reflect more generally, combines deliberative (persuasive and dissuasive) with epideictic (praise and blame) forms.[30]

COMMENTARY

GREETINGS (1:1–4)

Titus begins with an introduction uncharacteristically rich in theology (though recall Romans 1:1–7), perhaps in order to counteract the heresy in Crete. It is Pauline in nature, describing the author as both God's servant and Jesus Christ's apostle and combining themes of election, truth as knowledge plus morality, the hope of eternal life, and the progress of salvation history. The emphasis on godliness permeates the Pastorals; distinctive to these epistles is the description of *God as Savior,* which *may even form the unifying theme of Titus.*[31] As in Galatians, no thanksgiving appears. The problems of immaturity and ungodliness are serious enough that Paul must get straight down to business. "This formal greeting logically functions as a public legitimation of Titus in his role as Paul's delegate."[32]

INSTRUCTIONS FOR VARIOUS GROUPS IN THE CHURCH (1:5–2:15)

Concerning Elders (1:5–9) Quite different from modern, Western individuals, people in the ancient Mediterranean world were preoccupied with knowing their place in society, which was often unchangeable, and living a virtuous life within it. Part of the problem in Crete apparently involved role confusion, so Paul tries to help Titus straighten things out. These newly evangelized communities still need a full complement of elders, so Titus is charged with "appointing" (or, less likely, "ordaining") them (v. 5).[33] This matches the practice of Paul and Barnabas in Acts 14:23 but differs from 1 Timothy 3:1–7, in which the Ephesian congregation seemingly selects their own leaders. But if the churches in Crete were young and beset with heresy,

---

BTB 30 (2000): 145–57. The fit is remarkably apt, but the resulting outline corresponds less directly to the subdivision by themes reflected in our outline.

[30] Mark Harding, *Tradition and Rhetoric in the Pastoral Epistles* (New York: Peter Lang, 1998), 214–15.

[31] Bonnie Thurston, "The Theology of Titus," *HBT* 21 (1999): 177.

[32] Johnson, *Letters to Paul's Delegates,* 216. On "getting down to business," see p. 222.

[33] Knight, *Pastoral Epistles,* 288.

even among their leadership, then Titus's more "hands-on" role becomes perfectly understandable.[34]

The term "elder" is apparently interchangeable with "overseer" in verse 7 since the list of criteria for this leadership position spans verses 6–9.[35] Referring to someone holding this role or office as an elder (*presbuteros*; also translated "presbyter") reflects the respect for age, and the wisdom that often came with it, throughout the ancient world. Calling him an overseer (*episkopos*; also translated "bishop") represents his function. Elders already existed in Jewish synagogues as lay leaders, so Christianity was simply carrying over the practice from Judaism at this juncture.[36]

"A man whose children believe" (v. 6) is a misleading translation and would better be rendered, "a man whose children are faithful" (*pistos*), comparable to the respect for parents required of an overseer's children in 1 Timothy 3:4.[37] Verse 9 introduces a characteristic and distinctive expression in the Pastorals—"a trustworthy saying" (*pistos logos*) and describes the positive and negative theological tasks of church leaders in every era: encouraging believers by teaching sound (literally, "healthy") doctrine and discouraging heresy by refuting false teaching. We need an appropriate balance of both.

Concerning False Teachers (1:10–16) The description of the rebellious people in this paragraph reminds us of the Colossian heresy and will even more closely resemble the problems in Ephesus that 1 Timothy combats. There is a Judaizing element, involving circumcision (v. 10) and Jewish myths and commandments (v. 14) and a Gnosticizing (or at least Hellenizing) dimension, as the heretics claim to "know" God (as in Greek *gnōsis*) but deny him by their actions (v. 16). Seeking dishonest gain (v. 11) also fits a Hellenistic milieu more than a Jewish one. But the heresy seems to have a distinctively Cretan touch as well, as Paul quotes an unflattering proverb that was nevertheless widely recognized to be true, at least as a generalization (v. 12)! Crete was known already by the first century as a "resort of robbers and pirates,"[38] while "Cretize" had become a Greek synonym for lying, due to the Cretans' claim that they had Zeus's tomb (who of course, as a god, could not have died)![39] Paul's main concern is that the Cretan church shun asceticism (v. 15). As in Romans 14–15 and 1 Timothy 4, the principle that to the pure all things

---

[34] See esp. William D. Mounce, *Pastoral Epistles* (Nashville: Nelson, 2000), 386–87.

[35] The singular form of "overseer" is likely generic (Kelly, *Pastoral Epistles,* 231), despite attempts to argue that there was only one overseer per "church," with multiple elders as the leaders of the individual home congregations within each church.

[36] On these terms and their origin, see further Marshall with Towner, *Pastoral Epistles,* 170–81.

[37] Knight, *Pastoral Epistles,* 289–90. Cf. Norris C. Grubbs, "The Truth about Elders and Their Children: Believing or Behaving in Titus 1:6?" *Faith and Mission* (2005): 3–15.

[38] Hanson, *Pastoral Epistles,* 176. Cf. esp. Polybius, *Hist.* 6:46.3.

[39] Anthony C. Thiselton ("The Logical Role of the Liar Paradox in Titus 1:12, 13: A Dissent from the Commentaries in the Light of Philosophical and Logical Analysis," *BI* 2 [1994]: 207–23) thinks that this text employs the "liar paradox" (in which a person claiming always to speak the truth cannot but lie or vice-versa) to show how self-defeating it is not to live in ways that match one's ideology. But Reggie M. Kidd ("Titus as *Apologia*: Grace for Liars, Beasts, and Bellies," *HBT* 21 [1999]: 185–209) shows that there is no inherent contradiction in quoting a culture's self-critical proverb when it in fact represents a valid generalization.

are pure must be seen in the limited context of morally neutral matters such as food, drink, marriage, and so on.[40]

Concerning Men and Women of Various Ages (2:1–8)   Older men and women must live dignified, moral lives and become good examples to younger Christians (vv. 1–5). Again Paul refers to sound doctrine and several of the criteria that were used to select elders/overseers. In fact, most of these simply reflect character traits that all mature Christians should exhibit. The women in Titus's congregations seem to have been particularly susceptible to the false teaching (cf. 2 Tim. 3:6–7), so Paul encourages the more mature ones to instruct the less mature. As in Colossians and Ephesians, wives must submit to their husbands, but they also should become diligent "homeworkers" (from *oikourgos*; v. 5). The emphasis here is not on staying at home (which was usually taken for granted in antiquity) but on faithful work there.[41] Many wives in biblical cultures used their houses as places for plying trades or making crafts, which they sold to supplement their families' income (cf. the noble wife of Prov. 31). An entirely different Greek word not used here, except in a few late manuscripts, meant ones who "stayed at home" (from *oikouros*; i.e., without working).

The greatest need for young men[42] was self-control (v. 6). This remains true in our modern, sexually charged world more than ever. In his instructions to both women and men, Paul generalizes by referring to teaching and doing "what is good" (vv. 3, 7). In the second of these contexts, not only must teaching/doctrine be sound or healthy; this attribute is now applied to all speech (v. 8). Cultivating these virtues will minimize the amount of justifiable criticism believers receive from unbelievers and may even silence opponents (vv. 5, 9).

Concerning Slaves (2:9–10)   Verse 9 reads like a summary of Paul's injunctions to slaves in Colossians and Ephesians.[43] Verse 10a reminds us that theft was a common problem, whether or not that was the issue at stake with Onesimus in the letter to Philemon (see above, pp. 275–76). The last half of this verse presents the flip side of verse 8b. Not only should we minimize opportunities for others to speak evil of us; we should contextualize our presentations of the gospel in as culturally attractive packages as possible and then be sure our lives make our Savior equally attractive.

Concluding Rationale (2:11–15)   *Verses 5b, 8b, and 10b have reiterated the theme that fulfillment of proper role relationships helps to further the gospel and to squelch*

---

[40] "It should be observed that the Apostle is playing on the ritual and moral sense of *pure*. When modern people quote the apothegm, they usually take the word exclusively in the moral sense and deduce that the man who is himself pure need not fear contamination by anything impure. This is a dangerous half-truth, and far from Paul's meaning" (Kelly, *Pastoral Epistles*, 237).

[41] This behavior also contrasts with the younger Ephesian widows who were not working but gadabouts. Paul's teaching does not require a woman to work only at home, but it does give her duties in her home (Mounce, *Pastoral Epistles*, 411).

[42] According to Hippocrates's very precise division of human life into seven stages, the term used here for "young man" most closely approximates the word used for men from 22 to 28 years of age. "But there was also a rough division into young and old with the boundary set at the age of 40, and the NT writers appear to follow this" (Marshall with Towner, *Pastoral Epistles*, 239).

[43] The use of the harsher word *despotēs* for "master" may reflect a reference primarily to non-Christian masters, against whom slaves' desire to rebel would have often been the greatest (Knight, *Pastoral Epistles*, 314).

unnecessary objections to the Christian message and lifestyle.[44] *Verses 11–15 now sum up this larger section by referring to an even more fundamental principle. These things are good in and of themselves and what God requires* (v. 14, building on vv. 3b and 7a).[45] The word for "teaches" in verse 12 comes from the Greek *paideuō*, which often means to discipline but in this context perhaps connotes "educating in human culture."[46]

Having called God "our Savior" in verse 10 leads Paul naturally to review the principle of salvation by grace now unambiguously demonstrated in the atoning sacrifice of Jesus Christ (v. 11).[47] But as in Philippians 2:12–13 or Ephesians 2:8–10, Paul refuses to drive a wedge between faith and good works (which are different from the "works of the Law"). Sinners who are saved by grace alone are then increasingly transformed into godly people (v. 12). This process will be completed when Christ returns and believers are resurrected and glorified (vv. 13–14). Tucked into this section is a highly significant illustration of Granville Sharp's rule: two nouns paired with an "and," with the definite article only before the first, refer to the same entity. Thus in the expression, *tou megalou theou kai sōtēros hēmōn Iēsou Christou* ("the great God and Savior of us Jesus Christ"; v. 13b), Paul is describing Jesus not merely as Savior but also as God, a key affirmation of the deity of Christ.[48] Verse 15 repeats the twofold ministry of the pastor first presented in 1:9 and insists that Titus execute that ministry faithfully even if some become indignant.

CONCLUDING EXHORTATIONS: DO WHAT IS GOOD (3:1–11)

Following on from the theme of right role relationships, Paul encourages Titus to remind his congregations to be submissive to all duly constituted authorities and to display humility before everyone (vv. 1–2). Non-Christians of course may well not reciprocate; after all, Titus's young Christians can easily remember when they did not behave well either (v. 3). But when God brings salvation in Christ, he cleanses, regenerates, and renews people, entirely by his grace through the power of the Holy Spirit, to make them prepared to inherit eternal life (vv. 4–7).[49] The contrast between grace and works in this passage (disguised a bit by the NIV's translation, "things we had done" in v. 5) makes us think of Ephesians 2:8–9. But, again just as Ephesians 2:10 immediately proceeds to stress the good works that flow from salvation, so too

---

[44] On which, see esp. throughout Fee, *1 and 2 Timothy, Titus.*

[45] On which, see esp. throughout Knight, *Pastoral Epistles.*

[46] Johnson, *Letters to Paul's Delegates,* 241.

[47] The word for "appeared" here leads to our English term "epiphany." Combined with the reference to God as Savior, the expression would have called to mind the appearances of gods of healing or of deified emperors (Raymond F. Collins, *I & II Timothy and Titus,* 349).

[48] See esp. Murray J. Harris, "Titus 2:13 and the Deity of Christ," in *Pauline Studies,* eds. Donald A. Hagner and Murray J. Harris (Grand Rapids: Eerdmans, 1980), 262–77. When applied to pairs of singular, personal but non-proper nouns, Sharp claimed to find not a single exception to his principle in the large swath of Greek literature he surveyed, of which the New Testament was just a small portion. One could, of course, argue that "God" and "Savior" are being used as proper nouns here, i.e., equivalent to names, but this is not the most natural way to consider these terms.

[49] Verse 5 is sometimes taken as a reference to baptism, which then raises afresh the question of whether Paul is teaching baptismal regeneration or not. If baptism is in view, we are probably meant to treat this text exactly as we did Rom. 6:1–4. But the expression "washing of rebirth" is perhaps more naturally taken as referring to the cleansing that regeneration itself brings, rather than necessarily alluding to baptism at all.

here Paul adds that those who have trusted in God must devote themselves to doing good. This is how the church is built up rather than divided (v. 8).[50]

Verse 8 refers back to the first of the five "faithful" or "trustworthy" sayings scattered throughout the Pastorals (recall above, p. 343). This "saying" must include the preceding theological material about God's salvation, which in the Greek of verses 4–7 forms one uninterrupted sentence.[51]

Verses 9–11 return to the problem of the false teachers, introduced in 1:10–16. The "controversies" and "arguments" could refer to just about anything. The use of "genealogies" could imply Gnostic-like speculation about the evolution of the Godhead or Jewish concerns over tracing one's ancestry to determine what privileges might come with it. But "quarrels about the law" almost certainly mean debates over the interpretation of Torah (v. 9). Verse 10 suggests a process of church discipline akin to Matthew 18:15–18. After private and public warnings designed to bring people in line, it is better to let those dividing the church on fundamental theological issues do their damage elsewhere. Ironically, the disassociation commanded here may be even more sweeping than for unrepentant sexual offenders (see above, p. 174), yet how often today do congregations excommunicate the incurably factious? Yet verse 11 reiterates the judgment that the divisive bring on themselves.[52]

CLOSING (3:12–15)

Here appear the personal kinds of greetings and instructions that are difficult to square with pseudonymity. Tychicus in verse 12 would likely be the same man as the letter carrier of Ephesians, Colossians, and Philemon (see above, pp. 271–72). In verse 13, Apollos may be the same teacher we have encountered in Acts and 1 Corinthians. About Artemas and Zenas we know nothing else. Nicopolis was a city on the Greek mainland south of Corfu. Paul adds one more encouragement to "do good," in a context that could support the financial interpretation of the expression (v. 14). The problem of "unproductive" (literally, "fruitless") lives reminds us of the idle in Thessalonica. Perhaps a similar problem of clients "sponging off" their former patrons existed in Crete as well. Paul concludes with his final greetings and his customary grace (v. 15).

APPLICATION

Irrespective of where a Christian comes down on the debates between complementarians and egalitarians over gender roles, he or she must acknowledge that godly living in general is regularly characterized by submission to other people. The problems on Crete involved at least as much rebellion, independence, and self-centeredness as they did formal theological or moral error. Paul's antidote to the

---

[50] Winter (*Seek the Welfare of the City*) argues repeatedly that the expression "doing good" throughout the New Testament epistles often represents generous benefaction in particular.

[51] Collins (*1 & 2 Timothy and Titus*, 359–66) takes it to represent a primitive baptismal hymn.

[52] "Paul's point is that, since he has been solemnly warned by the church authorities, he must know that he is doing wrong and his own better judgment must therefore condemn him. Nothing can be done with a man who willfully persists in dividing the church's unity" (Kelly, *Pastoral Epistles*, 256).

false teachers and their ways includes humble, patient, kind, and generous deference to others. This is the appropriate lifestyle with which to thank God for his gift of unmerited salvation and to commend the Christian faith to a lost but watching world. More fundamentally, it defines what is inherently good in and of itself. Such a demeanor is diametrically opposed to fallen human nature and thus remains difficult even for redeemed people. To the extent that we are surrounded by the blatant in-your-face counterexamples of the dominant non-Christian cultures of our age, it becomes even harder to behave differently. We must therefore be ever vigilant in suppressing prideful desires and actions that seek our own advancement at the expense of others. There is no place in Christian living for a stubborn, rude insistence on one's own rights, though, as we saw in discussing Acts, it is often crucial to struggle, in the proper spirit, for the rights of others.

ADDITIONAL QUESTIONS FOR REVIEW

1. What confusion is Paul seeking to clarify for the congregation at Crete in Titus 1? What are the various roles highlighted in this church, and who should occupy each role?
2. What is the reason (repeated three times in Titus) for filling proper roles in the church? How does this role clarification apply to relationships beyond the church?
3. How does Paul tie the theme of God as Savior to ethical implications for believers who have been saved?
4. What type of attitude toward God and others is an appropriate response for the community of the saved?

SELECT BIBLIOGRAPHY

In addition to the works listed under "The Pastoral Epistles: General Introduction," above, see:

COMMENTARIES

Advanced

Quinn, Jerome D. *The Letter to Titus*. AB. New York: Doubleday, 1990.

1 Timothy: How to Pastor a Church and Turn It Away from Heresy

INTRODUCTION

P resumably at about the same time as he wrote Titus, Paul also wrote to Timothy in Ephesus. He had perhaps just been there himself, had definitely been in Macedonia, and may actually have been writing from that Greek province (1:3). *He gives guidelines for helping Timothy combat a form of heresy similar to that which afflicted Colossae* and, as we saw above (pp. 285–87), not unlike problems on the island of Crete. *But here, in addition to a clear Judaizing element, there almost certainly seems to be a Gnostic-like dimension (or at least Hellenistic features that would eventually evolve into Gnosticism).*[53] Thus while 1:7 refers to those who want to teach Torah but do not know what they are talking about, 4:1–5 addresses an ascetic dimension that forbids marriage (common in Hellenism but highly unusual in Judaism), while 6:20 explicitly opposes "what is falsely called knowledge" (*gnōsis*)—likely an allusion to a Gnosticizing element. When we recall that Ephesus was the nearest large city to Colossae, the commonalities between the false teachings in the two communities cause no surprise.

As with Titus, 1 Timothy would presumably have been intended to be read to the Ephesian church after Timothy had digested Paul's instructions. In this case, it appears that even the church leadership has been infected with the heresy; thus the more elaborate instructions for choosing overseers and deacons (3:1–13). The silencing of women in 2:12 is bound up with this issue, though exactly how continues to divide commentators (see below). The commands in 2:9–10 further suggest that a minority of *wealthy* women, the ones most likely to ascend to positions of leadership in Greek circles in the first place, caused a disproportionate amount of the problem.[54] Paul hopes to come soon to help improve the situation further, but does not know for sure if he will be able to make it, or, if he does, just how soon he can come (3:14–15a).

As with Titus, 1 Timothy appears to be a *mandate letter* (see above).[55] Its closest undisputed Pauline parallel may be 1 Corinthians, where we also saw Hellenistic philosophy, if not even proto-Gnosticism, afflicting the church.[56] An overall structure for the letter may be discerned if one recognizes that the body of the epistle addresses *the heresy Timothy must oppose and then offers three methods of accomplishing*

---

[53] Michael Goulder ("The Pastor's Wolves," *NovT* 38 [1996]: 242–56) plausibly envisions Jewish-Christian charismatic visionaries propounding proto-Gnostic mythology.

[54] Reggie Kidd, *Wealth and Beneficence in the Pastoral Epistles* (Atlanta: Scholars, 1990); Alan Padgett, "Wealthy Women in Ephesus: 1 Timothy 2:8–15 in Social Context," *Int* 41 (1987): 19–31.

[55] Johnson, *First and Second Timothy,* 91–97. On the other hand, Margaret M. Mitchell ("PTebt 703 and the Genre of 1 Timothy: The Curious Career of a Ptolemaic Papyrus in Pauline Scholarship," *NovT* 44 [2002]: 344–70) believes that parallels are not close enough to make this identification. Reading the papyrus that has generated this debate (which she prints) certainly demonstrates both the similarities and differences; a decision proves difficult.

[56] Johnson, *Letters to Paul's Delegates,* 214. Cf. further Philip H. Towner, "Gnosis and Realized Eschatology in Ephesus (of the Pastoral Epistles) and the Corinthian Enthusiasm," *JSNT* 31 (1987): 95–124.

this, before closing with a series of warnings.[57] Our outline may, therefore, proceed along the following lines:

I.   Greeting (1:1–2)
II. The Reason for the Letter: Stand Fast against False Teaching (1:3–20)
III. First Method: Careful Control over Church Worship and Leadership (2:1–3:16)
    A. Proper Attitudes to Outside Authorities (2:1–7)
    B. Proper Gender Roles for Leadership (2:8–15)
    C. Proper Criteria for Church Leadership (3:1–13)
        1. Overseers (3:1–7)
        2. Deacons (3:8–13)
    D. Conclusion (3:14–16)
IV. Second Method: Embrace True Godliness Rather Than Asceticism (4:1–16)
V.   Third Method: Proper Respect and Rules for Other Groups of People in the Church (5:1–6:2)
VI. Concluding Warnings (6:3–21)

COMMENTARY

GREETING (1:1–2)

The greeting in 1 Timothy is much shorter than its counterpart in Titus, reverting back to a more typical length for a Hellenistic letter opening. But the distinctive references to God as Savior[58] and to the addressee as Paul's true son in the faith are preserved. It is likely that both Titus and Timothy were led to the Lord by Paul; hence, the labels that he applied to them.

THE REASON FOR THE LETTER: STAND FAST AGAINST FALSE TEACHING (1:3–20)

Paul quickly jumps into the heart of the matter that has generated this epistle. Unlike Titus, 1 Timothy will contain a prayer of thanksgiving (1:12–17), but it does not appear immediately after the greetings, as in a conventional Greco-Roman letter. As with Titus, this may be due in part to the seriousness of the heresy that Paul and Timothy must oppose.[59] But it may also reflect the distinct character of a mandate letter, which does not follow conventional outlines closely at all. Verses 3–11 stress Timothy's responsibility to resist the false teaching afoot in his church. We have already noted the combination of Judaizing and Gnosticizing elements. The same options for genealogies remain here as they did with Titus (see above, p. 356); the myths that Paul links with them here (v. 4a) could likewise refer to Jewish narrative

---

[57] Cf. throughout Fee, *1 and 2 Timothy, Titus.*

[58] Again, central to the entire letter; see J. L. Sumney, "'God Our Savior': The Fundamental Operational Theological Assertion of 1 Timothy," *HBT* 21 (1999): 105–23.

[59] Collins, *I & II Timothy and Titus,* 24.

traditions (like many that developed in the intertestamental period) or to Gnostic-like speculations about the creation, fall, and salvation of the cosmos.[60] None of these stories represents a Christian worldview, so at best they prove "meaningless" (v. 6). At worst, they divide and distract from true Christian faith and love (vv. 4b–5). To the extent that they attempt to interpret the law, they only misinterpret it (v. 7).

Verses 8–11 proceed to explain the proper approach to the law. This paragraph meshes well with Paul's teaching in the undisputed letters.[61] The law was not given for speculative exposition but to address moral questions. It was especially given to sinners of all kinds to point out their plight and show them their need for the Savior (recall Gal. 3:19–4:7; Rom. 5:20–21).[62] The catalogue of sinners in these verses is representative, not exhaustive, and resembles other Jewish, Greco-Roman, and Christian vice lists. Particularly, it seems to follow most of the Ten Commandments in its sequence.[63] The word rendered "perverts" (from *arsenokoitēs*) is better translated "male homosexuals," inasmuch as it combines the two root words that mean "male" and "coitus."[64] As elsewhere, we must avoid the twin errors of either elevating any one of these sins above the others ("liars" are also on the list!) or denying that one or more of the practices is even sinful at all.

As Paul finally does offer a prayer of thanksgiving (vv. 12–17), he appropriately focuses on the salvation supplied by Christ as the remedy for the sins just sketched. As in 2 Corinthians 1:3–7, he thanks God not for his addressees but for God's work in his own life. After all, he now recognizes that his persecution of Christians before Jesus appeared to him on the Damascus Road flagrantly fought against God's people and purposes (v. 13). Thus it was by sheer grace that God chose to reveal himself to Paul so dramatically, to bring about a complete change of heart, and to commission him for the ministry that has now occupied the last thirty-plus years of his life (vv. 12, 14). Paul appends one of the "trustworthy sayings" that fits this context perfectly: it was saving sinners that formed Christ's central purpose for coming to earth (v. 15a; cf. Luke 19:10). Paul then reiterates how horrible his behavior had been (cf. 1 Cor. 15:9 and Eph. 3:8),[65] which merely magnifies God's grace and leads into a doxology (vv. 15b–17).

Rounding out this first main section, Paul comes full circle to where he began with his charge to Timothy to stand fast in the faith, combat the heresy, and avoid the apostasy that adopting the false teaching produces (vv. 18–20). The prophecies made about Timothy (v. 18) are referred to again in 4:14b in conjunction with what may have been a kind of ordination service and were apparently related to the gift of the Spirit that God bestowed upon him (4:14a), a gift that may well have combined

---

[60] Johnson, *First and Second Timothy,* 163.

[61] Stephen Westerholm, "The Law and the 'Just Man' (1 Tim 1, 3–11)," *ST* 36 (1982): 79–85.

[62] Knight, *Pastoral Epistles,* 83.

[63] Collins, *I & II Timothy and Titus,* 30. The word for "slave trader" (*andrapodistēs*) can also mean "kidnapper," thus explaining the sin involved even under the law, which allowed for slavery. See J. Albert Harrill, "The Vice of Slave Dealers in Greco-Roman Society: The Use of a Topos in 1 Timothy 1:10," *JBL* 118 (1999): 97–122.

[64] David F. Wright, "Translating *APΣENOKOITAI* (1 Cor. 6:9; 1 Tim. 1:10)," *VC* 41 (1987): 396–98.

[65] Intriguingly, v. 15b closes with the relative clause, *hōn prōtos eimi egō* (literally, "of whom I am first"). Given the unusual presence of a form of the verb "to be" in a context like this, it would appear to be emphatic. So it would appear that even the Christian Paul continues to recognize his total depravity apart from God's grace in Christ—a further confirmation that Rom. 7:14–25 makes best sense as referring to Paul's Christian experience.

exhorting (*paraklēsis*; much broader than NIV's "preaching") and teaching (*didas-kalia*).[66] The two men Paul cites as having rejected "faith and a good conscience" (v. 19) "have shipwrecked" *the* faith. While the definite article could have the sense of the possessive pronoun, it seems more likely that Paul is saying that they have brought discredit to Christianity rather than that they have lost their salvation.[67] A shipwreck does not always mean that a boat has sunk, but it does always imply that it is not going anywhere until it is repaired! For more on Hymenaeus and Alexander, see 2 Timothy 2:17–18 and 4:14. Handing them over to Satan echoes the language of 1 Corinthians 5:5 and is even more clearly remedial in this context, so excommunication rather than death must be in view.[68]

FIRST METHOD: CAREFUL CONTROL OVER CHURCH WORSHIP AND LEADERSHIP (2:1–3:16)

Proper Attitudes to Outside Authorities (2:1–7)

In a sense, the body of the letter begins here, as in 1 Corinthians 1:10, with Paul's *parakaleō* ("I urge" or "I appeal") formula. Chapter 3:14 demonstrates that Paul is thinking of the practice and organization of the local church throughout this section. *The basic principle he enunciates is prayer and peaceful submission to authority as the best testimony to an unsaved world* (2:1–7). There is a time and place for civil disobedience (see above), but this usually forms the exception not the rule.[69] Chapter 2:4 forms one of numerous Scriptures that distinguishes between what theologians have sometimes called God's decretive will and his permissive will. God *desires* all people to be saved but he does not decree that all *will* be saved, giving them permission to reject his offer.[70] One's salvation comes only through Jesus, who mediated between a perfectly holy God and sinful humanity by paying the ransom price to buy our freedom (vv. 5–6; cf. Mark 10:45; and recall on Rom. 3:24). Moreover, Paul was uniquely commissioned to bring this wonderful news especially to the Gentile world (v. 7; recall Acts 9:15, 22:21).

Proper Gender Roles for Leadership (2:8–15)

Second, men and women should play their appropriate roles in church worship and leadership (2:8–15). The men must pray without quarreling. Subordinate to that statement (in the Greek) is the participial clause, "lifting up holy hands" (v. 8). The manner simply reflects a common practice of the time; it is neither commanded nor proscribed. But Paul's actual command is clearly timeless in application. The bulk of the passage, however, turns to the women, undoubtedly because of the specifics of the problem in Ephesus (vv. 9–15). Paul has a prescription for their demeanor in worship, too. They must adorn themselves modestly and commend themselves to others by their godly behavior

---

[66] See further Marshall with Towner, *Pastoral Epistles,* 408–10.

[67] Mounce, *Pastoral Epistles,* 67.

[68] Knight, *Pastoral Epistles,* 112.

[69] In fact, prayer for rulers "was the Jewish and Christian way of combining the refusal to acknowledge earthly princes as divine—no matter what they claimed for themselves—and the duties of good citizenship within the given political order" (Johnson, *First and Second Timothy,* 194).

[70] Paul was also probably countering the narrower perspectives of Jews who believed God willed the salvation only of the righteous, as well as the convictions of those claiming *gnōsis* that no one was saved except the elite who fanned into flame the divine spark of knowledge within them. Cf. Kelly, *Pastoral Epistles,* 63.

rather than their outward appearance (vv. 9–10). The Greek of the last half of verse 9 reads literally, "not with braided hair *and* gold or pearls or costly dress." Wealthy Greco-Roman women often spent hours on their coiffure, weaving gems and precious stones into elaborately braided hair, announcing their wealth and status to all the world in so doing. Such ostentatious dress or adornment should not characterize Christian worshippers—again, a timeless principle.[71]

Verses 11–15 next call on the women of Ephesus not to supplant the male role of leadership in church. Verses 11–12 define this role as one of authoritative teaching. Verse 11 begins with the one positive command to the women, radical in Paul's day, literally, "they *must* learn."[72] Yet they should do so in an appropriately submissive spirit. The word for "quietness" does not mean "without speaking;" the same root also appears in 2:2 in which believers are to live "peaceful and *quiet* lives." Verse 12, at first glance, seems to make two separate prohibitions ("teach" and "have authority"), but they are probably intended as mutually defining (a figure of speech known as a *hendiadys*).[73] After all, Priscilla and Aquila taught Apollos (Acts 18:26), women apostles like Junia by definition would have taught multigendered audiences (see on Rom. 16:7), and women deacons like Phoebe obviously exercised delegated authority under the eldership over the rest of the congregation (see on Rom. 16:1–2). What is more, 1 Timothy 2 seems to be full of pairs of roughly synonymous expressions that say basically the same thing in two different ways (cf. vv. 1a,b; 2a,b,c; 3; 4; 7a,b; 8b; 9b; 11).

---

1 TIMOTHY 2:11–15

Women must learn (v. 11)

Paul's prohibition (v. 12)

Not a or b

    One not two practices (Payne)

    Both + or – (Köstenberger)

First rationale (v. 13)

(Second rationale ?) or setup for verse 15 (v. 14)

Balancing good news (v. 15)

The authoritative teaching role that Paul prohibits women from taking would thus be the office of the overseer or elder, inasmuch as 3:2 and 5:17 assign the combined functions of teaching and exercising authority uniquely to this office.[74] Alternately, one may point to various pre-Christian uses of the verb *authentein,* translated "to have authority" in the NIV, in a more negative sense such as "domineer" or "usurp authority" (KJV), in which case women (and presumably men as well) would be

---

[71] Hurley, *Man and Woman in Biblical Perspective,* 198–99.

[72] Aída B. Spencer, *Beyond the Curse: Women Called to Ministry* (Nashville: Nelson, 1985), 74.

[73] Similarly, Philip B. Payne, "*Oude* in 1 Timothy 2:12" (Atlanta: Unpublished paper delivered at the Evangelical Theological Society, 1986).

[74] Cf. Ann L. Bowman, "Women in Ministry: An Exegetical Study of 1 Timothy 2:11–15," *BSac* 149 (1992): 193–213.

forbidden merely to exercise authority *in an authoritarian way.*[75] But the grammatical construction in verse 12 of infinitive + *oude* + infinitive ("to teach or to have authority") elsewhere regularly pairs either two positive activities or two negative ones.[76] As long as the teaching in question refers to the ordinary transmission of the Christian faith, then the exercise of authority in view must be a healthy one as well. Obviously, Paul could be prohibiting false teaching, and then authoritarianism could work for the second verb, but elsewhere when he wants to specify false teaching he says precisely that, using a form of *heterodidaskaleō* (1:3; 6:3). So the ordinary, positive uses of both verbs are most likely what appear here. It is also possible throughout this passage to translate "man" and "woman" as "husband" and "wife." Then Paul's point would be that family structures should be modeled in the church (see above on Col. 3 and Eph. 5). This would limit Paul's restrictions to married women not exercising an authoritative teaching role over their husbands.[77]

Paul supplies his rationale for his instructions in verse 13, apparently based on the order of creation—Adam was created first.[78] Some commentators, however, think he is rebutting a Gnostic myth in which Eve was creator.[79] Verses 14–15 seem to supply the positive substitute for not holding the highest office in the church by highlighting God's appointed role or calling to women as a whole. Verse 14 has usually been taken as a second reason for Paul's prohibition in verse 12 or, more recently, as a further refutation of a Gnostic myth in which Eve did not sin at all. But the support for the latter comes exclusively from the third and fourth centuries,[80] while the former would make it inappropriate for mothers to teach their sons, lest the more "gullible" gender lead astray the most gullible age group! What is more, if Adam was not deceived, then it means that he sinned "with his eyes wide open," so to speak, scarcely a reason for giving him and his progeny a leadership role!

Perhaps, therefore, it is best to see verse 14 as merely a further thought triggered by the Genesis reference in the preceding verse. We might then paraphrase the flow of thought from verses 11–15 as follows: "Women (or wives) are not to hold the authoritative church teaching role because that is not a role for which they were created. In fact, things deteriorated for the woman after creation, when she fell through the deception of the serpent. But there is a bright side."[81] That silver lining then appears in verse 15. Here the Greek literally reads, "But *she* shall be saved through childbearing, if *they* remain in faith and love and holiness with modesty." The shift in number of the feminine pronouns in the English translation (the Greek merely

---

[75] E.g., Craig S. Keener, *Paul, Women and Wives* (Peabody: Hendrickson, 1992), 108–9.

[76] Andreas J. Köstenberger, "A Complex Sentence: The Syntax of in 1 Timothy 2:12," in *Women in the Church: An Analysis and Application of 1 Timothy 2:9–15,* ed. Andreas J. Köstenberger and Thomas R. Schreiner (Grand Rapids: Baker, rev. 2005), 53–84.

[77] Jerome D. Quinn and William C. Wacker, *The First and Second Letters to Timothy* (Grand Rapids and Cambridge: Eerdmans, 1999), 199–200.

[78] Consistent with the Jewish laws of primogeniture, in which the firstborn son inherited a double portion of his father's estate. Cf. further Mounce, *Pastoral Epistles,* 130–35.

[79] Most notably, Richard Clark Kroeger and Catherine Clark Kroeger, *I Suffer Not a Woman: Rethinking 1 Timothy 2:11–15 in Light of Ancient Evidence* (Grand Rapids: Baker, 1992).

[80] Sharon H. Gritz, *Women Teachers and the Mother Goddess at Ephesus* (Lanham: UPA, 1991), 157–58.

[81] Cf. further Craig L. Blomberg, "Not Beyond What Is Written: A Review of Aida Spencer's *Beyond the Curse,*" *CTR* 2 (1988): 410–16.

shifts from singular to plural verbs) suggests that the female gender as a whole is in view in verse 15a (with many individual exceptions), while all individual Christian women must follow verse 15b. "Saved" would then have the sense of "preserved" or "restored," as in 1 Timothy 4:16 and 2 Timothy 4:18.

This interpretation, encouraging many (though not all) women to focus on bearing and rearing children, would redress the imbalance created by the heresy afoot at Ephesus that was forbidding marriage (1 Tim. 4:3) and any similar imbalances in other cultures that do not adequately value the role of mothering as an inherently appropriate and fulfilling task for women.[82]

If the problem in Ephesus, as some have suggested, was that of women getting caught up in the teaching of this heresy, then the timeless application of these verses may be only that no one (of either gender) should teach heresy today either.[83] If verse 13 (or vv. 13–14) implies a timeless hierarchy, then valid application today must determine contemporary equivalents to an "overseer" or "elder." The bottom line for this interpretation would then be that the ultimately authoritative teacher in a given church should be male (or at least not a married woman teaching her husband). *In congregationally structured churches this would be the senior pastor*; in other forms of church government it might be a person "higher up" (e.g., a bishop or pope). Team ministry, however, is a more helpful model, even if there is one who ultimately supervises.[84]

In most evangelical churches, however, we have a long way to go before we come anywhere close to violating Paul's teaching, and we need to consider many more ways of getting women active in using all their gifts. One can exercise the gift of pastoring or deliver sermons as a preacher, for example, without holding the office of elder (or senior pastor) in a congregation. Finally, there is a desperate need for us to hold our views tentatively, admitting we could be wrong and agreeing to disagree in love and to tolerate diverse models among differently minded churches.[85]

Proper Criteria for Church Leadership (3:1–13)   *Overseers (3:1–7)*   If the leadership in the Ephesian church is not healthy, how can godly people be selected? Paul turns to this question, first considering overseers (vv. 1–7; recall on Titus 1:5–9) and then dealing with deacons (vv. 8–13). The position of overseer is a noble one and it is appropriate to aspire to it, as Paul's next "trustworthy saying" (v. 1) demonstrates.[86] Most of the criteria for these two offices remain self-explanatory and characterize most

---

[82] Somewhat similarly, cf. Andreas J. Köstenberger, "Ascertaining Women's God-Ordained Roles: An Interpretation of 1 Timothy 2:15," *BBR* 7 (1997): 107–44.

[83] As, e.g., in Linda L. Belleville, *Women Leaders and the Church: Three Crucial Questions* (Grand Rapids: Baker, 2000), 80.

[84] See esp. John R. W. Stott, *Issues Facing Christians Today* (London: Marshall Pickering, rev. 1990), 278–80.

[85] Unlike the two leading contemporary anthologies reflecting a more uncompromising complementarianism or egalitarianism. See, respectively, *Rediscovering Biblical Manhood and Womanhood*, eds. Piper and Grudem; and *Discovering Biblical Equality*, eds. Ronald W. Pierce and Rebecca M. Groothuis (Downers Grove: IVP, 2004). For an excellent example of the right spirit and for a mediating perspective very close to my own, see Sumner, *Men and Women.* Cf. also Robert L. Saucy and Judith K. ten Elshof, eds. *Women and Men in Ministry: A Complementary Perspective* (Chicago: Moody, 2001; Ronald and Beverly Allen, *Liberated Traditionalism* (Potland: Multnomah, 1985).

[86] See further J. Lionel North, "'Human Speech' in Paul and the Paulines: The Investigation and Meaning of ἀνθρωπίνος ὁ λόγος (1 Tim. 3:1)," *NovT* 37 (1995): 50–67.

mature Christians, even if they sometimes prove difficult to find! At the same time, they each counter a specific trait that the opponents of Paul's gospel in Ephesians or Crete have manifested.[87] "Above reproach" (v. 2) and having "a good reputation with outsiders," of course, cannot be absolutized, because Christians are sometimes falsely accused. The point is that they must provide no legitimate grounds for such accusations. The criterion of good family management (vv. 4–5) cannot require children of overseers to be Christians, since that is a decision every individual must make without coercion from others, nor can people blame parents for poor choices that adult children make after they have been given their independence. The word for "family" in both of these verses can also be translated "household" and mirrors the role of the father in Paul's day with those who resided with him and were expected by everyone in the culture to remain under his authority.[88]

Often these various criteria are inconsistently applied in the contemporary church. For example, some congregations pay little attention to Paul's words about overseers not being lovers of money (v. 3) or recent converts (v. 6). Conversely, "the husband of but one wife" (v. 2) has been overly scrutinized and often misinterpreted (see below). The two criteria that have no counterpart among the criteria for deacons are "able to teach" (the mastery of the content of the Christian faith, coupled with the ability to transmit it to others) and "hospitable" (v. 2). Hospitality has formed a key responsibility for ministers, historically, who have been expected to entertain church and community guests, though the practice has all but died out in many churches today.

What then of *mias gunaikos andra* (literally, "a man of one woman")? It is unlikely that Paul means an overseer must be married, for he would disqualify both himself and Jesus in the process! The dominant view in the early church was that he must never have had more than one wife, ruling out all the remarried. But this policy reflected the growing Hellenistic asceticism that encroached on the church and eventually led to Roman Catholic insistence on unmarried clergy. Quite differently, Paul permits and even encourages some who have been widowed to remarry (1 Cor. 7:9, 39; 1 Tim. 5:14), and it is improbable that he would urge something that would bar a person from church leadership. Is he then referring to those who were never divorced? This works only if one is prepared to exclude the widowed too, since nothing in the expression "one wife" implies "one wife in some circumstances but not in others." Perhaps, then, he means one wife at a time, ruling out polygamy. But polygamy was not widespread in the Greco-Roman world; it was extremely rare in the Jewish world; and the parallel phrase "wife of one husband" in 5:9 becomes almost unintelligible, since polyandry was virtually entirely unknown in the Roman Empire.

The only reasonable option left is to take the phrase as equivalent to: *currently characterized by marital fidelity if married, that is, a one-woman type of man.*[89] This

---

[87] Mounce, *Pastoral Epistles,* 156–58.

[88] Additionally, *teknon* normally, though not without exception, refers to a child still living at home; the combination of this term with "in subjection" reinforces that impression (cf. Knight, *Pastoral Epistles,* 161).

[89] Ed Glasscock, "'The Husband of One Wife' Requirement in 1 Timothy 3:2," *BSac* 140 (1983): 244–58.

interpretation fits the observation that the other criteria described one's current conditions, not necessarily lifelong practices, and it has support from such early authorities as Theodore of Mopsuestia, Theodoret, John Chrysostom, and Callistus.[90] It also fits Paul's emphasis in this context on being a good "family man" (v. 4), although it leaves unanswered the question of how long a person must have demonstrated fidelity to their current spouse (just as v. 10 leaves open how long a deacon must first be tested).

Deacons (3:8–13)   The largely similar criteria for deacons should discourage us from selecting these leaders on the basis of practical skills. They must be equally spiritual, even if the earliest model of such a division of labor followed certain "spiritual vs. practical" lines (Acts 6:1–6). The most we can say is that this is some kind of subordinate, "helping" or "serving" office. Who are the *gunaikas* (literally, "women") of verse 11? Some take them to be deacons' wives. But why then should the wives of overseers (the "higher" office) be left entirely unmentioned and unregulated? More likely these women are deaconesses.[91] Until Catholicism developed its monastic orders, somewhat as a substitute, deaconesses served almost universally throughout the early church. Parts of their ministries overlapped with the work of male deacons, while some of their other tasks were forbidden to men—for example, the visitation, pastoral care, catechizing, and superintending the baptism *of other women.*[92] The reinstatement of this division of labor might lead to fewer "fallen" male leaders today!

Conclusion (3:14–16)   Paul completes his discussion of this first method for countering the Ephesian heresy by reminding Timothy that these instructions substitute for his personal presence to guide the church (vv. 14–15). Functioning almost like a doxology, verse 16 presents a Christological confession of faith, perhaps hymnic in nature. The interpretation that takes the six poetic affirmations as sequential works well for the first five lines: incarnation, resurrection, exaltation, worldwide mission of the church, and response of believers. But "taken up in glory" more naturally describes the ascension and exaltation rather than Christ's second coming, in which case the sequence is destroyed. Perhaps, therefore, this "creed" combines three couplets, each of which pairs something that happened on earth with something that happens in heaven, irrespective of the order within each couplet (the order would be ABABBA).[93]

---

[90] For references, see C. H. Dodd, "New Testament Translation Problems II.," *BT* 28 (1977): 112–16. For a fuller and more recent defense of this view, cf. Sydney Page, "Marital Expectations of Church Leaders in the Pastoral Epistles," *JSNT* 50 (1993): 105–20. Johnson (*Letters to Paul's Delegates,* 143) adds, "The value Paul seeks is that of fidelity and responsibility."

[91] Thomas R. Schreiner, "Women in Ministry: A Complementarian Perspective," in *Two Views of Women in Ministry,* pp. 281–82; cf. Jennifer H. Stiefel, "Women Deacons in 1 Timothy: A Linguistic and Literary Look at 'Women Likewise . . .' (1 Tim 3.11)," *NTS* 41 (1995): 442–57. For argument for "wives" as a translation, see Mounce, *The Pastoral Epistles,* 202–4.

[92] Stephen Clark, *Man and Woman in Christ* (Ann Arbor: Servant, 1980), 117–23.

[93] See further D. J. MacLeod, "Christology in Six Lines: An Exposition of 1 Timothy 3:16," *BSac* 159 (2002): 334–48.

SECOND METHOD: EMBRACE TRUE GODLINESS RATHER THAN ASCETICISM (4:1–16)

Instead of promoting the asceticism encouraged by the heresy, which is ultimately demonic in origin (vv. 1–5), Timothy must nourish the Ephesian church on sound (literally, "healthy") doctrine (vv. 6–7). Bodily training has some value, but spiritual exercise makes one far healthier (vv. 8–10). If Timothy proves faithful in teaching and modeling these truths, he can expect the situation to improve (vv. 11–16). It is ironic that the two specific forms of asceticism mentioned here—prohibiting marriage and abstaining from certain foods (and probably drinks; cf. 5:23)—are precisely the two prohibitions that Catholics and Evangelicals, respectively, have often insisted on for the most "mature" of their members. The language of damaged consciences in verse 2 calls to mind the weak Christian brother or sister in 1 Corinthians 8–10 and Romans 14–15. The application of verses 4 and 5 is again limited to morally neutral matters and must not be applied to fundamentally immoral practices.[94] Anything else harks back to the non-Christian myths of the heresy, which Paul also calls "old wives' tales" (v. 7), a stock figure of speech not intended to demean all women, only gullible ones (and those of either gender who believe them)![95] The comparison between physical and spiritual exercise forms yet another "trustworthy saying," as verse 9 points out. Ironically, twenty-first-century people in many cultures, including many Christians, stress physical fitness far more than they do spiritual fitness.

Verse 10 seems to introduce a strange distinction between two kinds of salvation until we understand that *malista* in its five appearances in the Pastoral Epistles (1 Tim. 4:10; 5:8; 5:17; 2 Tim. 4:13; Titus 1:10) is best translated "namely," rather than "especially."[96] Verse 12 encourages the church, when it hears this letter read, not to despise Timothy for his youth (in a culture that highly respected old age; recall also 1 Cor. 16:10–11). But recall that a "young" person might mean merely under forty (above, see also Irenaeus, *Against Heresies* 2:22.5). Verse 14 supplies a rare biblical precedent for a form of ordination, which *was* practiced among the rabbis; compare also 5:22 and 2 Timothy 1:6.[97] It is impossible to know for sure if *tou presbuteriou* represents a subjective or objective genitive here. If the former, it would refer to the laying on of hands *by* the body of elders (or presbytery); if the latter, it would mean that the laying on of hands *made* Timothy an elder or member of the presbytery.[98]

---

[94] "In the Pastorals' vision of things, the good and clean conscience rejects both extremes, rampant lust and undue asceticism" (Collins, *I & II Timothy and Titus,* 114).

[95] Cf. Knight, *Pastoral Epistles,* 195.

[96] T. C. Skeat, "'Especially the Parchments': A Note on 2 Timothy IV.13," *JTS* 30 (1979): 173–77. For an attempted rebuttal, see Vern S. Poythress, "The Meaning of $\mu\acute{\alpha}\lambda\iota\sigma\tau\alpha$ in 2 Timothy 4:13 and Related Verses," *JTS* 53 (2002): 523–32. But it is precisely this verse for which Poythress offers no alternative other than to claim that "the commentaries show that other reasonable interpretations are possible" (576). Plus, he altogether skips 1 Tim. 5:8, where "one's own" and "one's household" most likely equal each other.

[97] More generally, see esp. Marjorie Warkentin, *Ordination: A Biblical-Historical View* (Grand Rapids: Eerdmans, 1982).

[98] But in light of a parallel Hebrew expression in Jewish practice, the latter seems more probable (Kelly, *Pastoral Epistles,* 108).

THIRD METHOD: PROPER RESPECT AND RULES FOR OTHER GROUPS OF PEOPLE IN THE CHURCH (5:1–6:2)

The nature of the heresy in Ephesus suggests that the leaders infected by it had adopted an elitist mentality so that proper attitudes to all groups of church members became crucial. Chapter 5:1–2 insists on *respect for the aged*[99] *and pure motives toward the youth,* principles still badly needed in our day and age. Verses 3–16 introduce another category of individual for which formal criteria are enumerated (vv. 9–10), *the "office" of widow,* clearly limited to a small selection of all the widows in the church. In a culture that insisted on a husband or father providing financially and legally for most women, becoming a widow could threaten one's very subsistence.[100] Where relatives could care for such women, Paul commands them to do so (v. 4). For those deemed too old to work (often identified as over sixty;[101] cf. v. 9) and without such help from family, the church was to provide (vv. 3, 5, 16b). Early on, such widows also developed special ministries of prayer, visitation, and teaching.

Verse 8a, therefore, says nothing about the man having to be the "breadwinner" in the family, but everything about the importance of relatives caring for needy family members, lest they have to "sponge" off the church (or today, off the state as well). Anything less is as audacious as denying the faith (v. 8b).[102] The order of widows who were truly on their own became an established part of the church for several centuries.[103] No valid hermeneutical principle allows us to dispense with similar responsibilities to care for the most dispossessed in our midst, even if the form of help may vary from one culture to the next.

On the other hand, a variety of factors, not least a young age, can lead widows to want to remarry, which apparently was precluded when one was enrolled in this particular "office" (vv. 6, 11–12). Even those who do not look for a new husband, knowing that the church is taking care of them, can make unwise use of their time (v. 13). Thus Paul encourages younger widows to go ahead and remarry and return to the standard roles for them of that day, so that their reputations, and even their faith, are not destroyed (vv. 14–15).[104]

Chapter 5:17–25 turns to *support for elders,* who are again linked with teaching and exercising authority by directing the affairs of the church (v. 17; literally, "standing over it"). Those who do their job well are worthy of "double honor," which no doubt included financial remuneration.[105] "Especially those whose work is preaching

---

[99] The word translated "older women" in v. 2 could also mean "women elders," but nothing in this context, which is all about different age groupings in the church supports the latter translation. Plus the corresponding word in the parallel passage in Titus 2:3 can mean only "old women."

[100] For nuancing and details, see Bruce W. Winter, "Providentia for the Widows of 1 Timothy 5:3–16," *TynB* 39 (1988): 83–99.

[101] Towner, *1–2 Timothy & Titus,* 116: "This age was the culturally recognized age of retirement, as well as, practically, an age at which remarriage was unlikely."

[102] Failing one's familial responsibilities does not equal apostasy, but for a believer not to live up even to "pagan standards of decency is virtually to deny the meaning of the Christian faith and to live as an unbeliever" (Mounce, *Pastoral Epistles,* 285).

[103] On which, see esp. Bonnie B. Thurston, *The Widows: A Women's Ministry in the Early Church* (Minneapolis: Fortress, 1989).

[104] On vv. 3–16 more generally, see further Jouette M. Bassler, "The Widows' Tale: A Fresh Look at 1 Tim 5:3–16," *JBL* 103 (1984): 23–41.

[105] Quinn and Wacker, *First and Second Letters to Timothy,* 450.

and teaching" could suggest two categories of elders—those who preach and teach and those who exercise only other kinds of authority—but why then would Paul have made ability to teach a criterion for overseers in 3:2? Are not all elders therefore overseers? But they were in Titus 1:6–7 and, even more tellingly, in Ephesus itself in Acts 20:17 and 28. It is better, again, to recognize that *malista* should be rendered "namely," rather than "especially," so that Paul is just referring to elders from two different perspectives rather than subdividing them into two different groups.[106]

Verse 18 affords Old Testament support for Paul's command to honor the faithful elders by developing an analogy with a farmer's treatment of oxen (Deut. 25:4; recall 1 Cor. 9:9), while also quoting Jesus' own words (see Luke 10:7), perhaps implying by this time that the Third Gospel was treated as Scripture as well.[107] Some would deny that such a development could occur so rapidly, while others cite it as proof that the epistle must come from a later generation. But if Luke, Paul's companion, really did write his Gospel by A.D. 62 (see above, p. 13), Paul might have read it almost immediately. And if subsequent generations of Christians agreed on its inspired character, why should Paul not have recognized that as well and said so sometime later in the same decade?[108]

His primary point in this context, however, deals with appropriate respect for elders. The flip side of honoring them properly is guarding against false or premature accusations. Verse 19 applies the principle of Deuteronomy 19:15, already utilized by Jesus in Matthew 18:16 and 19–20, to this process. "Witnesses" (from *martys*) here are those who "testify" against an elder, not necessarily those who actually saw some wrongdoing.[109] Nevertheless, elders must be held accountable and disciplined if necessary (v. 20), with complete impartiality (v. 21). One way to avoid having to discipline such leaders is not to ordain them to this office before they are ready for it (v. 22). But some character traits are more obvious than others, so it is not always possible to be sure about a person in advance (vv. 24–25).[110] Intruding into this context is the seemingly irrelevant injunction to Timothy to drink a little wine for medicinal purposes (v. 23). But the link may have been suggested by the command to purity in verse 22 and the likelihood that the heresy was promoting total abstinence.[111] Paul then implies that consuming small amounts of alcohol (contrast 3:3 and 8) need not make a person impure.

Finally, Paul considers *Christian slaves* (6:1–2). As in the domestic codes in Ephesians and Colossians, he commands respect for their masters. As in Titus, he stresses the positive impact such behavior will make on outsiders. Slaves with Christian masters who did not manumit them could easily have been tempted to

---

[106] Marshall with Towner, *Pastoral Epistles*, 612.

[107] Or that a saying from the oral traditions of Jesus' teachings was loosely appended to the scriptural text to illustrate the same point (Johnson, *First and Second Timothy*, 278).

[108] Cf. Knight, *Pastoral Epistles*, 234.

[109] Marshall with Towner, *Pastoral Epistles*, 618.

[110] Supporting this linkage between vv. 19–20 and 21–25, but based on parallels in Deut. 19:15–20, see J. William Fuller, "Of Elders and Triads in 1 Timothy 5.19–25," *NTS* 29 (1983): 258–63.

[111] Kelly, *Pastoral Epistles*, 95.

respect them less, for this very reason, whereas in fact their commitment to Christ makes them merit greater honor.[112]

Concluding Warnings (6:3–21)

One could think of verses 3–19 as comprising a final method of combating the heresy: avoiding the love of money. But unlike the previous main commands, this one does not address the false teaching and its effects, *per se,* but the attitudes some of the false teachers are displaying. Yet Paul does rehearse the dire consequences of worshipping mammon or money rather than God (Luke 16:13), while insisting that Timothy flee from temptations in this arena. One may thus treat this section as akin to the closing exhortations of the more traditionally structured Hellenistic letter body.[113] Verses 3–5 contrast the options starkly: either the heresy with the divisions it creates or the healthy teaching of the true gospel. The final clause of verse 5 presents an added dimension of the false teaching—not any further heterodoxy but part of its motivation. Most Greco-Roman religious teachers charged and/or received money for their ministry and apparently the leaders of the heresy in Ephesus did the same. The problem lay not in being paid for their services; Paul had already argued vigorously for full-time Christian leaders to be remunerated properly (1 Cor. 9:1–12a, 13–14). Rather, it was their conviction that they had the right to insist on this pay, which revealed their true loyalties.[114]

Playing on the word "gain," Paul insists that what brings spiritual status or right standing is "godliness with contentment" (v. 6). After all, we came into the world naked, and we will leave it unable to take any of our material possessions with us (v. 7; cf. Job 1:21). So we need to learn to be satisfied with the basics of life (v. 8). Otherwise, the craving always to acquire more can lead people in numerous destructive directions (v. 9). "For the love of money is a root of all kinds of evil" (v. 10a). This famous verse has unfortunately been mistranslated and misquoted throughout much of history. Neither Paul nor any other Scripture writer ever says that money itself is to blame; it is our covetous desire for it that can lead us away from the faith to our ultimate grief (v. 10b). Neither is the definite article present in the Greek before "root," and the grammatical structures in which the article is omitted even when a noun is definite do not appear here. So the love of money is one primary root of evil but not the only one. Finally, the plural expression, *pantōn tōn kakōn,* suggests "all kinds of evil," not necessarily every conceivable evil.[115] Notwithstanding these three caveats, dissatisfaction with one's present financial circumstances remains a major stimulus to sin and evil in the world.

Instead, Paul demands that Timothy shun such temptations and pursue godly character traits (v. 11), even when it is a struggle (v. 12a). Then he can assure himself that he is completing his Christian life properly, in accord with the pledg-

---

[112] Again, though Paul does not directly challenge the institution of slavery, his language suggests "the sort of reciprocity between master and slave that was at the heart of ancient *koinōnia*" (Johnson, *First and Second Timothy,* 290).

[113] Cf. Knight, *Pastoral Epistles,* ix.

[114] Cf. Quinn and Wacker, *First and Second Letters to Timothy,* 495.

[115] For all of these points, see Johnson, *First and Second Timothy,* 296.

es he made when he was converted (and, probably, baptized;[116] v. 12b). Recalling Timothy's confession leads Paul to reiterate his charge to keep his promises unwavering until Christ returns, just as Jesus himself refused to cave in before the Roman governor even when his life was on the line (vv. 13–14). We cannot know when the end will come, but we can trust God's timing because of his unsurpassable attributes and unique sovereignty and immortality, which should lead us into praise (vv. 15–16).[117]

Once Timothy ensures that his behavior models the right attitudes toward money, then he can command those who are well-to-do not to trust proudly in riches but in God (v. 17a). A key to preventing material possessions from becoming an idol is to give generous portions of them away. Our heavenly reward will more than compensate for what is "lost" in the process (vv. 18–19). Sandwiched between these two commands is a wonderful promise that reminds us that even this life need not reflect the asceticism that was promoted, paradoxically, by the same people who wanted to get rich from their teaching. God does generously give his people material goods for their enjoyment, particularly when they have demonstrated generosity and faithfulness with that with which he has already entrusted them (v. 17b).[118] Once again Paul personalizes this principle for Timothy, adding one more reminder to oppose the heresy that has been leading some away from genuine Christianity, and he closes by praying for God's grace to rest upon his younger colleague (vv. 20–21).

APPLICATION

Much of 1 Timothy repeats and expands the theology of Colossians and the practical applications of Titus. But there is a particular emphasis on the importance of the quality of Christian leaders here—an absolutely vital element for healthy churches. Plus there are important glimpses into distinctive women's ministries that should probably be recultivated, particularly the roles or responsibilities of deaconesses, older women, and widows. As in so many of Paul's letters, a clear contrast shines through between external lists of do's and don'ts versus inwardly generated holiness as the difference between heretical and true spirituality, a lesson several branches of the evangelical church today still desperately need to learn. This is hardly the bourgeois Christianity into which critics have accused the Pastorals of degenerating; if anything, these letters oppose the conventional morality, which so often takes the form of vices and virtues that can be legislated. Healthy, visible models of a Christian lifestyle accomplish so much more than lists of rules and regulations. And few arenas lack sufficient positive models more than the arena of stewardship.[119] It has rightly been claimed that one can learn a sizable amount about Christians' maturity by watching what they do with their wallets!

---

[116] Kelly, *Pastoral Epistles,* 142. The other main option is that it refers to his ordination.

[117] On the theme of the uniqueness of New Testament doxologies, esp. in expressing incomparable honor, see Jerome H. Neyrey, "'First,' 'Only,' 'One of a Few,' and 'No One Else': The Rhetoric of Uniqueness and the Doxologies in 1 Timothy," *Bib* 86 (2003): 59–87.

[118] For the right balance, see Johnson, *First and Second Timothy,* 315.

[119] I would like to think that I have made *some* progress in this arena; see my autobiographical reflections in Blomberg, *Neither Poverty nor Riches,* 247–53.

As for the parts of the letter that receive a disproportionate amount of contemporary attention—limitations on women in leadership, the criteria for certain office holders, and the proper exercise of church discipline—a balance of love and obedience is earnestly needed. Individual Christians, church leaders, and entire denominations too readily fall down on dogmatic positions—either firmly convinced that Timothy's instructions are merely situation specific and culture bound or equally sure of their precise, timeless applications. A considerably greater degree of humility in interpretation by both sides is in order.

ADDITIONAL QUESTIONS FOR REVIEW

1. Where is Timothy when he receives this letter? Where is Paul and what is he doing?
2. What heresy is afoot at the church that Timothy pastors? How is it similar and different from the heresy at Crete and Colossae?
3. What is the overall structure of 1 Timothy? How does the structure fit the response to the heresy?
4. What is Timothy's charge as a pastor? What are Paul's mandates for the way he fulfills these charges?
5. Name the principles that emerge with regard to women in leadership positions in the church in 1 Timothy 2:8–15. What specific features (words, grammar, syntax) in the text helps a reader arrive at these conclusions? How is verse 15 best interpreted and applied?
6. What are the criteria for church leadership for both overseers and deacons? How is the "husband of one wife" in 3:2 best understood in this context? What commands does Paul issue to those different groups in the church that hold no distinct leadership position?
7. What does Paul say about money in 1 Timothy 6? In light of this, how should both Timothy and the congregation handle their money?

SELECT BIBLIOGRAPHY

See the items listed in the bibliography for Titus that treat 1 Timothy as well. In addition, see:

COMMENTARIES

Advanced

Quinn, Jerome D., and William C. Wacker. *The First and Second Letters to Timothy.* ECC. Grand Rapids and Cambridge: Eerdmans, 2000.

Intermediate

Johnson, Luke T. *The First and Second Letters to Timothy.* AB. New York and London: Doubleday, 2001.

2 Timothy: Pass It On

INTRODUCTION

Paul is once again in prison, presumably for the second time in Rome, this time thanks to Nero's pogrom against Christians between A.D. 64 and 68. If 1 and 2 Timothy are inserted earlier into Paul's ministry in Acts than his two-year house arrest of 60–62, then of course 2 Timothy could fit at that juncture (Acts 28:30–31). But when he writes 2 Timothy, he wants Timothy to come to him quickly and to bring Mark along (2 Tim. 4:9, 11, 21), whereas Timothy and Mark were with Paul in Rome for at least part of his house arrest (Col. 1:1; 4:10; Philem. 21).[120] The conditions for the writing of 2 Timothy also appear to be more austere than they were during Paul's house arrest. Now he is literally in chains and hard to find (1:16–17). Church tradition places Paul in the Mamertine Prison, ruins of which can still be seen today, a wretched dungeon even by ancient standards.[121]

Second Timothy 4:6 suggests that Paul is convinced that death is near. The two winters alluded to in Titus 3:12 and 2 Timothy 4:21 mesh with the hypothesis of at least two years of freedom since the house arrest of Acts and a date of rearrest and execution during Nero's persecution. Now Paul has endured a preliminary hearing, which did not go well, humanly speaking (4:16; but cf. v. 17). The only remaining rescue he anticipates is the one that will take him to heaven (v. 18). *So he writes to pass the torch of his ministry in Ephesus on to Timothy in a final charge to bold witness for the gospel. This letter has been called Paul's last "testament,"[122] akin to the farewell discourses of key Old Testament figures. More technically, the epistle falls into the category of a "personal paraenetic letter,"* which exhorts someone to pursue one course of action and abstain from another.[123]

While the very fact of the letter's preservation led to its being read throughout the Christian world in church, this is the one epistle of Paul not designed in the first instance to be delivered aloud to a specific congregation. It was a personal charge to Timothy. Above all, it focuses on Timothy's character as he continues in Paul's footsteps. "It also reveals the faith and hope of a valiant apostle in the face of loneliness and adversity, just before he was executed."[124] Among the undisputed letters, Philippians provides the closest parallel.[125]

Second Timothy is also the one letter out of the three Pastorals that some scholars accept as authentic even while rejecting Pauline authorship for the other two.[126] More individuals' names appear here than in any New Testament epistle except for

---

[120] Kelly, *Pastoral Epistles*, 7.

[121] For a full list of the relevant early church traditions surrounding the composition of 2 Timothy, see Mounce, *Pastoral Epistles*, lxiii.

[122] Séan C. Martin, *Pauli Testamentum: 2 Timothy and the Last Words of Moses* (Rome: Gregorian University Press, 1997).

[123] Johnson, *First and Second Timothy*, 97.

[124] Ogden and Skinner, *Acts through Revelation*, 221.

[125] Ibid., 450.

[126] See esp. Michael Prior, *Paul the Letter-Writer and the Second Letter to Timothy* (Sheffield: JSOT, 1989).

Romans. Quite a few place names dot its pages as well.[127] While the contents of the other two Pastorals closely overlap, the topics in 2 Timothy largely differ. Whereas the styles of 1 Timothy and Titus match each other almost identically, there are a few notable differences in vocabulary and syntax in this third letter.[128] Because of all the personal references, 2 Timothy also best fits the fragment hypothesis (see above, p. 345). Marshall includes it along with 1 Timothy and Titus as "allonymous" (see above, pp. 347–48) because of the similarities with the latter two, despite observing that the case for authenticity could be strong if this epistle stood by itself.[129] Conversely, if a case for the authenticity of 1 Timothy and Titus can be made (above), the Pauline authorship of 2 Timothy becomes even more plausible. This is the position that we will adopt.

A simple, content-based outline of this short letter follows the chapter divisions that the church later inserted into 2 Timothy.

I.   Introductory Matters (1:1–18)
   A. Greetings (1:1–2)
   B. Thanksgiving and Call to Faithfulness (1:3–14)
   C. Bad and Good Models (1:15–18)
II. The Commitment That Faith Requires (2:1–26)
   A. Enduring Hardship (2:1–13)
   B. Working Hard to Be Approved (2:14–26)
III. Godlessness Described and Opposed (3:1–17)
   A. Depravity in the Last Days (3:1–9)
   B. The Antidote to the Depravity (3:10–17)
IV. Final Charge (4:1–22)
   A. Passing the Torch (4:1–8)
   B. Personal Matters (4:9–18)
   C. Final Greetings (4:19–22)

COMMENTARY

INTRODUCTORY MATTERS (1:1–18)

Greetings (1:1–2)   The beginning of verse 1 and the end of verse 2 match the corresponding parts of Paul's greeting in his first letter to Timothy exactly. In between, the wording varies just enough that, if these letters are pseudepigraphical, Paul's imitator has cleverly interwoven perfect parallelism with subtle changes. More likely this reflects Paul's own work, precisely because he is not slavishly copying himself but still adopting the same basic form.

Thanksgiving and Call to Faithfulness (1:3–14)   Unlike Titus and 1 Timothy, this final Pastoral Epistle launches immediately into the thanksgiving where we would

---

[127] For complete lists, see Collins, *I & II Timothy and Titus,* 178–80.
[128] See further Jerome Murphy-O'Connor, "2 Timothy Contrasted with 1 Timothy and Titus," *RB* 98 (1991): 403–18.
[129] Marshall with Towner, *Pastoral Epistles,* 85.

expect to find it. But only verse 3 is phrased in the form of a prayer. Yet verses 4–14 unfold seamlessly, as Paul proceeds to describe his longings (v. 4), memories (v. 5), and exhortations for Timothy (vv. 6–8, 13–14) that flow from his thanks, along with the undergirding theology (vv. 9–10) and personal model (vv. 11–12) that support his injunctions.

Paul is grateful as he remembers three generations of faithfulness in Timothy's family, first in Judaism and now in Christianity. We recall from Acts 16:1–3 that Timothy's father was Greek but his mother was Jewish. Now we learn her name, Eunice, as well as her mother's name, Lois (v. 5). It is not clear if Paul is also affirming that these two women came to Christian faith before Timothy did,[130] but in any event they have not succumbed to whatever form of Gentile religion Timothy's father would have preferred to impose on the family. Chapter 3:15 reinforces this impression as Paul points out how Timothy has learned about the Hebrew Scriptures from his infancy. So he now encourages his young friend and convert to use his spiritual gift(s) boldly in God's service (vv. 6–7). The reference to the laying on of hands in conjunction with this gift suggests that the same event is in view as in 1 Timothy 4:14, probably Timothy's ordination, which Paul could easily have participated in along with local leadership. There it appeared that his gift involved preaching and teaching; 2 Timothy 4:5 suggests that he had the gift of evangelism. Of course, he could have received more than one gift.

It is unfortunate that many people have concluded from these two verses (and perhaps 1 Cor. 16:10–11) that Timothy was a timid person in general. Paul's ministry faced enough hostility to give pause to the most courageous person. Acts and the Epistles portray Timothy remaining active as Paul's emissary nevertheless, and calls to courage rather than cowardice reflected stock charges by ancient philosophical and religious teachers as they appealed "to youthful sensitivity regarding honor and shame."[131]

So Paul tells Timothy not to be ashamed of bearing witness to Jesus or of the fact that Paul is again in prison (v. 8a). Timothy should remain holy, despite whatever pressures he feels to act otherwise, most notably to avoid persecution for his faith (vv. 8b–9a). After all, it is Christ to whom we all must ultimately answer, not any human authorities, because he alone is responsible for salvation (vv. 9–10). The theology of grace articulated here is as strong and clear as in any of the undisputed Pauline letters. Paul himself suffers for boldly preaching this message, and he remains unashamed because he trusts in the glorious outcome that awaits him in the future (vv. 11–12). So Timothy can surely imitate his teacher and spiritual father in this matter, too. Specifically, he must preserve the "sound teaching" of the true gospel (a recurring refrain throughout the Pastorals), guarding it as if it were a literal object entrusted to someone for safekeeping (vv. 13–14).[132] The interplay here between God's preserving

---

[130] More likely, Paul is not distinguishing in this context between the salvation by faith that Jews experienced before receiving the gospel and that which came to them in Christ. After all, he repeatedly makes the point in his letters how Abraham was the exemplar of faith for true believers in both communities. Cf. Johnson, *First and Second Timothy*, 342.

[131] Christopher R. Hutson, "Was Timothy Timid? On the Rhetoric of Fearlessness (1 Corinthians 16:10–11) and Cowardice (2 Timothy 1:7)," *BibRes* 42 (1997): 58.

[132] Or else the "deposit" is Paul's own life, which he has entrusted to God.

grace and human responsibility to persevere fits perfectly with what we have seen throughout the epistles surveyed thus far. God has the power to keep Timothy safe, spiritually speaking (v. 12), by means of the Holy Spirit who indwells him (v. 14b). As a result, Timothy must do all he can to remain faithful (vv. 13–14a).

BAD AND GOOD MODELS (1:15–18)   By way of illustration, Paul contrasts his companions in Asia Minor, who have deserted him (v. 15), with the household of Onesiphorus, which has faithfully and sacrificially ministered to him both when he was living in Ephesus and during his Roman imprisonment (vv. 16–18). Verse 15 can scarcely mean that the entire Ephesian church has apostatized; it more likely refers to those from Asia Minor who had most recently been with Paul in Rome.[133] Why Paul highlights Phygelus and Hermogenes is impossible to determine since we know nothing more about these two men. Clearly he prefers to dwell on the positive model of Onesiphorus's family, even if they proved the exception to the rule on that particular occasion.

THE COMMITMENT THAT FAITH REQUIRES (2:1–26)

Enduring Hardship (2:1–13)   *Chapter 2:1–2 encapsulates the thesis of this epistle.* As Paul is passing the torch of ministry to his disciple, Timothy, he wants him in general to be empowered by God's grace and specifically to keep the chain of godly leadership unbroken. Lasting results from any ministry of teaching and discipleship require the training of faithful successors who will in turn pass what they have learned on to others so that the pattern keeps repeating itself.[134] This responsibility, like faithful Christian service more generally, especially under difficult circumstances, demands the avoidance of entangling commitments that would distract or deter. Three analogies from ordinary human affairs make the point crystal clear—soldiers avoiding civilian pursuits, athletes spending extra time in training, and farmers working long hours in their fields (vv. 3–6). But in each case, Paul reminds Timothy of the rewards, expecting that he can draw his own parallels in the spiritual realm (v. 7). Believers who are serious about successful service to Christ will work harder than any other people, Christian and non-Christian alike, and yet avoid "spreading themselves too thin."

As elsewhere, Paul illustrates this single-minded devotion by appealing to the examples of Jesus and himself. Both men suffered greatly, but Jesus was rewarded by his resurrection and Paul looks forward to his coming eternal glory (vv. 8–10). "Such a conviction transforms victimization into victory."[135] Another "trustworthy saying" offers further support (vv. 11–13). This poetic quatrain combines synonymous with antithetical parallelism to stress the rewards of perseverance despite suffering. Of course, outright rejection of Christ leads him to reject us as well. But simple lapses

---

[133] Or that almost all of the Ephesian Christians "disassociated themselves from Paul during his arrest and imprisonment" (Mounce, *Pastoral Epistles,* 494).

[134] Knight (*Pastoral Epistles,* 391) links the teaching ministry here with the responsibility of the elders/overseers in 1 Timothy, concluding that Paul has elders in view here, too, but this may be overly narrowing the focus.

[135] deSilva, *Introduction,* 756.

THE CHAIN OF CHRISTIAN LEADERSHIP

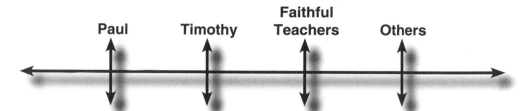

Paul   **Timothy**   **Faithful Teachers**   **Others**

Your ministry requires disciples who will train others to keep passing the torch.

Four Key Stages of 2 Timothy 2:2

in faith cannot separate us from him because, through the Spirit, he lives in believers and he cannot reject himself.[136]

Working Hard to Be Approved (2:14–26) Paul's encouragement to perseverance continues in this section. Here the controlling metaphor is a hard-working laborer approved by God. In spiritual matters the crucial backdrop for all acceptable service is responsible interpretation and application of God's Word (v. 15).[137] Herein lies the antidote to the destructive quarreling over semantics and the godless chatter of verses 14 and 16. Such behavior soon lands one in outright false teaching; apparently the Ephesian heresy is still lurking in the background (vv. 17–18a). Here Paul focuses on its denial of the resurrection. As in 1 Corinthians 15, "Christians" with Greek backgrounds were probably believing only in the immortality of the soul and not also in the resurrection of the body. Akin to later full-fledged Gnostics, they may also have developed an "overly realized eschatology," which asserted that the only kind of resurrection to which a believer could look forward was a spiritual one that occurred already in this life as people grasped the liberating knowledge of this elitist sect (v. 18b).[138] But God knows those who are truly his and will protect them from the heresy, even as they intentionally disassociate themselves from it (v. 19).

Moreover, as long as a person is alive, he or she can turn from damning beliefs and practices (vv. 20–26). Employing again the metaphor of honorable and dishonorable "vessels" (vv. 20–21; recall under Rom. 9:21–24), Paul reiterates the possibility and the urgency of those caught up in the heresy (or any other false system) to escape from the devil's snares and purify themselves by turning or returning to Christ.[139] Those not yet trapped should do everything possible to avoid the behavior of those

---

[136] Cf. Marshall with Towner, *Pastoral Epistles,* 740–42.

[137] The "rightly dividing" of the KJV misled many people into thinking Paul was talking about starting and stopping at proper places in the text, perhaps even with verse-by-verse commentary or exposition (notwithstanding the fact that versification was not added until the Middle Ages). The "correctly handles" of the NIV avoids this problem. Johnson (*First and Second Timothy,* 385) suggests "accurately delineate" to preserve the etymology of "rightly" plus "cut."

[138] Cf. ibid., 392–93. About Hymenaeus and Philetus we know nothing else.

[139] Clearly nothing implying the predestination of the lost appears in this context, making it less likely that it does in Romans 9 either. See above, p. 254. Cf. further Marshall with Towner, *Pastoral Epistles,* 763.

who have already been caught. Yet, despite the great dangers associated with the heresy, Paul recognizes that gentle rebuttals will work better than more combative ones. After all, if part of the problem involves too many arguments and quarrels, a polemical response will only perpetuate the debilitating pattern (vv. 22–26).

GODLESSNESS DESCRIBED AND OPPOSED (3:1–17)

Depravity in the Last Days (3:1–9)   The specific false teaching in Ephesus reminds Paul that godless thought and behavior will characterize the period preceding Christ's return (v. 1). But recall that the New Testament writers uniformly understood themselves to be living in those last days (Acts 2:17; James 5:3; 2 Pet. 3:3). The sins of verses 2–5, not limited to the overtly irreligious but present among those superficially religious as well (v. 5), have reappeared, to varying degrees, in every era and culture of history. The key thought that ties these sins together is that of misdirected love—toward oneself as the center of every aspect of life. Verses 6–9 seem to particularize the problems again, in light of the Ephesian heresy, by noting that spiritually immature women proved particularly susceptible to the false teachers' wiles.[140] These were probably the wealthy women who had the leisure time to learn from the false teachers but not the discernment to reject their message. But even then, Paul is convinced people will see through the charade, just as the Egyptian magicians in Pharaoh's court could imitate only the first few miracles that God worked through Moses and so were eventually exposed and destroyed. The basic story appears in Exodus 7:8–8:19; the names are furnished by later Jewish tradition (CD 5:17–19; Targum Ps.-Jonathan 1.3, 7.2).

The Antidote to the Depravity (3:10–17)   To counter the sins perpetuated by the false teachers, Paul stresses faithfulness to the gospel. Once again, he points to himself as a model that Timothy can follow, especially during persecutions, naming specifically the events described in Acts 13–14 in and around Timothy's hometown (vv. 10–11). Sooner or later, all godly believers will experience some sort of harassment or ostracism for their faith (v. 12). Indeed, things will get worse as what we might call the "last days of the last days" draw near (v. 13). But whatever the timetable, God's people can always stand firm by imitating faithful fellow Christians and letting scriptural values permeate their souls and guide their lives (vv. 14–17).

Verses 15b–17 are among the most important in the New Testament about the nature and purpose of the Bible, which of course for Paul, when he penned these words, would have been the Hebrew Scriptures or what Christians now call the Old Testament. Still, as the process of canonizing the New Testament unfolded, much of what Christians meant by including a book in this second testament is affirmed in these verses.[141] Scripture's primary purpose is to bring people to the salvation that is available in Christ. But their divine origin (*theopneustos* in v. 16 means more than merely "inspired" but "God-breathed" as in the NIV) makes them useful for in-

---

[140] The description of these particular women is not an affirmation about their gender as a whole, but about "the dilemma of women within a certain societal class in the Greco-Roman world" (Johnson, *First and Second Timothy,* 412). Similarly, Quinn and Wacker, *First and Second Letters to Timothy,* 725.

[141] See esp. Bruce, *The Canon of Scripture.*

struction and training in godly living, both positively and negatively, as well. While theologians have debated at length the nuances of the inspiration and inerrancy of Scripture,[142] Paul's primary emphasis here is on their relevance and their ability to produce spiritual maturity.

FINAL CHARGE (4:1–22)

Passing the Torch (4:1–8) Paul begins to wind up the last letter we know of that he ever wrote by calling Timothy once again to use his gifts faithfully regardless of the circumstances (vv. 1–5). "In season and out of season" (v. 2a) sums it up succinctly.[143] Even as these two men are already experiencing in their lives, Christian doctrine will become even more unpopular as the time of Christ's return draws near. People will believe just about anything, however mythical, except the truth (vv. 3–4). Different tactics will be required for different situations. Reasoned argument, direct confrontation, and positive help all play a role, combined with great patience and careful teaching (v. 2b). Above all, Timothy must remain faithful to his ministry of preaching and evangelism (vv. 2, 5).[144]

Soon Paul will have no further opportunity to remind Timothy of these responsibilities. Just before writing Philippians, Paul thought he might die and described the process as "being poured out like a drink offering" (Phil. 2:17). Here he repeats the identical expression (*spendomai*), but this time he realizes his end has truly come (2 Tim. 4:6). Just as he encouraged Timothy to "fight the good fight"[145] in 1 Timothy 1:18, now he avers that he has done precisely that. Changing the metaphor, he has finished the race. Either way, what he means is that he has "kept the faith" (v. 7). So he awaits his heavenly crown, which is the righteousness of eternal life, available to all who long for the parousia because they know they are Christ's (v. 8).

Personal Matters (4:9–18) "The end of Paul's final letter is a mixture of gloom and glory, of exasperation and exultation."[146] As in the undisputed letters, Paul inserts a variety of personal remarks and instructions before signing off for good.[147] Precisely because he knows his time is short, he hopes Timothy can come to him in Rome quite soon. With the coming of winter (v. 21), he will need his cloak, and he asks for parchment scrolls as well, probably a reference to the Hebrew Scriptures.[148] We are glad to hear he has been sufficiently reconciled with Mark that he wants him to come also. Luke alone remains his companion at the moment; others have left him, some by his commissioning and others for worldly motives. The cast of characters partly

---

[142] For a classic and accurate exposition, see Benjamin B. Warfield, *The Inspiration and Authority of the Bible* (Philadelphia: Presbyterian & Reformed, 1948), esp. pp. 131–66 and 245–96. The translation, "Every inspired Scripture is also profitable" is grammatically far less likely; see Marshall with Towner, *Pastoral Epistles,* 792–93.

[143] On which, see further Abraham J. Malherbe, "'In Season and out of Season': 2 Timothy 4:2," *JBL* 103 (1984): 235–43.

[144] On the latter, cf. Alastair Campbell, "'The Work of an Evangelist,'" *EQ* 64 (1992): 117–29.

[145] As an adjective modifying the noun "fight," "good" does not describe how Paul fought, but the nature of the battle. Translating these two words as "noble contest" perhaps erases the ambiguity best. Kelly (*Pastoral Epistles,* 208) renders the entire sentence, "I have fought in the noble match."

[146] Ogden and Skinner, *Acts through Revelation,* 223.

[147] Cf. further Malcolm C. Bligh, "Seventeen Verses Written for Timothy (2 Tim. 4:6–22)," *ET* 109 (1998): 364–69.

[148] Skeat, "2 Timothy 4:13."

overlaps the lists of names found at the ends of the various Prison Epistles, perhaps confirming that he is again in Rome, though not in the exact circumstances of those previous letters (vv. 9–13). The one new place name is Dalmatia (v. 9), the province that would have included Illyricum (cf. Rom. 15:19)

Paul singles out Alexander the metalworker as a particularly egregious opponent of whom Timothy should beware, too (vv. 14–15). It is tempting to assign this individual to the pagan guild of silversmiths in Ephesus who rioted in Acts 19:23–41, but we have no way of knowing this. After all, it is often professing Christians who cause the most trouble for Paul.[149] He also refers to a preliminary hearing in which no one supported him but, like Jesus on the cross (Luke 23:34), he still prays for the forgiveness of those who deserted him. What counted was the Lord's presence and empowerment as he proclaimed God's Word before this Gentile court (vv. 16–17). Of particular note is Paul's triumphant affirmation, in spite of it all, that the Lord will rescue him, not *from* dying, but *for* his eternal kingdom. A ringing "Amen" punctuates his burst of praise (v. 18).

Final Greetings (4:19–22)   The first four characters we have seen before; the other five appear only in these verses within the New Testament. A strong early church tradition names Linus as the second bishop of Rome after Simon Peter (Irenaeus, *Against Heresies* 3.3.3.). Paul blesses his spiritual son and wishes him grace one last time.

APPLICATION

Every local church is always only one generation away from potential extinction. Unless we are as concerned as Paul was to keep making disciples, training them in the faith, and leading them toward maturity, we have no guarantees that a Christian witness will continue in any given location after the current believers have all left or died off. Christ may have promised that nothing could destroy his church worldwide as a whole (Matt. 16:18), but Christian presence in various places throughout church history has often ebbed and flowed drastically over time. Nowhere does this observation prove more striking than in many of the communities Paul himself evangelized in what today is the country of Turkey. After more than thirteen hundred years of aggressive Muslim activity there, Christianity exists only in tiny pockets and by no means in every city in which Paul originally preached. Commitment to preserving and growing God's witness demands single-minded devotion, hard work, reliance on God's Word, and trust in his ultimate reward, while recognizing the likelihood of significant opposition in this life. If it does not materialize today, it will on some other day because all who desire to live according to God's desires will be persecuted. Long-term "Christians" who have never experienced any negative response to their faith should ask themselves if anyone really knows in detail what they believe. And if no one does, it is also worth asking if they even have genuine, saving faith.

---

[149] There is no good reason, however, to identify him with Alexander the Jew, referred to in Acts 19:33.

Faith-filled believers, on the other hand, will "pour themselves out" for the sake of Christ and humanity. This does not imply "workaholism" or require "burn out" but rather an unflagging commitment to one's calling and the exercise of one's spiritual gifts in the context of Christian nurture and renewal, so that one *can* serve God and others, whether or not in a professional capacity, throughout one's entire life.

ADDITIONAL QUESTIONS FOR REVIEW

1. What is the purpose and genre of 2 Timothy?
2. What circumstances generated this letter?
3. What is a good thesis statement of Paul's second letter to Timothy? What application does Paul's charge to Timothy have for church leaders today?
4. In view of 2 Timothy, what should be a leader's primary tasks? What is at stake if the instruction is not heeded?
5. What specific theological doctrines are addressed by key verses in 2 Timothy? What are those verses, and what do they contribute to the New Testament understanding of those doctrines?

SELECT BIBLIOGRAPHY

See the items listed in the bibliographies for Titus and 1 Timothy that treat 2 Timothy as well. In addition, see:

COMMENTARIES

Introductory

Stott, John R. W. *Guard the Gospel: The Message of 2 Timothy.* BST. Leicester and Downers Grove: IVP, 1973.

OTHER BOOKS

Martin, Séan. *Pauli Testamentum: 2 Timothy and the Last Words of Moses.* Rome: Gregorian University Press, 1997.

Prior, Michael. *Paul the Letter-Writer and the Second Letter to Timothy.* Sheffield: JSOT, 1989.

PART 3

OTHER NEW TESTAMENT WRITINGS

9

The Epistle of James: "Faith without Works Is Dead"

INTRODUCTION

AUTHORSHIP

Early church tradition (e.g., Origen, Jerome, Augustine, and the Council of Carthage) strongly supports the identification of the author of this book with James, the (half-) brother[1] of Jesus. There are three or four men by this name in the New Testament, but there are good reasons for eliminating the others. James the apostle, brother of John and son of Zebedee, was martyred under Herod Agrippa I in A.D. 44 (see Acts 12:1–2), probably too early in the development of the church to have written this letter. The other apostle by the name of James, the son of Alpheus, never attained any prominent position in the early church as far as we know. James the less (or "the little"), mentioned only as one of the sons of one of the Marys who was present at the crucifixion and the empty tomb, may well be the same person as the son of Alpheus. But if he is a different individual, we know nothing more about him.

James, the brother of Jesus (Mark 6:3 pars.), however, became an influential leader among the Jerusalem elders (Acts 12:17) and eventually the head of the Christian church there, at least by 49 (Acts 15:13). He apparently still held that position in about 57 when Paul returned to Jerusalem after his third missionary journey. Most have believed that this James did not become a follower of Jesus before the crucifixion, based on Jesus' attitude toward his nuclear family in Mark 3:31–34 and parallels and on his brothers' skepticism toward him in John 7:1–5. Of course it is possible, as the events unfolded that would lead Christ to the cross, that James began to change his attitude,[2] but the fact that Jesus singles him out for a special resurrection appearance (1 Cor. 15:7) suggests that he may have become a believer only at that time.

As we will see below, this same James is probably the brother of Jude, author of the second to the last book in the New Testament (Jude 1; cf. Mark 6:3). Early Christian tradition uniformly described him as a very pious man, given to much

---

[1] As Roman Catholicism developed, with its doctrine of the perpetual virginity of Mary, alternate understandings of "brother" developed as well, including the ideas that *adelphos* referred to a more distant relative of some kind or that Joseph had other children by a previous wife. But the most natural inference from Matthew 1:25 is that Joseph and Mary had other children after Jesus was born, and *adelphos* only very rarely means anything in *Koinē* Greek other than a physical or spiritual sibling.

[2] See esp. John Painter, *Just James: The Brother of Jesus in History and Tradition* (Columbia: University of South Carolina Press, rev. 2004).

prayer and devoted to a thoroughly Jewish form of Christian faith.[3] The apparent discovery of his ossuary in Jerusalem in the early twenty-first century[4] has revived international interest in a figure who was quite influential in early Christianity, even after his death, but who has been comparatively neglected in the centuries since.

Modern critics have frequently argued that this letter is pseudonymous, though not to the same degree, as with Ephesians or the Pastoral Epistles.[5] Reasons for rejecting James as author largely fall under two main headings.

First, it is alleged that his style of Greek is too good for an untutored carpenter's son writing in a second language. Yet more than three hundred years of Hellenistic influence in Israel, combined with James's possible use of an amanuensis who improved his style, make it difficult to say just what a Galilean Jewish construction worker could or could not have written.[6] Add to that the possibility of a later redactor making similar improvements, and the allegation does not get one very far.

Second, it is claimed that James's teaching is too Jewish; that is, that there is not enough distinctively Christian material in the epistle. Take away the two brief references to Jesus in 1:1 and 2:1, and there seems to be little that could not have been written by a non-Christian Jewish author. The audience is referred to as the twelve tribes (of Israel; 1:1), their congregations can be called synagogues (NIV "meeting"; 2:2), and there is no reference to the Holy Spirit in the letter at all (though see the NIV marg. on 4:5). In fact, it has been argued that "wisdom," quasi-personified, has replaced the role of the Spirit as it seems to do, at least in part, in Proverbs and other later Jewish wisdom literature.[7]

But an early Jewish feel to the letter is just what we would expect if it was an epistle written to Jewish believers in the first decades of the fledgling movement. James may seem different from other New Testament documents precisely because we have no other examples of early Christian literature from this period and branch of the church. At the same time, the letter is dotted with allusions to Jesus' teaching, especially in the Sermon on the Mount, so its Christian pedigree should not be questioned.[8] Ironically, the concerns that the letter is either too Greek or too Jewish largely cancel each other out![9]

---

[3] For a detailed presentation of the biblical and extrabiblical information we have about this James, see Hershel Shanks and Ben Witherington III, *The Brother of Jesus: The Dramatic Story and Meaning of the First Archaeological Link to Jesus and His Family* (San Francisco: HarperSanFrancisco, 2003), 91–223. Much more briefly, cf. James B. Adamson, *James: The Man and His Message* (Grand Rapids: Eerdmans, 1989), 19–24.

[4] In detail, Shanks and Witherington, *The Brother of Jesus,* 1–87; briefly, Craig A. Evans, *Jesus and the Ossuaries* (Waco: Baylor University Press, 2003), 112–22. There are, however, some reasons for doubting the authenticity of the full ossuary inscription, hence our use of the adjective "apparent."

[5] For a thorough discussion of the issues, see Luke T. Johnson, *The Letter of James* (New York and London: Doubleday, 1995), 89–123.

[6] See esp. the massive two-volume study by Martin Hengel, *Judaism and Hellenism* (London: SCM; Philadelphia: Fortress, 1974).

[7] J. A. Kirk, "The Meaning of Wisdom in James," *NTS* 16 (1969): 24–38. See the more nuanced evaluation and modification of this hypothesis by Mariam J. Kamell, "Wisdom in James: An Examination and Comparison of the Roles of Wisdom and the Holy Spirit in James" (Denver Seminary: M.A. Thesis, 2003).

[8] See the helpful charts in Peter H. Davids, *The Epistle of James* (Exeter: Paternoster; Grand Rapids: Eerdmans, 1982), 147–48. For detailed unpacking, see Patrick J. Hartin, *James and the Q Sayings of Jesus* (Sheffield: JSOT, 1991).

[9] For a thorough demonstration that the letter ascribed to James could well have been penned by a Palestinian Jewish-Christian not long after A.D. 40, in conjunction with pervasive eschatological presuppositions of that milieu, see Todd C. Penner, *The Epistle of James and Eschatology* (Sheffield: SAP, 1996).

DATE

If the letter is authentic rather than pseudonymous, then it must be dated prior to the martyrdom of James, the brother of Jesus, in A.D. 62 (see Josephus, *Antiquities* 20.9.11). Perhaps the most vexing theological problem of this epistle throughout Christian history has been its relationship to the writings of Paul. Does James's teaching about faith needing to be supplemented with works contradict Paul's insistence that salvation comes by grace through faith apart from human works? We will discuss this issue below (pp. 397–98); here what is relevant is the question of whether James is consciously responding to Paul, or perhaps to a misinterpretation of Paul. If he is, then we probably need to allow enough time for the major letters of Paul to have circulated some, and we are looking at a date close to the end of James's life, probably at the beginning of the decade of the 60s.[10] If he is writing independently of Paul, then he likely composed this epistle between 44 and 49. Before Peter's departure from Jerusalem in 44, James probably did not have enough authority or reputation to be sending out a missive of this nature, whereas after the Apostolic Council in 49, he would have known Paul's teaching well enough that he could not have been writing independently of it.[11]

Many commentators, skeptical of James's authorship, place this epistle in the last third of the first century.[12] Those who think the brother of Jesus did write the letter, including almost all evangelicals, are fairly evenly split between the early and late dates, though the most recent round of scholarship is increasingly favoring an early date. While an outright contradiction between James and Paul seems unlikely, it is quite imaginable that the antinomian factions Paul has to address in several of his letters could have distorted his emphasis on faith versus the works of the law and claimed that good behavior was optional for Christian believers. James would then have had to rebut this distortion soundly. On the other hand, if this were the case, one wonders if he would not have clarified his terms a bit more, so that his rebuttal would sound less like an outright contradiction. It is also arguable that the quarrelling with which James's audience is involved, especially in 4:1–4, indicates a date just before James's death, as frustration with Rome's abuse was approaching a boiling point.

But it is probably better to opt for the early date when James could not yet have known how Paul would word things in his letters. James's epistle, addressed only to Jewish Christians, likely did not circulate nearly as widely around the empire as Paul's letters did, and there is no reason James should have reproduced the exact wording of his letter at the Apostolic Council. So it is more conceivable that Paul wrote later than James, but without knowing the seeming discord that his wording

---

[10] So, e.g., Ralph P. Martin, *James* (Waco: Word, 1988).

[11] So, e.g., Douglas J. Moo, *The Letter of James* (Grand Rapids and Cambridge: Eerdmans; Leicester: IVP, 2000).

[12] It is possible, though, to argue for a post-Jamesian date and thus for pseudonymous authorship, yet see the quarrelling in the book fit the period of A.D. 62–66 as tensions grew between Jews in Palestine and Syria and the Roman "imperialists." See esp. David H. Edgar, *Has God Not Chosen the Poor? The Social Setting of the Epistle of James* (Sheffield: SAP, 2001).

would generate.[13] *If James was written in the second half of the 40s, then it is almost certainly the earliest of the New Testament or any other Christian documents of which we know.*

AUDIENCE AND CONTEXT

The "early and late rains" of 5:7 (NIV: "autumn and spring rains") characterize only the eastern half of the Roman Empire and best fit the climate of Israel or Syria at the eastern end of the Mediterranean Sea. The setting of rich unbelievers oppressing poor Christians (2:6–7) in an agricultural context (5:1–6) fits the practice of many Jewish (and a few Roman) landlords who owned large farms in Palestine and Syria and relied on what today we might call migrant workers for their labor, many of whom were often unfairly treated. *Given the uniformly Jewish tenor of the letter, there is no reason not to take the reference to "the twelve tribes scattered among the nations" in 1:1 entirely literally and to understand James's audience to be largely poor and exploited Jewish Christian day-laborers, probably in Syria, in an unspecified number of local congregations.* Given the tension in the early church between Christian and non-Christian Jews, such marginalization could well have been exacerbated for these hired hands who claimed to be both Jewish and Christian.[14] It is possible to view the *diaspora* of this verse (masked in the NIV by the translation "scattered") as the scattering of Jewish believers after the stoning of Stephen (Acts 8:1), in which case some of the addressees might have remained within Israel. But the far more common use of "diaspora" in the first century applied the expression to Jews living outside the land.

GENRE AND STRUCTURE

A quite different approach to James analyzes it as an "apostolic letter" or "encyclical" to the entire diaspora.[15] On this view, James had the authority to address Jewish Christians throughout the entire Roman Empire and did so in this document. This view, however, runs the risk of "intercepting the text," as Elsa Tamez describes it,[16] by failing adequately to account for the situation-specific details in the letter that would not have been true of all Jewish believers at that time and by muting the strident calls for punishment against the oppressors and for liberation of the oppressed. Nor do any of the other New Testament epistles even hint at James's influence in any wide swath of the empire; even the much larger and well-established Jewish leadership did not wield that much power (recall Acts 28:21).

An older form-critical school of thought, associated particularly with Martin Dibelius, viewed James as the closest New Testament analogy to Old Testament

---

[13] See further Davids, *James,* 2–22. Davids accounts for the features that point some to a later date by postulating the influence of a redactor who subsequently edited the document a little (12–13), while Patrick J. Hartin (*James* [Collegeville: Liturgical, 2003], 25) suggests a close associate of James, with excellent Greek, writing in his name shortly after his death to churches in the diaspora who recognized his authority.

[14] See further ibid., 28–34. Cf. also throughout Elsa Tamez, *The Scandalous Message of James: Faith Without Works Is Dead* (New York: Crossroad, rev. 2002).

[15] So esp. Richard Bauckham, *James* (London and New York: Routledge, 1999), 11–28; cf. Donald J. Verseput, "Genre and Story: The Community Setting of the Epistle of James," *CBQ* 62 (2000): esp. 99–102.

[16] Tamez, *James,* 1–11.

and intertestamental Jewish *wisdom literature* and therefore assumed that, just as in Proverbs or Sirach, no tightly knit structure need be present. This approach viewed James as compiling some of Jesus' sayings, other proverbs, minihomilies, and his own thoughts into a group of small, unified passages without any necessary overarching outline. It was clear that in a number of places, James moved from one text to the next by "catchwords," terms from one verse that were repeated (or alluded to by synonyms) in the subsequent verse and that generated the next thought. For example, in 1:2 "trials" is echoed in verse 3 by "testing." "Perseverance" links verses 3 and 4. "Not lacking" in verse 4 leads to "lacking" in verse 5. Asking connects verses 5 and 6a, while doubting appears in verses 6a, 6b and 7. One cannot identify catchwords to link every verse in the letter, but there are a striking number of other examples, and one can understand why many perceived a more "stream of consciousness" kind of writing to James's narrative flow.[17]

A CHIASTIC OUTLINE OF JAMES

Introduction (1:1)	A	B	C
3 Key Themes Statement 1	Trials (1:2–4)	Wisdom (1:5–8)	Riches/Poverty (1:9–11)
3 Key Themes Statement 2	Temptation (1:12–18)	Speech (1:19–26)	The Dispossessed (1:27)
Expansion of Theme C			Riches vs. Poverty and the Dispossessed (2:1–26)
Expansion of Theme B		Speech and Wisdom (3:1–4:17)	
Expansion of Theme A	Trials/ Temptations (5:1–18)		
Conclusion (5:19–20)			

More recently, this approach has been widely rejected in favor of one that sees James as a purposeful theologian with an overarching structure in mind (just as form criticism in Gospels studies has largely given way to redaction and even literary criticism). Unfortunately, there is no widespread agreement as to the specific outline. Several proposals of *an extended chiastic structure,* however, hold out considerable promise. We will adopt, with minor modifications, one that has become best-known through the commentary of Peter Davids. In it, chapter 1 presents the three key

---

[17] Cf. throughout Martin Dibelius, *James,* rev. Heinrich Greeven (Philadelphia: Fortress, 1976).

themes of the book twice through rapidly.[18] Then chapters 2–5 elaborate each of these themes in reverse order, with a brief conclusion at the end. Whether or not James intended anything this precise, this kind of outline has the merit of accurately highlighting three crucial themes in the letter. If it *is* largely on target, it suggests that the central theme of wealth and poverty is the most important of the three, a point usually missed in the (wealthy!) Northern and Western hemispheres!

   I. Greetings (1:1)
  II. Statement of Three Key Themes (1:2–11)
       A. Trials in the Christian Life (1:2–4)
       B. Wisdom (1:5–8)
       C. Riches and Poverty (1:9–11)
 III. Restatement of the Three Themes (1:12–27)
       A. Trials/Temptations in Relation to God (1:12–18)
       B. Wisdom in the Area of Speech (1:19–26)
       C. The "Have-Nots" and the Responsibility of the "Haves" (1:27)
  IV. The Three Themes Expanded (2:1–5:18)
       A. Riches and Poverty (2:1–26)
           1. Favoritism Condemned (2:1–13)
           2. The Problem of Faith without Works (2:14–26)
       B. Wisdom and Speech (3:1–4:17)
           1. The Dangers of the Tongue (3:1–12)
           2. Unspiritual vs. Spiritual Wisdom (3:13–18)
           3. The Two Kinds of Wisdom Illustrated: Violence vs. Humility (4:1–12)
           4. Boastful Speech (4:13–17)
       C. Trials and Temptations (5:1–18)
           1. External Persecution (5:1–6)
           2. A Patient Response (5:7–12)
           3. Sickness (5:13–18)
   V. Closing (5:19–20)

COMMENTARY

GREETINGS (1:1)

Little needs to be added here that has not already been presented in our introduction above. That James does not call himself an apostle fits our identification of this man. Some find it surprising that he does not stress his family ties to Jesus, but if he

---

[18] See Davids, *James,* 22–29. An intriguing alternative sees essentially the same three themes introduced twice in 1:1–21 (though labeling the third theme as "the great reversal"), but then finds in 5:7–20 a double presentation of (a) an exhortation to endure; (b) an OT example; and (c) the confirmation of wisdom. In between, the three elements of 1:19 are unpacked: (1) "quick to hear" (1:22–2:26), (2) "slow to speak" (3:1–18), and (3) "slow to anger" (4:1–5:6). See Robert W. Wall, *Community of the Wise: The Letter of James* (Valley Forge: Trinity, 1997). For a thorough survey of recent approaches, see Mark E. Taylor, "Recent Scholarship on the Structure of James," *CBR* 3 (2004): 86–115.

did not come to faith during the earthly life of his special brother, such reticence is understandable.

STATEMENT OF THREE KEY THEMES (1:2–11)

Trials in the Christian Life (1:2–4)   James begins with the theme of trials, no doubt because of the poverty and the socioeconomic and religious oppression that his audience was experiencing. His first command may be the most challenging in the entire letter: "Consider it pure joy . . . whenever you face trials of many kinds" (v. 2). The joy James has in mind, of course, cannot be an emotion, because emotions cannot be commanded (and "no discipline seems pleasant at the time"—Heb. 12:11). Instead, it must refer to a deeply seated contentment that we can choose to adopt, born from the conviction that God is working for our good in the difficult circumstances, bringing us along the path toward maturity (vv. 3–4).[19] The fact that James uses the verbs "consider" and "know" demonstrates further that *he is talking about a mind-set rather than a feeling.*

Wisdom (1:5–8)   Second, James introduces the theme of wisdom. He may still have the context of trials in view, though his principles are scarcely limited to that context. When we need wisdom, we must ask God in faith, not doubting (vv. 5–6). The doubter is *dipsychos,* literally, "double-souled" (v. 8), and will not receive the wisdom he or she requests (v. 7). This unusual Greek word does not appear in any pre-Christian literature that we know of, so it may well be that James coined it.[20] It appears again in 4:8, where it refers to someone not wholeheartedly committed to God. There is thus no support here for the "name it and claim it" theology that pretends God will give us everything we ask for if we just believe strongly enough. James's point is not that we must know *how* our prayers will be answered in advance; rather, we must be certain of *who* will answer them. *We must make sure that we are trusting in the God of Jesus Christ rather than any other god.*[21]

Riches and Poverty (1:9–11)   Third, James introduces the theme of riches and poverty, the specific problem responsible for producing the trials of the Christians to whom he is writing. The major exegetical question in these verses is whether both the poor and rich are "brothers," that is, fellow Christians. The term appears explicitly only in verse 9, where it is modified by the adjective *tapeinos.* This is not the most common New Testament word for "humble," and more likely means someone in "humble" or even "humiliating" *circumstances.* Such Christians can be thankful at least for their eternally valuable spiritual possessions. Some commentators think

---

[19] Cf. Wall, *Community of the Wise,* 48. "Perfection" in this context does not first of all mean the sinlessness that will be ours in the life to come, but a maturity that is significantly achievable in this life. The same is true of Jesus' teaching in Matt. 5:48, to which James appears to be alluding. See Patrick J. Hartin, "Call to Be Perfect through Suffering (James 1, 2–4): The Concept of Perfection in the Epistle of James and the Sermon on the Mount," *Bib* 71 (1996): 477–92. This approach is then fleshed out in idem, *A Spirituality of Perfection: Faith in Action in the Letter of James* (Collegeville: Liturgical, 1999).

[20] Stanley E. Porter, "Is *Dipsuchos* (James 1,8; 4,8) a 'Christian' Word?" *Bib* 41 (1990): 469–98.

[21] Cf. George M. Stulac, *James* (Leicester and Downers Grove: IVP, 1993), 43: "The *doubt* then is a vacillation between self-reliance and God-reliance."

that verses 10–11 describe only the non-Christian rich, but this requires the admonition for them to take pride in their low position to reflect bitter irony.

In other words, what James is really commanding would be the exact opposite of the literal meaning of his words. But he does this nowhere else in his letter; indeed his clearest examples of irony mean exactly what they say (5:1–6). *So it is better to understand the term "brother" carrying over to James's comments about the rich,* in which case he is reminding them of the temporal and transient nature of their wealth. Instead of boasting in their material possessions, they should glory in their lowly, dependent condition before the God of the universe.[22]

RESTATEMENT OF THE THREE THEMES (1:12–27)

Trials/Temptations in Relation to God (1:12–18) James begins again with the topic of trials (v. 12), but turns quickly to talk about temptation (vv. 13–18). The same Greek word *peirasmos* can be translated either way, depending on the context. *One set of external circumstances can either be a "trial" that believers allow to help them mature or become a seduction to sin.* Our response is what proves determinative.[23] Those who prove faithful under trials will receive the heavenly crown, which is eternal life (v. 12). Those who become bitter or give in to some other type of sin should not blame God, because he does not directly cause evil, and even the evil he allows he intends to use for some good purpose (recall Rom. 8:28). Moreover, each believer has the power through the Spirit to resist temptations (recall 1 Cor. 10:13). Therefore, when Christians give in to temptations, they have only themselves to blame (vv. 13–14).[24] But unchecked sin can have disastrous consequences and in a worst-case scenario demonstrates that a person never truly was saved (v. 15). Intriguingly, neither does James here permit believers to blame the devil for their sins, even though he will later show that he knows all about the devil's attacks (4:7).

If God does not cause evil, then everything he produces must be good and perfect (vv. 16–17). Preeminent among his good gifts is the regeneration that comes through the message of the gospel. As in Paul's writings, James can envision people's conversions to Christ like the early fruits on a plant or tree that prove harbingers of a much greater harvest to come (v. 18).[25]

Wisdom in the Area of Speech (1:19–26) One might imagine that this section is not really about wisdom at all; at least the term itself does not appear here. But when we see speech and wisdom juxtaposed in 3:1–12 and 13–18, we suspect that they are linked in James's mind. The contents of 1:19–26 certainly describe wise speech. If the actual words for "wise" or "wisdom" are not used, the good deeds "done in the

---

[22] See further Blomberg, *Neither Poverty nor Riches,* 149–51.

[23] Cf. Douglas J. Moo, *The Letter of James* (Grand Rapids: Eerdmans; Leicester: IVP, 1985), 71–72.

[24] Cf. Joel Marcus, "The Evil Inclination in the Epistle of James," *CBQ* 44 (1982): 606–21.

[25] The upshot of vv. 2–18 is thus to highlight two possible patterns of behavior in response to *peirasmoi* (the plural form). Difficult external circumstances can be viewed positively as God's testing, designed to create in us perseverance, the end result of which is maturity/perfection. Or they can be viewed negatively as temptations caused by our own evil desires, which can lead to sin and ultimately to death. Cf. Stulac, *James,* 54. Obviously, James calls us to choose the former rather than the latter pattern.

humility that comes from wisdom" (3:13) clearly permeate these verses. *The three main points of this subsection appear in verse 19: we "should be quick to listen, slow to speak and slow to become angry."* Verses 20–21 elaborate the rationale and means for not becoming upset quickly. The "implanted word" (v. 21), like the "word of truth" in verse 18, refers to the gospel planted in us at the time of our new birth.[26] Verses 22–25 unpack the theme of being quick to listen. James's point is not just that we hear carefully what others and especially God are saying to us, but that we then obey his word.

As absurd as the thought is of people seeing something wrong with their faces after looking in a mirror and then leaving without attending to the problem, so also hearing God's word and immediately ignoring it proves ludicrous (vv. 22–24).[27] Wise persons will instead continually obey "the perfect law that gives freedom" (v. 25), that is, the gospel as the fulfillment of Torah, precisely because it liberates and blesses in ways the Old Testament law by itself could not.[28] Finally, verse 26 amplifies the theme of slowness to speak. Sooner or later those who talk too much and too quickly, without carefully listening to others and to God, will just get themselves into trouble with what they say (cf. 3:1–12).[29]

The "Have-nots" and the Responsibility of the "Haves" (1:27)   Verse 27 reintroduces the theme of the dispossessed. Verse 26 ended with a reference to worthless "religion," implying a term (*thrēskeia*) that normally referred to outward systems of rituals or morality. Here James contrasts this futility with a paradigm of godly behavior that reflects acceptable Christian service. In so doing, he combines two dimensions of the Christian religion that have often been separated or even seen as at odds with each other.[30] On the one hand, *believers must be involved with the neediest people of our world,* including those who are physically and materially the neediest, as widows and orphans in biblical cultures often were. On the other hand, *they must separate themselves from the world's sin* (not from its sinners!) by keeping themselves morally pure in the midst of the corruption around them.

THE THREE THEMES EXPANDED (2:1–5:18)

Riches and Poverty (2:1–26) *Favoritism Condemned (2:1–13)*[31]   James now elaborates his concern for the disparity between rich and poor. He begins by sketching

---

[26] So almost all contemporary commentators. For a revival of the idea that this *logos* is a law (similar, though not identical to the Stoic law of reason) implanted in all of humanity at creation, see Matt A. Jackson-McCabe, *Logos and Law in the Letter of James* (Leiden and New York: Brill, 2001). For him, this logos finds its written expression in the Jewish Torah, which is then the perfect law of liberty of v. 25, directly contrary to Paul's understanding of the law.

[27] The use of a mirror as a metaphor for moral self-examination was well known in ancient Judaism and Hellenism. See Luke T. Johnson, "The Mirror of Remembrance (James 1:22–25)," *CBQ* 50 (1988): 132–45.

[28] Or, more precisely, to "the law of Moses as interpreted and supplemented by Christ" (Moo, *Letter of James* [2000], 94).

[29] On the meaning and structure of this section, cf. esp. William R. Baker, "James," in William R. Baker and Paul Carrier, *James-Jude* (Cincinnati: Standard, 1990), 29.

[30] See, e.g., Ronald J. Sider, *One-Sided Christianity?* (Grand Rapids: Zondervan; San Francisco: HarperSanFrancisco, 1993).

[31] For a comprehensive analysis of this passage as an elaboration of a theme as taught in Greco-Roman rhetorical handbooks, see Wesley H. Wachob, *The Voice of Jesus in the Social Rhetoric of James* (Cambridge and New York: CUP, 2000).

a portrait of gross favoritism toward a wealthy person and discrimination against a poverty-stricken one (vv. 1–4). This all takes place in "your meeting" (v. 2), but the noun here in Greek is *synagōgē* or "synagogue." James uses the regular word for "church" (*ekklēsia*) in 5:14, so it is possible that he has a different kind of assembly in mind here. Given that Jews frequently used their synagogues for courts to settle intramural disputes, especially property-related matters, it is tempting to suggest that something similar is going on in James's congregations (recall also Paul's injunctions in 1 Cor. 6:1–11). There are even passages in the rabbinic literature that require identical dress for courtroom procedures (b. Sheb 31a; *Deut. Rab.* 5.6 on 16:19), which would make the discrepancies here that much more heinous. Moreover, much of James's language is judicial in nature—most notably, "favoritism" in verse 1 and "discriminated" and "judges" in verse 4. *If this is a Christian courtroom rather than a normal worship service, then the litigants are likely both Christians, further evidence that James could envision a rich Christian, even if this one is neither treating others nor being treated properly.*[32]

James next supplies the rationale for his outrage against the kind of favoritism just depicted (vv. 5–7). This is precisely the behavior that has already caused so much suffering for the poor Christians he is addressing. The wealthy non-Christian landlords are dragging the poor day-laborers into court (v. 6), undoubtedly to force them to repay various debts, a common scenario in the first century that often landed those unable to pay in debtors' prison. By their words and their actions, these rich persons are blaspheming the very name of Christ (v. 7). Yet for the most part, believers in the first century were among the poorer classes (recall 1 Cor. 1:26–29). If favoritism were ever justified, it would be for the sake of the shabbily-dressed person of verse 2, not his rich counterpart (cf. v. 5). At the same time, verse 5 must be read in its entirety. This text does not support liberation theology's "preferential option for the poor" irrespective of an individual's faith, but rather promises a full kingdom inheritance to poor people "who love him [God]."[33]

Furthermore, the law itself condemned favoritism (vv. 8–11). The "royal law" (which could mean the "supreme law," but also "the law of the kingdom") includes the second part of Jesus' double love-command: "love your neighbor as yourself" (v. 8; Lev. 19:18), which clearly carries over into the New Testament age as well.[34] If certain people protest that they have kept the other fundamental moral laws of Scripture, James replies that it only takes one transgression to become a lawbreaker (vv. 9–11). Fortunately, Christians will not be judged by the law or all would be condemned. Rather, they will stand before God on judgment day, acquitted due to Christ's merits and mercy (again, "the law that gives freedom"; v. 12). As in Jesus'

---

[32] See esp. Ronald B. Ward, "Partiality in the Assembly: *James* 2:2–4," *HTR* 62 (1969): 87–97.

[33] James "stops short of an unqualified idealization of poverty as the distinguishing mark of membership" in the community. It is "faith that is the mark" (Sophie Laws, *The Epistle of James* [London: Black; New York: Harper & Row, 1980], 103). Verse 5 is also "an observation of reality: the poor are more inclined toward God than are the rich" (Baker, "James," 50). Of course there are exceptions, but this principle has remained remarkably consistent as a broad generalization across the various eras and cultures of Christian history. At the same time the main point of vv. 1–4 is to combat partiality, which reverse discrimination as a *permanent* policy scarcely accomplishes. Cf. Nancy J. Vyhmeister, "The Rich Man in James 2: Does Ancient Patronage Illumine the Text?" *AUSS* 33 (1995): 265–83.

[34] Moo (*Letter of James* [1985], 94) thus equates the royal law with "the entire will of God for Christians."

parable of the unforgiving servant (Matt. 18:23–35) and even in the context of the Lord's Prayer itself (Matt. 6:9–15), one who has experienced God's lavish mercy in Christ will by definition show similar mercy to others.[35] Those who never do so could not have been saved and thus will experience merciless judgment. But for believers, undeserved mercy triumphs over deserved judgment (v. 13).

The Problem of Faith without Works (2:14–26)   Ever since Martin Luther puzzled over verses 18–26 and ventured the opinion that James was a "right strawy epistle" because it seemed to contradict Paul's emphasis on salvation by faith alone, the context of these verses has largely been neglected. This subsection actually begins with an illustration of "workless" faith (vv. 14–17), which continues to unpack the topic of rich and poor. James produces another extreme illustration, though both here and in verses 1–4 he may well have had actual incidents he had heard of in mind. This time his sketch portrays a Christian lacking adequate food or clothing who goes to a fellow believer who is in a position to help his brother or sister, but does absolutely nothing at all except to wish them well (vv. 15–16).[36] This kind of faith without works is dead, that is, non-existent (v. 17). The rhetorical question with which this paragraph begins ("Can such faith save?") employs the Greek negative particle *mē*, which means that the answer is "no."

Verses 18–26 anticipate and answer a potential objection: aren't faith and works separable? James denies this possibility (v. 18). The demons believe that God exists and that he alone is God, but they hardly worship him and certainly are not saved (v. 19).[37] They have the "faith by itself" that verse 17 decried. By way of contrast, Abraham and Rahab in Old Testament times demonstrated their righteous standing before God by their good deeds (vv. 20–26). James even goes so far as to deduce from these illustrations that people are justified by works (*ex ergōn*) and not by faith alone! Not surprisingly, many skeptics have argued that this is one of the clearest examples in all of Scripture of a flat-out contradiction (recall Rom. 3:28 and 4:3). But we must recognize that Paul and James use the terms "faith" and "works" in different ways. As Joachim Jeremias so memorably put it, *Paul speaks of Christian faith* (trust in Christ) *and Jewish works* (obeying the law so as to justify oneself), *while here James deals with Jewish faith* (pure monotheism) *and Christian works* (good deeds that flow from salvation).[38] Both authors agree that true commitment to Christ will, of necessity, lead to a transformed lifestyle (recall Gal. 5:6).[39] As Augustine phrased it centuries ago, "Paul said that a man is justified through faith without the works of the law, but not without those works of which James speaks"

---

[35] Cf. William Dyrness, "Mercy Triumphs over Justice: James 2:13 and the Theology of Faith and Works," *Themelios* 6.3 (1981): 14.

[36] It was situations like this one that led to the "pauper's dish" in every local synagogue, which included funds to help the most destitute in each congregation. See Johnson, *James,* 238.

[37] All agree that vv. 18–19 contain a question and an answer, but there is little agreement on the extent of each and who is responsible for each position. For an attempt to break the impasse, see Craig L. Blomberg and Mariam J. Kamell, *The Epistle of James* (Grand Rapids: Zondervan, forthcoming).

[38] Joachim Jeremias, "Paul and James," *ET* 66 (1955): 568–71.

[39] John G. Lodge, "James and Paul at Cross-Purposes? James 2,22," *Bib* 62 (1981): 213.

(*On the Christian Life* 13).[40] More specifically, in light of James 1:26–27, James may be combating the substitution of certain rituals in Christian life and worship for the necessary deeds of mercy (recall 2:13) that define true piety.[41]

JAMES AND PAUL ON FAITH AND WORKS		
	James	**Paul**
Faith	Jewish	Christian
Works	Christian	Jewish

Wisdom and Speech (3:1–4:17) *The Dangers of the Tongue (3:1–12)* James begins his expanded treatment of wise speech by referring to the power and potential of people's words for great influence.[42] Because of the status accorded rabbis in Jewish circles, too many in James's congregations may have been aspiring to an analogous role of teacher in their Jewish-Christian circles. So James cautions against too many of them filling this position because of the great responsibility that goes with it (v. 1). One can apologize for ill-chosen words and even be forgiven, but some damage may never be undone. *The larger the teacher's sphere of influence, the more an error can mislead and a sin can hurt* and, because we all remain sinners, sooner or later all teachers stumble (v. 2a).[43]

Indeed, the tongue unleashes great power for both good and ill, more generally, in its capability for duplicity, unique in all creation (vv. 2–12). Verses 2b–5a liken the power of the tiny tongue to affect an entire person to the role of a bit in a horse's mouth and of a ship's rudder. Verses 5b–8 turn to the tongue's overtly destructive power. Evil or careless speech is like the spark of fire that kindles an entire forest, potentially corrupting one's whole life in both this world and the next (vv. 5b–6). Representatives of every branch of the animal kingdom can be domesticated, but the human tongue, controlled by a supposedly superior creature, can never be tamed

---

[40] Or to use the language of mathematics and philosophy, good deeds are a necessary but not a sufficient condition for salvation. Except in the very unusual cases of "deathbed" conversions, people in whom the Spirit has truly come to reside will give some kind of visible evidence of the transformation that the Spirit initiates. And if we could read people's minds, including those of people with very little time left to demonstrate this transformation, we would see changed thoughts and attitudes that are part of the fruit or works of salvation as well. More simply, "True faith always results in faithfulness" (Robert L. Millet, *Grace Works* [Salt Lake City: Deseret, 2003], 118). Cf. esp. John F. MacArthur, "Faith according to the Apostle James," *JETS* 33 (1990): 13–34.

[41] Donald J. Verseput, "Reworking the Puzzle of Faith and Deeds in James 2.14–26," *NTS* 43 (1997): 97–115.

[42] The most detailed, helpful analysis of these themes appears in William R. Baker, *Personal Speech-Ethics in the Epistle of James* (Tübingen: Mohr, 1993); for a popular-level counterpart, see idem, *Sticks and Stones: The Discipleship of Our Speech* (Downers Grove: IVP, 1996).

[43] Teachers, both ancient and modern, inhabit settings in which they experience virtually every kind of temptation to speak sinfully: "arrogance and domination over students; anger and pettiness at contradiction or inattention; slander and meanness toward absent opponents; flattery of students for the sake of vainglory" (Johnson, *James*, 263).

(vv. 7–8)! James increases the irony in verses 9–12 by lamenting how people can curse others and praise God in the same breath. Yet all human beings, even as yet unredeemed ones, are created in God's image as creatures he infinitely values. Once again, nature itself models greater consistency, as springs of water and fruit-bearing trees produce only one predictable product.[44]

Unspiritual vs. Spiritual Wisdom (3:13–18)   The concept of wisdom explicitly returns in these verses, as James turns from speech to more general behavior. Unspiritual wisdom, which comes from the world, the flesh, and the devil (v. 15), is characterized by self-centeredness (vv. 14, 16). *Spiritual wisdom, however, which comes from God, is above all else pure* (v. 17) and then full of winsome traits such as humility, peacemaking, compassion, sincerity, and the like, all of which lead to the good deeds that characterize truly redeemed persons (vv. 13, 17–18).[45]

The Two Kinds of Wisdom Illustrated: Violence vs. Humility (4:1–12)   The self-centeredness that characterizes unspiritual wisdom easily leads to violence (vv. 1–6). Instead of asking God for what they need, people fight one another for what they want (vv. 1–2). A few scholars date James in the early 60s because they take these verses literally and think that some of the violence associated with the Zealot movement had infiltrated the church.[46] But the language may be metaphorical, just as we often use it today, for intense divisions or disputes in the church. Of course, a natural reply to James's line of reasoning would be that Christians don't always get what they want (or even need) from God. James's response in this context is twofold.

First, sometimes they just have not asked (v. 2b) or asked long enough (the Greek present tense may suggest continuous action). Second, they often ask with wrong, self-centered motives (v. 3). This latter explanation probably accounts for more unanswered prayer than we care to admit. Even such seemingly noble requests such as good health (so we can serve Christ better), good finances (so we can care for our families properly) or a good job (so we can exercise our spiritual gifts) too easily can turn out to be motivated by the even more fundamental yet ultimately selfish desires to feel good, be able to buy what we want, and gain a good reputation with others.

Verses 4–6 stun James's listeners. Can he really be saying that Christians are (metaphorically) adulterous, cozying up to the world but hating God and becoming his enemy? Perhaps only a minority in his congregations fit the bill and, as with the author of Hebrews (see below), he does *not* take for granted that everyone involved in church is necessarily saved. Luke Johnson, however, sees *4:4 as equivalent to the thesis verse for the entire letter,*[47] in which case James would not necessarily be saying that anyone to whom he is writing *is* completely alienated from God, merely

---

[44] "James seems more interested in personal character than in professional competency. What finally decides the value of the teacher's faith is whether he is 'wise and understanding' [see v. 13] rather than merely orthodox" (Wall, *Community of the Wise,* 162).

[45] Comparing chaps. 2 and 3, we learn that "the malicious speech of an insider has the same deleterious effect upon the community's life as that provoked by the rich outsider who hauls the poor believer before the law-court in order to shame those who follow" (ibid., 187).

[46] See esp. Martin, *James,* 144.

[47] Johnson refers to the "call to conversion" in 3:13–4:10 as "the thematic heart of the composition" and to 4:4 as "the most perfect expression of James' 'voice'" (*James,* 88).

that these are the logical corollaries of starting down a path in this direction (recall 1:15).

Verse 5 proves notoriously difficult to translate as the two (!) variant renderings in the NIV margin demonstrate. Is *pneuma* ("spirit") the subject or object of the envy/longing, and is it the Holy Spirit or a human spirit to which James refers? Because *epipotheō* in every other New Testament use carries the wholly positive connotations of a godly longing, not always attributable to a human's spirit, and because God is the only possible subject of "caused to dwell," the most common understanding of verse 5b is "God jealously longs for the spirit he caused to dwell in us" (TNIV; NIV mg).[48] Thus James would be contrasting God's desire to keep us close to himself with our tendency to rebel, and he is undergirding it by citing Scripture. But what Scripture? No Old Testament text reads like this (or like any of the alternate translations). Probably he has the larger theme of God's jealousy for his people in mind, as reflected in texts like Exodus 20:5; 34:14 and Zechariah 8:2.[49]

Instead of quarreling with one another or imitating the covetousness and pride of the world, believers must submit to God and humble themselves before him (4:7–10). This paragraph unleashes a barrage of staccato-like commands that enhances the seriousness of James's injunctions. No one dare claim that "the devil made me do" any particular kind of sin, because he coerces no one. We sin only when we yield to Satan's temptations rather than staying close to God; if we resist the devil he will flee from us (vv. 7–8a). In verse 8b, James applies the Old Testament language of ritual purity to the arena of moral purity.[50] His worldly listeners must refrain from mocking God's standards and must repent of their sin (vv. 9–10).

Verses 11–12, at first glance, seem at best loosely connected to the preceding material, but in fact they tie together the entire section on wisdom and speech thus far. In the context of the primarily verbal fights of verses 1–2, it would have been easy to misrepresent one's opponents and slander them. But to do so would have been to bear false witness against them, in violation of one of the fundamental moral commandments of the Old Testament (Exod. 20:16) that carries over into the New Testament age (Luke 18:20). Such behavior implicitly sets oneself up as a judge over others and even the law itself, when only God may legitimately function in this way. This is the "wisdom" of the world, flesh and devil (3:15), which stands in utter contrast to the heavenly wisdom that Christians should display (3:17), by which they learn to control their tongues (3:1–12).

Boastful Speech (4:13–17)   The last subsection of this part of James's letter contrasts wise and foolish planning (4:13–17). The relevant principles are illustrated with an example from the small merchant, middle class of the Roman Empire, which had the mobility to ply their wares out-of-town as well as close to home. Today we would call them traveling businesspeople. Planning a whole year in advance was

---

[48] See Moo, *Letter of James* (2000), 188–90.

[49] A very attractive alternative, however, is the possibility that 4:5b–6a reflects a paraphrase of the "Scripture" James is citing, which is then rendered *literally* in vv. 6b–c with the quotation of Prov. 3:34 (LXX); see Craig B. Carpenter, "James 4.5 Reconsidered," *NTS* 47 (2001).

[50] Davids, *James,* 166.

about as far ahead as most people ever managed in the ancient Mediterranean world, dependent as they were on the vicissitudes of the annual seasons. But even life itself could be cut off or drastically changed in a moment, so any confident pronouncements about what the coming days or months would hold reflected arrogant boasting (vv. 13–14, 16).[51] Despite all of the technology that enables modern people to control their environments in many ways, this principle remains unchanged. The godly alternative is not to give up planning, but to leave room for the Lord's will to overturn ours (v. 15).[52] That James could have expected his readers to act this way reinforces our convictions that his readers are Christians and that he recognizes that some believers can be moderately well-to-do. This paragraph also gives *a third answer to the question of why we do not always get what we want from God (recall vv. 2–3)—it may simply not be his will.*

JAMES ON PRAYER

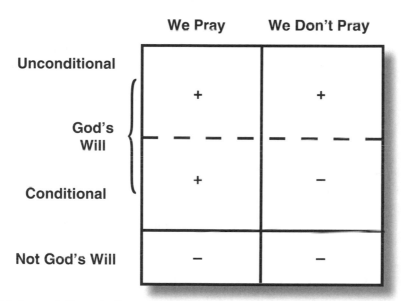

Trials and Temptations (5:1–18) *External Persecution (5:1–6)* At last James returns to the theme with which he began his epistle. First, he takes up the specific circumstances of oppression in which many in James's church found themselves (5:1–12). He assures them that those who cause their trials—the exploitation by the rich landlords—will be judged severely (vv. 1–6). These self-indulgent people are clearly not Christians, but their living in luxury while indifferent to the plight of the oppressed offers a strong warning to all who would act similarly while still claiming to be believers. Verse 1 begins with the identical literary apostrophe as 4:13, but that does not mean the same audience is in view. In the earlier passage James encourages

---

[51] J. Alec Motyer (*The Message of James: The Tests of Faith* [Leicester and Downers Grove: IVP, 1985], 161) observes that the three verbs in vv. 14–15 warn against a presumptuous attitude that denies, respectively, our ignorance, frailty, and dependence.

[52] Ibid. Kurt A. Richardson (*James* [Nashville: Broadman & Holman, 1997], 201) calls vv. 13–17 "one of the most important biblical sources for a Christian ethic of business." Not to involve God in our planning amounts to "practical atheism" (James B. Adamson, *The Epistle of James* [Grand Rapids: Eerdmans, 1976], 180).

corrective action; here he calls the godless wealthy to bemoan their coming judgment and condemnation.[53] Verses 2–3a could contain prophetic perfect tenses in light of the future tenses in verse 3b, but they make even more sense as true past tenses. Precisely because these material possessions are *unused* surplus, they have rotted, corroded, and become moth-eaten.[54]

The landlords' refusal to pay timely, decent wages to their farmhands becomes that much more heinous, since they have more than enough resources to do so (vv. 4–5). *As throughout the Bible, acquiring wealth is not necessarily bad, but not giving generously from one's wealth always proves culpable.* Verse 6 probably does not refer to literal but to judicial murder—condemning to debtors' prison those who could not pay the extravagant taxes or rents they were often charged. Eventually many would just die there.

A Patient Response (5:7–12)   It would have been easy for Christians to imitate the Zealots and try to rebel or lash out at their oppressors in some way. Or, to the extent that they could not get at the landlords themselves, they could at least displace their anger and take out their frustrations on one another. James counsels a quite different approach (vv. 7–11).[55] On the one hand, he encourages his audience to look to the future and remember Christ's imminent return (vv. 7–9). However long Christ may seem to delay from a human perspective, his second coming and vindication of his people will occur quickly from eternity's perspective. Patience, like a farmer's waiting for the two periods of rain that would enable spring and fall plantings to yield a harvest in due season, will eventually pay rich dividends. Grumbling against one another will only turn God's judgment on them instead.

On the other hand, James also commands his listeners to look to the past and remember the examples of the patience and perseverance of the prophets and Job (vv. 10–11). But James has not swung the pendulum from the violent extreme of the Zealots to the quietist extreme of many Essenes, who withdrew from society and simply prayed to God to intervene supernaturally to right the wrongs of the world. What he calls attention to about the prophets is how they "spoke in the name of the Lord." And the prophets' approach to the injustice of their days was bold denunciation, even when it meant condemning the reigning king's behavior. Likewise, Job persistently protested his innocence of any sin serious enough to justify the horrible afflictions that befell him. And God eventually vindicated him at the expense of his counselors, whose traditional theodicies (explanations for the evil that he suffered) had failed. *So while James eschews violence, he scarcely supports passivism; God's people have the responsibility to speak powerfully against the injustice of the world that impoverishes some people so that the rich may get richer!*[56]

Even more so than with 4:11–12, 5:12 seems at first unrelated to anything that comes before or after it. In fact, there may be a very direct tie-in with the oppres-

---

[53] The "'last days' (*eschatais hēmerais*) are not the anticipated retirement years of the rich, but the time of God's judgment" (Johnson, *James,* 301)!

[54] Davids, *James,* 176.

[55] Moo, *Letter of James* (1985), 170.

[56] Cf. Adamson, *James: Man and Message,* 257; Martin, *James,* 197.

sion described in 5:1–6. Then, as now, one of the most common ploys to attempt to stave off bankruptcy, foreclosure, or even more severe punishments such as debtors' prison, was to promise to pay up in the near future if the debtor would be given just a little more time. In many instances, however, such promises were highly unrealistic and qualified as rash vows. Swearing to do something one would be unable to do just brought further discredit to oneself and to the entity, including God, by which one swore. People should rather develop a reputation of being so trustworthy that they do not have to take any special measures to convince others that they will do what they say.[57]

JAMES'S "MILITANT PATIENCE" (5:10–11)

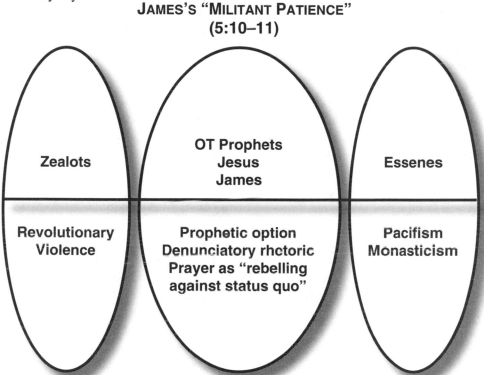

Zealots	OT Prophets Jesus James	Essenes
Revolutionary Violence	Prophetic option Denunciatory rhetoric Prayer as "rebelling against status quo"	Pacifism Monasticism

Sickness (5:13–18) Perhaps even more common than external persecution and harassment are the trials that result from bodily illness. This passage is one of the most important in all of Scripture on the believer's proper response to severe or prolonged sickness. Once again, James enjoins faithful prayer, this time as the primary antidote for suffering. Various terms for prayer occur seven times in these six verses, an important fact to remember before one gets caught up in the details of the ritual of anointing. But in serious enough situations (indicated here by the fact that the sick person summons the elders who pray over him or her, suggesting someone who is at the time bedridden),[58] anointing with oil should be applied as well. Several words

---

[57] Cf. further William R. Baker, "'Above All Else': Contexts of the Call for Verbal Integrity in James 5.12," *JSNT* 54 (1994): 57–71.

[58] Motyer (*James,* 193–94) notes three other reasons for seeing the illness or injury as extremely serious: the word for "sick" can also mean completely worn out, the elders do all the praying, and the only faith that is mentioned also belongs to the elders.

in this passage can refer to either physical or spiritual sickness and healing, leading some interpreters to think that only the latter is in view. But verses 15b–16 demonstrate that only *some* of these illnesses are caused by sin (in which case confession is needed), while rabbis often used oil to anoint physically sick people ceremonially, so it is best to see physical disease as in view throughout.[59] Others have argued that the anointing with oil reflected a primitive form of medicine, but again the rabbinic parallels suggest otherwise, not to mention the fact that even the ancients knew that oil could help only a fairly limited range of bodily afflictions.

But what then do we do with verse 15a: "The prayer offered in faith will make the sick person well"? *We have to remember that James assumes we have already read and remember 4:15, in which God's will may well overrule ours.* As Douglas Moo aptly phrases it, "A true prayer of faith, then, always includes within it a tacit acknowledgment . . . that it is *God's* will that must be done."[60] James obviously knew that even the most pious of God's people eventually died, and many of them died from illnesses, so 5:15 dare not be taken with the "health-wealth" heresy as if the only reason for Christians not to be healed is their own lack of faith. At the same time, this passage offers no support for the traditional Catholic sacrament of extreme unction or last rites. While some of those who summon their elders may be close to the point of death, nothing suggests that all are, and the point of this ceremony is to pray for healing, not to prepare a person for death!

The anointing with oil must also be distinguished from the ministries of those who have the gift of healing (1 Cor. 12:30). None of the criteria for elders ever included having this particular gift. Why then involve the elders? Probably because they were the duly commissioned pastoral leaders of the church, and the ceremony described here is meant as a way of keeping the sick person connected with his or her congregation, whereas faith healers typically had an itinerant ministry, at best loosely connected to one local assembly. Lest anyone doubt the potential of the anointing ceremony with prayer, James reminds his readers of how Elijah's prayers stopped the heavens for three and one-half years and then brought a deluge of rain on the drought-ridden land afterward (vv. 17–18; cf. 1 Kings 17–18).[61]

CLOSING (5:19–20)

James's comparatively abrupt ending reminds us that his letter does not follow standard Hellenistic epistolary form, but falls more into the genre of wisdom literature. *Still, these verses form a fitting conclusion, reminding his audience of a key task of the Christian life—to restore sinners from error and save them from spiritual death.* Wherever one comes down on the Calvinist-Arminian debate over the perseverance of the saints will typically dictate how one assesses the situation portrayed here. "Wandering from the truth" translates a verb (*planaō*) that can mean to lead astray, mislead or deceive, and in the passive voice, as here, to go astray, be mistaken, be misled, or wander about. Nothing in this passage resolves the debate over

---

[59] See esp. Gary S. Shogren, "Will God Heal Us: A Re-examination of James 5:14–16a," *EQ* 61 (1989): 99–108; John C. Thomas, "The Devil, Disease, and Deliverance: James 5.14–16," *JPT* 2 (1993): 25–50.

[60] Moo, *Letter of James* (1985), 182.

[61] On which, see Keith Warrington, "The Significance of Elijah in James 5:13–18," *EQ* 66 (1994): 217–27.

whether this is someone who has been a true Christian (or even a professing one) or not.

ADDITIONAL QUESTIONS FOR REVIEW

1. Who are the possible authors of James? Who of these is the most likely candidate, and why?
2. To whom was the epistle of James written, and to what year should it be dated? What are the issues surrounding the epistle's date?
3. What recurring themes provide structure to James's letter? Summarize James's main idea about each of these three key themes as they are presented throughout the epistle.
4. What is James's point about the relationship between faith and works in 2:14–26? How can his teaching be harmonized with Paul's teachings on the relationship between the two?
5. What actions will characterize a person who has received God's wisdom? What actions and behaviors will Christian behavior necessarily exclude?
6. For James, how are salvation and stewardship related? How is the position of twenty-first-century American Christians different from the situation of the intended audience? Which portions of James's epistles are especially pointed and disconcerting to the American church? Why?
7. How does James answer believers' frustrations at not getting what has been requested of God? What reasons does James give for unanswered prayers? How do these themes tie in with James's advice on praying for the sick? What are some key exegetical issues to understand regarding the prayer offered in faith for the sick in James 5?

APPLICATION

Perhaps no other New Testament document as pointedly demonstrates the contrast between biblical and nominal Christianity. Indeed, the very fact that Protestants in general and Evangelicals in particular have squirmed as much as they have when reading "faith without works is dead" shows the neglect of large swaths of biblical teaching in favor of an overemphasis on Paul, accompanied by a selective, one-sided reading of him. Dietrich Bonhoeffer's famous discussion of "cheap grace" in his classic writing, *The Cost of Discipleship*,[62] unfortunately could have applied to numerous branches of the church throughout its history and today, not just to the majority of German Christians who co-operated far too easily with the Nazi regime. One of the reasons the Church of Jesus Christ of Latter-day Saints (also known as the Mormons) takes issue with evangelical theology is because of the perception that

---

[62] New York: Collier, 1959.

we promote easy believism: a person can accept Jesus as Savior, go out and live like the devil and still be saved.[63]

So too, liberal Christianity often rejects a more conservative form of faith because of the impoverished social ethic they discern among evangelicals, particularly in the United States, or at least a very narrow one, focusing perhaps solely on pro-life and anti-gay issues, rather than on poverty, health care, the environment, relief work for the victims of natural disasters and wars, as well—issues that all receive far greater amounts of attention in the Bible. Liberation theology grew out of Roman Catholicism in the 1960s as a protest against a very traditionalist form of the Catholic faith, which *did* emphasize good works, perhaps even too much, but not the kinds of deeds that would challenge unjust social systems, structures, and governments that perpetuated a huge divide between the haves and the have-nots of the Third World, particularly in Latin America.[64]

Evangelicals have taken great strides in the last fifty years to improve and become more balanced in several of these arenas, though more so outside the U.S. than within, and more so on some issues than on others. Intramural evangelical debates illustrate both the positive steps that have been taken and the misguided opposition against them. John MacArthur's emphasis in several of his writings on "Lordship Salvation" displays in detail how there is no biblical warrant for accepting Jesus as Savior by grace through faith without simultaneously submitting to him as Lord or ultimate Master. Of course, new believers can never know all that God will ask of them over the course of a lifetime when they are just beginning that pilgrimage, but those who think they can accept a free gift of salvation without likewise submitting to Jesus as best they understand his demands and without repenting when they fail to live up to them are not truly becoming Christians.[65]

Saving faith leads inevitably, over time, to transformed living, if the Holy Spirit has truly taken up residence in a person. That transformation may look different in its details for every believer, and it is not without many fits and starts and even serious lapses. But true believers will come back to God, submit afresh to his Spirit, and continue to mature again. Financial concern for the poor and needy will often be a prime "exhibit" of this changed life. If no such change ever occurs, we have serious reason to question any profession of salvation. It *is* possible to be rich and Christian, according to James, but it is *not* possible to be a rich Christian without being generous with one's wealth in helping the needy.[66]

---

[63] See, e.g., Richard R. Hopkins, *Biblical Mormonism: Responding to Evangelical Criticism of LDS Theology* (Bountiful, UT: Horizon, 1994), 130–36.

[64] On James, see esp. Tamez, *Scandalous Message*; and Pedrito U. Maynard-Reid, *Poverty and Wealth in James* (Maryknoll: Orbis, 1987).

[65] See p. 397 above. Cf. also John F. MacArthur Jr., *The Gospel according to Jesus* (Grand Rapids: Zondervan, rev. 1994; idem, *The Gospel according to the Apostles* (Nashville: Word, 2000).

[66] See throughout Blomberg, *Neither Poverty nor Riches*.

SELECT BIBLIOGRAPHY

COMMENTARIES

Advanced

Davids, Peter H. *The Epistle of James*. NIGTC. Exeter: Paternoster; Grand Rapids: Eerdmans, 1982.

Dibelius, Martin. *James,* rev. Heinrich Greeven. Hermeneia. Philadelphia: Fortress, 1976.

Johnson, Luke T. *The Letter of James*. AB. New York and London: Doubleday, 1995.

Martin, Ralph P. *James*. WBC. Word: Waco, 1988.

Intermediate

Blomberg, Craig L., and Mariam J. Kamell. *The Epistle of James*. ZEC. Grand Rapids: Eerdmans, forthcoming.

Brosend, William F., II. *James and Jude*. NCBC. Cambridge and New York: CUP, 2004.

Hartin, Patrick J. *James*. SP. Collegeville: Liturgical, 2003.

Laws, Sophie. *The Epistle of James*. BNTC. London: Black; Peabody: Hendrickson, 1980.

Moo, Douglas J. *The Letter of James*. PNTC. Leicester: IVP; Grand Rapids: Eerdmans, 2000.

Wall, Robert W. *The Community of the Wise: The Letter of James*. NTinCont. Valley Forge: Trinity, 1997.

Introductory

Baker, William R. "James." In William R. Baker and Paul K. Carrier, *James-Jude*. SBS. Cincinnati: Standard, 1990.

Motyer, J. Alec. *The Message of James: The Tests of Faith*. BST. Leicester and Downers Grove: IVP, 1985.

Sleeper, C. Freeman. *James*. ANTC. Nashville: Abingdon, 1998.

Stulac, George M. *James*. IVPNTC. Leicester and Downers Grove: IVP, 1993.

Tidball, Derek. *Wisdom from Heaven: The Message of the Letter of James for Today*. Fearn, Ross-shire, Scotland: Christian Focus Publications, 2003.

OTHER BOOKS

Adamson, James B. *James: The Man and His Message*. Grand Rapids: Eerdmans, 1989.

Baker, William R. *Personal Speech-Ethics in the Epistle of James*. Tübingen: Mohr, 1995.

Bauckham, Richard. *James: Wisdom of James, Disciple of Jesus the Sage*. London and New York: Routledge, 1999.

Chilton, Bruce, and Jacob Neusner, eds. *The Brother of Jesus.* Louisville and London: WJKP, 2001.

Cheung, Luke L. *The Genre, Composition and Hermeneutics of the Epistle of James.* Carlisle: Paternoster, 2003.

Edgar, David H. *Has God Not Chosen the Poor? The Social Setting of the Epistle of James.* Sheffield: SAP, 2001.

Hartin, Patrick J. *James and the Q Sayings of Jesus.* Sheffield: JSOT, 1991.

Hartin, Patrick J. *A Spirituality of Perfection: Faith in Action in the Letter of James.* Collegeville: Liturgical, 1999.

Maynard-Reid, Pedrito U. *Poverty and Wealth in James.* Maryknoll: Orbis, 1987.

Painter, John. *Just James: The Brother of Jesus in History and Tradition.* Columbia: University of South Carolina Press, rev. 2004.

Penner, Todd C. *The Epistle of James and Eschatology.* Sheffield: SAP, 1996.

Shanks, Hershel, and Ben Witherington III. *The Brother of Jesus: The Dramatic Story and Meaning of the First Archaeological Link to Jesus and His Family.* San Francisco: HarperSanFrancisco, 2003.

Tamez, Elsa. *The Scandalous Message of James: Faith without Works Is Dead.* New York: Crossroad, rev. 2002.

Wachob, Wesley H. *The Voice of Jesus in the Social Rhetoric of James.* Cambridge and New York: CUP, 2000.

Bibliography

Mills, Watson E. *James.* Lewiston and Lampeter: Mellen, 2001.

10

The Epistle to the Hebrews: The Superiority of Christ

INTRODUCTION

GENRE

Despite its traditional title as an epistle, only the ending of this book resembles a letter. It begins with a lofty theological prologue (1:1–4), while interspersing doctrine and ethics throughout the rest of the document in discrete segments. The author describes the work itself as "a word of exhortation" (13:22), an expression found elsewhere in the New Testament only in Acts 13:15, where it refers to a sermon. The same is true of its use in the extrabiblical, fourth-century Christian work known as the Apostolic Constitutions (8:5). So it is best to think of Hebrews as *the written form of (or substitute for) a preached message.*[1]

RECIPIENTS

The original audience for the message has traditionally been identified as one or more groups of Jewish Christians; hence, the title "to the Hebrews." No other superscription was ever given the book in early Christian history, and the contents for the most part fit this identification. The document is replete with Old Testament quotations and imagery and is designed to demonstrate the superiority of the Christ to every other key Jewish figure and institution.

Of course, the frequency of these features in some of Paul's letters addressed to predominantly Gentile-Christian communities shows that other kinds of audiences could have been in view as well. Some modern scholars have indeed argued for a more Gentile orientation of either author or audience (or both), noting particularly a method of reasoning that seems more akin to the Greek philosopher Plato or the Hellenizing Jew Philo, who merged Jewish thought with Greek philosophy for the sake of commending Judaism to the Gentiles. Perhaps most noteworthy in this respect is the comparison of earthly and heavenly tabernacles in 8:1–6, with parallels to Plato's famous allegory of the cave in which earthly realities are but shadows of heavenly substances. It is also sometimes argued that passages like 3:12, warning against turning "from the living God," or 6:1 on moving on from "elementary teachings" and "acts that lead to death" are not expressions that a Jewish author (or even

---

[1] William L. Lane, "Hebrews: A Sermon in Search of a Setting," *SWJT* 28 (1985): 13–18. Andrew Trotter (*Interpreting the Epistle to the Hebrews* [Grand Rapids: Baker, 1997], 79) concludes that Hebrews is "a complex literary form, basically a sermon but clearly reconstructed as an epistle."

a Gentile author appreciative of Judaism as preparatory for Christianity) would have used to describe those adhering to non-Christian Judaism.[2]

Since the discovery of the Dead Sea Scrolls after World War II, however, the pendulum has swung back among the majority of scholars to reading Hebrews in light of Jewish backgrounds. Some have even found distinctive similarities between these Essene writings and the epistle. For example, the Qumran sectarians looked for a priestly as well as a kingly Messiah, and Hebrews is the only New Testament document to develop the theme of Christ as high priest. One Qumran document, 11QMelchizedek, equates this priestly Messiah with Melchizedek, priest of Salem at the time of Abraham (Gen. 14:18–20). Elsewhere among the Dead Sea Scrolls, Melchizedek appears as an exalted figure, including as the archangel Michael. Meanwhile, Hebrews 7 develops a comparison between Jesus and Melchizedek at length, even though no other New Testament document refers to this obscure Old Testament figure.

The founder of Qumran, known merely as "the Teacher of Righteousness," was repeatedly likened to a prophet like Moses, and Hebrews compares Jesus and Moses as well (esp. 3:1–6), though this comparison is not unique to this letter. Finally, Hebrews 6:2 strangely refers to "baptisms" in the plural, which could tie in with the daily ablutions practiced at Qumran.[3] At the same time, there are other ancient Jewish writings that envision a priestly Messiah, talk about Melchizedek or the eschatological prophet, or describe multiple baptisms, so none of these arguments proves conclusive.

Probably the most balanced conclusion is to allow for several possibilities. *A largely Jewish-Christian composition of the original audience seems most likely. But there may well have been Gentile believers mixed in. And among those of Jewish background, some could easily have come from sectarian roots, like the tightly knit communities of the Essenes.*[4] The earlier the date (see below), the more likely the readers were predominantly, if not even exclusively, Jewish. The later the date, the more likely the distinctively Jewish features of the letter did not necessarily determine the make-up of the audience.

---

[2] For a full analysis of the question, see Ronald Williamson, *Philo and the Epistle to the Hebrews* (Leiden and New York: Brill, 1970). Cf. also James W. Thompson, *The Beginnings of Christian Philosophy: The Epistle to the Hebrews* (Washington: CBAA, 1982).

[3] C. Spicq, "L'épitre aux Hébreux: Apollos, Jean-baptiste, les héllenistes, et Qumran," *RevQ* 1 (1959): 365–90. For a demonstration of later Essene influence in Rome on 1 Clement and the Shepherd of Hermas, see E. Glenn Hinson, "Essene Influence in Roman Christianity: A Look at the Second-Century Evidence," *PRS* 19 (1992): 399–407. On the other hand, a plausible case has been made for an Ebionite background (Jewish Christians known to us from second-century testimony, who did not believe in Christ's deity but thought an angelic power possessed him from his baptism to his passion), if we can assume they were in existence already in the mid-first century. See Michael Goulder, "Hebrews and the Ebionites," *NTS* 49 (2003): 393–406.

[4] See esp. F. F. Bruce, *The Epistle to the Hebrews* (Grand Rapids: Eerdmans, rev. 1990), 3–9. David A. deSilva, in several writings, now summarized in his socio-rhetorical commentary on Hebrews (*Perseverance in Gratitude: A Socio-Rhetorical Commentary on the Epistle "to the Hebrews"* [Grand Rapids and Cambridge: Eerdmans, 2000], 2–23) stresses that the main conclusions we can draw about the make-up of the audience is that they are in positions of marginalization in their world, having to deal with the disgrace or shame of being a Christian, but that links with Judaism or explicit persecution are more precarious. For a full survey of possible backgrounds, see Lincoln D. Hurst, *The Epistle to the Hebrews: Its Background of Thought* (Cambridge and New York: CUP, 1990).

AUTHOR

The author of this letter is unknown. The ancient manuscripts do not attribute it to anyone, either in the text of the epistle itself or in any appended superscriptions or postscripts. The postscript in some editions of the KJV that refers to Paul as author is not based on any of the oldest manuscripts and, therefore, should not form part of what Christians believe to be the words God inspired.[5] Pauline authorship was simply a common conviction in the Middle Ages passed on by the KJV translators from various late manuscripts that had added the reference at the end of the letter. Indeed, the various early Church Fathers who did ascribe the letter to Paul did so largely to support their convictions of its apostolic authority, not because they had actual evidence that Paul wrote it. The earliest Patristic testimony is, in fact, very divided in its opinion.

In addition to Paul, candidates for author included Luke (based on alleged stylistic parallels with his writings), Barnabas (a "Levite"—accounting for the interest in the priesthood and in exhortation—recall the meaning of his nickname in Acts 4:36), and Clement of Rome (based on similarities with his later letter known as 1 Clement). Latin/Catholic writers were much slower than Greek/Orthodox ones even to countenance the possibility of Pauline authorship, in part because of their opposition to its supposed hard line against apostates. Early collections of New Testament books find Hebrews inserted in many different locations, within and after the avowedly Pauline letters. The most common Protestant proposal, first popularized by Martin Luther in the 1500s, attributes authorship to Apollos, based on his reputation for eloquence and thorough knowledge of the Old Testament (Acts 18:24-28) and his upbringing in Alexandria, with its "school" of exegetical interpretation similar to that found in this letter. Even the parallels with Qumran could have been picked up in Alexandria, because there was an Essene community there.

Others, in the last three centuries of "modern" scholarship, have suggested Silas, Philip, and even Priscilla. There are some similarities between Hebrews and 1 Peter, and Silas has been understood by some as the amanuensis who helped account for the good Greek style of the latter (1 Pet. 5:12). Philip, the deacon, was one of the original Hellenistic Jewish-Christian leaders, whose thought may have mirrored Stephen's and thus been more radical and willing to embrace Greco-Roman philosophy akin to some readings of Hebrews. Priscilla, finally, has been suggested to account for the letter's anonymity, since a woman in those days would have lacked credibility if she had published in her own name. Chapter 11:32, however, rules out this last option, unless it too is a very subtle fiction, since it employs a masculine participle modifying the "I" that refers to the author.

It is fair to say that Paul remains the least probable suggestion of all, however, for four main reasons. (1) No other letter of Paul is anonymous, while 2 Thessalonians 3:17 suggests that Paul affixed his name to all his letters. (2) The style and form of argument are entirely different from all of Paul's other letters, including the disputed

---

[5] Based on the specific body of early church testimony that *did* suggest Pauline authorship, later scribes added this claim into that family of medieval manuscripts known as the Textus Receptus, from which large portions of the KJV were translated, and then published in 1611.

ones, and these differences prove far greater than the differences between the undisputed Paulines and the so-called deutero-Pauline epistles. (3) Chapter 2:3 shows that the author learned the gospel second-hand rather than via a direct encounter with the risen Lord. Finally, (4) none of the other letters attributed to Paul was ever debated in the ancient discussions about the New Testament canon, while Hebrews was, precisely because the question of authorship was unresolved.

Already around A.D. 200, Origen declared that *only God knew who wrote this epistle, and that conclusion remains the safest.*[6] But all the suggestions, ancient and modern, preserve a link with Paul, since biblical are some very Pauline touches here and there, and any of these proposals would be adequate to establish apostolic authority. Apostolicity did not mean that a book was written by one of the twelve closest followers of Jesus; otherwise Mark and Luke would have been disqualified (and Paul, too, strictly speaking, though he at least called himself an apostle in the broader sense—see above, p. 190). Rather it meant that the author was connected to one of the apostles and wrote within the period of time in which one or more of the apostles were still living.[7]

DATE AND PLACE

The juxtaposition of Romans and Hebrews in some ancient canonical sequences is best explained if it was believed the letter was addressed to Christians in Rome. Clement's awareness of the letter in Rome in the 90s accords with this conviction. Chapter 13:24 fits well with this belief, too, as the author sends greetings from "those from Italy." While this could mean that the author is in Italy writing to somewhere else, and suggestions of both Jerusalem and Alexandria have been made periodically throughout church history,[8] it would be a bit unusual to refer to all the Christians in a huge Roman province greeting a specific congregation. More naturally, someone writing to Rome from elsewhere, accompanied by a handful of Italian Christians known to his audience, would phrase his greetings this way.[9]

The references to Hebrews in 1 Clement (see esp. 36:1–5) and to Timothy in Hebrews 13:23 require a first-century date for this letter. Debates as to whether it predates or postdates A.D. 70 usually center on the lack of any reference to the temple's destruction and to the use of present tenses with reference to the sacrificial system. Yet while both of these arguments could support the earlier date, the first is an argument from silence and the second phenomenon is paralleled in numerous rabbinic texts centuries later. Moreover, the greater interest in the rituals of the

---

[6] For elaboration on all of the major options discussed here regarding authorship (and several minor ones not discussed), see Paul Ellingworth, *The Epistle to the Hebrews* (Carlisle: Paternoster; Grand Rapids: Eerdmans, 1993), 3–21; on canonization, cf. pp. 34–36. For an even more recent survey of scholarly opinion on authorship, along with defenses of Apollos, Luke, and (even) Paul, respectively, see Simon Kistemaker, "The Authorship of Hebrews," George H. Guthrie, "The Case for Apollos as the Author of Hebrews," David L. Allen, "The Authorship of Hebrews: The Lukan Proposal," and David A. Black, "Who Wrote Hebrews? The Internal and External Evidence Reexamined," *Faith and Mission* 18 (2001): 57–69, 41–56, 27–40, and 3–26.

[7] Cf. Klein, Blomberg, and Hubbard, *Introduction to Biblical Interpretation,* 115.

[8] For a vigorous defense of Jerusalem, see Carl Mosser, "No Lasting City: Rome, Jerusalem and the Place of Hebrews in the History of Earliest 'Christianity'" (St. Andrews: Ph.D. thesis, 2004).

[9] Cf. further R. McL. Wilson, *Hebrews* (London: Marshall, Morgan & Scott; Grand Rapids: Eerdmans, 1987), 9–12.

tabernacle, antedating even the construction of Solomon's temple, could reflect the recognition that literal sacrifices in the Jerusalem temple were no longer possible. The seemingly harsh attack on the priesthood in this letter could also be interpreted in two different ways—reflecting either the polemic of two living communities in debate with each other or the rhetoric of an era after one's opponents were no longer around to defend themselves. The same is true of 8:13. The first half of the verse could suggest a post-70 date, by calling God's first covenant "obsolete," while the second half might suggest pre-70 writing, because "what is obsolete and aging will soon disappear" (but apparently has not quite done so yet).[10]

More decisive, however, is 12:4. Here the author declares, "In your struggle against sin, you have not yet resisted to the point of shedding your blood." This appears to be a reference to the fact that no one in the audience has yet been martyred for their Christian faith, even though persecution is increasing. In other words, the struggle against sin is the community's response to the sin of persecution; few sins that individuals themselves can commit lead to their own bloodletting if resisted too long! *If these believers lived in Rome, they would have begun to be martyred during Nero's persecution in and around the imperial capital beginning in A.D. 64. The reference to the prior confiscation of their property in 10:32–34 would also fit well with Claudius's banishment of the Jews from Rome in 49, rescinded with his death in 54. Combining all this data together, the most persuasive case for date and provenance finds the author writing to one or more larger Jewish-Christian house churches in Rome (rather than to the entire church in the city) just prior to A.D. 64.[11]*

STRUCTURE AND THEME

This epistle's "big idea" highlights *the supremacy of Jesus as the Messiah over all other things Jewish, presumably to discourage these professing Jewish Christians from reverting back to a form of Judaism less distinctively Christian so as to escape the growing threat of persecution and martyrdom under Nero.*[12] Each main section of the letter body compares Christ to a different individual or institution, alternating between theological affirmations and ethical implications, to warn against the eternal punishment that wholesale apostasy would trigger.[13] *Thus Christology and soteriology form the two major theological concerns of the author,* and the resulting outline resembles the following:

---

[10] Craig R. Koester (*Hebrews* [New York and London: Doubleday, 2001], 50–54) surveys many of these and related points, concluding that any date between 60 and 90 is possible.

[11] See esp. William L. Lane, *Hebrews 1–8* (Dallas: Word, 1991), li–lxvi.

[12] Cf. throughout David Peterson, *Hebrews and Perfection* (Cambridge and New York; CUP, 1982). For an outstanding narrative reconstruction of what life might have been like for one of these Jewish Christians, see George H. Guthrie, *Hebrews* (Grand Rapids: Zondervan, 1998), 17–18.

[13] Cf. Trotter, *Hebrews,* 81–94. A much fuller study of Hebrews' structure, coming to somewhat different conclusions, is George H. Guthrie, *The Structure of Hebrews: A Text-Linguistic Analysis* (Leiden and New York: Brill, 1994; Grand Rapids: Baker, 1998). For yet one more plausible option, cf. also Cynthia L. Westfall, *A Discourse Analysis of the Letter to the Hebrews: Relationship between Form and Meaning* (London and New York: T & T Clark, forthcoming). Perhaps the most famous proposal for Hebrews' outline is the elaborate chiasmus of Albert Vanhoye (*Structure and Message of the Epistle to the Hebrews* [Rome: PIB, 1989], but many of the supposed points of correspondence seem very general.

I. Prologue (1:1–4)
II. The Central Thesis: Asserting the Supremacy of Christ (1:5–12:29)
    A. Over Angels (1:5–2:18)
        1. In Sovereignty (1:5–14)
        2. First Resulting Warning (2:1–4)
        3. In Suffering (2:5–18)
    B. Over Moses (3:1–4:13)
        1. Servant vs. Son (3:1–6)
        2. Second Resulting Warning (3:7–4:13)
    C. Over Other Priests (4:14–7:28)
        1. The Fundamental Exhortation (4:14–16)
        2. Comparisons with Aaron and Melchizedek (5:1–10)
        3. Third Resulting Warning (5:11–6:12)
        4. Comparisons with Levi and Melchizedek (6:13–7:28)
    D. Over the Old Covenant (8:1–10:39)
        1. Obsolescence of the Mosaic Covenant (8:1–10:18)
        2. Fourth Resulting Warning (10:19–39)
    E. Over Previous "Heroes of the Faith" (11:1–12:29)
        1. The Cloud of Witnesses (11:1–12:13)
        2. Fifth Resulting Warning (12:14–29)
III. Concluding Exhortations (13:1–21)
IV. Letter Closing (13:22–25)

COMMENTARY

PROLOGUE (1:1–4)

Hebrews begins with a paragraph of some of the loftiest Christology in the whole New Testament. In contrast with the varied and repeated communications from God in past times, Jesus has become his decisive revelation to humanity "in these last days" (vv. 1–2a), another reminder of how the New Testament writers understood the end times to have begun with Christ's first coming. Jesus is scarcely just a prophet, like those of old, but God's very Son. This sonship is defined by the actions predicated of him in the rest of the prologue. The emphasis here is not on subordination or inferiority, as often with earthly children, but on *an exact equivalence between God and Christ.* Jesus inherits the universe, which God in fact created through him (v. 2b). He is his Father's mirror image and providentially sustains the cosmos moment by moment (v. 3a). And most significantly for humanity, he offered the atoning sacrifice for our sin problem, after which he was again exalted and reunited with his Father at the closest position possible to God himself (v. 3b). If anyone previously doubted that he was superior even to the most exalted angel, this "resumé" should settle things once and for all![14] Verse 4 thus bridges to the first main comparison the author wants to develop, namely, Christ and the angels.

THE CENTRAL THESIS: ASSERTING THE SUPREMACY OF CHRIST (1:5–12:29)

Over Angels (1:5–2:18) *In Sovereignty (1:5–14)* Jesus is superior to the order of beings that in Jewish thought were next only to God—the angels. He is superior first with respect to his sovereignty. Hebrews defends this claim by means of *seven Old Testament quotations,* six taken to refer to Christ and one to the angels. When one looks up these passages, it is not always easy to see how one could interpret them as the author did. In some cases, at least a few Jewish commentators had already taken them as messianic texts. Second Samuel 7:14, cited in Hebrews 1:5b, is the least controversial. Nathan's promise to David to create an eternal kingdom from his descendants had not yet been fulfilled, so that many Jews understood this prophecy to refer to the messiah (cf. esp. 4QFlor 10:11, 18–19, which had already linked this text with the next one Hebrews cites).[15] While Psalm 2:7, cited in verse 5a, might refer to a mortal king, his universal sovereignty described throughout the psalm, if not rhetorical hyperbole, naturally suggests someone greater. At least the psalms of Solomon 17:21–18:7 had already determined this. Psalm 45:6–7, quoted in verses 8–9, creates the problem of appearing to address God but then speaking of a second individual called "God, your God." Again, the initial vocative could be exaggerated language for God's anointed monarch in Israel, but we can certainly understand why Jews as well as Christians could take the text as describing Messiah (cf. *Targum Ps. Jonathan* 45:2).[16]

The precedent for taking Psalm 110:1, quoted in verse 13, as messianic comes from Jesus himself (Mark 12:35–37 pars.). There Christ asks the temple crowds, in essence, who is this other "Lord" who speaks to "my Lord"? Jesus accepts the Jewish tradition and Psalmic superscription at face value, that David is the author of this psalm. There are no merely human lords above David, so the exalted figure in between Yahweh and the king must be Messiah.[17] A similar logic may be at work in the use of Psalm 102:25–27 in Hebrews 1:10–12. In the LXX, the consonants are revocalized so that once again we find God addressing God.[18] The strangest citation, at first glance, is the form of Deuteronomy 32:43 used in Hebrews 1:6. This clause does not even appear in the MT but only in the LXX, yet with the discovery of the Dead Sea Scrolls a Hebrew version of it has appeared (4Q Deut 32). Even then, there is no way to identify more than one divine figure in the passage or its

---

[14] The sequence of predicates about Jesus comes full circle, from exaltation, to creation, to eternal existence, to conservation of creation, to death and entrance into the heavenly sanctuary and back to exaltation again. See John P. Meier, "Structure and Theology in Heb 1,1–14," *Bib* 66 (1985): 189.

[15] Lane, *Hebrews 1–8,* 25.

[16] See further Murray J. Harris, "The Translation of *Elohim* in Psalm 45:7–8," *TynB* 35 (1984): 65–89; and idem, "The Translation and Significance of ὁ θεὸς in Hebrews 1:8–9," *TynB* 36 (1985): 129–62.

[17] There are pre-Christian Jewish hints of a messianic interpretation, but none is unambiguous. Post-Christian Judaism developed an unambiguously messianic interpretation, however. The text may well have been intended as typological, as well as prophetic. See Herbert W. Bateman IV, "Psalm 110:1 and the New Testament," *BSac* 149 (1992): 438–53.

[18] Perhaps even indicating that the Hebrew originally read that way. See Philip E. Hughes, *A Commentary on the Epistle to the Hebrews* (Grand Rapids: Eerdmans, 1977), 67, n. 38.

immediate context, and that figure is clearly Yahweh. But he is providing atonement, and the notion of Messiah rescuing God's people is hardly foreign to the Hebrew Scriptures (see esp. Isa. 52:13–53:12).[19] Once Jesus' disciples became convinced that his resurrection had vindicated his claims that his crucifixion would atone for humanity's sins, it would have been natural for them to assume that he was in view in Old Testament texts prophesying God's redemption for humanity.[20]

The lone text involving just the angels (Heb. 1:7) cites Psalm 104:4. While the word rendered "angels" here somewhat more naturally refers to "winds" (*pneumata*), the former translation is not impossible, particularly since *pneumata* frequently also means "spirits." And angels were often viewed as spirits (cf. v. 14).[21] Thus if anyone was tempted to seek refuge from persecution in Judaism, thinking that the angels could save them or delighting in the intertestamental apocalyptic writings that ascribed great power and majesty to the angelic host, Hebrews calls them to abandon such foolish notions.[22]

First Resulting Warning (2:1–4)   The first of Hebrews' five warning passages follows naturally. The gospel message spoken by Jesus demands our full attention, lest we begin to drift away, however slowly or imperceptibly (v. 1). The verb here (*parareō*) could also be used for a ring that slips unnoticed off one's finger.[23] After all, the Mosaic Law, believed in Jewish tradition to have been mediated by angels (recall above on Acts 7:53 and Gal. 3:19), itemized punishments for all violations (v. 2). How much more, then, shall we face judgment if we ignore the message mediated by someone greater than the angels (v. 3a)? The problem of whether the author of Hebrews believed that a true Christian could lose or forfeit his or her salvation is one that plagues every one of the warning passages, and we will explore it in greater detail under 6:4–8 below. Here the writer concludes this shortest of the five warnings by stressing reasons for continuing to believe Jesus' message. These Christians learned it from those who directly heard Christ, while God further confirmed its truth through miraculous signs and other spiritual gifts (vv. 3b–4).[24]

In Suffering (2:5–18)   Even more extraordinary than the Messiah's superiority to angels in sovereignty is his superiority in suffering. Clearly this was by far the less expected characteristic of his "job description." Hebrews begins this section by reminding the listeners that it was humans as his unique image-bearers (not angels) to

---

[19] Though again, only a small minority of pre-Christian Judaism seems to have taken the passage this way, rather than applying it to Israel corporately.

[20] Cf. C. F. Keil and F. Delitzsch, "The Fifth Book of Moses," in *Commentary on the Old Testament,* vol. 1 (Grand Rapids: Eerdmans, repr. 1985), 491–92. Cf. further Gareth L. Cockerill, "Hebrews 1:6: Source and Significance," *BBR* 9 (1999): 51–64.

[21] See further Ellingworth, *Hebrews,* 120.

[22] For a good book-length study of the uses of the Old Testament in Hebrews 1, see Herbert W. Bateman, *Early Jewish Hermeneutic and Hebrews 1:5–13* (New York: Lang, 1997). More briefly, cf. Stephen Motyer, "The Psalm Quotations of Hebrews 1: A Hermeneutic-Free Zone?" *TynB* 50 (1999): 3–22. On the various approaches to Hebrews' use of the Old Testament throughout the epistle, see George H. Guthrie, "Hebrews' Use of the Old Testament: Recent Trends in Research," *CBR* 1 (2003): 271–94.

[23] Bruce, *Hebrews,* 66.

[24] Nothing in the aorist tense of "confirmed" in v. 3 suggests that any of the miraculous signs have ceased or were entirely in the past. This simple Greek aorist tense merely describes certain things that happened prior to the time of the writing of Hebrews.

whom God initially entrusted the task of stewarding the earth (Gen. 1:27–28). Psalm 8:4–8 would later rehearse those truths in majestic poetry, marveling that God would grant such frail creatures so noble a responsibility (Heb. 2:5–8a).[25] But because of the fall and humanity's ongoing sin, creation is not properly subject to mortal men and women (v. 8b). Instead, the Messiah, born "a little lower than the angels" just like human beings, had to die for our sins (v. 9) in order to begin the process of restoring us to our rightful role in the cosmos.

Verse 10 describes this death as making him "perfect through suffering." The Son of God was ontologically perfect already, but he had not fully experienced all stages of human life until he died. So now he acquired an additional kind of perfection as well, one that some understand as a fulfillment, completion, or consecration (based on the meaning of *teleioō*).[26] This experience further enables him to identify with other human beings, all of whom must die sooner or later, and with believers in particular, who will be resurrected and exalted with him after their deaths (v. 11). Three more Old Testament quotes buttress these wonderful truths (vv. 12–13).[27]

Verses 14–18 spell out two additional implications of Christ's death. *First, Jesus has conquered death, and therefore the domain of the devil, to free all those held captive by it.* This aspect of the work of Christ has come to be known as the "classic" view of the atonement. Fear of death was widespread in the religions of the ancient Mediterranean world,[28] though most of them did not directly attribute that fear to Satan's activity. Nevertheless Jews and Christians alike believed that he was its indirect cause. *Second, by taking upon himself full humanity and temptability, he has not only made full provision for the forgiveness of sin, but knows intimately what temptation to sin feels like* (see esp. Matt. 4:1–11 pars.).

Over Moses (3:1–4:13) *Servant vs. Son (3:1–6)* Hebrews' second major comparison highlights Christ's superiority to the great lawgiver of Israel, Moses. This paragraph likens their differences to those between a servant and a son. Both were faithful to their missions, leading their followers or "households" (vv. 1–2). But Moses was faithful *within* his house, whereas Christ was the *builder* of the house, that is, the Creator (vv. 3–6). This holds true whether one takes "house" to mean "family" or "dynasty," and both may well be intended.[29] Jesus was also a heavenly sent messenger ("apostle") and high priest (v. 1), as well as God's very Son (v. 6),

---

[25] Nothing in either the psalm's or Hebrews' use of it refers to the Messiah. "Son of man," as in most of its Old Testament uses outside of Daniel 7:13–14, merely means a human being. "Man" and "son of man," like the lines in which they appear, exhibit simple synonymous parallelism. See, e.g., Gerald H. Wilson, *Psalms,* vol. 1 (Grand Rapids: Zondervan, 2002), 204–5.

[26] Leon Morris, "Hebrews," in *Expositor's Bible Commentary,* ed. Frank E. Gaebelein, vol. 12 (Grand Rapids: Zondervan, 1981), 27. Morris adds, "There is a perfection that results from actually having suffered" that "is different from the perfection of being ready to suffer."

[27] Space prevents a discussion of every use of the Old Testament in Hebrews. Here the larger messianic contexts of Psalm 22 and Isaiah 7–9 undoubtedly come into play in the interpretation of the specific verses.

[28] See esp. Peter G. Bolt, "Life, Death, and the Afterlife in the Greco-Roman World," in *Life in the Face of Death: The Resurrection Message of the New Testament,* ed. Richard N. Longenecker (Grand Rapids and Cambridge: Eerdmans, 1998), 51–79. For a detailed comparison of superstitious and godly fear in Hebrews, see Patrick Gray, *Godly Fear: The Epistle to the Hebrews and Greco-Roman Critiques of Superstition* (Atlanta: SBL, 2003; Leiden and Boston: Brill, 2004).

[29] deSilva, *Perseverance in Gratitude,* 137.

while Moses was only a servant (v. 5; based on Num. 12:7). Sons can inherit authority over households where servants cannot. Professing Christians, therefore, should not imagine that revering Moses rather than Jesus can bring them the spiritual inheritance they would want.[30]

Second Resulting Warning (3:7–4:13)　The logic of 2:1–3a reemerges. Faithless Israelites were severely punished in Moses' day, so those who harden their hearts against the gospel, announced by a far greater messenger, can expect only more fearful retribution (3:7–19). The author's concern that some in the Jewish-Christian community in Rome might commit apostasy reminds him of the warnings in Psalm 95:7–11 to the Israelites not to rebel against God as their ancestors did during the wilderness wanderings (vv. 7–11, 15). He was struck by the use of "today" in this psalm, demonstrating God's timeless concern that his people not fall away. Yet he also knows a day of judgment is coming when it will be too late to repent, so he warns his listeners to encourage one another to faithfulness "as long as it is called Today" (v. 13).[31]

The language of verse 14 does not settle the Calvinist-Arminian debate over what the Reformers called the perseverance of the saints. Both sides would have agreed that the way one determines who the true saints or believers are is to see who perseveres to the end.[32] But, as in Moses' day, as also in the first century, and indeed in every era of human history, many who abandon faith have been active in the community of God's people and have at the very least given the appearance to outsiders of being true believers. But if they die in disobedience and unbelief, they are lost (vv. 16–19).

Chapter 4:1–3a, however, may be seen as swinging the pendulum in the direction of the Calvinist interpretation. Here the author's language less naturally suggests someone who had truly believed. Instead, the writer is concerned lest anyone "be found to have fallen short of" God's promise of eternal rest (v. 1). Likewise, in verse 2, the problem with the rebellious Israelites in the wilderness generation was that they did not "combine" the hearing of God's word "with faith." Other manuscripts read, "because they did not share in the faith of those who obeyed" (NIV marg.), but either way the point seems to be that they never experienced full, saving faith.[33] Thus God declares with an oath that they will never enter his heavenly rest, whereas "we who have believed enter that rest" (v. 3a).

The author of Hebrews now develops the concept of "rest" in several stages (vv. 3b–11). From the accounts of creation, we learn that God rested on the seventh day (Gen. 2:2). This might have been all that Scripture would say about the topic (vv. 3b–4). Much later, however, Joshua would lead the Israelites into the Promised Land as God was providing them with rest from their enemies (v. 8). Later still, Psalm

---

[30] This remains true even for those who were convinced that Moses was more exalted even than the angels because of the intimacy he was perceived to have with God. It was still not on a par with Christ's union with his Father. See further Mary R. D'Angelo, *Moses in the Letter to the Hebrews* (Missoula: Scholars, 1979), 91–131.

[31] On the use of Psalm 95 throughout this section, see esp. Peter E. Enns, "Creation and Re-Creation: Psalm 95 and Its Interpretation in Hebrews 3:1–4:13," *WTJ* 55 (1993): 255–80.

[32] See esp. Schreiner and Canaday, *The Race Set Before Us*; cf. also Gerald Borchert, *Assurance and Warning* (Nashville: Broadman, 1989).

[33] P. Hughes, *Hebrews,* 157.

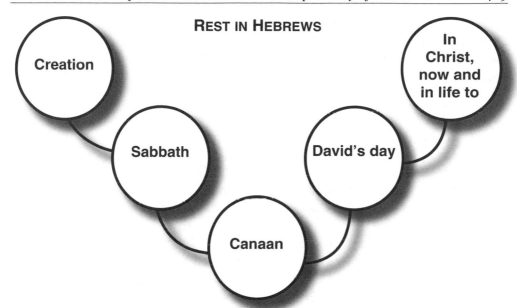

REST IN HEBREWS

Creation

Sabbath

Canaan

David's day

In Christ, now and in life to

95 would continue to offer rest for those in right relationship with God (vv. 5–7), and our author rightly recognizes that nothing has transpired since then to rescind this offer. *It is appropriate, therefore, to speak of people who become Christians as entering into God's rest, a kind of "Sabbath-rest" that is not tied to a particular day of the week or frequency of celebration but continues endlessly, even into the age to come.* We should move heaven and earth, so to speak, to ensure that we enjoy this incredible experience (vv. 9–11).[34]

Or, if threats motivate better than rewards, we are reminded of God's judgment that lies ahead and are assured that nothing we have done will escape it (vv. 12–13). The "word of God" in this context is not Scripture, but God's pronouncement of judgment or acquittal on a person based on the absence or presence of faith. Because God's knowledge remains all-encompassing, his insights and verdicts penetrate even to those parts of the human being otherwise usually thought to be inseparable.[35] Verse 12 offers no support for the trichotomous division of the human person into body, soul, and spirit; if we were to separate soul and spirit here, we would have to argue for a sixfold division of soul, spirit, joints, marrow, thoughts, and attitudes! The point here is not anthropological but eschatological.[36]

A number of theological corollaries follow from the warnings in 3:7–4:13. To begin with, the writer is not looking ahead to a literal return of Jews to the land of Israel, but sees the Old Testament promises of rest in the land fulfilled spiritually when men and women turn to Christ.[37] Second, Sabbath-keeping is no longer equated

---

[34] Khiok-Khng Yeo, "The Meaning and Usage of the Theology of 'Rest' (Κατάπαυσιν and σαββατισμός.) in Hebrews 3:7–4:13," *AJT* 5 (1990): 2–33.

[35] For an excellent application of this text to seminary students, see A. T. Lincoln, "God's Lethal Weapon (Hebrews 4:11–13)," *Themelios* 3 (1977): 1–3.

[36] Cf. Koester, *Hebrews,* 274.

[37] As is consistent with the rest of the New Testament teaching on this topic; see esp. W. D. Davies, *The Gospel and the Land* (Berkeley: University of California, 1974).

with ceasing from work one day in seven, but with resting in Christ throughout one's Christian life (cf. Matt. 11:28–30).[38] Third, there is continuity as well as discontinuity between the testaments. Hebrews can speak of the Israelites in the wilderness as also having had "the gospel" preached to them (4:2a), without thereby implying that they knew all the details that were disclosed only in New Testament times.[39]

Over Other Priests (4:14–7:28) *The Fundamental Exhortation (4:14–16)* Hebrews' third comparison proves the most extensive of all. Here the author demonstrates Christ's superiority over the entire Old Testament priestly system. These three verses begin this section with the implications of what will be demonstrated: *Jesus' high priesthood is neither temporary nor merely human, so he can offer his followers access into God's very throne room, empathizing with any kind of weakness we experience.* So they should hold fast to their professions of faith, pray to God for all their needs, and expect to receive mercy and grace. The expression, "has gone through the heavens," probably draws on the same multitiered imagery that we have seen before in 2 Corinthians 12:2 and Ephesians 2:2.[40] Christ's complete sinlessness, despite experiencing the full range of human temptations, is clearly taught in verse 15: "one who has been tempted in every way, just as we are—yet was without sin." But because every other human who has ever lived was able to sin when tempted, Jesus must have been "peccable" (able to sin) as well.

Much of Christian theology has often denied one or the other of these propositions. Conservatives are prone to say that Jesus, even in his human nature, never could have sinned, in which case his temptations were unlike ours. Liberals often deny Christ's sinlessness, in which case his death could not have substituted for ours; he would have been dying for his own sins. Millard Erickson captures the correct balance by affirming both Jesus' sinlessness and his peccability, adding that "while he could have sinned, it was certain that he would not."[41] This gives believers great assurance about Jesus' empathetic abilities. After all, "the Sinless One knows the force of temptation in a way that we who sin do not. We give in before the temptation has fully spent itself; only he who does not yield knows its full force."[42]

Comparisons with Aaron and Melchizedek (5:1–10) Chapter 5:1–10 provides the first of two sections comparing and contrasting Jesus' priesthood with the corresponding Old Testament institution, administered by the descendants of Levi through Aaron, and likening it ultimately to the priesthood of Melchizedek (cf. also 6:13–7:28).[43] Here the focus is primarily on the Aaronic priesthood; later the relationship with Melchizedek will be elaborated. Verses 1–4 mention three characteristics of Jewish priests: (1) these men represented all the people in offering the sacrifices that atoned for sin (v. 1); (2) they dealt gently with fellow sinners since they were

---

[38] See esp. A. T. Lincoln, "Sabbath, Rest and Eschatology in the New Testament," in *From Sabbath to Lord's Day*, ed. D. A. Carson (Grand Rapids: Zondervan, 1982), 197–220.

[39] For similarities and differences, cf. Lane, *Hebrews 1–8*, 98.

[40] Though we do not need to try to determine how many the author had in mind. See Bruce, *Hebrews*, 115.

[41] Millard Erickson, *Christian Theology* (Grand Rapids: Baker, rev. 1998), 735–37, with quote on p. 736.

[42] Morris, "Hebrews," 46.

[43] On the continuity and discontinuity between the two priesthoods, see Susan Haber, "From Priestly Torah to Christ Cultus: The Re-Vision of Covenant and Cult in Hebrews," *VSNT* 28 (2005): 105–24.

subject to similar weakness (vv. 2–3); and (3) they did not appoint themselves but were selected by God (v. 4).[44]

Hebrews next describes Christ fulfilling the same three criteria in reverse order (vv. 5–10). Jesus did not appoint himself; God selected him (vv. 5–6). Again Psalm 2:7 provides support, but so does Psalm 110:4, which will be expounded at length in chapter 7. Jesus was subject to the weakness of being human, even if not sinful, to the point of having to learn by human experience what it meant to be obedient (vv. 7–9a).[45] Here our author alludes to the story of Gethsemane (Mark 14:32–42 pars.), in which Christ demonstrated his utter humanity in longing to avoid the cross, just as any other rational person would desire. Yet he submitted to God's will when it became clear there was no other way. The end of verse 7 has puzzled many readers, as it claims that "he was heard because of his reverent submission," as if God had finally agreed to save him from crucifixion. But then all the references in this book to his atoning death would make no sense. More likely, the point is that God renewed his promise to Jesus to raise him up after his death and vindicate his mission.[46] Finally, Jesus' sacrifice provided salvation for all who followed him (vv. 9b–10).

Third Resulting Warning (5:11–6:12)   Here appears the central warning in this letter, not only as the third out of five, but as the most theologically pivotal as well. Chapter 5:11–6:3 laments the readers' moral and doctrinal immaturity; they should have progressed further in the Christian life by now. They should be teaching others, but they need to relearn the basics of the gospel instead. Rather than eating spiritual meat like adults, they must still drink spiritual milk like babies.[47] That some are seriously considering reverting back to Judaism (and that others may have already done so) demonstrates that they do not understand the exclusive source of true righteousness and cannot distinguish which path in life alone leads to eternal goodness (5:11–14). But the writer of Hebrews wants to be able to move them along to the next level, so that he no longer has to rehearse foundational Christian truths. These include repentance and faith rather than the works of the law as the means of salvation, Christian rather than Jewish baptism,[48] and the opportunity to look forward to resurrection life rather than eternal judgment (6:1–3).

Chapter 6:4–12 thus stresses the impossibility of repentance after one commits full-fledged apostasy. Perhaps no other passage in Scripture has provided more support for those who believe that true Christians can renounce their faith and be lost.[49]

---

[44] On the formative influence of the Pentateuchal laws for the priesthood on our author's thought here, see William Horbury, "The Aaronic Priesthood in the Epistle to the Hebrews," *JSNT* 19 (1983): 43–71.

[45] On the two different kinds of perfection involved, see above (p. 417). "There is a certain quality involved when one has performed a required action—a quality that is lacking when there is only a readiness to act. Innocence differs from virtue" (Morris, "Hebrews," 50).

[46] Ellingworth, *Hebrews*, 286–91. For a survey of other solutions, and in defense of a variation of this one, see James Swetnam, "The Crux at Hebrews 5, 7–8," *Bib* 81 (2000): 347–61.

[47] The imagery may have been taken over from patterns of education common in the ancient Mediterranean world. See Harold W. Attridge, *The Epistle to the Hebrews* (Philadelphia: Fortress, 1989), 162.

[48] This probably accounts for the plural "baptisms," while the laying on of hands in this context most likely also describes an aspect of baptismal rituals. See Koester, *Hebrews*, 305.

[49] For one of the strongest defenses of this interpretation, in light of all the relevant data of Hebrews, see Scot McKnight, "The Warning Passages of Hebrews: A Formal Analysis and Theological Conclusions," *TrinJ* 13 (1992): 21–59.

Some have seen this text as a merely hypothetical warning, but the tone seems too severe for that. Others have taken the author's threats to refer to loss of reward in heaven rather than loss of salvation, but the imagery of verses 7–8 points to hell as the ultimate danger.[50] Part of the difficulty doubtless stems from the fact that the readers are Jewish Christians living in a time and place in which the boundaries between non-Christian and Christian Judaism were far less clear than in most subsequent eras of church history. While the verbs in verses 4–5 ("enlightened," "tasted," "shared") all readily sound as if they refer to true believers, parallels inside and outside of the Bible show that they can describe people who have only a close association with something without having fully embraced it.

Similarly, to "be brought back to repentance" (v. 6) can mean to be brought again to the threshold of salvation. It is not as unlikely as many commentators suggest that the writer of Hebrews feared that at least some in his congregations had never sufficiently committed themselves to Christ so as to guarantee their perseverance during unprecedented persecution.[51] The wording of 2:3; 3:19; 4:2; 10:39; and 12:25 at least hints at the possibility that this author would have argued that those who flagrantly and unrepentantly renounce their professions of faith in Christ never were truly saved.[52]

But whichever perspective one adopts, it is important to recognize that Calvin and Arminius both agreed that Hebrews holds out no eternal hope for those who repudiate Christ and never change their mind in this life. Those two Reformers disagreed over what such behavior demonstrates about people's prior state, but they agreed about their eternal destiny. At the same time, other texts that speak of this "unforgivable sin" (Mark 3:29 pars.) make it clear that these are people who implacably oppose God. Scripture never depicts a scenario where a person who *wants* to repent is refused forgiveness. Moreover, immediately after this dire warning in verses 4–8, verses 9–12 proceed to express the author's continuing confidence in at least a majority of the people in his congregations. He believes that their attitudes and behavior in the past show that they *are* really saved, and he simply encourages them to "keep on keeping on" even as times get tougher. After all, the Reformation doctrine of the perseverance of the saints means that those who persevere show themselves to be genuine saints. "Once saved, always saved" may express a Christian truth in simple fashion, but often the only way to determine who was saved is to see who stayed saved![53] Whatever optimism the author of Hebrews has about the majority, he wants to be sure that "each" of them shows equal diligence (v. 11), suggesting he is less confident about the current state of a minority of his addressees.

---

[50] For a concise survey of the interpretive issues and options, see Guthrie, *Hebrews,* 223–32.

[51] David Mathewson ("Reading Heb 6:4–6 in Light of the Old Testament," *WTJ* 61 [1999]: 209–25) reinforces this point with reference to the Old Testament analogies cited.

[52] For a detailed defense of this viewpoint in light of each of the key expressions in vv. 4–6, see Roger Nicole, "Some Comments on Hebrews 6:4–6 and the Doctrine of the Perseverance of God with the Saints," in *Current Issues in Biblical and Patristic Interpretation,* ed. Gerald F. Hawthorne (Grand Rapids: Eerdmans, 1975), 355–64. Cf. also Wayne Grudem, "Perseverance of the Saints: A Case Study from Hebrews 6:4–6 and the Other Warning Passages in Hebrews," in *The Grace of God, the Bondage of the Will,* ed. Thomas R. Schreiner and Bruce A. Ware, vol. 1 (Grand Rapids: Baker, 1995), 133–82.

[53] Or, with deSilva (*Perseverance in Gratitude,* 221), the people described in Heb. 6:5 cannot be saved, since "salvation" for Hebrews is only finally determined at the end of one's life or when Christ returns.

Comparisons with Levi and Melchizedek (6:13–7:28)   Our author returns to his comparisons between Jesus' priesthood and those of Aaron and Melchizedek, though this time focusing more on Levi, the patriarch from whom the Jewish priests descended centuries before Aaron's day. He also develops in detail the analogies between Jesus and Melchizedek at which he has thus far only hinted. Chapter 6:13–20 picks up on the optimism of verses 9–12 and the promise believers will inherit (v. 12) to stress that God can be trusted absolutely to keep all his promises. Just as human beings make oaths to certify their commitments, God himself swore that he would bless Abraham and his progeny (Gen. 22:17), from which the entire plan of salvation eventually unfolded (vv. 13–15). People, of course, swear by a higher power, whereas God could not take an oath by any power higher than himself, because no such power exists. So he simply swore by himself!

Combine the oath (God's trustworthiness) with the character of the person by whom the oath was sworn (his immutability or infallibility), and we have "two unchangeable things" (v. 18) that guarantee his purposes will be accomplished.[54] All this should greatly encourage believers to continue to trust in Jesus even as days grow dark, especially when they remember Christ's atoning crucifixion, which perfectly fulfilled the same function as the high priest did annually on the Day of Atonement, when he entered the Holy of Holies (vv. 17–20).

Chapter 7 proceeds finally to unpack the concept of Jesus as an eternal high priest after the order of Melchizedek. Obviously, via his human lineage, he could not have qualified even to be an ordinary priest, because he was from the tribe of Judah rather than Levi. But Melchizedek represented a different way to become a high priest. Verses 1–10 point out the superiority of this Melchizedekian priesthood.[55] This obscure religious leader in otherwise pagan, Canaanite Salem (the precursor to Jerusalem) somehow had knowledge of "God Most High," the God of Abraham (v. 1a).[56] Abraham, in turn, acknowledged his subordinate role to this priest by tithing him his spoils from battle (vv. 1b–2a; recall Gen. 14:18–20). Both Melchizedek's name and the city in which he ministered have meanings that Hebrews considers significant pointers to his unique role (v. 2b).

Most telling of all, his priesthood is described as eternal: without mother, father, genealogy or beginning or end of life, he remains a priest forever "like the son of God" (v. 3). The word "like" makes it improbable that Hebrews' author thought that Melchizedek *was* the preincarnate Christ; rather, he was drawing an analogy between the two individuals.[57] The first part of this verse should probably be interpreted, "without *record* of father or mother, without *record* of the genealogy," and so

---

[54] Or, more simply, his oath and his promise (Lane, *Hebrews 1–8*, 152).

[55] On which, see esp. Bruce A. Demarest, *A History of Interpretation of Hebrews 7,1–10 from the Reformation to the Present* (Tübingen: Mohr, 1976).

[56] The standard evolutionary explanation of the development of religion—from early polytheism to late monotheism—cannot account for such anomalies. But the history of Christian mission is dotted with examples of peoples encountering the gospel, explaining that it meshed with ancient traditions that claim they had once known the one, true God but lost this knowledge through rebellion. Melchizedek could well have been one of a handful of people in his society who had preserved this knowledge. See Don Richardson, *Eternity in Their Hearts* (Ventura: Regal, rev. 1984).

[57] Koester, *Hebrews*, 349.

forth (cf. GNB). The point is not that Melchizedek had no parents or never died, but that he did not derive his priesthood from ancestral credentials or pass it on to any descendants.[58] On this model, Christ, too, could be considered a high priest.

But if Jesus is at least on the level with Melchizedek, then he is superior to the entire Old Testament priesthood. Verses 4–10 make this point by a somewhat convoluted argument that can be rephrased as follows: By giving his tithe to Melchizedek, Abraham demonstrated his own subordinate role. But the Old Testament priesthood came from the descendants of Levi, one of Abraham's great-grandchildren. So the Levitical priests likewise must have been subordinate to Melchizedek and any other priests of his kind. If Jesus, then, is a priest of Melchizedek's kind, then the Levitical priesthood is subordinate to Jesus as well.[59]

The rest of the chapter unfolds a second argument to demonstrate the inferiority of the Jewish priests. The very fact that a second model, that of Melchizedek, was picked up by Psalm 110:4 as descriptive of the Messiah shows that the priests from the tribe of Levi left something to be desired (vv. 11–28). Psalm 110, of course, was the same psalm that demonstrated the Messiah's superiority to Israel's kings (v. 1, cited in Heb. 1:13).[60] Hebrews 7:11 sets out the basic claim; verses 12–17 simply unpack it and reiterate the logic implicit in verses 4–10. But what was wrong with the old priesthood and the law that prescribed it? For one thing, it could not fully perfect people and, therefore, might as well have been useless, because God's presence may be entered only by those who are perfectly righteous and holy (vv. 18–19). Second, it was not instituted with the kind of oath one finds in Psalm 110:4 concerning the Melchizedekian priesthood, so it has not been as solemnly guaranteed (vv. 20–22).

Third, its priests, being mortal, died and had to be replaced, whereas Jesus' priesthood remains permanent (vv. 23–24). Fourth, as a result, Jesus provides complete and eternal salvation for his followers, always interceding for them from heaven,[61] in a way temporary, earthly priests never could do (v. 25). Fifth, the Old Testament priesthood was officiated by sinful people, qualitatively no different than those for whom they offered their sacrifices. Jesus, on the other hand, was utterly holy and sinless (vv. 26, 27b–28a). Finally, therefore, unlike the sacrifices legislated in the Torah that had to be repeated daily, Jesus' sacrifice was once for all, perfectly efficacious and never to be repeated (vv. 27a, 28b).

---

[58] It is often thought that Hebrews was relying on the rabbinic principle that what was not recorded in the Torah did not in fact exist. It may be, rather, that he was following a different rabbinical concept that when a pagan turns to Judaism he has no *legal* father. Melchizedek obviously had parents, but "he did not have the right of kingship or priesthood on account of his descent" (M. J. Paul, "The Order of Melchizedek [Ps 110:4 and Heb 7:3]," *WTJ* 49 [1987]: 207).

[59] And, of course, Hebrews' point is not that Jesus is just on a par with Melchizedek but that he is even greater. See esp. Jerome H. Neyrey, "'Without Beginning of Days or End of Life' (Hebrews 7:3): Topos for a True Deity," *CBQ* 53 (1991): 439–55.

[60] Deborah W. Rooke ("Jesus as Royal Priest: Reflections on the Interpretation of the Melchizedek Tradition in Heb 7," *Bib* 81 [2000]: 81–94) sees a tradition of sacral kingship here that can readily be applied to Jesus as well as Melchizedek.

[61] The picture is not one of a subordinate courtier pleading before a reluctant authority, but of an enthroned priest-king, "asking what he will from a Father who always hears and grants his request" (Bruce, *Hebrews,* 174).

Over the Old Covenant (8:1–10:39) *Obsolescence of the Mosaic Covenant (8:1–10:18)*[62]   From comparing the two priesthoods, it is a natural next step to compare the old and new covenants. Jeremiah had prophesied about a new covenant (Jer. 31:31–34), Jesus had applied Jeremiah's language to the wine at the Last Supper that symbolized his blood-letting death (Luke 22:20), and now Hebrews draws a further conclusion: the Mosaic covenant must be old and on the verge of disappearance (8:13).[63] The writer, in fact, makes two main points throughout these three chapters: (1) the Old Testament tabernacle prefigured a superior, more heavenly form of worship;[64] and (2) the Mosaic legislation has given way to a superior, more internalized ethic.[65] Chapter 8 introduces both of these emphases. Verses 1–5 describe the typological significance of the tabernacle, employing a "cosmological dualism" between earth and heaven, while verses 6–13 quote the prophecy about the need for a new covenant, employing "eschatological dualism" between old and new ages.

JESUS AS A PRIEST LIKE MELCHIZEDEK (HEBREWS 7)

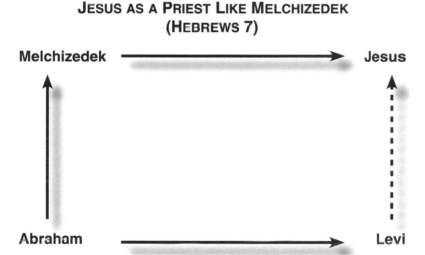

Because earthly priests served in a literal, physical sanctuary, they were never as exalted as Christ, who returned to God's right hand in what can be thought of as a heavenly sanctuary (vv. 1–5). Like Plato and Philo, the author of Hebrews envisions earthly objects as mere copies or shadows of heavenly realities and thus inferior to them. But his most direct inspiration comes from Exodus 25:40, which commanded the Israelites to build their sanctuary exactly according to the pattern God gave Moses on Mount Sinai, a pattern that is interpreted as corresponding to

---

[62] On the overall narrative flow of this section, cf. Gareth L. Cockerill, "Structure and Interpretation in Hebrews 8:1–10:18: A Symphony in Three Movements," *BBR* 11 (2001): 179–201.

[63] Graham R. Hughes (*Hebrews and Hermeneutics* [Cambridge and New York: CUP, 1979], 66–74) observes that discontinuity between the covenants is most highlighted in Hebrews' theological sections; continuity, in the ethical sections.

[64] On which, see esp. Susanne Lehne, *The New Covenant in Hebrews* (Sheffield: JSOT, 1990).

[65] Or in more sociological language, shifting from a community with "strong group, strong grid" to one with "weak group, weak grid." See Richard W. Johnson, *Going Outside the Camp: The Sociological Function of the Levitical Critique in the Epistle to the Hebrews* (London and New York: SAP, 2001).

those heavenly realities (v. 5b).[66] Perhaps this is why the writer chose to compare the tabernacle and not the temple with its heavenly counterpart, since no other text so explicitly draws a connection between the later Jerusalem temple and any corresponding entity in God's throne room.

But just as with the priesthood, the conclusion is drawn that an imperfect copy must give way to a better one. Because the instructions for the tabernacle were found in the law by which God's covenant with Moses was established, it is natural to expect a new covenant to enshrine the more perfect provisions for the ministry that Jesus inaugurates (vv. 6–13). Verses 6–7 make this point exactly. *Verses 8–12 then present the longest uninterrupted Old Testament quotation in the New, with Jeremiah's prophecy of the new covenant.* The covenant is still with the house of Israel (v. 8), though it is clear that for Hebrews the true Israel is as much the multiethnic church of Jesus Christ, combined with Old Testament believers, as it was for Paul (see esp. 11:40). But it will not result in the same kind of faithlessness as Israel displayed (v. 9; another good reason for believing Hebrews does not affirm the possibility of apostasy among genuine Christians). Rather, it will eventually produce a fully internalized ethic (v. 10), precisely what Jesus' moral instruction regularly promoted. Nor will the new covenant demand the same kind of elite, priestly class of intermediaries to offer religious instruction, because God's people will enjoy an untainted relationship with him (v. 11).[67]

Above all, this covenant will bring the full and final forgiveness of sins (v. 12). Verse 13 by itself could be taken as a statement of complete discontinuity between the old and new covenants, but the language of 10:1 ("the law is only a shadow of the good things that are coming"), reminiscent of Colossians 2:17, suggests that Hebrews follows the same "promise-fulfillment" scheme as the rest of the New Testament.[68]

Chapter 9 elaborates the two theses introduced in chapter 8. Verses 1–14 compare the earthly and heavenly tabernacles. The main point of this material is that even the holiest places and practices of the Jewish religion, described at length in verses 1–10, could not provide what Christ did—complete and final salvation (vv. 11–14). The detailed description of the furniture of the tabernacle (vv. 1–5a; v. 5b)[69] and of its ritual (vv. 6–10) could suggest that the readers were not as familiar with

---

[66] Alternately, perhaps "copy" in v. 5 should be translated as "preliminary sketch," so that a horizontal or temporal parallelism (more than a vertical or spatial parallelism) is in view already here too. See Lincoln D. Hurst, "How 'Platonic' are Heb. viii.5 and ix.23f?" *JTS* 34 (1983): 156–68.

[67] Cf. P. Hughes, *Hebrews,* 301–2. Obviously, in the "church age" teaching will be needed; the letter to the Hebrews is providing precisely that, but believers for the first time permanently indwelt by the Holy Spirit will not have to be told repeatedly to "know the Lord," as if being empowered afresh each time.

[68] The language of imminence, nevertheless, points to complete fulfillment in the future, even though Hebrews recognizes the new age to have begun and the old age to be in the process of passing away. This is the same "already but not yet" structure that characterizes both Jesus and Paul. Cf. Marie E. Isaacs, *Reading Hebrews and James* (Macon: Smyth & Helwys, 2002), 199.

[69] The golden altar of incense (v. 4a) was in fact not located in the Holy of Holies but in the court immediately outside (Exod. 30:6). It is hard to imagine a Jewish author (or anyone else as steeped in the Old Testament and its ritual regulations as this author) not knowing as basic a feature of the tabernacle arrangement as this. Donald Guthrie (*The Letter to the Hebrews* [Leicester: IVP; Grand Rapids: Eerdmans, rev. 1983], 180) may thus well be correct in arguing that the verb translated "had" here actually means "belonged," just as 1 Kings 6:22 describes this altar as belonging to the inner sanctuary even while not actually positioned in it. For detail, cf. Harold S. Camacho, "The Altar of Incense in Hebrews 9:3–4," *AUSS* 24 (1986): 5–12.

these features as Jews typically would have been. More probably, the writer is again stressing the careful attention to detail that the Israelites paid. Despite a long history of Christian allegorization of all of these elements, nothing in the text itself moves us in that direction.[70] Instead, everything serves the climactic point of verses 8–10 that, *despite all this elaborate care, the efficacy of these sacrifices was temporary and incomplete, awaiting the arrival of the new order of things.*

Christ's sacrificial death, on the other hand, provided permanent and complete atonement for sin, as his exaltation and return to his Father's right hand brought him into a heavenly sanctuary analogous to the earthly tabernacle, yet lacking its imperfections (vv. 11–14). By offering his own fully human blood, he perfectly qualified as a representative for human beings, something animal sacrifices and their blood could never accomplish. This is not to say that faithful Jews under the Mosaic covenant perceived that their sins were not properly dealt with, merely that the repetition of the ceremonies reminded the people that new sins required new sacrifices.[71]

Verse 15 forms a bridge to the next subsection of 8:1–10:19. The author has finished his discussion of the two tabernacles and returns to the contrast between the covenants, interweaving language about inheritance and ransom that he has used earlier. But his primary purpose in reintroducing covenantal terminology is to set the stage for a play on the Greek word *diathēkē,* which could mean both "covenant" and "will."[72] Thus, in verses 16–17 he shifts to the second of these meanings to exploit the fact that people receive the inheritance stipulated in a will only when the testator dies. Similarly, the Mosaic covenant/will required the deaths of animals to put it into practice, with the sprinkling of their blood comprising a central part of the ceremonies that symbolized the forgiveness of sins (vv. 18–22). Going all the way back to Leviticus 17:11 and the principle that a creature's life is in its blood, Jews and Christians alike came to believe that a death in which blood was actually shed was the requirement for atonement.

Our author, therefore, repeats for emphasis two of the points he has already made about Christ's superior sacrifice (vv. 23–28). It formed the heavenly antitype of the earthly ritual (vv. 23–24), and it was performed once for all time (vv. 25–28). This latter point leads to two corollaries. First, if Jesus' death provided full and final atonement, then the "end of the ages" must have arrived (v. 26b). Again we see first-century Christians believing that they lived in the end times! Second, unlike the situation during the Mosaic covenant, there will be no further opportunities to avoid judgment since there are no additional provisions to be made for salvation. *Verse 27 thus is one of the most important texts in Scripture to refute any "second-chance-*

---

[70] Instead of looking for symbolism in each item of tabernacle furniture, we should follow the author's established points of correspondence between the earthly and heavenly tabernacles, and between the old and new covenants. "The outer tent is to the Holy of Holies as the earthly tent is to the heavenly tent," while "the daily sacrifices are to the Day of Atonement as the levitical sacrifices altogether are to the sacrifice of Christ" (Steve Stanley, "Hebrews 9:6–10: The 'Parable' of the Tabernacle," *NovT* 37 [1995]: 398).

[71] William L. Lane, *Hebrews 9–13* (Dallas: Word, 1991), 225.

[72] On the other hand, John J. Hughes ("Hebrews IX 15ff. and Galatians III 15ff.," *NovT* 21 [1979]: 27–96) argues that the word means "covenant" even in these verses, as in every other use in Hebrews, and that the author is referring to the representative deaths of sacrificial victims when covenants were ratified. This view has become increasingly popular in the last quarter-century.

after-death" theology. As long as people live, they may always repent and turn to Christ. But once they die, their decisions are final and all that remains is to stand before God on judgment day. Then those, but only those, who have believed in this life can look forward to eternal salvation (v. 28).[73]

Undoubtedly, the writer of Hebrews realized the difficulty of inculcating all these comparatively new concepts among staunchly Jewish Christians, so he reiterates the imperfections of the old sacrificial system (10:1–10) and the perfections of the new covenant (vv. 11–18) one last time. The law formed but a transient shadow of the coming permanent realities because the sacrifices had to be repeated daily, seasonally, and annually (vv. 1–4). Verse 2 does not mean that faithful Jews continued to feel guilty about sins for which they had already offered sacrifices, but that again they recognized they had to keep offering sacrifices for each new round of sins. Verses 5–7 provide scriptural support (Ps. 40:6–8) for the author's argument. Christ did not come to the world to offer the kinds of sacrifices that Leviticus commanded, but to perform God's will by offering up his entire body himself (cf. vv. 8–10).[74]

That the temporary Old Testament sacrifices gave way to Jesus' perfect sacrifice leads to one more precious truth: his people now embark on the journey of being made holy, even if they reach their destination only in the life to come. After all, Christ himself has to wait until he returns to earth before he sees his enemies fully vanquished (vv. 11–14). Jeremiah had predicted this process, too, in God's determination both to declare believers legally free of blame (v. 17; citing 31:34) and to begin to actually make them more obedient (v. 16; citing 31:33). Sandwiched around these two quotations are another reminder that God's Spirit testifies through Scripture (v. 15) and the converse of an earlier affirmation. If a once-for-all sacrifice creates complete forgiveness, then full forgiveness likewise demonstrates no further need for sacrifices (v. 18).[75]

Fourth Resulting Warning (10:19–39) If no other religious system, not even pre-Christian Judaism, made full provision for the atonement of sin, then abandoning the Christian way could never be the right choice for a person to make no matter how bleak the circumstances might seem. Verses 19–39 thus issue an urgent call to perseverance. The immense privileges of the new covenant must be welcomed (vv. 19–25) by taking advantage of the new intimacy of access to God that Christ's death provided, purifying us fully, unlike the ritual immersions of Judaism (vv. 19–22), by faithfulness to our professions of belief and hope in Jesus (v. 23) and by corporate worship and fellowship, encouraging one another to love and good deeds (vv. 24–25). If even under growing persecution the author of Hebrews insisted that Christians "not give up meeting together" (v. 25a), how much greater disgrace it is

---

[73] Cf. Ronald H. Nash, "Restrictivism," in *What About Those Who Have Never Heard?* ed. John Sanders (Downers Grove: IVP, 1995), 108.

[74] For the seemingly strange use of Psalm 40 in these verses, see Bruce, *Hebrews,* 239–43. The tradition of David as spokesman led naturally to its attribution to "great David's greater Son," while "ears" may have been changed to the more understandable "body" by synecdoche.

[75] For a demonstration of the relevance of these claims and their uniqueness among the teaching of all other world religions, see William D. Spencer, "Christ's Sacrifice as Apologetic: An Application of Heb 10:1–18," *JETS* 40 (1997): 189–97.

when believers in less dangerous settings think they can go it alone in the Christian life or treat regular gatherings with fellow believers casually as an option only if nothing else intrudes on their schedules.[76]

By way of contrast, verses 26–39 depict the dire consequences of spurning the privileges of the new covenant. These verses contain as harsh, "judgmental" language as any in the New Testament.[77] Commentators typically interpret verses 26–31 to match their understanding of 6:4–6. A superficial reading of the text certainly favors the Arminian belief in the possibility of forfeiting (or repudiating) salvation. But again, receiving "the knowledge of the truth" (v. 26) does not necessarily imply that someone has acted on it by genuinely trusting in Christ, nor does trampling "the Son of God underfoot" or insulting "the Spirit of grace" (v. 29) have to portray something that only a Christian could do.

The hardest clause to deal with from a Calvinist perspective reads, "who have treated as an unholy thing the blood of the covenant that sanctified them." But "sanctification" does not always mean growth in Christian living, as so often in Paul, but can mean merely a "setting apart" of some kind. In 9:13, it is clearly used in the ritual sense of outward cleansing only, and that may be how our author is using the term here too.[78] But as with 6:4–8, whether a person was or was not a Christian before rejecting the faith is not the ultimate issue. Either way, both Calvinists and Arminians agree such a person is lost. *The main idea of this paragraph is that eternal judgment is so dreadful that we should avoid it at all costs* (vv. 27–28, 30–31).[79]

Verses 32–39 round out this section. Much as the writer qualified his threats in 6:1–8, with the hope that his readers would indeed persevere and demonstrate themselves to be truly saved, so also here he tempers his dire warnings with praise for these Jewish Christians' faithfulness after Claudius's edict expelled them from Rome and confiscated their property about fifteen years earlier (vv. 32–34; recall above, p. 413). As a result, he can encourage his listeners to persevere once again, reminding them also that, after what will represent a comparatively short period of suffering from an eternal perspective, Christ will return to judge their oppressors and lead his followers into glorious, endless bliss (vv. 35–39). A quotation from Habakkuk (2:3–4) clinches his argument.

Over Previous "Heroes of the Faith" (11:1–12:29) *The Cloud of Witnesses (11:1–12:13)* Chapter 10 ends by reminding the readers of the principle of living by faith, so it is natural to move to an explanation and series of illustrations of that faith. Throughout most of chapter 11, one might imagine that the author has finished making his point about Jesus' supremacy. But along the way he frequently comments about how these models of faith did not receive in this life everything God

---

[76] "The reason the meetings of the assembly are not to be neglected is that they provide a communal setting where mutual encouragement and admonition may occur" (Lane, *Hebrews 9–13*, 290). On "The Old Testament Concept of Solidarity in Hebrews" more generally, see the article so entitled by G. W. Grogan, *TynB* 49 (1998): 159–73.

[77] Famous for inspiring the eighteenth-century American theologian, pastor, and revivalist, Jonathan Edwards, to write his celebrated sermon, "Sinners in the Hands of an Angry God."

[78] Grudem, "Perseverance of the Saints," 177.

[79] deSilva (*Perseverance in Gratitude*, 344, n. 20) observes that this text describes "not the person who is Christian on the outside but refuses to be transformed on the insid [*sic*]; rather, it describes the person who shrinks back from being seen as Christian on the outside because of what that identification costs in a hostile society."

had promised them (see esp. vv. 13–16). By verses 35–38a, he is listing categories of people whose experience on this planet was downright miserable despite their faith (v. 39). And why was this? Verse 40 gives the answer: "God had planned something better for us so that only together with us would they be made perfect." In other words, the community of faith would not be complete until after Jesus had fulfilled his mission so that his followers could be included in that community along with believers of previous ages. So the theme of Jesus' superiority continues after all.

THE SUPERIOR PRIESTHOOD OF CHRIST (ACCORDING TO HEBREWS)	
Levitical Priesthood	**Jesus' Priesthood**
many in number	one
finite	eternal
foreshadowed salvation	completes salvation
offered by sinners, and for own sin	offered by sinless one, not for self
repeated	once for all
under temporary old covenant	under permanent new covenant
in earthly sanctuary	in heavenly sanctuary
barriers to access to God	intimacy with God
blood of goats and bulls	his own blood
outward cleansing	inward cleansing
conscience still guilty	full forgiveness
incomplete sacrifice for incomplete sanctification	complete sacrifice for complete sanctification

Before beginning what has often been called the "roll call" of Old Testament saints, our author provides an important definition of faith (v. 1). The KJV translates very literally: "Now faith is the substance of things hoped for, the evidence of things not seen." But what does this mean? The NIV's rendering is understandable but unrealistic—"being sure of what we hope for and certain of what we do not see." Certainty by definition excludes any doubt, and no believer has ever gone very long without various doubts! Instead, the author's point is that faith substitutes for the actual experience of things still in the future to show that there is reason to believe they will one day occur, especially when present reality seems to contradict such hope. *More simply, faith means believing God's promises about the future despite the appearances of the present.*[80] The Old Testament affords numerous examples (v. 2).

---

[80] "Hebrews addresses the contradiction between the promise of glory and the experience of reproach in the world" by producing examples of cases in which things have turned out well though seemingly 'contrary to reasonable expectation'" (Koester, *Hebrews*, 469–70, citing Aristotle for the last phrase).

Verses 3–38 thus proceed to unleash a barrage of illustrations of this kind of faith from Jewish history.[81] The series begins with God's act of creating the universe out of nothing, a perfect example of One who trusted that something he did not see at one moment would come into existence in the next by his very command (v. 3).[82] Long before the writing of Hebrews, Jews had debated what made Abel's sacrifice but not Cain's acceptable to God (Gen. 4:3–7). Without getting into specifics, our writer simply affirms that Abel in some way trusted God more and so brought him a more acceptable offering (v. 4).[83] We know even less about Enoch's life, except that God "translated" him to heaven without him having to die first because he had "walked with God" (Gen. 5:24). Hebrews reasonably interprets this walk as a life of faith (v. 5). Before moving on to the next illustration, the author generalizes by stressing that faith is a prerequisite for anyone who would please God and that it will be rewarded by him (v. 6).

The next set of examples proves easier to understand. Clearly Noah exercised amazing faith by building an ark on dry land to prepare for a flood, the magnitude of which the world had never before seen (v. 7; cf. Gen. 6:13–7:1). Abraham demonstrated robust faith by following God's call to leave his home and travel to a far country, the location of which he did not yet know, and to live as a stranger in a strange land even after he arrived there, as did his children and grandchildren (vv. 8–9; cf. Gen. 12:1–9). Perhaps even more remarkable was his willingness to believe that God would enable his wife and him to conceive a child at ages ninety and one hundred, respectively, from whom God would raise up enough descendants to populate the entire land of Canaan (vv. 11–12; cf. Gen. 18:1–10, 16–19; 21:1–5). But of course, none of the patriarchs would live to see all this happen (v. 13). While they could believe that God would fulfill his promises long after their deaths, their personal hope had to be for some kind of life after death with God (vv. 10, 14–16).[84] What else could possibly have motivated Abraham to obey the seemingly absurd command to sacrifice his only son Isaac, heir to the promise, unless he believed God could raise him from the dead and so continue to fulfill his plan for human history (vv. 17–19; cf. Gen. 22:1–19)?

---

[81] For detailed analysis, see Pamela M. Eisenbaum, *The Jewish Heroes of Christian History: Hebrews 11 in Literary Context* (Atlanta: Scholars, 1997). She stresses the author's emphasis on the "non-national" or "transnational" nature of these heroes' experiences, often explicit or at least implicit in the text, but in other cases inferred from diaspora Jews' (and Gentiles') somewhat parallel experiences.

[82] This text is often cited as support for the doctrine of *creatio ex nihilo,* but "not made out of what was visible" leaves the door open for the universe to have been "made out of that which was invisible," as in those worldviews that believe God molded the universe out of invisible pre-existing particles. But in context, v. 2 forms a chiasm—literally, "by faith we understand: to have been created [A] the world [B] by the word of God [C] so that not out of the visible [C] what is seen [B] has been made [A]." In other words, the unseen preexisting entity from which God created the cosmos was his own word! See Ellingworth, *Hebrews,* 568.

[83] Gen. 4:7a had already explained, "If you do what is right, will you not be accepted?"

[84] It is often asserted that the patriarchs could not possibly have believed in life after death, and especially not bodily resurrection, since no text in Genesis clearly teaches these doctrines and they seemed to have emerged only gradually over the entire Old Testament period. Yet every surrounding nation and culture believed in an afterlife, so it would be astonishing if Abraham, from Ur of the Chaldees, and his descendants did not. Moreover, the Egyptians clearly believed in bodily resurrection, with their mummification and elaborate tombs, so one can scarcely say that religion in general had not "evolved" to that level. Cf. Murray J. Harris, *From Grave to Glory: Resurrection in the New Testament* (Grand Rapids: Zondervan, 1990), 31–36.

The writer to the Hebrews moves on to briefer examples of similar faith in the lives of Isaac, Jacob, and Joseph. Isaac had to trust that Rebekah was really hearing from God when she was told that the younger of his twin boys would inherit God's blessings (v. 20; Gen. 25:23). Jacob needed even greater discernment at the end of his life as he divided up God's various blessings among his twelve sons (v. 21; Gen. 49:1–28).[85] Joseph obviously hoped against hope when he insisted that his bones be taken to the Promised Land, even though that event would not occur for another four centuries (v. 22; Gen. 50:25).

The second character on whom our author dwells in greater detail is Moses. Moses' parents exercised great faith by defying Pharaoh's edict to kill all newborn Israelite boys and saw God miraculously place the child in Pharaoh's own household (v. 23; Exod. 1:15–2:10). Moses himself rejected all the creaturely comforts of the elite family that brought him up in order to identify with his people, even though that meant leaving Egypt after he killed an Egyptian who was beating a fellow Hebrew (vv. 24–27; Exod. 2:11–25). Strong faith was likewise needed to believe that God would not destroy the firstborn Hebrews along with their Egyptian counterparts, that fleeing Egypt would actually lead to the people's freedom and that the Red Sea[86] would part as the people started to walk into it and not swallow them up as it subsequently did their pursuers (vv. 28–29; Exod. 11–14).[87]

Much more quickly, we are reminded of the faith of Joshua and the Israelites who marched around Jericho for seven days, waiting for God to knock its walls down (v. 30; Josh. 6). So, too, Rahab the prostitute believed that God was with the invading Hebrews and that they would protect her, even if she defied her own leaders by welcoming the Hebrew spies and lying about where they went (v. 31; Josh. 2). Our author realizes he could go on at length but believes he has made his point adequately. So he simply lists another half-dozen individuals by name, mentions the prophets as a group, summarizes a variety of their heroic exploits, and makes special mention of the mothers whose sons Elijah and Elisha raised from the dead (vv. 32–35a). But abruptly he shifts to the opposite extreme. Some equally faith-filled people experienced only persecution, suffering, and torture, not even enjoying the foretastes of God's promises with which most of their contemporaries in Israel had been blessed (vv. 35b–38).[88] And even the latter had clearly received only a small part of the full inheritance awaiting them (v. 39).

Why would God delay the process for so many centuries? Put simply, the Messiah had not yet come, and therefore the new covenant, which would bring all the greater blessings that Hebrews has so far highlighted, had not yet been inaugurated. In other

---

[85] The last half of v. 21 relies on the LXX of Gen. 47:31, which is quite different from the MT. On the various possible explanations, see Moisés Silva, "The New Testament Use of the Old Testament: Text Form and Authority," in *Scripture and Truth,* ed. D. A. Carson and John D. Woodbridge (Grand Rapids: Zondervan, 1983), 147–65.

[86] Again following the LXX rather than the MT and its "Sea of Reeds." But the latter shallower area flowed into the former, so there is no necessary contradiction.

[87] In fact, all the examples from Moses' life speak directly to the situation of Hebrews' audience by commending faith instead of fear. See Isaacs, *Hebrews and James,* 133.

[88] Not all of the categories of sufferings listed here appear in the Old Testament. The author appears to have relied on extrabiblical traditions as well, for example, the Martyrdom of Isaiah, in which that prophet was sawn in two (cf. v. 37). Those who were tortured after refusing release (if they violated their faith) in v. 35 were probably the Maccabean martyrs (see esp. 2 Macc. 6–12).

words, *God knew what a vastly larger number of people would become believers only during that later age, and he wanted them to be born and to have a chance to become a part of his "forever family."* Chapter 11:40 should humble all contemporary Christians and make them profoundly thankful for God's marvelous grace that waited so long so that they could be included as heirs to his incredible promises.[89] Full resurrection life, moreover, for all God's people of both covenant periods would be made possible only through the Messiah's death and resurrection.[90]

With all these models to inspire them, surely the Christians to whom Hebrews was written could "hang in there" a little longer and endure whatever persecution Rome might initiate (12:1–13). Verse 1 envisions the heroes of chapter 11 as "a great cloud of witnesses" surrounding these Jewish Christians, perhaps cheering them on like spectators in a stadium, but certainly inspiring them as the testimony of their lives is recalled. Of far greater importance, however, is the model of Jesus himself, who was willing to suffer even the agony and disgrace of crucifixion for our sakes. Because he has been reenthroned next to Yahweh, he can empower all those who focus exclusively on him to endure whatever hostility may come their way. As both "author" (or "pioneer") and "finisher" or ("perfecter") of our faith, he sees the process of preserving us through from beginning to end (vv. 2–3).[91] And Hebrews reminds his listeners that to date no one has yet been martyred in their community at all (v. 4).

What is more, God can use believers' suffering, even when it is more immediately caused by his enemies, to discipline and train his spiritual children (vv. 5–13).[92] Proverbs 3:11–12 taught the same thing centuries earlier (vv. 5–6), while ordinary human experience with biological parents and children reinforces this truth (vv. 7–11).[93] Of course, analogies between divine and human behavior always break down sooner or later. Some human discipline turns abusive, but our author's point is not that God engages in divine child abuse! Yet if moderate discipline balanced with love can train biological children to become well-behaved, how much more should we believe that God can use hardships to make us, his spiritual children, more holy! Therefore, we should exercise our spiritual limbs so that we are strengthened to run the race to which he has called us (vv. 12–13).

Fifth Resulting Warning (12:14–29) For the last time, Hebrews issues one of its solemn warnings against refusing God's plan of salvation. Sandwiched between a brief positive exhortation in verse 14 and a concluding call to worship God with thanksgiving and reverence in verses 28–29 is a stern admonition not to miss out on the wonderful blessings of the new covenant and suffer the horrors of eternal punishment (vv. 15–27). Bitterness can keep people from God, so it must be shunned

---

[89] Cf. further deSilva, *Perseverance in Gratitude*, 424.

[90] Gareth L. Cockerill, "The Better Resurrection (Heb. 11:35): A Key to the Structure and Rhetorical Purpose of Hebrews 11," *TynB* 51 (2000): 232–33.

[91] Wilson, *Hebrews*, 220.

[92] On which, see esp. N. Clayton Croy, *Endurance in Suffering: Hebrews 12:1–13 in Its Rhetorical, Religious, and Philosophical Context* (Cambridge and New York: CUP, 1998).

[93] The expression "Father of spirits" probably derives from "the God of the spirits of all flesh" (i.e., living beings) in Num. 16:22 and elsewhere. It does not naturally suggest the concept of preexisting spirits before their embodiment in human beings (Koester, *Hebrews,* 529).

(v. 15). So can sexual immorality, not because it is the unforgivable sin, but because so many people want to live a lifestyle contrary to God's standards (without recognizing that even in this life they only end up hurting themselves and others in the process) that they fail to become his followers (v. 16a). But any wholesale rejection of God's will, like Esau selling his birthright (Gen. 25:29–34), can prove equally disastrous (vv. 16b–17; cf. Gen. 27:30–40).[94]

How ironic this all is, for in the age of the new covenant what is offered to humanity is not a terrifyingly holy mountain (Mt. Sinai) that cannot be touched, as at the outset of the Mosaic covenant (vv. 18–21; cf. Exod. 19:12–13; Deut. 9:19). Instead God invites people to approach the heavenly archetype of the temple mount in Jerusalem (Mt. Zion) without terror and join the glad assembly of all believers from every era of history in the presence of Christ and all the holy angels (vv. 22–24).[95] Who on earth would want to refuse so incredible an offer? Yet people do, and then they must be alerted to what else an omnipotent God has promised—the dissolution of the cosmos as we know it, followed by new heavens and earth for the redeemed and the lake of fire (or hell) for everyone else (vv. 25–27; cf. Hag. 2:6 for the imagery and Rev. 21–22 for the elaboration).

CONCLUDING EXHORTATIONS (13:1–21)

Although the writer of Hebrews has interspersed exhortations and warnings throughout his epistle, he now groups together a series of concluding admonitions much as the more standard letters of Paul do. Verses 1–6 appear to be united around the theme of love, a perennially crucial responsibility, but all the more when a community is undergoing persecution.[96] Believers should treat one another with familial love (v. 1) but also show hospitality to strangers, particularly when one does *not* know who they are. They might well turn out to be bearers of glad tidings, as in Genesis 18–19 (v. 2). Applying the Golden Rule (Matt. 7:12), Christians should love and, therefore, help their spiritual brothers and sisters who have been imprisoned for their faith, just as they would want to be loved and helped if they were imprisoned (v. 3). Love of spouses demands exclusivity in sexual relationships (v. 4), while true contentment amid the changing circumstances of life requires believers not to love money. If God will never abandon them, then it ultimately matters little how much property remains (v. 5). Moreover, they need not fear persecution or even martyrdom, since the Lord will help them through it and bring them safely to glory afterwards (v. 6).

---

[94] Thus "society's goods stand in a value relation to God's reward similar to that of a single meal to a birthright" (deSilva, *Perseverance in Graatitude,* 462).

[95] As in chaps. 3–4, it is telling that our author mentions nothing of any hope for his audience of Jews to return to the land of Israel to experience the literal fulfillment of various Old Testament prophecies (most notably the rebuilding of the temple). Rather, his approach to the Old Testament imagery here is fully "spiritualizing," as he moves straight from this life to "heaven." Cf. esp. Marie E. Isaacs, *Sacred Space: An Approach to the Theology of the Epistle to the Hebrews* (Sheffield: JSOT, 1992). For this Sinai-Zion contrast in vv. 18–24 as "a hermeneutical key to the epistle," see Kiwoong Son, *Zion Symbolism in Hebrews* (Milton Keynes and Waynesboro, Ga.: Paternoster, 2005), subtitle.

[96] deSilva, *Perseverance in Graatitude,* 485.

Verses 7–17 may be loosely unified by the topic of good and bad leadership.[97] Both verses 7–8 and verse 17 commend good leaders, using the broadest term in the New Testament for such persons (*hēgemenoi*; from the verb for "govern"), so that no specific office is necessarily in view.[98] Christians should remember past leaders who taught God's word but also lived it, even when that led to hardships and perhaps death. The same Jesus who promises present help came to their aid, too, and will strengthen future believers equally powerfully (vv. 7–8).[99] Such people deserve the cooperation and respect of those over whom they have authority, particularly because they must give account to God for the leadership they have exercised over those very people (v. 17).

The words translated here as "obey" (from *peithō*) and "submit" (from *hupeikō*) are not the same ones used in the domestic codes in Colossians and Ephesians. "Obey" may, in fact, be too strong a rendering of a verb that in the passive voice (as here) can also mean "be persuaded," "pay attention to," "listen to" or "be a follower of."[100] "Submit," on the other hand, is the standard rendering of the second verb, which reminds us that God's people must voluntarily subordinate themselves to all their leaders, male and female, not just those in specific roles or offices that are reserved for men. We may discern here further implications of the mutual submission commanded in Ephesians 5:21.

In between this inclusio appears the warning not to follow the false teaching that wants to move these congregations back to full-fledged Judaism (vv. 9–16).[101] They must stand fast in God's grace, not trusting in the Jewish dietary laws or seasonal festivals, because these are fulfilled in Christ (vv. 9–10). One more time, the author reminds them that all this has come about because of the final and permanent sacrifice of Jesus on the cross, which took place "outside the camp," so to speak, of Jerusalem (vv. 11–12). Even if it means following in his footsteps, Christians must be prepared to accept whatever shame their faith brings them, because they know that this world is not their true home (vv. 13–14).[102] They should offer sacrifices, but not those of burnt or bloodied animals. Rather, they offer a metaphorical sacrifice of praise—acknowledging their God even when it costs them and treating others kindly even when abused (vv. 15–16).

As the letter nears completion, we learn for the first time that there may be one or more coauthors of the epistle. Verse 18 shifts to the first-person plural, though this need not refer to anyone other than the author and "those from Italy" who are with him (cf. v. 24). The singular form returns in verse 19, suggesting a primary author in any event, who desires prayer that he might live honorably and be able to see his congregations in Rome soon. Verses 20–21 bring this section to a close with a

---

[97] Cf. ibid., 508.

[98] Cf. Lane, *Hebrews 9–13*, 526.

[99] Verse 8 thus has nothing to do with the idea that methods of Christian worship and service should continue unchanged from one generation to the next, regardless of their relevance, as is sometimes alleged.

[100] Koester (*Hebrews,* 572) thus prefers the translation "heed."

[101] Or to leave it more decisively if they have never done so in the first place. See Norman H. Young, "'Bearing His Reproach' (Heb 13.9–14)," *NTS* 48 (2002): 243–61.

[102] Hebrews thereby calls its audience to forego both a people and a place, both Judaism and Jerusalem. See Peter Walker, "Jerusalem in Hebrews 13:9–14 and the Dating of the Epistle," *TynB* 45 (1994): 39–71.

beautiful doxology perfectly tailored to the circumstances. The God who is invoked is the One who established the everlasting new covenant through Jesus, the Good Shepherd, who died for humanity's sins and was raised by his Father. Thus he can now empower his followers to perform God's will and please him in every walk of life (vv. 20–21).

LETTER CLOSING (13:22–25)

Despite the fact that the letter would take an hour or so to read aloud as a sermon, it remains brief (v. 22), at least in comparison with some ancient orations.[103] Apparently Timothy has been imprisoned but recently released, and if he meets up with the author the two will come to Rome together (v. 23). Finally, our writer greets all his addressees again, singling out the leaders for special mention during these tough times and pronouncing his grace upon all of the believers in his congregations (vv. 24–25).

APPLICATION

No other New Testament document presents as strong or sustained an emphasis on both the perfect deity *and* the perfect humanity of Christ. Only with this precise combination of natures could Jesus have offered an eternal, once-for-all sacrifice on the one hand and a representative, vicarious sacrifice on the other. As it stands, this is exactly the form of atonement he provides, thereby rendering any other supposed form of atonement obsolete, irrelevant, and impotent. Only through Christ's crucifixion can anyone find redemption.

Hebrews' audience was tempted to lapse back into a temporarily safe form of "civil religion" (in their case, Judaism) to avoid persecution, but in so doing, whether they realized it or not, they risked renouncing faith in Jesus and placed themselves in danger of being damned. Western Christianity today counts large numbers of nominal adherents who identify with the movement, but just to the extent that it is socially acceptable. It may be that only the crucible of suffering or persecution can prove the reality of a person's profession of faith. If so, a huge percentage of self-identified believers in the Western world remain untested, at least to the extent that many Christians throughout church history and in other parts of the world today have been tried. Others, who have already abandoned their professions under less severe circumstances, have shown that they never had saving faith to begin with.

Repentance always remains possible so long as the breath of life resides within a person. Still, without the ability to forecast the time of one's physical demise, no one who needs to repent and turn (or turn back) to Jesus dare delay. Hebrews asserts that Jesus' supremacy over all other religious institutions and figures, even among the people group that represented God's elect nation until the establishment of the new covenant, makes it ludicrous, indeed eternally perilous, to adopt any other religion, philosophy, or worldview besides Christianity.

---

[103] deSilva, *Perseverance in Gratitude*, 513.

One important form of immunization against the temptation to apostatize is regular biblically based devotions (and devotion). God's Word is powerful; even the Old Testament points to Christ whether literally or typologically. Full understanding of Scripture requires the insights of the entire church, just as believers are meant to gather regularly in assemblies of worship, prayer, mutual encouragement, and scriptural instruction.

ADDITIONAL QUESTIONS FOR REVIEW

1. What are the hypotheses for the authorship of Hebrews, and which hypothesis is most likely, given the evidence?
2. What is the relationship of the date of Hebrews to the make-up of its audience? What date is most likely for Hebrews? What was the historical context of the audience and the writer?
3. Identify the central thesis of the letter to the Hebrews. What is the author trying to encourage his audience to do? What structural features of the letter help to achieve this goal?
4. What do the comparisons of Christ to each of the institutions mentioned in Scripture convey about Jesus? To what institutions is Christ compared?
5. How are some of the more difficult uses of Old Testament Scripture in the comparison of Christ to the angels used in Hebrews 1 best understood?
6. What theological issue plagues every warning passage in Hebrews? What are the different camps and their interpretations of this issue? Which warning passages are the most helpful to solving the debate, and why? No matter how one settles the issue, what is the central truth the author wishes to emphasize in the warning passages, especially Hebrews 6:4–12?
7. What are the full implications of Christ's suffering and death according to Hebrews 2? What benefits does humanity gain from his death in both this life and in the life to come?
8. How does Jesus' priesthood differ significantly from the priesthood of merely human priests? With what examples does the author assert the superiority of Jesus to the entire Old Testament priesthood?
9. What specific features of the new covenant under Christ are superior to the old covenant under Moses?
10. What would be a good clarification to the NIV translation of the definition of faith in Hebrews 11? Which examples of the heroes of the faith received sustained attention, and for what reasons? What was the purpose of "the roll call of faith" for the audience of Hebrews that is often missed by contemporary Christians in comfortable settings? How is this purpose reinforced by the opening verses of Hebrews 12?

SELECT BIBLIOGRAPHY

Commentaries

Advanced

Attridge, Harold W. *The Epistle to the Hebrews.* Hermeneia. Philadelphia: Fortress, 1989.
Ellingworth, Paul. *The Epistle to the Hebrews.* NIGTC. Carlisle: Paternoster; Grand Rapids: Eerdmans, 1993.
Koester, Craig R. *Hebrews.* AB. New York and London: Doubleday, 2001.
Lane, William L. *Hebrews,* 2 vols. WBC. Dallas: Word, 1991.

Intermediate

Bruce, F. F. *The Epistle to the Hebrews.* NICNT. Grand Rapids: Eerdmans, rev. 1990.
deSilva, David A. *Perseverance in Gratitude: A Socio-Rhetorical Commentary on the Epistle "to the Hebrews."* Grand Rapids and Cambridge: Eerdmans, 2000.
Hughes, Philip E. *A Commentary on the Epistle to the Hebrews.* Grand Rapids: Eerdmans, 1977.
Wilson, R. McL. *Hebrews.* NCB. London: Marshall, Morgan & Scott; Grand Rapids: Eerdmans, 1987.

Introductory

Guthrie, Donald. *The Letter to the Hebrews.* TNTC, rev. Leicester: IVP; Grand Rapids: Eerdmans, 1983.
Guthrie, George H. *Hebrews.* NIVAC. Grand Rapids: Zondervan, 1998.
Hagner, Donald A. *Encountering the Book of Hebrews.* Grand Rapids: Baker, 2002.
Isaacs, Marie E. *Reading Hebrews and James.* Macon: Smyth & Helwys, 2002.
Lane, William L. *Call to Commitment: Responding to the Message of Hebrews.* Nashville: Nelson, 1985.

Other Books

D'Angelo, Mary R. *Moses in the Letter to the Hebrews.* Missoula: Scholars, 1979.
deSilva, David A. *Despising Shame: Honor Discourse and Community Maintenance in the Epistle to the Hebrews.* Atlanta: Scholars, 1995.
Dunnill, John. *Covenant and Sacrifice in the Letter to the Hebrews.* Cambridge and New York: CUP, 1993.
Gelardini, Gabriella, ed. *Hebrews: Contemporary Methods—New Insights.* Leiden and Boston: Brill, 2005.
Hurst, Lincoln D. *The Epistle to the Hebrews: Its Background of Thought.* Cambridge and New York: CUP, 1990.
Isaacs, Marie E. *Sacred Space: An Approach to the Theology of the Epistle to the Hebrews.* Sheffield: JSOT, 1992.

Käsemann, Ernst. *The Wandering People of God: An Investigation of the Letter to the Hebrews.* Minneapolis: Augsburg, 1984.

Lehne, Susanne. *The New Covenant in Hebrews.* Sheffield: JSOT, 1990.

Lindars, Barnabas. *The Theology of the Letter to the Hebrews.* Cambridge and New York: CUP, 1991.

Peterson, David. *Hebrews and Perfection.* Cambridge and New York: CUP, 1982.

Rhee, Victor (Sung-Yul). *Faith in Hebrews: Analyses within the Context of Christology, Eschatology, and Ethics.* New York: Peter Lang, 2001.

Salevao, Iutisone. *Legitimation in the Letter to the Hebrews: The Construction and Maintenance of a Symbolic Universe.* London and New York: SAP, 2002.

Scholer, John M. *Proleptic Priests: Priesthood in the Epistle to the Hebrews.* Sheffield: JSOT, 1991.

Thompson, James W. *The Beginnings of Christian Philosophy: The Epistle to the Hebrews.* Washington: CBAA, 1982.

Trotter, Andrew H. *Interpreting the Epistle to the Hebrews.* Grand Rapids: Baker, 1997.

BIBLIOGRAPHY

Mills, Watson E. *Hebrews.* Lewiston and Lampeter: Mellen, 2001.

11

1 Peter: Perseverance Despite Persecution

INTRODUCTION

AUTHORSHIP

First Peter 1:1 claims that this letter was written by Peter, the apostle of Jesus. The only Peter who appears in the New Testament is Simon Peter, the leader of the Twelve, who was promised the keys to the kingdom (Matt. 16:16–19), denied his Lord three times (Mark 14:66–72 pars.), was reinstated by Christ after the miraculous fish catch on Lake Galilee (John 21:15–19), and served as chief apostle and missionary, particularly to the Jews, during the first twelve chapters of Acts. He and Paul vigorously opposed each other in Antioch over the issue of Judaizing (Gal. 2:11–15) but were later reconciled, personally and theologically (Acts 15:1–29). Early church tradition claimed that Peter was crucified upside down by Nero in Rome in the mid- to late-60s.[1] No alternatives to Petrine authorship of this letter were ever suggested in antiquity, and numerous early Christian sources agreed that Peter was the author (see esp. Irenaeus, *Against Heresies* 4.9.2; Tertullian, *Scorpiace* 12; and Origen, cited by Eusebius, *Church History* 6.25.8).[2] Some writers have detected various similarities between the style and contents of 1 Peter and Peter's various sermons in Acts or sayings in the Gospels.[3]

Nevertheless, various modern scholars have denied that Peter could have written this epistle. The vocabulary and style are alleged to be too polished a form of Greek for a Jewish fisherman writing in a second language. The persecution implied in 4:12 (literally "the fiery trial," as if Christians were being burned at the stake) and 5:9 ("throughout the world") is too intense and widespread to fit a date during Peter's lifetime, in which the only imperial persecution unleashed against Christians occurred in and around Rome under Nero (64–68). Burning people by fire scarcely occurred on any widespread basis. Still other concerns involve the apparent dependence of 1 Peter on Paul's letters, especially the Prison Epistles, including those often alleged to be post-Pauline, and the lack of much direct reference to Christ's life and teachings in this letter.[4]

---

[1] The standard survey of Peter's life according to early Christian documents is Raymond E. Brown, Karl P. Donfried, and John Reumann, *Peter in the New Testament* (Minneapolis: Augsburg, 1973). A more recent discussion that focuses more on post-New Testament literature, orthodox and unorthodox alike, is F. Lapham, *Peter: The Myth, the Man and the Writings* (London and New York: SAP, 2003).

[2] For these and other primary sources, see J. Ramsey Michaels, *1 Peter* (Waco: Word, 1988), xxxii–xxxiv.

[3] E.g., Martin, *New Testament Foundations,* vol. 2, 330–31.

[4] For a full catalogue of arguments for and against Peter's authorship of this book, see John H. Elliott, *1 Peter* (New York and London: Doubleday, 2000), 118–30.

On the other hand, it is possible that an amanuensis, skilled in Greek, accounted for the polished style, though, even more so than with James, it is virtually impossible to determine today how skilled in Greek a first-century Jew traveling throughout the Hellenistic world over several decades like Peter could have become (esp. if one does not mistranslate Acts 4:13 as implying the apostles' illiteracy).[5] "With the help of (*dia*) Silas" in 1 Peter 5:12 has often been taken as indicating that Peter dictated his letter to his Greek companion, who could have greatly improved its style, but more recent research casts doubt on this interpretation. Parallel expressions elsewhere do not normally indicate help in letter writing, merely in delivering an epistle.[6]

As for the persecution, the fiery trial may be a metaphor for intense suffering without literal flames, as in the NIV's rendering, "painful trial," in 1 Peter 4:12.[7] Moreover, no period within the first 150 years of Christian history saw empire-wide persecution of believers; this would take place only much later. Yet 1 Peter is quoted by early- and mid-second-century Christian writers, so we know it had to have been written by then. Chapter 5:9 is much more likely referring to unofficial, local harassment of believers, such as Christians received from both Jews and Gentiles throughout the book of Acts in the first generation of church history.[8] After all, the one specific elaboration of the persecution in the letter describes Christians' pagan acquaintances abusing them for no longer engaging in debauched partying with them (4:4), precisely the local kind of rejection that believers could experience anywhere irrespective of imperial policies or attitudes.

With respect to the relationship between 1 Peter and Paul's letters, it is doubtful that direct dependence can be established; the parallels prove closest in the sections on submitting to authorities, commonplace injunctions among *Haustafeln* of the day. Next most common are theological and Christological parallels in passages that have often been deemed to reflect early Christian creeds and confessions—the type of material that was widely affirmed in the primitive church.[9] And, as in James, even if there are no exact quotations of the Jesus traditions, there are numerous allusions to the kinds of things Jesus did and said in the Gospels.[10] Thus, even though pseudonymity is affirmed by a slight majority of current scholars, roughly comparable to the situation with Colossians among the deutero-Paulines, the case remains unproven and *traditional claims of authorship can still be accepted.* Indeed, even among commentators unwilling to go this far, proposals of a "Petrine circle" of Peter's disciples as responsible for this letter have grown in popularity. But no adequate criteria

---

[5] On the other hand, Karen H. Jobes (*1 Peter* [Grand Rapids: Baker, 2005], 325–38) determines that the letter contains enough "Semitic interference" in the syntax to suggest that Greek was not the first language of the author.

[6] E. Randolph Richards, "Silvanus Was Not Peter's Secretary: Theological Bias in Interpreting διά Σιλουάνου ἔγραψα in 1 Peter 5:12," *JETS* 43 (2000): 417–32.

[7] Thomas R. Schreiner, *1, 2 Peter, Jude* (Nashville: Broadman & Holman, 2003), 219.

[8] I. Howard Marshall, *1 Peter* (Leicester and Downers Grove: IVP, 1991), 23, 171.

[9] J. N. D. Kelly, *A Commentary on the Epistles of Peter and of Jude* (London: Black; New York: Harper, 1969), 11–15.

[10] See esp. Robert H. Gundry, "'Verba Christi' in 1 Peter: Their Implications concerning the Authorship of 1 Peter and the Authenticity of the Gospel Tradition," *NTS* 13 (1966–67): 336–50; idem, "Further *Verba* on the *Verba Christi* in First Peter," *Bib* 55 (1974): 211–32.

exist for distinguishing this origin of the epistle from more straightforward Petrine authorship (or from more "random" pseudonymity either).[11]

SETTING

Chapter 5:13 announces that "she who is in Babylon, chosen together with you, sends you her greetings." But Old Testament Babylon lay in ruins, and only a small village existed nearby in New Testament times. No other ancient documents ever suggest that Christianity had reached this area this early (or that it would reach there for several centuries), and Babylon was a long way from the addressees who lived in what we would call western and central Turkey (1:1). Given that Revelation uses "Babylon" as a code word for Rome (Rev. 17:5), that Peter ended his apostolic career in Rome and that Mark came to Rome to be with Paul in the mid-60s (2 Tim. 4:11; probably also Col. 4:10) and is with Peter as he writes this letter (1 Pet. 5:13), it seems likely that *Peter is writing from Rome.*[12]

An older generation of scholars frequently suggested that the more specific setting for the use of significant portions of 1 Peter was a baptismal liturgy.[13] More recent commentators recognize this hypothesis as "possible," but lacking enough external evidence to deem it "probable." Even so, it is clear that there are several Christological creeds or confessions of the kind we saw scattered about Paul's letters, especially in 1:19–21; 2:21–25; and 3:18–22, that would be very appropriate for new believers to learn and recite as they encapsulate fundamental doctrine about the person and work of Christ. Scholars also agree that Peter is using numerous sources and traditions throughout his letter— note also the *Haustafel* in 2:13–3:7—but they recognize that identifying these without new comparative evidence seems to remain outside our reach.[14]

DATE

Those who find 1 Peter pseudonymous usually date the letter to the time of the Roman emperor Domitian, in the late 80s or early 90s just before his short-lived but intense persecution of Christians in the mid-90s,[15] while some place it as late as the hostilities under Trajan in the 110s.[16] A few stress the lack of explicit imperial persecution and date the epistle to the comparatively peaceful era of the 70s or 80s.[17] If Peter indeed wrote this letter, however, then it is best dated to the early- or mid-60s, *just before or just as the Neronic persecution began.* It is true that Peter left Jerusalem around A.D. 44 (Acts 12:17), could have traveled through the provinces

---

[11] For a survey and critique of recent proposals, see David G. Horrell, "The Product of a Petrine Circle? A Reassessment of the Origin and Character of 1 Peter," *JSNT* 86 (2002): 29–60.

[12] So almost all commentators, whether or not they accept Petrine authorship. See, e.g., Paul D. Achtemeier, *1 Peter* (Minneapolis: Fortress, 1996), 353–54.

[13] See esp. throughout Edward G. Selwyn, *The First Epistle of St. Peter* (London: Macmillan, rev. 1947; Grand Rapids: Baker, 1981).

[14] Which likewise undermines the main, older theories for 1 Peter as a composite document. See Achtemeier, *1 Peter,* 58–62.

[15] So, e.g., Ernest Best, *1 Peter* (London: Marshall, Morgan & Scott, 1971; Grand Rapids: Eerdmans, 1981), 63–64.

[16] E.g, Francis W. Beare, *The First Epistle of Peter* (Oxford: Blackwell, 1970).

[17] E.g., Elliott, *1 Peter,* 134–38.

CHURCHES OF THE REVELATION

REV. 2–3

- City
- Cities of the Seven Churches
- Major road

John writes Revelation encouraging Christians to remain faithful.

he addresses very soon thereafter, and could have arrived in Rome already in the later 40s or during the decade of the 50s. But solid external tradition does not place him in the imperial capital until the 60s. At the same time, if the traditions of Peter's martyrdom under Nero are accurate, the letter cannot be dated after that emperor's suicide in 68.[18] Chapter 3:13–14 suggests that persecution for one's faith is still viewed as possible but not probable, while 2:13–17 reminds us of Romans 13:1–7 with its positive attitude toward submission to the governing authorities. All this suggests a date of *63 or early 64,* perhaps very close in time and circumstances to the epistle to the Hebrews.[19]

RECIPIENTS

The recipients of 1 Peter were scattered throughout *Pontus, Galatia, Cappadocia, Asia, and Bithynia,* five Roman provinces connected by roads that could have allowed couriers to pass this letter, and copies that would be made of it, from each region of modern-day Turkey to the next in the order they are listed (1:1). Despite the language of election and dispersion (1:1–2), reminiscent of James 1:1, it is doubtful if Jewish Christians comprised more than a minority of Peter's audience. Gentiles predominated throughout these parts of the ancient world, and it is unlikely that Jews would ever have been described as living the lascivious lives of dissipation that pagans practiced (4:4). Chapter 2:10 reinforces the impression that *a majority were Gentile Christians* by referring to the recipients as once no people, but now a part of the people of God. Compare also the descriptions of these believers' past lives in 1:14 and 18.[20]

In several writings, John Elliott has argued in detail that at least a significant number of the "aliens and strangers" (2:11) to whom 1 Peter is addressed (cf. 1:1) should be taken as literal refugees—persons involuntarily displaced from their homelands. The terms *paroikai* and *parepidēmoi* do most commonly mean "resident aliens" and "visiting strangers" in a geographical and ethnic sense. Earthquakes, famines, wars, and similar upheavals certainly did displace many residents in the Roman Empire in the first century, while persecution or harassment for one's Christian faith may have driven others to leave their homes.[21] But there is also good biblical precedent for understanding such language metaphorically. Because this world is not Christians' true home (recall Phil. 3:20 and Heb. 11:13–16), all of them can be thought of as aliens and strangers wherever they live.[22] Moreover, the very process of converting from Judaism or one of the Greco-Roman religions to Christianity produced enough initial disorientation and reorientation that new believers could have felt particularly

---

[18] For a concise catalogue of these and other extrabiblical traditions about Peter's life, see Edgar Hennecke, *New Testament Apocrypha,* ed. Wilhelm Schneemelcher, vol. 2 (London: Lutterworth; Philadelphia: Westminster, 1965), 45–50. Curiously, almost all of the material on the early traditions about the activities of each of the apostles is omitted from the revised edition of 1992.

[19] Cf. Wayne Grudem, *The First Epistle of Peter* (Leicester: IVP; Grand Rapids: Eerdmans, 1988), 35–37.

[20] Cf. Achtemeier, *1 Peter,* 50–51.

[21] See esp. John H. Elliott, *A Home for the Homeless* (Philadelphia: Fortress; London: SCM, 1981).

[22] See esp. Moses Chin, "A Heavenly Home for the Homeless: Aliens and Strangers in 1 Peter," *TynB* 42 (1991): 96–112.

"homeless for a while."[23] So it is impossible to determine what percentage of Peter's audience may have been literal refugees.[24]

Genre and Outline

First Peter is the first of the non-Pauline letters to both begin and end like a true Hellenistic epistle. In between, the body of the letter intersperses doctrine and ethics, more like Hebrews than like most of Paul's epistles. But unlike Hebrews, the exhortational material begins and dominates each main section, with the theological material subsequently and much more briefly providing the rationale for Peter's commands. The Christological confessions or creeds, in particular, function in this fashion. The first major section of the letter body reflects a strong call to holiness and a concern that Peter's congregations care for one another as the surrounding society falls apart or proves hostile to them (1:13–2:10).[25] The second major section, however, simultaneously stresses the need to preserve right relationships in family and society as an evangelistic witness to a fallen world (2:11–4:19).[26] Together, both of these objectives are designed to give the persecuted believers hope in the midst of suffering. Chapter 4:19 ("So then, those who suffer according to God's will should commit themselves to their faithful Creator and continue to do good") may well form the thesis statement of the letter, summarizing these twin strands of emphasis.[27]

This overall structure does not neatly conform to one particular subgenre of letter. Ramsey Michaels creates the label "an apocalyptic diaspora letter to Israel."[28] Paul Holloway focuses more on function than form and finds significant parallels to a letter of consolation.[29] Like James, 1 Peter reflects the address of a key Jewish Christian leader writing to more than just a single community of Christians. The application of the language of God's elect (see esp. 1:1; 2:5, 9), no longer strictly to literal Jews but to the church of Jesus Christ of whatever ethnic composition, is one of the important theological developments of this epistle.

   I. Greeting (1:1–2)
  II. Blessing (1:3–12)
 III. First Response to Suffering: Creating a Holy Community (1:13–2:10)
     A. Call to Holy Living (1:13–25)
     B. Creation of Vibrant Community (2:1–10)
 IV. Second Response to Suffering: Winsome Witness in Society (2:11–4:19)
     A. Good Conduct for the Sake of Evangelism (2:11–12)
     B. Specific Examples of Submitting to Authorities (2:13–3:7)
       1. Citizens with Government (2:13–17)

---

[23] Torrey Seland, "Παροίκους καί Παρεπιδήμους: Proselyte Characterizations in 1 Peter?" *BBR* 11 (2001): 239–68.

[24] Jobes *(1 Peter,* xi *et passim)* argues that many of the original readers were literal refugees from Rome including Jewish Christians expelled by Claudius but that Peter's language quickly lent itself to a more spiritualizing application as well.

[25] See esp. John H. Elliott, *The Elect and the Holy* (Leiden and New York: Brill, 1966).

[26] See esp. David L. Balch, *Let Wives Be Submissive: The Domestic Code in 1 Peter* (Chico: Scholars, 1981).

[27] Grudem, *First Epistle of Peter,* 184.

[28] Michaels, *1 Peter,* xlvi-xlix.

[29] Paul A. Holloway, "*Nihil inopinati accidisse* — 'Nothing Unexpected Has Happened': A Cyrenaic Consolatory *Topos* in 1 Pet 4.12ff." *NTS* 48 (2002): 433–48.

COMMENTARY

GREETING (1:1–2)

In addition to Peter's description of the locations and nature of his audience, discussed above (p. 445), this greeting contains an important incipient trinitarian reference to the God who brought these believers into fellowship with himself. The order, "Father, Son and Holy Spirit" has not yet become standard, but the functions of each person match the kinds of things said about them already in Paul: God through his foreknowledge elects, Christ's blood makes possible believers' obedience, and the Spirit lives in people to enable ongoing sanctification.[30]

BLESSING (1:3–12)

As in 2 Corinthians, the Jewish form of *berakah* ("blessing") replaces an explicit word of thanksgiving at the beginning of the prayer section. Despite the necessary punctuation in English translations, these ten verses all form one long Greek sentence, with the main point of praising God for our salvation (vv. 3, 9, 10). Peter's primary focus is on the certainty of our future hope for an imperishable inheritance (vv. 4–5), which can inspire us to endure and even to rejoice during whatever sufferings this life may throw our way (v. 6). The complementary nature of God's sovereignty and human perseverance emerges in characteristic biblical form with God's power shielding believers as they exercise faith in him.[31] Like the refining fires of a kiln removing the dross from the precious elements that are preserved, suffering enables us to focus on the eternal realities that alone will last and to recognize a positive, purging value of the tests that afflict us (vv. 7–9).

But Peter also casts a backward glance, reminding believers of the advantage they have over people of past eras, and even angels, who longed to understand more details about Old Testament prophecies concerning the climax of God's salvific plan for humanity (vv. 10–12). A major debate surrounds the translation of *tina ē poion*

---

[30] Although sanctification throughout the New Testament can also encompass the beginning of the process at the time of initial salvation. See esp. David Peterson, *Possessed by God* (Leicester and Downers Grove: IVP, 1995).

[31] On which, see esp. I. Howard Marshall, *Kept by the Power of God* (London: Epworth; Minneapolis: Bethany, 1969).

kairon in verse 11—does it mean "what and what kind of time" (i.e., the time and circumstances of the Messiah's ministry) or "who and what time" (i.e., the identity and timing of that ministry)? Despite the popularity of the former perspective, the grammar allows for both, and it is difficult to imagine the prophets not wanting to know who the Messiah would be as well as when he would come.[32] But of course neither of these details was revealed, except for the general conviction that it was a future age beyond the lifetimes of the prophets which would see the fulfillment of their predictions (v. 12).

FIRST RESPONSE TO SUFFERING: CREATING A HOLY COMMUNITY (1:13–2:10)

Call to Holy Living (1:13–25)[33]   Chapter 1:13–25 begins the body of Peter's letter by describing the overall Christian lifestyle: be holy, just as God is holy, just as Jesus was holy—even when this entails suffering. Verses 13–16 sum up God's will in terms of the Levitical holiness code (see esp. Lev. 19:2). Proper living, of course, begins with right thinking, so we must be mentally prepared and self-controlled by focusing fully on our ultimate destiny in Christ.[34] Then the desire for holy behavior will outweigh the temptation to give in to evil desires, despite the fact that the latter often bring pleasure and help avoid pain in the short-term.

Verses 17–21 unpack the rationale for this ethic: we have been redeemed from a worldly lifestyle. Plus we must give account to a God who is both judge and father. The first role inspires a healthy fear of the last day; the second tempers that with the reminder that our true home and family are not on this earth and that God is waiting to welcome those who are his into a completely loving relationship with him.[35]

Embedded in this paragraph is Peter's *first Christological confession* (vv. 19–21; cf. above) that expands on the nature of the redemption Jesus provided. Like the sacrificial lambs of Old Testament ritual, Jesus provided an atoning death for the sins of humanity, a provision decided on ages ago but only recently completed with the inauguration of the end times in the first century. In all these affirmations, Peter is fully consistent with what we have already studied in Acts, Paul, and Hebrews.

The purification of our lives, which begins at conversion, leads to obeying the truth and loving one another (recall Eph. 4:15). Peter encourages his congregations to let this process continue and deepen, once again recognizing their wonderful eternal futures now that they have been born again through the power of the gospel (vv. 22–24). This world in general, like human lives on this earth in particular, remains fragile and fading compared with eternal verities such as God's revelation (v. 25; quoting Isa. 40:6–8). This contrast between the transient and the permanent would undoubtedly have strengthened the beleaguered Christian community facing the

---

[32] And this comports with general New Testament usage. See G. D. Kilpatrick, "1 Peter 1.11: *TINA H ΠΟΙΟΝ KAIPON*," *NovT* 28 (1986): 91–92.

[33] For a detailed analysis of this passage as the theological basis for the ethics of the entire letter, see Jacob Prasad, *Foundations of the Christian Way of Life according to 1 Peter 1, 13–25: An Exegetico-Theological Study* (Rome: PIB, 2000).

[34] Elliott (*1 Peter*, 355) suggests, as an idiomatic English equivalent to v. 13a, "having rolled up the sleeves of your mind."

[35] Marshall (*1 Peter*, 53–54 n.), however, notes that the biblical role of "father" should also inspire reverence, perhaps even more than the metaphor of judge does, precisely because of the combination of images of authority and care.

seemingly limitless power and glory of Rome. Indeed, all human "strength, power, wealth, beauty [and] glory . . . will quickly fade," but "Christians who have been 'born anew' . . . will live with God forever."[36]

Creation of Vibrant Community (2:1–10)   Chapter 2:1–10 concentrates more specifically on how to grow in Christian living, especially via the formation of a holy community. To this end, Peter develops two metaphors—craving pure, spiritual milk (vv. 1–3) and building the spiritual house (vv. 4–10). Verse 1 employs the word picture of "putting off" (*apothemenoi*—NIV "rid") vices as one would remove dirty clothing. The sins enumerated "are not the grosser vices of paganism, but community-destroying" sins that would have most tempted a persecuted community in a society marked by factious rivalries, social competition, and conflict.[37] Instead, these Christians should crave the "milk" that enables them to mature in their faith (vv. 2–3). In 1 Corinthians 3 and Hebrews 5, milk was used as a negative metaphor equivalent to baby food; here it functions as a positive metaphor for that which nourishes believers throughout their lives.

The word translated "spiritual" (*logikos*) has generated protracted controversy. Its two most common meanings were "rational" (cf. English "logical") and "spiritual" (more in the sense of metaphorical vs. literal). But the use of *logos* in 1:23, combined with the twofold appearance of *rhema* in 1:25 (both meaning "word") could suggest that we should translate according to the adjective's etymology and speak of the "pure milk of the Word [of God]."[38]

Verses 4–10 develop the corporate nature of God's people, as they grow, even more directly. From verses 4–8, Peter thinks of Christians collectively as a building made up of individual, living stones fitted together to form a house of sacrifice, that is, a temple. But both the edifice and the offerings are metaphorical, not literal (v. 5). Christ himself, of course, is the cornerstone, a truth Peter finds foreshadowed in Isaiah 28:16, Psalm 118·22,[39] and Isaiah 8:14, in that order. The first of these texts was taken by the Jewish targum to refer to "King Messiah"; the similar language in the second two texts, combined with their references to a Davidic king and to God in their original contexts, make it natural for Peter to apply them in like fashion.

Moreover, he may recall Jesus' similar teaching after the parable of the vineyard (Mark 12:1–11 pars.) in which Christ already referred to himself with this cornerstone imagery. Together, these Old Testament quotations indicate a dual role for Jesus, as he promises to honor his followers but threatens to shame those who reject him. The last half of verse 8 in English could sound like support for predestination to damnation, but the Greek uses a neuter relative pronoun for "which," suggesting

---

[36] Grudem, *First Peter*, 93.

[37] Peter H. Davids, *The First Epistle of Peter* (Grand Rapids: Eerdmans, 1990), 80.

[38] Dan G. McCartney, "λογικός in 1 Peter 2,2," *ZNW* 82 (1991): 128–37. Karen H. Jobes ("Got Milk? Septuagint Psalm 33 and the Interpretation of 1 Peter 2:1–3," *WTJ* 64 [2002]: 1–14) hears echoes of Ps. 33:9 (LXX) and thinks Peter has merged the metaphor of tasting the goodness of the Lord with the metaphor of new birth to refer to the new reality established in a believer by the resurrection of Jesus.

[39] It makes no sense, with the NIV, to translate *kephalēn gōnias* in v. 7 as "capstone," after rendering *akrogōnaion* in v. 6 as "cornerstone," especially given the description in v. 8 that this is a stone over which people can trip (hardly what one would do with the top of an archway)! The TNIV has corrected this by using a "cornerstone" throughout.

the entire previous clause as its antecedent.[40] In other words, unbelievers are not individually predestined to disobey God, but it is a prearranged principle that those who do disobey will stumble (i.e., spiritually fall).[41]

The next two verses apply an array of Old Testament metaphors for Israel to the multiethnic church of Jesus Christ (vv. 9–10). Combined with similar descriptions in verse 5, it is clear that Peter sees substantial overlap between the two entities (though not necessarily exact identity). It is the worldwide body of Christian believers, not Israel or the Jewish people, who are now the elect people of God.[42] From verse 5, Martin Luther developed his famous doctrine of the priesthood of all believers (as opposed to just the priests of medieval Catholicism). This application seems justified, but the context here is not one that stresses individualism (as in the modern Baptist offshoot known as "soul competency"), but the joint role of all Christians together mediating God's grace to a fallen world.[43]

SECOND RESPONSE TO SUFFERING: WINSOME WITNESS IN SOCIETY (2:11–4:19)

Good Conduct for the Sake of Evangelism (2:11–12)   From the inwardly focused theme of building a holy community, Peter shifts to a complementary task of the church, particularly in a hostile world—godly, outward behavior in order to maximize a positive impact and to minimize a negative response among the unbelieving people in society. Verses 11–12 introduce these two purposes, which will then be illustrated via a *Haustafel* like those we have seen in Colossians and Ephesians. Moral lives remain a powerful testimony to unbelievers, leading some to become Christians, so that they will be praising God on judgment day (v. 12).[44] Of course, various other people will inevitably continue to accuse Christians unjustly.[45]

Specific Examples of Submitting to Authorities (2:13–3:7)   *Citizens with Government (2:13–17)*   The first of Peter's three examples of the relationships between authorities and subordinates in his domestic code differs from what Paul included in his *Haustafel* (though recall Rom. 13:1–7). Christian subjects (today we would say citizens, but few first-century Christians were actually Roman citizens) must submit to "every human creation" (v. 13a; the literal rendering of what the NIV translates as "every authority instituted among men"). But in the context of treating kings and governors (vv. 13b–14a), Peter is obviously not talking about every possible person who might ever assume power over another, but about duly constituted

---

[40] Achtemeier, *1 Peter,* 162,

[41] Cf. Norman Hillyer (*1 and 2 Peter, Jude* [Peabody: Hendrickson, 1992], 64): "Peter's meaning is that stumbling to disaster is the inevitable consequence of persistently refusing to obey Christ."

[42] Cf. Achtemeier (*1 Peter,* 69), who adds, "Israel as a totality has become for this letter the controlling metaphor in terms of which its theology is expressed."

[43] See esp. Elliott (*1 Peter,* 449–55), who may, however, have swung the pendulum a little too far away from Luther's approach altogether.

[44] Davids, *First Epistle of Peter,* 97 (*contra* those who see the "day he visits us" as something that could happen during the normal course of events in this age).

[45] For outstanding reflections on both of these phenomena, see Miroslav Volf, "Soft Difference: Theological Reflections on the Relation Between Church and Culture in 1 Peter," *ExAud* 10 (1994): 15–30.

political authorities.[46] Like Paul before him, Peter speaks only of the positive role of government here; even imperial regimes are better than anarchy and chaos.

When it functioned according to its own mandate, Roman government had two basic roles: to reward benefactors and punish criminals (v. 14b).[47] But Peter himself had practiced civil disobedience when the demands of Israel's authorities contravened God's law (Acts 4–5), so we must understand "for the Lord's sake" in verse 13 as meaning something like "whenever human laws do not dishonor God's laws." It is also just possible that *hos huperechonti* (NIV "as the supreme authority") should be interpreted as "when he is superior," that is, when (and only when) the king's demands reflect morality or justice qualitatively superior (to the all-too-frequent immorality and corruption).[48]

Objections to Peter's teachings which point out that Christians are free from laws other than God's are in principle valid, but believers must be concerned for the effect of their behavior on a fallen world (vv. 15–16). Verse 17 generalizes and rounds out the paragraph by ending with another command to honor (from *timaō*) the king. But before Peter gets there, he relativizes that command some by also insisting that believers honor (again from *timaō*) everyone, which includes loving their Christian brothers and sisters, and by reserving the strongest verb (*phobeisthe*; fear, reverence) for God.[49]

Slaves with Masters (2:18–25) The second two parts of Peter's *Haustafel* return to relationships that Paul had discussed in his domestic codes as well. Our comments on Ephesians 6:1–9, Colossians 3:20–25, and Philemon should thus also be consulted. Concerning slaves and masters, Peter emphasizes even more than Paul the virtue of unjust suffering (vv. 18–20). "With all respect" in verse 18 is too weak a rendering of *en panti phobē* ("in all fear"), which probably has God rather than the master as its implied object (cf. the ends of vv. 19 and 20).[50] As his example of submission to harsh suffering, Peter naturally turns to Jesus and inserts his *second Christological confession* (vv. 21–25). While the crucifixion was much more than a model for Christians to emulate (most notably, we cannot atone for the sins of the world!), it was exemplary nevertheless (v. 21). We can refuse to trade insults with others or to threaten to retaliate when abused. In so doing we can remain sinless, not absolutely but at least in those specific situations (vv. 22–23a). And we can do so in the same way Jesus did, by reminding ourselves that we can wait for the vengeance a just God will exact from those who oppress us and never repent of their sins (v. 23b).[51] Indeed, if it were not for his atoning death, which makes possible the

---

[46] Schreiner, *1, 2 Peter, Jude*, 128.

[47] Winter (*Seek the Welfare of the City*, 25–40) demonstrates the prominent role of awarding civic honors to generous, private benefactors in the task of "commending those who do right."

[48] Recall under our discussion of Romans 13:1.

[49] "In what is apparently mild irony Peter has put the emperor on the same level as 'all people'" (Grudem, *First Epistle of Peter*, 123). The NIV obscures this by translating the first use of *timaō* as "show proper respect" rather than "honor."

[50] Achtemeier, *1 Peter*, 194–95.

[51] Marshall (*1 Peter*, 97) stresses that this text is about not retaliating when persecuted. Securing justice for the oppressed is a different matter, which the Bible regularly calls on God's people to pursue.

forgiveness of our sins and the transformation of our lives, we would still be straying from God as much as our unsaved enemies are (vv. 24–25).

Echoes of Isaiah 53 resound throughout this confession, while verse 22 quotes that chapter directly (see Isa. 53:9). The imagery of wandering sheep comes from Isaiah 53:6, which naturally leads to the label of Jesus as Shepherd (v. 25), but Peter's reinstatement as one commissioned three times to tend Christ's flock (John 21:15–17) may lie in the background, too.

Wives with Husbands (3:1–7)   The final section of Peter's *Haustafel* turns to the relationship between husbands and wives. In verses 1–6, Peter has in mind especially Christian wives of non-Christian husbands, who would no doubt be greatly tempted not to submit to their spouses in numerous areas! After all, they were breaking from cultural convention the moment they refused to retain the religion of their husbands.[52] "In the same way" (v. 1a) does not mean "as if you were slaves," but "here is another example" of the principles Peter is discussing. After all, the expression reappears in verse 7, addressed to husbands, where it does not even refer to the subordinate party in the relationship (cf. also 4:5 where *no* command to anyone to submit has preceded the call, "in the same way be submissive").[53]

Verses 1b–2 do not imply that wives should never present their unbelieving husbands with the verbal proclamation of the gospel but that they should not nag them with it.[54] Reverent lives may be the most powerful witness of all. But the application of these commands cannot be limited to mixed marriages, since Peter writes "if any of them do not believe," implying that others will believe. Indeed, wives' submission should be much easier within a Christian marriage in which husbands heed verse 7.

Verses 3–4 remind the wealthy women of Asia Minor that their proper beauty must be internal rather than external (recall 1 Tim. 2:9), a principle that again is not limited to the immediate audience being addressed. As with his instructions for slaves, Peter backs up these commands by appealing to an exemplary model, in this case "the holy women of the past." Most notable among them was Sarah, Abraham's wife (vv. 5–6). The only place in Genesis where she calls her husband *kurios* ("master" or "lord") is in 18:12, in which she also mocks the notion that she will bear a son in her old age. Nothing in this context illustrates obedience to her husband or even to God! But perhaps Peter has in mind two separate incidents, with the reference to obedience alluding to Sarah's willingness to comply with Abraham's instructions to pose as his sister in Genesis 12:10–20, despite the trouble it eventually got him in.[55]

Either way, it is important to see that Sarah's obedience is merely one illustration of the broader principle of Israel's matriarchs submitting to their husbands, which suggests that obedience *per se* is just one way of demonstrating submission, along

---

[52] Schreiner, *1, 2 Peter, Jude,* 153.

[53] Cf. Hillyer, *1 and 2 Peter, Jude,* 92.

[54] After all, 3:15 would appear to reflect the more timeless, contrasting principle. See Jeannine K. Brown, "Silent Wives, Verbal Believers: Ethical and Hermeneutical Considerations in 1 Peter 3:1–6 and Its Context," *WW* 24 (2004): 395–403.

[55] Aída B. Spencer ("Peter's Pedagogical Method in 1 Peter 3:6," *BBR* 10 [2000]: 107–19) well defends the latter option, concluding that "*obedience per se* is not the focus but rather pure conduct" (p. 116).

with silent witness, focusing on inward adornment, and so on. Other situations may require different tactics. The word for "fear" in verse 6a is not the common *phobos* but the rare *ptoēsis*—an act of intimidation or even terror. Thus this fear probably refers to the wives' natural fear of the punishment unsaved husbands might unleash on them.[56]

Although the immediate context of many mixed marriages in which the wife was far more likely to convert than the husband dictated a much longer set of instructions for wives, husbands in any context dare not neglect verse 7. Here only *Christian* husbands may be expected to know about Peter's injunctions. "Be considerate as you live" may more literally be translated as "dwelling together according to knowledge," almost in the sense of showing empathy for one's wife. The "weaker partner" (literally, "vessel") was often taken during church history as referring to women's ontological or even moral inferiority, a view rightly abandoned by almost all scholars today. After all, this same verse stresses the absolute equality of man and woman in God's sight as co-heirs of his undeserved gift of salvation. The majority now assume the expression to refer to the generally slighter physiques of most women, but this hardly applies in every marriage.

Popular Christian psychology has at times tried to turn the adjective into a compliment, claiming it refers to wives' greater sensitivity, but there is no lexical support for this meaning for *asthenēs*. The view that best fits the meaning of the word and its immediate context is the *voluntarily adopted position of vulnerability* a Christian woman puts herself in by submitting to her husband,[57] which the husband dare not abuse, lest God refuse to answer his prayers!

More General Principles Concerning Undeserved Suffering (3:8–4:6) *A Submissive, Nonretaliating Spirit (3:8–12)* There is no consensus as to where the larger section that began in 2:11 ends. No further categories appear of specific kinds of people submitting to their leaders, however, so it would seem that Peter has shifted gears to more general principles of deferring to others. Yet the repetition in 3:9 about not trading insults (recall 2:23) suggests that we are still on the same main topic. Chapter 3:8–4:6 is broadly unified by the theme of believers submitting to injustice, though the actual verbs for submission do not reappear as they did throughout 2:13–3:7. The first subtheme under this heading involves repaying evil with good rather than with more evil. It is hard enough at times to live in harmony with fellow Christians (v. 8), since they can still deeply hurt us,[58] but harder still when the non-Christian world tempts us to supplant the role of God as judge by retaliating for the atrocities it can unleash against us. But Jesus in the Sermon on the Mount/

---

[56] Davids (*1 Peter,* 121) combines the insights of these last three sentences to conclude that the wives "are subordinate, but their subordination is revolutionary in that they are subordinate not out of fear or desire for social position or other human advantage but out of obedience to Christ, who treats them as full persons and allows them to rise above the threats and fears of this age."

[57] Combining insights from Grudem (*First Epistle of Peter,* 144) and Davids (*First Epistle of Peter,* 123).

[58] "Modern Western concepts of individualism tend to trump commitment to community. Where commitment is found, it is often evaluated in terms of individual needs. An individual whose needs are no longer met by a community terminates the commitment and seeks a new and more obliging group. Such thinking runs counter to the qualities of 3.8. Like-mindedness implies a willingness to conform one's goals, needs, and expectations to the purposes of the larger community" (Jobes, *1 Peter,* 216).

Plain (Matt. 5:43–48; Luke 6:27–36) commands love for enemies in language close enough to Peter's to suggest that he may be alluding to Christ's words here (v. 9).[59] Plus Psalm 34:12–16 reinforces Jesus' and Peter's injunctions in the context of the suffering of the righteous, including the resident alien (vv. 10–12).

The Unlikelihood of Suffering for Doing Good (3:13–17)   The rhetorical question of verse 13, combined with the fourth-class condition (using the rare optative mood) in verse 14a, a construction sometimes called the "future less probable," suggests that Peter still does not think it all that likely that Christians will be persecuted as long as they do good.[60] But he also recognizes that it can happen, in which case they must not be afraid but continue to honor Christ and lovingly explain why they believe what they believe (vv. 14b–16a). As in 2:12, this will lead some to change their attitudes toward Christians and perhaps even embrace their faith (v. 16b). As in 2:20, suffering for wrongdoing accomplishes little, but persevering through unjust suffering can be God's will as he accomplishes some greater good (v. 17).

The Example of Jesus (3:18–22)   Peter now appends the *third and lengthiest Christological confession* of his epistle. Its main purpose is clear: suffering can have a purifying effect on us, just as Jesus' death provided purification for us (4:1, recall 1:7). But some of the details remain obscure. Historically, this passage became the most commonly cited prooftext for the clause in the Apostles' Creed (not in the original third-century form, but added in the eighth century) about Christ's descent into hell. Yet it is doubtful that it actually teaches this doctrine. Verse 18a is clear enough. Christ's crucifixion provided a vicarious, substitutionary atonement that enables people to be reconciled with God. But after that, interpretation becomes more difficult. The approach we will sketch here, however, does reflect a fair majority of contemporary commentators across the theological spectrum.[61]

Verses 18b–19a could be translated, "He was put to death in the body but made alive in the spirit, through which also he went and preached . . ." (NIV marg.), in which case Peter would be describing the activity of Christ's spirit during the period that his body lay entombed awaiting his resurrection. But the middle part of this excerpt could just as easily be translated, "but made alive by the Spirit, through whom . . ." (NIV), in which case the time of the preaching will have to be determined by other elements of the passage. Verses 19–20 introduce us to the key crux. What is the preaching to the spirits in prison who disobeyed in Noah's day, and who are these spirits? Is this a second chance at salvation for someone? Probably not (recall Heb. 9:27). The verb used here is not *euangelizō* ("evangelize") but *kērussō* ("proclaim"

---

[59] Elliott, *1 Peter,* 606–9. This spirit of non-retaliation has proved influential in the twentieth-century nonviolent ideologies (and largely nonviolent protests) of as diverse figures as Mohandas Gandhi in India, Martin Luther King Jr. in the USA, Cory Aquino in the Philippines, the East German Lutheran candlelight vigils just before the fall of the Iron Curtain, and public prayer meetings and mass rallies in Ukraine after a fraudulent election there in 2004.

[60] Or, as a variation of this view, that he does not know how much persecution any individual believer may experience, while recognizing the growing threat on the horizon more generally. Cf. Schreiner, *1, 2 Peter, Jude,* 179.

[61] For a history of the interpretation of 3:18–22 and a defense of the position adopted here, see William J. Dalton, *Christ's Proclamation to the Spirits: A Study of 1 Peter 3:18–4:6* (Rome: PIB, rev. 1989). More recently, cf. Andrew J. Bandstra, "'Making Proclamation to the Spirits in Prison': Another Look at 1 Peter 3:19," *CTJ* 38 (2003): 120–24. On the weaknesses of this view, see esp. David G. Horrell, "Who Are 'The Dead' and When Was the Gospel Preached to Them? The Interpretation of 1 Pet 4.6," *NTS* 49 (2003): 70–89.

or "announce a message"). Is this a *first* chance at salvation for Old Testament saints who had not yet heard about Jesus? Again, probably not, because the word "spirits" elsewhere in the New Testament, when not qualified by an explicit modifying phrase, always means angels or demons.

Most likely, this is an announcement by Christ to the demons of the victory his death has wrought over them. When did this happen? Given that "went" in verse 19 translates the identical form of the aorist passive participle as "has gone" in verse 22 (*poreutheis*), that early Christians believed in an unseen realm between heaven and earth in which angels and demons did battle (recall on 2 Cor. 12:2 and Eph. 2:2), and that verse 22 explicitly talks about Christ's subjection of both good and evil spirits, it seems probable that all this took place as part of his ascension from earth to heaven.[62]

Verses 20–21 also contain puzzling references to Noah's generation and to baptism. If the imprisoned spirits were demons, then Peter presumably saw them as the power behind that unusually wicked race of Noah's day (cf. Jude 6; 2 Pet. 2:4).[63] Mention of Noah triggers a typology concerning two kinds of salvation "through" water—Noah and his family being physically preserved as the ark floated atop the flood and Christians demonstrating their spiritual salvation by brief immersion into the waters of baptism. Verse 21a is often cited out of context by those who believe in baptismal regeneration, but verse 21b makes it plain that baptism is the external sign (the "pledge" or "response") of an inward change of heart ("a good conscience").[64]

The Victory His Atonement Makes Possible for Us (4:1–6)   Whatever details of the previous passage remain unclear, Peter's main purpose in incorporating this confession is to encourage believers that they can withstand suffering just as Christ did, and that it can help them rid their lives of sin, at least progressively if not absolutely (4:1–3).[65] Of course our unsaved neighbors will not understand why we abandon the seemingly fun sins that they still commit, but one day they will be judged for them (vv. 4–5).[66] Verse 6 presents the next exegetical crux. The Greek reads simply, "for this reason the gospel was also preached to the dead . . ." Is this referring back to the same event as 3:18–22 depicts? Does this support a second chance at salvation after

---

[62] The next most probable understanding of this passage is that Christ was preaching the need to repent through Noah to the generation that ultimately was destroyed in the flood and thus wound up in hell. See esp. Wayne Grudem, "Christ Preaching through Noah: 1 Peter 3:19–20 in the Light of Dominant Themes in Jewish Literature," *TrinJ* 7 (1986): 3–31. As for the common view throughout church history that "Christ descended into hell," this would seem to run afowl of Christ's word on the cross to one of the criminals crucified with him that he would be with him that very day in Paradise (Luke 23:43). Cf. further John Yates, "'He Descended into Hell': Creed, Article and Scripture," *Churchman* 102 (1988): 240–50, 303–15.

[63] This approach does not require us to understand Gen. 6:1–2 as referring to demons literally having sexual relationships with human women, as in some ancient Jewish traditions. But diabolical designs could be seen behind the intentions of human chieftains or aristocrats (another ancient meaning of "sons of God") inappropriately multiplying wives to themselves. See esp. Meredith G. Kline, "Divine Kingship and Genesis 6:1–4," *WTJ* 24 (1962): 187–204.

[64] Marshall, *1 Peter,* 130–31.

[65] Others take "he who has suffered in his body" as referring to *Christ's* absolute victory over sin or see "is done with sin" in a legal rather than experiential sense. But the former is less apt in a context about the believer's response, while the latter reads Pauline theology into the writing of a different author who does not elsewhere employ that category. See further Elliott, *1 Peter,* 714–18.

[66] The Greek in v. 4 for "plunge with them into the same flood of dissipation" is particularly vivid. Kelly (*The Epistles of Peter and Jude,* 170) likens the imagery to "the euphoric stampede of pleasure-seekers"!

death even if 3:18–22 does not? The rest of the verse introduces a contrast between being judged in the flesh by other humans (presumably, including those condemned to die by persecutors) and being made alive by God in the spiritual realm (including resurrection). This supports the interpretation that the NIV makes explicit by adding the word *now*: the gospel was preached to people while they were alive, so that they became believers, which in turn guaranteed them eternal life even if they were martyred.[67]

Exhortational Summary (4:7–11) This paragraph reminds us of many of the closing sections of exhortational material at the end of Paul's letter bodies. Peter summarizes several key concepts in quick, staccato fashion. As with Paul, the potential for this age to end at any time creates an urgency for Christian living. Love remains central, enabling us to overlook the many sins of others, especially those committed against us. Believers should identify their spiritual gift(s) and exercise them faithfully. Paul's lists of gifts are much fuller (recall under 1 Cor. 12, Rom. 12, and Eph. 4); Peter has arguably fitted them all under two headings (perhaps reflecting the division of labor in Acts 6:1–7)—gifts of speaking (prophecy, teaching, tongues, wisdom, etc.) and gifts of service (administration, hospitality, faith, giving, etc.).[68] The doxology with which this section ends has suggested to many commentators that the body of the letter concludes at this juncture. Yet Jewish writers tend to lapse into praise for God in the middle of sections as well (recall Rom. 9:5 and see throughout the rabbinic literature), while verse 19 reads like a summary of all of Peter's main points; hence, the outline we have adopted here.

Doctrinal Summary (4:12–19) Peter now returns to where he began in the letter's thanksgiving. Suffering need not seem strange; it can even lead to rejoicing and blessings (vv. 12–14). The motif of the messianic woes (see above on Col. 1:24) may also lie behind Peter's thought here.[69] But again, we must be sure that we are not suffering for wickedness of our own but as Christians (vv. 15–16). This need not be limited to hostility directly related to our faith; God can use sickness contracted simply as part of life in a fallen world in the same ways as persecution. But a sexually transmitted disease or an arrest for some criminal offense does not reflect God's purifying blessings in the same way! Verses 17–18 remind Peter's readers of God's action in Ezekiel 9:6, in which judgment began at God's temple in Israel, an event that Malachi 3:1 expected to recur.[70] As harsh as God's temporal response to his own people's sins was, imagine the terror that his eternal judgment of unbelievers will engender (and cf. Prov. 11:31). Christians can rest content that God will avenge

---

[67] See esp. Elliott, *1 Peter*, 731–40. Wisdom of Solomon 3:1–6 provides a particularly close parallel. The other main options defended throughout church history, in decreasing frequency and with decreasing order of probability, include (a) offering full, Christian salvation to Old Testament saints; (b) offering a chance at salvation to those who never heard the gospel in this life; and (c) offering a second chance at salvation even for those who had heard the gospel in this life but had not accepted it.

[68] Schreiner, *1, 2 Peter, Jude*, 215.

[69] See esp. Mark Dubis, *Messianic Woes in First Peter: Suffering and Eschatology in 1 Peter 4:12–19* (New York: Peter Lang, 2002).

[70] See esp. Dennis E. Johnson, "Fire in God's House: Imagery from Malachi 3 in Peter's Theology of Suffering (1 Pet. 4:12–19)," *JETS* 29 (1986): 285–94.

all the evil directed against them (and elsewhere) and continue to follow both main principles for coping with suffering—*loyalty to God and service to others* (v. 19).[71]

FINAL EXHORTATIONS (5:1–11)

Although Peter's letter has contained major sections of exhortation throughout, he now gathers one final section of parenesis together before concluding with another doxology and amen. If there is any link with what has come before, it may be that the elders have a special role in preparing the household of God for the coming judgment mentioned in 4:17–18. Chapter 5:1–5 resembles one more segment of a domestic code, this time involving church elders and those under their care and authority. The major portion of this material deals with the responsibilities of the elders (vv. 1–4). Peter could have asserted his apostolic authority at this point, but precisely because he wants to enjoin servant leadership, he stresses his role as a fellow elder with them, a unique eyewitness of Christ's crucifixion to be sure, but one, like them, who will share in Christ's resurrection glory (v. 1). The upshot is an appeal from a peer rather than an authoritarian dictum.[72]

Verse 2a reproduces the pattern noted in Acts 20—elders (presbyters) are also shepherds (pastors) and overseers (bishops).[73] Verses 2b–3 present a threefold contrast. These church leaders must not serve under compulsion, for material gain or autocratically, but willingly, eager to give of themselves to others and modeling the behavior they want to instill in their "flock." If that produces too little glory in this life, they can look forward to an eternity of glory in the life to come, after Jesus, the "Chief Shepherd," returns (v. 4). Yet even this title for Christ, found nowhere else in the Bible, reminds elders that they are merely "undershepherds" under the true leader of the church.

The natural opposite of an older person (*presbuteros*) is a younger one (*neoteros*)—verse 5. But if elders in verses 1–4 were officeholders, are "youngers" official roles as well? Probably not! Precisely because of the ambiguity in the term *presbuteros,* derived from the tradition of usually appointing older men as elders, the submission of the rest of the congregation to its leaders can be described in the terms Peter employs here.[74] Alternately, Peter may be singling out for special mention those who were most likely to rebel against the leadership. Either way, by the second half of the verse, he is clearly addressing the entire church, quoting Proverbs 3:34, just as James did in James 4:6. This promise to the humble leads naturally to a call for humility before God and the invitation to cast all our cares on him as the alternative to worry and a means for eventual exaltation (vv. 6–7).

---

[71] Michaels (*1 Peter,* 274–75) explains the overall thrust of this section as reminding believers that their ultimate vindication does not produce present, unadulterated bliss. Suffering must first purify them, but God remains sovereign throughout the whole process.

[72] Elliott (*1 Peter,* 847) observes that Peter's wording tempers but does not erase the existing authority structures. Recall our comments on Eph. 5:21–33 above.

[73] An important work by R. Alastair Campbell (*The Elders: Seniority within Earliest Christianity* [Edinburgh: T & T Clark, 1994]) on elders in the New Testament world defends the close link between age and leadership role and also challenges the equation of elders and overseers. The former proves more persuasive than the latter.

[74] Leonhard Goppelt, *A Commentary on 1 Peter* (Grand Rapids: Eerdmans, 1993), 350–52.

Finally, Peter calls on his audience to resist the devil through alert self-control. Suffering does not automatically purify us; we can choose to become embittered or vindictive and blame God instead. But we can be encouraged by the fact that no Christians ever remain exempt from suffering forever, and God has frequently empowered many to heroic acts of resistance and endurance that usually make our complaints pale in comparison (vv. 8–9). After what is only a blip on the radar screen of eternity, the suffering will give way to unending glory, a precious truth that likewise empowers us to "hang in there," as well as to give God all praise (vv. 10–11).

CLOSING (5:12–14)

As noted in the introduction (p. 442), all that we can infer with any confidence about Silas's role from verse 12 is that he was the letter carrier, though of course he *could* have been an amanuensis given enough freedom to produce the good Greek style of the letter. It is just that the phrase "with the help of Silas" probably implies nothing one way or the other about the latter possibility. "Encouraging" and "testifying" reflect the ethical and doctrinal sections of the epistle, regularly interspersed in that order (recall above, p. 446). The use of Babylon in verse 13 to stand for Rome (recall above, p. 443) also reflects a more negative, balancing view of the government than that disclosed in 2:13–17. That Mark is with Peter in Rome meshes well with the testimony of the Church Fathers that Mark wrote his Gospel based on Peter's memoirs.[75] The Jewish greeting of peace (without the more Hellenistic "grace") fits Peter's more conservative Jewish-Christian background (v. 14).

APPLICATION

Depending on which main section of the letter body one stresses, one may read 1 Peter in two quite different ways. One way focuses on Peter's call to the church to look after one another during difficult times, and thus to provide what John Elliott has stressed throughout his numerous works on this letter and encapsulated in the title of one of his books as *a home for the homeless*.[76] The other way highlights Peter's calls to submit to social structures and winsomely witness to Christian faith in the midst of a fallen but watching world. Here the title of Bruce Winter's study, adopting a portion of Jeremiah 29:7, nicely summarizes Peter's emphasis—*seek the welfare of the city*.[77] These two approaches are complementary, not contradictory, as 4:19 demonstrates.

In a world with many literal and spiritual refugees, and with increasing "culture wars" between Christians and the non-Christian society around them, both emphases remain absolutely crucial for God's people. As a church, we must provide for the hurting people of the world in ways that few governments ever do, by meeting spiritual as well as physical needs, while at the same time participating actively as law-abiding citizens working for all the good "within the system" that we can. Times

---

[75] See Blomberg, *Jesus and the Gospels,* 123.

[76] See p. 445 above.

[77] See p. 451 above.

of growing persecution against God's people should drive us to emphasize both of these principles even more than at other times.[78]

ADDITIONAL QUESTIONS

1. On what basis can the authorship of 1 Peter be attributed to the apostle Peter? What are modern scholarship's claims about the authorship of 1 Peter? How is the apparent relationship between 1 Peter and Paul's letters explained?
2. What other details of introduction to 1 Peter are most disputed? Which details are most secure? Explain why in each case.
3. Identify the major emphases of each of the two major sections in 1 Peter. Based on these two emphases, what is a good thesis statement for the entire epistle?
4. How does Peter cast suffering in a positive light in his epistle? What can godly living in the midst of suffering accomplish?
5. What rationale does Peter give for living holy lives? How is the community essential for fostering holy living? How does Peter's emphasis on the priesthood of believers differ from Martin Luther's Reformation emphasis on the same subject?
6. For Peter, what is the ultimate purpose and outcome of intentionally fostering a holy community? How do Peter's household codes fit into this purpose? How can Peter's illustration from the life of Abraham and Sarah be understood to demonstrate the submission of wives to husbands when that was not how the story functioned in its original context? What is the best interpretation of women as the "weaker partner" in marriage?
7. What are the key affirmations of each of Peter's Christological confessions? Summarize a succinct Christology according to Peter.
8. How is the difficult passage in 1 Peter 3:18–19, which affirms the preaching of Christ to the spirits in prison, best interpreted? What can be said of this passage offering a second chance at salvation to those who have previously refused the gospel?
9. Concluding his epistle, what attitude does Peter advise when one is faced with suffering or persecution? What is the potential spiritual danger of becoming embittered in the midst of suffering? What are the main principles for coping with suffering that will ultimately allow for purification and holiness of believers?

SELECT BIBLIOGRAPHY

COMMENTARIES

Advanced

Achtemeier, Paul D. *1 Peter.* Hermeneia. Minneapolis: Fortress, 1996.
Elliott, John H. *1 Peter.* AB. New York and London: Doubleday, 2000.

---

[78] For a sociological study of how this all fits together in the world of Peter's addressees, see Steven R. Bechtler, *Following in His Steps: Suffering Community and Christology in 1 Peter* (Atlanta: Scholars, 1998).

Jobes, Karen H. *1 Peter.* BECNT. Grand Rapids: Baker, 2005.

Michaels, J. Ramsey. *1 Peter.* WBC. Waco: Word, 1988.

Selwyn, Edward G. *The First Epistle of St. Peter.* London: Macmillan; rev. 1947; Grand Rapids: Baker, 1981.

Intermediate

Best, Ernest. *1 Peter.* NCB. London: Marshall, Morgan & Scott, 1971; Grand Rapids: Eerdmans, 1982.

Davids, Peter H. *The First Epistle of Peter.* NICNT. Grand Rapids: Eerdmans, 1990.

Goppelt, Leonhard. *A Commentary on 1 Peter.* Grand Rapids: Eerdmans, 1993.

Kelly, J. N. D. *A Commentary on the Epistles of Peter and Jude.* BNTC/HNTC. London: Black; New York: Harper, 1969.

Schreiner, Thomas R. *1, 2 Peter, Jude.* NAC. Nashville: Broadman & Holman, 2003.

Senior, Donald P., and Daniel J. Harrington. *1 Peter, Jude and 2 Peter.* SP. Collegeville: Liturgical, 2003.

Introductory

Boring, M. Eugene. *1 Peter.* ANT. Nashville: Abingdon, 1999.

Grudem, Wayne A. *The First Epistle of Peter.* TNTC, rev. Leicester: IVP; Grand Rapids: Eerdmans, 1988.

Marshall, I. Howard. *1 Peter.* IVPNTC. Leicester and Downers Grove: IVP, 1991.

McKnight, Scot. *1 Peter.* NIVAC. Grand Rapids: Zondervan, 1996.

OTHER BOOKS

Balch, David L. *Let Wives Be Submissive: The Domestic Code in 1 Peter.* Chico: Scholars, 1981.

Bechtler, Steven R. *Following in His Steps: Suffering, Community and Christology in 1 Peter.* Atlanta: Scholars, 1998.

Campbell, Barth L. *Honor, Shame, and the Rhetoric of 1 Peter.* Atlanta: Scholars, 1998.

Elliott, John H. *A Home for the Homeless.* Philadelphia: Fortress; London: SCM, 1981.

Martin, Troy W. *Metaphor and Composition in 1 Peter.* Atlanta: Scholars, 1992.

Seland, Torrey. *Strangers in the Light: Philonic Perspectives on Christian Identity in 1 Peter.* Leiden and Boston: Brill, 2005.

Talbert, Charles H., ed. *Perspectives on 1 Peter.* Macon: Mercer, 1986.

BIBLIOGRAPHY

Casurella, Anthony. *Bibliography of Literature on 1 Peter.* Leiden and New York: Brill, 1996.

Dubis, Mark. "Research on 1 Peter: A Survey of Scholarly Literature Since 1985," *CBR* 4 (2006): 199–239.

12

The Epistle of Jude:
"Contend for the Faith"

INTRODUCTION

RELATIONSHIP WITH 2 PETER

It is quite possible that considering Jude at this point breaks the chronological sequence of the non-Pauline epistles that we are otherwise trying to follow. But it is natural to treat Jude with 2 Peter, because there seems to be a literary relationship between these two short epistles. *Much of the imagery, detail, and even specific wording of Jude closely matches that of 2 Peter 2.* More specifically, 2 Peter 2:1–3:3 repeats eighty of the 311 words of Jude 4–18 within its 426 words.[1] *It is usually assumed that Jude is the earlier of the two,* because (1) there would have been little need for Jude had 2 Peter already been written, and (2) Jude follows a more carefully structured and obviously Jewish form of argument, much more so than we would expect if Jude were the document borrowing from and modifying 2 Peter.[2] So we interrupt the canonical and (perhaps) the chronological progression from 1 to 2 Peter with our treatment of this brief letter.

DATE

Following the consensus of scholars, therefore, the date of the composition of Jude must precede that of 2 Peter. Assuming 2 Peter is authentic (see below, pp. 473–75), Jude must have preceded Peter's death, which occurred some time during Nero's persecution of Christians in A.D. 64–68. How much earlier than the mid-60s is anybody's guess. *The early 60s reflect a common and cautious suggestion,* given the flurry of apostolic writing that occurred during this decade and the ready access that many Christians had to apostolic documents (and that the various Christian leaders had to one another) by that time. The similarities between the false teachers combated in Jude and 2 Peter further points to a similar date for the two letters, and 2 Peter cannot be earlier than 1 Peter in about A.D. 63. But the Jewish nature of the letter and the apocalyptic milieu of many of Jude's examples could suggest a date

---

[1] Terrance Callan, "Use of the Letter of Jude by the Second Letter of Peter," *Bib* 85 (2004): 43.

[2] See esp. Richard J. Bauckham, *Jude, 2 Peter* (Waco: Word, 1983), 3–17. Douglas J. Moo (*2 Peter, Jude* [Grand Rapids: Zondervan, 1996] 16–18) tentatively opts for Jude's dependence on 2 Peter because he thinks Jude 17–18 quotes 2 Pet. 3:3. But most scholars believe that both of these verses refer to repeated apostolic prophecy concerning the rise of immoral skeptics in the last days and that Jude's reference to "the apostles" demonstrates that he is not precisely quoting any one specific source.

as early as the 40s or 50s. Alternately, if Jude or 2 Peter is pseudonymous, a date between 70 and 90 would seem likely.[3]

JUDE	2 PETER 2
"Certain men . . . have secretly slipped in . . . godless men, who . . . deny . . . our only Sovereign and Lord" (v. 4).	"False teachers . . . will secretly introduce . . . heresies, even denying the Sovereign Lord" (v. 1).
The angels who did not keep their positions . . . these he has kept in darkness. . . for judgment" (v. 6).	"God did not spare the angels when they sinned . . . putting them in gloomy dungeons to be held for judgment" (v. 4).
"Sodom and Gomorrah . . . gave themselves up to sexual immorality . . . They serve as an example" (v. 7).	"Sodom and Gomorrah . . . made them an example of what is going to happen to the ungodly" (v. 6).
"These dreamers pollute their own bodies, reject authority, and slander celestial beings. But even the archangel Michael . . . disputing did not . . ." (vv. 8–9).	"Those who follow the corrupt desire of the sinful nature and despise authority . . . are not afraid to slander celestial beings, yet even . . . angels do not" (vv. 10–11).
"What things they do understand by instinct, like unreasoning animals— these are the very things that destroy them" (v. 10).	"They . . . are like brute beasts, creatures of instinct . . . to be . . . destroyed" (v. 12).
"Balaam's error . . . blemishes . . . along clouds without rain, blown along by the wind . . . for whom blackest darkness has been reserved forever" (vv. 11–13).	"Blemishes . . . the way of Balaam . . . springs without water and mists driven by a storm. . . . Blackest darkness is reserved for them" (vv. 13–17).

SETTING

The circumstances that produced this epistle remain equally vague. The letter was most readily accepted in Alexandria in early church history, beginning with the late-second-century Clement, who hailed from there. That Egyptian city has thus

---

[3] For a representative cross-section of perspectives, see Schreiner, *1, 2 Peter, Jude*, 409, n. 31.

been frequently suggested as the location of the Christians to whom Jude writes. A significant Jewish-Christian community developed there, but the same is the case with Syria and Asia Minor, which have also been put forward as popular options. A recent suggestion has proposed that the author's use of 1 Enoch indicates he was writing from Palestine, where that work was best known.[4] *The antinomian nature of the heresy* afflicting the church(es) Jude addresses, however, more *likely represents Gentile influences more common in the Jewish diaspora* than in Israel, so at least the audience seems to have been outside of the "holy land."

Who the specific false teachers were proves equally mystifying. An older generation of scholarship frequently suggested Gnostics of some kind, based on these teachers' rejection of fundamental Mosaic morality and the comparisons and contrasts between these heretics and angels and demons (vv. 6, 9, 14)—an area of particular interest in Gnosticism.[5] But apocalyptic Judaism demonstrated at least as much interest in angels, both righteous and fallen, while licentious leaders unfortunately crop up in all religions, however law-oriented they may be. The analogies between the false teachers and others who did not respect proper positions or persons of authority (vv. 6, 7, 8, 10) could point to overly autocratic leaders, as with the powerful in many settings throughout history who violate sexual norms while still wanting to keep their posts and avoid disciplinary action.[6]

Furthermore, these teachers were probably "charismatic," in the sense of claiming to be uniquely empowered by the Spirit and thus able to do whatever they wanted without regard for anyone else's reaction. Jude 8 appears to indicate that they specifically supported their claims by reference to dreams or visions that they had experienced.[7]

AUTHORSHIP

The first verse of this letter claims that "Jude, a servant of Jesus Christ and a brother of James," authored the epistle. Because the James who regularly appears without further description in the New Testament is the (half) brother of Jesus (see above, p. 387), this *Jude is most likely another (half) brother of Christ*. Mark 6:3 refers to such an individual by the name of Judas (*Ioudas*), precisely the name that reappears in Jude 1:1. The diminutive form common in English translations merely reflects a translational device to avoid confusion with Judas Iscariot, the disciple who betrayed Jesus. Two other followers of Jesus with the name of Judas appear in the New Testament—one of the Twelve (Luke 6:16; Acts 1:13), who is called Thaddeus in parallel accounts (Mark 3:18; Matt. 10:3); and Judas Barsabbas, who accompanied Paul, Barnabas, and Silas to Antioch to deliver the Apostolic Decree from Jerusalem (Acts 15:22). The Judas to whose home Saul went for instruction by Ananias of Damascus (Acts 9:11) may likewise have been a believer, but we are

---

[4] Jonathan Knight, *2 Peter and Jude* (Sheffield: SAP, 1995), 32.

[5] See classically, Rudolf Bultmann, *Theology of the New Testament*, vol. 1 (London: SCM; New York: Charles Scribner's Sons, 1951), 170.

[6] Cf. Michel Desjardins, "The Portrayal of the Dissidents in 2 Peter and Jude: Does It Tell Us More about the 'Godly' Than the 'Ungodly'?" *JSNT* 30 (1987): 89–102.

[7] Schreiner, *1, 2 Peter, Jude*, 414.

never explicitly told. Ancient church tradition, nonetheless, never associated any of these men with the letter of Jude.

Like the author of James, then, the Jude who wrote this letter likely came to faith only after the resurrection (cf. John 7:5 with Acts 1:14), but then embarked on itinerant ministry, perhaps even accompanied by his wife (cf. 1 Cor. 9:5). Jude's family may well have become quite prominent in first-century Christianity. Eusebius (*Church History* 3.19.1–3.20.7) quotes Hegesippus as recounting how the emperor Domitian summoned Jude's grandsons at the end of the first century because they were related to Jesus and of Davidic descent. He apparently viewed them as a threat to his kingdom, but they reassured him that they were but ordinary "working-class" men, tilling the earth and anticipating a heavenly rather than an earthly kingdom.[8]

Objections to the early church's conviction concerning the authorship of Jude have centered primarily on the conviction that the letter reflects the *"early Catholicism"* of the end of the first century. This thought world is often viewed as consisting of (1) fading hope for Christ's return, (2) the increasing institutionalization of the church, and (3) the crystallization of faith into a fixed body of doctrine.[9] Verse 3 (referring to "the faith that was once for all entrusted to the saints") could easily fit with characteristic (3), while verse 17 (instructing the readers to "remember what the apostles of our Lord Jesus Christ foretold") could match item (2). But "the faith" in question is the gospel, not later church tradition, and "Paul often spoke of 'faith' as the specific content of his preaching of the gospel (Rom. 10:8; Gal. 1:23) and as the confession of his churches (1 Cor. 16:13; Gal. 6:10)."[10]

As for verse 17, these predictions scarcely suggest that the apostles have died. After all, they began predicting (and experiencing) the emergence of false teachers even as they were founding and following-up on churches early in the first Christian generation (cf. esp. Galatians). Moreover, element (1) does not apply at all to Jude; verses 6, 21, and 24 make it clear that Jude still exercised a lively hope for Christ's return.

GENRE AND STRUCTURE

J. Daryl Charles likens Jude to the "word of exhortation" that frequently described early Christian sermons (see above, p. 409), highlighting the rhetorically powerful figures of speech, alliteration, and other devices designed to communicate the passionate urgency Jude felt for contending against these false teachers.[11] J. N. D. Kelly likens Jude to a "polemical tract," thinking more of literary than rhetorical forms,[12] while Richard Bauckham finds at least the body of the letter (vv. 5–19) akin to Jewish *midrash,* with Jude's repeated reference to and commentary on specific texts and

---

[8] See Richard Bauckham, *Jude and the Relatives of Jesus in the Early Church* (Edinburgh: T & T Clark, 1990), 94–106. He provides both a translation and a thorough analysis of the text in question.

[9] James D. G. Dunn, *Unity and Diversity in the New Testament* (London: SCM; Philadelphia: Westminster, 1977), 341–66.

[10] Jerome H. Neyrey, *2 Peter, Jude* (New York and London: Doubleday, 1993), 55.

[11] J. Daryl Charles, *Literary Strategy in the Epistle of Jude* (Scranton: University of Scranton Press; London: Associated University Presses, 1993). Donald P. Senior and Daniel J. Harrington (*1 Peter, Jude and 2 Peter* [Collegeville: Liturgical, 2003], 178–79) identify Jude as "a letter with features both of a Jewish sermon and of a Greek/Latin speech."

[12] Kelly, *The Epistles of Peter and of Jude*, 228.

themes of the Hebrew Scriptures and intertestamental literature.[13] Whatever the merits of Bauckham's overall generic label, his commentary does seem to have captured the major subdivisions of the epistle, on which the following outline heavily relies:[14]

I. Introduction (vv. 1–4)
    A. Greeting (vv. 1–2)
    B. Occasion (vv. 3–4)
II. Description and Denunciation of the False Teachers (vv. 5–19)
    A. Their Immorality (vv. 5–7)
    B. Their Blasphemy (vv. 8–10)
    C. Their Leadership (vv. 11–12a)
    D. Their Lawlessness (vv. 12b–13)
    E. Their Judgment (vv. 14–16)
    F. Their Fulfillment of Apostolic Predictions (vv. 17–19)
III. How the Churches Must Respond (vv. 20–23)
    A. Within Themselves (vv. 20–21)
    B. To the Interlopers (vv. 22–23)
IV. Doxology (vv. 24–25)

COMMENTARY

INTRODUCTION (VV. 1–4)

Greeting (vv. 1–2) Verse 1 extends the most general of all the New Testament's epistolary greetings, but clearly Jude has a specific audience in mind, even if he does not identify them more precisely. Verse 2 presents his distinctive triplet of attributes he hopes will characterize his readers—"mercy, peace and love"—but all are as appropriate as Paul's or Peter's typical combinations.

Occasion (vv. 3–4) The next two verses explain that Jude had originally hoped to write a different kind of letter but, upon learning of the false teachers troubling his audience, changed directions. Presumably the original plans would have resulted in a more upbeat, dispassionate treatise, encouraging his readers with the benefits of Christian salvation (v. 3a), but instead he pens a more polemical, combative text (v. 3b). As in Galatians and Titus, the severity of the problems leads to the omission of any form of thanksgiving. Nevertheless, as in Galatians, 2 Corinthians 10–13, and Philippians 3 (the three most polemical texts in Paul's letters, all warning against the Judaizers), Jude does not directly address the heretics but uses this urgent tone to warn the believers in danger of being led astray by them. Denouncing unbelievers seldom wins them over to Christ; if anything it alienates them further from genuine

---

[13] Bauckham, *Jude, 2 Peter* 3–5. Even when Jude refers to incidents clearly described in the Old Testament, he regularly betrays awareness of later Jewish traditions about those incidents. See Thomas Wolthuis, "Jude and Jewish Traditions," *CTJ* 22 (1987): 21–41.

[14] Bauckham, *Jude, 2 Peter*, 5–6. For a slightly different analysis based on rhetorical criticism, see Duane F. Watson, *Invention, Arrangement, and Style: Rhetorical Criticism of Jude and 2 Peter* (Atlanta: Scholars, 1988), 29–79. For Watson, vv. 1–3 form the introduction; v. 4, the central point; vv. 5–16, the proof; vv. 17–23, the resulting instructions; and vv. 24–25, the doxology (though using the more precise and technical Latin terms).

faith.[15] But warning believers not to be misled by others may at times have to adopt denunciatory rhetoric, especially if they have "secretly slipped in" to a Christian congregation (v. 4a).

In the case of Jude's audience, the false teachers are promoting a godless, immoral lifestyle, probably appealing to God's grace that frees them from the law. Likely, they still claim to be Jesus' followers, but their behavior and its justification amount to a "practical denial of Christ" (v. 4b).[16] The rest of Jude's letter does not describe their false doctrine in order to refute it, but offers an *ad hominem* and *ad hoc* attack on their character, marshaling numerous analogies from the notoriously wicked characters of Jewish history and tradition.

DESCRIPTION AND DENUNCIATION OF THE FALSE TEACHERS (VV. 5–19)

Their Immorality (vv. 5–7)   Jude's first three analogies refer to sexually immoral people depicted in the Old Testament, in each case intertwined with God's faithful in damaging ways. (1) The Israelites destroyed in the wilderness demonstrated their unbelief in a variety of rebellions, none more infamous than the lascivious gathering associated with the worship of the golden calf (v. 5; cf. Exod. 32). (2) The angels who fell from heaven were believed to have been involved in some way with the procreation of the particularly wicked race destroyed by the flood in the time of Noah (v. 6; cf. Gen. 6).[17] (3) The citizens of Sodom and Gomorrah were so caught up in homosexuality that Lot's family had to be supernaturally protected by the Lord's angels, lest they as his guests or his two virgin daughters be raped by the townspeople (v. 7a; Gen. 19). Since only the last of these examples involves homosexuality, we cannot infer that Jude's opponents were necessarily gay, just that they were promoting serious sexual sin of some kind.[18] All three examples do, however, stress God's eternal judgment against such sinners if they fail to repent and come to faith (v. 7b).

Their Blasphemy (vv. 8–10)   The next characteristic of the false teachers that Jude highlights is their blasphemy (from *blasphemeō*; NIV "slander" in v. 8). Here he develops only one analogy, from the pseudepigraphical Jewish work known as the Assumption of Moses. In it, the story is told of how the archangel Michael refused to slander the devil in a dispute between them over whether or not Moses deserved an honorable burial (since he had been a murderer and lost out on the promise of entering Canaan but still was a great leader, miracle worker, lawgiver, and prophet). This work has been lost but was referred to by numerous ancient writers as forming the

---

[15] Cf. Bauckham, *Jude, 2 Peter*, 32. Far better is a dialogical approach; cf., e.g., John R. W. Stott and David L. Edwards, *Evangelical Essentials: A Liberal Evangelical Dialogue* (Leicester and Downers Grove: IVP, 1988); Stephen E. Robinson and Craig L. Blomberg, *How Wide the Divide? A Mormon and an Evangelical in Conversation* (Downers Grove: IVP, 1997). Sometimes this process enables one to see that one's conversation partner is a believer after all, and that one has drawn the parameters of one's own faith too narrowly; in almost every case it helps one to clarify where the most fundamental differences between faith communities lie as well as where significant agreements appear.

[16] Moo, *2 Peter, Jude*, 231.

[17] See above, p. 463. This need not imply that angels literally copulated with human women, though some Jewish traditions did interpret the text this way. For a close parallel to the binding of these demons, see 1 Enoch 10:4–6.

[18] Cf. further Bauckham, *Jude, 2 Peter*, 54.

end of the larger, intertestamental work known as the Testament of Moses, much of which *has* been preserved.[19] Jude's point was not that Christians should treat Satan gently, but that all judgment is reserved for the Lord (v. 9). Rebuking Satan in the Lord's name also echoes God's own language in Zechariah 3:2.

Does Jude's appeal to these stories in the pseudepigrapha mean he believes these documents to be inspired? Hardly! Paul quoted pagan poets and prophets without making that assumption about them (Acts 17:28; Titus 1:12). But does Jude think that at least these specific accounts narrate actual historical events? We have no way of knowing. Jewish and Christian preachers, ancient and modern, have often appealed to well-known works of fiction, citing excerpts that illustrate key lessons they want to draw, without explicitly reminding their congregations of what everyone already knows about their literary genre. Today a speaker might well enjoin an audience to persevere in their Christian commitment with the same tenacity displayed by Frodo in his quest to destroy Sauron and the forces of darkness in Middle Earth, confident that the listeners would recognize the allusion to the trilogy of novels by J. R. R. Tolkein, known as *The Lord of the Rings* (or the three movies inspired by them).[20] Indeed, one can draw an even closer parallel. Like Lord Sauron, Jude's opponents were setting themselves up as incontestable authorities (v. 8), especially if they were judging God's law, but in so doing were also setting themselves up for divine condemnation (v. 10).

Their Leadership (vv. 11–12a)   Three more Old Testament analogies in verse 11 illustrate the false leadership of the heretics: (1) *Cain*—in the Hebrew Scriptures he was known primarily as the first murderer, but in Jewish tradition he became a paradigm of false teaching,[21] and one second-century Gnostic sect called itself the Cainites; (2) *Balaam*—despite initially resisting bribes offered to him so that he might curse Israel, he eventually used his leadership role as a pagan prophet to seduce the Israelite women (cf. Num. 31:16 with chap. 25; cf. also Rev. 2:14);[22] and (3) *Korah*—Moses' rival in Numbers 16 was eventually swallowed up by the earth, later becoming a "classic example of the antinomian heretic."[23] These three analogies thus support the charge of verse 12a that the false teachers are "shepherds who feed only themselves." The word translated "blemishes" also means "reefs" and may well reflect the danger of believers shipwrecking their faith if they continue to allow these men to participate with them in as holy an event as the love feast or *agapē* meal—a shared Christian meal culminating in the Lord's Supper.[24]

Their Lawlessness (vv. 12b–13)   In this short section, Jude employs four analogies from the natural world of phenomena that violate standard patterns of behavior, one from each of the major portions of the universe as conceived of by the

---

[19] On Jude's use of this tradition and those from 1 Enoch, see esp. J. Daryl Charles, "Jude's Use of Pseudepigraphal Source-Material as Part of a Literary Strategy," *NTS* 37 (1991): 130–45.

[20] Cf. Moo, *2 Peter, Jude*, 250.

[21] "The archetypal sinner and the instructor of others in sin" (Bauckham, *Jude, 2 Peter*, 79).

[22] Jude may also be implying that the opponents were "wandering prophets who spoke to make money" (Schreiner, *1, 2 Peter, Jude*, 463).

[23] Ibid., 83.

[24] Cf. Kelly, *The Epistles of Peter and Jude*, 270–71.

ancients—air, earth, water, and the heavens: clouds that produce no rain; trees that survive the summer without yielding fruit and then are uprooted; wild waves of the sea; and the planets, whose appearance like wandering stars gave them their name, in Greek and English. Similar unnatural (i.e., lawless) behavior further condemns the false teachers.

Their Judgment (vv. 14–16)   Now Jude quotes 1 Enoch (1 En. 1:9) explicitly. This widely used work of intertestamental Jewish apocalyptic was probably well known to Jude's audience. Here Jude actually declares that "Enoch, the seventh from Adam, prophesied" about the false teachers when he spoke of God's coming judgment, in the company of his myriads of angels, to destroy and punish the wicked.[25] But still, this language does not mean Jude believed 1 Enoch to be inspired (as far as we know, no other Jews did). Rather, he could well have imagined that this text unwittingly reflected a divine truth, much like Caiaphas was said to have prophesied unknowingly in John 11:51. Nor need he have believed that the historical Enoch actually wrote these words. The phrase "seventh from Adam" actually comes from 1 Enoch itself (60:8) and thus helps to identify Jude's source; it need not be an affirmation of authorship.[26] What Jude *does* believe is that the text of 1 Enoch that he excerpts reflects a true statement.[27] In fact, its teaching fundamentally agrees with Zechariah 14:5.

Their Fulfillment of Apostolic Predictions (vv. 17–19)   Some commentators would end the major body of the letter after verse 16, observing that verses 17–23 hang together by means of the two parallel introductions that read literally, "but you beloved," in verses 17 and 20. But verses 17–19 are still describing the false teachers, whereas verses 20–23 turn to the proper behavior of Jude's listeners. Verses 17–19 are thus best seen as concluding the letter body by explaining the existence of these heretics in the first place. They have fulfilled the various apostolic warnings that such errorists would emerge (e.g., Acts 20:29–31; 2 Thess. 2:1–4; 2 Tim. 3:1–8). Though they undoubtedly claim to be led by God's Spirit, Jude flatly denies this allegation and attributes their behavior to their carnal, fallen human natures.[28]

HOW THE CHURCHES MUST RESPOND (VV. 20–23)

Within Themselves (vv. 20–21)   Jude closes the letter by encouraging his readers to build up each other and themselves in faith through prayer (v. 20). They must exhibit love and mercy rather than vindictiveness as they await God's ultimate reward for their faithfulness and judgment on those who are troubling them (v. 21).[29] These verses unobtrusively make mention of God, the Lord Jesus Christ, and the Holy

---

[25] The fourfold repetition of "ungodly" in v. 15 and the four expressions for the sins of speech in v. 16 create one of the most emphatic censures possible (Neyrey, *2 Peter, Jude*, 78).

[26] Cf. Schreiner, *1, 2 Peter, Jude*, 471.

[27] Charles (*Literary Strategy in the Epistle of Jude*, 165) speaks of the passage's "illustrative function."

[28] Knight (*2 Peter and Jude*, 51) notes how damning a charge this would have been in a religious milieu in which virtually all religious leaders claimed to have the S/spirit of God or the gods.

[29] Indeed, Jude's overall pattern is to laud his readers while censuring the opposition, a rhetorical strategy designed to persuade the former to reject the latter. See Stephan J. Joubert, "Persuasion in the Letter of Jude," *JSNT* 58 (1995): 75–87.

Spirit, too, offering another reminder that trinitarian thought emerged at a remarkably early stage in Christian history.

To the Interlopers (vv. 22–23)   To the opponents, or to those infected by them, the church's behavior must vary depending on the specific circumstances. Those who are simply starting to doubt orthodoxy should be dealt with tenderly and graciously, with encouragement. Those who have all but committed apostasy should be snatched, as it were, from a fire and not allowed to be influenced any further by the errorists. Others will fall somewhere in between these two ends of the spectrum. Pastoral ministry and counseling require great sensitivity to what will most likely help each individual rather than some "one-size-fits-all," programmed approach to complex issues.[30]

DOXOLOGY (VV. 24–25)

Brief though Jude's letter is, it closes with one of the fullest and most inspiring of New Testament doxologies. Acknowledging that ultimately it is only God who can empower us to live as we need to, Jude closes with praise and the prayer-wish that God through Christ be worshipped as alone retaining all "glory, majesty, power and authority." The letter thus ends as it has begun; despite the strong warning against falling into heresy and immorality, God calls and preserves those who are truly his.[31] Here, too, appears one of the clearest New Testament statements of the eternality of the Deity from all eternity past extending forever into the future.

APPLICATION

One might sum up the abiding relevance of Jude with the slogan, "tolerance has its limits."[32] In an age of pluralism, in which at times the only thing not tolerated is intolerance, Jude sends sharply countercultural signals. His strategy, too, is out of vogue—he does not argue rationally, but emotionally, denouncing the false teachers' behavior more than their theology. But herein lies a key to the application of this little letter. Wrong theology (beliefs about God, Jesus, human nature, etc.) may damn a person, but it is impossible to prove this in the "public square." American freedom of religion, like God's creation of human beings with free will, allows for people to choose damning worldviews that hurt no one but themselves. But in the realm of gross interpersonal violations, like the sexual immorality, autocratic leadership, abusive rhetoric, and materialistic manipulation that characterized Jude's opponents, God's people have the responsibility to intervene and take firm action. We should staunchly oppose Islam's mistreatment of women, Hinduism's demeaning

---

[30] On the combination of the urgency of the need and the disgust over the opposition reflected here, see Watson, *Invention, Arrangement, and Style,* 46. On the textual variations and the different possible ways of grouping the clauses in vv. 22–23, see, most recently, Joel S. Allen, "A New Possibility for the Three-Clause Format of Jude 22–3," *NTS* 44 (1998): 133–43.

[31] See further Schreiner, *1, 2 Peter, Jude,* 447.

[32] Cf. Carson and Moo, *An Introduction to the New Testament,* 694: "The atmosphere of postmodernism in which the church now lives requires us to guard vigilantly against the temptation to welcome heresy in the name of 'tolerance.'"

of the "untouchable" caste, and the demon-worship in various forms of animism that lead its practitioners to mutilate themselves or sacrifice children to their gods. But we should equally strongly denounce and protect our people from supposedly Christian leaders who abuse our children, refuse to submit to reasonable accountability mechanisms, or teach heresy in a harsh, divisive spirit (*contra* both parts of Eph. 4:15a).

If we want to emulate Jesus and Paul, we will give outsiders the benefit of the doubt that they have at least some good motives and try to woo them to Christ (and hence to Christian truth) through forms of outreach characterized by compassion and love. But the more we are convinced that those who are perpetrating serious heresy or unethical living are genuine believers, the more we need to take harsher measures, not merely to protect our people from their abuse, but also to clearly distinguish their actions and beliefs from true Christian ethics and theology in the eyes of a watching world.

ADDITIONAL QUESTIONS FOR REVIEW

1. Why are Jude and 2 Peter treated together? What is their relationship?
2. What can be said of the setting and date of Jude? What are some of the features of Jude that have caused scholars to doubt an early date, or authorship by Jesus' half brother Jude? How can these criticisms be answered?
3. What is the nature of the heresy that Jude is refuting? Name a few specific examples of notorious figures from Jewish history Jude uses to denounce the false teachers.
4. How can the use of pseudepigrapha in Jude's letter and cultural influences such as prophets and poets in Pauline letters be justified? What can be said of the inspiration of such documents? How can teachers apply this principle to their own teaching?
5. What specific suggestions does Jude give for combating these false teachings? How should Christians encourage one another, and how should they deal with heretics? How does this apply to Christian ministries today when they find their message compromised by those who would teach less than the full truth of the gospel?

SELECT BIBLIOGRAPHY

In addition to the works listed under James or 1 Peter that also treat Jude, see:

COMMENTARIES

Advanced

Bauckham, Richard J. *Jude, 2 Peter.* WBC. Waco: Word, 1983.

Bigg, Charles. *A Critical and Exegetical Commentary on the Epistles of St. Peter and St. Jude.* ICC. Edinburgh: T & T Clark, 1901.

Mayor, Joseph B. *The Epistle of S. Jude and the Second Epistle of S. Peter.* London and New York: Macmillan, 1907.

Intermediate

Hillyer, Norman. *1 and 2 Peter, Jude.* NIBC. Peabody: Hendrickson, 1992.
Moo, Douglas J. *2 Peter, Jude.* NIVAC. Grand Rapids: Zondervan, 1997.
Neyrey, Jerome H. *2 Peter, Jude.* AB. New York and London: Doubleday, 1993.

Introductory

Green, Michael. *The Second Epistle General of Peter and the General Epistle of Jude.* TNTC, rev. Leicester: IVP; Grand Rapids: Eerdmans, 1987.
Knight, Jonathan. *2 Peter and Jude.* NTG. Sheffield: SAP, 1995.
Kraftchick, Steven J. *Jude, 2 Peter.* ANTC. Nashville: Abingdon, 2002.
Lucas, Richard C., and Christopher Green. *The Message of 2 Peter and Jude: The Promise of His Coming.* BST. Leicester and Downers Grove: IVP, 1995.

OTHER BOOKS

Bauckham, Richard. *Jude and the Relatives of Jesus.* Edinburgh: T & T Clark, 1990.
Charles, J. Daryl. *Literary Strategy in the Epistle of Jude.* Scranton: University of Scranton Press; London: Associated University Presses, 1993.
Lyle, Kenneth R. *Ethical Admonition in the Epistle of Jude.* New York: Lang, 1998.
Reese, Ruth Anne. *Writing Jude: The Reader, the Text, and the Author in Constructs of Power and Desire.* Leiden and New York: Brill, 2000.
Watson, Duane F. *Invention, Arrangement, and Style: Rhetorical Criticism of Jude and 2 Peter.* Atlanta: Scholars, 1988.

2 Peter: "Where Is the Promise of His Coming?"

INTRODUCTION

AUTHORSHIP AND GENRE

Most of the New Testament writings that many modern scholars find pseudonymous were uncontested in antiquity. With 2 Peter, however, doubts have circulated from the earliest periods of church history on. As a result, *no other New Testament document has received as sustained a challenge to its traditional authorship claims as this one. Ancient objections* included lack of sufficient, external attestation; a dramatic difference in style from 1 Peter; and thoroughly Hellenistic theology (Eusebius, *Church History* 6.25.11, citing Origen; see also 3.3.1, 4; 3.25.3–4). The earliest unambiguous witness to Petrine authorship (and the only second-century testimony in this category) is the Acts of Peter (ca. A.D. 180).[1] Whereas 1 Peter is written in rather good Greek, 2 Peter contains some of the most awkward grammar in the New Testament—touches of high-blown classical style mixed with very "un-Greek" barbarisms.[2] The seemingly Hellenistic theology even goes to the "extreme" of speaking about Christians participating "in the divine nature" (1:4), reminiscent of pagan *apotheosis*—humans becoming gods.[3]

Additional modern objections have included 2 Peter's relationship with Jude and theological developments seemingly requiring at least a late first-century date, after Peter's death in the mid- to late-60s. Under the former heading, the question is raised as to why the leader of the Twelve would want to borrow from as "lesser a light" as Jude, if the common assumption of 2 Peter's dependence on Jude is accepted (see above, p. 461). In the latter category appear three issues of particular prominence: (1) the problem of the delay of Christ's return (see esp. 3:3–10) seems too severe to have arisen within the first Christian generation, especially given the reference to the believers' ancestors in 3:4; (2) 2 Peter 3:2 seems to recall a previous apostolic era;

---

[1] Bauckham, *Jude, 2 Peter*, 162–63.

[2] Cf. Kelly, *The Epistles of Peter and of Jude*, 235–36. Terrance Callan ("The Style of the Second Letter of Peter," *Bib* 84 [2003]: 202–24), on the other hand, finds significant parallels with the Nemrud-Dagh inscription from Commager in northern Syria and with the description of the "grand Asian style" described by Demetrius (*On Style*, 38–124), a style deliberately designed to appeal to the emotions and impress on the listeners the importance of the topic.

[3] This was also the most influential text in the development of the Eastern Orthodox doctrine of deification, though unlike various pagan counterparts, it was never understood as humans sharing in God's unique ontological nature. So Donald Fairbairn, *Eastern Orthodoxy Through Western Eyes* (Louisville and London: WJKP, 2002), 79–95; and Daniel B. Clendenin, *Eastern Orthodox Christianity: A Western Perspective* (Grand Rapids: Baker, 1994), 117–37.

and (3) the letter closes with a reference to a collection of Paul's letters as Scripture (3:15), a conviction that would have taken some considerable time to develop after those epistles were written.[4]

Nevertheless, a case for the authenticity of 2 Peter can still be mounted.[5] *First,* the external attestation for the letter is still better than for any of the disputed documents considered for the canon of the New Testament but ultimately rejected.[6] The two New Testament Apocrypha ascribed to Peter (an apocalypse and a gospel) were particularly sharply denounced in the early church. *Second,* if an amanuensis was responsible for the good Greek of 1 Peter (see above, p. 442), then 2 Peter could reflect the best Peter could do with Greek as a second language (or perhaps he used two different secretaries—see already Jerome, *Epistle* 120.11). *Third,* if Peter was impressed with the material Jude had used against similar false teachers, there is no reason he should not have been content to borrow and reuse some of it.

Fourth, the delay of the parousia was a problem already in the 50s (recall 1 Thessalonians), and the ancestors referred to in 3:4 are almost certainly Old Testament leaders—the consistent meaning of "our fathers" elsewhere in the New Testament—especially because the author is speaking about an attitude that stresses the supposed uniformity of history "since the beginning of creation."[7] *Fifth,* 3:15 does not indicate how many letters of Paul were considered Scripture, and there is no reason why a collection of his earliest letters written, say, by the mid-50s could not have been viewed as Scripture by at least some Christians within a decade. The same features that convinced second-century believers of their canonicity were already present,[8] and with Peter and Paul both spending a number of years in the 60s in or near Rome, Peter in particular might have come to appreciate the inspired nature of Paul's writings, especially his letter to the Romans, before a majority of the Christians of his day did.

In addition to these responses to the case against Petrine authorship, the following points should be noted. (1) The author of this epistle makes claims that suggest he was an eyewitness of the transfiguration (1:16). If he were not Peter, then it is hard to see this claim as anything but an intentional effort to deceive his readers. (2) The very differences in style and format between the two letters are also hard to square with theories of pseudonymity; recall that one of the major reasons 2 Thessalonians and Ephesians are often considered deutero-Pauline is their supposedly slavish imitation of 1 Thessalonians and Colossians, respectively. (3) Especially puzzling is the address in 1:1, in which the author uses the name *Sumeōn Petros* (Simeon Peter), found elsewhere in the New Testament only in Acts 15:14. This looks far more like an authentic signature than an attempt to imitate the style of 1 Peter, in which the

---

[4] Cf. Knight, *2 Peter and Jude*, 15–20.

[5] Two of the more extended defenses include Guthrie, *New Testament Introduction,* 811–42; and E. M. B. Green, *2 Peter Reconsidered* (London: Tyndale, 1960).

[6] In detail, see "Appendix D: Lists and Catalogues of New Testament Collections," in *The Canon Debate,* ed. Lee M. McDonald and James A. Sanders (Peabody: Hendrickson, 2002), 591–97.

[7] Hillyer, *1 and 2 Peter, Jude,* 214.

[8] Cf. further Bruce, *Canon,* 255–69. Of course, not enough time would have elapsed to demonstrate the widespread usefulness of each of Paul's works, but otherwise all the criteria of canonicity would have been met.

apostle simply calls himself *Petros* (1:1).[9] (4) Finally, a meticulous comparison of 1 and 2 Peter discloses numerous similarities in wording as well as the obvious differences in style.[10]

A mediating view, argued particularly cogently by Richard Bauckham, postulates that 2 Peter was a posthumously compiled "last testament" of Peter.[11] This was a well-known ancient genre, usually though not necessarily pseudepigraphical, adopting a literary device arguably not intended to deceive readers concerning the true author. Chapter 1:15 could suggest that Peter began the process of preparing this letter and had arranged for a successor to complete the work if death prevented him from doing so. Bauckham believes that the author was "an erstwhile colleague of Peter's, who writes Peter's testament after his death, writing in his own way but able to be confident that he is being faithful to Peter's essential message."[12] Tertullian (*Against Marcion* 4:5) and the Mishnah (*Berakoth* 5:5) both suggest that at least by A.D. 200 it was considered acceptable in both Christian and Jewish circles for a pupil to publish in his master's name. Whether this was the case a century earlier remains uncertain. Nothing in principle prevents the proponent of a high view of Scripture from incorporating this form of a hypothesis of pseudonymity (or what Marshall would call allonymity; recall under the Pastorals above, pp. 347–48); it is just unclear that there are any unambiguous parallels to this device that we know were accepted by Christians in the early-second or late-first centuries.[13] At the same time, it does appear that the genre and contents of a *testament* most closely match what we find in this epistle.

OTHER CIRCUMSTANCES

If at least a core of this epistle is Petrine, then it must be dated *prior to 68,* as already noted with 1 Peter above (p. 445). If its final form is due to one of Peter's disciples, a later first-century date is likely. Proponents of pure pseudonymity often suggest the early-second century and some have proposed a date as late as the middle of the second century. But possible allusions to 2 Peter in early- to mid-second-century Christian writings make this less likely.[14] If 3:1 does refer back to 1 Peter, then 2 Peter is obviously addressed to at least part of the first letter's audience in what today is western and central Turkey.[15] If it refers to some lost letter, then we have no way of determining the location of the audience. Because Peter writes 1 Peter from Rome, because he dies in Rome, and because no early church traditions

---

[9] Schreiner, *1, 2 Peter, Jude,* 260–1.

[10] For detailed lists comparing 2 Peter with 1 Peter and with several other early Christian writings, see J. B. Mayor, *The Epistle of S. Jude and the Second Epistle of S. Peter* (London and New York: Macmillan, 1907), lxviii–cxiv.

[11] With variations, cf. Bauckham, *Jude, 2 Peter,* 131–35, 158–62; Denis Farkasfalvy, "The Ecclesial Setting of Pseudepigraphy in Second Peter and Its Role in the Formation of the Canon," *Second Century* 5 (1985): 3–29; and J. Ramsey Michaels, "Peter, Second Epistle of," in *International Standard Bible Encyclopedia, Revised,* ed. Edgar W. Smith, vol. 3 (Grand Rapids: Eerdmans, 1986), 816–18.

[12] Bauckham, *Jude, 2 Peter,* 147. He later suggests Linus, Peter's successor as bishop of Rome (see also 2 Tim. 4:21), as a plausible candidate for this task (pp. 160–61).

[13] Likewise Schreiner, *1, 2 Peter, Jude,* 274; Green, *The Second Epistle General of Peter and the General Epistle of Jude,* 33.

[14] Bauckham (*Jude, 2 Peter,* 158) thus proposes 80–90 for the most likely date.

[15] The similarities between the two books' opening verses and additional scattered parallels makes such usage quite likely. See Tord Fornberg, *An Early Church in a Pluralistic Society: A Study of 2 Peter* (Lund: Gleerup, 1977), 13–15.

place him elsewhere during the 60s, *the letter probably comes from Rome.* If 1 Peter was written just as Nero's persecution was beginning (or at least looming on the horizon), then *2 Peter probably was penned after Nero's persecution had already begun, as the apostle became convinced that Jesus' prophecy that he would die a martyr's death (John 21:18–19) was soon to be fulfilled.*[16]

As with Jude, counteracting false teachers with libertine lifestyles forms the key purpose for this letter. In 2 Peter, however, a doctrinal foundation for this immorality clearly emerges—the denial of the parousia and, therefore, of final judgment.[17] This could fit the overly realized eschatology of certain Gnostic or proto-Gnostic errorists (recall under 1 Cor. 15), but it is hardly limited to that ideology. Jerome Neyrey has pointed to significant parallels with Epicurean philosophy,[18] while Daryl Charles shows how the false teachers could have been Stoics.[19] That the Epicureans and the Stoics held opposite views on numerous fundamental tenets merely demonstrates how little we actually know about the false teachers Peter opposed![20] Indeed Peter couches his response in the form of predictions of future problems, as if the heretics were not yet around, but he frequently shifts to present-tense descriptions, making it clear the false teaching is already afoot.[21]

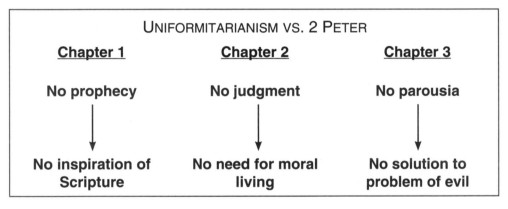

STRUCTURE

One main doctrinal error emerges in each of the three chapters of 2 Peter, each of which appears to derive from the heretics' denial of Christ's return (or at least of a cataclysmic divine intervention accompanying it[22]): *the denial of the inspiration of Scripture* (refuted in 1:16–21), *the denial of basic Christian morality* (attacked in 2:1–22) *and the denial of final judgment* (rebutted in 3:1–10). Enclose these three

---

[16] Moo, *2 Peter, Jude*, 25.

[17] Bauckham (*Jude, 2 Peter*, 154–55) refers to this as "eschatological skepticism" fueling "moral freedom."

[18] Neyrey, *2 Peter, Jude*, throughout.

[19] J. Daryl Charles, *Virtue amidst Vice: The Catalog of Virtues in 2 Peter 1* (Sheffield: SAP, 1997).

[20] The same conclusion results when one attempts to locate the milieu of the letter (based on internal evidence alone) any more precisely than between the mid-first and early-second centuries. See in detail Michael J. Gilmour, *The Significance of Parallels between 2 Peter and Other Early Christian Literature* (Leiden and New York: Brill, 2002).

[21] Callan, "Use of the Letter of Jude," 62–63.

[22] Edward Adams, "Where Is the Promise of His Coming? The Complaint of the Scoffers in 2 Peter 3.4," *NTS* 51 (2005): 106–22.

sections in various components of letter openings and closings, and an outline like the following results.

I. Opening Remarks (1:1–15)
    A. Greeting (1:1–2)
    B. God's Promises and Demands (1:3–11)
    C. Testamentary Disposition (1:12–15)
II. Letter Body (1:16–3:10)
    A. The Certainty of the Parousia Is Defended (1:16–21)
    B. The Denial of the Parousia Brings Severe Judgment (2:1–22)
    C. The Delay of the Parousia Is Explained (3:1–10)
III. Closing Remarks: Resulting Implications for Christian Living (3:11–18)

COMMENTARY

OPENING REMARKS (1:1–15)

Greeting (1:1–2) The opening verses of 2 Peter contain striking similarities and yet significant differences from 1 Peter that make more sense as the work of a single versatile author than as the product of pseudepigraphy. Peter is now Sim(e)on Peter (see above, pp. 474–75), not just an apostle but also a servant of Jesus. The end of 1 Peter 1:2 reappears verbatim ("Grace and peace be yours in abundance"), but it is expanded with "through the knowledge of God and of Jesus our Lord." The deity of Christ is implied in the phrase "our God and Savior Jesus Christ" as in 1 Peter 1:2,[23] but without mention of the Spirit there is no incipient trinitarianism, only binitarianism.

God's Promises and Demands (1:3–11) This segment reflects the ancient patron-client relationship of benefaction (recall above, p. 168).[24] The section resembles the contents of some letter thanksgivings more than anything in Jude did, but this time the unique genre of a testament does not lead to the expectation of a formal introductory prayer. As one soon to face martyrdom, Peter naturally wants to reassure his churches that they have everything they need to enable them to live a faithful Christian life in Jesus (v. 3), even if Peter is no longer available to guide them. Jesus' power thus enables believers to "participate in the divine nature" (v. 4a). This expression is undoubtedly the most controversial line in the whole book (see above, p. 473), but the immediate context explains its meaning. Verses 3, 4b and 5–9 are all speaking clearly about moral living over against sinful behavior. We can share God's moral attributes but not his ontological ones.[25] Nothing in this letter even remotely hints at Christians becoming omnipresent, omnipotent, or omniscient.

---

[23] Hillyer, *1 and 2 Peter, Jude,* 158. Terrance Callan ("The Christology of the Second Letter of Peter," *Bib* 82 [2001]: 253–63) finds here an important intermediate step between pure monotheism and full-blown trinitarianism.

[24] Neyrey, *2 Peter, Jude,* 145.

[25] See, in detail, James M. Starr, *Sharers in Divine Nature: 2 Peter 1:4 in Its Hellenistic Context* (Stockholm: Almqvist and Wiksell, 2000).

It may be that the false teachers had used an expression like partaking of divinity for more sweeping claims and that Peter takes it up but redefines it, thus accounting for the unusual terminology. It may also be that "partners of the deity" is a better rendering of the Greek *theias koinōnoi phuseōs* than "participa[nts] in the divine nature," not in the sense of equal status with God but as coworkers with God for his covenant purposes who live eternally as God does.[26]

Verses 5–9 itemize the virtues in which believers must grow if they are to be effective partners with God. The specific list in verses 5–7 does not appear to follow a sequence that requires its elements to remain in the order given, but, in such lists, first and last items were often the most emphatic. That works well here, too, with "faith" and "love." Faith is also the required prerequisite for the other virtues to be truly Christian, while love well summarizes the intended outcome.[27] That the person who lacks these virtues is both "nearsighted and blind" (v. 9) sounds odd until we realize that the word from which we get our English *myopic* could also mean "with eyes shut." Believers who are not growing are not inherently blind, they just have closed their eyes to the truth for a time![28] Those who are making progress are likewise making their "calling and election sure" (v. 10), a reminder that God's predestining choice never operates apart from free human response. Such believers will also never fall, in the sense of committing full-fledged apostasy, but will be warmly welcomed into the fullness of God's kingdom in the life to come (v. 11).[29]

Testamentary Disposition (1:12–15)   To this end, Peter prepares his audience so that even after he has died, and even though they have already learned the fundamentals of the faith, they will be reminded again and again of key Christian principles. On the possible significance of this paragraph for the circumstances surrounding the publication of this letter, see above (p. 475). Whether or not the letter was completed before Peter's death, it is obvious that he anticipates the possibility that he might not have enough time to do everything he would like to prepare his readers for his departure, so he "will make every effort" (v. 15) to get them ready as long as his life lasts.

LETTER BODY (1:16–3:10)

The Certainty of the Parousia Is Defended (1:16–21)   It is possible that the body of the letter itemizes three problems with the false teachers Peter is combating: denial of the inspiration of Scripture, an immoral lifestyle, and denial of Christ's return and final judgment. But more likely, all three of these issues form part of the one main problem of questioning the belief in Christ's return, as elucidated in 3:4. Peter, therefore, points particularly to his experience of the transfiguration (Mark 9:2–8 pars.) as a foreshadowing of Christ's return in glory and insists that this story is no mere myth (vv. 16–18). *Muthoi* (v. 16) can simply mean "stories" but frequently

---

[26] See further Al Wolters, "'Partners of the Deity': A Covenantal Reading of 2 Peter 1:4," *CTJ* 25 (1990): 28–44; idem, "Postscript to 'Partners of the Deity,'" *CTJ* 26 (1991): 418–20.

[27] Cf. further Bauckham, *Jude, 2 Peter,* 185.

[28] Cf. further Moo, *2 Peter, Jude,* 48.

[29] Cf. further Schreiner, *1, 2 Peter, Jude,* 305.

connoted something "untrue or unseemly;" "rationalist thinkers in the ancient world commonly criticized the stories of fantastic postmortem punishments in the underworld as myths fabricated for moral and social control of naive people."[30]

The reality of Peter's experience with Jesus, however, renders the Old Testament prophecies about the Day of the Lord, now recognized as including the parousia of Christ, that much more certain (vv. 19–21). Thus all professing Christians should carefully heed the words of the prophets, not disparaging them, just as people follow a light to find their way out of a dark place, until Christ, the morning star, returns. After all, no scriptural prophecy can be interpreted simply according to personal whim, as the false teachers undoubtedly were doing, because it is not of merely human origin. Instead God, through his Spirit, inspired Scripture's human authors and illuminates their interpreters when they truly follow his Spirit rather than their own.[31]

The Denial of the Parousia Brings Severe Judgment (2:1–22) If Christ is not returning because there is no supernatural end to the world as we know it, then there is no final judgment and there is no ultimate reason for not seeking temporal pleasure and power, even if it requires immoral behavior. Logic like this led the false teachers Peter opposes to indulge in all the sins that chapter 2 denounces. Here Peter clearly shows his dependence on Jude, borrowing a majority of the analogies Jude had used in his letter, while inserting additional comments and modifying the imagery in ways that fit his slightly different situation and that break up the tightly knit midrashic structure of Jude (see above, p. 461). Because much of this material has already been discussed in connection with Jude, we will limit our comments to the most distinctive sections.[32]

Verse 1 introduces the discussion of the false teachers as if they were a forthcoming phenomenon. But the chapter shifts from the future tense in verses 1–10a to the present in 10b–22, suggesting that such individuals had already begun to infiltrate the congregations addressed. Peter adds to Jude's language of denying their sovereign Lord the clause "who bought them," which suggests either that these are true Christians who lose their salvation or that the scope of Christ's atonement is not limited to the "elect." In view of verses 20–22 (see below), the latter conclusion is preferable. The term for hell in verse 4 comes from the word *tartarus,* not used elsewhere in Scripture but known from Greek mythology as "the subterranean abyss in which rebellious gods, nefarious human beings, etc., were punished,"[33] an apt label for the experience of the demons after they fell. Verse 5 refers to Noah as "a preacher of righteousness." The Genesis account does not explicitly describe Noah acting in this capacity, but what else would he have told the people during the long years of

---

[30] Neyrey, *2 Peter, Jude,* 175.

[31] Many interpreters debate whether Peter is affirming the divine origin or the divine interpretation of Scripture here, but it seems unnecessary to pit the one against the other. God's role in both processes is affirmed.

[32] H. C. C. Cavalin ("The False Teachers of 2 Pt as Pseudo-Prophets," *NovT* 21 [1979]: 263–70) plausibly suggests that more of an emphasis on the false *teaching* corresponds to the repeated comparisons with false *prophets* in the Old Testament. Cf. also Terrance Callan, "Use of the Letter of Jude by the Second Letter of Peter," *Bib* 85 (2004): 42–64.

[33] Kelly, *The Epistles of Peter and Jude,* 331.

constructing the ark? Jewish traditions later regularly applied this epithet to Noah (cf., e.g., Josephus, *Antiquities* 1.74).

More puzzling is the label for Lot as "a righteous man who was distressed by the filthy lives" of the townspeople of Sodom and Gomorrah (v. 7). After all, in Genesis 19:8, he volunteers to give up his virgin daughters to the lascivious crowd. But, however one explains this bizarre offer, he was trying to protect and thus demonstrate proper hospitality to his angelic visitors, and we have no indication that this is anything other than a single lapse in what otherwise was a more exemplary life that qualified his family and him for being rescued from the destruction of those two towns.[34] The belief about the torment Lot experienced in his soul (v. 8) may well have derived from the LXX of Genesis 19:16 with one small punctuation change.[35]

Verse 13 represents an application of the Old Testament *lex talionis* (or "tit for tat" judgment), which remains God's punishment for unbelievers even in the New Testament age. Whatever homosexual sins may have been called to mind by the earlier references to the "filthy lives" that surrounded Lot (v. 7), verse 14 explicitly refers to adultery, confirming our earlier notion that sexual sin *per se,* though not necessarily of one particular kind, characterized the false teachers in Peter's churches. A different element of the Balaam narratives is highlighted here, too (vv. 15–16): his temptation to sell his prophetic services for money, leading to God's rebuking him by speaking through his own donkey (Num. 22:21–41).

Verses 18–19 make explicit what remained implicit in Jude. The heretics not only bring destruction on themselves, but threaten to lead others into slavery to sin as well. Verse 20, at first glance, appears to describe those who are caught up in the heresy as once having been genuine believers. But verse 22 applies two proverbs to them that point in the opposite direction. Just as dogs return to their vomit and pigs to wallowing in the mud, so someone who has never truly repented may sound and act like a Christian for a while, but ultimately will reassert his original damning beliefs and behavior.[36] Verse 21 is hard to square with any belief in annihilationism, because ceasing conscious existence at death can scarcely be a worse fate for one person than for another. But if hell is some form of conscious punishment, but in greatly varying degrees according to one's understanding of God's will (Luke 12:47–48), then Peter's words make perfect sense.

The Delay of the Parousia Is Explained (3:1–10)   The key philosophical underpinning of the false teachers' denial of Christ's return is naturalism or uniformitarianism (vv. 3–4), remarkably similar to the modern-day atheist's conviction that this world simply proceeds by analyzable scientific laws without any supernatural interruptions. Peter replies that this worldview overlooks two great events in human history that have already disproved it: the creation of the world from nothing and the worldwide flood (vv. 5–6). Interestingly today, the big-bang theory of the

---

[34] See esp. T. Desmond Alexander, "Lot's Hospitality: A Clue to His Righteousness," *JBL* 104 (1985): 289–91. Wis. 10:6 likewise calls Lot "a virtuous man."

[35] John Makujina, "The 'Trouble' with Lot in 2 Peter: Locating Peter's Source for Lot's Torment," *WTJ* 60 (1998): 255–69.

[36] Cf. esp. Schreiner, *1, 2 Peter, Jude,* 365.

universe's origin closely resembles *creatio ex nihilo,* while evidence for an ancient flood of enormous proportions continues to grow.[37] But even in Peter's day, people had the Scriptures, penned by Old Testament prophets[38] and New Testament apostles,[39] which witnessed to these events (vv. 1–2). Rejection of this testimony can lead only to final judgment (v. 7).

This judgment will be accompanied by the next great supernatural conflagration—the destruction of the present universe and the creation of new heavens and new earth (vv. 7, 10b, 12b–13; cf. Isa. 65–66; Rev. 21–22). For those who think that thirty-five years or so from the death of Christ form too much of a delay until his return (or for those who think that almost two thousand years are too long!), they must recognize the principle enunciated already in Psalm 90:4 that a thousand years are like a day in God's sight—his perspective on time is vastly different than ours (v. 8). Can any finite period of time be considered too long from the vantage point of eternity?[40] But the reason for God's perceived delay in bringing about the events of the end of this world as we know it, which Jesus' second coming will unleash, is that then there will be no further opportunity for anyone to repent. God wants everyone (but will not coerce anyone) to be saved (v. 9). But eventually there will be an end to his patience, and the Day of the Lord will come without warning for those who are unprepared (recall 1 Thess. 5:2 and cf. Matt. 24:43).

CLOSING REMARKS: RESULTING IMPLICATIONS FOR CHRISTIAN LIVING (3:11–18)

As with Pauline exhortation after theology, but without a formal letter closing, Peter ends with the ethical implications of his instruction. Believers must live holy, grace-filled lives according to true doctrine (vv. 11, 14 and 18)—diametrically opposite to what the false teachers are doing. As more are saved, the end will loom ever nearer (vv. 12a and 15a), but since we do not know what that "full number" is (Rom. 11:25) we cannot use this fact to predict the timing of the end.[41] Finally, Christians must guard against those who distort the Scriptures, like the false teachers were apparently doing (vv. 15b–17a). The specific reference to Paul may well point to their misrepresenting his teaching about grace, as in 1 Corinthians 6:12. Such safeguards

---

[37] Transcending the debate between old-earth and young-earth creationists, who tend to support only their preferred theories and scorn the alternatives, is the rapidly growing intelligent design movement, on which, see, e.g., William Dembski's numerous books, esp. *The Design Inference* (Cambridge and New York: CUP, 1998). Cf. David T. Tsumura, "Genesis and Ancient Near Eastern Stories of Creation and Flood: An Introduction in *I Studied Inscription from Before the Flood*," *Ancient Near Eastern, Literary and Linguistic Approaches to Genesis 1–11,* ed. Richard S. Hess and David T. Tsumura (Winona Lake, Ind., Eisebrauns, 1994), 27–57.

[38] Green (*The Second Epistle General of Peter and the General Epistle of Jude,* 139–40) observes that the plural term for "prophets" in the New Testament elsewhere always refers to Old Testament prophets, so one should not argue that these are New Testament prophets of a past age, thus requiring a post-Petrine date for 2 Peter.

[39] Similarly, "your apostles" does not mean that the writer of this letter is not an apostle, merely that other apostles have had a more formative influence on the churches addressed. Recall the problems in 1 Cor. 1:12 of various congregations or individuals aligning themselves with the different Christian leaders who had most influenced them. Cf. Schreiner, *1, 2 Peter, Jude,* 371.

[40] Interestingly, several pre-Christian Jewish sources likewise appeal to this text and/or principle to explain the perceived delay of the Day of the Lord, prophesied by numerous Old Testament prophets from the eighth century B.C. onward as "at hand." See Richard Bauckham, "The Delay of the Parousia," *TynB* 31 (1980): 3–36.

[41] For elaboration, see Schreiner, *1, 2 Peter, Jude,* 380.

will form the foolproof antidote against apostasy (vv. 17b–18). The language of these last two verses reiterates themes from the beginning of the epistle, creating an inclusio around the entire letter.[42]

APPLICATION

Second Peter provides the classic New Testament answer to the problem of evil. Why does God delay in righting all the wrongs of the world? Every Christian should have at least this one answer memorized—based on 2 Peter 3:9: He waits because the only way he can do away with all evil is to do away with this world as we know it, and cf that will mean an end to the opportunity for anyone more to be saved. So while he delays we must do all we can to bring as many as we can to Christ, thus giving meaning to this otherwise unjust world, which will eventually be destroyed. Of course, it is also important to stress that God has already done the most important thing in dealing with the problem of evil by sending Jesus to die an atoning death for the sins of humanity so that any who truly turn to him can be forgiven of the evil to which they have personally contributed. Scripture testifies to all these truths, and its stories narrate things that actually happened, not like legends or myths.

False teachers, however, will arise in every age to dispute or radically redefine scriptural teaching to suit their personal fancies. Surprisingly often, as with Peter's opponents here, though couched in the guise of "we know that such-and-such never happened," their real motive will be their unwillingness to adopt biblical morality, which then requires them to reject the historic Christian understandings of final judgment. True Christians must avoid such distortions of the faith "like the plague," because, if unchecked, they prove damning. At the same time, they do so right in the midst of the pagan world, not by withdrawing from it.[43] The looking inward to the community in 1 Peter 1:13–2:10 is altogether missing in this epistle.

ADDITIONAL QUESTIONS FOR REVIEW

1. Why has the authorship of 2 Peter been so contested? What arguments can be marshaled in favor of authorship by the apostle Peter?
2. What can be plausibly inferred about the remaining introductory issues for this epistle? What remains more or less uncertain?
3. What three heretical assumptions are battled in the letter body of 2 Peter? What is the logical outcome of each of these denials according to Peter? Which one of these denials most resembles a fundamental tenet of modern atheism?
4. How do Peter's arguments against the root philosophical problem 2 Peter addresses remain effective today against modern equivalents to each of the three false doctrines addressed?
5. What are the ethical implications of the truth of the coming parousia for believers?

---

[42] Cf. further Moo, *2 Peter, Jude,* 206–7.
[43] See Robert W. Wall, "The Canonical Function of 2 Peter," *BI* 9 (2001): 64–81.

6. What is the appropriate response to the problem of evil based on 1 Peter 3:9? How do the denials made by the opponents in 1 Peter reflect some of the same opposition to the gospel we see in people today?

SELECT BIBLIOGRAPHY

In addition to the works listed under 1 Peter or Jude that also treat 2 Peter, see:

Charles, J. Daryl. *Virtue amidst Vice: The Catalog of Virtues in 2 Peter 1*. Sheffield: SAP, 1997.
Fornberg, Tord. *An Early Church in a Pluralistic Society: A Study of 2 Peter.* Lund: Gleerup, 1977.
Green, E. M. B. *2 Peter Reconsidered.* London: Tyndale, 1960.

BIBLIOGRAPHIES

Snyder, John. "A 2 Peter Bibliography," *JETS* 22 (1979): 265–67.
Hupper, William G. "Additions to 'A 2 Peter Bibliography,'" *JETS* 23 (1980): 65–66.
Bauckham, Richard J. "2 Peter: A Supplementary Bibliography," *JETS* 25 (1982): 91–93.
Gilmour, M. J. "2 Peter in Recent Research: A Bibliography," *JETS* 42 (1999): 673–78.

14

THE EPISTLES OF JOHN: THE TESTS OF LIFE

1 John: Countering the Secessionists

INTRODUCTION

AUTHORSHIP

Like Hebrews, 1 John is formally anonymous. No verse in the letter ever refers to the author by any name or description. But numerous early Christian writers referred to the author of this epistle as "John." Among the earliest were Tertullian, Clement of Alexandria, and Origen.[1] The style and vocabulary of this letter is very close to that of the two labeled 2 John and 3 John, though with a few very minor differences. With a little more variation, 1 John also reasonably closely resembles the Gospel in diction and syntax.[2] Some of these parallels are very striking. For example, only the Gospel and 1 John ever use the terms *paraklētos* ("Paraclete") for the Holy Spirit or *monogenēs* ("One and Only") for Jesus. The Greek of these documents is among the "easiest" in the New Testament and typifies the *koinē* Greek that a Jew learning a second language might have been expected to write.

Other common themes or terms include life, light, belief, witness, truth, abiding, keeping the commandments, and loving one another. Thus while some scholars try to distinguish between the author of the Gospel and the writer of 1 John, and a very small handful separate the writer of 1 John from the author of 2 and 3 John (who calls himself "the elder," on which see below, p. 500),[3] a fair cross-section of commentators acknowledge the probability that all four of these documents came from the same hand.[4]

But who is this writer? Papias's early second-century testimony (quoted by Eusebius in *Church History* 3.9.3–4) states, "I took care to search out according to the words of the elders what Thomas or James or John or Matthew or any other of

---

[1] For full details and these and other pieces of evidence for authorship, see Donald W. Burdick, *The Letters of John the Apostle* (Chicago: Moody, 1985), 7–37.

[2] For both of these observations, see, e.g., Werner G. Kümmel, *Introduction to the New Testament* (Nashville: Abingdon, 1975), 442–45, 449–51; John R. W. Stott, *The Epistles of John* (Leicester: IVP; Grand Rapids: Eerdmans, rev. 1988), 28–30.

[3] For arguments for both of these verdicts, see Raymond E. Brown, *The Epistles of John* (Garden City: Doubleday, 1982), 19–30.

[4] For helpful tables of word frequencies in each part of the New Testament of key words that link the Fourth Gospel and the three Johannine epistles, see John Painter, *1, 2, and 3 John* (Collegeville: Liturgical, 2002), 62–70.

the disciples of the Lord, and what Aristion and the elder John, the disciple of the Lord, would say." This quotation could be understood as referring to two different men named John, the latter an elder in the church in the early-second century separate from the apostle and son of Zebedee. This explanation could account for why the author of 2 and 3 John describes himself in the opening verses of those letters as "the elder," as well as why early church tradition associated these letters with someone named John.[5] It would not account for the lack of any name or label in 1 John, however, and it is just as possible that Papias mentions the apostle John twice, as belonging to two different groups, since he is the only living apostle at the turn of the century and an elder in his local church(es) as well.[6]

Many scholars speak of a Johannine school or community that edited (or produced) the literature traditionally ascribed to John in several stages of composition and/or redaction. It is plausible to postulate at least some minimal editing of the Gospel, in light of the multiple witnesses mentioned in John 21:24–25. One reasonable hypothesis suggests that the Gospel was published in final form just after John died, which would explain the inclusion of 21:20–23 to dispel false rumors about what Christ had promised John. The editor(s) could well have added all of chapter 21, given the appearance of 20:31 as an end to the Gospel, along with the third-person references to the beloved disciple scattered throughout John. But the substantial core of the writing would still have come from the apostle (21:24).[7] But many theories are far more elaborate than this, involving up to nine stages of composition between the Johannine heart of the Fourth Gospel and the final form of the first epistle.[8] At best, such theories rely on educated guesswork; at worst, on creative imagination with scarcely any objective constraints.[9] In view of the strong claims in 1 John 1:1–4 that the author is speaking for a group of people who had actually seen, heard, and touched Jesus, *the traditional ascription of authorship to the apostle John, the beloved disciple and one of the three closest followers of Jesus, still seems defensible.*[10]

CIRCUMSTANCES

Tradition also identifies the recipients of the Johannine literature as the Christian congregations in and around Ephesus toward the end of the first century (probably in the 90s). From the internal evidence of 1 John, the Johannine community clearly is troubled by false teaching that denies the full humanity of Christ, claims sinless

---

[5] See esp. Martin Hengel, *The Johannine Question* (London: SCM; Philadelphia: Trinity, 1989). For a defense of this figure as the person who penned the Apocalypse, see John J. Gunther, "The Elder John, Author of Revelation," *JSNT* 11 (1981): 3–20.

[6] See further Craig L. Blomberg, *The Historical Reliability of John's Gospel* (Leicester and Downers Grove: IVP, 2001), 23–26.

[7] See, e.g., Colin G. Kruse, *The Letters of John* (Leicester: IVP; Grand Rapids: Eerdmans, 2000), 1–3; idem, *The Gospel according to John* (Leicester: IVP, 2003; Grand Rapids: Eerdmans, 2004), 28–29.

[8] So John Ashton, *Understanding the Fourth Gospel* (Oxford: Clarendon, 1991), 163–66. In addition to the eight stages he discerns behind the Gospel of John would be the formation of 1 John as the ninth stage.

[9] For a "middle-of-the road" representative of a four-stage view of the composition of the Gospel and 1 John, which is as cogent as any of the less traditional perspectives, see throughout Rudolf Schnackenburg, *The Gospel according to John*, 3 vols. (London: Burns & Oates, 1968–82); and idem, *The Johannine Epistles* (New York: Crossroad, 1992).

[10] Kruse, *The Letters of John*, 9–14.

perfectionism, and yet promotes certain lifestyles that transgress the law. This picture fits ancient descriptions of the proto-Gnostic teacher, Cerinthus, ministering in and around Ephesus at the same time as the aged apostle (Irenaeus, *Against Heresies* 1.26.1, 3.11.1). A particularly well-known story ascribed to Polycarp, disciple of John the apostle, depicts John going to the local public bath-house in Ephesus. "Perceiving Cerinthus within, [he] rushed out of the bath-house without bathing, exclaiming, 'Let us fly, lest even the bath-house fall down, because Cerinthus, the enemy of the truth, is within'" (Irenaeus, *Against Heresies* 3.3.4).

Avoiding the temptation to lump together too quickly somewhat different movements, we may suggest, with Rudolf Schnackenburg, that 1 John has to combat false teachers who are splitting the church(es) and taking followers with them (see esp. 2:19) over three at least partially related ideologies: *incipient Gnosticism, docetism, and Cerinthianism.*[11] From the first of these could have come the notion that lawless living was compatible with spiritual maturity; from the second, that Christ only seemed to be human while being fully God; and from the third, that the Spirit descended on Jesus at the baptism and withdrew before his crucifixion because God could not truly suffer and die as a human being (contrast 5:6 and see below, pp. 495–96). At the same time, we cannot exclude all mention of the Jewish opposition that plagued the Ephesian church when the Fourth Gospel was penned. The emphasis on Jesus as the Christ, the Messiah, continues, which even some Jewish supporters of Jesus found hard to accept, to say nothing of the larger Jewish community as a whole.[12]

GNOSTIC DOCTRINES VS. JOHN'S TESTS OF LIFE		
Perfectionism	vs.	Keep the commandments
Antinomianism	vs.	Keep the commandments and love
Docetism	vs.	Belief in Christ's full humanity

It is interesting to compare 1 John with the Gospel of John in another respect. Whereas the Fourth Gospel has a much more consistent and explicit focus on the deity of Jesus than the Synoptics have, in 1 John more of an emphasis on his humanity

---

[11] Schnackenburg, *The Johannine Epistles*, 23.

[12] Stephen S. Smalley, *1, 2, 3 John* (Waco: Word, 1984), xxiii. Judith Lieu ("What Was from the Beginning: Scripture and Tradition in the Johannine Epistles," *NTS* 39 [1993]: 458–77) believes that numerous texts in these three letters can be seen as exposition of Old Testament teaching on sin, confession, and forgiveness; Cain, sin, and righteousness; and darkness, blindness, and stumbling. She proposes that "the letter is not just 'Jewish' but reflects a tradition of Biblical interpretation and application" (p. 461).

appears (doubtless because of the docetists John is combating). In the Gospel, commentators perceive a strong "law-grace" dichotomy; in the epistle, lawkeeping is reaffirmed (against the false teachers' immoral behavior). In the Gospel, John highlights "realized eschatology"—eternal life or death as beginning already now in the present age; in the epistle, a futurist emphasis dominates (perhaps vs. the Gnosticizing idea that salvation is *fully* accomplished already in this life). Finally, while the Gospel contains comparatively little, over against the Synoptics, about the atoning significance of Jesus' death, in 1 John the topic reappears in more detail (balancing out the proto-Gnostic lack of emphasis on this theme). If the Fourth Gospel was written with one eye on growing Gnostic-like tendencies, but with Jewish polemical concerns more directly in view, *it could easily be that the Gnostic problem grew worse as the false teachers latched on to some of John's emphases and distorted them, exaggerating and applying them in one-sided ways that required John's letters to reassert the balancing doctrines of Christian faith that were being neglected.*[13] Gary Burge phrases matters provocatively by suggesting that "it was the letters of John—1 John in particular—that redeemed the Fourth Gospel for the New Testament we possess today."[14]

EMPHASES IN JOHN'S WRITINGS

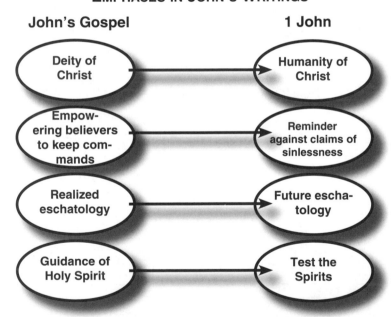

If this hypothesis has any merit to it, then we must assume that the epistles were written after the Gospel. If the Gospel of John was written in the late 80s or early 90s,[15] then the epistles should probably be dated to some time in the 90s as well. But if the epistles were not reacting to a one-sided appropriation of the Gospel or if

---

[13] See esp. Raymond E. Brown, *The Community of the Beloved Disciple* (New York: Paulist, 1979), 93–144.

[14] Gary M. Burge, *The Letters of John* (Grand Rapids: Zondervan, 1996), 26.

[15] See Blomberg, *The Historical Reliability of John's Gospel*, 41–44.

the Gospel is dated to the 60s, following a minority view, then the door is left open for dating the letters to any time between the 60s and the 90s.[16] One later Christian tradition that fits well with a date when John would have been quite elderly is recorded by Jerome early in the fifth century in his commentary on Galatians (6.10). When he could no longer walk for himself, he would be carried into church by his disciples and spoke only the words, "Little children, love one another." After hearing this injunction repeatedly, he was asked why he never said anything else and replied, "Because it is the Lord's command, and if this only is done, it is enough" (Jerome, *Commentary on Galatians* 6.10).

GENRE AND STRUCTURE

First John bears few formal similarities to a letter. It contains neither a typical letter opening nor an identifiable closing. It does not follow any discernible epistolary structure. Some scholars fail to discern much of *any* structure! Suggestions for its genre have included "homily," "diatribe," "informal tractate," "paper," and "pastoral encyclical." The circular nature of the last of these possibilities—a doctrinal declaration intended for a series of congregations—could account for the lack of personal remarks at the beginning and end.[17] An older era of scholarship sometimes tried to parcel up 1 John into discrete sources supplemented by later redaction, but this approach has been recognized today as fruitless.[18] *The purpose of the letter appears to be summed up in 1 John 5:13—to assure true believers of their salvation in light of the dissension and heresy afoot,* though in such a context a polemical as well as pastoral motive necessarily obtains.[19] What *is* clear about the structure is that John repeatedly cycles through *three key themes, which together form what have been called "the tests of life": loving one another, keeping the commandments, and believing in Jesus as fully God and fully human.*[20] While recognizing that it may impose more structure on this "epistle" than John originally intended, we suggest an outline along the following lines:

I. Prologue (1:1–4)
II. The Tests of Life: Cycle One (1:5–2:27)
    A. Sin vs. Obedience (1:5–2:6)
    B. Love for One Another (2:7–17)
    C. Correct Christology (2:18–27)
III. The Tests of Life: Cycle Two (2:28–4:6)
    A. Sin vs. Righteousness (2:28–3:10)

---

[16] I. Howard Marshall, *The Epistles of John* (Grand Rapids: Eerdmans, 1978), 48.

[17] Kruse, *The Letters of John,* 28–29.

[18] For examples and the problems with them, see Marshall, *The Epistles of John,* 27–30.

[19] Cf. further Daniel L. Akin, *1, 2, 3 John* (Nashville: Broadman & Holman, 2001), 32.

[20] After the commentary so entitled by Robert Law (Edinburgh: T & T Clark, 1909). Duane F. Watson ("Amplification Techniques in 1 John: The Interaction of Rhetorical Style and Invention," *JSNT* 51 [1993]: 99–123) discusses John's repetitive style in detail. Recently, several commentators have opted for a much simpler two-part outline that sees, after the prologue of 1:1–4 and before the concluding remarks of 5:13–21, two main sections unpacking the concepts of God as *light* and our responsibility to walk in the light (1:5–3:10) and of God as *love* and our responsibility to walk in love (3:11–5:12). See, e.g., Akin, *1, 2, 3 John,* 47–48. While these themes without question recur, it is even less clear than with our more detailed outline if all that is grouped under these broad headings really was intended to illustrate them.

B. Love for One Another (3:11–24)

C. Correct Christology (4:1–6)

IV. The Tests of Life: Cycle Three (4:7–5:21)

A. Love for One Another (4:7–21)

B. Correct Christology (5:1–15)

C. Sin vs. Life (5:16–21)[21]

THE TESTS OF LIFE (1 JOHN)

	Cycle 1	Cycle 2	Cycle 3
Keeping God's commandments	1:5–2:6	2:28–3:10	5:16–21
Loving one another	2:7–17	3:11–24	4:7–21
Believing in Jesus as the God-man	2:18–27	4:1–6	5:1–15

Each test entails the other two (3:23–24)

COMMENTARY

PROLOGUE (1:1–4)

This opening paragraph reminds the reader of the prologue of John's Gospel (John 1:1–18), even though it is considerably shorter.[22] The Son existed from the beginning with the Father (recall John 1:1–2, 18) but became incarnate, enabling his first followers to see, hear, and touch him, thereby confirming his genuine humanity (recall John 1:14). Their role now is to testify to what they have experienced (recall John 1:6–8, 15)—that Jesus is the bringer of eternal life (recall John 1:4). Proclaiming this good news completes the process of producing joy in both the preachers and their audience because of the fellowship Jesus enables between God and humanity and among redeemed humans themselves.[23]

---

[21] For a slightly different division of the text, but following the same pattern of three cycles of the three tests, see Stott, *The Epistles of John,* 61.

[22] Wendy E. Sproston ("Witnesses to What Was ἀπ᾽ ἀρχῆς: 1 John's Contribution to Our Knowledge of Tradition in the Fourth Gospel," *JSNT* 48 [1992]: 43–65) highlights these and other parallels between the epistle and the Gospel, arguing that both utilized common tradition. Common authorship explains them even better!

[23] The goal of proclaiming the gospel, therefore, is not merely salvation of individuals, but the creation of the fellowship of God's people ("the church"). The nature of that proclamation remains authoritative, "for the Christian message is neither a philosophical speculation, nor a tentative suggestion, nor a modest contribution to religious thought, but a confident affirmation by those whose experience and commission have qualified them to make it" (Stott, *The Epistles of John,* 68).

THE TESTS OF LIFE: CYCLE ONE (1:5–2:27)

Sin vs. Obedience (1:5–2:6) The first test of life is the test of obeying God's commands (2:3). Synonymous with this is John's metaphor of "walking in the light" (1:7) rather than in darkness. The false teachers afflicting the Ephesians were promoting a kind of sinless perfectionism that John must debunk. Such a claim itself is sinful because it is so wrong and misleading. Obedience in this context involves confession of that sin so that fellowship with God may be restored (1:9). Chapter 1:5 thus begins the body of this letter with the affirmation that God is wholly light—a fully reliable source of illumination for how to live. Verses 6–10 proceed to present and deny three false inferences from this premise that the Gnostic-like teachers seem to have been making, once they divorced inward spirituality from external morality.[24] (1) One's relationship can be separated from his or her lifestyle (v. 6). (2) It is possible to achieve a state of sinlessness as a Christian (v. 8). (3) Some had in fact achieved this state quite awhile ago (v. 10). After each of these verses, John intersperses the positive remedy: walking as God directs us to do (v. 7),[25] confessing our sins (v. 9), and recognizing Jesus as having made the necessary atonement for the forgiveness of those sins (2:1–2).

The false teachers in Ephesus were probably not claiming to have eradicated the sinful nature that fallen humanity inherits but rather to have not committed actual sins for some significant period of time, perhaps ever since they had received the "enlightenment" they thought their belief system provided them.[26] Other eras of church history have been infected by this similar deception. "Perfectionism has always had an attraction for the pious, for intellectuals, for those who are confident they have mastered the basics. 1 John teaches that perfection consists in obeying God's word, that and nothing else (2:5)."[27] True Christian belief leads to a recognition of the need to obey all of God's commands, living like Jesus, outwardly as well as inwardly (2:3–6).

Love for One Another (2:7–17) The second test of life involves loving one another. Indeed, God's commands can be summed up in the one command to love (vv. 7–11). This is both an old and a new command (vv. 7–8). It formed the heart of the law (recall Jesus citing Deut. 6:4 and Lev. 19:18 in Mark 12:29–30 par.—on loving God and neighbor) and thus embodied an ancient principle. But Jesus' coming had taken God's love to a new level and thus proves even more crucial for *Christian* fellowship. Those who claim to be Christians while merely dividing the church and failing to love the believers around them disclose the emptiness of their claims. True Christian love, on the other hand, prevents apostasy (vv. 9–11). The use of "brother" throughout the epistles of John refers to a fellow member of the professing Christian community, but some of them turn out to be fakes.[28]

---

[24] Cf. Marianne Meye Thompson, *1–3 John* (Leicester and Downers Grove, IVP, 1992), 44.

[25] "But such works of man, no matter what their quantity or qualitiy, in no way alter the fact that we are saved by the grace of Christ—by and through unearned divine assistance" (Millet, *Jesus Christ*, 8).

[26] Kruse, *The Letters of John*, 66, 70.

[27] Gerard S. Sloyan, *Walking in the Truth: Perseverers and Deserters* (Valley Forge: Trinity, 1995), 18.

[28] Cf. Akin, *1, 2, 3 John*, 98.

All segments of that community bear the responsibility to live as John is enjoining them (vv. 12–14). The three different terms with which John addresses his congregations here most likely refer to his entire audience ("dear children"—the term he uses elsewhere when speaking to everyone to whom he is writing, e.g., 2:1, 18, 28; 3:7, etc.), then broken down into those who are older and those who are younger (either biologically or spiritually or both).[29] Although English translations usually render all uses of the verb "I write" here in the same way, the first three use the Greek present tense while the second three use the aorist (simple past) tense. But these do not refer to some previous communiqué; John merely shifts from stressing what he is saying at the moment to what his entire letter has implied.[30]

Christian love further involves not loving the fallen world order and all its transient attractions (vv. 15–17). The three paradigmatic temptations of verse 16 remind us of the temptations faced by Adam and Eve in the garden and by Jesus in the wilderness.[31] Literally, this triad reads "the lust of the flesh, the lust of the eyes and the pride of life." The paraphrase of the original Living Bible captures the flavor more forcefully with its rendition: "the craze for sex, the ambition to buy everything that appeals to you, and the pride that comes from wealth and importance."

Correct Christology (2:18–27) The third test of life involves correct Christology. The false teachers John is opposing are actually "antichrists," foreshadowing *the* antichrist of end times (v. 18). These teachers, like some of their followers, have seceded from the Christian community, thereby demonstrating that they did not truly belong to it (v. 19). Calvinists regularly see this as one of the clearest verses in Scripture to resolve the questions of how to "diagnose" what happens when someone commits apostasy.[32] These teachers, however, are claiming a unique anointing of the Spirit that John disputes. Such an anointing is the prerogative of *all* Christians and occurs whenever someone trusts in Jesus (vv. 20–21).[33] The secessionists' fundamental doctrinal error is in denying Jesus as the Christ (v. 22), a denial that may point to Jewish and not just Hellenistic influence in the heresy.[34] Second-century sectarian Jewish-Christians known as Ebionites denied that Jesus was the divine Messiah, but maintained that one could still be Christian by worshipping the Father. If this mentality had already appeared in Ephesus by the end of the first century, John's reply makes perfect sense—*one cannot have the Father without a correct understanding of the Son* (v. 23).

The antidote to incorrect Christology is simply to remain faithful to the truth as these believers had originally learned it (vv. 24–27). Verse 27 cannot be taken abso-

---

[29] So, e.g., Smalley, *1, 2, 3 John*, 69–71.

[30] Cf. Stanley E. Porter, *Verbal Aspect in the Greek of the New Testament, with Reference to Tense and Mood* (New York: Peter Lang, 1989), 229–30.

[31] See the chart in Blomberg, *Jesus and the Gospels*, 223. Akin (*1, 2, 3 John*, 108) finds the parallels "too striking to be insignificant."

[32] E.g., Gordon R. Lewis and Bruce A. Demarest, *Integrative Theology*, vol. 3 (Grand Rapids: Zondervan, 1994), 202, 205, 223.

[33] John's "anointing" is equivalent to Paul's "baptism" of the Spirit (1 Cor. 12:13) and may reflect a deliberate play on words (*chrisma*) with the term "antichrist" (*antichristos*), which he may have coined. Cf. Burge, *The Letters of John*, 128.

[34] Smalley, *1, 2, 3 John*, 113.

lutely; after all, John is teaching his readers through this very letter! But his point is that they do not need any esoteric or elitist teaching to supplement what they have already learned. They don't need to be taught anything new that contradicts the truth, but simply to remain loyal to the basics. Other ideologies may well lead them astray.[35]

THE TESTS OF LIFE: CYCLE TWO (2:28–4:6)

Sin vs. Righteousness (2:28–3:10) If the first cycle described the need to keep God's commands in terms of obedience rather than sin, this cycle speaks of righteousness rather than sin. Indeed, the concept of "doing righteousness" unifies this section (2:29; 3:7, 10). The "like parent, like child" principle shows that one who does what is right in the way God is righteous is truly born of him (2:9). Of course, in this life we can only partly emulate our heavenly Father, but in the life to come, we will be transformed in ways we cannot yet understand (2:28; 3:1–3). Then "we shall be like him" (3:2)—not ontologically but morally. "Believers can never be *equal* to Christ, since He is infinite and they are finite; but they can and will be *similar* to Him in holiness and in resurrection bodies."[36] Chapter 3:4–10, however, appears to make an even stronger claim. Because believers have been purified from sin—defined as lawbreaking—by the cleansing of Christ's atoning death, they no longer sin. Those who do sin do not know him (vv. 4–6)! Verses 7–10 pursue this sharp dualism: sinners show that they are the devil's offspring while those born of God do not sin. Doing righteousness and loving others indicate that a person is a Christian.

But how can John say these things after equally vigorously affirming that anyone who claims never to sin tells a blatant lie (1:6–10)? The NIV masks the stark language of the original Greek but points to the correct solution. The string of present tense verbs in these verses implies that "no one who lives in him *keeps on* sinning," and that "no one who *continues to* sin has either seen him or known him" (3:6; cf. also v. 9: "no one who is born of God *continues to* sin"). In other words, "sin is not the identifying characteristic of those who live" in Christ.[37] They still sin but not as the dominant pattern of their life. But this type of relative "sinlessness" fundamentally differs from that of the Gnostics, because it opposes lawlessness (v. 4). Gnostics were notorious for seeing the law (and the God!) of the Old Testament as evil and, therefore, they remained unconcerned with keeping all of God's commands.

Love for One Another (3:11–24) The end of verse 10 sets up John's second discussion of Christian love. Once again, this is the message Christians have heard "from the beginning" of their walk with the Lord (v. 11), not like the divisive teaching of the heretics who have only lately arrived. Verses 12–18 proceed to contrast the negative model of hate exhibited by Cain (vv. 12–15) with the positive model of love displayed

---

[35] Cf. Thompson, *1–3 John*, 82.

[36] Burdick, *The Letters of John the Apostle*, 234.

[37] Thompson, *1–3 John*, 95. The root meaning of the present tense in Greek, especially in moods outside the indicative, was to refer to ongoing or continuous action. The family imagery John applies throughout this letter may account for much of the apparently absolute language. Children's responsibility to uphold their family's honor was a powerful motivator in the ancient Mediterranean world. See J. G. van der Watt, "Ethics in First John: A Literary and SocioScientific Perspective," *CBQ* 61 (1999): 491–511. Other possible solutions to this apparent contradiction are surveyed in Brown (*The Epistles of John*, 411–16).

by Christ (vv. 16–18). Cain's hatred for his brother led him to become the first murderer; Jesus' love for humanity allowed him to be murdered. We should expect the world to hate us as they hated Christ (v. 13; recall John 15:18–25), but we should lay down our lives for one another if necessary (v. 16; recall John 15:9–17). The next most powerful demonstration of the genuineness of our love comes when we share from the surplus of our material possessions to help those in need (v. 17).[38]

This kind of love can powerfully reassure us of our salvation when we are tempted to doubt it (vv. 19–24). So often it is some of the most obedient, loving Christians with tender consciences and hidden insecurities who agonize over whether they truly "believe" in Jesus properly. Here is where the other two tests of life can help them see the transformation that Christ has wrought in their years of walking with him (vv. 19–20).[39] When we recognize that God does not condemn us, we do not need to condemn ourselves and we may come before him confidently with our requests (vv. 21–22). Like many other seeming "blank checks" in Scripture, verse 22 must be read in the context of the whole document in which it appears; elsewhere 1 John 5:14 insists that we must ask according to God's will. *Verses 23–24 round out this segment by showing how interchangeable the three tests are*: his command is to believe and love. Love equals obedience plus having Christ live in us.[40] And the indwelling Spirit testifies to all these realities.

Correct Christology (4:1–6)   The second cycle culminates with John's second discussion of proper belief. Obedience and love by themselves cannot save a person if one is not already trusting in the Jesus of the Gospels. The false teachers, of course, claimed that this was exactly what they were doing, but by denying the true humanity of Christ, their assertions proved unfounded. If, in insisting that Jesus is also the Christ, John is countering Jewish "believers" denying the divinity of Jesus, then we have an implicit reminder here of the other key doctrine that we must affirm about this "God-man" (vv. 1–3).[41] When we do, when God's Spirit truly lives within us, then we can discern true from false spirits, prophets, or teachers (vv. 4–6). This is because "the one who is in you [the Spirit] is greater than the one who is in the world [the devil]"—a truth that should be applied to every dimension of spiritual warfare.[42] But the principle only works when *we take care to "test the spirits" and do not gullibly believe everyone who claims to have a message from God* even while failing to pass one or more of these tests of life (v. 1).

---

[38] "John is not saying that the wealthy alone are required to share their possessions with others; *every* Christian who is in a position to help others materially is required (responsibly!) to do so" (Smalley, *1, 2, 3 John*, 196).

[39] Cf. Marshall, *The Epistles of John*, 197–98.

[40] Cf. Sloyan, *Walking in the Truth*, 39–40.

[41] Or to combine these truths and further unpack them, "behind these words John is urging three things about our belief: (1) that the man Jesus of Nazareth is indeed the divine Word of God; (2) that Jesus Christ was and is fully divine as well as fully human; and (3) that Jesus is the sole source of eternal life since he alone reveals the Father to us and atones for our sins" (Burge, *The Letters of John*, 174–75).

[42] On which, see esp. Clinton E. Arnold, *3 Crucial Questions about Spiritual Warfare* (Grand Rapids: Baker, 1997).

THE TESTS OF LIFE: CYCLE THREE (4:7–5:21)

Love for One Another (4:7–21)   The third cycle does not present the tests of life in the same order as in the other two, and references to more than one of the tests appear in each subsection. Still, 1 John does seem to subdivide into three segments with one of the tests dominant in each. John mentions "love" in every verse from 7 through 21 except 13–15. Much of this section reinforces themes already introduced in the letter—our behavior as the sign of our new birth (vv. 8–9); God's amazing love for us, which enables us to love others sacrificially as well (vv. 10–12, 16–17a); the role of the Spirit in giving us assurance (v. 13); our testimony to Jesus and the inseparability of Jesus and the Father (vv. 14–15); and the incompatibility of claims to love God while repeatedly hating one another (vv. 19–21).

Verse 7 must be kept within this larger context. There is more to God than love, but love is a crucial and central attribute. Conversely, not all who show love do so from Christian motives; "here it is likely that love is being presented as the *effect* of new birth from God, and the knowledge of God, rather than as their *cause*."[43] Verse 8a nicely illustrates the Greek grammatical principle that in a sentence of the form "x is y," where x and y are nouns and one but not the other has the article preceding it, the noun with the article is usually the subject. In other words, "God is love" is an irreversible statement. Love is not God, "as if any display of affection suddenly qualifies as divine"![44] Verse 9 calls to mind its more famous counterpart in John 3:16. Verses 13–14 reflect further incipient trinitarianism. Verses 15–16 show how correct Christology leads to love, while verse 21 points out how love is obedience to God's commands. Clearly we have much more than an emotion in view here, since emotions usually cannot be commanded (recall under 1 Cor. 13). Indeed, throughout the Bible love for God is usually not nearly so much an emotional experience as obedience to his commands.

The main new element in this section is the theme that love expels the fear of judgment from the believer (vv. 17b–18). Death holds terror for those who think they have no further existence or that they do but that it might be unpleasant. Truly believing in the biblical concept of judgment day could heighten this terror, but for believers it should only be something they anticipate with the joy of people who have been forgiven of their sins and await their glorious heavenly reward. But in our fallen humanity, the subjective appropriation of these truths is not always easy!

Correct Christology (5:1–15)   Chapter 5:1–5 provides another good summary of the interrelationship of the three tests of life. True believers acknowledge both Father and Son and demonstrate interpersonal love and obedience to the commandments. Still, faith takes priority by producing the victory over the evil world system (v. 4); love and obedience flow from that faith without the burden that those who try to work their way into God's favor feel (v. 3).[45] The paragraph spanning verses 6–12

---

[43] Smalley, *1, 2, 3, John,* 238.

[44] Burge, *The Letters of John,* 187. Cf. further D. A. Carson, *The Difficult Doctrine of the Love of God* (Wheaton: Crossway, 2000).

[45] Cf. Ogden and Skinner, *Acts through Revelation,* 296: "Salvation is only through Christ. . . . One cannot merit anything in and of oneself."

is clearly unified by the theme of testimony to Jesus as the Christ and Son of God. But some of the details remain puzzling. What does it mean that Jesus came by water and blood (v. 6)? In light of Cerinthian teaching (above, p. 487), John is probably emphasizing that the Spirit was with Jesus not merely at his baptism and throughout his ministry, but even on the cross to the very moment of his death.[46]

Verses 7b–8a reflect one of the most famous textual variants in church history, known as the Johannine Comma ("comma" here meaning a short part of a book). No known Greek manuscript prior to A.D. 1400 ever contained these words, so they are appropriately relegated to a footnote in the NIV. In fact, nowhere else in any printed edition of the New Testament is a textual variant with such meager attestation ever even included, even in a footnote. But the addition had crept into the Latin tradition in late copies of the Roman Catholic Vulgate and proved influential because of its trinitarian language. When the Catholic Reformer Erasmus was compiling his critical text of the Greek New Testament in 1520, he left this "comma" out and was criticized by various Catholic authorities for so doing. After replying that no Greek manuscript that he knew of contained these words, one was procured that seems clearly to have been altered based on the Latin tradition but Erasmus gave in and included the material. Translators of the KJV, relying heavily on Erasmus, preserved the extra words as well, but all knowledgeable modern translations rightly omit them. Claims that this omission reflects a "liberal" bias against the doctrine of the Trinity are just historically uninformed.[47]

What then does the remaining text mean that the Spirit, water, and blood agree in their human and divine testimony about God's Son, Jesus Christ (vv. 7–9)? Simply put, *the historical events of Jesus' baptism and crucifixion, the subsequent inspiration of the Spirit in guiding the apostles to speak and write of Christ, and the faithful tradition of the church communicated to the next generation all converge to testify to the truth.*[48] John is convinced that this truth is credible and compelling. Ultimately, people must choose either to accept this testimony or to reject it; there are no intermediate options. Those who accept it find eternal life; those who do not accept it call God a liar and do not find life (vv. 10–12).

Verses 13–15 conclude this segment and include a purpose statement for the entire epistle. As with John 20:31, it is easy to imagine John ending his document at this point, but he will append one more short section. Whereas the purpose of his Gospel was to encourage those with no faith to believe (or those with some faith to believe even more),[49] here he writes to believers to assure them of eternal life. But the present tense of "believe" in verse 13 remains crucial. John is not promising salvation to those who at some point in the remote past have made some superficial profession of faith but have not demonstrated anything of the tests of life—correct Christology, love, or obedience to God's commands—in the intervening years. To those who are

---

[46] E.g., Kruse, *The Letters of John*, 178.

[47] For full details, see Brown, *The Epistles of John*, 775–87.

[48] Thompson, *1–3 John*, 133.

[49] See Blomberg, *Jesus and the Gospels*, 169.

currently believing, however, he promises that God will answer their prayers, of course with the caveat that they are within the Father's will (vv. 14–15).[50]

Sin vs. Life (5:16–21) The theme of sin reappears once more, this time as John distinguishes between "mortal sins"—those that lead only to spiritual death—and lesser ones that can be forgiven. If the term "brother" here must refer to true Christians, then John either envisions the loss of salvation for some or refers merely to physical death (as with Ananias and Sapphira). But if, as we have seen earlier, it means "fellow member of the community," then those who "continue to sin" (v. 18) as the characterizing feature of their lifestyle (recall on 3:6 and 9), as presumably the false teachers who have left the church in Ephesus do, demonstrate simply that they were never true believers in the first place. As elsewhere in Scripture, the only unforgivable sin is the sin of persistent unbelief from which one never repents.[51]

Reading verses 16–21 too rapidly can lead to a seriously mistaken inference from John's commands. He clearly encourages believers to pray for those who have sinned in ways not leading to spiritual death. But does not verse 16 also suggest that they should *not* pray for those who have committed mortal sins? Actually, what John writes is that he is *not saying* that people *should* pray in those situations, rather than *saying* that they should *not* pray. In other words, he is just not discussing the situation of what to do with people who have so hardened their hearts that they never will repent.[52] But since we do not have God's ability to know who may have crossed such a line, we must pray for everyone on the assumption that they may still have a chance!

Verses 18–20 reinforce John's promises of security for the believer. Despite the wiles of the devil, who controls the entire unregenerate portion of humanity, God is so much stronger that he can protect us, just as his Son gives us full insight into the nature of God and the ability to know him. But none of this means that the devil cannot have a powerful, negative effect on us, if we let him. So the warning of verse 21 remains apt. While this verse seems an abrupt way to end this "letter" that does not entirely resemble a letter, idolatry is the "catch-all" label for the worship of anything other than the true and living God of the universe. This is what John is convinced the false teachers were promoting, this is what Jews believed all Gentile religion reflected, and, if Jesus incarnated the true God of the cosmos, then the literal idols or statues of gods and goddesses that Gentiles worshipped incarnated the deities of false religions. *The verse is thus an appropriate summary of what John's audience should be doing after all.*[53]

---

[50] "The divine life given to the Christian believers must become life with God and with the brothers and sisters. It is a life that requires constant vigilance" (Schnackenburg, *The Johannine Epistles*, 247).

[51] See esp. Tim Ward, "Sin 'Not Unto Death' and Sin 'Unto Death' in 1 John 5:16," *Churchman* 109 (1995): 226–37. Cf. further Smalley, *1, 2, 3 John*, 299; Akin, *1, 2, 3 John*, 210.

[52] See esp. Randall K. J. Tan, "Should We Pray for Straying Brethren? John's Confidence in 1 John 5:16–17," *JETS* 45 (2002): 599–609.

[53] See esp. Terry Griffith, *Keep Yourselves from Idols: A New Look at 1 John* (London and New York: SAP, 2002). Cf. also Julian Hills, "'Little Children, Keep Yourselves from Idols': 1 John 5.21 Reconsidered," *CBQ* 51 (1989): 285–310.

THE JOHANNINE COMMUNITY

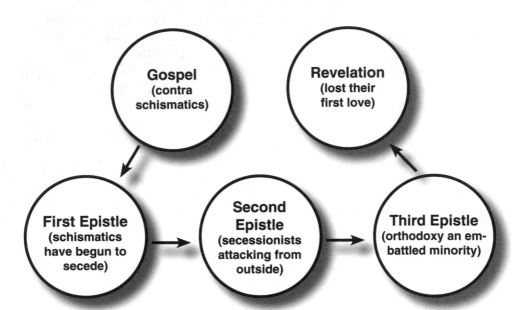

2 John: The Secessionists
Attack from Outside

INTRODUCTION

A t first glance, this letter seems to be written to an otherwise anonymous
Christian woman and her family who are warned not to give hospitality to
false teachers in their home. On closer inspection, a good case can be made
for taking this as a *house church*, as it has often been understood throughout church
history: (1) Israel and the church are regularly personified in the feminine gender
throughout Scripture. (2) That this "lady" is loved by "*all* who know the truth" (v. 1)
makes more sense if she is a church than if she is a private individual. (3) The greetings from "the children of her chosen sister" (v. 13) are more natural as a reference
to a "sister" church. Why would biological offspring of a literal sister send greetings
but not their (even more beloved) mother? (4) The alternation from singular to plural
"you's" throughout the letter makes little sense if John is addressing a literal woman
and her children, but fits well if the "lady" stands for the church as a whole, with
the "children" (John's characteristic form of address to fellow Christians) as individual members. Two other alternatives occasionally suggested for which there is no
positive evidence are that (a) either Electa ("the elect") or Kyria ("lady") is a proper
noun; and (b) the woman is a pastor. The external evidence for 2 John is scantier
than for 1 John, but it includes several of the same writers: Irenaeus, Clement of
Alexandria, Eusebius, and Jerome.[54]

The similarities of content and problems addressed in 2 John suggest it was writ-
ten at roughly the same time as 1 John to the same community. Perhaps 1 John was
an encyclical that made the rounds of all the house churches in or near Ephesus,
while 2 John was addressed just to one particular home congregation.[55] Some have
suggested that 2 John preceded 1 John, because in 2 John it seems that the false
teachers still have access to the church (v. 10), whereas in 1 John they had clearly
seceded (2:18–19; cf. 4:1).[56] On the other hand, 2 John 7 also seems to imply secession. *It is perhaps somewhat more likely that 2 John follows 1 John, because*
the original problem leading to the secession had emerged from within the church,
whereas in 2 John 10 the false teachers are now attacking from outside the church,
trying to come back and do further damage to it.[57]

It is difficult to label 2 John any more specifically than as an *exhortational or*
parenetic letter.[58] It has the length and form of a typical personal epistle, but takes on
a public character by being addressed to a house church. While attempts at detailed

---

[54] For external and internal evidence, succinctly summarized, cf. further Stott, *The Epistles of John*, 19–20, 28–30.

[55] Kruse, *The Letters of John*, 40.

[56] See, e.g., Marshall, *The Epistles of John*, 10–11.

[57] Cf. Brown, *The Epistles of John*, 70.

[58] Duane F. Watson, "A Rhetorical Analysis of 2 John according to Greco-Roman Convention," *NTS* 35 (1989): 107.

rhetorical analysis of this "flyleaf" have been made, a simpler outline seems appropriate:

I. Greetings (vv. 1–3)
II. Letter Body (vv. 4–11)
III. Closing (vv. 12–13)

COMMENTARY

GREETINGS (VV. 1–3)

Much of the content of these verses has been dealt with in the introduction above. If this is John, the son of Zebedee, his use of the term "elder" fits both his office and age and functions more tenderly than the formal title "apostle." Because he was largely respected and well loved, he did not need to assert apostolic authority more explicitly. The truth, of course, refers to the gospel message and perhaps even to God himself in his Spirit. The combination of truth and love in these opening greetings is striking and reminiscent of Ephesians 4:15. At times, unity cannot be preserved when some in a Christian gathering are denying fundamental truth, as in Ephesus. But even confrontation and discipline must be undertaken in as loving a way as possible. The "Golden Rule" (Matt. 7:12) comes into particular focus here (cf. Gal. 6:1–2).

LETTER BODY (VV. 4–11)

Verses 4–6 do not form either a prayer or a thanksgiving, but they do resemble the second section of more typical Hellenistic (including Pauline) letters by expressing joy for the faithfulness of "some" of the Christians in this congregation. Commentators debate whether this implies that "others" are not remaining faithful, a point we know to be true from the second part of the letter body anyway. Two of the three tests of life reappear in these verses—love and obedience to the commandments. As in 1 John 2:7–8, these love commands are both old (Mosaic) and new (distinctively Christian). Here appears the doctrinal basis for the exhortations to come.[59]

Verses 7–11 proceed to the heart of the problem, offering a stern warning. Here the third test of life comes into play—correct Christology. John urges the congregation to beware of the secessionists (v. 7). True Christians who are led astray by these false teachers risk losing the reward of seeing their work in building up the church not come to full fruition (v. 8). Those who actually join up with the secessionists demonstrate that they are not true Christians at all. The verb "runs *ahead*" in this verse was used by some Gnostics to assert their maturity. John, in essence, maintains

---

[59] Urban C. von Wahlde, "The Theological Foundation of the Presbyter's Argument in 2 Jn (2 Jn 4–6)," *ZNW* 76 (1985): 209–24.

that such running runs *away* from the gospel altogether.[60] Verses 10–11, if written to a house church, imply that the Christians must not allow their worship services to be used as a platform for the false teachers. "Welcoming" often implied financial help for itinerant missionaries, and this, too, should be withheld from the secessionists. There is no justification, therefore, for using this text to tell Christians to close the door on people of other religions who come to one's home to share their faith. How would they ever hear (or see modeled) the gospel of Christ's love in us if we always acted this way?[61]

CLOSING (VV. 12–13)

The length of this letter, like that of 3 John, approximates what would have fit on one normal sheet of papyrus. John limits himself to this much, planning to supplement his conversation when he next comes in person to worship with them. The end of verse 12 recalls 1 John 1:4. On verse 13, see the introduction to 2 John above (p. 499).

---

[60] "The phrase 'going beyond' the teaching of Christ (προάγων) rather than 'remaining in' it (μένων ἐν) as received in the tradition has led to the description of the dissidents as 'progressives.' Most progressives in a movement are a vanguard exploring new frontiers, but when they progress past a core teaching that may not be abandoned, however sublime they may think their new position, they cannot be praised" (Sloyan, *Walking in the Truth*, 65).

[61] Cf. Akin, *1, 2, 3, John*, 233.

3 John: The Secessionists Take Over Inside?

INTRODUCTION

This final Johannine epistle is written to one otherwise unknown Christian named Gaius, again presumably in and around Ephesus near the end of the first century.[62] The author again identifies himself as "the elder," almost certainly the same individual as the person who wrote 2 John. Gaius apparently provided hospitality to true Christians in their itinerant ministries. Inns in the ancient world were notorious for their incivility, so this was an important role for early Christians of some means to play. In addition to providing bed and board, such hosts often donated funds as well to pay for past or future travel expenses.[63] In this case, John writes Gaius to encourage him in this ministry (vv. 5–8) and in his adherence to orthodoxy in the midst of the onslaught of the false teachers (vv. 3–4). Diotrephes, who may well be one of these teachers (see below, p. 504–5) and the opponent of true Christians, provides the "foil" for Gaius (vv. 9–10).

Again, the order of the letters is uncertain. There is no unambiguous reference to the false teaching behind 1 and 2 John anywhere in this brief letter. That fact could argue for a date before either or both of the Johannine epistles.[64] On the other hand, Diotrephes has often been linked with the false teaching in some way, in which case *3 John could reflect a stage of deteriorating relations in which some of the schismatics had returned to at least one house church and now gained the upper hand.*[65] That all the other letters in the New Testament addressed to individuals were also intended for the larger Christian congregation of which they were a part (or related to in some way) could suggest that a house church of some kind lay behind Gaius as well. Yet there is nothing in the letter that positively points in this direction, as there is in Philemon, the Pastorals, or 2 John. So perhaps this truly is a personal letter, intended initially only for Gaius, but recognized by subsequent generations of Christians as valuable and significant as John's other letters and thus equally worthy of preservation and canonization. One might think of a letter of this length and nature as somewhat equivalent to a (somewhat detailed) postcard sent in our modern world. A simple tripartite division again seems most helpful:[66]

---

[62] Elsewhere in the New Testament we read of men named Gaius from Macedonia (Acts 19:19), Derbe (20:4), and Corinth (16:23), but there is no reason to equate any of these with the addressee of 3 John. Gaius was a common Greek name.

[63] On hospitality in the ancient Mediterranean world and its significance for 3 John, see Bruce J. Malina, "The Received View and What It Cannot Do: III John and Hospitality," *Semeia* 35 (1986): 171–94.

[64] For a plausible case for the sequence, 1 John, 3 John, 2 John, see Judith M. Lieu, *The Second and Third Epistles of John: History and Background* (Edinburgh: T & T Clark, 1986); for 3 John, 2 John, 1 John, see J. Christopher Thomas, "The Order of the Composition of the Johannine Epistles," *NovT* 37 (1993): 68–75.

[65] Smalley, *1, 2, 3 John,* xxx–xxxii. Marshall (*The Epistles of John,* 9–14) is more cautious, noting no unambiguously doctrinal link with the false teachers of 1 and 2 John and envisioning Diotrephes as a prophet or teacher to whom John had delegated some oversight, but who then overstepped his leadership role.

[66] For a much more detailed analysis, see Duane F. Watson, "A Rhetorical Analysis of 3 John: A Study in Epistolary Rhetoric," *CBQ* 51 (1989): 479–501.

COMMENTARY

GREETINGS (VV. 1–2)

These verses include a formal salutation (v. 1) and a brief prayer (v. 2), thus reverting to the conventional Hellenistic letter form. The same combination of love and truth reappears as in 2 John 1–2. The most striking feature about John's prayer is his petition that Gaius's physical health might be as good as his spiritual health. Would that most of us were healthy enough spiritually to make this a desirable prayer![67]

LETTER BODY (VV. 3–12)

John begins the body of his letter by commending Gaius for his ministry of hospitality for traveling Christian ministers (vv. 3–8). As in 2 John 4, he is grateful to learn about his recipient's faithfulness to Christian doctrine and behavior, insisting that nothing gives him greater joy (vv. 3–4). He encourages Gaius to continue his gracious generosity for itinerant preachers, even those he does not personally know. Sending them on their way "in a manner worthy of God" in verse 6 probably implies financial support (recall above, p. 233),[68] while verse 7a harks back to the early days of Acts when believers referred to Jesus' "name" as almost an independent entity or power itself (but probably deriving from Jewish reluctance to utter divine names). Verse 7b reflects the frequently hostile environment of the first century, one that has not always afflicted Christians in the same way in every time and place since. But John Stott derives the timeless application from this half–verse that "Christians should finance Christian enterprises which the world will not, or should not be expected to, support. . . . There are many good causes which we *may* support; but we *must* support our brothers and sisters whom the world does not support."[69]

Second, John warns against the negative example of Diotrephes (vv. 9–10). The letter alluded to in verse 9 cannot readily be equated with any other canonical document; it has most likely been lost.[70] Probably Diotrephes had some connection with the false teachers. Many commentators have tried to be more specific, linking him with the growing institutionalization of the church (and so, e.g., involved in a power play with the last of the more "charismatic" apostles). Some have even argued that he was the defender of orthodoxy against a heterodox Johannine community, but

---

[67] Cf. Akin, *1, 2, 3 John*, 240. It was natural for Hellenistic prayers to contain a health-wish, even as those praying recognized that such health was not always God's (or the gods') will. Nothing here supports the notion of the "prosperity gospel" that God always wants believers to enjoy good physical health. This view seems to have originated only in the mid-twentieth-century in the teachings of Oral Roberts. See Heather L. Landrus, "Hearing 3 John 2 in the Voices of History," *JPT* 11 (2002): 81–82.

[68] Thompson, *1–3 John*, 160.

[69] Stott, *The Epistles of John*, 227. This, of course, is different from accepting unsolicited support from non-Christians for Christian causes, which seems entirely appropriate so long as those donors are clear precisely what their funds are supporting.

[70] Kruse, *The Letters of John*, 226.

there is no actual evidence to support this.[71] The most we can know for sure is that "he love[d] to be first" (v. 9). Personal ambition alone causes enough church divisions![72] In any case, we should understand Diotrephes as evicting true believers from his congregation and preventing other genuine Christians from entering.

Finally, John commends the positive example of an otherwise unknown Demetrius (vv. 11–12). We know even less about him, save that he is "well spoken of by everyone" (v. 12). Gaius would have known more, so John does not need to spell out the details. Psychologically and spiritually, it is always good to balance warnings against bad models with the presentation of good models whom Christians can emulate. The "blanket" statements in verse 11b must be understood as in 1 John 3:6 and 9 and in the context of all three tests of life. Obviously unbelievers do good things, but not in the fullest sense of "good," which ultimately must include serving and pleasing the one God of the universe, incarnated in Jesus.[73]

CLOSING (VV. 13–14)

As in 2 John 12, the elder explains that he will save most of his remarks for a face-to-face meeting (vv. 12–13a). John's conclusion twice uses a unique name for fellow Christians: "the friends." Perhaps the term derived from John 15:13. This term has played a prominent role in the history of the Quaker movement as a synonym for believers in this particular denominational tradition. Stott suggests that the command to greet these friends by name "surely means each local fellowship was to be sufficiently small and closely knit for the pastors and the members to know each other personally and be able to greet each other by name."[74] Of course, such fellowships can be created within a larger congregation, but the point remains that every believer should be a part of such a smaller group.

APPLICATION

John's tests of life provide an important safeguard against a truncated view of Christianity. It is easy to imagine that correct belief about Jesus is all that is necessary for salvation. James, of course, reminded us that faith inevitably leads to good works (his equivalent to John's emphasis on obeying the commandments). Paul stressed that faith works itself out through love (Gal. 5:6), and love reappears as a test of life in John's letters, too. When professing Christians aren't sure if they have "believed" enough, looking at the way the Spirit has transformed them into more loving and obedient people than they had been previously can often reassure them. But when "belief" is not accompanied by a transformed life, however slow or fitful in its growth, then we have reason to doubt the presence of true Christianity altogether.

---

[71] Most notably Ernst Käsemann, in an influential German article, "Zum johanneischen Verfasserproblem," *ZTK* 48 (1951): 292–311. See also Georg Strecker, *The Johannine Letters* (Minneapolis: Fortress, 1996), 202–63.

[72] Cf. Margaret M. Mitchell, "'Diotrephes Does Not Receive Us': The Lexicographical and Social Context of 3 John 9–10," *JBL* 117 (1998): 299–320.

[73] Cf. Brown, *The Epistles of John*, 721.

[74] Stott, *The Epistles of John*, 234.

If the historical sequence of the letters of John corresponds to their canonical sequence, then we can reconstruct a somewhat depressing deterioration of the Johannine church—from Gnostics (or proto-Gnostics, or Gnostic-like opponents, etc.) seceding (1 John), to attacks from outside by those same individuals (2 John), to successful inroads in the church as a result of those attacks (3 John). Revelation 2:1–7 confirms that the church was hard hit as a result of all of this, and by the end of the second century Christian influence had seriously waned in and around Ephesus. And this in the community that had received more apostolic ministry during the first century than any other! Yet there is actually an encouraging, albeit backhanded, application from all of this. If a ministry can die out with all that positive input, then we can take heart when we give it our best "shot" in ministry, and the results, humanly speaking at least, seem to be a failure. It is not necessarily our fault! We should do all we can in the power of the Holy Spirit, but then leave the results to God.

ADDITIONAL QUESTIONS FOR REVIEW

1. What external and internal evidence support the apostle John (or the author of the Fourth Gospel), as the author of 1, 2, and 3 John as well? What are some of the specific similarities between John's Gospel and John's epistles? Why is there some dispute as to whether the same author penned these works?

2. What heresies are affecting the church to which John writes? Whose teachings are propagating the heresies, and what are these heresies' key features, beliefs, and divergences from genuine Christian belief?

3. What is a plausible structure of 1 John, and what recurring themes produce this structure? Combine these themes to form a summary statement of what John thinks it means to be truly Christian.

4. In what ways are the purposes of the Johannine epistles different from the purposes of John's Gospel? How does a discussion of the tense of the Greek verb "believe" in 1 John 5:13–15 affect a person's understanding of one of these key purposes and how is one's understanding of the doctrine of "eternal security" affected?

5. How does John define "love?" Specifically, how does a Christian effectively love God? How does he or she rightly love others? How do these definitions differ from the way we often use the word "love" in twenty-first-century Western culture?

6. To whom is 2 John addressed? Is this a literal or a metaphorical addressée? What evidence in the text points to this interpretation?

7. If the canonical sequence of John's letters indeed follows the historical sequence, what can be inferred about the state of the church(es) to which John writes? Reconstruct the events that may have been occurring within and outside of the church.

8. What backhanded encouragement does the progression of events identified in the last question offer for practical ministry?

SELECT BIBLIOGRAPHY

COMMENTARIES

Advanced

Brown, Raymond E. *The Epistles of John*. AB. Garden City: Doubleday, 1983.

Schnackenburg, Rudolf. *The Johannine Epistles: Introduction and Commentary*. New York: Crossroad, 1992.

Smalley, Stephen S. *1, 2, 3 John*. WBC. Waco: Word, 1984.

Strecker, Georg. *The Johannine Letters*. Hermeneia. Minneapolis: Fortress, 1996.

Intermediate

Akin, Daniel L. *1, 2, 3 John*. NAC. Nashville: Broadman & Holman, 2001.

Burdick, Donald W. *The Letters of John the Apostle*. Chicago: Moody, 1985.

Kruse, Colin G. *The Letters of John*. PNTC. Leicester: IVP; Grand Rapids: Ecrdmans, 2000.

Marshall, I. Howard. *The Epistles of John*. NICNT. Grand Rapids: Eerdmans, 1978.

Painter, John. *1, 2 and 3 John*. SP. Collegeville: Liturgical, 2002.

Introductory

Burge, Gary M. *The Letters of John*. NIVAC. Grand Rapids: Zondervan, 1996.

Rensberger, David. *1 John, 2 John, 3 John*. ANTC. Nashville: Abingdon, 1997.

Sloyan, Gerard S. *Walking in the Truth—Perseverers and Deserters: The First, Second, and Third Letters of John*. NTinCont. Valley Forge: Trinity, 1995.

Stott, John R. W. *The Epistles of John*. TNTC rev. Leicester: IVP; Grand Rapids: Eerdmans, 1988.

Thompson, Marianne Meye. *1–3 John*. IVPNTC. Leicester and Downers Grove: IVP, 1992.

OTHER BOOKS

Brown, Raymond. *The Community of the Beloved Disciple*. New York: Paulist, 1979.

Griffith, Terry. *Keep Yourselves from Idols: A New Look at 1 John*. London and New York: SAP, 2002.

Lieu, Judith M. *The Second and Third Epistles of John: History and Background*. Edinburgh: T & T Clark, 1986.

Lieu, Judith M. *The Theology of the Johannine Epistles*. Cambridge and New York: CUP, 1991.

Neufeld, Dietmar *Reconceiving Texts as Speech Acts: An Analysis of 1 John*. Leiden and New York: Brill, 1994.

von Wahlde, Urban C. *The Johannine Commandments: 1 John and the Struggle for Johannine Tradition*. New York: Paulist, 1990.

BIBLIOGRAPHY

Mills, Watson E. *The Letters of John*. Lewiston and Lampeter: Mellen, 1993.

15

The Book of Revelation: God's Plans for Cosmic History

INTRODUCTION

AUTHORSHIP

C ritical scholarship commonly rejects the church's historic claim of *Johannine authorship* for the book of Revelation. Stylistic and theological differences from the Gospel and epistles of John are usually viewed as most decisive. For example, the noun and verb for "love" (*agapē, agapaō*) appear 44 times in the Gospel, 52 times in the epistles, but only 6 times in Revelation. "Believe" (*pisteuō*) occurs 98 times in the Gospel, 9 times in the epistles, but not at all in Revelation. Revelation also contains numerous solecisms (grammatical irregularities not attributable to any known rules or patterns of Greek writing) that are absent from the other books attributed to John. The third-century bishop of Alexandria, Dionysus, expressed his own doubts about the apostolic authorship of this document, in large measure due to his suspicion of the millennial theology contained within it and his dislike of apocalyptic literature more generally.[1]

At the same time, this is the only one of the five books ascribed to John that actually contains the name "John" within its text. So if any of the books have a claim to apostolic authorship, it should be this one. On the other hand, this John is identified as servant, brother, and prophet (1:1, 4, 9; 22:8), but never apostle or elder. In keeping with the resurgence of an appreciation of the Jewish origins of the bulk of the New Testament literature, many scholars today are prepared to accept the labels the text uses and to concede that the writer of this document was a Jewish-Christian prophet named John, perhaps even from Palestine, but they still distinguish him from the apostle by the same name.[2] After all, the Gospel and the epistles do *not* refer to their author as John. Because Revelation never specifies which John is its author, this line of argument is entirely reasonable.

Nevertheless, we may not need to jettison early church tradition quite so quickly. Justin Martyr (*Dialogue* 81.15), Irenaeus (*Against Heresies* 4.14.1, 5.26.1), Tertullian (*Against Marcion* 3.14, 24), and Clement of Alexandria (*Miscellanies* 6.106–7, *Tutor* 2.119) all affirmed that the apostle wrote the Apocalypse, and there are no competing ancient traditions concerning authorship. The differences in vocabulary can be

---

[1] For these and other arguments, see Robert H. Mounce, *The Book of Revelation* (Grand Rapids: Eerdmans, rev. 1998), 8–15.

[2] See, e.g, Richard Bauckham, *The Theology of the Book of Revelation* (Cambridge and New York: CUP, 1993), 2.

attributed to genre and contents. Revelation does not have the evangelistic or catechetical purposes of encouraging belief that the other Johannine writings have; the period of time described reflects God's judgment far more than his love. The rugged style could reflect the nature of John's visions—trying to describe the indescribable—or the ecstasy of the prophet, or the nonuse of an amanuensis or redactor or the noninvolvement of the "Johannine school" (see above, p. 486).[3] And the overall vocabulary and level of writing of Revelation are still more like the other writings of John than unlike them (or like any of the other New Testament documents).

For example, only in these five books does a logos Christology appear, or "Lamb of God" as a title for Jesus, or the use of Zechariah 12:10 as a prophecy fulfilled by Jesus (cf. John 19:37; Rev. 1:7). Revelation also shares with the other writings ascribed to John a distinctive emphasis on testimony, eternal life versus eternal death, spiritual hunger and thirst, and the theme of conquest.[4]

SETTING

The most widely adopted setting for Revelation is the short-lived but at times intense Domitianic persecution from 94 to 96. Irenaeus (*Against Heresies* 5.30.3) and Eusebius (*Church History* 3.18–20, 5.8.6) explicitly refer to the latter part of Domitian's imperial reign, which overall lasted from 81 to 96 (cf. also Victorinus, Clement of Alexandria, and Origen). John's brief exile on the island of Patmos (1:9) fits the mid-90s well, whereas there is no evidence of Christians being banished from their homelands by the government prior to this date. The policy during this period seems to have been to arrest only those Christians specifically turned into the authorities by others and usually only when a charge of some other crime (however trumped up) accompanied the betrayal. Even then, imprisonment (or banishment for Christian leaders so that they would exert less influence) rather than death formed the usual penalty. And the edict against believers was rescinded by Nerva, Domitian's successor, in 96.[5] Moreover, little in Revelation requires *direct* governmental hostility. Informal Roman harassment and local pagan cultural disdain for Christians from the mid-first to the early-second centuries proved pervasive and could account for much of what John's churches were currently experiencing.[6]

Various historical references scattered throughout Revelation also fit the 90s best. By this time, Laodicea has recovered from the earthquake that shattered it in the early 60s. Tension with various branches of Judaism has reached a fever pitch,

---

[3] Moreover, not all of the infelicities of the Greek of Revelation may be as awkward as they first seem, when a broader survey of Hellenistic Greek is conducted. See Stanley E. Porter, "The Language of the Apocalypse in Recent Discussion," *NTS* 35 (1989): 582–603.

[4] Cf. G. R. Beasley-Murray, *The Book of Revelation* (London: Marshall, Morgan & Scott, rev. 1978; Grand Rapids: Eerdmans, 1981), 34. Sometimes different words for the same concepts appear in Revelation *vis-à-vis* the Fourth Gospel, but, unnoticed by many writers, seldom without the same words also recurring in both documents at one point or another. See Peter Whale, "The Lamb of John: Some Myths about the Vocabulary of the Johannine Literature," *JBL* 106 (1987): 289–95.

[5] Particularly in light of the arguments by Leonard L. Thompson (*The Book of Revelation: Apocalypse and Empire* [Oxford and New York: OUP, 1990], 95–115), many scholars have begun to claim that Domitian barely persecuted any Christians at all. This trend does provide a necessary pendulum swing against an older consensus that exaggerated the severity of this persecution, but it now underestimates what went on. For a brief but balanced assessment, see Ben Witherington III, *Revelation* (Cambridge and New York: CUP, 2003), 5–10.

[6] Thomas B. Slater, "On the Social Setting of the Revelation to John," *NTS* 44 (1998): 232–56.

leading to the *birkath ha-minim* ("blessing" [as a euphemism for "curse"] on the heretics, particularly Christians)—a nineteenth prayer inserted into the synagogue liturgy, accompanied by the expulsion of Christian Jews from the synagogues and their membership rosters. Thus John can label the Jewish assemblies in Ephesus and Philadelphia as synagogues "of Satan" (2:9; 3:9). By this time, too, the belief in certain pagan circles of a Nero *redivivus* (come back to life) prevailed—imagery that seems to lie behind the portrayal of the anti-Christian beasts in chapters 12–13. The church in Ephesus had declined in prominence (as in 2:1–7), Gnosticism was on the verge of becoming full-blown (as perhaps in 2:24), and the famine of 92 formed the background of the imagery of 6:6.[7]

A small number of usually very conservative scholars, however, do argue for a date in the 60s, in part due to silence about the destruction of Jerusalem in A.D. 70 and to the assumption that the references to the temple in chapter 11 imply that it is still standing. Some appeal to a minority tradition in the early church that John was martyred at an early date. Many point to imagery throughout Revelation that mirrors events in the life of Nero, though all this does is establish that the setting can be no *earlier* than Nero's reign.[8] Some think the mystery of the seven kings in 17:9–11 (see below, p. 546) is best solved by this dating. Others seemingly just *want* an early date to be correct so they can defend their "preterist" approach to the book (see below, pp. 518–19), by which almost everything except for the new heavens and earth of chapters 21–22 can be taken as referring to events completed by 70.[9] But the external and internal evidence for a later date (and a later martyrdom for John) remains far stronger, not to mention the fact that persecution under Nero (64–68) scarcely involved Christians outside the province of Italy.[10]

On either date, the addressees are clear: *seven Christian congregations in Asia Minor* (today western Turkey), listed in a sequence that corresponded to the order in which a traveler would have come to them, following a series of roads in a very roughly shaped oval and beginning with Ephesus on the Aegean coast (1:4, 11). This, of course, was the area in which John had ministered (see above, pp. 486–87). John's desire may have been that a visitor to Patmos from the mainland whom he could trust would deliver the scroll first to the Ephesians, who would make a copy for themselves and then send the document down the road to the next community addressed. That church would then repeat the process, as would the next, until all seven congregations had received a copy of the book. Why these seven churches were selected cannot be answered with certainty—not all of the communities were equally important by any means. Perhaps it was the ease of delivery combined with John's recognition that they represented a fair spectrum of healthy to unhealthy churches

---

[7] For these and related arguments, cf. esp. Grant R. Osborne, *Revelation* (Grand Rapids: Baker, 2002), 6–9.

[8] From a quite different perspective, J. Christian Wilson ("The Problem of the Domitianic Date of Revelation," *NTS* 39 [1993]: 587–605) questions the entire Patristic tradition of claims about John's writings and Domitianic persecution and tries to coordinate the references to the five kings who have fallen in 17:10 with the list of emperors beginning with either Julius or Augustus, thus ending with either Claudius (right before Nero) or Nero himself.

[9] See esp. Kenneth L. Gentry, Jr., *Before Jerusalem Fell: Dating the Book of Revelation* (Tyler, Tex.: Institute for Christian Economics, 1989).

[10] For a theory of a two-stage composition of the documentary allowing the strengths of the cases for each date to be combined, see Robert B. Moberly, "When Was Revelation Conceived?" *Bib* 73 (1992): 376–93.

in his world (see further below, pp. 521–25). Perhaps they were the churches he knew best, forming the heart of the "Johannine community." Certainly several of them were home to key pagan competitors of Christianity, most notably the imperial cult.[11]

The heart of John's message was to assure these Asian Christians that the harassment and persecution (or even simply the fear of each) that they experienced fit in with God's plan, with current events portending the greater tribulation to come just before Christ's return.[12] But to those who "overcame," who remained faithful in confessing Christ, God would provide ultimate victory and recompense, even as he would judge and utterly destroy their enemies. No matter how bleak things look in this life, God remains in control. One day, Jesus will triumph, and the only thing that will matter is if we are on his side or not!

LITERARY GENRE

Revelation is a hybrid of three well-known Jewish and Greco-Roman genres.[13] Most foundationally, as the very title and first word of the book indicate, this is an *apocalypse (apokalypsis)*. Apocalyptic literature was common in other Jewish and Christian sources, including parts of Ezekiel, Daniel, Zechariah, and Jesus' Olivet Discourse (Matt. 24–25 pars.). In the intertestamental literature, 1 Enoch, 4 Ezra, and 2 Baruch are among the most well-known and important Jewish apocalyptic books, especially for interpreting Revelation.[14] Apocalyptic varied widely in form, but frequent features included (a) the extensive use of symbolism, often with outlandish or grotesque creatures and cosmology, much like our modern political cartoons;[15] (b) the depiction of past, present, and/or future events of world history leading up to a decisive intervention on the part of God to right the injustices of society and to reward God's faithful people; and (c) the assurance to those people in a setting of crisis or perceived crisis that evil would not ultimately maintain the upper hand.[16]

Thus there is no way of predicting in advance how literal or figurative such a work will be. Each potential symbol will have to be interpreted in light of its historical background and how the original audience would most likely have understood it. In the case of John's apocalypse, this background includes the *Old Testament*,[17] *intertestamental literature, and current or recent events in the cities of Asia Minor*

---

[11] On the pervasiveness of emperor worship and its significance for interpreting Revelation, see Steven J. Friesen, *Imperial Cults and the Apocalypse of John* (Oxford and New York: OUP, 2001).

[12] Cf. esp. Adela Yarbro Collins, *Crisis and Catharsis: The Power of the Apocalypse* (Philadelphia: Westminster, 1984).

[13] Cf. Dave Mathewson, "Revelation in Recent Genre Criticism: Some Implications for Interpretation," *TrinJ* 13 (1992): 193–213.

[14] For an excellent anthology of noncanonical Jewish and Christian apocalypses, see Mitchell G. Reddish, ed., *Apocalyptic Literature: A Reader* (Peabody: Hendrickson, 1995).

[15] Beasley-Murray, *Revelation,* 16–17.

[16] An oft-quoted technical definition of apocalypse is that of John J. Collins, "Introduction: Toward the Morphology of a Genre," *Semeia* 14 (1979): 9—"a genre of revelatory literature with a narrative framework, in which a revelation is mediated by an otherworldly being to a human recipient, disclosing a transcendent reality which is both temporal, insofar as it envisages eschatological salvation, and spatial insofar as it involves another, supernatural world."

[17] "Revelation contains more references to the Old Testament than any other document in the New Testament, even if these parallels are often allusive" (Stephen S. Smalley, *The Revelation to John* [London: SPCK; Downers Grove: IVP, 2005], 9).

of John's day. Numbers, though, are almost always symbolic, especially sevens and their multiples (standing for completeness or universality—based on the seven days of creation) and twelves and their multiples (standing for the twelve tribes of Israel and/or the twelve apostles—to designate God's people as a whole).[18] At the same time, Revelation differs from most apocalyptic literature of the ancient world by *not* being (a) pseudonymous; (b) retrospectively historical (representing prophecy *ex eventu,* i.e., after the event); or (c) morally dualistic and unrelentingly pessimistic in worldview.[19] And, to the extent that other apocalyptic writings were not necessarily based on actual visions or revelations experienced by the authors but a literary device for communicating ineffable truth, this apocalypse differs by being founded on objective experiences of the Lord disclosing himself to John.

Ben Witherington captures the right balance between literal revelation and symbolic interpretation: "What John heard he may have transcribed almost verbatim, but what he saw he had to describe and thus draw on his existing mental resources. When one sees images and symbols in odd combinations, one must grope for analogies to describe the experience (hence the repeated use of the phrase 'it was like')."[20]

Revelation also combines elements of two other genres that make its apocalyptic form distinctive—prophetic and epistolary literature. As *prophecy* (1:3), John refers to real future events, even if he often describes them in highly symbolic garb. When John addresses the present situation of the churches, he does so in part so that the churches that need to repent will do so and take the necessary steps to bring about the changed world that God desires already in their day, however imperfect it may remain. In other words, Revelation partakes of the same "already but not yet," inaugurated kingdom theology that characterizes the rest of the New Testament.[21] It also implicitly challenges the evil, imperial structures of Rome that illicitly claim divine authority, just as prophets in many eras have confronted kings and rulers when they overstepped their God-ordained authority.[22]

As an epistle (cf. the form of 1:4–5), which itself contains seven shorter individualized letters to each of the seven churches (chaps. 2–3), the book is rooted in the distinctive backgrounds and current events at the end of the first century for each of the Asian communities in which the seven churches are located. The entire document is written to these congregations to give them hope in specific historical circumstances. *This means that the most fundamental hermeneutical principle to follow in interpreting Revelation is to look for meanings that could have been intelligible to first-century Christians in Asia Minor, not hidden meanings decipherable*

---

[18] See esp. Richard Bauckham, *The Climax of Prophecy* (Edinburgh: T & T Clark, 1993), 22–37; cf. Frederick J. Murphy, *Fallen Is Babylon: The Revelation to John* (Harrisburg: Trinity, 1998), 24–27.

[19] For a more extensive list, see Leon Morris, *The Book of Revelation* (Grand Rapids: Eerdmans, rev. 1987), 25–27.

[20] Witherington, *Revelation,* 36.

[21] On Revelation as prophecy, see esp. Frederick D. Mazzaferri, *The Genre of the Book of Revelation from a Source-Critical Perspective* (Berlin and New York: de Gruyter, 1989).

[22] See esp. Allan A. Boesak, *Comfort and Protest: Reflections on the Apocalypse of Patmos* (Philadelphia: Westminster, 1987); Elizabeth Schüssler Fiorenza, *The Book of Revelation: Justice and Judgment* (Philadelphia: Fortress, 1985).

only by people centuries later who think they might be living in the days immediately prior to Christ's return.[23]

This conclusion is sometimes disputed by those who cite Daniel 12:4, 8–10 in the Old Testament's most famous prophetic-apocalyptic work. There the prophet was told by God to seal up his scroll because people would fully understand his words at a much later date, and then only those who were "wise." But Revelation 22:10 intentionally contrasts with this outlook, as God commands John, "Do not seal up the words of the prophecy of this book, because the time is near." Those who think that the more than 1,900 years that have elapsed since John wrote refute this claim should consult the discussion of 2 Peter 3:8–9 above.[24]

STRUCTURE AND OUTLINE

Parts of the structure of John's apocalypse present themselves straightforwardly. Chapter 1 introduces the volume, chapters 2–3 form the letters to the seven churches, 4–5 depict a vision of heavenly praise, and 6–19 form the backbone of the book with its three series of seven judgments portrayed as seals, trumpets, and bowls of God's wrath. Chapter 20 envisions the millennium, while chapters 21–22 portray the eternal state—new heavens and new earth. The most complex structural debate surrounds the relationship of the three sets of judgments in chapters 6–19, especially since various segments of text, which have often been called "interludes," intervene in between each series (7:1–17; 10–11:14; 12:1–14:20). The interludes do not advance the progress toward judgment day any and sometimes appear like historical flashbacks or even "flash-aheads."

The simplest understanding of the three sevens finds in them a purely consecutive or *chronological* sequence. This nicely accounts for the growing intensity and severity of the judgments as one progresses from the first set to the third. For example, the seal judgments appear to affect at most one-fourth of the earth (6:8), the trumpets consistently torment one-third of the planet (8:7, 8, 9, 10, 11, 12), while no geographical restrictions attach themselves to the bowl judgments (16:1–21). On the other hand, the sixth judgment in each sequence seems out of chronological order, bringing us to the very threshold of the end of the world, describing cosmic upheavals that could not allow the current universe to remain in existence (6:12–17; 9:13–21; 16:17–21). Yet in each case, John's narrative continues for some time as if heavens and earth had not been convulsed as violently as these plagues describe.[25]

---

[23] Cf. Fee and Stuart, *How to Read the Bible for All Its Worth,* 254.

[24] For a thorough overview of all three of these genres as they apply to Revelation, see David E. Aune, *Revelation 1–5* (Dallas: Word, 1997), lxx–xc. A fourth genre sometimes viewed as coming into play is that of drama. James L. Blevins (*Revelation as Drama* [Nashville: Broadman, 1984]) argues, for example, that the apocalypse was intended to be acted out on stage in seven scenes. Closely related is the suggestion that the structure and function of the book is one related to the liturgy of the worship of the Christian community. Cf. José A. Filho, "The Apocalypse of John as an Account of a Visionary Experience: Notes on the Book's Structure," *JSNT* 25 (2002): 213–34; with Paulo A. de Souza Nogueira, "Celestial Worship and Ecstatic-Visionary Experience," *JSNT* 25 (2002): 165–84.

[25] Marko Jauhiainen ("Recapitulation and Chronological Progression in John's Apocalypse: Towards a New Perspective," *NTS* 49 [2003]: 543–59), however, argues that the sixth seal ushers in "the Day of the Lord," while the sixth trumpet marks the end of the time during which unbelievers may still repent. Thus he accounts for the unusual upheavals associated with these judgments without abandoning a chronological approach.

As a result, many have seen the three sevens as *recapitulative,* each describing the same period of great tribulation from different angles. But this makes the growing intensity from one set to the next hard to explain. Perhaps the best option, therefore, is the third. *The sixth judgment in each series does, from one perspective, bring us close to the end, but the seventh in each set does not so much advance the chronology but introduce the next series.* Or, better put, it contains the next series. It would be as if someone put a magnifying glass on the seventh seal and then was able to observe the seven trumpets lurking within, and likewise with the seventh trumpet disclosing the seven bowls. This has often been called *the telescopic perspective.*[26]

APPROACHING THE ABYSS

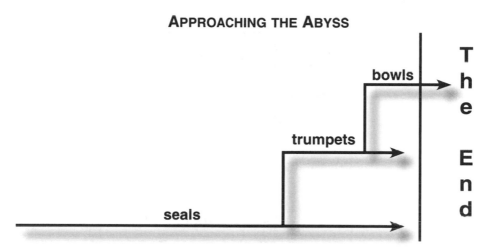

A much simpler three-part outline to the entire book has often been found embedded in 1:19. Here Christ commands John to "write, therefore, what you have seen, what is now and what will take place later." A natural interpretation of this instruction, assuming Revelation is the result of John's obedient response, is that *chapter 1 depicts what he already has seen by the time of this command. Chapters 2–3 (and possibly 4–5 since their only temporal indicator is that they take place after Christ's atonement—5:5–6)[27] then reflect "what is now," with their present assessments of the spiritual states of the seven churches. Chapters 6–21, finally, move ahead to describe events that are still future from John's perspective.* This approach has fallen out of

---

[26] Or yet another way to think of this approach is to imagine a person walking toward a cliff (the first five seals), taking a peek over it (the sixth seal), shrinking back in horror, following a path parallel to the cliff for awhile, then walking toward it again from a much closer starting point (the seventh seal, introducing the first five trumpets), looking over the edge again (the sixth trumpet), shrinking back again, but following another path parallel to the cliff even further, then walking toward it one last time from an even closer starting point (the seventh trumpet, introducing the first five bowls), looking over the edge one last time (the sixth bowl) only to be finally pushed off it (the seventh bowl). This is not a diagram I invented, but I have been unable to locate where I first discovered it. For helpful charts depicting all three approaches to structure (much more simply!), see H. Wayne House, *Chronological and Background Charts of the New Testament* (Grand Rapids: Zondervan, 1981), 146.

[27] Chap. 4:1 relates that a heavenly voice promised John he would be shown "what must take place after this." But that promise is fulfilled only as the Lamb begins to open the seals in 6:1. Chaps. 4–5 comprise hymnic praise for God and the Lamb, which has probably taken place in heaven ever since Jesus' resurrection.

favor in recent times, but it still seems defensible.[28] Others focus on what they believe are seven main sections, sometimes viewed as chiastic in arrangement corresponding to the frequency of the number seven as a symbol of completeness throughout the book.[29] At the risk of imposing too little rather than too much structure on John's apocalypse, we propose an outline that is largely topical, breaking the text into segments of one to three chapters each and then subdividing accordingly.

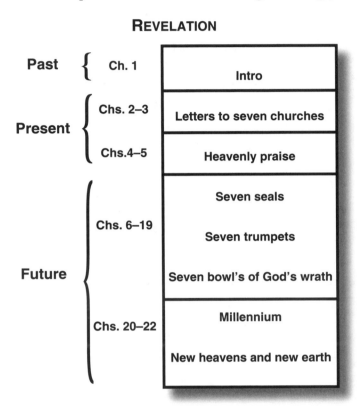

REVELATION

Past	Ch. 1	Intro
Present	Chs. 2–3	Letters to seven churches
	Chs. 4–5	Heavenly praise
Future	Chs. 6–19	Seven seals / Seven trumpets / Seven bowl's of God's wrath
	Chs. 20–22	Millennium / New heavens and new earth

I. Introduction (1:1–20)
   A. Prologue (1:1–3)
   B. Greetings and Dedication (1:4–8)
   C. John's Commission (1:9–20)
II. Letters to the Seven Churches (2:1–3:22)
   A. Ephesus: Losing Your First Love (2:1–7)
   B. Smyrna: Persevering Despite Difficult Circumstances (2:8–11)

---

[28] John F. Walvoord, *The Revelation of Jesus Christ: A Commentary* (Chicago: Moody, 1966), 47–49. The major objection to this perspective is that material related to past, present, and future appears in *each* section of the book, but that hardly prevents us from identifying a *dominant* time period present in each. The most common proposal today interprets this verse as dividing the book into two tenses: "what you have seen" anticipates the completion of the entire set of revelations, then subdivided into present ("what is now") and future ("what will take place later"). G. K. Beale (*The Book of Revelation* [Carlisle: Paternoster; Grand Rapids and Cambridge: Eerdmans, 1999], 152–70) thoroughly summarizes and critiques these and other main options, proposing an approach that sees all three clauses of 1:19 as referring to the entire book.

[29] See the survey of approaches in ibid., 127–37.

INTERPRETIVE APPROACHES

The number of different approaches and combinations of approaches to Revelation makes it impossible to treat all of the possible options to interpreting each passage as we proceed through this book. All we can do is to highlight the perspective adopted here and point readers to other literature that explains all the options in more detail.

Millennial Grid   One interpretive debate is over the role of the one-thousand-year period described in 20:4–15. *Premillennialists* see Christ returning before this golden age of human history. *Postmillennialists* reverse that sequence of events. *Amillennialists* view the millennium either as spiritual and coinciding with the present reign of Christ in believers' hearts (and in heaven) or with the new heavens and new earth still to come. As will be explained below (p. 550), it is hard to see how a chronological break can be inserted between 19:21 and 20:1, as is necessary on either the standard amillennialist or postmillennialist views. The rebellion at the end of the millennium (20:11–15) makes it hard to equate this period with the eternal state. That leaves the premillennialist approach as the one followed here. But premillennialism subdivides into *dispensational* and *classic/historic* premillennialism, especially on the basis of the timing of the rapture.[30]

Relationship of Rapture and Tribulation   Typically post-, a- and classic premillennialism all support a *posttribulational* rapture. That is to say, the catching up of believers into the air to meet the descending Christ (recall 1 Thess. 4:17 and discussion there) is concurrent with Christ's final descent to earth—what is usually called the "second coming." Dispensational premillennialists, on the other hand, are normally *pretribulational,* seeing a secret rapture of believers from the earth to heaven before the period depicted as the "great tribulation," which itself immediately precedes the second coming. A few premillennialists of either kind have also championed a *midtribulational* rapture, particularly based on their understanding of chapter 11 (see below, p. 536). Here the church lives through the first half of the tribulation on earth but is exempt from the second half. In recent times, some premillennialists have modified this approach to what they call a *pre-wrath* rapture, because their main concern is that the church not experience God's wrath poured out on earth, not that it be exempt from the entire tribulation. But they do not pretend to know exactly when during the tribulation this removal has to occur.

We have already argued for a posttribulational rapture based on the only biblical text that actually uses the term from which "rapture" is derived (see above, pp. 147–48). We will see that this approach makes best sense here, while noting in the commentary why the texts in Revelation often taken to teach a different perspective do not in our opinion point in such directions.[31]

Historical Perspective   The final major interpretive decision that must be made is whether Revelation supports *futurism*—viewing the events of chapters 6–19 as still future from John's perspective (and largely still future from our perspective today as well); *preterism*—seeing them as fulfilled in the events leading up to and including A.D. 70 and thus referring to events during John's lifetime that are now in the distant past from our perspective; *historicism*—understanding them as progressively fulfilled throughout church history, with only the worst still in the future from

---

[30] For the various approaches, see esp. Robert G. Clouse, ed., *The Meaning of the Millennium: Four Views* (Downers Grove: IVP, 1977); Millard J. Erickson, *A Basic Guide to Eschatology: Making Sense of the Millennium* (Grand Rapids: Baker, rev. 1999).

[31] For the various views, see esp. Richard Reiter, ed., *The Rapture: Pre-, Mid- or Post-Tribulational* (Grand Rapids: Zondervan, 1984); Marvin J. Rosenthal, *The Pre-Wrath Rapture of the Church* (Nashville: Nelson, 1990).

our perspective; or *idealism*—taking the events as symbolic of the timeless struggle between good and evil throughout the church age.[32]

There is no question that the struggle depicted throughout Revelation is reenacted frequently in church history and even in world history, so that the idealist and historicist perspectives capture key truths. Likewise, numerous first-century events more specifically corresponded to a number of the judgments depicted throughout John's apocalypse. If John wanted his first-century congregations to understand something of the ineffable visions he experienced, he would naturally use imagery from the events of his day to help them grasp the significance of those visions. But to the extent that all three of these views typically deny a still-future, more-awful fulfillment of the judgments depicted throughout this book or a discrete period of unparalleled tribulation ushering in the parousia, we have to demur and adopt a primarily *futurist* perspective, while recognizing elements of truth in the other three approaches, too.[33]

Trends in Christian History It is interesting to observe that historic premillennialism dominated the pre-Augustinian church of the first three centuries of Patristic writings, though some amillennialism can be found there, too. From Augustine on, the Roman Catholic church became overwhelmingly amillennial. Some of the Protestant Reformers preserved this perspective; others began to return to premillennialism. Postmillennialism has been the least-held of the three views throughout church history, but it has come to the fore particularly in times of great missionary movements and the expansion of the church. Then it seems as if God's Spirit wants to use Christians to usher in the millennium even before the parousia. Nineteenth-century Christianity in Western Europe and North America formed the greatest heyday for postmillennialism. Postmillennialism has tended to take a preterist approach; amillennialism, an idealist approach; and premillennialism, a futurist or, occasionally, a historicist approach.

Dispensationalist premillennialism and, specifically, a pretribulational rapture is largely the product of the Plymouth Brethren denomination, founded by J. Nelson Darby in Scotland in the 1830s and subsequently transplanted to America, where it flourished, particularly through the study Bible notes penned by C. I. Scofield and the voluminous writings of Lewis Sperry Chafer, founder of Dallas Theological Seminary. Dispensationalism also spawned countless Bible colleges in the U.S. and abroad, making its interpretive approaches to Scripture well known throughout conservative Christianity worldwide. In more recent decades, and at a very popular level, especially through the "non-fiction" writings of Hal Lindsey and the "Left Behind" novels of Tim LaHaye and Jerry Jenkins, it has led to an approach to Revelation that sees its prophecy fulfilled in current events. But then other approaches have produced their accounts of how the same prophecies were being fulfilled in their eras,

---

[32] For parallel readings of the apocalypse from each of these four perspectives, see Steve Gregg, *Revelation: Four Views—A Parallel Commentary* (Nashville: Nelson, 1997). For a comparison of preterist, idealist, progressive dispensationalist (much closer to historic than to dispensationalist premillennialist), and classic dispensationalist approaches, see C. Marvin Pate, ed., *Four Views on the Book of Revelation* (Grand Rapids: Zondervan, 1998).

[33] Cf. Osborne, *Revelation*, 21–22.

all throughout history. The only indisputable observation about these claims is that, to date, *100 percent of them have proved wrong, a fact that should warn us against putting any stock in any author's specific scenario.*[34]

COMMENTARY

INTRODUCTION (1:1–20)

Prologue (1:1–3)   Like the Gospel of John and 1 John, the Apocalypse begins with a Christ-centered prologue. Here, though, the focus is more on the nature of the revelation John is receiving. "Made it known" in verse 1 is literally "signified," alerting the reader to the fact that this communication will be by means of signs and symbols.[35] The nearness of the end announced here must be interpreted as in 2 Peter 3:8 and Psalm 90:4. It also reminds us of what we have consistently seen from Acts 2:17 onward—that the last days began at Pentecost and have continued ever since. This is also the only book in the New Testament that explicitly promises a blessing to those who read it and take it to heart, so we neglect it at our peril, even as we strive to interpret it rightly rather than abusing it as so many have.

Greetings and Dedication (1:4–8)   John extends to the seven churches the Greek greeting of "grace" and the Jewish blessing of "peace," both Christianized by coming from the triune God—the eternally existing Father, "the sevenfold [i.e., complete] Spirit" (see NIV marg.)[36] and Jesus Christ (vv. 4–5a). He then offers a doxology specifically to Christ in gratitude for the atonement he has wrought and the kingdom he has created for believers who now have direct priestly access to the Father (vv. 5b–6). These verses suggest what will become clearer as the book unfolds: its theology is much richer than just affirmations about the end times.[37] With respect to eschatology, the central tenet appears in verse 7: *Christ will return to earth in triumph in a universally public, visible way, and everyone will mourn.* In Zechariah 12:10, this text clearly refers to the mourning of repentance by believers, but, as Jesus uses it in Matthew 24:30, it may involve the sorrow of judgment for unbelievers as well. Verse 8 is important because its concepts will be repeated in verses 17–18, this time not of the Lord God but of Jesus, a clear indicator of the deity of Christ.[38]

John's Commission (1:9–20)   John rounds out his introduction by describing the events that led him to put ink to papyrus in penning this document. Just as the per-

---

[34] For more on the various perspectives throughout church history, see esp. Arthur W. Wainwright, *Mysterious Apocalypse: Interpreting the Book of Revelation* (Nashville: Abingdon, 1993).

[35] Cf. Osborne, *Revelation*, 55.

[36] The other way to translate this expression is as "the seven spirits," understanding them as an angelic host surrounding God, but since these "spirits" are elsewhere said to be "of God and of the Lamb" (3:1; 4:5; 5:6), it is better to see them as a representation of the Holy Spirit in all his fullness. See esp. Bauckham, *The Theology of the Book of Revelation,* 110–15.

[37] See esp. Graeme Goldsworthy, *The Gospel in Revelation* (Exeter: Paternoster, 1984; Nashville: Nelson, 1985).

[38] An intriguing feature of the Jehovah's Witnesses' New World Translation of the Bible is that, while more obvious texts affirming the full deity of Jesus have been reworded so as to obscure this doctrine, no change has been introduced into these passages, so that even the NWT can be used to demonstrate Christ's divinity.

secution of Domitian has begun to affect some in his audience, John too has been exiled to Patmos and is a "companion in the suffering" that is theirs in Jesus as a result of their common faith (v. 9). One Sunday, in the context of (private?) worship, John had some ecstatic experience, which included a vision of the exalted "son of man"—that is, Jesus in his role as depicted in Daniel 7:13–14.[39] This Son of man appeared among seven lampstands (v. 12), which stand for the seven churches (v. 20). The individual items of this vision—Jesus' robe, sash, hair, eyes, and so on (vv. 13–16), should not be given independent allegorical significance. Together, though, they create a powerful picture of Christ the glorious, majestic judge.[40] After identifying himself (vv. 17–18), Jesus commissions John to write this book. If verse 19 is not a reference to a past-present-future outline of the document (see above, p. 515), then "what you have seen" may anticipate the entire volume, with its visions of what is both present ("what is now") and future ("what will take place later").[41]

The seven stars that stand for the "angels" of the seven churches have perennially puzzled commentators. The word *angelos* means "messenger," so some have imagined letter carriers or pastors, but elsewhere in the New Testament the expression always refers to supernatural beings, so most believe John is alluding to the Jewish idea, probably behind 1 Corinthians 11:10 (recall above, p. 515), of angels watching over churches at worship.[42] In any event, it is clear that the messages he is about to write are for the actual churches in Asia Minor.

LETTERS TO THE SEVEN CHURCHES (2:1–3:22)

All seven letters are very similarly structured. *The general pattern is address, identification of the speaker (Christ), commendation, criticism, threat of judgment, call to hear, and promises to those who "overcome," that is, who remain loyal to Jesus in hard times.* Parallels to imperial edicts suggest that these letters signify God's royal commands taking precedence over Caesar's claims.[43] Two churches receive no criticism: Smyrna and Philadelphia. Two receive no formal commendation: Sardis and Laodicea. The seven churches thus reflect the full spectrum of faithfulness and faithlessness present in every age of church history.[44]

Ephesus: Losing Your First Love (2:1–7)   Those who remained orthodox despite the intrusion of heretics (recall under the Epistles of John, pp. 486–89) had won the theological war but lost the battles of behavior and spirit. Nothing is known about

---

[39] See Blomberg, *Jesus and the Gospels,* 405–7, and the literature there cited.

[40] Arguably portrayed in similar fashion to exalted angels, as a bridge between pure Jewish monotheism and full-orbed post-New Testament trinitarian thought. See esp. Peter R. Carrell, *Jesus and the Angels: Angelology and the Christology of the Apocalypse of John* (Cambridge and New York: CUP, 1997).

[41] See, e.g., Mounce, *Revelation,* 62.

[42] Cf. further Jürgen Roloff, *Revelation: A Continental Commentary* (Minneapolis: Fortress, 1993), 38–40.

[43] David E. Aune, "The Form and Function of the Proclamations to the Seven Churches (Revelation 2–3)," *NTS* 36 (1990): 182–204; Nestor P. Friedrich, "Adapt or Resist? A Socio-Political Reading of Revelation 2.18–29," *JSNT* 25 (2002): 185–211.

[44] The most accurate and detailed work of background information on these seven cities to help us decipher the unique visions God tailored for each of them is Colin J. Hemer, *The Letters to the Seven Churches of Asia in Their Local Setting* (Sheffield : JSOT, 1986). Somewhat more user-friendly are the two books by Roland H. Worth Jr., *The Seven Cities of the Apocalypse and Roman Culture* and *The Seven Cities of the Apocalypse and Greco-Asian Culture* (New York: Paulist, 1999).

the Nicolaitans (v. 6), except that the name means "conquer the people" in Greek. In 2:15, they are linked with the idolatrous and immoral supporters of Balaam, whose name interestingly means the same thing in Hebrew. The Ephesians are called to repent and do the works they did at first (v. 5), an indicator that forsaking their first love (v. 4) is not primarily a statement about their lack of emotional fervor but a problem with the practical outworking of their faith.[45] They clung to truth better than they loved God or others; compare many "heresy hunters" today! The threat of their removal—the demise of the church in Ephesus—came true near the end of the second century in conjunction with the overall decline of the city.[46] The promise of the tree of life (v. 7) stands in stark contrast with the Artemis cult oak tree-shrine in town and the asylum it offered.

Smyrna: Persevering Despite Difficult Circumstances (2:8–11)   Here is the first of the two churches for which John offers no condemnation. Stressing Jesus' deity and resurrection are important (v. 8) in countering a strong imperial cult in Smyrna. This city also called itself "first" among Asian cities and viewed itself as "resurrected" in 290 B.C. after it had been destroyed by an invading Lydian king.[47] On the "synagogue of Satan" (v. 9), recall above, page 511. This language is not to be generalized to all Jews. "Those who say they are Jews and are not" refers to those whose activity in persecuting Christians belies their ethnic and spiritual heritage.[48] Smyrna is where Polycarp, disciple of the apostle John, would be martyred approximately thirty years later, with Jews gathering wood for fuel for the stake on which Polycarp would be burned, even though it was the Sabbath (*Mart. Polyc.* 13.1, 17.2)! The ten-day persecution (v. 10) probably employs a round number for a short, limited period of suffering (recall Dan. 1:12–14).[49] An inscription in Smyrna with the identical syntax speaks of another such period lasting five days.[50] Despite their faithfulness, God gave them no guarantee of outward blessing in this life. But overcomers would receive a garland wreath—an appropriate symbol of their heavenly reward in a community well known for such a crown as an emblem of its beauty—rather than experiencing the "second" (i.e., eternal, spiritual) death.

Pergamum: Mixing Faith and Immorality (2:12–17)   Pergamum formed a center for Zeus worship, Asclepian healings, and the imperial cult, any or all of which could be in view when John speaks of Satan's throne (v. 13).[51] Nothing else is known

---

[45] In fact, given the context of the Johannine community's struggle with false teachers, it seems more likely that it is love for the wayward church member, not love for God, that they most need to recover (Murphy, *Fallen Is Babylon*, 115–16).

[46] Though see Osborne, *Revelation*, 108–9. It is not certain whether attempts to prevent the silting over of the Ephesian harbor that led to the city's decline were successful or not.

[47] Ibid., 128.

[48] Cf. further Beasley-Murray, *Revelation*, 82. He adds, "Never was opposition so extreme as at Smyrna." Mark R. J. Bredin ("The Synagogue of Satan Accusation in Revelation 2:9," *BTB* 28 [1999]: 160–64) adds the suggestion that the Christians' unwillingness to pay the tax to Rome that kept Jews exempt from persecution exacerbated the tensions with the synagogue.

[49] Roloff, *Revelation*, 48–49.

[50] Hemer, *The Letters to the Seven Churches*, 69–70. Sjef van Tilborg ("The Danger at Midday: Death Threats in the Apocalypse," *Bib* 85 [2004]: 12) observes that gladiatorial games with men or beasts fighting condemned criminals could last from three to thirteen days and fit well with the kind of suffering described here.

[51] Mounce, *Revelation*, 79.

about the martyr Antipas, but obviously this church has remained partly faithful to Jesus. But they have indulged in food sacrificed to idols, obviously in the context of pagan worship, which is said to have included sexual relations like those with a pagan temple's priests or priestesses in hope of achieving union with the god(s) or goddess(es) (v. 14; for the allusions to Balaam and Balak, see Num. 24:14; 31:16). Recall the condemnations in 1 Corinthians 10:1–22. On the Nicolaitans, see above on Revelation 2:6. The immorality here, however, as so often in the Old Testament, could of course be a metaphor for the unfaithfulness the idolatry reflected. The reward for the overcomer includes the hidden manna—the "bread of life" that Jews believed would be restored in the end times and that Jesus spiritually provided in his own person and ministry (John 6:30–59). A white stone could be used as an admission ticket to a feast, a vote of acquittal in a court, a sign of initiation into a religious group, and a magical amulet offering permanent protection for its possessor.[52] All of these uses find their spiritual analogies in the Christian's future hope. The new name reflects the believer's regeneration, already begun now but only fully completed when Christ returns.

Thyatira: Confusing the Devilish with the Divine (2:18–29) To a center of trade guilds, John naturally refers to Jesus as one who appears in "blazing fire" and "burnished bronze" (v. 18) like various pots after surviving a kiln.[53] Thyatira, like Pergamum, exhibited key elements of faith and service (v. 19) but disastrous disobedience centering on idolatrous food and sexual immorality. This time John compares the city with Old Testament Queen Jezebel, Ahab's wicked wife, against whom judgment was prophesied and executed (vv. 20–23; cf. 1 Kings 21:23 and 2 Kings 9:33). "Satan's so-called deep secrets" (v. 24) may refer to the Gnostic-like idea that one has to experience evil deeply in order to show one is immune to it.[54] Like someone smashing the beautiful pottery that Thyatira produced, Christ will destroy those in the church there who do not repent (v. 27). The morning star could refer to Venus, the symbol of Roman sovereignty, and/or Christ himself (see 22:16; cf. Num. 24:17).

Sardis: Almost Totally Dead (3:1–6) The state of the church in Sardis matched the condition of the city. Both were in eclipse, but neither was willing to admit it (v. 1). Jesus as the only one who could truly hold on to them or preserve them contrasted sharply with the almost impregnable hilltop fortress of the town, which had nevertheless twice fallen to enemies when the guards failed to keep watch (under Cyrus and Antiochus III).[55] Where one next expects a commendation, one finds none, though verse 4 will acknowledge a few faithful followers in the church. But here John proceeds immediately to a strong rebuke and call to repent, lest Jesus come surprisingly and suddenly in judgment (vv. 2–3; recall 1 Thess. 5:2 and Matt.

---

[52] Cf. Aune, *Revelation 1–5,* 190–91.

[53] Aune (ibid., 201) notes the prominence in Thyatira of associations of "clothiers, bakers, tanners, potters, linen workers, wool merchants, slave traders, shoemakers, dyers, and copper smiths [*sic*]."

[54] Cf. further Osborne, *Revelation,* 162–63.

[55] Ibid., 174, 177.

24:43 par.). Unlike the watchmen who let down their guard, the Christians in Sardis must remain vigilant.

The double negative, "never blot out," creates a strong assurance that those who overcome will be guaranteed eternal life. Their immorality ("soiled clothes") will be replaced by righteousness ("dressed in white"; vv. 4–5).[56] For the book of life imagery, see originally Exodus 32:32–33. Christ's promise also strongly contrasts with the excommunication Jewish Christians were experiencing from the synagogues, where their names were blotted out of a membership register. Acknowledging someone's name before the Father and his angels appears to allude to Jesus' saying in Luke 12:8–9 and parallel.

Philadelphia: Obedient and Faithful (3:7–13)   Here is the most positive of all the letters. Unlike Smyrna, which was faithful yet persecuted, Philadelphia is faithful and visibly blessed, with an open door to enter God's kingdom and to help others enter with them, despite little strength in and of themselves (vv. 7–8).[57] But nothing suggests the Philadelphian church was *more* obedient than the one in Smyrna. God alone in his sovereignty determines when outward blessing is and isn't appropriate for Christian perseverance and service. The parallelism with Smyrna is furthered by another reference to a "synagogue of Satan" (v. 9; recall 2:9). Verse 10 provides the key crux in this letter. Does being kept "from the hour of trial that is going to come upon the whole world" refer to the preservation of Christians by removing them from the place of tribulation or by protecting them in its midst? Grammatically, the expression could mean either. Proponents of a pretribulational rapture obviously opt for the former, while posttribulationists prefer the latter. Interestingly, the only other use of the verb *tēreō* ("keep") with the preposition *ek* ("from") in the New Testament occurs in John 17:15, in which Jesus prays for his followers to be protected from trouble, even while they remain on earth.

But if this is an allusion to the great tribulation at the end of human history, it is the only such reference in these letters to the seven churches. Every other detail in them clearly applies to their contemporary context at the end of the first century. So perhaps the "hour of trial" here refers merely to coming empire-wide persecution of Christians (another established meaning of "whole world" in a Roman context). Is it merely a coincidence that the church in Philadelphia remained until 1392, long after the churches in the other six cities had been destroyed, several by the Islamic invasions beginning in the seventh century?[58] Verses 11–12 proceed to promise to make the overcomers pillars of God's new temple in the new Jerusalem. Of course this is a metaphor for a firm grounding, since the new Jerusalem contains no literal temple (21:22). It also formed an apt image for Philadelphians, who were so used to earthquakes in the area shaking the pillars of their temple and other stone structures that most of them lived outside the city walls.

---

[56] J. William Fuller, "'I Will Not Erase His Name from the Book of Life' (Revelation 3:5)," *JETS* 26 (1983): 297–306.

[57] Hemer, *The Letters to the Seven Churches,* 162.

[58] Cf. Aune, *Revelation 1–5,* 240; Craig S. Keener, *Revelation* (Grand Rapids: Zondervan, 2000), 154.

Laodicea: Undrinkable and Useless (3:14–22) This is the most negative of the seven letters. The church in town was like its water supply, proverbial for its lukewarmness (v. 15). Laodicea did not have its own fresh water supply, so it had to be piped in either from the clear, cold mountain streams near Colossae or from the therapeutic hot springs near Hierapolis. Either way, by the time the aqueducts reached Laodicea, the water had become insipid. Thus hot and cold are both *positive* metaphors in this passage, over against the disgusting state of the Laodiceans (v. 16).[59] The city was also famous for its wealth (it rebuilt itself without Roman aid after an earthquake in A.D. 60), its black wool industry, and a medical school that produced eyesalve. By way of contrast, verse 17 declares the Christians there to be "wretched, pitiful, poor, blind and naked." They must buy spiritual "gold," "white clothes," and "salve" for their eyes in order to reverse this state of affairs (v. 18).[60]

The call for the Laodiceans' repentance (v. 19) utilizes the famous metaphor of opening a door so that Jesus can come in and eat with them (v. 20). Although derivatively this can be a powerful image for a person receiving Christ into his or her heart for the first time, in this context John is clearly referring to the church *collectively* welcoming Jesus *back* into their midst.[61] His patient knocking contrasts with the forced entry of Roman officials coming through the impressive triple gate in the city walls and requiring lodging in this wealthy town.

Eugene Peterson nicely captures the essence of what is praised and condemned in each of the churches, which can help us find analogous groups of Christians in other times and places who require similar promises and threats. "The churches are affirmed for untiring, unflagging, and vigilant work (Ephesus); for brave suffering (Smyrna); for courageous witness (Pergamum); for growing and developing discipleship (Thyatira); and for brave steadfastness (Philadelphia)." But "they are corrected for abandoning their first zestful love of Christ (Ephesus); being indifferent to heretical teaching (Pergamum); being tolerant of immorality (Thyatira); being apathetic (Sardis); letting luxurious riches substitute for life in the Spirit (Laodicea)."[62]

In addition, Richard Foulkes stresses that the "eruption" of the message of Jesus into lives of the members of the seven churches leaves nothing intact. It insists on vital changes not only at the individual level (plenty of religions in and around Ephesus accepted personal conversion to a particular cult that did not discredit the other religious options of the day), but also at the social level of "structures that enslave and deceive the people. That is to say, the religious aspect of life is so interrelated with other aspects, economic, civic, and legal—even in our so-called 'secular' world—that a religious change effected by Jesus would have to affect the rest of existence."[63]

---

[59] See esp. M. J. S. Rudwick and E. M. B. Green, "The Laodicean Lukewarmness," *ET* 69 (1957–58): 176–78; and Stanley E. Porter, "Why the Laodiceans Received Lukewarm Water (Revelation 3:15–18)," *TynB* 38 (1987): 143–49.

[60] Cf. further Beasley-Murray, *Revelation,* 103, 106.

[61] Tim Wiarda, "Revelation 3:20: Imagery and Literary Context," *JETS* 38 (1995): 203–12.

[62] Eugene H. Peterson, *Reversed Thunder: The Revelation of John and the Praying Imagination* (San Francisco: Harper & Row, 1988), 51, 52.

[63] Ricardo Foulkes, *El Apocalipsis de San Juan: Una lectura desde América Latina* (Buenos Aires: Nueva Creación; Grand Rapids: Eerdmans, 1989), 30 (translation mine).

HEAVENLY PRAISE (4:1–5:14)

For God (4:1–11) In his vision, John is now caught up to the heavenly throne room, where he will be shown future events (which seemingly begin in 6:1). But first he receives a glimpse of the very antechamber of God himself (chap. 4). The "open heaven" of verse 1a, along with a heavenly guide and visionary transport are all standard features of apocalyptic, so there is no reason to imagine that John stands for the entire church being raptured here, as in classic dispensationalism.[64] "After this" in verse 1b, nevertheless, does support the futurist interpretation of the bulk of the rest of the book. The veiled description of God and the details of his surroundings should not be allegorized; the elements of verses 2–6 combine to create a magnificent picture of the wealth, beauty, majesty, sovereignty, power, and purity of the Lord. The twenty-four elders and four living creatures resemble the cherubim and seraphim of Ezekiel 10:14 and Isaiah 6:2. The "elders" are linked with other heavenly creatures throughout the book of Revelation (4:6; 5:5, 11; 7:11; 19:4) and are distinguished from those redeemed from the earth (5:8; 7:13–14; 11:18; 14:3), so they should most likely be viewed as angelic spokespersons.[65] That there are twenty-four of them could suggest they represent and/or guard the entire people of God throughout time led by the twelve sons/tribes of Israel and the twelve apostles. But the number could also come from the twenty-four divisions of priests and levitical singers in 1 Chronicles 24–25 and indicate a leadership role in heavenly worship.[66]

Verses 6b–11 introduce us to precisely that worship. Here it is directed to God, ceaselessly praising him for his holiness, eternality, creation, and providence. Honoring him as "Lord God Almighty" directly challenged Domitian's claims to those same three titles. That the elders cast their crowns before the throne (v. 10) has often been taken as proof that believers receive varying degrees of reward (crowns) in heaven. But if the elders are angels, then this picture teaches nothing about *believers'* rewards. And even if they do represent the church, the fact that they turn their rewards back over to their heavenly father ultimately makes them all equal again anyway.[67] Indeed, the main point of the chapter is not about the exaltation of anyone other than God himself. Only he is worthy to receive all glory and honor.

For the Lamb (5:1–14) Chapter 5 continues this theme but transfers the praise to the slain Lamb, who alone can open the scroll that will narrate end-time events. At first, an apparently insoluble problem appears: no one in the universe is worthy to break the seals that keep the scroll wrapped up with its prophecies hidden (vv. 1–4). A scroll written on both sides was often an imperial edict.[68] Breaking the seals of a

---

[64] The word "open" is actually the perfect passive form of the verb, literally, "having been opened." "This may suggest that the door has been permanently opened as a result of Christ's death and resurrection for perennial access of believers to God" (Witherington, *Revelation,* 116).

[65] See, e.g., George E. Ladd, *A Commentary on the Revelation of John* (Grand Rapids: Eerdmans, 1972), 75.

[66] Cf. esp. Mounce, *Revelation,* 121–22.

[67] Worship "reminds us that whatever else our calling or gifts now [are], all Christians become the same as God's worshipers; the eternal future leaves little place for gifts now valued, but our devotion to God will always rise" (Keener, *Revelation,* 180).

[68] Indeed, the entire chapter echoes Roman emperor worship but demonstrates that Christ not Caesar merits this tribute. See J. Daryl Charles, "Imperial Pretensions and the Throne-Vision of the Lamb: Observations on the Function of Revelation 5," *CTR* 7 (1993): 85–97.

scroll could refer to the legal execution of its contents. In this case, a sacrifice for sin must be paid before the devil can be conquered and Christ's perfect kingdom established. But as John begins to lament this state of affairs, the announcement comes that "the Lion of the tribe of Judah, the Root of David, has triumphed" and can open the scroll (v. 5). A king descended from the regal family and tribe is obviously the Messiah. But although the Christ is called a *lion,* when John turns to look at this figure he sees a slaughtered but revivified *lamb* at the center of God's throne, with seven horns and eyes that represent the sevenfold (i.e., Holy) Spirit (recall above, p. 520), by whom the Messiah is omnipresent. That the Spirit comes from God completes the incipient trinitarian reference (v. 6).

Taking the scroll is the necessary prelude to opening it. But before events progress, the angelic hosts burst into a litany of praise for the Messiah's atonement, which has enabled people to be redeemed from every ethnic and linguistic grouping on earth. This praise crescendos as the Lamb is presented, exalted, and enthroned—a complete coronation ceremony (vv. 7–14).[69] The suffering servant has indeed become the warrior-king.[70] That every creature in the universe praises the Lamb (v. 13) does not imply that all are saved. Isaiah 45:23–24 sets the precedent for the forced worship of God by his enemies who will simultaneously be shamed (cf. Phil. 2:10–11; Col. 1:20; Eph. 1:21–23). The glimpse of heavenly glory awaiting all God's people that chapters 4–5 provide prepares John for the visions of the more awful events that must precede this glory and gives his readers the "big-picture" perspective necessary to keep them faithful during the tough times soon to come.[71]

SEVEN SEALS AND THE FIRST INTERLUDE (6:1–8:5)

The First Six Seals (6:1–17)   The heart of the book of Revelation presents twenty-one judgments of God on the world, in three groups of seven items each. The first of these sets is represented by seven seals, which have to be removed from a scroll so that it can be unrolled. The imagery of a scroll of God's judgments (cf. 5:2–5) harks back to Old Testament precedents (most notably Ezek. 2:9–3:3). Because the seals must be peeled off before the scroll can be read, it is most natural to take most of these first judgments as *the prelude to the end-time horrors* (later labeled the "great tribulation"—7:14), rather than as part of those horrors themselves.[72] The parallels with a number of the events that Jesus predicted in the Olivet Discourse (see Mark 13:7a, 8 pars.) as items which did *not* signal the end (v. 7b) reinforce this impression. Indeed, the first four seal judgments, also represented by four horses and riders, reminiscent of Zechariah 1:8–11, depict tribulation that has often occurred throughout the course of history: militarism, warfare, famine, and death (Rev. 6:1–8).

---

[69] Beasley-Murray, *Revelation,* 126. Mounce (*Revelation,* 134) calls this "one of the greatest scenes of universal adoration anywhere recorded."

[70] Donald Guthrie, *The Relevance of John's Apocalypse* (Exeter: Paternoster; Grand Rapids: Eerdmans, 1987), 46–51. But, as Aune (*Revelation 1–5,* 368) notes, the figure of a dying lamb (as at Passover or in Isaiah 52–53) is fused with the image of a warrior ram in apocalyptic texts such as in Daniel 8.

[71] "Praise puts persecution, poverty and plagues into perspective; God is sovereignly bringing about his purposes, and this world's pains are merely the birth pangs of a new world" (Keener, *Revelation,* 182).

[72] Ladd, *Revelation,* 95–96, 98.

The first seal (vv. 1–2) offers the only significant ambiguity among the first four. Because in 19:11 Christ himself will appear as a rider on a white horse, some have taken this seal as his positive conversion of the nations. But since every other one of the twenty-one symbols of judgment is unrelentingly negative, we should probably recognize here the Roman symbol of *imperial militarism and conquest.* The bow (as in "bow and arrow") was an image of combat, especially among the Parthians, neighbors of Rome to the northeast of their empire.[73] The Greco-Roman sun god, Apollo, likewise was believed to fight with a bow. But the powers of humans and "gods" will prove impotent against Yahweh's powerful judgment.[74]

The second seal (vv. 3–4) clearly portrays *warfare.* The third seal (vv. 5–6) represents *famine,* closely paralleling the conditions that followed a drought in A.D. 92. A whole day's wages were needed to buy normal daily rations of wheat and barley, while the olive trees' and grapevines' roots (which extend deeper into the soil) were still able to get enough water to grow fairly well.[75] God's mercy is clearly limiting the amount of suffering unleashed here. The fourth seal (vv. 7–8) predicts *death* by warfare, famine, and plague. The text is sometimes read as if it prophesied that one-fourth of humanity would be killed. But John actually writes that the horse and rider are "given power over a fourth of the earth." How many are killed in this portion of the world in which the judgment is unleashed is unspecified.[76]

The fifth seal breaks the pattern of active judgments depicted by horses and their riders. Instead, this seal releases *the cries of Christian martyrs,* who ask how long it will be until God avenges their deaths.[77] The reply is that they must wait a little longer as even more will yet be martyred (vv. 9–11). But as "souls" close to God's presence, they receive white robes, symbolizing their heavenly purity. The only actual plague represented by the fifth seal, thus, is the assurance that the plagues of seals one to four must continue, as indeed they have in many times and places of Christian history.[78]

With the sixth seal, we move from events that prepare the way for the great tribulation to what reads as if the tribulation has begun and is coming to its climax (vv. 12–17). These are events, which even if not taken literally, are so cosmic in their scope and destruction, that John's point must be that the world as we now know it cannot continue (vv. 12–14). Such imagery in other Jewish apocalyptic literature at times does not refer to the literal dissolution of the universe, but to a completely new socio-political era of God's rule on earth.[79] The turmoil created is at least as wide-

---

[73] Murphy, *Fallen Is Babylon,* 205.

[74] See further Allen Kerkeslager, "Apollo, Greco-Roman Prophecy, and the Rider on the White Horse in Rev 6:2," *JBL* 112 (1993): 116–21.

[75] Justo L. González and Catherine G. González, *Revelation* (Louisville and London: WJKP, 1997), 48–49.

[76] Cf. Ladd, *Revelation,* 101.

[77] Some question the morality of these calls for vengeance, but God's justice is the flip side of his love. Still, only he can avenge with complete fairness, so we must call on him to do so, rather than trying to take vengeance into our own hands. Recall Deut. 32:35, in which God reserves vengeance for himself (cf. Ps. 94:1, Rom.12:19, and numerous other texts in which God promises to avenge his people).

[78] Despite its uniqueness as the only "prayer of supplication" in the Apocalypse, this seal plays an integral role in tying together what the book teaches about judgment and vindication. See John P. Heil, "The Fifth Seal (Rev 6, 9–11) as a Key to the Book of Revelation," *Bib* 74 (1993): 220–43.

[79] N. T. Wright, *The New Testament and the People of God* (London: SPCK; Minneapolis: Fortress, 1992), 280–86.

spread as, and probably more so than, what we imply when we use equally metaphorical expressions such as "all hell broke loose" or "she turned the world upside down." As discussed above, this is probably a "flash-ahead" to the threshold of the end, just before Christ returns and makes all things new.[80] Whatever literal events are implied, they produce extreme terror and the desire for death based on the misguided conviction that death would end their torture (vv. 15–17). The "wrath of the Lamb" is a delicious oxymoron for Jesus' role in this setting!

The 144,000 and the Numberless Multitude (7:1–17)   Before describing the seventh seal, John inserts two segments of another vision of heaven. Verses 1–8 depict the sealing of 144,000 people. Before the next plague can be unleashed, God ensures that his "servants" still on earth are protected from his coming wrath (vv. 1–3; cf. Ezek. 9:4–6). The seal may also signify God's ownership of his followers. So it is obvious that there are believers on earth during the tribulation that is about to come. What is disputed is if this is a description of the entire Christian church or just a small segment of it—for example, Jewish Christians—who (or a selection of whom) alone are not raptured or who come to faith when they see the entire church raptured. At first glance, interpretations taking these to be literal Jews would seem far more probable. This passage perhaps affords the strongest support for a pretribulational rapture of any biblical text. The group announced in verses 4–9 is heralded as taken from the tribes of Israel—12,000 from each of the twelve tribes. On the other hand, in the vision of verses 9–17, John sees a numberless multitude from every ethnic group on earth (v. 9), that has "come out of the great tribulation" (v. 14), presumably the raptured, multiethnic church of Jesus Christ.[81]

On closer inspection, however, various features of this chapter cast doubt on this interpretation. The *first* is the unique list of tribes in verses 5–8. Nowhere else in any ancient Jewish literature does this exact list of names (in any sequence) reappear, with the tribe of Dan missing and with Joseph mentioned but only in conjunction with one of his two sons (Manasseh but not Ephraim), among whom his land was apportioned. This could be the first indicator that this is not a fully literal description of ethnic Israel.[82] *Second,* the 144,000 reappear in 14:1–5 without any ethnic limitations and having general Christian characteristics (see also below, p. 543). *Third,* John never actually has a vision of the 144,000. Verse 4 explains that he "heard" this intoning of the number sealed from each tribe. After hearing such a description, one would expect John to look to see the group just announced. This is precisely what he does at the beginning of verse 9 and what he sees is the numberless multitude. *It would appear that this vision is intended to present the same group just described in more Jewish terms.*[83]

---

[80] Cf. Witherington, *Revelation,* 135–36.

[81] This is the classic dispensationalist approach. See, e.g., Robert L. Thomas, *Revelation 1–7* (Chicago: Moody, 1992), 487.

[82] For a detailed survey of attempts to make sense of this unique list, see Richard Bauckham, "The List of the Tribes in Revelation 7 Again," *JSNT* 42 (1991): 99–115. Cf. also Christopher R. Smith, "The Portrayal of the Church as the New Israel in the Names and Order of the Tribes in Revelation 7.5–8," *JSNT* 39 (1990): 111–18.

[83] See, e.g., Roloff, *Revelation,* 98.

We dare not forget that the identical phenomenon occurred already in 5:5–6. There John was told to look and see the Lion of Judah, but when he looked he saw a Lamb that appeared as if it had been slain. No greater difference could be imagined in the imagery of John's world than between the powerful king of the beasts and a slaughtered baby sheep. And yet both refer to the same reality—Jesus himself (see above, p. 527).[84] It is entirely conceivable, therefore, that the numbered members of the tribes of Israel and the numberless multiethnic multitude are likewise meant to depict the same entity—the church—from two quite different yet complementary perspectives. On the one hand, the church is the ultimate fulfillment of God's original intentions for Israel. On the other hand, it is literally made up of a much vaster number of people from every ethno-linguistic group on earth.[85]

Verses 9–17 also contrast with verses 4–8 by showing the company of all the redeemed in heaven, no longer on earth. But to label them "those who have come out of the great tribulation" more naturally suggests that they first lived through it than that they were exempt from it altogether.[86] Their white robes (vv. 9, 13) call to mind the martyrs' reward in 6:11. Having been washed and made white by the blood of the Lamb (v. 14) presents another striking oxymoron, but Christ's atonement does in fact make his followers perfectly clean, at least after the end of their earthly lives. Not surprisingly, such a wonderful destiny leads to the redeemed, alongside the angelic host, bursting into praise for their salvation (v. 10), for the magnificence of the God who made it possible (v. 12) and for their eternal state (vv. 15–17). Whatever suffering they have experienced in this life will be wiped away, never again to recur. The Lamb morphs into a Shepherd who guides his people to places of eternal refreshment![87]

The Seventh Seal (8:1–5)   At last, John is allowed to learn about the seventh seal. But instead of it unleashing plagues, cries for vengeance, or cataclysmic upheavals, as with the first six seals, all that happens is *prolonged heavenly silence* (cf. Zech. 2:13), *followed by what might be called cosmic sound effects and visual aids* such as those associated with "natural" disasters throughout human history. Only in this case, it seems that the thunder and lightning begin on earth and reverberate into heaven. That both the silence (v. 1) and the later theatrics (vv. 3–5) sandwich a reference to the seven angels with the seven trumpets supports our earlier suggestion that the seventh seal does not introduce some new judgment but merely prepares the way for and encompasses the entire next series of trumpet judgments (recall above, pp. 514–15).[88]

---

[84] Cf. the parallel dual imagery throughout Revelation of Christ's followers as both triumphant warriors and persecuted martyrs. See esp. Stephen Pattemore, *The People of God in the Apocalypse* (Cambridge and New York: CUP, 2004).

[85] Cf. Philip E. Hughes, *The Book of Revelation* (Leicester: IVP; Grand Rapids: Eerdmans, 1990), 94–95. The fully multicultural nature of heaven suggests the mandate to work for multicultural *churches* as well as a universally multicultural church in this age. See Justo L. González, *For the Healing of the Nations: The Book of Revelation in an Age of Cultural Conflict* (Maryknoll: Orbis, 1999).

[86] Cf. Ladd, *Revelation*, 117–18.

[87] Cf. further Kirsten Nielsen, "Shepherd, Lamb and Blood: Imagery in the Old Testament—Use and Reuse," *ST* 46 (1992): 121–32.

[88] For details, see J. Ramsey Michaels, *Interpreting the Book of Revelation* (Grand Rapids: Baker, 1992), 56–58.

SEVEN TRUMPETS AND THE SECOND INTERLUDE (8:6–11:19)

The First Six Trumpets (8:6–9:21) From Joshua's famous march around Jericho to apocalyptic texts such as 1 Corinthians 15 and 1 Thessalonians 4–5, trumpets frequently function as harbingers of judgment in Scripture. *At last we are ready for the great tribulation itself,* as recounted in the scroll that can now be unrolled to disclose the coming judgments of God (v. 6). As with the first four seals, the first four trumpet judgments prove closely parallel (vv. 7–12). *They also resemble the plagues on the Egyptians during the contest between Moses and Pharaoh. This parallelism suggests that, even at this late date, their purpose is to stimulate the wicked to repent.* The conclusion of this section (9:20–21) confirms this intent in a backhanded way. Even despite the trumpet judgments, the earth's wicked do not repent—which suggests they still had the opportunity to do so.[89]

The first trumpet judgment involves *hail mixed with bloody fire*; the second, *a fiery mountain catapulted into the sea turning it into blood*; the third, *a fiery star turning the fresh water sources into blood*; and the fourth, *a plague darkening the light associated with sun, moon, and stars* (vv. 7–12). In each case, one-third of the targeted areas on earth are affected. Whatever else this fraction may signify, it is obviously more than the one-fourth of the earth mentioned in 6:8. Yet despite the intensification of judgment, only a minority of the world is afflicted by God's plagues.[90] How literal all of these descriptions are is impossible to determine. Some of the visions of course include phenomena that could not literally occur, for example, darkening exactly one-third of the sun. The imagery involved is a staple of (non-literal) apocalyptic prophecy. John is no doubt describing as accurately as he can what he saw in his visions, but that is different from those visions being exact reproductions of coming events. Rather, as frequently in apocalyptic literature, they are symbols for real events that may literally look quite different, but whose purposes and consequences are equally awful.[91]

The fifth and sixth trumpets (also called the first and second woes) are of a different nature (8:13–9:21). *First, John sees armies of locusts grotesquely portrayed, whose origin is the Abyss* (9:1–2). This suggests that he is viewing a demonic horde rather than merely human warfare.[92] Locust plagues were all too common in the ancient Middle Eastern world, and Joel 2:1–11 had already provided prophetic precedent for a locust plague that morphed into armies in battle. But still God is limiting the havoc these diabolical creatures can wreak. They must not harm any plants (whereas in 8:7 all the grass on earth was destroyed, a further reminder that these are not always prophecies of the literal events that must occur). More importantly, they cannot harm any of the believers who were sealed in 7:4. And they cannot kill

---

[89] Cf. Beasley-Murray, *Revelation,* 156, 167.

[90] Keener, *Revelation,* 272.

[91] Robert H. Mounce, *The Book of Revelation* (Grand Rapids: Eerdmans, 1977), 302–3. For some reason, this explanation has been deleted from the revised edition, even though the author's position on this issue does not seem to have changed.

[92] David E. Aune, *Revelation 6–16* (Nashville: Nelson, 1998), 527.

unbelievers but must limit their torture to a five-month period, appropriate for this vision since this length of time reflected the standard life cycle for locusts (v. 5a).[93]

Nevertheless, they are able to inflict agonizing suffering on the people they can hurt during this period (v. 5b–6). The irony is that Satan, called the Destroyer in verse 11, has turned on his own, as evil always does sooner or later. John next depicts the demonic locust-warriors with a series of similes, undoubtedly groping for analogies with which to describe the indescribable (vv. 7–10). The composite picture somewhat resembles the Parthian armies with their armored horses decked out in long flowing manes and their riders shooting arrows behind them as well as in front of them to combat anyone attacking from any side. At times, they swung maces around behind their horses as well.[94] But, again, we must not think of them as merely human armies; to do so would be to "demythologize" or take the supernatural element out of the text.[95]

Second, John hears the command to release four angels prepared to kill a third of humanity (vv. 13–16). Their *modus operandi* involves, literally, "two myriads of myriads" of mounted troops. A "myriad" (Gk. *muriados*) could mean ten thousand or just a very large number. That the steeds breathed out fire, smoke, and sulfur, all elements associated with hell, suggests that these are every bit as demonic a form of creature as the locusts were. Attempts to identify these hordes as human armies, from a country large enough to have two hundred million troops, thus misses John's point altogether. *But if the creatures are demonic, then the warfare may well be spiritual warfare, and the death of one-third of humanity could just as easily be spiritual as physical death* (vv. 17–19).[96] Amazingly, even though so large a portion of the world's people are judged, the remaining unbelievers continue to pursue their idolatry and immorality (vv. 20–21).

The Little Scroll (10:1–11) As with the seal judgments, a hiatus occurs between John's narration of the sixth and seventh items in the series of trumpet judgments. The interlude contains two discrete visions. The first discloses an angel with a "little scroll" (*bibliarion*—the diminutive form of the word used in 5:1). The angel is depicted with heavenly majesty reminiscent of Jesus himself (v. 1). But Jesus is nowhere else referred to as an angel in Scripture, so he is unlikely to be in view here. The details of the angel's appearance should not be allegorized. Because the word for this scroll in verse 2a is different from the one used earlier and because it seems to refer to a new stage in God's revelation ("you must prophesy *again*"—10:11), most scholars assume its contents correspond to those of 11:1–13—the vision John receives after ingesting the scroll and before the trumpet judgments resume.[97] A few, however, have suggested that this is part of the bigger scroll and plan of God earlier

---

[93] Ibid., 530.

[94] George B. Caird, *The Revelation of Saint John the Divine* (London: Black; New York: Harper & Row, 1966), 122.

[95] "John would no doubt have laughed at attempts to identify this horde with a group of human beings for he is talking about powers and principalities" (Witherington, *Revelation,* 154).

[96] Aune (*Revelation 6–16,* 539), who observes that huge armies of destroying angels appear twice in the Babylonian Talmud (*b. Shabbat* 88a; *b. Pesahim* 112b). In the latter passage, "180 thousand angels of destruction go out every night," obviously to wreak spiritual rather than physical havoc.

[97] E.g., Mounce, *Revelation,* 202.

unrolled.[98] That the angel's feet span land and sea (v. 2b) suggests, on either interpretation, the universal significance of this revelation.

When the angel gives a shout, John hears loud voices described as "seven thunders" (v. 3). But when he dutifully begins to record their words, as he has done with all of the other revelations of God thus far, he is commanded to "seal up" what they have said and not write them down (v. 4). Jewish apocalyptic elsewhere at times included one hidden revelation among numerous public ones (in the New Testament, cf. the entirely private revelation to Paul in 2 Cor. 12:1–4).[99] In light of the main idea of verses 5–7 that there will be no more delay, one could imagine the seven thunders disclosing judgments avoided that God might have unleashed had he allowed for more time before the end, but we have no way of being sure.[100] The elaborate, formal oath of verses 5–6 makes this affirmation that much more solemn and certain.

Whereas Daniel had been told that the outcome of his prophecy was sealed up until the end, implying that the end was not yet imminent (Dan. 12:9), John is told to seal up what he had heard because the end *is* imminent. Whereas the fifth seal replied to the martyrs' cry for vengeance with the command to wait a little longer (6:9–11), now we have once again been brought to the threshold of the end (as with the sixth seal in 6:12–17). At the same time, eight more judgments remain to be narrated, so it would appear that we have a second "flash-ahead" that does not in fact lead immediately to the final consummation of all things.[101]

What John is now commanded to do with the little scroll directly reflects Ezekiel's commissioning centuries earlier (see esp. Ezek. 3:3, 14). In his vision, John has the angel tell him to eat the scroll, warning him that it will turn his stomach sour even though it tastes sweet as honey (vv. 9–10). In other words, the coming judgments he must proclaim about the fate of the whole world (v. 11) will prove bitter-sweet. For believers the end will mean salvation; for unbelievers, judgment. Some of the bitterness may also involve the persecution believers must endure before their vindication. As will become clearer in chapters 11–14, three themes pervade this long "interlude" before the seven bowl judgments are narrated: *(1) God's people are exempt from his wrath, (2) but they do not necessarily escape human and diabolical persecution; (3) nevertheless, God will ultimately right all the wrongs of this age by bringing eternal life to those who support him and eternal death to those who oppose him.*[102]

ADDITIONAL QUESTIONS FOR REVIEW

1. What are some of the challenges to attributing the authorship of Revelation to the same person who wrote the Fourth Gospel and the Johannine epistles? What internal and external evidence bolsters the argument that attributes Revelation to this same author?

---

[98] See esp. Bauckham, *Climax of Prophecy*, 243–57.

[99] Cf. Aune, *Revelation 6–16*, 562–63.

[100] E.g., Caird, *Revelation*, 126.

[101] The KJV translation, "time will be no more," misleads, for that is true only in the eternal state (if even then).

[102] Cf. Murphy, *Fallen Is Babylon*, 260.

2. Revelation is a hybrid of what three well-known Jewish and Greco-Roman genres? How is Revelation similar to other ancient apocalyptic writings, and how does it differ? What hermeneutic principle does Revelation's epistolary nature demand?

3. The three series of sevens presented in Revelation have been variously understood. Which of the three options provides the explanation of the events of Revelation?

4. What simple outline of the entire apocalypse does Revelation 1:19 offer? How does such an understanding aid a reader in appropriately interpreting the images and metaphors offered throughout Revelation?

5. Perhaps more so than any other New Testament writing, Revelation demands several interpretive decisions that dictate the understanding of this book as a whole. What are these interpretive issues, and what are the major views within each of these issues?

6. What is the pattern of structure in each of the seven letters to the churches? Who do the churches represent? Summarize the central idea of Christ's message to each of the seven churches and the principle applicable to today's church. What relevant historical information surrounding each letter helps a modern interpreter better understand the author's originally intended meaning?

7. How are the metaphors of Christ as both Lion and Lamb to be understood throughout Revelation? How is this figure unique among all the inhabitants of heaven?

8. What is the intended purpose of the seals in Revelation? What elements in the text itself and from the Old Testament help interpreters arrive at this conclusion? Answer the same questions for the trumpets.

9. What three significant themes pervade the interlude of the little scroll in Revelation 10?

The Two Witnesses (11:1–14) The second vision John sees before the sounding of the seventh trumpet involves two individuals, called simply God's "witnesses," who bear a striking resemblance to Moses and Elijah in their miracle-working powers, but who are crucified and resurrected just like Jesus was. Most commentators acknowledge that this is the hardest chapter in the entire Apocalypse to interpret in terms of detail, though main themes remain reasonably clear. Whether the entire church or just Jewish Christians (or post-rapture Christians) live through the tribulation, it is natural to view these two witnesses as symbolic or representative of all God's faithful, witnessing followers during this awful period at the end of human history as we know it. Outside scholarly circles, however, many prefer to imagine two literal individuals, possibly including the literal Moses and Elijah returned from heaven.[103]

John's prophecy here begins with a vision of the Jerusalem temple and a command to measure it and count its worshippers (v. 1). As in Zechariah 2:2, these ac-

---

[103] See Osborne (*Revelation,* 417–24) for a presentation and discussion of the full range of interpretation. On the possibly more widespread Moses typology in the Apocalypse, see Peder Borgen, "Moses, Jesus, and the Roman Emperor: Observations in Philo's Writings and the Revelation of John," *NovT* 38 (1996): 145–59.

tions symbolize God's protection. Verse 2 shows what happens to the outer court that is not measured—it is given up for destruction. In the 90s, John's audience would immediately have thought of the destruction of the temple in A.D. 70 (cf. esp. Luke 21:24). But at that time, the entire temple was razed, not just the outer precincts, so the protection of the inner courts and holy place must be spiritual, not literal. If God could depict the entire fellowship of believers as 144,000 Jews, it is not hard to imagine him describing his church as the temple; indeed that is the consistent meaning of the word *temple* throughout the epistles of Paul and Peter (see above, pp. 156–57; cf. also p. 450). In this case, the inner-outer contrast would suggest inward (spiritual) protection despite outward (physical) persecution. And once again, the church could be seen as the faithful remnant of Israel.[104]

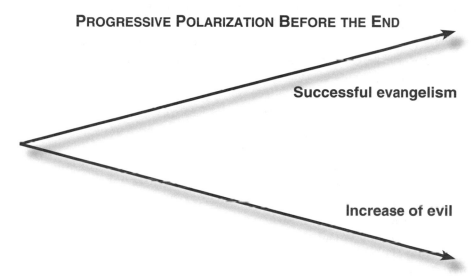

PROGRESSIVE POLARIZATION BEFORE THE END

Successful evangelism

Increase of evil

The two witnesses will prophesy for 1,260 days. At thirty days per month, this number equals forty-two months or three and one-half years. The length of time comes originally from Daniel 9:27 and 12:7, referring to the last period of time before all of Daniel's prophecies are fulfilled. This period of time will recur in Revelation 12:6, 14; and 13:5. Given that seven is the number of completion or perfection throughout Revelation (and much of the Bible), the most obvious significance of three and one-half is that it is half of seven—an incomplete period that does not represent God's perfect or complete word on a topic. Evil has the penultimate say, but the tribulation gives way to God's judgment and vindication, which discloses his final verdict on human history.[105] Given that the trampling of the temple's outer court initiates this 1,260-day period, it would seem best to equate it with the "church age," or at least that period of time from the temple's destruction in A.D. 70 until the outpouring of faith among the Jewish people that occurs just before Christ's return.[106]

---

[104] Keener, *Revelation*, 288–89.
[105] Cf. Roloff, *Revelation*, 130.
[106] Keener, *Revelation*, 287.

The ministry of the two witnesses finds them prophesying in sackcloth, the ancient garb for mourning, in this context no doubt lamenting the sins of the world in its rebellion against Christ and calling it to repentance. In verse 4, the olive trees recall symbolism used in Zechariah 4:6 for the activity of God's Spirit, while the lampstands hark back to Revelation 1:20 where they were said to represent the churches. Both of these images appear to confirm the suggestion that *the two witnesses portray the church of Jesus Christ boldly testifying to the gospel through the power of the Spirit in these last days.*[107] Even as the impact of evil grows, so too do the positive effects of proclaiming the good news of God's plans, just as Moses' plagues on the house of Pharaoh led to the exodus. Likewise, Elijah's calling down fire from heaven led to the destruction of the prophets of Baal, and his prophesying both drought and rain set in motion the events that would ultimately lead to the downfall of the evil reign of Ahab and Jezebel (thus the imagery of vv. 5–6 here).[108]

In the short run, however, the witnesses must suffer the consequences of their spiritual warfare against the powers of evil. They are martyred by demonic forces (v. 7) and disgraced by the lack of any burial of their bodies. Meanwhile the peoples of the world gloat over their demise (vv. 8–10). According to verse 8, all this takes place in "the great city" (a first-century term for Rome), "which is figuratively called Sodom and Egypt" (places of gross immorality and oppression of God's people in Old Testament times), "where also their Lord was crucified" (obviously Jerusalem). Since no location could be more than any one of these four places at a time, the point is obviously not to identify a site but to liken the persecution suffered by the church to that inflicted on Old Testament and New Testament believers alike, and even Jesus himself.[109] The three and one-half days the witnesses lie unburied is again obviously only a penultimate period of time, because it gives way to the resurrection and ascension of the witnesses to heaven (vv. 11–12). In the same way that Jesus was vindicated, believers too can look forward to ultimate resurrection and eternal life with God in the heavenly realms.

For some who see a strict sequential chronology throughout the Apocalypse, this "rapture" of the saints, coming (on this view) half-way into the trumpet and bowl judgments, has given rise to the midtribulation perspective on the timing of the rapture. But if the sixth trumpet brought us to the threshold of the end, this picture could just as easily support the posttribulational view. Because pretribulationists have concluded that the church has already been raptured earlier, they must take the witnesses as individual saints (or representative of the small number of believers who do live throughout the tribulation). For this position, the resurrection of the witnesses teaches nothing about the timing of the rapture.

After the witnesses' resurrection and ascension, a severe earthquake destroys a tenth of the "great city." Because seven thousand are killed, we may be meant to think of a community of about seventy thousand people, approximately the size of

---

[107] "Revelation repeats the Great Commission but places it deliberately in the context of tribulation and suffering." So David E. Holwerda, "The Church and the Little Scroll (Revelation 10, 11)," *CTJ* 34 (1999): 148.

[108] Cf. Beasley-Murray, *Revelation,* 183–85.

[109] Osborne (*Revelation,* 433) thus describes this picture as "an amalgamation of Jerusalem and Rome into one unholy capital city of the Antichrist."

first-century Jerusalem. If this is the Jewish capital city being depicted here, perhaps the conversion of the survivors stands for the outpouring of faith among Jews just before Christ returns (cf. Rom. 11:25–26).[110] But without any more explicitly Jewish imagery in verse 13, it is very hard to be confident of this suggestion. Some scholars even doubt that "giving glory to the God of heaven" means more than "fessing up" to one's deeds, as with the parallel expression in Joshua 7:19 addressed to Achan.[111] On any interpretation, though, we do have an additional example of the remedial nature of God's judgment, even this late in his plan of events for bringing history to a close. He is giving fallen humans every opportunity to repent if they would choose to do so. But that time will soon be past; the seventh trumpet points to the inexorable march to the end (v. 14).[112]

THE TRIBULATION

7 YEARS?

Powerful testimony	Persecution
of believers	of believers

OR

3 1/2 YEARS?

God's judgment on unbelievers

Powerful testimony by believers

and

Persecution by Satan of believers

Believers are exempt from God's wrath
Believers are not exempt from Satan's wrath

The Seventh Trumpet (11:15–19) As with the seventh seal, no new plague accompanies the seventh trumpet, reinforcing our earlier suggestion that it introduces and encompasses all seven of the final series of bowl judgments. Triumphant voices in heaven praise God because the fullness of his kingdom is about to be established (vv. 15–17), which will usher in the day of judgment—rewarding God's servants and punishing his enemies (v. 18). *Cosmic sound effects—heavenly thunder, lightning,*

---

[110] See esp. Ladd, *Revelation*, 159–60.

[111] Contrast Osborne (*Revelation*, 433–35), who sees the conversion of some from all nations implied here, with Mounce (*Revelation*, 223–24), who sees this only as their acknowledgment of their complicity in the persecution of the church.

[112] R. Dalrymple ("These Are the Ones . . . [Rev 7]," *Bib* 86 [2005]: 396–406) identifies four foci for the righteous in chap. 11: divine protection, witness, enduring persecution, and vindication. The first two of these characterize the 144,000 in Rev. 7:1–8; the last two, the numberless multitude in 7:9–17, further supporting the equation of these two groups.

hail, and an earthquake—accompany this last trumpet, but nothing suggests they are felt on earth at this point (v. 19).[113]

THE SATANIC TRINITY: RISE AND IMPENDING FALL (12:1–14:20)

The Dragon (12:1–17) Yet another interlude begins here because the seven bowls of God's wrath are not depicted until chapters 15–16. But chapters 12–14 are a long-enough section with a coherent-enough theme of their own that they form much more than an interlude. Together they narrate the apex of spiritual warfare, with the devil's worst attack against humanity (chaps. 12–13) ultimately failing to accomplish its objectives. His followers are vanquished, while even more people actually enter the kingdom (chaps. 14). *Chapters 12–13 form a unified whole by describing, in turn, the three members of what has been called the Satanic trinity—counterparts to, but also parodies of, the Father, Son, and Holy Spirit.* Chapter 12 portrays the head of this trinity: the dragon (v. 3), who stands for Satan (v. 9).

Once again John's attention is directed to heaven. This time he sees the glorious portrait of a woman surrounded by the sun, moon, and stars (v. 1). One thinks of the dream Joseph had in Genesis 37:9–11, which symbolized his entire family (and hence Israel as a whole) doing obeisance to him. This woman is in labor (v. 2); birth pangs regularly referred to the "messianic woes" or tribulation that Jews believed would precede the advent of the Messiah.[114] When the woman does give birth (v. 5), she brings forth a boy who is said to fulfill prophecy associated with the Messiah (v. 5a; cf. Ps. 2:9). This would make us think the woman must be Mary or perhaps the nation of Israel as a whole. But in verse 17, the dragon wars against the woman and her other offspring, in a context that refers to the persecution of believers. So the woman probably represents the entire "messianic community."[115]

The dragon's heads and horns make us think of the prophecies of Daniel 7–8 about coming empires that would fight against God's people. The crowns suggest pretensions of royalty and power, parodying God himself. The dragon's tail flinging a third of the stars from heaven (v. 4a) to earth may build on Jewish tradition about the fall of those angels who became demons.[116] Meanwhile, the dragon waits in heaven to devour the woman's child as soon as he is born (v. 4b). The child is protected from this fate, however, and the vision moves directly from Christ's birth to his ascension to heaven (v. 5; recall 11:12). Christ's followers, however, have to flee, but God protects them for the same 1,260-day period first introduced in 11:2–3 (v. 6). Given that chapter 12 has begun with a flashback to Jesus' first advent, we cannot simply add the two three-and-one-half-year periods of time together. More likely they both refer to the same interval between the first and final generations of Christian history.

It is unclear when the war in heaven next described took place. Verse 4 makes it appear that the demons have already been swept from heaven when Messiah is

---

[113] Ladd (*Revelation,* 164) explains that the lightning, thunder, earthquake, and hail "are conventional ways of expressing majesty and power attending the manifestation of the divine presence."

[114] See esp. in the Qumran Hymns (1QH 3:1–11); cf. Murphy, *Fallen Is Babylon,* 282–83.

[115] Mounce, *Revelation,* 231.

[116] Osborne, *Revelation,* 461.

born, leading some to see verses 7–9 as a prehistoric fall of Satan and his minions. Yet verse 4 also depicts Satan in heaven when the Christ child comes into this world, suggesting that at least *his* fall takes place later. In Luke 10:18, Jesus replies to the reports of the successful ministry of the seventy (or seventy-two) disciples by declaring, "I saw Satan fall like lightning from heaven."[117] Of course, the fluidity of apocalyptic metaphor means that John may not intend to answer this question at all! At any rate, we have already learned that John believes that the decisive death blow to the devil dealt with the crucifixion and resurrection of Jesus (recall chapter 5), a point made even more explicit in verses 10–11. But like a snake with its head cut off, wriggling out of control in its death throes, the fatally wounded devil thrashes about violently on earth, doing as much damage as possible in the comparatively short period of time left before he expires altogether (v. 12).

Verses 13–17 return to the battle between the dragon and the woman. His pursuit in verse 13 corresponds to her flight in verse 6 (note the references to the desert in both vv. 6 and 14a). Thus the time, (two) times and half-a-time in verse 14b match the three and one-half years of verse 6 and once again roughly equate to the church age. The attack continues in verse 15, until the protection of verse 16 emerges. But the persecution against believers ("those who obey God's commandments and hold to the testimony of Jesus") continues throughout the church's history (v. 17).[118]

The First Beast (13:1–10)   Next John sees a beast coming out of the sea, often a place of terror in the ancient world. Its horns and heads resemble those of its "father," the dragon, who has delegated it authority, and both pictures draw on imagery from Daniel 7 of what 1 John 2:18 called the Antichrist (vv. 1–2). The clearest indication that this beast is a parody of Jesus comes in verse 3a, in which it appears to have had a fatal wound that has been healed. But John phrases things so as to suggest the appearance may not match reality. The beast tries to look like Christ but has not actually experienced a crucifixion and resurrection. Still, he fools enough individuals, so that people from around the whole world who had worshipped the dragon will worship the beast as well (vv. 3b–4). John's audience would have undoubtedly thought of Domitian's blasphemous claims to be God, along with the traditions that he (or someone else soon to appear) was Nero come back to life.[119]

The Antichrist exercises his authority for forty-two months. Now, for the first time, a period described as three and one-half years seems to refer to the great tribulation at the end of the church age (v. 5). But because the earlier three and one-half years were not a literal length of time, there is no reason that the tribulation must last this literal period of time either.[120] The point is rather to show the parallelism between the tribulation characterizing all of Christian history and that which emerges at the very end of the age. Calamity may intensify in nature right before the end, but it need not be qualitatively different from what has gone on in earlier eras (vv. 6–7a).

---

[117] Cf. Witherington, *Revelation*, 171.

[118] Keener (*Revelation*, 327) has incisive words about the willingness to face martyrdom that will be needed to reach those parts of our world most resistant to the gospel.

[119] Mounce (*Revelation*, 251) sums up this imagery: "The worship of a satanically inspired perversion of secular authority is the ultimate offense against the one true God."

[120] Cf. Ladd, *Revelation*, 180.

The Antichrist's blasphemy and authority have the same broad influence over people from all ethnic groups, just as Jesus' followers eventually come from all of those groups, too (vv. 7b–8a; recall 7:9).

As the Great Commission is fulfilled, hostility against the church intensifies. As persecution increases, more and more people become believers. *The sign that we are living in the very end times is neither the Christianization of the world, nor the unparalleled horrors of the day, but the progressive* polarization *of good and evil, as each increases through the power of Christ and the power of the enemy, respectively.* Verse 8b makes it clear that the world winds up divided into two camps—those whose names have been written from the creation of the world in the book of life (NIV marg.) and those who choose to worship the beast.[121] The time is now so short and the destinies of each group of people so certain that John encourages patient endurance for the faithful, even if suffering or martyrdom becomes inevitable (vv. 9–10).

The Second Beast (13:11–18)   The third member of the Satanic trinity is depicted as a beast from the land (13:11–18). This beast parodies the Holy Spirit. Just as God's Spirit is fully one with the Father and the Son, this land beast looks like a lamb (the Antichrist, parodying the Lamb of God) and speaks like a dragon (Satan, parodying God himself) (v. 11). Just as the Holy Spirit exercises the authority of Jesus and empowers people to worship him, so too the land beast exercises the first beast's authority to enable people to worship it (v. 12). Just as the Spirit produced tongues of heavenly fire and filled the disciples so that they might work miraculous signs at Pentecost, the land beast likewise calls down fire from the skies and manufactures counterfeit signs to deceive those who are not God's chosen (vv. 13–14a). Just as the emperors had statues of themselves erected, this beast orders those he has deceived to build an image of the Antichrist, into which he breathes life, comparable to the Spirit's role in "quickening" humans (v. 14b–15).[122] That "all who refused to worship the beast" were killed cannot refer to every single Christian, because the very next two verses describe living Christians experiencing an economic boycott against them. Perhaps this phrase refers to those who publicly held fast to their faith when turned in to the authorities (recall above, p. 510).[123]

The final action of the land beast that John sees has become by far the most famous. Unbelievers of any socioeconomic class receive some kind of mark on their right hands and foreheads, which alone entitles them to trade in the marketplace (vv. 16–17). Just as believers were sealed with a mark on their foreheads before the

---

[121] Although the syntax favors the translation, "all whose names have not been written in the book of life belonging to the Lamb that was slain from the creation of the world," this hardly yields any coherent meaning. God's plan of salvation by means of Christ's death was set up from before the creation of the world, but Jesus was hardly put to death at that point. The NIV margin is an acceptable translation and produces the best conceptual sense. It is also interesting to note that no corresponding statement attaches to those who worship the beast, perhaps again implying only single predestination (cf. above, pp. 254, 309).

[122] Indeed, the imperial cult produced a number of partial parallels to the signs and wonders described in this context through various mechanical devices and forms of trickery. See Steven J. Scherrer, "Signs and Wonders in the Imperial Cult: A New Look at a Roman Religious Institution in the Light of Rev 13:13–15," *JBL* 103 (1984): 599–610.

[123] Osborne (*Revelation*, 516) likewise calls attention to this parallel practice of Pliny fifteen years later.

tribulation began (7:3), the Satanic opposition parodies God's sealing with a mark on its followers, too. While no identical ancient practices have been discovered, trade guilds in the Greco-Roman world did restrict certain business transactions to their members (cf. also Ezek. 9:4–7).[124] This "mark of the beast" is said to equal the beast's name or the number of his name. When calculated, that number is 666. One thinks at once of the ancient Hebrew and Greek use of letters for numerals and the corresponding *gematria* that assigned esoteric significance to the sum of the numbers corresponding to the letters of someone's (or something's) name.

כ	י	ט	ח	ז	ו	ה	ד	ג	ב	א
20	10	9	8	7	6	5	4	3	2	1

ת	ש	ר	ק	צ	פ	ע	ס	נ	מ	ל
400	300	200	100	90	80	70	60	50	40	30

ר	ס	ק		מ	ו	ר	נ	**NRWN QSR**
200 +	60 +	100		50 +	6 +	200 +	50	

From early days in Christian history, the suggestion has been made that 666 stands for Nero Caesar, since the Hebrew consonants קסר נרון (NRWN QSR) add up to this sum. The problem with this identification is that it works only in Hebrew, while Revelation was written in Greek and Nero would have spoken Latin. In addition, it works only when a less common spelling of Nero's name is used, adding an extra "n" to the end of his name.[125] Perhaps the more likely suggestion is that just as seven is the perfect number in much of Revelation's symbolism, 777 would be the number for the perfect triune Godhead. *The number 666 would then form a natural way to symbolize the Satanic trinity's attempt to imitate and parody the true Father, Son, and Holy Spirit, always seeming to come close, but never quite measuring up.*[126]

Attempts to perform *gematria* in some modern language on the name of a contemporary figure thus miss the point of John's symbolism altogether. So, too, do those who look for some literal mark that could be placed on people's bodies, or who equate the mark of the beast with credit cards, computer chips, or the World Wide Web—because the sixth letter of the Hebrew alphabet was *W*! Indeed, even attempts to identify the Antichrist with some awful, godless person or movement in any age distract from the faithful Christian living to which biblical apocalyptic

---

[124] Edwin A. Judge, "The Mark of the Beast, Revelation 13:16," *TynB* 42 (1991): 158–60. Philip A. Harland ("Honouring the Emperor or Assailing the Beast: Participation in Civic Life among Associations (Jewish, Christian and Other) in Asia Minor and the Apocalypse of John," *JSNT* 77 [2000]: 99–121) stresses the parallels between John's churches and voluntary Greco-Roman associations more generally, noting the likelihood that some of these Christians even participated in the trade guilds.

[125] A few manuscripts, however, have 616, which is the sum of the consonants with the extra "n" removed, so at least some scribes believed Nero was in view.

[126] See, e.g., Beasley-Murray, *Revelation*, 219–21.

consistently calls believers. The history of Jewish and Christian speculation on who this figure might be makes for fascinating reading—dozens of proposals have been preserved—but again thus far 100 percent of them have proved wrong, which at the very least should inspire extraordinary caution before suggesting (or believing anyone else's suggestion about) another candidate![127] After all, since Satan is not omniscient, and since only God knows the timing of the end, the devil must have an "antichrist" ready in every era, lest that turn out to be the time God has appointed for the consummation of all things.[128]

If we want to point fingers at anyone, we should perhaps turn them on ourselves. Peterson's applications are so profound that they deserve to be quoted at length.

> How do we protect ourselves from organized deceit? St. John is blunt; use your heads. Figure out what is going on. Most of the conspicuous religion that is in vogue at any one time in the country derives from the land beast. Expose these religious pretensions. This religion has nothing to do with God. Get its number: it is a *human* number. This is not divine mystery, but a confidence man's patter: it is religion that makes a show, religion that vaunts itself; religion that takes our eyes off the poor and suffering and holy Christ. In the language of numbers, 666 is a triple failure to be a 777, the three-times perfect, whole, divine number. It is a recurring characteristic of this land-beast religion that it is commercialized. It requires huge budgets to maintain itself. It manipulates us economically, getting us to buy and sell at its bidding, marketing advice, solace, blessing, solutions, salvation, good feelings. The devil's strategy here is not the black mass, but the mass market.[129]

The Lamb's Victory over the Satanic Trinity (14:1–20) *The 144,000 Revisited (14:1–5)* Despite the deception and terror the dragon and the two beasts produce, their glory will prove short-lived. Chapter 14 breaks into three parts that describe the redemption of God's people (vv. 1–5), the judgment of those who have accepted the mark of the beast (vv. 6–13), and the "harvest" of the earth (vv. 14–20). This third scene appears to contrast the conversion of people from every nation with the judgment of unbelievers from the identical cross-section of people groups (vv. 14–20). Together these three scenes prepare the way for the revelation of the final seven plagues in chapter 15.

The 144,000 of verses 1–5 are obviously the same group as in 7:1–8.[130] The seal on their foreheads (7:3) is now specified as the names of the Father and the Lamb inscribed there (14:1). The sound like rushing waters recalls the description of Christ's voice in 1:15. But the noise morphs into the sound of harps, and John recognizes the angelic creatures around God's throne singing a new song, which only the redeemed could join in singing (vv. 2–3). Verse 4 has perplexed many readers; in our modern

---

[127] Cf. esp. Bernard McGinn, *Antichrist* (San Francisco: HarperSanFrancisco, 1994).
[128] Keener, *Revelation,* 342–43.
[129] Peterson, *Reversed Thunder,* 126.
[130] Beasley-Murray, *Revelation,* 222.

world it can sound misogynist.[131] But being "defiled with women" almost certainly employs the same metaphorical range as the Old Testament frequently does when describing the faithlessness of God's people as adultery or whoredom against the Lord.[132] The metaphor "firstfruits" has suggested to some that only martyrs are in view here, experiencing ahead of time the glorious future ultimately awaiting all believers. But firstfruits could also represent the glorification of the believers who live during the tribulation as the first installment of the resurrection and perfection (cf. v. 5) of all of God's people from all time. At any rate, nothing appears here as in chapter 7 to suggest the idea that these must be literal *Jewish* Christians.[133]

The Three Angels (14:6–13) Verses 6–13 disclose three angels making final pro-nouncements about salvation and judgment, though the emphasis here lies clearly on judgment. The first angel continues the fulfillment of the Great Commission, calling people to "fear God and give him glory," in a context where this command clearly refers to true worship (vv. 6–7), supporting our earlier suggestion that conversion was in view in 11:13. The second angel proclaims the imminent judgment on the evil empire that the Satanic trinity established, here referred to for the first time as Babylon, reminiscent of the archenemy of Israel centuries earlier (v. 8). But the heart of this subsection involves the third angel's declaration of the condemnation on those who received the mark of the beast (vv. 9–11). What they thought was giving them the privilege to trade in this world's goods turns out to damn them to eternal torment![134] The sulfur and smoke may again be metaphors, but the reality behind them is clearly an agonizing one.

It is hard to square the clear statement that they will have "no rest day or night" (v. 11) with the annihilationist view of hell, whereby unbelievers simply die and cease conscious existence (as their eternal separation from God). While it does not diminish believers' suffering any, the knowledge that their persecution is almost completed and that their oppressors will pay far more dearly should help them en-dure whatever they must yet go through on earth (v. 12). Then they can look forward to the very eternal rest that will escape their tormentors (v. 13).[135]

---

[131] As alleged esp. by Tina Pippin (*Death and Desire: The Rhetoric of Gender in the Apocalypse of John* [Louisville: WJKP, 1992]) for the entire book of Revelation.

[132] See esp. Elizabeth Schüssler Fiorenza, *Revelation: Vision of a Just World* (Minneapolis: Fortress, 1991), 88. She plausibly sees the specific faithlessness in this case being participation in the imperial cult. Cf. Ruben Zimmermann, "Die Virginitäts-Metapher in Apk 14:4–5 im Horizont von Befleckung, Loskauf und Erstlingsfrucht," *NovT* 45 (2003): 45–70.

[133] Even the reference to Mt. Zion cannot be to the earthly hill on which the Jewish temple sat, because these believers, like the Lamb, stand before God's throne. John's usage is analogous to the heavenly Mt. Zion in Heb. 12:22.

[134] On the radical reversal of who accrues the world's honor and shame here and who gains God's approval and disapproval, see David A. deSilva, "Honor Discourse and the Rhetorical Strategy of the Apocalypse of John," *JSNT* 71 (1998): 79–110. Unpacking this theme in detail for this specific passage and showing how John stresses the supplanting of Rome by Jesus as the true Judge and Benefactor to whom his churches must relate, see idem, "A Sociorhetorical Interpretation of Revelation 14:6–13," *BBR* 9 (1999): 65–117.

[135] "Some may ask if we can really rejoice in heaven if we know the eternal fate of the damned (14:10–11). But the purpose of recording this announcement is to assure oppressed Christians of their coming vindication (14:12). For those of us who generally face a much lesser level of oppression, the image may not strike us as cause for celebra-tion. To fully capture the spirit of the text, we need to enter into the sufferings of our oppressed brothers and sisters elsewhere in the world" (Keener, *Revelation*, 380).

The Two Harvests (14:14–20)   Commentators debate whether both scenes in this subsection (vv. 14–16, 17–20) depict the judgment of unbelievers or whether the first portends the conversion of the nations. To the extent that the sickle-wielding harvester represents the farmer in Jesus' parable of the seed growing secretly (Mark 4:26–29), he would offer a positive image of the reaper of the fruit of God's kingdom. To the extent that John is being pointed directly back to the similar picture in Joel 3:13, the portrait would be one of judgment. Given that the 144,000 were called firstfruits at the beginning of this chapter, it seems more natural to see these as the remaining fruits, creating an inclusio around the entire subsection.[136] Verses 17–20, however, unambiguously promise judgment on God's enemies via the metaphor of the winepress of God's wrath. Like the trampling of human feet on grapes already squeezed through a cylinder and coming out the bottom of a winepress, to get the last amount of juice possible out of them, the supporters of the dragon and the two beasts will be condemned "for all they're worth." The metaphor gives way to the reality symbolized at the end of verse 20, as the grapes turn to blood and rise as high as horses' bridles over an area roughly equivalent to the territory of Israel in the first century.[137]

SEVEN BOWLS (15:1–16:21)

Heavenly Praise Prepares for the Bowl Judgments (15:1–8)   More heavenly praise and joy among believers accompany the onset of the last seven plagues. God's people stand in his throne room (recall 4:6), holding harps and singing "the song of Moses . . . and the song of the lamb" (recall 14:2–3). The kind of praise that Israel bestowed on Yahweh after the exodus (Exod. 15) is now Christianized (vv. 3b–4). The worship offered by all nations reinforces our conclusion that 14:14–16 depicted the conversion of people from all the world's ethnic groups. Here appear the true "united nations" and perfect racial reconciliation.[138] Verses 5–8 turn from highlighting the worship of God to portraying his glory. Just as the Israelite tabernacle and temple on earth figuratively housed God's glory, so too this heavenly sanctuary, strikingly revealing perfectly pure angels with perfectly disgusting plagues, is filled with smoke-like incense "from the glory of God," completely filling the enclosure and thus preventing anyone else from entering.

The Bowl Judgments Unleashed (16:1–21)   At last the final seven judgments representing God's wrath on unbelievers are poured out on the earth (v. 1). The first five resemble one another and, as with the first four trumpet judgments, remind us of the plagues Moses inflicted on the Egyptians—*sores, the seas and fresh water both turning to blood, sunscorching and darkness* (vv. 2–11). This time, however, there are no limitations on the percentage of the world afflicted (see esp. v. 3). Still, God's purpose is remedial, as verses 9–11 confirm in a backhanded way, by observing

---

[136] Cf. esp. Bauckham, *Climax of Prophecy,* 238–337. For the view that both scenes refer to the judgment of believers, see esp. Eckhard J. Schnabel, "John and the Future of the Nations," *BBR* 12 (2002): 243–71.

[137] Ladd, *Revelation,* 202. On the other hand, 1,600 may have been used because it "is the square, multiplied by 100, of 4, the number which expresses the wholeness of the world (cf. 7:1). The meaning would then be that the destruction encompasses the entire world in all its regions" (Roloff, *Revelation,* 178).

[138] Osborne, *Revelation,* 573.

people's refusal to repent.[139] One of the angels reminds John that God is completely just in these judgments, because the people affected are precisely those who have tormented God's people and martyred many of them (verses 5–6).[140]

As in the previous two series of judgments, the sixth item differs noticeably from the previous five. Bowl number six *dries up the Euphrates River* (Israel's ideal border to the northeast), preparing the way for empires from that direction to cross over without difficulty (v. 12). Readers in the Roman Empire at the end of the first century would have again thought at once of the Parthians.[141] Out of the Satanic trinity's "mouths" now emerge three frogs (again reminiscent of the plagues on Egypt), explicitly identified as symbolizing demonic spirits that disperse to trick all of the fallen world powers into gathering for a great battle (vv. 13–14) in a place known as Armageddon (v. 16). The Hebrew underlying this word, transliterated from John's Greek, is *har magedon*—the mount of Megiddo. A small village-fortress stood atop a large hill at that site in the first century overlooking the Valley of Jezreel, notorious as the location of various battles in Old Testament times (see Judg. 5:19; 2 Kings 9:27; 2 Chr. 35:22). But the expression had probably become proverbial for any place where a great, decisive battle could be fought, just like today we refer to someone "meeting their Waterloo" after the battlefield where Napoleon finally was defeated in 1815.[142]

Before John can describe what actually happens when the kings begin to fight, he reminds his readers how suddenly and soon Christ will return (v. 15) and hears the seventh angel cry, "It is done" (v. 17). One cannot help but think of Christ's penultimate words from the cross, "It is finished" (John 19:30). As with the sixth seal, it seems that the entire cosmos is coming unraveled (Rev. 16–21). God's enemies try unsuccessfully to escape the horrors, while the great city representing the Satanic, anti-Christian end-times empire, along with all of its satellite cities, collapses. This final "flash-ahead" allows John to narrate the demise of this empire and lament for it in the next two chapters before returning in 19:19 to the scene of the kings of the earth gathered for the final battle introduced here.

THE CONQUEST OF THE EVIL POWERS BY CHRIST'S KINGDOM (17:1–20:15)

The Demise of the Evil End-Times Empire (17:1–18:24) *Religious and Political Dimensions (17:1–18)* Chapter 17 portrays the evil empire of the last days as a harlot who had fornicated with the kings of the earth (vv. 1–2).[143] John thus again combines the images of immorality and idolatry to suggest a blasphemous anti-Christian mix of politics and religion. John's readers would of course have thought of Rome

---

[139] Keener, *Revelation*, 400.

[140] Cf. Mounce, *Revelation*, 294: "The judgment of God is neither vengeful nor capricious. It is an expression of his just and righteous nature."

[141] Cf. Aune, *Revelation 6–16*, 893.

[142] Alan F. Johnson, "Revelation," in *Expositor's Bible Commentary*, ed. Frank E. Gaebelein, vol. 12 (Grand Rapids: Zondervan, 1981), 552.

[143] Here and in chap. 21 appear the respective climaxes of two closely contrasting symbols that punctuate the Apocalypse—Babylon, the prostitute, and the New Jerusalem, the bride of Christ. See Gordon Campbell, "Antithetical Feminine-Urban Imagery and a Tale of Two Women—Cities in the Book of Revelation," *TynB* 55 (2004): 81–108. For a book-length equivalent of sorts, see Barbara R. Rossing, *The Choice Between Two Cities: Whore, Bride, and Empire in the Apocalypse* (Harrisburg: Trinity, 1999).

under Domitian. Verses 3–6a shift the scenery, but the reality represented remains the same. Now the prostitute masquerades as a queen with adornment and accoutrements of royalty. She likewise sits astride a scarlet beast (the color again denoting royalty and/or blood) described like the Antichrist of 13:1. Despite the apparent beauty and power surrounding both creatures, from God's perspective they represent only abomination and filth (v. 4). Both also have blasphemous names emblazoned on their foreheads, with the harlot again being labeled Babylon (recall 14:8). Verse 6a explains the most horrible sin she has committed—martyring believers.[144]

After recoiling from this disgusting vision, John receives an elaborate explanation of it (vv. 6b–18). The beast is again a parody of the eternal Godhead who fails to imitate it fully. Instead of being one who was, is, and is to come (recall 1:4), the beast "once was, now is not, and yet will come" (v. 8). John's readers would also recall the *Nero redivivus* legends; one day Nero would appear again to reclaim his throne, absent though he currently was from the political landscape.[145] The book of life imagery likewise reappears, this time without any hint of people being blotted out. Instead, those who are unbelievers are simply those whose names were not written in this book from the days of creation, a more predestinarian motif than suggested by 3:5.

Verses 9–11 appear at least as cryptic as the mysterious number 666 in 13:18. Just like there, a call for wisdom is followed by a puzzling use of numbers. The Antichrist, reminiscent of Nero, is associated with the city that sits on seven hills—a common way of referring to Rome and its topography.[146] He is also the eighth king who somehow belongs to a series of seven kings, of which "five have fallen," one currently reigns, and the final one will last only a short while. No attempt to match this series with emperors of first-century times (esp. with either Nero or Domitian as the sixth) makes very much sense or has commanded any consensus acceptance.[147] So again the symbolism is probably just that of seven as the complete number. By saying that the sixth king currently reigns, John implies that, from God's perspective, the time until the end is short. The description of the eighth king suggests that the Antichrist, too, is a political power broker, but more overtly demonic.[148]

A short-lived alliance joins ten other political powers to the Antichrist and his supporters. Again, the number is probably one of completeness, though it is interesting that Rome was divided into ten provinces at this time.[149] These combined forces will persecute Christ's followers, but they will ultimately be defeated (vv. 12–14). In

---

[144] Roloff (*Revelation,* 197) observes that two aspects characterize the appearance of the woman riding the beast—"luxurious voluptuousness and arrogant lasciviousness," and that "the murder of witnesses to Jesus becomes for the empire the final, heightened triumph of its godlessness."

[145] Gilles Quispel, *The Secret Book of Revelation* (New York: McGraw-Hill, 1979), 96.

[146] David E. Aune (*Revelation 17–22* [Nashville: Nelson, 1998], 920–22) notes that a late-first-century coin depicts the goddess Roma as a warrior, sitting on seven hills with her foot dipped in the Tiber River—all possible background imagery for this reference.

[147] For seven different approaches, see Osborne, *Revelation,* 618–20.

[148] Mounce, *Revelation,* 316–18.

[149] It is certainly exegetically unwarranted and theologically perverse to equate these ten powers with the European Economic Union, which for many years had ten members. Today they number roughly twenty-five and, even when they were smaller, European believers were quietly accomplishing significantly Christian undertakings through that organization. See Fred Catherwood, *Pro-Europe?* (Leicester: IVP, 1991).

the process, evil turns on itself again, as with the fifth and sixth trumpets (chap. 9). Moreover, we are reminded that God behaves asymmetrically with respect to good and evil. Instead of the devil and he being equal but opposing forces, as in various other ancient religions and modern "Star Wars" theology (with its light and dark sides of "the force"), God's power always remains superior and his purposes are always accomplished, in spite of wicked people and powers thinking they can rule freely and unchecked (vv. 15–18).

Economic Dimensions (18:1–24)   Chapter 18 supplements the picture of the previous chapter by adding the announcement of "Babylon's" demise (vv. 1–3), a call for God's people to separate themselves from her (vv. 4–8), and a lament by the world's power brokers for her fall (vv. 9–19). But God's people have reason to rejoice (v. 20), particularly because this overthrow of evil is a complete, everlasting defeat (vv. 21–24). By the end of the chapter there can be no doubt as to the finality of it all.

Verses 1–3 repeat crucial imagery from chapter 17, with one key addition—Babylon's "excessive luxuries." To the extent that one looks at wicked earthly governments in any age as possibly developing into the final end-times empire, *one must look not merely for politically powerful entities that persecute Christians and blaspheme the triune God, but also for those who amass vast amounts of material wealth.* No nation qualifies better today as the most politically powerful and economically wealthy in our world than the United States. And as the values of our Judeo-Christian heritage continue to erode and as it is harder today to witness for Jesus in the public sector in this country than even in the former Soviet Union, we scarcely need to point fingers beyond our own shores if we are looking for examples of the harlot or the beast.[150]

When these circumstances converge, Christians must separate themselves from the abominations, not necessarily geographically but behaviorally, so that they do not receive an identical judgment for their sins (vv. 4–8). Yet in just about any major moral arena, the statistics in America today scarcely disclose a differentiation between believers and unbelievers, while Christians' economic responsibilities command far too little attention in evangelical preaching and teaching. Craig Keener's applications could hardly be more pointed and accurate:

> Today over one billion people subsist on the equivalent of less than one dollar a day, and matters are only growing worse. The economic gap between rich and poor countries has doubled since 1960; the richest 20 percent of the world's population has gone from absorbing 70 percent

---

[150] Perhaps no more powerful exposé of these parallels exists than the poem by Julia Esquivel, "Thanksgiving Day in the USA," in *Threatened with Resurrection* (Elgin: Brethren, 1982), 79–91. As I write the first draft of these words on Thanksgiving Day 2004, little has changed since 1980. Our sophisticated weaponry is killing hundreds, if not thousands, in Iraq rather than in Central America, but the rationale remains unchanged. Interestingly, during the Clinton administrations in the U.S. from 1992–2000, many right-wing Christians confidently believed that the U.S. was slipping further and further into the morass predicted by Revelation here. During the Bush administrations of 2000 to the present, many find such thoughts blasphemous. Both reactions are exaggerated and show the problems that result when trying to read Revelation too closely as the prophecy of events being fulfilled *uniquely* in the very time or culture of any particular reader. But sooner or later perennial trends of every era will come to a climactic fulfillment.

of the world's income in 1960 to nearly 83 percent by the 1990s; the poorest 20 percent dropped from 2.3 percent to 1.4 percent in the same period, so that the income ratio of richest to poorest changed "from 30 to 1 in 1960 to 59 to 1 in 1989." Because we have many Christians here and because citizens of our nation and shareholders in our corporations have a voice, one would hope that more Christians would work to make things more equitable on behalf of our brothers and sisters struggling in many other nations. . . .

More to the specific point, we consume luxury goods often at the expense of others' resources (cf. 18:12–13). The lifestyle of the average middle-class American family compared to that of the world's billion poorest people is roughly equivalent to that of a medieval aristocrat compared with his serfs.[151]

And can we honestly say that we do not imitate the arrogance of the harlot in verse 7 in all the arguments we use to rationalize away our enormous expenditures on ourselves at the cost of the destitute and dying whom we could be helping at home and especially overseas?

Verses 9–19 can be summarized prosaically in one sentence. The wealthy and the merchants of the world bemoan the loss of their ability to "shop till they drop"! Verses 11–13 read like a bill of sale on an ancient Roman dock. Of Pliny's list of the twenty-seven most expensive items in the empire in the early second century, eighteen appear here. But after the luxuries, most of them imported to Italy from the subjugated people groups in the empire, come staples, too: wine, olive oil, flour, wheat, cattle, sheep, horses, and carriages. The climactic lowlight of the list comes in verse 13 with "the bodies and souls of men"—the Roman slave trade.[152] Verses 14–17 summarize the loss of wealth, repeating all the themes of verses 9–10 to create an inclusio around this luxurious bill of sale. Verses 18–19 depict the sailors who transported the goods across the Mediterranean joining the merchants in bemoaning the loss of the "great city" and her wealth. Peterson powerfully points out that

in Whore-worship they got everything they wanted, their lives overflowed with things, and now it is gone, wasted, up in smoke. They are bereft of everything they were promised and invested in and enjoyed. It is not their businesses that have collapsed, but their religion, a religion of self-indulgence, of getting. Now it is gone: salvation-by-checkbook is gone, god-on-demand is gone, meaning-by-money is gone, religion-as-feeling is gone, self-as-(temporary)-god is gone. They are left with

---

[151] Keener, *Revelation*, 442–43.

[152] See further Bauckham, *Climax of Prophecy*, 338–83; J. Nelson Kraybill, *Imperial Cult and Commerce in John's Apocalypse* (Sheffield: SAP, 1996).

nothing but themselves, of whom after a lifetime in the whorehouse, they know nothing.[153]

But unlike current American Christians, the believers in ancient Rome were for the most part poor. So the demise of the empire promised them a new chance economically as well as religiously. Rejoicing was appropriate (v. 20), now that the harlot and the beast were judged. Like the decisive drowning of a millstone in the open sea, the finality of Babylon's destruction is declared one last time (v. 21). Even the ordinary events of life and happiness have vanished (vv. 22–23a), as the spell that entrapped so many in worshipping earthly delights and that led to the martyrdom of both prophets and saints has been broken (vv. 23b–24). The ultimate culture of narcissism has collapsed![154]

The Establishment of Christ's Kingdom (19:1–20:15) *The Parousia (19:1–20:3)*   The fall of "Babylon" gives rise to a litany of heavenly hallelujahs (vv. 1–8) for God's triumph over his enemies. The fully righteous vengeance that only God can execute has at last fallen on those who corrupted the earth and martyred God's people, and the punishment will be everlasting. The company of the redeemed already in the presence of God praises him (vv. 1–3), as do the angels (v. 4). Then both groups together with one magnificent voice glorify him together in anticipation of the wedding feast of the Lamb (vv. 6–8)   the culmination of Isaiah's prophecy of an eschatological banquet (Isa. 25:6–8)—already foreshadowed in Jesus' table fellowship with sinners and in several of his parables. A beatitude for the feast's invitées and a further asseveration of divine truthfulness (v. 9) understandably lead John to respond in worship. But he errs by doing obeisance before the angelic messenger, a fellow servant of Christ, rather than before God himself. So the angel rebukes him, reminding him to worship only God. He then adds, "For the testimony of Jesus is the spirit of prophecy" (v. 10). This puzzling statement has been taken by some in charismatic circles to mean that true Christian witnesses always prophesy. But such a claim would be irrelevant in this context. Far more likely, the angel means that true Christian prophets (like John) must recognize that no one but Jesus can occupy center stage in their proclamations.[155]

With this refocus of his vision, John is now ready to see the revelation of Christ returning to earth from heaven (19:11–20:3). Contrary to the symbolism of the first seal (6:2), this time the rider on a white horse can be only Jesus. His names and attributes echo God's perfections; his appearance suggests royalty and purity. The one who died like a sacrificial lamb returns as a divine warrior to slay his enemies and rule over them (vv. 11–16). His name recalls his depiction in John 1:1 as the Word of God, the quotation of Psalm 2:9 reiterates Revelation 2:27, and the metaphor of the winepress of God's wrath recalls 14:18–20. Explicitly challenging the blasphemous claims of Domitian, John proclaims Christ, not Caesar, as "King of kings and Lord

---

[153] Peterson, *Reversed Thunder,* 148. For a detailed chapter of practical suggestions for modern capitalist societies on how believers can avoid this fate, see Wes Howard-Brook and Anthony Gwyther, "Coming Out of Empire Today," in *Unveiling Empire: Reading Revelation Then and Now* (Maryknoll: Orbis, 1999).

[154] Cf. Osborne, *Revelation,* 659.

[155] Cf. Witherington, *Revelation,* 234 For a "both-and" approach, see Smalley, *Revelation,* 487.

of lords" (v. 16).[156] Just as the Satanic trinity had parodied the triune God, so Christ will host a meal for his enemies that parodies the wedding feast of the Lamb: "the great supper of God" (v. 17).[157] But its guests will be carrion-eating birds who gorge themselves on the flesh of the fallen enemies of God, no matter how powerful they may have seemed in this world (v. 18; cf. Ezek. 39:18).

With verse 19, we pick up the story where we left it in 16:16—the godless rulers of the earth gathered together in Armageddon to make war against God's people. Now John explicitly mentions the beast or Antichrist as present, just as he spells out the ungodly army's intention to fight against Christ and his followers. After being exposed to so many movies and novels, paintings and poems about this final battle, it is worth actually reading what the Bible says about it! Astonishingly, *there is no battle at all, at least not in the conventional sense of human warfare with casualties on both sides over a prolonged period of time.*[158] Rather, as we hold our breath awaiting the beginning of the combat, we read that the beast and the false prophet (the unholy spirit or third demonic being) are captured and thrown alive into the lake of fire (v. 20). So, too, their followers are killed and their corpses consumed (v. 21). Christ vanquishes his enemies without his followers striking or suffering a single blow![159]

Amillennialists and postmillennialists have to interpret 20:1–6 as a flashback to Christ's first coming, just like virtually all commentators recognize a comparable flashback in 12:1–9. There certainly are parallels between 20:1–6 and first-century events: the binding of Satan, the division of humanity into the supporters and opponents of Jesus, and the beginning of new, spiritual life for his followers. Their reigning with Christ could then be seen as the spiritual victory they have in him throughout their lives and the "church age." The freeing of Satan for a short time at the end of this period will then correspond to the havoc he wreaks during the tribulation as just described throughout the previous chapters of the Apocalypse. He will likewise deceive the nations and gather their armies for battle against God's elect, only to be judged by God's supernatural intervention and condemned along with all his followers (vv. 7–15).

On the other hand, it is much harder to introduce a literary seam and chronological break between 19:21 and 20:1 than between 11:19 and 12:1. At that earlier suture, an entirely different scene ensued; here we have just been told of the demise of two-thirds of the Satanic trinity, and now we learn of the fate of the remaining third—the

---

[156] Osborne, *Revelation*, 686.

[157] Aune, *Revelation 17–22*, 1063.

[158] The army accompanying Christ "is never said to fight. In fact, they are wearing ceremonial garments not armor or battle gear. Christ does whatever fighting is required, and that by his word" (Witherington, *Revelation*, 243).

[159] "One of the unintended and unhappy consequences of St. John's Armageddon vision is that it has inflamed the imaginations of the biblically illiterate into consuming end-time fantasies, distracting them from the daily valor of dogged obedience, sacrificial love, and alert endurance. This is exactly what St. John did not intend, as even a cursory reading of his Revelation makes evident. When people are ignorant of the imagery of prophets and gospels, and untutored in the metaphorical language of war in the story of salvation, they are easy prey for entertaining predictions of an end-time holocaust at Mount Megiddo in Israel, conjured up from newspaper clippings on international politics. Jesus told us quite clearly that the people who make these breathless and sensationalist predictions are themselves the false Christs and false prophets that they are pretending to warn us against (Matt. 24:23–26)" (Peterson, *Reversed Thunder*, 165)!

devil. Chapter 19:19–20:3 belong together as one, uninterrupted paragraph describing how all three demonic creatures meet a violent fate when Jesus comes back from heaven. On this reading, Christ returns *before* the millennium of verse 3 begins.[160] Whether this is a literal one thousand years is less a matter of concern. This large, round number could be used simply to denote the character rather than the length of this period—what has been called "the sabbath rest of history."[161]

The Millennium (20:4–15)[162]　The first two-thirds of verse 4 comprise one giant sentence in the Greek. In breaking it up in English translation, the NIV misleads the reader into thinking that only those who were beheaded (or perhaps, by synecdoche, martyred in any fashion) will be resurrected to live throughout the millennium. The Greek, however, reads more literally that John saw those "beheaded . . . because of the word of God and those who had not worshipped the beast." In other words, all of the redeemed—*both* those who had previously died and gone to heaven and returned with Christ *and* those who lived to see his parousia—will receive their resurrection bodies at the same time, just as 1 Thessalonians 4:15–17 promised. Only those who died as unbelievers must await the end of the millennium for their resurrection (v. 5); believers reign with Christ in a "golden age" of peace and righteousness on earth (v. 6).[163]

This kind of premillennial interpretation, however, faces several difficult questions. Who is left on earth for the saints to rule? Who remains to rebel at the end of the "thousand years"? In 19:21 "the rest of" the unbelievers aligned with Satan and his forces were killed. Two possible answers suggest themselves: (1) The entire "battle" could be spiritual, so that these beast worshippers are simply confirmed in their spiritual rebellion, never again able even to consider repenting. Or, perhaps more likely, (2) the people killed here do die physically but are simply the soldiers in the beast's armies (cf. v. 19), not every living unbeliever on the planet.[164] Why does God then give these people one more chance to rebel, at the end of the millennium?

Presumably, he does so to demonstrate that, even when the right of free choice is again briefly restored to them, they inevitably choose evil and warfare against God, demonstrating that their final condemnation is perfectly just.[165] Does this then

---

[160] For a detailed list of exegetical arguments here for seeing the millennium after the return of Christ, see Keener, *Revelation*, 464–65. Cf. also Beatrice S. Neall, "Amillennialism Reconsidered," *AUSS* 43 (2005): 185–210.

[161] George R. Beasley-Murray, "Premillennialism," in *Revelation: Three Viewpoints* (Nashville: Broadman, 1977), 67. The idea is that just as Psalm 90:4 can speak of a day as a thousand years in God's sight, so John could be given the vision of a Sabbath-day's rest lasting for a comparable period. There is evidence of some ancient Jews and Christians believing that human history would last for six thousand years followed by a millennium of rest. The irony of modern Christians appealing to this belief to argue that the millennium must begin somewhere around A.D. 2000 is that not even young-earth creationists any longer adopt the approach to Scripture that just calculates all of the references to years, without allowing for any gaps, and deduces that God created the universe in about 4000 B.C. Even the strictest of today's creationists concede that the earth has been in existence well over six thousand years.

[162] Cf. also J. Webb Mealy, *After the Thousand Years: Resurrection and Judgment in Revelation 20* (Sheffield: JSOT, 1992).

[163] Keener (*Revelation*, 467) explains, "Because John envisions the whole church needing to resist the world system, he can portray the church as a martyr church, though his wording can allow for others who have withstood the beast but were not specifically martyred."

[164] Osborne, *Revelation*, 688.

[165] This is the closest Scripture ever comes to the plausible, though ultimately unprovable, view of C. S. Lewis, in his wonderful novel *The Great Divorce*, that even those already suffering the horrors of hell would not choose to leave and go to heaven were the opportunity offered to them, because of their lack of capacity to enjoy it.

suggest that the millennium is a time when believers walk around in resurrected bodies alongside unbelievers in mortal bodies, and isn't that so odd as to be unbelievable? It is odd, to be sure, but if we believe that Jesus bodily rose from the grave (not to mention the resurrection of select other saints in Matt. 27:51–53), it has already happened once as Jesus repeatedly appeared to his not-yet-resurrected followers.[166] That it should happen again on a more widespread basis is only quantitatively, not qualitatively, different.

But what of the saints' experiences in heaven? Isn't it anticlimactic in the extreme to be enjoying perfect happiness in a disembodied intermediate state directly in God's presence and then have to be brought back to a still imperfect earth, however much better it may be during the millennium than before? It all depends. Disembodied happiness is scarcely all that God originally intended for his creatures; his designs for humanity are not complete until his people are once again holistic entities, reunited in perfectly glorified bodies and souls. And nothing in this chapter (or in the various Old Testament prophecies often assumed to depict this same period of time) suggests that the happiness of God's people in the millennium is in any way tarnished simply because the new heavens and new earth have not yet come. That we even raise this question shows how Platonized many Christians really are. We think that disembodied bliss—the immortality of the soul—is all that we have to look forward to—when, as N. T. Wright puts it so powerfully, the true Christian hope is "[resurrection] life *after* life after death."[167] Moreover, God created *this* world and all its creatures "good," while he created humanity "very good" (Gen. 1). Despite our sin and the proliferation of evil, he will vindicate those original creative purposes for *this* world, before proceeding to fashion an entirely re-created cosmos.

Chapter 20:7–15 describes the final insurrection and judgment at the end of the millennium. Verses 7–10 depict the final release of Satan from his imprisonment in the abyss, so that he may "deceive the nations" all over the world one last time (vv. 7–8). Here these nations are referred to as Gog and Magog, names John reuses from Ezekiel 38. To the extent that an identifiable place was in view, Ezekiel was probably referring to Gyges of Lydia, in what today would be southwestern Turkey. Despite claims to the contrary in some popular Christian "prophecy handbooks," there are no geographical or etymological links between these terms and any locations in either the former Soviet Union or present-day Russia.[168] Moreover, by John's day, the expressions had most likely become as proverbial as "Armageddon"; after all, Lydia (or even southern Russia) would scarcely have been viewed as one of the far corners of the earth in Roman times.

What is more, only on an amillennial or postmillennial recapitulative interpretation do Gog and Magog have any relevance for events *prior* to Christ's return. On a premillennial interpretation (which is usually what such prophecy handbook writers profess), these names refer to the extremities of the earth only at the *end* of the

---

[166] Cf. Ladd, *Revelation*, 268.

[167] Wright, *The Resurrection of the Son of God*, 31 *et passim*.

[168] In Ezek. 38:2, Gog appears as the chief prince of Meshech and Tubal. These "are not the original forms of Moscow and Tobolsk! (They are the Hebrew names of the East Anatolian groups known to classical historians as the Moschi and the Tibareni.)" (Mounce, *Revelation*, 372, n. 5).

millennium! But just as with the nations prepared to do battle at Armageddon, these armies merely prepare for warfare. Instead of actually attacking God's people, fire from heaven devours them. The dragon, Satan, joins the beast and the false prophet in the lake of fire (recall 19:19–21) to experience unending torment.[169]

At this juncture, the wicked dead are resurrected, judged, and likewise banished forever to hell, in what John sees as "the great white throne judgment" (vv. 11–15). The basis for their condemnation is intriguing. The imagery of books reappears. On the one hand, one book apparently has a record of all of the deeds of humanity (vv. 12–13). So the wicked are judged on the basis of what they have done. On the other hand, the book of life reappears, too, and if anyone's name was not found written there, they were likewise condemned (vv. 12, 15). So both God's failure to include them among the elect and their evil deeds damn them.[170] Attempts to further define the relationship of these two causes to each other must go beyond anything the text outlines here.

NEW HEAVENS AND NEW EARTH (21:1–22:21)

The Eternal State (21:1–22:6)   In "Babylon" humanity tries to create paradise on earth apart from God and fails utterly. For those who resist the urge and wait on him, God promises to remake earth and heaven to create the most perfect paradise conceivable for his people to enjoy for all eternity. If there is to be a dissolution of the universe by fire (2 Pet. 3:10), this would be the logical time and place for it. But after the old heaven and earth come new ones (v. 1a), as prophesied as far back as Isaiah 65:17–25 (though there a few imperfections remained that have vanished here). The lack of any sea (v. 1b) is not to disappoint those who love to sail or fish. In John's day, the sea was frequently a source of terror. People drowned, ships sank, great storms unleashed their fury, and, worst of all, demons were believed to dwell there.[171] In striking contrast, the eternal state will contain nothing to cause "death or mourning or crying or pain" (v. 4).

Phrased positively, a holy city will descend from the new heaven to adorn the new earth. Whereas we began in a garden, we will end in a city—*God's people in perfect community*.[172] That the city is called the new Jerusalem suggests the fulfillment of all the promises to Israel as well as to humanity in this revelation.[173] But the city is also a bride (just as Yahweh and Christ are portrayed as bridegrooms to their

---

[169] "Those who are offended by such teaching have too low a realization of the terrible nature of sin and the natural response that divine holiness must have toward it" (Osborne, *Revelation,* 717).

[170] Having adopted the view that only martyrs are resurrected during the millennium, Mounce (*Revelation,* 377) assumes that the rest of the Christian dead are judged here and that their names *do* appear in the book of life. While possible, it is interesting that nothing is said explicitly to this effect, only about those whose names did *not* appear in the book.

[171] Cf. Aune, *Revelation 17–22,* 1119.

[172] Many people imagine the life to come as some private, idyllic paradise, but God envisions teeming masses of humanity living with one another! In this fallen world of course such cities produce great evils, but in the new cosmos sin will be abolished. "We enter heaven not by escaping what we don't like, but by the sanctification of the place in which God has placed us" (Peterson, *Reversed Thunder,* 174).

[173] Cf. Celia Deutsch, "Transformation of Symbols: The New Jerusalem in Rv 21,1–22,5," ZNW 78 (1987): 106–26. The image has already appeared as a "heavenly Jerusalem" in Gal. 4:26 and Heb. 12:22. For a detailed study of this theme and of Revelation 21–22, see Phichan Lee, *The New Jerusalem in the Book of Revelation* (Tübingen: Mohr, 2001).

followers throughout the Old and New Testaments, respectively). It is the people rather than the place who form the focus of attention (v. 2).[174] Greatest of all, God's redeemed will have an unequaled, intimate interpersonal communion with him (v. 3). That all this happens because the city descends from heaven suggests that the eternal state is entirely the creation of God rather than humanity (v. 5a).[175] Little wonder John is told to write all this down (v. 5b), though here more than anywhere else he must have felt the impotence of imperfect, finite language to describe magnificent, infinite perfection!

Just as in 16:17, John hears the solemn pronouncement, "It is done." God reiterates his eternal titles introduced first in 1:8. Echoing Isaiah 55:1, he offers free, living water to the thirsty (v. 6). To all those who "overcame" (recall the end of each of the seven letters in chaps. 2–3), he promises this incredible inheritance (v. 7). But verse 8 reminds us that hell still exists in this new cosmos. The litany of sinners here correlates directly with those who persecuted Christians in their mortal lives and/or refused to acknowledge Jesus under threat of persecution (v. 8).[176]

The rest of this section elaborates on the details of the new Jerusalem. Verses 9–14 describe its brilliance and its reflection of God's glory. The twelve gates hark back to the twelve tribes of Israel, just as the twelve foundations of the city represent the twelve apostles (vv. 12, 14). God's covenant people from both Old and New Testament times are now indissolubly united. The dimensions of the city make it a perfect cube of astronomical height (vv. 15–17). The only building of this shape well known in the ancient Mediterranean world was the Holy of Holies in the Jerusalem temple. The absence of any literal temple in the new Jerusalem (v. 22) could suggest that the entire city, the whole community of God's redeemed, now functions like the high priesthood in having direct access to God. The length of twelve thousand cubits again suggests the symbolism of completeness (recall 7:5–8).[177] The precious jewels on the foundations (vv. 19–20) remind us of Aaron's breastplate in Exodus 28:17–20, which was bedecked with many of the identical gems, appropriate for an entire priestly community.[178] The rest of the walls, gates, and streets of the city were likewise made up of the most valuable and beautiful of metals. Royalty may also be denoted by the streets of gold; purity is explicitly in view with the comparison of the gold to glass (vv. 18, 21).

If believers all have priestly access to God, God in Christ remains the eternal sacrifice. Thus, as Jesus predicted as far back as John 2:19, "the Lord God Almighty and the Lamb are [the city's] temple" (Rev. 21:22). So, too, their light replaces any need for the literal sun or moon to shine on this holy community (v. 23). At the same

---

[174] Cf. Robert H. Gundry, "The New Jerusalem: People as Place, Not Place for People," *NovT* 29 (1987): 254–64.

[175] Keener, *Revelation*, 486.

[176] See the itemized list of elements and their explanation in ibid., 489–90.

[177] Witherington (*Revelation*, 268) deduces that "there is no more division of secular and sacred. The whole city is a holy temple, for God is with his people throughout the city and they are his temple." With respect to the twelve thousand cubits, he also notes that the surface area of the city would approximate "the whole of the Mediterranean crescent from Jerusalem to Spain," and that "John then would be suggesting that the new creation is coterminous with the new people of God or their new community" (p. 269).

[178] Keener, *Revelation*, 496.

time, in some fashion not at all spelled out, continuity with the old order remains. The entities once called "nations" (or, better, "ethnic groups") and their rulers somehow still exist; that which was redeemed brings its "splendor," "glory and honor" into the new Jerusalem (vv. 24, 26; cf. throughout Isa. 60).[179] While the city is still conceived of as having walls, like all great urban centers in John's world, its gates are never shut because no dangers remain from which the community needs to be protected. The terrors of the night are likewise absent (v. 25). Like verse 8, however, verse 27 alludes to the fact that the wicked still exist, but in hell they can no longer harm these paradise-dwellers in any way.

While John observes no sea in the new earth, he does view the river of life flowing from God's throne down through the middle of the city (22:1). One thinks especially of the river associated with Ezekiel's new temple (Ezek. 47:1–12). This parallel, combined with the role of the entire city as a new "holy of holies," suggests that the true fulfillment of Ezekiel's prophecy comes in the eternal state, not in some literal, rebuilt edifice in a Jewish-led nation of Israel.[180] Like the river, the tree(s) of life nourish(es) God's people, always bearing enough fruit to sustain them abundantly (v. 2a). Those who needed healing are now made whole.[181] The "throne of God and of the Lamb" are no longer located just in heaven; they, too, have a counterpart on the new earth (vv. 1, 3b).

The reference to "service" raises tantalizing questions about what kinds of activity we will engage in for eternity but leaves them unanswered. *Latreuō* here may mean just "worship." At any rate, the intimate relationship we will have with God now justifies the metaphor of seeing "his face," which was always previously forbidden on penalty of death. His name on our foreheads indicates identification and ownership (v. 4). Verse 5 repeats the thoughts of 21:23, perhaps because they are so amazing, and concludes with our eternal reign. Verse 6 creates an *inclusio* with 21:5 concerning the trustworthiness of God's words and another with 1:1 on how soon all this will occur.

Closing (22:7–21)   Three times in this closing, Jesus himself echoes this refrain by repeating, "Look/Yes, I am coming soon" (vv. 7a, 12a, 20).[182] The beatitude of v. 7b picks up the theme of 1:3, only now the blessing is not merely for the one who reads this prophecy, but for the one who obeys its teachings (a reminder that prophecy is often more forthtelling than foretelling). Verses 8–9 create a reprise of 19:10. Those who doubt that John could have made this same mistake twice must

---

[179] Dave Mathewson ("The Destiny of the Nations in Revelation 21:1–22:5: A Reconsideration," *TynB* 53 [2002]: 121–42) surveys the major options, concluding that John's language highlights "the nations who will be converted in the future in fulfillment of the OT prophecies (Is. 2:2–5; 60)." But unlike the emphasis throughout Bauckham (*Climax of Prophecy*), Mathewson does not see John's emphasis on universal salvation superseding or taking priority over his similar emphasis on universal judgment. The two must be allowed to stand together.

[180] Keener, *Revelation*, 497.

[181] There is no verb in the Greek, so we must supply the form of "to be" that most fits the context. Given the absence of any curse in the very next statement, it is impossible to believe that John thought anyone *still* needed to be healed in the New Jerusalem. The translation should read, "And the leaves of the tree *were* for the healing of the peoples." Nor does the text support universalism, merely the fulfillment of the Great Commission. Cf. ibid., 511; Osborne, *Revelation*, 772.

[182] Beale (*Revelation*, 1135) points out that the next main event in salvation-history after Pentecost is the parousia, so it will always be "soon" no matter how many years elapse.

have an unrealistic perspective on Christian sanctification *and* must fail to appreciate the overwhelming temptation to bow before one revealing such unimaginable splendors. Verse 10a contrasts with both 10:4 and Daniel 12:4 (on which, see above, p. 533). Verses 10b–11 suggest that the end is so close that it is too late to change people's ways (recall 13:10),[183] though this cannot be meant absolutely, since people do repent, and have additional chances to repent that they do not take advantage of, in several places throughout the Apocalypse.[184]

As in chapter 1, Jesus can be the beginning and the end, exactly as God can (v. 13). Verses 14–15 form an inclusio with 21:7–8. For the first time in the entire book, Jesus now identifies himself by name, as well as by three distinctive messianic titles, all rooted in the Hebrew Scriptures (v. 16). The only proper, commonsensical response to this overwhelming revelation, by any who hear what the Spirit and God's people have said, is to "come" and accept the invitation to partake freely of eternal life (v. 17). Astonishingly, however, some will still refuse.

Worse still, some will add to or delete from the words of this prophecy. God's response will be to deny them any share in the life to come so powerfully depicted here (vv. 18–19). These warnings ultimately derive from Deuteronomy 4:2 and cannot have yet referred to the whole canon of Scripture. In John's context, they apply strictly to the book of Revelation itself. But part of what the early church meant by subsequently canonizing twenty-seven different documents and creating a New Testament was that all of the books should be treated with this same reverence.[185] Those who substantively change God's Word concerning the "who and how" of salvation and judgment cannot count on being his people. The liturgical responses of the last verse and a half of the book affirm this truth one final time, pray for Christ's speedy return, and pronounce a shortened form of the grace of 2 Corinthians 13:14 on all believers.

APPLICATION

Instead of reading Revelation as if it were a handbook on current events, we must try to understand the timeless truths, promises, and warnings that the apocalyptic symbolism intends to communicate. While one generation will indeed see the climactic fulfillment of the events prophesied in John's apocalypse, preceding generations will undergo many similar, penultimate fulfillments. God has not given us (nor did he intend to give us) a sufficiently detailed road map to enable us to be sure of when the ultimate fulfillments are at hand, precisely because the type of things that he predicts happen in part again and again in anticipation of the "grand finale." Our task is not to preach or listen to sermons, to write or read books, or to attend to any other media that claim to know what Jesus repeatedly said we cannot know—the times and seasons of the final realization of the reality behind all these symbols. *What we must do is to focus on the central claim of the book that ultimately, despite*

---

[183] Roloff, *Revelation*, 251.

[184] Osborne, *Revelation*, 786.

[185] Cf. Peter Balla, "Evidence for an Early Christian Canon (Second and Third Century)," in *The Canon Debate*, ed. Lee M. McDonald and James A. Sanders (Peabody: Hendrickson, 2002), 375.

all of the diversity in humanity, there are only two possible destinies for people—one indescribably wonderful and one unimaginably horrible. How one responds to Jesus (the Lamb who is also a Lion) makes all the difference in the universe as to how we experience eternity.

Meanwhile, human history is going somewhere; and every event, no matter how awful, remains under God's sovereign guidance. These truths should provide strong encouragement for believers in all kinds of adverse circumstances. If we cannot estimate the timing of Christ's return, we can at least anticipate the nature of the days just before it. It will be one of greater polarization of good and evil than ever before in history, as God's powerful word goes forth to the ends of the earth, with people of every major ethnic group on the planet coming to faith. At the same time, those who reject Christ's offer of salvation will oppose believers with unprecedented persecution, while God in turn unleashes his wrath on unbelievers with plagues and disasters of record magnitude. Not surprisingly, true Christians in this context may be described as overcomers![186] Those who truly are saved will indeed endure to the end, but they will demonstrate that salvation precisely by their endurance. The compensation in the new heavens and new earth, however, is magnificent.

Blaise Pascal's famous "wager" applies here if ever. If atheism is right and Christianity wrong, all Christians can lose are their physical lives, whereas if atheism is wrong and Christianity right, atheists can suffer horribly, banished from the presence of God and all things good forever. If some other world religion is right and Christianity wrong, most Christians still stand a reasonable chance at a good afterlife, because all other religions at one level or another boil down to salvation by works. And true Christians demonstrate many good works as their lives are increasingly conformed to the image of Jesus. But if it all depends on grace through faith, then people of all other religions or ideologies must renounce any attempt to merit God's favor and must throw themselves entirely on his mercy, believing that he alone can save them, uniquely through the cross of Christ. Believers likewise triumph not in life but in death. Their subsequent victory over death makes everything in this life pale in comparison. To reapply the contemporary advertising slogan, "We can have it all!" But to get it all, we must accept God's terms and await his perfect timing.

ADDITIONAL QUESTIONS FOR REVIEW

1. How does one best respond to the repeated claim that we are most certainly in the final generation because of either the evil in the world or the increased evangelization of previously unreached people groups? What is an exegetically sound principle for determining when the end of days might come? Consider chapter 11 in particular.

2. Compare the Satanic trinity of Revelation 12–14 to the Godhead. In what ways does the Satanic trinity attempt to mimic the holy Trinity? Show how each

---

[186] David Scholer ("Breaking the Code: Interpretive Reflections on Revelation," *ERT* 25 [2001]: 304–17) shows how the book applies more as a manual on discipleship, particularly during intense suffering, than as a "cryptogram" of current or coming events.

member of the Satanic trinity parodies one of the members of the holy Trinity. What is the main theme that the vision of the Satanic trinity is communicating to its readers?

3. What is the relationship of the seals and the trumpets to the bowls? What portion of humanity is affected by each of them, and how did the author intend the specific numbers mentioned to be understood? Discuss the interludes and their significance in each of these series of seven judgments.

4. What visions depict the political, religious, and economic dimensions of the great evil empire of the end-times? Into what more prosaic truths do they translate?

5. What is John's description of the final battle at Armaggedon? How does this depiction differ from what is often portrayed in the media or in stories loosely based on Revelation's events? How are believers prepared and armed for the battle that will finally depose Satan and evil?

6. What are some of the key ideas and passages in Revelation that premillennialists, postmillennialists, and amillennialists use to support their positions. Analyze the events of Armageddon based on these three interpretations. According to each camp's interpretation, when did/will Armageddon occur? Reading Revelation 19:19–20:3 as one paragraph, in which the Satanic trinity is defeated at once, favors which millennial interpretation?

7. What are some of the difficulties of a premillennial interpretation of Revelation 20? How are these difficulties best resolved?

8. With all of its cryptic language and puzzling imagery, what is the central claim that believers must understand from Revelation concerning the end of human history? How does this differ from the way many people have used Revelation, both in our generation and in previous generations?

SELECT BIBLIOGRAPHY

COMMENTARIES

Advanced

Aune, David E. *Revelation*, 3 vols. WBC. Dallas: Word, 1997–98.

Beale, Gregory K. *The Book of Revelation*. NIGTC. Carlisle: Paternoster; Grand Rapids and Cambridge: Eerdmans, 1999.

Osborne, Grant R. *Revelation*. BECNT. Grand Rapids: Baker, 2002.

Smalley, Stephen S. *The Revelation to John*. London: SPCK; Downers Grove: IVP, 2005.

Thomas, Robert L. *Revelation*, 2 vols. Chicago: Moody, 1992–96.

Intermediate

Beasley-Murray, G. R. *The Book of Revelation*. NCB, rev. London: Marshall, Morgan & Scott, 1978; Grand Rapids: Eerdmans, 1981.

Caird, George B. *A Commentary on the Revelation of Saint John the Divine*. BNTC/ HNTC. London: Black; New York: Harper, 1966.

Hughes, Philip E. *The Book of Revelation*. PNTC. Leicester: IVP; Grand Rapids: Eerdmans, 1990.

Johnson, Dennis E. *Triumph of the Lamb: A Commentary on Revelation*. Phillipsburg, N.J.: Presbyterian and Reformed, 2001.

Keener, Craig S. *Revelation*. NIVAC. Grand Rapids: Zondervan, 2000.

Mounce, Robert H. *The Book of Revelation*. NICNT, rev. Grand Rapids: Eerdmans, 1998.

Murphy, Frederick J. *Fallen Is Babylon: The Revelation of John*. NTinCont. Harrisburg: Trinity, 1998.

Reddish, Mitchell G. *Revelation*. SHBC. Macon: Smyth & Helwys, 2001.

Roloff, Jürgen. *The Revelation of John: A Continental Commentary*. Minneapolis: Fortress, 1993.

Witherington, Ben, III. *Revelation*. NCBC. Cambridge and New York: CUP, 2003.

Introductory

Kovacs, Judith, and Christopher Rowland, with Rebekah Callow. *Revelation*. BBC. Oxford and Malden, Mass.: Blackwell, 2004.

Metzger, Bruce M. *Breaking the Code: Understanding the Book of Revelation*. Nashville: Abingdon, 1993.

Michaels, J. Ramsey. *Revelation*. IVPNTC. Leicester and Downers Grove: IVP, 1997.

Morris, Leon. *The Book of Revelation*. TNTC, rev. Leicester: IVP; Grand Rapids: Eerdmans, 1987.

Peterson, Eugene H. *Reversed Thunder: The Revelation of John and the Praying Imagination*. San Francisco: Harper & Row, 1988.

OTHER BOOKS

Bauckham, Richard. *The Climax of Prophecy*. Edinburgh: T & T Clark, 1993.

Blevins, James L. *Revelation as Drama*. Nashville: Broadman, 1984.

Blount, Brian K. *Can I Get a Witness? Building Revelation through African American Culture*. Louisville: WJKP, 2005.

Boesak, Allan A. *Comfort and Protest: Reflections on the Apocalypse of John of Patmos*. Philadelphia: Westminster, 1987.

Collins, Adela Yarbro. *Crisis and Catharsis: The Power of the Apocalypse*. Philadelphia: Westminster, 1984.

Court, John M. *Myth and History in the Book of Revelation*. London: SPCK, 1979.

Dawn, Marva J. *Joy in Our Weakness: A Gift of Hope from the Book of Revelation*. Grand Rapids and Cambridge: Eerdmans, 2002.

Duff, Paul B. *Who Rides the Beast? Prophetic Rivalry and the Rhetoric of Crisis in the Churches of the Apocalypse*. Oxford and New York: OUP, 2001.

Fiorenza, Elizabeth Schüssler. *The Book of Revelation: Justice and Judgment*. Philadelphia: Fortress, 1985.

Friesen, Steven J. *Imperial Cults and the Apocalypse of John*. Oxford and New York: OUP, 2001.

Goldsworthy, Graeme. *The Gospel in Revelation*. Exeter: Paternoster, 1984; Nashville: Nelson, 1985.

Koester, Craig R. *Revelation and the End of All Things*. Grand Rapids and Cambridge: Eerdmans, 2001.

Kraybill, J. Nelson. *Imperial Cult and Commerce in John's Apocalypse*. Sheffield: SAP, 1996.

Michaels, J. Ramsey. *Interpreting the Book of Revelation*. Grand Rapids: Baker, 1992.

Pate, C. Marvin, ed. *Four Views on the Book of Revelation*. Grand Rapids: Zondervan, 1998.

Rhoads, David, ed. *From Every People and Nation: The Book of Revelation in Intercultural Perspective*. Minneapolis: Fortress, 2005.

Slater, Thomas B. *Christ and Community: A Socio-Historical Study of the Christology of Revelation*. Sheffield: SAP, 1999.

Smalley, Stephen S. *Thunder and Love: John's Revelation and John's Community*. Milton Keynes: Word, 1994.

Thompson, Leonard L. *The Book of Revelation: Apocalypse and Empire*. Oxford and New York: OUP, 1990.

Wainwright, Arthur W. *Mysterious Apocalypse: Interpreting the Book of Revelation*. Nashville: Abingdon, 1993.

BIBLIOGRAPHY

Muse, Robert L. *The Book of Revelation: An Annotated Bibliography*. New York: Garland, 1996.

SUBJECT INDEX

AUTHOR INDEX

SCRIPTURE INDEX